MAJOR LEGAL SYSTEMS
IN THE
WORLD TODAY

AUSTRALIA AND NEW ZEALAND
The Law Book Company Ltd.
Sydney : Melbourne : Perth

CANADA AND U.S.A.
The Carswell Company Ltd.
Agincourt, Ontario

INDIA
N.M. Tripathi Private Ltd.
Bombay
and
Eastern Law House Private Ltd.
Calcutta and Delhi
M.P.P. House, Bangalore

ISRAEL
Steimatzky's Agency Ltd.
Jerusalem : Tel Aviv : Haifa

MALAYSIA : SINGAPORE : BRUNEI
Malayan Law Journal (Pte.) Ltd.
Singapore

PAKISTAN
Pakistan Law House
Karachi

MAJOR LEGAL SYSTEMS

IN THE

WORLD TODAY

An Introduction
to the
Comparative Study of Law

RENÉ DAVID

Professeur honoraire à la Faculté de
Droit et de Science politique
de l'Université d'Aix-Marseille

JOHN E. C. BRIERLEY

Sir William Macdonald
Professor of Law
McGill University, Montreal

Third Edition

LONDON
STEVENS & SONS
1985

First edition by René David
published in France in 1964 by
Librairie Dalloz of
11 & 14 rue Soufflot, Paris, France
and printed in France
Eighth edition 1982

First English edition by René David and John E. C. Brierley 1966
Second edition   1978
Third edition   1985

Published by Stevens & Sons Ltd. of
11 New Fetter Lane, London.
Computerset by Promenade Graphics Ltd.,
Cheltenham and printed in Scotland.

British Library Cataloguing in Publication Data

René David
  Major legal systems in the world today:
  introduction to the comparative study of law.—
  3rd ed.
  1. Comparative law
  I. Title   II. Brierley, John E.C. III. Les
  grands systèmes de droit contemporains. *English*
  342   K583

  ISBN 0 420 47340 8
  ISBN 0 420 47350 5 Pbk

PREFACE TO THE FIRST ENGLISH EDITION

The publication in English of my book on the major systems of contemporary law gives me great pleasure—and for a reason I do not hesitate to state here. I am convinced that it is absolutely essential at the present time to develop comparative legal studies, and I believe that this book, such as it has been conceived, provides the necessary basis for a study of comparative law.

I wish to thank Professor C. M. Schmitthoff, on whose initiative the publishers first became interested in the English-language publication of the work.

I would also especially like to thank Professor John E. C. Brierley, who was kind enough to undertake the translation and adaptation. To do so it would not have sufficed, as the uninitiated might think, to be thoroughly conversant with English and French. It was also necessary to be a comparatist and to understand the many legal terms peculiar to the different systems studied. Few people could have translated what I have written with as much understanding as Professor Brierley has. To show my appreciation of the very considerable and intricate work that he has carried out, it seemed to me only just that this work appear under our two names—although this alone cannot repay my debt of gratitude.

October 1966   R.D.
Montreal

Note to the Third English Edition

This is a translation and adaptation of Professor René David's *Les Grands systèmes de droit contemporains* which was originally based on the second French edition of 1966, published by Librairie Dalloz in the series known as *Précis Dalloz*. It has been revised largely in the light of changes made by Professor David and Professor Camille Jauffret-Spinosi in the eighth French edition of 1982.

The adaptation to an English readership has involved certain changes in the text itself as well as alterations and additions to the notes and bibliography.

J.E.C.B.

TABLE OF CONTENTS

TITLE III

Structure of the Law

PART THREE

THE COMMON LAW

TITLE I

PART FOUR

OTHER CONCEPTIONS OF LAW
AND THE SOCIAL ORDER   453

TITLE I

Muslim Law   455

TITLE II

Law of India   484

TITLE III

Laws of the Far East   516

TITLE IV

Laws of Africa and Malagasy   547

APPENDIX I

BIBLIOGRAPHICAL INFORMATION 577

APPENDIX II

USEFUL INFORMATION AND REFERENCES 610

LIST OF ABBREVIATIONS

ABGB	Allgemeines Bürgerliches Gesetzbuch für Österreich
A.C.	Law Reports, Appeal Cases (U.K.)
Alb. L.J.	Albany Law Journal (U.S.A.)
All E.R.	All England Law Reports (1936) (U.K.)
Amer. Bar Assoc. J.	American Bar Association Journal
Am. J. Comp. L.	American Journal of Comparative Law
Amer. J. of Int'l. Law	American Journal of International Law
Ann.	Annales/Annals
Arbitration Law J.	Arbitration Law Journal (U.S.A.)
BGB	Bürgerliches Gesetzbuch
Bull.	Bulletin
Bull. civ.	Bulletin civil des arrêts de la Chambre civile de la Cour de Cassation (France)
Cal. L.R.	California Law Review (U.S.A.)
Cambridge L.J.	Cambridge Law Journal (U.K.)
Can. Bar Rev.	Canadian Bar Review
Cass. civ.	Judgment of the Cour de Cassation Chambre civile (France)
Ch.	Law Reports, Chancery Division (1891–) (U.K.)
Col. L.R.	Columbia Law Review (U.S.A.)
Cornell L.Q.	Cornell Law Quarterly (U.S.A.)
Cranch	Cranch, United States Supreme Court Reports (1801–1805)
Dal. L.J.	Dalhousie Law Journal (Canada)
Duke L.J.	Duke Law Journal (U.S.A.)
Eliz.	Elizabeth
E.R.	The English Reports
Ex. D.	Law Reports, Exchequer Division (1875–1880) (U.K.)

F.	Federal Reporter (U.S.A.)
F.2d	Federal Reporter (Second Series)
Fla. L. Rev.	University of Florida Law Review (U.S.A.)
Fordham L.R.	Fordham Law Review (U.S.A.)
Geo. Wash. L.R.	George Washington Law Review (U.S.A.)
Harvard Int. L.J.	Harvard International Law Journal (U.S.A.)
Harv. L. Rev.	Harvard Law Review (U.S.A.)
H. L. Deb.	House of Lords, Debates (U.K.)
H.R.N.J.	Hage Raad, Nederlandsche Jurisprudentie (Netherlands)
I.L.R.	Indian Law Reports
Ind. App.	Indian Appeals (U.K.)
Int. and Comp L.Q.	International and Comparative Law Quarterly (U.K.)
J. Comp. Leg.	Journal of Comparative Legislation and International Law (U.K.)
J. dr. africain	Journal de droit africain
Journ. dr. int.	Journal de droit international (France)
J. of African Law	Journal of African Law (U.K.)
J.S.P.T.L.	Journal of the Society of the Public Teachers of Law (U.K.)
K.B.	Law Reports, King's Bench (U.K.)
L.Q.R.	Law Quarterly Review (U.K.)
Louisiana L.R.	Louisiana Law Review (U.S.A.)
L.R. Ind. App.	Law Reports, Indian Appeals (1872–1950)
McGill L.J.	McGill Law Journal (Canada)
M.H.C.R.	Madras High Court Reports (1862–1875)
Mich. L.R.	Michigan Law Review (U.S.A.)
Moo. Ind. App.	Moore's Indian Appeals (1836–1872)
Nouv. Rev. hist. de droit	Nouvelle Revue historique de droit français (France)

N.E. 2d	North Eastern Reporter, Second Series (U.S.A.)
N.Y.	New York (State) Court of Appeals Reports
N.Y. 2d	New York (State) Court of Appeals Reports, Second Series
N.Y.S.	New York State Reporter, New York Supplement (National Reporter)
N.Y.S. 2d	New York Supplement Reporter, Second Series (National Reporter)
N.Y.U. Law Rev.	New York University Law Review (U.S.A.)
N.Z.U.L. Rev.	New Zealand University Law Review
Pat.	All Indian Reporter, Patna.
Q.B.	Law Reports, Queen's Bench (U.K.)
Rabels Z.	(Rabels) Zeitschrift für ausländisches und internationales Privatrecht
Rep. N.Y. State Bar Assoc.	Reports of the New York State Bar Association
Rev.	Revue/Review
Rev. crit. dr. int. privé	Revue critique de droit international privé (France)
Rev. dr. int. et dr. comp.	Revue de droit international et de droit comparé (Belgium)
Rev. dr. int. légis. comparée	Revue de droit international et de législation comparée (France)
Rev. dr. public	Revue de droit public et de la science politique en France et à l'étranger (France)
Rev. int. dr. comparé	Revue international de droit comparé (France)
Rev. jur. et pol. d'outre-mer	Revue juridique et politique d'outre-mer (France)

Rev. jur. et pol. ind. et Coop.	Revue juridique et politique, indépendence et coopération (France)
Rev. soc. Law	Review of Socialist Law (Netherlands)
Rev. trim. dr. commercial	Revue trimestrielle de droit commercial (France)
Rev. tun. droit	Revue tunisienne de droit (Tunisia)
Riv. dir. comm.	Rivista di diritto commerciale (Italy)
RGZ	Entscheidungen des Reichsgerichts in Zivilsachen
R.S.F.S.R.	Russian Soviet Federated Socialist Republic
S.C.R.	Supreme Court Reports (India)
Sov. Gos. i Pravo	Sovetskoe Gosudarstov i Pravo (U.S.S.R.)
S.S.R.	Soviet Socialist Republic(s)
Trav. Comm. fr. dr. int. privé	Travaux de la Commission de réforme du droit international privé (France)
Tulane L.R.	Tulane Law Review (U.S.A.)
U.S.	United States Supreme Court Reports
U. of Pa. L.R.	University of Pennsylvania Law Review (U.S.A.)
U.S.S.R.	Union of Soviet Socialist Republics
Vict.	Victoria
Wheat.	Wheaton, United States Supreme Court Reports (1816–1827)
Wisconsin L.R.	Wisconsin Law Review (U.S.A.)
W.L.R.	Weekly Law Reports (U.K.)
Wm.	William
Yale L.J.	Yale Law Journal (U.S.A.)
ZPO	Zivilprozessordung

INTRODUCTION

1. Outline

The majority of introductory works on comparative law published up to the present time have, for the most part, concentrated on defining the purpose of comparative law and emphasising the value, as well as the difficulty, of comparative law studies. While these topics continue to be of interest, there is no purpose in pursuing them here. Consequently, the first section of this Introduction will briefly summarise and explain, from an historical point of view, the different concepts which have been developed concerning the nature and the usefulness of comparative law.[1]

The second section of the Introduction is devoted to the idea of the "legal family" (*famille juridique*). It explains how, despite the diversity of laws encountered in the world today, it is possible to concentrate on the presentation of certain "models," certain laws which can be considered typical and representative of a family which groups a number of laws. On the basis of these considerations, the third section provides a preliminary sketch of the major legal families themselves.

SECTION I—COMPARATIVE LAW

2. Development of comparative law

There have always been studies of foreign laws and recourse to comparison in legal scholarship.[2] The comparison of laws, at least in their geographical diversity, is as old as the science of law itself. Aristotle (384–322 B.C.), in considering what form of political community would be best, studied 153 constitutions of Greek and

---

[1] For more details, *cf.* especially the first part of David (R.), *Traité élémentaire de droit civil comparé* (1950). *Adde* Gutteridge (H. C.), *Comparative Law* (2nd ed., 1949).

[2] See Hug (W.), The History of Comparative Law," 45 Harv. L. Rev., 1027–1070 (1932), and Pound (R.), *Comparative Law in the Formation of the American Common Law* in *Acta Academiae Universalis Jurisprudentiae* (1928); Sarfatti (M.), *Les premiers pas du droit comparé* in *Mélanges Maury*, II, p. 237 (1960). Ancel (M.), *Utilité et méthodes du droit comparé* (1971).

1

other cities in his treatise, *Politics*; Solon (*c.* 640–558 B.C.), when
drafting the Athenian laws, we are told, proceeded on the same
basis; the decemvirs appointed in 451–450 B.C. to draw up the law
of the XII Tables for Rome are also supposed to have carried out
comparative law enquiries in the Greek cities. In the Middle Ages,
Canon law and Roman law were compared, and in sixteenth-
century England the respective merits of the Canon law and the
Common law were debated. The comparison of customary laws in
continental Europe was the basis of the formulation of the principles of a "common customary private law" (*droit commun coutumier* in France; *Deutsches Privatrecht* in Germany). Montesquieu
(1689–1755) attempted, through comparison, to penetrate the
spirit of laws and thereby establish common principles of good
government.

Many historical precedents can therefore be invoked. But the
development of comparative law, as a science, is rather more
recent. Only in the last century was its importance recognised, its
method and aims systematically studied, and the term itself *comparative law (droit comparé)* received and established in usage.

The reasons for this late development of comparative law as an
independent science are not difficult to identify. For many previous centuries, the science of law was devoted to discovering the
principles of just law, that is to say law conforming to the will of
God, to nature and to reason, and there was little concern for positive law or the law as it applied in fact. Local or customary law was
of importance to practitioners and the legislative measures of ruling sovereigns were of interest to governments of other countries,
but neither was of any real significance to those who as thinkers in
the universities meditated upon and wrote about law. Positive law
in either form was neglected in the universities. There the principal study, one thought more noble and more suitable to true legal
training, was the search for just rules that would be applicable in
all countries. This search, which was to reveal the true science of
law, was best carried out in the study not of the various national or
local laws but rather in that of Roman law and Canon law, the only
laws common to the whole of the civilised (*i.e.* Christian) world.

It was, then, only in the latter part of the nineteenth century that
the desirability and later the necessity of comparing national European laws emerged, little by little. This development occurred
after the breakdown of the notion of a *ius commune* or law of

universal application, which was brought about by the nationalism engendered by the adoption of national codifications and the implantation of these national laws as the proper subject-matter of legal studies in the universities. In France especially, after the Napoleonic codification, it was thought that the new codes had given final expression to law in terms having universal value. Other nations had only to follow the model provided them; those who adopted the codes could find the answer to any problem by means of their simple exegesis. Legal writing, in prevailing thought, was typified by the famous quip of the French jurist Beugnet—"Gentlemen, I do not teach the civil law; I only teach the Napoleonic Code."[3] There was no place for comparative law.

The development, in the second half of the century, of comparative law, as such, was the logically inevitable aftermath of this nationalisation of the idea of law which had ascendancy in the first part of the nineteenth century. It was, moreover, rendered necessary, and even urgent, by the unprecedented expansion in more modern times of international relations and contacts of all kinds.

3. Beginnings of comparative law—its importance now

Comparative law has developed enormously since the beginning of the twentieth century. Not much more than 35 or 40 years ago it was seen as a rarefied field for dilettantes; today comparative law studies are admitted to be a necessary part of any legal culture and training.

The beginning of comparative law in the nineteenth century was, naturally enough, taken up with discussions attempting to define its aims and nature, to establish its place among the sciences, to characterise its methods, possible applications and general usefulness. Was it an autonomous *body* of legal knowledge or simply a *method*—the "comparative method"—applied to established legal science? Was it a field distinct from comparative legal history, general legal theory and the sociology of law? In what precise areas of law would comparison be especially useful and what laws could properly, and with profit, be compared? What dangers were there in comparative law studies? Discussions of this sort constituted the basis of the first published works on the sub-

---

[3] "Messieurs, je n'enseigne pas le droit civil; je ne connais que le code Napoléon!"

ject which appeared in various countries, and they were items on the agenda of the first International Congress of Comparative Law held in Paris in 1900.[4] A belated echo of them is even to be found in more recent publications.

It was, of course, only natural that such questions preoccupy those first confronted with the phenomenon "comparative law." What teaching orientation it should have and what direction research under this new classification should take were important matters to clarify. But now that comparative law is firmly established, these early discussions have lost a good deal of interest and need not delay us. Today, two important challenges do however remain: first, the general utility of comparative law must be underscored, be it only to convince those who remain sceptical; and secondly, means must be found to assist those who want to use comparative law for their own several purposes.

The present usefulness of comparative law can be analysed under three heads: it is relevant in historical and philosophical legal research; it is important in order to understand better, and therefore to improve, one's own national law; and it assists in the promotion of the understanding of foreign peoples, and thereby contributes to the creation of a context favourable to the development of international relations.

4. Legal history, legal philosophy, general legal theory

1. It was in relation to legal history, the philosophy of law and general legal theory, that comparative law was first recognised, in the nineteenth century, as having importance. Following upon Montesquieu (1689–1755), who has been called (not without some exaggeration) the father of comparative law, it became fashionable in the nineteenth century in the light of Darwinian theory and ideas of progress then current, to trace vast historico-philosophical tableaux of the evolution of law. The legal systems of various peoples were studied in order to demonstrate, in an historical perspective, the progress of humanity. Primitive tribal custom was cited as evidence of the origin of law and contrasted to the laws of peoples of more advanced civilisations. Sir Henry Maine

---

[4] *Congrès international du droit comparé.* Procès-verbaux des séances et documents (1905–1907). Only jurists of continental Europe participated. One Englishman, Sir Frederick Pollock (1845–1937), represented the world of the English legal tradition.

(1822–1888) in England and Josef Kohler (1849–1919) in Germany were prestigious examples of scholars in this tradition,[5] and it was in this spirit that the first chair in France in "comparative legislation" was established in the Collège de France in 1831. Oxford's chair in "historical and comparative jurisprudence" was first taken up in 1869. Comparative law was thus recognised as a factor in legal education.[6]

While this type of generalisation is no longer pursued today, the potential contribution of comparative law to studies in legal history and philosophy is still very considerable. So long as the necessary precautions are observed, the study of primitive tribal law can assist in the search for the origins of the idea of law, or in order to provide a better understanding of certain institutions and rules of ancient law. Early Roman law, early Germanic law and feudal law have been clarified in many respects through the use of comparative law.

Turning to legal philosophy, comparative law is useful in pointing out the variations which exist in the very concept of law itself. It introduces us to societies where the western notion of law is altogether unknown, or where law is synonymous with force and sometimes even the symbol of injustice, or again where law is intimately linked to religion and takes on its sacred character. A history of the philosophy of law could undoubtedly be limited to a description of the nature and role of law in some defined part of humanity. But since philosophy itself is a science of general ideas, it need hardly be emphasised how narrow and barren a philosophy of law would be which merely took one national law or a series of related national laws into account. Comparative law manifestly has a crucial role to play in the development of legal philosophy.

Jurisprudence or general legal theory can also benefit from comparative studies. The historical origins of the classifications known to any system, the relative character of its concepts, the political and social conditioning of its institutions, all these are really understood only when the observer places himself outside his own legal system, that is to say when he adopts the perspective of comparative law. A person studying the French legal system, for

---

[5] Maine's *Ancient Law* was first published in 1861.
[6] The American Bar Association founded a section on International and Comparative Law in 1910.

example, may be tempted to attribute a necessary character to the distinctions, which within it seem so natural, between "public law" and "private law," "civil law" and "commercial law, "imperative" and "suppletive" legislation, "moveable" and "immoveable" property, etc. Comparative law shows that these notions are not known everywhere, or are in decline, or may even have been abandoned in legal systems claiming some relationship with French law itself. A renewed study of such "national" characteristics which goes beyond the question of their historical origins and examines their real significance and continued justification can thus be stimulated by a comparative law perspective. This last observation is no less true of the working legal concepts of any legal system, to which an inevitable character is often attributed. And such an attitude, in some countries, has led on occasion to the sacrifice of the real objectives of law in favour of the maintenance of a merely logical and internal conceptual coherence. Comparative law can contribute to the re-education of those having such views.

The same considerations apply to the sources and methods of a legal system. Codification and enacted law (*loi*) are exalted within the general theory of French law; they are held up as "progressive" modes for giving expression to legal rules in a democratic state. Judicial decisions and doctrinal writings, in this context, are seen as no more than means of applying, or commenting upon, the law. Comparative law shows this to be nothing other than a bias, an exaggeration, even a fiction, because it demonstrates that there are other countries no less democratic than France which reject codification and, as *un*democratic, any increase in the role of legislation. Comparative law also reveals, on the other side of the picture, that there are states which we would characterise as not truly democratic and, therefore, hypocritical, where these same forms of legal expression are used. The truth can be more clearly established through comparative reflections of this nature.

5. Understanding and improving national law

2. Comparative law is useful in gaining a better understanding of one's own national law and in the work of improving it.

Legislators have always made use of comparative law in the framing of legislation and in its practical improvement. It was not by accident that "comparative legislation" (*législation comparée*) took hold in the last century. The concern of those who founded the Societé de législation comparée in France in 1869, the English Society of Comparative Legislation in 1895 and the chairs of comparative legislation in various universities, was to study the many new codes adopted throughout the world in order to see whether suggestions for the improvement of national legislation might be forthcoming. In fact similar circumstances created similar needs and attitudes, and legislative developments have followed very substantially similar paths in most European countries for the last hundred years. In commercial law, criminal law, labour law, the law of social security, and even in family law, procedure and administrative law, there has been, in a very concrete way, a true concordance of legislative development and not merely a generally similar tendency. In periods of 20, 10 or even fewer years, a reform carried through and found beneficial in one country is introduced elsewhere, with such modifications as may be found necessary because of local conditions or other special considerations which ensure its smooth integration into the legal system of the new country. The English cheque, the German limited liability company, the Swedish matrimonial property regime of participation in acquests, the suspended sentence originating in the Belgian *sursis* in criminal cases, are all examples of institutions that have been used as models in the development of legislation in other countries. And this use of comparative law will undoubtedly be increasingly frequent in the years ahead, as the feeling grows that law, through new legislation, is an instrument for transforming society rather than merely a means of maintaining order within it. Any issue of one of the many comparative law reviews or quarterlies[7] will indicate the extent to which there is real interest in foreign legal development through the exchange of information, the reporting of events of one kind or another and critical writings, all of which act as a source of inspiration for ideas advanced in other countries.[8]

---

[7] *Cf.* below, Appendix I.

[8] The media manage to contribute to the current fashion of comparative law by reporting how the consumer is protected in Sweden, how the fight against pollution is carried on in the U.S.A., etc. Carbonnier (J.), "A beau mentir qui vient de loin, ou le mythe du législateur étranger," *Mélanges T. J. Dorhout Mees* (1974), pp. 61–66 (*Verzekeringen van vriendschap*); *Essais sur les lois* (1979), p. 191.

But the use of comparative law as a means of improving one's national law is open to courts and legal commentators as well as legislators. Legislation (*loi*) may well have a national character but law (*droit*) is never to be identified solely with legislation. The science of law is in its very nature transnational. Whatever is enacted, written or adjudged in one country of the same structure and tradition as our own can influence the way in which our own law is explained, interpreted or even renewed, quite apart from legislative interventions. Here, too, many examples can be cited. The phenomenon is especially evident in English-language countries where judicial decisions ("case law") are an essential ingredient of the law. The decisions of English courts, for example, have very great influence upon Canadian, Australian or New Zealand judges, and are freely cited; and, inversely, some decisions of the highest courts of the Commonwealth countries are cited in English courts with an authority almost equal to that they would enjoy had they been rendered in English courts. This is also true of decisions of the French Supreme Court (*Cour de cassation*) or the Council of State (*Conseil d'Etat*) which have been treated as weighty precedents in other countries in which French law is considered to be something of a model.

The use of comparative law may well be generally less in doctrinal writing and judicial decisions than it is in the framing of legislation. But jurists of any country can profit from a study of foreign legal thought and find, in the experience of others, useful material for the better serving of justice in their own countries. The further development of comparative law studies can only help in this work. It forms part moreover of that general scheme of things tending to promote better international understanding.

6. International understanding: international law

3. Comparative law is helpful in the understanding of foreign peoples; it thereby assists in the creation of a healthy context for the development of international relations. Today this third interest attaching to comparative law studies has, perhaps, become predominant.

First, as to public international law. Modern world conditions require that this part of the law be completely re-thought: over and above mere peaceful co-existence between nations, new forms of

co-operation must develop on technical matters and upon regional
and even world-wide scales.[9] It is clear that these relationships will
not be established, or develop as they should, if we remain ignorant of the laws in which different countries give expression to their
sense of justice and regulate, in the light of their respective political views, a variety of state structures.[10] In the sixteenth century,
Henry VIII created university chairs in Roman law with a view to
training diplomats to represent England in European countries
where the legal tradition was principally Romanist. Today diplomats of any nation and those negotiating trade agreements and
international conventions must, in the same way, be ready to
understand the outlook of others and know in what manner, and
with what arguments, they can hope to be persuasive. These persons will not really measure up to their task if, in their reasoning,
they are unable to appreciate the thinking of their foreign counterparts or if they speak and act as though they were dealing with persons from their own country. For example, in negotiations with the
United States or Canada, it is essential to know something of the
constitutional law of these countries so that one can appreciate, in
particular, the limitations under which their federal authorities
really operate. Again, in dealing with the Soviet Union, it is essential to understand that, living as he does in a society organised differently from any western nation, the Soviet representative will
have doubts and concerns and see questions and problems where a
westerner may have none at all. The same is all the more true of
dealings with representatives of far eastern countries who, with
their very different intellectual processes, contemplate law and
international relations in a manner very different from those in
western countries. Comparative law can also be a factor in promoting a better understanding between different countries within
regional schemes or communities of cooperation, as well as in certain federal states or the various political and economic groupings
established in Europe and on other continents.

One of the sources of public international law, mentioned in the
statute of the Permanent Court of International Justice, is stated
to be "general principles of law recognized by civilized nations"—

[9] Friedmann (W.), *The Changingr Structure of International Law* (1964).
[10] The constituent document of UNESCO advocates the study of foreign laws and the comparative law method on a world-wide scale with a view to promoting mutual understanding
(art. 3).

the interpretation of this provision can only be based in comparative law.[11]

7. Private international law

Comparative law is as important to the development of a coherent private international law as it is to public international law. Private international law today does lack coherence. It is made up, essentially, of "conflict rules" which in each state determine whether its courts are competent to hear a dispute with a foreign element and then to which national law the dispute will be subject. This approach would be satisfactory were all countries to adopt uniform rules for finding the answers. But conflicts of laws and conflicts of jurisdictions are, in reality, most often resolved in any given country without paying heed to any of the rules applying elsewhere. The result is that international relations are, in one country or another, subject to different systems and rules. Two unfortunate consequences flow from this present state of affairs: there is uncertainty about the result of litigation and conflicting solutions to the same problem may be established from one country to another.

A principal task of contemporary jurists is to end this anarchy. Since international relations are growing in number and importance every day, it is essential that the framework of these relations be put on a proper basis. Agreement must be reached so that one and the same international relation will everywhere be subject to the same rule in all national laws. States must promote and accept uniform rules in this domain. But while international conventions are the obvious means of doing so, the national courts of each country can help as well by taking into account the way in which the problem put to them is resolved by the legislation or courts of other countries.

8. International unification of law

It may well be easier, or in the long run more practical, to attempt to reach international agreement on the substantive legal rules applicable to such international relations, rather than to attempt to unify the national conflict rules. The international unifi-

---

[11] Art. 38 : 3. The Court was re-constituted in 1946 as the International Court of Justice.

cation of the law touching international legal relations is undoubtedly a major contemporary challenge.[12] There are those who, rooted in nineteenth-century thinking, decry such an ambition as pure fantasy. But it may be more fanciful to think that the present anarchy in international relations can be tolerated any longer in the modern world. It is not, after all, a matter of replacing any one national law with a uniform supra-national law enacted by some world-wide legislator; without going so far, some progress towards a gradual improvement of international relations can be made through a variety of other techniques such as international conventions and model contracts and clauses. A measure of international unification of law is required now and more will be necessary in the future. And the harmonisation[13] implied by international unification cannot be carried out without the help of comparative law. It is the means whereby the points of real agreement and disagreement between national laws can be revealed and the limits to any unification, geographical or otherwise, which have to be recognised, can be established. It is, moreover, the means whereby different technical approaches can be reconciled so that the efforts to bring about unification will be as successful as possible in present circumstances.

9. Role of comparatists

Comparative law is thus called upon to play an important part in the renewal of legal science and in the creation of a new international law, one capable of responding to modern world conditions. But underscoring the use of comparative law in this way does not go far enough. Comparatists can also assist jurists in their special fields of expertise. Comparative law is not reserved territory for a select few. Any person using a given national law must be made to understand that comparative law can help him to arrive at a better understanding of his own law, assist in its improvement,

---

[12] An International Institute for the Unification of Private Law (UNIDROIT) was set up in Rome in 1926 under the aegis of the League of Nations.

[13] While the goal of *unification* has remained in recent years in respect of new areas (such as the legal regulation of space, atomic activity and television) where there is no rooted tradition and the advantages of unification are obvious, and while it is still of interest in respect of some other subjects (such as Maritime Law where there has always been desire for uniformity), it has become rather more common recently to speak of the *harmonisation* of national laws: Zweigert (K.), *Europäische Zusammenarbeit im Rechtswesen* (1955).

and that it opens the door to working with those in other countries in establishing uniform conflict or substantive rules or at least their harmonisation. For most, no doubt, comparative law will really be a method—"the comparative method"—employed to assist them in achieving their own particular objectives. For others, however, when their principal concern is the study of foreign laws and the comparison with their own national law, it will have the status of a *science*, an autonomous branch of legal knowledge. In other words, alongside those who, in their own fields, may make use of comparative law, there is need for a category of jurists who can properly be termed "comparatists." Their principal task is to prepare the ground, so to speak, in order that others can, with profit, adopt the comparative method in their specific fields.

The comparison of different laws is, in effect, sometimes difficult. One must be aware of certain dangers, particularly of language and vocabulary,[14] and of a number of rules of simple prudence that it is wise to observe. For some time this aspect of comparative law was not very obvious, even to those in the field, because the range of laws in which the work was first carried on was very limited. No special preparatory training in comparative law was necessary so long as one was dealing only with laws of the same "family," those of the same general tradition and with the same structure and methods and operating in generally similar social and economic contexts. It is not necessary to be a comparatist to *understand* other laws in the same tradition.

But today's world is not that of yesterday. We are, more and more, in contact with persons who have been trained in traditions wholly different from those in the West. They reason according to methods and use concepts quite different from our own. Their view of the world and their concept of law are not ours. There is, therefore, a need for comparatists who, in order to maximise the usefulness of such encounters, will draw attention to the difficulties and dangers which lawyers everywhere are likely to encounter in such exchanges, and the manner in which spokesmen from different countries can best understand their foreign counterparts and be understood by them. The realisation that there is such a

---

[14] As Professor Otto Kahn-Freund said in his inaugural address when assuming the chair in Comparative Law at Oxford (May 12, 1965), one must learn not to be lured by homonyms and not to be afraid of synonyms, (1966) 82 L.Q.R. 40 at p. 59.

need explains, in large part, the significant world-wide modern development of comparative law courses and university institutes devoted to study and research in comparative law.[15]

10. Comparative law and sociology of law

Some have considered comparative law as no more than an aspect of the sociology of law. While not adopting this view here, it must be recognised that there are between them many points of contact and some common ground. Both seek to identify the extent to which law determines man's behaviour and the place law has in the social order.

Those living in societies where law is highly esteemed and regarded as a suitable instrument to regulate the most varied aspects of social relations are inclined to think that this is so in all countries, or at least in those having attained comparable development. We are also prone to think that only positive law is a reality—we forget that duality which existed for centuries between law as taught in the universities and legal rules as applied by the courts.

When considering a foreign law, we must however bear in mind that the manner in which such law is presented in its formal sources is not necessarily the only factor conditioning social relations in that country. Some consideration which with us is only of secondary importance may, in another country, be a factor of much greater importance; conversely, legal rules and procedures we consider essential may elsewhere play a role so minor as to be negligible, their place being taken by other non-legal factors. For example, the rules of *giri* in Japanese law, the *Fomba* in Malagasy, the arbitral function of some religious or community group, the fear of public opinion, or the control of a political party, all these may make of the law itself nothing more than a façade from which real social life is more or less divorced. This may well occur even in countries where law is held in high esteem but nonetheless seen as an ideal that is, in actual practice, unattainable; such is the case in many countries where Muslim law applies. And the same pheno-

---

[15] Rabel (E.), "On Institutes for Comparative Law" 47 Colum. L. Rev. 227 (1947). *Cf.* on the subject of the teaching methods in comparative law, Garner (J. F.), "The Use of the Comparative Method in University Courses in Law" (1970–1971) J.S.P.T.L. 134; von Mehren (A.), "An Academic Tradition for Comparative Law?" (1971) Am. J. Comp. L. 624; Sereni (A. P.), "On Teaching Comparative Law" 64 Harv. L. Rev. 770 (1951). Neville Brown (L.), "A Century of Comparative Law in England: 1869–1969" 19 Am. J. Comp. L. 232 (1971).

menon can be observed, in contrary fashion, in countries where law is downgraded; such is the case in countries of the Far East where good citizenship means settling disputes through conciliation rather than having recourse to law and court action, which are shameful. Even in the West it is of course clear that law alone does not reflect the full reality of social life—not all misdemeanours are prosecuted, not all taxes owing are collected, and not all judgments are put into execution. Many administrative, commercial or professional practices and religious, political and social factors influence individual behaviour. Law, taken alone and considered only in its strict theory, would give a false view of the way in which social relations, and the place therein of law, really operate.

11. Sources of law

Turning now to the formal sources of law—legislation, custom, judicial decisions, doctrinal writings, equity—a very different role is assigned to each in different legal systems. A first thing to realise when taking up the study of foreign law is that our own notions about the relationship of these different sources are not always those received elsewhere, and that therefore our reasoning methods for determining the applicable rule may not be the same. Law in one country for example may well have a religious or sacred character, and the legislator is thus denied the right to change it. Some other may view law as no more than a model, with respect to which custom is a natural derogation. Elsewhere judicial decisions can enjoy an authority going well beyond the range of persons who were impleaded at trial. Certain general principles of justice may, in other countries, be invoked to correct the application of the strictly formal rules of law, and so on.

Such general notions of any legal system must be known. One must also be aware that on such matters as the sources of law and rules of interpretation, the explanations furnished by general legal theorists do not always reflect the true nature of things. Formal doctrine in France, for example, holds to the tradition that judicial decisions (*la jurisprudence*) are not a source of law; it is nonetheless true that the decisions of the *Cour de cassation* or the *Conseil d'Etat* can have, in some circumstances, an authority in fact hardly less than that attributed to legislation. In England, one may say even today that legislation has something of an "exceptional" character about it because the legal system is cast primarily in a judicial mode of thought: and yet in England statutes are no less numerous than in France, and their authority is, in reality, no less than that attaching to French enacted law. English statutes are moreover, in many instances, no longer so literally or so restrictively interpreted as the classic canons of statutory construction would have it. It remains true to say however that English lawyers, unlike their French counterparts, are not at ease in the presence of legislative enactment that has not yet been the object of judicial interpretation. Islamic doctrine, as a final example, denies the authority of the legislator to change the legal rules which form the sacred core of Muslim law. But this prohibition does not rule out the possibility that the sovereign authority is able to put some legal rule into check or subordinate its application to a variety of conditions, without, for all of that, violating orthodox doctrine.

12. Structure of law

This last observation respecting the sources of law suggests a further range of differences between legal systems which must be underscored. Each system has concepts through which its rules are expressed and categories within which they are organised. And the legal rule itself in each of them is expressed in a particular way. The study of any legal system supposes that there is an awareness of such structural differences.

The balancing of opposing interests, and the organisation of justice which the law seeks to bring about, can be achieved in different ways. The protection of private persons against arbitrary governmental or administrative action can, for example, be confided to the courts in some countries and in others to internal administrative mechanisms, parliamentary commissions, or mediators. Rules of evidence, in one country, fulfil the function devolving to rules of form in some other country. The condition of the surviving spouse may be defined as a consequence of the matrimonial property regime in one law and elsewhere as part of the law of inheritance. Incapable persons may be protected by a system involving a representative of the incapable or by the technique of the trust. Sentencing may be a function of the judge or of penitentiary authorities.

The comparatist must call attention to these different ways of seeing things and point out the need to envisage, first and foremost, the *problem* that is to be studied in the light of the foreign system rather than the scope of any of the particular concepts. One must therefore be wary of questionnaires, a simplistic method of comparative law analysis. Even the most "exact" answer in response to a questionnaire may give an entirely false view of any given law to the person making use of it, unless of course he takes all those factors and rules not covered by the questionnaire into account as part of the total and more complex reality.

The absence of an exact correspondence between legal concepts and categories in different legal systems is one of the greatest difficulties encountered in comparative legal analysis. It is of course to be expected that one will meet rules with different content; but it may be disconcerting to discover that in some foreign law there is not even that system for classifying the rules with which we are familiar. But the reality must be faced that legal science has developed independently within each legal family, and that those categories and concepts which appear so elementary, so much a part of the natural order of things, to a jurist of one family may be wholly strange to another. This is true even as between those trained in a continental law and the Common law, without going so far as to invoke Muslim law. Some matter of primary importance to one may mean nothing, or have only limited significance, to another. A question put by a European jurist, for example, to an African on a matter of family organisation or land law may well be totally incomprehensible if it put to him in terms of European institutions.

It falls therefore to comparatists, by way of general studies of foreign social and legal structures, to create the conditions necessary for fruitful dialogue. It behoves them to explain the mentality, the thought processes and the concepts which shape a foreign legal system, and to establish, in the largest sense, "dictionaries" of legal science, so that those who do not, as it were, speak the same language can in the end come to understand one another.

13. Conclusion

Comparative law has a primary role to play in the science of law. It can enlighten the understanding of the place and significance of law by drawing upon the experience of all nations. At a more practical level, it can contribute to the better organisation of international relations by showing where agreement is within reach and by suggesting modes of international co-operation. Finally, with respect to national or internal law, it broadens the perspective of those seeking ways to bring about its improvement by inviting them to consider new ideas.

But for comparative law to fulfil the role that falls to it, jurists everywhere must abandon the practice of concentrating solely on the study of their own national law and, where appropriate, must adopt the comparative method. Each, in his field, will undoubtedly benefit by such a change in approach. Much, it is true, remains to be done to bring about such an enlargement of attitude. The practical value of comparative law has only recently been recognised; comparative studies endeavouring to widen horizons and to rekindle a sense of universalism are still imperfect. Many today, even though recognising the value of comparative law, are loath to take up the comparative method because they have not had any initiation to the study of foreign law. The new generation is now receiving this training in many countries; it is, indeed, more aware of contemporary world realities, more sensible to the need for the co-existence of nations, and more unwilling to accept that legal science be down-graded—as Jhering (1818–1892) once deplored[16]—to the level of a merely local or provincial jurisprudence. It is of course normal that legal practitioners, in their daily work, should limit their outlook to their own national law and its political boundaries. But there is, on the other hand, no true science of law unless it aspires to be universal in scope and in spirit. Comparative law is only one element in this new universalism so important today, but it has and will continue to have in time to come a primary part to play in the progress of law.

Section II—The Idea of a Family of Laws

14. Diversity of contemporary laws

Each political society in the world has its own law, and it often happens that several laws co-exist within the same state. Thus, in

---

[16] *Geist des romanischen Rechts*, pp. 12, 14 *et seq.*

addition to a federal law there may be laws of states, provinces or districts as in the United States, Canada or Switzerland. There are moreover laws of communities that have no political organisation at all, such as Canon law, Muslim law, Hindu law and Jewish law. There is as well international law which attempts to govern relations between states and international commerce on a world-wide or regional scale.

The purpose of this book is to supply a guide for a first examination of these many laws for those who, whatever their reason, wish to be introduced to a particular foreign law. The very diversity of laws poses a problem which at first sight may appear insurmountable; since the laws of the world are expressed in many different languages and forms, and since they have evolved in societies where the social organisation, beliefs and social manners are so very different, how can they be satisfactorily presented in a work of this limited scope? There is a factor which simplifies the task. In law, as in other sciences, one can detect the existence of a limited number of types or categories within which this diversity can be organised. Just as the theologian or political scientist recognises types of religions or governmental regimes, so too the comparatist can classify laws by reducing them to a limited number of *families*. Without therefore attempting to explain the detail of each individual law, our objective can be carried out by limiting the discussion to those general characteristics of the several legal families to which, in the end, all contemporary laws belong. The idea of a family of laws and the definition of contemporary legal families in the world today must therefore be explained.

15. Variable and constant elements in law

The diversity of laws in the modern world is a fact. But what is the real significance of this phenomenon and how is it revealed?

The general legal practitioner whose sphere of operation is limited to his own national law will undoubtedly answer by saying that different *rules* are laid down and applied in various countries; the diversity is clearly visible because rules of law do in fact differ: Swiss law and Soviet law differ because the age of majority is established at 20 years in one country and 18 years in the other; one law admits divorce and another does not, and so on. But the diversity of laws does not really reside in the fact that different national laws may on a variety of topics have different rules of this kind. It is a superficial and indeed false view to see law as being only composed of the totality of such rules. The law of any country will, of course, be concretely manifested at any given time by means of just such a series of rules—the juridical phenomenon which they represent is, however, far more complex. Each law in fact constitutes a *system*: it has a vocabulary used to express concepts, its rules are arranged into categories, it has techniques for expressing rules and interpreting them, it is linked to a view of the social order itself which determines the way in which the law is applied and shapes the very function of law in that society.

"Three words from the legislator and entire libraries can go to the pulp mill," said a German author of the mid-nineteenth century.[17] The thought behind this quip is however incorrect. With the possible exception of revolutionary upheavals, there are features of the law which can only be changed at the slow rhythm at which the civilisation of the country itself, the sense of justice of its citizens, its economic structure, language and social manners themselves are changed. It is true that the legal practitioner must be wary of legal treatises and works which are out of date because the particular legal rules themselves may have changed. But the teaching of law is only possible because the law is constituted by something more than these changing rules. What is asked, or should be asked, of the law student is not that he learn, by heart, and in all their detail, all the rules in force during his time as student: that will be of little service to him in his later professional life when many of those rules will have changed. Of far greater importance to the student will be a knowledge of the structure within which the rules and concepts are organised, the meaning of these categories and concepts, and the relationship of the rules among themselves. The legislators may, indeed, with a stroke of the pen modify the actual legal rules, but these other elements and features nonetheless subsist. They cannot be so arbitrarily changed because they are intimately linked to our civilisation and ways of thinking. The legislators can have no more effect on them than upon our language or our reasoning processes.

Despite changes in the rules as they exist at any moment, then, there is a continuity in the law which draws upon a range of

---

[17] Kirchmann (J.), *Die Wertlosigkeit der Jurisprudenz als Wissenschaft* (ed. 1936), p. 25.

elements subjacent to those rules. The work of the American Roscoe Pound (1870–1964) has made this especially clear.[18] The sense of historical continuity which these elements engender enables us therefore to consider law as a science and makes possible the teaching of law.

16. Criterion for the classification of laws into families

When endeavouring to determine the families into which different laws can be grouped, it is preferable to take into consideration these constant and more fundamental elements rather than the less stable rules found in the law at any given moment. There is agreement among comparatists on this point. The classification of laws into families should not be made on the basis of the similarity or dissimilarity of any particular legal rules, important as they may be; this contingent factor is, in effect, inappropriate when highlighting what is truly significant in the characteristics of a given system of law.

These characteristics can be identified by examining those fundamental elements of the system through which the rules to be applied are themselves discovered, interpreted and evaluated. While the rules may be infinitely various, the techniques of their enunciation, the way in which they are classified, the methods of reasoning in their interpretation are, on the contrary, limited to a number of types. It is therefore possible to group laws into "families" and to compare and contrast them when they adopt or reject common principles as to substance, technique or form.

This grouping of laws into families, thereby establishing a limited number of types, simplifies the presentation and facilitates an understanding of the world's contemporary laws. There is not, however, agreement as to which element should be considered in setting up these groups and, therefore, what different families should be recognised. Some writers base their classification on the law's conceptual structure or on the theory of sources of the law; others are of the view that these are technical differences of secondary importance, and emphasise as a more significant criterion either the social objectives to be achieved with the help of the legal system or the place of law itself within the social order.

---

[18] See in particular *An Introduction to the Philosophy of Law* (1922).

To establish the existence of legal families, it is certainly possible to select only one or the other of these two criteria. The two considerations seem equally decisive for the purposes of classification. From the technical standpoint, it is advisable to ask whether someone educated in the study and practice of one law will then be capable, without much difficulty, of handling another. If not, it may be concluded that the two laws do not belong to the same family; this may be so because of differences in the vocabularies of the two laws (they do not express the same concepts), or because the hierarchy of sources and the methods of each law differ to a considerable degree. This first criterion, no matter how essential, is nevertheless insufficient, and it should be complemented by the second consideration. Two laws cannot be considered as belonging to the same family, even though they employ the same concepts and techniques, if they are founded on opposed philosophical, political or economic principles, and if they seek to achieve two entirely different types of society. The two criteria must be used cumulatively, not separately.

Neither of them, to be sure, is very clear-cut. A minor difficulty for one person might be a major problem for another; the average jurist, to whom we are bound to refer, is only an abstraction. It is, moreover, often a matter of opinion whether the idea of the world and society (*Weltanschauung*) which dominates each law is sufficiently different to justify their classification into two distinct families. One cannot aspire to mathematical exactitude in the social sciences. But it should be noted in passing that the comparatist must, of necessity, place himself on a sufficiently high plane in order to make some classification.

These discussions, however, if pushed too far, do not make very much sense in the end. The idea of a "legal family" does not correspond to a biological reality: it is no more than a didactic device. We are attempting no more than to underscore the similarities and differences of the various legal systems—and, in that light, almost any systematic classification would serve the purpose. The matter turns upon the context in which one is placed and the aim in mind. The suitability of any classification will depend upon whether the perspective is world-wide or regional, or whether attention is given to public, private or criminal law. Each approach can undoubtedly be justified from the point of view of the person proposing it and none can, in the end, be recognised as exclusive.

SECTION III—LEGAL FAMILIES IN THE WORLD TODAY

17. Outline

What, then, are the major contemporary legal families found in the world today?

There would appear to be three at least which occupy an uncontested place of prominence: the Romano-Germanic family, the Common law family and the family of Socialist law. These three groups, whatever their merits and whatever their extension throughout the world, do not however take into account all contemporary legal phenomena. There are other systems, situated outside these three traditions or sharing only part of their conception of things, which prevail in a large number of contemporary societies and in their regard too a number of observations will be made.

18. Romano-Germanic family

A first family may be called the Romano-Germanic family. This group includes those countries in which legal science has developed on the basis of Roman *ius civile*. Here the rules of law are conceived as rules of conduct intimately linked to ideas of justice and morality. To ascertain and formulate these rules falls principally to legal scholars who, absorbed by this task of enunciating the "doctrine" on an aspect of the law, are somewhat less interested in its actual administration and practical application—these matters are the responsibility of the administration and legal practitioners. Another feature of this family is that the law has evolved, primarily for historical reasons, as an essentially *private* law, as a means of regulating the private relationships between individual citizens; other branches of law were developed later, but less perfectly, according to the principles of the "civil law" which today still remains the main branch of legal science. Since the nineteenth century, a distinctive feature of the family has been the fact that its various member countries have attached special importance to enacted legislation in the form of "codes."

The Romano-Germanic family of laws originated in Europe. It was formed by the scholarly efforts of the European universities which, from the twelfth century and on the basis of the compilations of the Emperor Justinian (A.D. 483–565), evolved and developed a juridical science common to all and adapted to the conditions of the modern world. The term *Romano-Germanic* is selected to acknowledge the joint effort of the universities of both Latin and Germanic countries.[19]

Through colonisation by European nations, the Romano-Germanic family has conquered vast territories where the legal systems either belong or are related to this family. The phenomenon of voluntary "reception" has produced the same result in other countries which were not colonised, but where the need for modernisation, or the desire to westernise, has led to the penetration of European ideas.

Outside Europe, its place of origin, these laws although retaining membership in the Romano-Germanic family nonetheless have their own characteristics which, from a sociological point of view, make it necessary to place them in distinct groups. In many of these countries it has been possible to "receive" European laws, even though they possessed their own civilisations, had their own ways of thinking and acting and their own indigenous institutions, all of which ante-date such reception. Sometimes the reception has left some of these original institutions in place; this is particularly clear in the case of Muslim countries where the reception of European law and the adhesion to the Romano-Germanic family have been only partial, leaving some legal relations subject to the principles of the traditional, local law. The old ways of thinking and acting peculiar to these countries may also mean that the application of the new law is quite different from what it is in Europe. This question is particularly important in the case of the countries of the Far East, where an ancient and rich civilisation existed long before the reception of western law.

Finally, with respect to the countries of Africa and America, it will also be necessary to ask whether their geographical conditions

---

[19] The term "Romanist laws" (*droits romanistes*) also employed upon occasion, *brevitatis cause*, is useful, but obscures the fundamental role played by medieval scholarship in the system's formation; it also hides the fact that the present content of the legal rules in this family is quite different from what it was in those of Roman law. The term *civil law*, used in the English-speaking world to indicate that these laws derive, by origin, from Roman law itself, and in particular the *Corpus Iuris Civilis*, raises the same objection; and the fact that the words *civil law* (as a translation of *ius civile*) are also used in other contexts is a further reason for not employing them here. The expression *continental law* (*droit continental*), formerly frequent in England, has lost its value since Europe is no longer the only area of importance in the world where this sytem prevails.

and population distribution, creating conditions entirely different from those in Europe, have not led to the development of laws substantially different from their European models.

19. Common law family

A second family is that of the Common law, including the law of England and those laws modelled on English law. The Common law, altogether different in its characteristics from the Romano-Germanic family, was formed primarily by judges who had to resolve specific disputes. Today it still bears striking traces of its origins. The Common law legal rule is one which seeks to provide the solution to a trial rather than to formulate a general rule of conduct for the future. It is, then, much less abstract than the characteristic legal rule of the Romano-Germanic family. Matters relating to the administration of justice, procedure, evidence and execution of judgments have, for Common law lawyers, an importance equal, or even superior, to substantive legal rules because, historically, their immediate preoccupation has been to re-establish peace rather than articulate a moral basis for the social order. Finally, the origins of the Common law are linked to royal power. It was developed as a system in those cases where the peace of the English kingdom was threatened, or when some other important consideration required, or justified, the intervention of royal power. It seems, essentially, to be a *public* law, for contestations between private individuals did not fall within the purview of the Common law courts save to the extent that they involved the interest of the crown or kingdom. In the formation and development of the Common law—a public law issuing from procedure— the learning of the Romanists founded on the *ius civile* played only a very minor role. The divisions of the Common law, its concepts and vocabulary, and the methods of the Common law lawyer, are entirely different from those of the Romano-Germanic family.

And as with the Romano-Germanic family, so too the Common law has experienced a considerable expansion throughout the world—and for the same reasons: colonisation or reception. The observations made with respect to the Romano-Germanic family apply with equal value. But here again a distinction between the Common law in Europe (England and Ireland) and that outside Europe must be made. In certain extra-European countries, the

Common law may have been only partially received as in the case, for example, of certain Muslim countries or India; and where it was received, attention must be given to its transformation or adaption by reason of its co-existence with the tradition of previous civilisations. A different environment has, in any event, created differences between the Common law of the countries where it originated and that of those into which it was imported. This observation is particularly true with respect to the Common law family because it groups some countries such as the United States and Canada where a civilisation different in many respects from that of England has developed. The laws of these countries enjoy a largely autonomous place within the family.

20. Relations between these two families

Over the centuries there have been numerous contacts between countries of the Romano-Germanic family and those of the Common law, and the two families have tended, particularly in recent years, to draw closer together. In both, the law has undergone the influence of Christian morality and, since the Renaissance, philosophical teachings have given prominence to individualism, liberalism and personal rights. Henceforth, at least for certain purposes, this reconciliation enables us to speak of one great family of *western* law.[20] The Common law retains, to be sure, its own particular structure, very different from that of the Romano-Germanic system, but the methods employed in each are not wholly dissimilar; above all, the formulation of the legal rule tends more and more to be conceived in Common law countries as it is in the countries of the Romano-Germanic family. As to the substance of the law, a shared vision of justice has often produced very similar answers to common problems in both sets of countries.

The inclination to speak of a family of western law is all the stronger when one considers that the laws of some states cannot be annexed to either family, because they embody both Romano-Germanic and Common law elements. The laws of Scotland, Israel, the Union of South Africa, the Province of Quebec and the

---

[20] David (R.), "Existe-t-il un droit occidental?" in *Mélanges Hessel E. Yntema* (*Twentieth Century Comparative and Conflicts Law*), 1961.

Philippines would fall into this group.[21] And lastly, but from
another point of view, the Romano-Germanic and Common law
families are included in the same deliberately ignominious term of
"capitalist" or "bourgeois laws" by jurists of the socialist camp,
made up of the Soviet Union and those countries that have used its
law as a model or which, like the U.S.S.R., profess an adherence
to Marxist-Leninist teachings.

21. Family of socialist laws

The Socialist legal system makes up a third family, distinct from
the first two. To date, the members of the socialist camp are those
countries which formerly belonged to the Romano-Germanic
family, and they have preserved some of the characteristics of
Romano-Germanic law. Thus, the legal rule is still conceived in
the form of a general rule of conduct; and the divisions of law and
legal terminology have also remained, to a very large extent, the
product of the legal science constructed on the basis of Roman law
by European universities.

But apart from these points of similarity, there do exist such differences that it seems proper to consider the Socialist laws as
detached from the Romano-Germanic family—the socialist jurists
most decidedly do—and as constituting a distinct legal family, at
least at the present time. The originality of Socialist law is particularly evident because of its revolutionary nature; in opposition to
the somewhat static character of Romano-Germanic laws, the proclaimed ambition of socialist jurists is to overturn society and
create the conditions of a new social order in which the very concepts of state and law will disappear. The sole source of Socialist
rules of law resides therefore within the revolutionary work of the
legislature, which expresses popular will, narrowly guided by the
Communist Party. However, legal science as such is not principally
counted upon to create the new order; law, according to Marxism-
Leninism—a scientific truth—is strictly subordinate to the task of
creating a new economic structure. In execution of this teaching,
all means of production have been collectivised. As a result the

---

[21] Unfortunately, the laws of these "mixed jurisdictions" have not been dealt with in this
work. Certain relevant bibliographical information has however been included in Appendix I.
Adde Smith (T. B.), "The Preservation of the Civilian Tradition in Mixed Jurisdictions," in
Yiannopoulos (A. N.), *Civil Law in the Modern World* (1965), pp. 3–26.

field of possible private law relationships between citizens is extraordinarily limited compared to the pre-Marxist period; private law has lost its pre-eminence—all law has now become public law. This new concept removes from the very realm of law a whole series of rules which jurists of bourgeois countries would consider legal rules.

The family of Socialist laws originated in the Union of Soviet Socialist Republics where these ideas prevailed and a new law has developed since the 1917 Revolution. However, the laws of the socialist or people's republics of Europe and Asia must be classed as groups distinct from Soviet law. These laws belong to the Socialist family, but in those of the first group a greater persistence of characteristics properly Romano-Germanic is detected, while in those of the second it is useful to enquire how these new concepts are reconciled in practice with the principles of Far Eastern civilisation which governed such societies before the Socialist era.

22. Other systems

The three families just described, each of which has numerous variants, are undoubtedly the three principal families of law existing in the contemporary world. Strictly speaking there is no law in the world today which has not drawn certain of its elements from one or other of these families. Some even hold the view that all other systems, no more than survivors from the past, will ultimately disappear with the passing of time and the progress of civilisation.

This attitude however proceeds from a rather naïve sense of superiority and is really no more than an hypothesis. It does not acknowledge an observable reality in the modern world. All contemporary states have, it is true, taken over a number of western ideas either because it was necessary to preserve their independence or because it was useful in their internal development. It does not follow that the older ways of thinking which, not so very long ago, were widely accepted in these different societies have been totally abandoned. Everyone will recognise the superiority of western technology; opinions differ however on the superiority of western civilisation taken as a whole. The Muslim world, India, the Far East and Africa are far from having adhered to it without reservation. These countries remain very largely faithful to philosophies in which the place and function of law are very different from what they are in the West. A true picture of law in contemporary world society would be incomplete without taking these considerations into account.

In non-western societies the governing social principles to which reference is made are of two types. On the one hand law is fully recognised as being of great value but the law itself is framed in a different concept than it is in the West; on the other, the very notion of law is rejected, and social relations are governed by other extra-legal means. The first view is that of Muslim and Hindu societies, while the latter is that adopted in countries of the Far East and large parts of Africa and Malagasy.

23. Muslim, Hindu, and Jewish laws

The attitude of the Muslim, Hindu and Jewish communities about the law is easily understood by a western jurist, even though the definition of law itself in western jurisprudence has always given rise to difficulties and no single definition has so far elicited any general acceptance. One of the fundamental reasons for this lack of agreement is the debate between the proponents and adversaries of the notion of "natural law." But it is because the idea of "natural law" exists that we are able to understand the starting premise of these other systems.

In this debate, law is held by some to be no more than the body of rules that are *really* observed, the application of which is entrusted to the courts. This is the view today in our western universities in which our national laws are taught. But law may also be seen as a model of ideal behaviour, one not to be confused with the actual rules by which individuals act and which courts apply. European universities, in their pre-nineteenth-century tradition, paid very little attention to national or customary laws of the time and taught, almost exclusively, an ideal law constructed on the basis of Roman law. In Muslim countries, in the same way, more attention is given to the model law linked to the Islamic religion than to local custom (treated as a phenomenon of fact) or the laws and decrees of the sovereign (treated as merely administrative measures) and neither of these is thought to possess the full dignity of law. The same can be said of Jewish law and, in a very different context, Hindu law.

Law, then, whether linked to a religion or corresponding to a particular way of thinking about the social order, is not in either case always necessarily observed by private persons or applied by courts. It may nonetheless exert considerable influence on both—"righteous" men may endeavour to rule their own lives according to what they consider to be truly the law. A student of western societies may well, in a positivist perspective, concentrate attention upon the rules enacted by legislatures and applied by courts or, alternatively, in a sociological perspective, classify as law only those rules which are really observed as a matter of practice. This difference in approach is not a source of any real inconvenience, because in western societies there is a large degree of equivalence between justice, positive law and social manners. The same cannot however be said of non-western societies where "rules of law" (in the western sense) remain unorganised, fragmentary and unstable, and where there is a general feeling that true law is to be found elsewhere than in legislation, custom or judicial decisions. Without taking sides in the debate between positivists and advocates of natural, Muslim and Hindu laws, therefore, must be included within the major contemporary legal systems. Jewish law, despite its historical and philosophical interest, must be omitted because its sphere of influence is incomparably less than the other two.[22]

24. Far East

The situation in the Far East, especially China, is completely different. Here there is no question of studying an ideal law distinct from rules laid down by legislators or simply followed in practice; here the very value of law itself has traditionally been put into question.

In the West, and in Islamic and Hindu communities, law is held to be a necessary part of, indeed a basis for, society. Good social order implies the primacy of law: men must live according to law and, where necessary, be prepared to fight for the supremacy of law; administrative authorities, no less than any other part of

---

[22] Canon law, as such, has been omitted as well but for different reasons: unlike Muslim law, it has none of the features of a revealed law, nor does it purport to encompass all human relationships. It is essentially the public law of that society constituted by the Roman Catholic Church; "private law" matters affecting the Church are left by Canon law to the regulation of the national laws of individual states (*Ecclesia vivit sub lege romana*), although Canonists do formulate principles which, to satisfy Christian morality, secular laws in Christian states should put into effect and which the faithful should in any case observe.

society, must act legally; courts must ensure that law is respected. Law, a mirror of justice, is in this conception superior even to equity itself; outside the law, there can only be anarchy, or arbitrariness, chaos or, the rule of force. Law is therefore venerated, the courts are temples of justice, the judges its oracles.

Far Eastern countries reject this view. For the Chinese, law is an instrument of arbitrary action rather than the symbol of justice; it is a factor contributing to social disorder rather than to social order. The good citizen must not concern himself with law: he should live in a way which excludes any revendication of his rights or any recourse to the justice of courts. The conduct of individuals must, unfailingly, be animated by the search for harmony and peace through methods other than the law; man's first concern should not be to respect the law. Reconciliation is a greater value than justice; mediation must be used to remove conflicts rather than invoking law to resolve them. Laws may exist to serve as a method of intimidation or as a model; but law is not made with a view to being really applied, as in the West. Scorn is reserved for those who aspire to regulate matters according to law or whose preoccupation is its study or application, and who thereby defy convention and accepted proprieties.

Countries of the Far East have, traditionally, held the view that law is only for barbarians. The Chinese communist regime and the westernisation of Japan have not fundamentally changed this conception rooted as it is in their ancient civilisations. In China the communist regime rejected the legal codes drawn up after the fall of imperial rule along western lines and, after some brief hesitation, then repudiated the Soviet method of building communism. The techniques finally adopted for doing so have given up to the present time a very narrow place to law. Codes on the European model have been instituted in Japan but, generally speaking, the population makes little use of them; people abstain from using the courts and the courts themselves encourage litigants to resort to reconciliation; and new techniques have been developed for applying—or removing the need to apply—the law.

25. Black Africa and Malagasy Republic

The preceding observations regarding the Far East apply as well to the black African countries and the Malagasy Republic (Madagascar). There too, in milieux in which the community's cohesion prevails over any developed sense of individualism, the principal objective is the maintenance or restoration of harmony rather than respect for law. The western laws adopted in Africa are often hardly more than a veneer—the vast majority of the population still lives according to traditional ways which do not comprise what we in the West call law and without heed to what is very often nothing more than an artificially implanted body of rules.

PART ONE

THE ROMANO-GERMANIC FAMILY

26. Characteristics of this family

The first family of laws found in the world today is the Romano-Germanic.

The Romano-Germanic family has a long history. It is bound up with the law of ancient Rome, but an evolution of more than a thousand years has greatly changed its substantive and procedural rules, and also its very concept of law and of the rule of law since the time of Augustus (63 B.C.–A.D. 14) or Justinian (A.D. 483–565).[1] The laws of the Romano-Germanic family are the continuators of Roman law whose evolution they have perfected; they are in no sense a copy of it; indeed, many of their elements come from sources other than Roman law.

At the present time, the Romano-Germanic family is spread throughout the entire world. Far exceeding the boundaries of the ancient Roman Empire, it has in particular conquered the whole of Latin America, a large part of Africa, the countries of the Near East, Japan and Indonesia. Part of this expansion is owed to colonisation and part to the legal technique of *codification*, generally adopted by the Romanist laws of the nineteenth century, which has facilitated its reception.

The dispersion of the system, and the very technique of codification which tends to create a confusion between law (*le droit*) and enacted legislation (*la loi*), make it difficult to detect the element

---

[1] English law is, in many respects, closer to Roman law than the Romanist laws themselves are today, in the sense that it has duplicated, though quite autonomously, the same general evolution: the primary importance of the forms of action, the casuistic character of the legal rule and the suspicion of general formulae and systematisation. *Cf.* Buckland and McNair, *Roman Law and Common Law* (2nd ed., 1952); Thomas (J. A. C.), "Roman Law" in *An Introduction to Legal Systems* (1968), ed. by Derrett (J. D. M.); Peter (H.), *Römisches Recht und Englisches Recht* (1969). "English jurisprudence in all its ignorance of Roman law breathes nevertheless the air of ancient Roman law. There is the same manipulation .with form, the same pedantry, the same roundabout means and make-believe transactions; and neither is there any lack of fictions," Jhering observed (as quoted by Zweigert (K.) and Siehr (K.), *Jhering's Influence on the Development of Comparative Legal Method* 19 Am. J. Comp. L. 215 (1971).

linking what at first sight appear to be simply so many distinct national laws. The study of the Common law and the Socialist laws will nevertheless underscore even more vividly the unity which, despite appearances, really does exist among these many and varied laws.

As in other families, this unity does not therefore exclude a certain amount of diversity. To establish a degree of order within the family, it may thus be necessary to recognise secondary groupings—Latin, Germanic or Scandinavian laws, laws of Latin America, and so on. This question will have to be asked under each of the headings devoted to the Romano-Germanic family in which, successively, consideration will be given to the historical formation of the system, essential to an understanding of its present characteristics, to its structure and, lastly, to its system of sources and methods.

TITLE I

HISTORICAL FORMATION OF THE SYSTEM

27. Outline

The Romano-Germanic system of law was formed in continental Europe and is principally centred there today even though, because of the phenomena of expansion and reception, many non-European countries have adhered to it or borrowed certain of its elements.

The Romano-Germanic system as such appeared in the thirteenth century. Previously there undoubtedly existed some of the elements from which it was formed, but it is premature to speak of a system, or perhaps even of law, until that time. A period of incubation preceded the thirteenth century during which its elements accumulated, but any effort at synthesis and any idea of system were lacking. A second period begins with the renaissance of Roman law studies in the universities—an essential phenomenon, the significance and implications of which will be discussed. For five centuries the system was to be dominated by the writings of jurists under whose influence the practice of law was itself to evolve. In conjunction with the Natural Law School, these doctrinal authors prepared the ground for the following period—the present one—in which the system appears to be dominated by legislation. Finally, having studied its European development, a final chapter will be devoted to the expansion of the Romano-Germanic family beyond Europe to other continents.

CHAPTER I

CUSTOMARY LAW PERIOD

28. Reign of Roman law: its decline

Before the thirteenth century, what picture can be drawn of European law? The existing elements, from which the system was to be constituted, were essentially of a customary character at this time. The Roman Empire had created a brilliant civilisation and Roman genius had constructed a legal system without precedent. It is not necessary to describe here either the system or its history. If we place ourselves at the beginning of the thirteenth century, the Roman Empire had ceased to exist in the West for many centuries. The invasions of many peoples, especially Germanic tribes, had put an end to it in the fifth century. Subsequent to these invasions, the Romanised peoples on the one hand and the invaders on the other continued to live side by side, each according to their own laws, for some time. After the conversion of the Germanic peoples to Christianity, the populations drew together little by little in their ways of life; but this fusion took place very gradually, and only as territorial customs and nascent feudalism came to supplant the primitive principle of the personality of laws.

There do exist some documents which can be referred to for an idea of the state of Roman law or that of the so-called "barbarian laws." In the East, and to a certain extent in Italy, Roman law, in theory at least, is represented by the compilations of Justinian (*Code, Digest, Institutes*, published from 529 to 534 and completed by a series of *Novels*) and, in France and the Spanish Peninsula, by the *lex romana visigothorum* or *Breviary of Alaric* (promulgated in 506). Some barbarian laws, for the most part of Germanic tribes, had been drafted as of the sixth century; and for the laws of the different Slavic or Nordic tribes, the process continued until the twelfth century.[1]

These documents, however, give a very poor idea of the law as really applied in Europe in the twelfth century. The barbarian laws only regulated a part, and often a very small part, of the social relationships we now consider to be governed by law. On the other hand, the Roman compilations, even in the simplified version of Alaric, soon became too scholarly and complicated: it was a *scholars' law* and was modified and replaced by a *popular* or *vulgar law* spontaneously applied in fact by the people. No one bothered to reduce these laws to writing since their sphere of application was purely local.

However there were two compilations of interest: the *Edict of Theodoric* (500) in Italy, and the *Fuero Juzgo* in Spain (compiled in 654 and revised in 694 at the Eighth and Seventeenth Councils of Toledo). The principle of the personality of laws, while admitted in other countries, was rejected by the Ostrogoth chieftains of Italy and the Visigoths of Spain who tried to achieve a fusion of the laws applicable to their subjects of Germanic and Latin origin.[2] But these efforts failed in Italy as a result of the invasion of the Lombards (565) and in the Spanish Peninsula with the invasion of the Arabs (711). Apart from these efforts, the public authorities did nothing to attempt to reduce the existing law to written form; they restricted themselves to intervening on certain specific points, and in matters generally more related to public than private law (as, for example, the Frankish *capitularia*), and private initiative did not fill the hiatus.

Why, indeed, would such work be undertaken at that time? In the West, during the Dark Ages, there was no teaching of law; and, even for practical purposes, the knowledge of law was of little use. What we might call the law of the time was made up of rules which individuals of different regions observed, more or less spontaneously, in their personal relationships, but it is doubtful that

---

[1] The laws of the Germanic tribes, drafted mostly in Latin, were published in the collection *Monumenta Germaniae Historica* (1826–1909).

[2] In the East, where the Empire still existed, Justinian's compilations were, in the same way, neglected in favour of simpler and more accessible memorials of Roman law: the *Ecloga* of Leo the Isaurian (740) and the *Procheiron* of Basil the Macedonian (870). The efforts of Leo VI (the Wise, 866–912) to revive the law of Justinian in 900 by compiling the *Basilica* led only to a temporary renaissance, and as a matter of practice earlier or later works were employed. *Cf.* Svoronos (N.), *La "Synopsis major" des Basiliques et ses appendices* (1964).

these "rules of behavior" could even be characterised as rules of law. No social authority was desirous—or even capable—of enforcing respect for them; and for individuals finding a competent court would have been the first difficulty; proceedings were dominated by appeals to the supernatural and by a system of non-rational proof; the judicial execution of judgments was not assured. Why then study and refine the rules of law, when success for one party or another depended on such means as a judgment from God, the oath of the parties, wager of law (*compuragtion*) or trial by battle and ordeals (*ordalies*), or when it may further have turned merely upon the discretion of some local authority? What was the use of obtaining a judgment if authorities were not obliged, or prepared, to put the force at their command to the benefit of the successful litigant?

In the shadows of the Dark Ages, society had returned to a more primitive state. Some law might still exist—an indication that it did is furnished not only by the compilations just mentioned but also by the existence of a number of institutions designed to enunciate the law (Frankish *rachimbourgs*, Scandinavian *laghman*, Icelandic *eôsagari*, Irish *brehons*, Anglo-Saxon *withan*)—but the reign of law had ceased. Between individuals and between social groups, disputes were resolved by the law of physical force or by the discretionary authority of the leader.

Doubtlessly more important than law at this time was some form or technique of arbitration which sought not so much to give to each his due according to fixed and pre-established rules, but rather to maintain the solidarity of the group, assure peaceful coexistence between rival groups and restore peace in the community or society. Even the ideal of a society founded on the notion of the "rights" of individuals was largely abandoned; should not a Christian society seek to base itself more upon ideas of brotherly love and benevolence? Saint Paul (d. A.D. 67), in his *First Epistle to the Corinthians*, extolled love of one's fellow man instead of justice, and recommended that the faithful submit to the arbitration of their spiritual leaders or brothers, rather than resort to the tribunals of the pagans. Saint Augustine (354–430) defended the same ideas. In Germany, as late as the sixteenth century, it was said: *Juristen, böse Christen*—jurists are bad Christians; if it was applied above all to the Romanists, the adage nonetheless included all jurists: law itself was considered a bad thing.

29. Renaissance of the idea of law

The creation of the Romano-Germanic family of law is linked to the renaissance of the twelfth and thirteenth centuries in western Europe. This revival was evident in all spheres; one of its important aspects was in the realm of law. The new society, with the growth of cities and commerce, became conscious once again of the need for law to assure that order and security which would ensure social progress. The ideal of a Christian society founded on brotherly love was abandoned; the City of God was not to be created on earth. The Church itself admitted this by distinguishing more clearly between the religious society of the faithful and secular society, between external and internal conscience (*for externe* and *for interne*), and by drawing up at this time a private law of the Church, Canon law.[3] By the thirteenth century religion and morality were no longer confused with civil order and law; law was given a role of its own, an autonomy which has henceforth characterised western modes of thought ahd civilisation.

The idea that society must be ruled by law was not of course entirely new. It was admitted, in so far as private relationships were concerned, by the Romans. But in the twelfth century, the return to this notion was revolutionary. Philosophers and jurists demanded that social relations be based on law, and that the arbitrariness which had existed for centuries come to an end. They wanted a new law founded on justice which Reason could reveal; they rejected for private dealings appeals to the supernatural. The movement which occurred in the twelfth and thirteenth centuries was just as revolutionary as that of the eighteenth century which advocated the substitution of democracy for the rule of personal power, or that of the twentieth century which purported to substitute the Marxist formula of social organisation for the anarchy of the capitalist regime. Secular society must be founded on the law: and the law must permit the realisation of order and progress in that society. These ideas became governing principles in western Europe in the twelfth and thirteenth centuries and they have remained uncontested until the present time when Marxist theory put them again into question.

---

[3] Le Bras (G.), "Naissance et croissance du droit privé de l'Eglise" in *Mélanges Petot* (1959), pp. 329–345.

The germination of the Romano-Germanic system which took place in the twelfth and thirteenth centuries was in no way a result of the affirmation of a political power, nor the effect of centralisation brought about by a sovereign authority. The Romano-Germanic system thereby differs from English law where the development of the Common law was bound up with the progress of royal power and the existence of strongly centralised royal courts. Nothing similar is to be observed in continental Europe. On the contrary, the Romano-Germanic system took shape at a time when there was not only no European political unity but when even the very idea that it might, or should, be otherwise bordered on the fanciful: indeed, at the time, it was clear that the efforts of the Papacy or the Holy Roman Empire would not succeed in reconstituting the unity of the Roman Empire on a political basis. The Romano-Germanic system *was never founded on anything but a community of culture.* It came into being and continued to exist *independently of any political considerations*—a point to be fully realised and emphasised.

The principal means of spreading the new ideas favouring the renaissance of law were the new centres of culture then created in western Europe; an essential role devolved to the universities, of which the first and most illustrious was the University of Bologna in Italy. It is therefore appropriate to examine first of all the work of the universities and how, spanning the centuries and neglecting mere political frontiers, they drew up a scholarly law common to all Europe. The popular or vulgar laws, applied by the courts and varying from state to state and region to region, will be examined next; in conclusion, it will be indicated how these same laws were influenced in varying degrees by the *ius commune* taught in the universities.

SECTION I—IUS COMMUNE OF THE UNIVERSITIES

30. The law as a model of social organisation

In a university the law cannot be considered only in its purely practical aspects. The university professor is interested in principles of justice and methods for discovering those principles, how law can conform to morality and how society can function properly, and not simply in technical matters or how in practice rules found to be just can in fact be put into effect. What interests him in the law is the search for real justice; this is as true today as it ever was.[4]

The medieval universities considered the law as a model of social organisation and aspired to formulate the essence of justice rather than to impart to students a mastery of legal technique. The purpose of the study of the law was not to state which solution the courts would give to a trial in fact; and subjects such as procedure and evidence were left to practitioners and administrators. Law was to tell judges how they should decide in justice. It prescribed the rules which just men must observe in their social behaviour. The law, like morality, was a *Sollen* (what ought to be done), not a *Sein* (what is done in practice). The teaching of law adopted this view, therefore, that law was linked to philosophy, theology and religion. Could one conceive of a teaching of morality which merely states the current morality of individuals in their daily behaviour, without bothering to instruct how life should be lived? The same thing seemed natural for law.

Moreover, how would it have been possible in the Middle Ages to teach the law based on what we, today, call positive law? This, in most countries, was in a chaotic, uncertain, fragmented and sometimes primitive condition. Italy and France, where the model of the new study originated, had no national law; in these countries, where feudalism prevailed, no general sovereign exercised a controlling influence. The same was true of Spain and Portugal where the kings were no more than chieftains of a precarious coalition against the Muslims. In England, the Common law had barely begun to emerge and to displace local custom. Unless they were to remain schools of local procedure, without prestige, influence or power, the universities had to teach something other than the local law. Moreover, it was precisely in order to rise above this local law and abandon the inadequate rules of customary law that this renaissance of the study of Roman law came about. No European university, therefore, took as the basis of its teaching the local or

---

[4] A difference today, however, is that we tend to think of the law within the framework of "social sciences"—in its relation to political science, economics, and sociology. In the Middle Ages, when the world was dominated by a religious spirit, there was a greater tendency to consider it in the framework of morality—and therefore in its relation to philosophy, theology or divinity.

regional positive customary law; this, in the eyes of the university, gave no expression to justice and was not law. *"Non est proprie ius, sed fex"* said a German author somewhat bluntly.

31. Prestige of Roman law

Any real hesitation on this point was impossible because, in the face of the diversity and primitiveness of the local customs, one law offered itself for study and admiration to both students and professors. This was Roman law. It was readily available: the compilations of Justinian explained its rules in a language conserved and popularised by the Church and used by all chancelleries and scholars: Latin. Roman law was the issue of a brilliant civilisation extending from the Mediterranean to the North Sea, from Byzantium to Brittany and, in the minds of contemporaries, it evoked with nostalgia the lost unity of Christendom.

But Roman law—by which the Church had lived, and upon which its Canon law, with only simple amendments and appendices, was based—was open to criticisms. Was it not the product of a pagan world, an aspect of a civilisation unaware of Christ, linked to a philosophy different from that of the Gospels, the church fathers and Christianity? To build society on Roman law, to take it as a model, was this not to turn aside from divine law and to seek justice at the expense, and in ignorance, of brotherly love?

Saint Thomas Aquinas (1225–1274), at the start of the thirteenth century, was to eliminate this criticism. His work, renewing that of Aristotle (384–322 B.C.) and showing that the pre-Christian philosophy based on Reason was to a very large extent in conformity with divine law, had the effect of "exorcising" Roman law. It constitutes the final rejection of any pretension to build secular society upon an apostolic model dominated by the notion of brotherly love. One can see in Saint Thomas the architect of the law's secularisation; after his teaching, the last obstacle to the renewal of the study of Roman law was removed.[5]

---

[5] Villey (M.), *Leçons d'histoire de la philosophie du droit* (2nd ed., 1962), pp. 43–49 and 203–219. The teaching of Roman law was however prohibited in the Université de Paris in 1219 by Honorius III in the bull *Super Specula* at the request of Philippe-Auguste who saw it as giving support to the claims of the Holy Roman Emperor. But the prohibition was never absolute throughout France, not even in the *pays de coutumes*; and the teaching of Roman law was formally re-established in Paris by Louis XIV in the Edict of St-Germain-en-Laye in 1679. *Cf.* below, para. 40.

32. Teaching of national laws

The basis, therefore, of all legal teaching in all European universities was Roman law and alongside of it, Canon law. This was as true in continental Europe as in the British Isles or in Scandinavian countries. Only at a much later period was the teaching of national law taken up in the universities. Swedish law was taught at Uppsala from 1620 and a chair of French law was created at the Sorbonne in Paris in 1679, but in most countries the national law was not the object of scholarly attention until the eighteenth century: in 1707 at Wittenberg, the first university of the Empire to teach the *Deutsches Recht*, in 1741 in Spain, in 1758 at Oxford and in 1800 at Cambridge, England, and in 1772 in Portugal. Until the nineteenth century, and the period of national codifications, instruction in Roman law remained therefore the basis of legal education and national law occupied an altogether secondary place. It is important to realise these facts, and the undisputed place of Roman law in the universities over the centuries, in order to appreciate the phenomenon of the renaissance of Roman law studies; its significance went considerably beyond the University of Bologna on the one hand or the twelfth and thirteenth centuries on the other.

33. The usus modernus pandectarum

The teaching of Roman law in the universities underwent an evolution: a succession of "schools" appeared, each having its own emphasis and methods of commenting upon and explaining the Roman law texts. A first school, that of the *glossators*, endeavoured to fix the original meaning of the Roman laws as given in Justinian's compilations. Some of the Justinianic texts were however abandoned even at this stage because they dealt with certain institutions (such as slavery) that had disappeared or because some other subjects were henceforth ruled by Canon law (such as marriage, wills). The school of the glossators reached its height in the middle of the thirteenth century with the work of Accursius (1182–1263) who, in his Great Gloss, recast the efforts of his predecessors into a treatise comprising approximately 96,000 explanatory glosses. With the school of the *post-glossators* in the fourteenth century a new tendency appeared and an altogether different work was accomplished: Roman law was expurgated and adapted and used for entirely new developments (such as commercial law and conflict of laws). Its presentation was, at the same time, systematised in a way which contrasts vividly with the chaos of the *Digest* and the casuistic, empirical spirit of the Roman jurisconsults. The methods of the Roman jurists were abandoned by these medieval scholars: they no longer merely sought to rediscover the Roman solutions, but endeavoured to continue, perfect and complete Roman legal scholarship by using Roman law to explain rules adapted to the society of their own time.[6]

As a result, the Roman law taught in the universities in the fourteenth and fifteenth centuries moved further and further away from the original model; it was a modernised Roman law, adapted to new circumstances—a *usus modernus Pandectarum*. Under this title a vastly changed Roman law, influenced principally by Canon law (admission of the principle that agreements are binding, *pacta sunt servanda*), was taught. In the scholastic method of the time the opinions of the authors—Bartolus (1313–1357), Baldus (1327–1400), Azo (1150–1230) and others—were presented in relation to a problem and the appropriate solution identified by taking into account the *communis opinio doctorum*. Some exception to this occurred in France, where the school of the *humanistes* triumphed in the sixteenth century. French scholars were able to indulge in the luxury of attempting to restore the purity of the Roman law because in France that body of rules came to be seen as only "written reason" (*ratio scripta*) and, when necessary, nothing prevented its open rejection in favour of more reasonable solutions which were, in many instances, similar in any event to those recommended by the *usus modernus Pandectarum*. In Spain and Portugal, the full evolution of Roman law was retarded by a "law of citations" which, in doubtful cases, imposed the observance of the opinions of a number of earlier commentators. In Germany, on the other hand, the progressive work of the school of *post-glossators* was continued by that of the *pandectists*, resulting

---

[6] The substitution of the idea of rights (*droits subjectifs*) derived from the will to that of the classical idea of a natural law founded on justice, totally transformed the basis of law as admitted by the Romans. Villey (M.), *Cours d'histoire de la philosophie du droit*, 1962–1963 ("le franciscanisme et le droit"), mimeographed; *adde* Ullmann (W.), *The Individual and Society in the Middle Ages* (1966) where the development of the idea of the individual as a *citizen* rather than a *subject* is examined.

in that momument to Romanist scholarship which is so little Germanic, the German Civil Code (BGB) of 1896.

34. Ius commune and common law

The preceding discussion contributes to an understanding of Roman law as the *ius commune* of the Romano-Germanic system. It is an edifice of European scholarship which aspired essentially to provide jurists with the framework, vocabulary and methods to orient them in the search for just solutions. But the work of the universities can really only be fully understood by reference to a concept of natural law. The law faculties attempted to articulate, with the help of Roman law, rules which best expressed a sense of justice and a well ordered society, the existence of which was required by the very nature of things. The universities did not purport to elaborate a system of positive law; moreover, they did not have the status necessary to determine which rules in each country judges and practitioners would necessarily have to apply. Today these features are of great interest because we are once again speaking in terms of the European community and of European law.[7] The Romano-Germanic system united the peoples of Europe while respecting their diversity—and, without this diversity, Europe would not be what it is and what we hope it may be.

The *ius commune* (*droit commun*, or *Gemeines Recht*) of continental Europe was thus very different in nature from English Common law, by which is meant the uniform law applied in the English royal courts as opposed to the local customs which existed before the Common law arose.[8] The flexibility of this European *ius commune* and its purely persuasive authority should be noted as well. In England the rigidity of the Common law, a system of positive law linked to procedural considerations, made necessary the elaboration of other rules, called *rules of equity*, intended to complete and correct the Common law. Such a need was never felt in the Romano-Germanic family and, as a result, its member-countries knew nothing of the fundamental English distinction between Common law and Equity. The idea of a strict law which is

---

[7] *Nouvelles perspectives d'un jus commune européen*, Colloquium at the Institut universitaire européen de Florence, May 1977.

[8] David (R.), "Droit commun, jus commune, common law," *in Studi in memoria di Tullio Ascarelli* (1968) Vol. I, pp. 345–363.

not "equitable" ran counter to the very idea of law as conceived by the universities; such a law could clearly not be suggested as a model; in fact, in the eyes of the European universities, it would not even have qualified as law at all.

35. Law and reason: the natural law school

Systematised and adapted by jurists to the needs of society, the law taught in the universities from the time of the post-glossators moved further and further away from the law of Justinian to become a law which, because it was founded on Reason, was suited for universal application. The care once taken in the universities to respect Roman law gradually gave way to a concern for discovering and teaching the principles of a fully *rational* law. A new school, the Natural Law School, triumphed in the universities in the seventeenth and eighteenth centuries.

The Natural Law School which dominated thought at this period departed in several respects from the thinking of the post-glossators. It abandoned the scholastic method and furthered the systematisation of the law by casting it in logical propositions, in imitation of the sciences.

The idea of a divinely inspired natural order of things was moreover put aside in favour of basing the whole social order upon a consideration of man himself—individual "natural rights," deriving from the very personality of every citizen, were emphasised. The concepts of personal rights and the rule of law dominated all legal thought.[9] The Natural Law School, despite its name, considered law to be not so much a natural phenomenon, but rather the product of reason. It therefore rejected the classical notion of an order of things deriving from divine will and nature, and treated man as the only reality. It followed that man's reason was to be the sole instrument for establishing the just rules of an immutable, universal law common to all people for all time.[10] These ideas reinforced the merging tendency of local and regional customs.

---

[9] Villey (M.), "Abrégé du droit naturel classique," in *Archives de philosophie du droit,* VI: *La réforme des études de droit. Le droit naturel* (1961), pp. 25–72; *Seize essais de philosophie du droit* (1968); "Contro l'umanesimo nel diritto," (1967) *Rev. int. di filosofia del diritto* 670–682.

[10] The new statutes of the University of Coïmbra, prescribed by the Marquis of Pombal in 1772, stated that instruction was henceforth to be given on the basis of comparative law, as drawn from the general principles of jurisprudence of civilised peoples, rather than on that of Roman law.

Thus it came about that the exaltation of reason, and the new role recognised as attaching to enacted law, prepared the way for codification.

The Natural Law School completely changed, therefore, the nature of legal science—its philosophy changed the basis of the law, its resort to legislation and its development of logical propositions revolutionised its methods, and its influence on the substance of private and public law was considerable.

In private law, the Natural Law School was not however revolutionary; it did not globally reject the work of the post-glossators which to the leading jurists of this period, Grotius (1583–1645) from the Netherlands, Domat (1625–1696) in France, Stair (1619–1695) in Scotland and Hugo (1764–1844) somewhat later in Germany, appeared to be based on reason. The Roman law of the universities (*usus modernus Pandectarum*) and Natural Law became in the end one and the same. Grotius, in his *Introduction to the Jurisprudence of Holland*, one of the first legal works written in a vernacular language on the continent,[11] does not justify the application of Roman law in the Netherlands on the basis of principal or subsidiary reception of Roman law, but on the basis of the conformity of Roman law to Natural Law and to Reason. The same justification is at the basis of the *Institutions* of Stair, through whose work Scots law was systematised and Scotland very largely penetrated by Roman law in the seventeenth century.[12] Domat writes in the same way in the preface to his book *Les loix civiles dans leur ordre naturel:* " . . . all the Rules of the Roman law which are received with us, consist almost wholly of the Laws of Nature, and but very few of them are Arbitrary Laws."[13] The Natural Law School required that an end be put to certain retro-

---

[11] *Inleiding tot de Hollandsche Rechtsgeleertheyd* (1631). The work was published in Dutch, with an English translation, by Lee (R. W.), *The Jurisprudence of Holland* (1926).

[12] Stair (J. D.), *The Institutions of the Law of Scotland* (1681).

[13] "Tout ce qu'il y a dans le droit romain qui soit de notre usage, ne consiste presque qu'en droit naturel, et ne comprend que peu de lois arbitraires." The English version cited in the text is drawn from the translation *The Civil Law in its Natural Order* by William Strahan (London, 1722); a reprint of the second edition of the above (1737) was published by Luther S. Cushing (Boston, 1850 & 1861) but without the author's preface. Domat's work, published 1689–1694, is principally a work on Roman law, although this is often forgotten. The author intended, as he says, to render the study of the Roman laws easy and agreeable, by exposing in a systematic fashion—following their natural order—the unorganised solutions to be found in Justinian's compilations. In his second volume, concerning public law, Domat was nevertheless led to abandon Roman law, because "it contains much fewer Rules of the Publick Law, and there is hardly in it one Rule concerning several matters that are of the greatest Importance in Publick Law"; he finds "the Materials for Rules" by appealing to the "Principles of Natural Equity."

gressive and mechanical methods employed in the application of Roman law and that its rules only be received when doing so was not contrary to reason, justice, or the ideas and needs of society such as they were conceived in the seventeenth and eighteenth centuries. The School in no wise demanded the abandonment of Roman law; it advocated a new and more progressive method in its application and interpretation. It was a question of adopting the attitude of a country like France in which Roman law was received only as "written reason" (*raison écrite*) rather than that of some other countries (such as Italy, Spain and Portugal) where the *communis opinio doctoram* was to be followed obligatorily. Natural Law neither invented nor offered any practical system to take the place of Roman law; its action applied only to points of detail and served more as a means for the harmonisation of solutions already admitted in different parts of Europe and, if need be, their modernisation, than as a new basis for such solutions.

It was altogether different, however, in the field of public law. Here the principles of Roman law never served as a model.[14] Rome knew neither constitutional nor administrative law: the areas of government and administration on the one hand, and that of law on the other, had always been considered distinct. In the same way, Roman penal law, little developed in the work of Justinian, was not taught in the universities, and any influence it did have was more nefarious than beneficial.[15] The Natural Law School completed the secularising work of the universities by proposing models, deduced from the principles of Reason as understood in the seventeenth and eighteenth centuries, for constitutions, administrative practice and criminal law. These rational models were to a large degree inspired by English example, for even though the Common law at this time had not been able to equal the perfection of Roman law in private law, English law, as an issue of the relations between the Crown and subjects, had reconciled administrative and police powers with the liberties of individual subjects better, or so it seemed, than any other.

The Natural Law School demanded that, in addition to the private law founded on Roman law, Europe formulate what it there-

---

[14] Schultz (F.), *Principles of Roman Law* (1936).
[15] Esmein (A.), *Histoire de la procédure criminelle en France* (1882).

tofore had lacked because of the universities' very absorption in the Roman law: a public law giving effect to the natural rights of man and guaranteeing the liberties of the individual.

SECTION II—NATIONAL OR REGIONAL LAWS

36. Return to the idea of law

Like other movements in the realm of ideas, the revival of Roman law in the universities ran the risk of remaining wholly academic. The universities advocated a new system of social organisation; they maintained that secular society should be ruled by law and they affirmed that the best law, and the only intellectually conceivable one, was Roman law as they had refashioned it. However, the people, the leaders and, above all, the judges who were principally responsible at this time not only for the application but also the determination of the applicable law had to be convinced. To what extent, then, were the ideas taught in the universities actually accepted, and in what way did their proposed model become the positive law of different European countries?

The idea that society should be ruled by law was an established one by the thirteenth century. The Fourth Lateran Council was an event of particular importance indicating very clearly the need felt at this time to return to the idea of law. Its decision in 1215 to prohibit clerics from taking part in procedures in which recourse would be made either to ordeals or to the judgment of God marks a decisive turning point. Civil society could not be ruled by law so long as trials were resolved by appeals to the supernatural; the very study of law was not of any great practical interest if the solutions to disputes were to be left to a non-rational system of proof. The decision of the Lateran Council to reject this vestige of the past resulted in the adoption in continental Europe of a new, rational procedure for which the Canon law served as model[16]; its decision thus paved the way for ushering in the reign of law.

The renaissance of the twelfth and thirteenth centuries

---

[16] Another type of procedure, involving trial by jury, was adopted in England as a result of the decision of the Council, perhaps because of the absence of officials able to apply the canonical procedure. *Cf.* Hamson (C. J.) and Plucknett (T. F. T), *The English Trial and Comparative Law* (1952).

involved—more, it required—the renaissance of the idea of law. The decision of the Lateran Council clearly expressed these new ideas and feelings. It did not, however, indicate how the idea of law was to be rediscovered, nor upon what basis the new law was to be constructed.

37. Possible future developments

The universities, in which the renaissance of Roman law studies had occurred, proposed a solution: reinstate the law of Rome. Another solution, however, was conceivable: develop a new law on the basis of existing customs or, in the absence of such customs, on the basis of court decisions. The alternative was either to adapt what already existed or, as need be, make something altogether new. As will be seen, the second solution prevailed in England where a new system, that of the Common law, was created. The conditions peculiar to England prevented its courts from thinking of law in the way indicated by the universities, because English procedure, in particular, did not allow the law to be freely developed in the light of moral and policy considerations. Roman law was, perhaps, the best law and what ought to have applied, but in England this was nonetheless an impossibility.

Mention should also be made of the effort of the school of law at Pavia which proposed Lombard law as a model instead of Roman law. This endeavour, however, ended in failure; Lombard law did in fact hold its ground and expand somewhat in Italy but it never passed beyond the frontiers of that country and, outside of Pavia, no university adopted it as a basis for teaching.[17]

Thus in the countries of continental Europe, unlike England, the solution proposed by the universities prevailed. It was in this way that the Romano-Germanic family came into existence: it is made up of countries which, to a varying although always large extent, were influenced by the teachings of the university law faculties on the concept of law, its form of presentation and research techniques and often in its very rules.

On the European continent, again unlike England, a more flex-

---

[17] Calasso (F.), *Introduzione al diritto commune* (1951). Cappelletti (M.), Merryman (J. H.), and Perillo (J. M.), *The Italian Legal Systema. An Introduction* (1965). The *Liber Papiensis* which was the basis of the teaching at Pavia was made up of the *Edict of Rothari* (643), which in 388 chapters was the most complete memorial of the law of a Germanic tribe, and a number of capitularies taken from the *Capitulare italicum*.

ible procedure permitted the teachings of the universities to bear full fruit and Romanisation of the law to take place. After the Lateran Council, and in imitation of Canon law, a new and more rational and also more sophisticated written rather than oral procedure was admitted in continental Europe. This innovation produced fundamental and decisive changes in judicial organisation. The Carolingian system, in which the judge simply directed procedures (*Richter*) whereas aldermen or "law-finders" (*Scabini, Schöffen*) stated what the custom was and rendered the decision, was gradually abandoned. From the thirteenth to the sixteenth centuries, the administration of justice passed into the control of jurists trained in universities according to the Roman law tradition. Since law was administered by jurists, the law as taught in universities exercised a considerable influence. To understand this, it is necessary to consider the circumstances of the period. In the Middle Ages, law had neither the certainty nor the comprehensive character that it has acquired today. Its evolution was not directed by governments; their task at this time was essentially one of police regulation. Nor was law, conceived as the expression of what is just (*id quod justum est*), identified with the command of an often still-disputed sovereign. Because of this, the responsibility for the discovery and formulation of legal rules fell to the courts as guided by doctrinal writers. In these conditions, the model law taught by the universities was never, in any sense, the idealised work of contemplative thinkers having no relationship with, or influence upon, legal practice. As a result of the prestige of the universities—everywhere, that is, where universities existed—the principles of law taught by them were either received or at least exercised some influence. There was only one exception—England.

38. Revival of Roman law studies and its reception[18]

The renaissance of the studies of Roman law did not necessarily imply, as already suggested, its complete reception. The renewal of these studies had, above all, the effect of restoring to Europe a feeling for the dignity and importance of law in assuring order and

---

[18] See for a good summary Hazeltine (H. D.), "The Renaissance and the Laws of Europe" in *Cambridge Legal Essays* (1926), p. 139. Vinogradoff (P.), *Roman Law in Medieval Europe* (3rd ed., de Zuleuta, 1961).

promoting social progress. This feeling does not exist as a matter of course and it had, in fact, died out in Europe after the fall of the Roman Empire. As in the Far East and in primitive societies, confidence was placed in techniques of mediation and arbitration and in the search for a peaceful solution through compromise and equity much more than through law. But the universities believed in the mission of law and its essential role in society. This primary point is independent of the content of Roman law or its actual reception: the renaissance of the studies of Roman law is first and foremost, if not the renewal of the idea of law itself, at least the renewal of the idea of the rule of law, that is to say that law is the very basis of civil order.

The renewal of Roman law scholarship also meant that the law's vocabulary, the divisions into which rules are arranged and the concepts used, were to be the vocabulary, divisions and concepts of the science of the Romanists. The divisions of private and public law, the classification of rights as real and personal, the notions of usufruct, servitude, fraud, prescription, mandate and the contract for services, all these became the divisions and notions upon which jurists, once trained in the Roman law school, were to reason. The renewal of Roman law studies is the principal event marking the birth of the Romano-Germanic family. Historically, the countries which belong to this family are those where jurists and legal practitioners drew their conception of law, as well as the basis for their method of approach and reasoning, from the Roman law tradition.

It is of little consequence that the basic stuff of the law—the rules, in fact—might have been taken from local, non-Roman sources. The reception of the Roman rules themselves is something quite different and, all things considered, secondary in importance. The universities never purported to impose Roman solutions. They were never supranational institutions entrusted with applying the law. They merely stated how the law could be envisaged and, starting from Roman rules, they endeavoured to show what, according to them, was the best law and how a knowledge of it might be attained. Their work was one of persuasion only—not that of imposing uniformity by means of authority.[19]

---

[19] Quite different was the formation of the Common law, a uniform system for the whole of England, which the royal courts of Westminster imposed by displacing local customs. Contrary to the usual assumption, it is in continental Europe that a respect for tradition can best be seen, whereas England rejected it. The formation of the Common law was a revolution; on the continent tradition and local customs were spared.

39. Necessary evolution of custom

Although the renaissance of Roman law studies is distinct from the reception of Roman law, it is equally true that almost everywhere the influence of the universities resulted, to some extent, in an increase in the authority of Roman law rules and the rules derived from it.

While the law applied in practice was not changed, it is evident that it was, in the first place, looked at with a more critical eye. It could not subsist in the new society unless it truly constituted a *law*, and unless it exhibited those qualities of certainty, territorial generality and conformity to justice which, in the opinion of the time, characterised law. And to conform to justice, it was necessary that the law be adaptable to the circumstances of a period of social change.

The local customs, sometimes varying from village to village, were condemned. They were only acceptable in a closed society; too difficult to ascertain or to prove, they only survived when regrouped so as to permit greater geographical application and when their rules were made readily available through written compilations. Otherwise they were inevitably doomed to disappear— and in this event they were most often replaced, in practice, by the schoolmen's law of the universities. The progress of Roman law was, then, only contained when confronted by major statements of customary law such as those which appeared in the thirteenth century, in France with the work of Beaumanoir (1250–1296), or in Germany with the *Mirror of Saxons* (*Sachsenspiegel*). Its progress was also limited either by new legislative compilations, such as the *Siete Partidas* of thirteenth century Spain, or simply by the redaction of customs in the mid-fifteenth century as directed by the French *Ordonnance de Montil-lez-Tours* (1454).

These compilations—redactions of, or commentaries on, the customary laws—require some comment. The striking thing about most of them, especially those of France,[20] is their fragmentary character. The customs only deal with those social relationships already in existence before the thirteenth century: family relations, land law and inheritance. In these areas the old rules could be retained. But the customs offered no basis whatsoever for the

---

[20] See for example the *Coutume de Paris*, Olivier-Martin (F.), *Histoire de la Coutume de la Prévôté et Vicomté de Paris* (1922).

development in new areas. They were appropriate for the constitution of a *ius civile* in the strict sense—the law of a localised community—but they were not suitable to the formation of a *ius gentium*, a law in other words embracing those relationships reaching beyond the territorial limits within which they apply.[21]

The law taught in the universities, on the other hand, was not linked to the past in the same way and was transnational; it was a work of Reason and placed above local contingencies or traditions. In all those cases where a *new* law was needed, to govern the relations between foreigners for example and to be acceptable to them, recourse was had to Roman law. The customs were the law of *closed societies* bound by tradition; the law of the universities was the law of an *open society*, one turned towards the future. Therein lies the reason for its expansion and, in various places, for its reception.

40. Means of expansion of the continental Roman Common law

Expansion and influence, or reception? Both formulae are employed, without necessarily indicating a greater Romanisation of the law in one area or another. Between a law applied in principle but subject to certain exceptions and a law applied to supplement gaps, there is little real difference. The important thing is the number of exceptions, or the extent to which the indigenous body of law is complemented either by the authority or the persuasive force of Roman law.

In France, for example, Roman law was admitted everywhere as an authority of Written Reason—*imperio rationis* and not *ratione imperii*, because the king of France was emperor in his own kingdom and did not recognise the obligatory character of Roman, or as they were then considered, "imperial" laws. However, the same term covered two distinct realities, depending upon whether it was applied in the south of France (*Midi*), the land of "written" law (*pays de droit écrit*), or in the north (*pays de coutumes*) where "customary" law prevailed.

In principle, Roman law had been received throughout the Holy Roman Empire and was therefore applicable as law, although cus-

---

[21] The same phenomenon is to be noticed in the Muslim countries and in India and Africa where only those rules relating to personal status (*statut personnel*) are sufficiently evolved to subsist today.

tom (*Landrecht* or *Stadtrecht:* regional or municipal laws) could derogate from it. But there were other parts of the Empire, such as the Swiss Cantons and those countries subject to the *Mirror of Saxons*, where the reception did not take place and where, as a result, Roman law only prevailed as written reason (*ratio scripta*). But there appears to have been no major difference between them with respect to the real influence of Roman law. The same observation applies to Spain where Roman law was received in Catalonia, but only prevailed as written reason in Castile: the *Siete Partidas* had borrowed so much from Roman and Canon law that the result was very similar.

More important than these affirmations was the influence of judicial organisation and procedure. In France the penetration of Roman law was hampered by the existence of the procedure *enquête par turbes*, a technique for the judicial determination or proof of the content of customary law.[22] And from the beginning of the fourteenth century, even before the post-glossators had begun adapting Roman law, the *Parlement de Paris*, a new central royal court equipped to do similar work, was established.[23]

In Scandinavian countries the penetration of Roman substantive law was halted because there the law was already unified and custom already reduced to writing on a national scale.[24]

In Germany and Italy, on the other hand, there were no such obstacles. There were no procedures for determining the relevant customary law rule and the judges were uninstructed in it. In Italy, in the thirteenth century, itinerant judges were often expressly selected from outside the locality in the hope that they would be independent and impartial. In sixteenth century Germany there developed a practice producing similar results, that of sending the record of the litigation to university law faculties (*Aktenversendung*). The organisation of the courts was, at the time, in great disorder; there were more than 2000 courts in Saxony alone. In order that justice be rendered, the dossier of the case would be sent to a university (*Spruchfakultät*) which, removed from the place of trial,

---

[22] The *enquête* was adopted by royal ordinance in 1270 as the means of proving custom before the *Parlement de Paris*.

[23] The organisation of the *Parlement de Paris* is described by Dawson (J.), *The Oracles of the Law* (1968), pp. 273 *et seq.*

[24] *Judske Lov* of Valdemar Seir (1241) in Denmark, the *General Code* of Magnus Lagaböte (1274) in Norway and Iceland, and the *General Law for Towns* and *General Law for the Country* of Magnus Eriksson (1350) for Sweden and Finland.

would say how the case should be decided. This practice necessarily meant that Roman law had a preponderant influence because the judges, uninformed about local custom, willingly made use of the *communis opinio doctorum.* In Germany, a deeply divided country, Roman law was applied in order to supply a common basis to judicial decisions.[25]

41. Official and private compilations

The progress of Roman law, or rather that of Romanist scholarship, was made concrete and official in numerous countries by private or official compilations of regional custom carried out from the thirteenth to the eighteenth centuries. Doubtless the original and principal aim of these compilations was merely to fix the content of regional custom. And, as already suggested, these redactions of custom did impede, to some extent, the progress of Roman law. But their effect in this sense was limited. There were, in fact, two alternatives. The draftsmen of the customs might merely fix the content of the custom, in which case their work made evident all its gaps, archaisms and insufficiencies. No one custom could purport to be the complete system needed to regulate the variety of new relationships which the law was bound to take into account. For this reason, therefore, the custom inevitably had the appearance of a "special law," that of a corrective to a system whose main principles were to be found elsewhere. Such was the case of the French customs drafted in the second half of the fifteenth and the first half of the sixteenth centuries by order of Charles VII (1403–1461) (*Ordonnance de Montil-lez-Tours,* 1454). On other occasions, however, the draftsmen attempted to present the custom as a comprehensive system, adequate in all instances. This was only possible through a large amount of creative work which in fact most often involved the importation of Roman law principles. Such was notably the case in the *Siete Partidas.* In this compilation the king of Castile, Alphonsus X (the Wise, 1252–1282) took up the Spanish tradition of the *Fuero Juzgo;* he wished to harmonise the customary rules of Castile and the rules of Roman and Canon law, advocated by the university and the Church. More so than other compilations of the same period, the

---

[25] Dawson (J.), *The Oracles of the Law* (1968) pp. 196 *et seq.*

Siete Partidas was a work of law reform. Drafted in 1265, it was clearly ahead of its time, although only in 1348, it would seem, did it receive the force of law by virtue of the Ordinance of Alcalà. Its influence, outside its country of origin, Castile, was considerable throughout Spain and Portugal. To a large extent it contributed to the Romanisation of the rules of Spanish and Portuguese law.

The mere wish to present the custom as being regional, rather than simply local, inevitably led the draftsmen to ignore local particularities; there is no doubt that faced with several variations they opted in favour of what was most in harmony with the Roman rules.

As time passed, the Roman law scholarship emerged more and more as the science of law itself; Roman law, as taught in the universities, became the "written reason" of the Christian world. Its growing influence is even more evident in the revised versions of the customs. In France, as in Germany, the later reform of the customs or municipal laws brings this out even more clearly. The only exceptions were the codifications which occurred in Norway (1683), Denmark (1687), and in Sweden and Finland (1734); exception must also be made in the case of the orthodox Christian countries which at this time were without universities and cut off from the rest of the Christian world.

42. French parlements

To what extent did judicial decisions have an influence upon legal development in countries of the Romano-Germanic family?

In France, from the close of the twelfth century, royal justice was organised at the local level through the bailiffs' and seneschals' courts (*bailliages*, *sénéchaussées*) and, from the middle of the thirteenth century, a specialisation in judicial affairs developed within the *Curia Regis*. The *Parlement* of Paris and, later, those of the provinces, were at one and the same time royal courts and involved in the government of the kingdom. They were not bound to observe either immemorial custom or Roman law. Their place in the organisation of things, linked as it was to royal prerogative, enabled them to depart from the application of strict law and draw on other sources in order that equity be made to prevail. French judges thus considered themselves not bound by the university teaching tradition of Roman law. Legal scholarship and governing the country were not seen as one and the same thing. The French *parlements*, in their efforts to modernise French law, took all kinds of sources into account. Roman law exercised its influence in some respects, in the law of contract for example, but while it was admitted to be "written reason" it was never taken to be a *droit commun* or "common law"—that, in France, was the role of the *jurisprudence* or judicial decisions of the *parlements*, the many published collections of which reveal the importance that was attached to them. And especially in the sixteenth and seventeenth centuries, their *arrêts de règlement*, that is to say decisions having a general authority and revealing how the *parlement* would dispose of a future case, were frequent. These touched upon matters of procedure and judicial administration for the most part but they also settled many questions of private law. Judicial "precedents," often cited, played a role in France no less and probably more important than they did in England at this time. The *jurisprudence* of the *parlements* became, in eighteenth century France, a "customary common law" (*droit commun coutumier*) distinct in many respects from Roman law.[26]

43. The Deutsches Privatrecht

In Germany the situation was altogether different. The break-up of the Holy Roman Empire (Austria, Germany, the Netherlands) and the social decline of the thirteenth century brought about a disintegration of centralised judicial organisation. The imperial court (*Reichshofgericht*) that remained in place was very limited in its effectiveness because of the many immunities to its jurisdiction conceded by the emperor; it had no fixed seat, no permanent judges, no means of enforcing its judgments. A new imperial court, the *Reichskammergericht*, set up in 1495 by the Emperor Maximilian (1493–1519), had only a very partial success as well. Thus, while judicial decisions in the different German states, in other words at a wholly local level, had some importance, a German legal system never really evolved on the basis of decided cases—and the way was open for the reception of Roman law.

---

[26] Dawson, *op. cit.* pp. 307, 342, 348. The author observes that in France the most influential jurists were practitioners rather than professors of law. No law professor is to be found among those who drafted the French *Code civil* of 1804.

A "German" private law (*Deutsches Privatrecht*) only developed in relation to a much more limited number of subjects than in France. Before reception there was, however, some growth in the new law of the towns which, especially with the organisation of the Hanseatic league, had expanded significantly. This might conceivably have produced a common German private law, in commercial matters for example, because it was established usage for one town to adopt the statutes of another and, when a question of their interpretation arose, to seek consultation of the court (*Oberhof*) of such town. But the practice was abandoned in the sixteenth century when the German princes, each in his own principality, exerted a monopolistic control over judicial administration.[27] Moreover the *Oberhöfe* at this time fell under the control of academics.

In the eighteenth century a number of German writers attempted to systematise "German" law and thereby rival the *ius commune* or *Gemeinrecht* which Roman law then was. But this effort came too late; Roman law was solidly implanted and the sphere of the *Deutsches Privatrecht* remained limited to sundry institutions. German law as such was never "de-Romanised" and then "nationalised" as a whole.

Even more typical was the effort of the Historical School in the nineteenth century. This school affirmed the need for a spontaneous development of the law, similar to that in social customs and language, adapted to the original elements of civilisation in each country. But, by a curious reversal of attitudes, Savigny (1779–1861), the recognised leader of this school, managed to justify the reception of Roman law by means of these same premises, and to advocate an even stricter application of Roman law in Germany; in fact, according to him, those imbued with national feeling in law were the very jurists who advocated the application of Roman law. "To want to eliminate the Roman law by creating a code," concluded Saleilles (1855–1912),[28] "would have been [at the end of the nineteenth century] to create a German Code without German law," so true was it at this time that Roman law had become the national law of Germany. It has often been pointed

---

[27] Dawson, *op. cit.* pp. 157 *et seq.* It is to be noted that the *Oberhöfe* were rarely appeal courts. The practice of the *Aktenversendung*, as explained in para. 40 above, was only abolished finally in 1879 upon the promulgation of the Ordinance of Civil Procedure (ZPO).

[28] Saleilles (R.), *Introduction à l'étude du Code civil allemand* (1904), p. 8.

out that the French Civil Code contains more Germanic elements than the German Civil Code.[29] The Roman imprint is even more obvious and indisputable in the Austrian Civil Code (ABGB) of 1811.

44. Latin countries

The positive laws closest to Roman law were to be found in countries where the populations had always lived according to Roman law established as a general custom and quite apart, therefore, from any reception. Roman law thus became, quite naturally, the "common law" of Italy, Spain and Portugal and, to some extent, of the south of France (although French legal historians have lately realised that very little is known about the law actually applied in the *pays de droit écrit*). On the Iberian peninsula the *Siete Partidas* contributed to the authority of Roman law, at the expense of local custom which derogated from it. But the danger in these countries was that through too great an attachment to the teachings of the post-glossators the law itself would atrophy. A reaction, therefore, set in under the influence of the Natural Law School against the excessively mechanical techniques of the earlier period which had required a strict observance of the *communis opinio doctorum*.

In Savoy in 1729 and in Naples in 1774, legislation prohibited judges from referring to the opinions of the doctors in their decisions, which in the absence of any applicable legislative text were thenceforth to be founded on "reason."[30] The same development took place in Portugal. Legislation of 1769 prompted by the Marquis de Pombal (the *lei da boa razão*) freed judges from the strict duty of following the opinions of Accursius and Bartolus and the *communis opinion doctorum* as required by seventeenth century ordinances.[31] These opinions were only to be cited in future when they conformed to right reason (*boa razão, recta ratio*), that is to say "to essential, intrinsic and unalterable truth" from which

[29] Mitteis (H.), "Die germanischen Grundlagen des französischen Rechts," *Zeitschrift der Savigny-Stiftung für Rechtsgeschichte, Germanische Abteilung* (1943), Vol. 63 pp. 138 *et seq.*; Koschaker (P.), *Europa und das römische Recht* (1947), p. 140.

[30] Gorla (G.), "I tribunali supremi degli Stati italiani fra i secoli XVI e XIX" *in La formazione storica del diritto moderno in Europea. Atti del terzo Congresso internazionale della Società italiana di storia del diritto* Vol. I (1977), p. 447–532.

[31] Ordinance of 1603, preamble to Book III, Title 64 *in fine*. These measures were confirmed in 1643.

both divine law and the laws of man drew the moral and civil laws of Christianity. Apart from them judges were referred to those other rules which, with the consent of all, were established by international law to direct and govern all civilised peoples.

45. Legislation

As a source of law throughout the period under consideration, legislation is only of secondary importance. In the view of things accepted in the middle ages, the law existed independently of the commands of those vested with sovereign authority; the monarch was not qualified either to create or to modify the law. His role was one of simple administration; only in order to organise and facilitate the administration of justice could he intervene in the formulation of a law he did not create. By means of ordinances, edicts and administrative practices of one kind or another deriving their authority from royal prerogative, the sovereign could correct certain judicial lapses, organise courts of justice and regulate procedure but he did not, properly speaking, make laws.[32] In the twelfth century, the great Canon law scholar Gratian (d. *circa* 1159) insisted that for a law to be valid it must be confirmed through usage—an idea which remained predominant for a long time.

In this view of things, then, the ordinances issued by royal authorities in this whole period played an important part in the development of administrative structures, in what today we would call "public law," and in criminal law which was then linked to police regulation. In Germany at this period the only imperial law of any widespread or real importance was the *Carolina* of 1532 dealing with criminal law. On the whole, however, legislation was of no great significance in the development of private law. Ruling sovereigns were generally well disposed towards custom in the sense that they did not aspire even to modify it. The French kings, in particular, made it their business to see that regional customs were reduced to writing in order that they might be preserved. It is therefore incorrect to imagine that they were predisposed to favour Roman law because it re-enforced or justified their absol-

---

[32] This idea is well established in Muslim thinking: the sovereign, by his *Kānūns*, can only provide for the application of legal principles already established, independently of him, by other and different sources. Hindu law draws a similar distinction. *Cf. infra.* Part Four.

ute sovereignty. The extent to which private law was in fact modified was really due to royal interventions in procedural matters—the importance of the substitution to the old oral procedures of a written procedure, inspired by the canonical model, which did facilitate the reception of Roman law, has already been emphasised. Even the absolute French monarchs did not consider themselves entirely free to change private law. They gave up any idea of attempting to unify French private law, as recommended by doctrinal writers. There were no more than a dozen or so royal *ordonnances* or *édits* on private law subjects prior to 1789.[33] The sixteenth century French *ordonnances* (Villers-Cotterets, 1539; Moulins, 1566) deal only with procedure and evidence. Those of Colbert (1619–1683) in the seventeenth century touched only on matters of judicial administration and police (*Ordonnances sur la procédure, sur le commerce, sur la marine*); they did not touch upon the private law as such. The *Ordonnances* of D'Aguesseau (1688–1751) in the eighteenth century did deal with private law (gifts, wills), but it was felt necessary to present them as being fundamentally a systematised explanation of the rules already accepted by custom; the king did not consider he could change the law solely according to his will alone.

In the eighteenth century the Natural Law School broke with this tradition. It did not go so far as to recognise the omnipotence of the sovereign or to attribute the character of law to commands resulting from an arbitrary exercise of his will. But the School was ready to see a legislator in the sovereign it allotted to him the function of reforming the law in order to reject past errors and establish the authority of rules which fully conformed to reason. Through the force of these ideas, the countries of the European continent moved towards the new formula of codification, very different from that of the earlier compilations. This marks the beginning of the modern period in the history of the Romano-Germanic family of laws, a period in which the legislators took the leading role in the work of discovering and developing the law.

---

[33] Arnaud (A. J.), *Les origines doctrinales du code civil français* (1969), p. 5.

CHAPTER II

THE PERIOD OF LEGISLATIVE LAW

46. Growth of public law

The Natural Law School achieved two spectacular successes. The first of these was to bring about a recognition of the law's new role in the sphere of relations between those who govern and those who are governed, between the authority of the state and private individuals. Roman law had formulated the distinction between public and private law, but this was done in order to leave public law, if indeed it existed, aside[1]—in other words, jurists prudently avoided this reserved and dangerous area. The Natural Law School put an end to this taboo. Since the eighteenth century, jurists have extended their investigations to public law subjects, and have succeeded since the French Revolution in building a legal structure parallel to that of traditional private law. But the degree of success has varied: it has, generally speaking, been considerable in criminal law; middling in administrative law; and somewhat mixed in constitutional law.

47. Codification

The second notable success of the Natural Law School was codification. Codification, however revolutionary it may have appeared, was nonetheless the natural fulfilment of the universities' ideas and endeavours over the centuries.[2] For 600 years the universities had taught a law which they presented as a model of justice. Much effort had been expended in imbuing jurists with this idea. Now they were convinced of its excellence and considered the local laws no more than an archaic survival of an obscure past,

---

[1] Schultz (F.), *Principles of Roman Law* (1936); Jolowicz (H. F.). *Roman Foundations of Modern Law* (1957).
[2] *Cf.* in general, Vanderlinden (J.), *Le concept de code en Europe occidentale du XIIIe au XIXe siècle* (1967).

a *ius asininum* alongside the model law of the universities. Why not, under the aegis of Reason whose light was at last clearly visible everywhere, take the decisive and now obvious step? Why not make the model law of the universities, completed and refined by the Natural Law School, the living, real and *applied* law of different countries? On this point the Natural Law School marks a turning point in history; for the first time there was a willingness to make a real law of the taught but ideal law. Again for the first time, it was admitted that the sovereign is capable of defining law and of reforming it as a whole. True, this power is accorded him in order to expound the principles of natural law. But as Cambacérès (1753–1824), principal legal adviser to Napoleon, once admitted, it would be easy to change this purpose, and legislators, apart from any consideration for "natural laws," could use this power to transform the basis of society.[3]

Codification was the technique which eventually enabled the ambition of the Natural Law School to be realised. It consolidated the evolution of Romanist scholarship over the centuries, and systematically expounded the law as suited to eighteenth century society—a law, therefore, to be adopted on the practical as well as the theoretical level, and one whose organisation was a far cry from the chaotic compilations of Justinian.

Codification not only served to fuse theoretical and practical law; it also put an end to the all too frequent archaisms, to the fragmentation of the law, and to the multiplicity of customs, often a drawback in practice and, by this time, impossible to justify in theory. Codification is thus to be distinguished from the official or private compilations of the preceding centuries. These had occasionally, and very quietly in some cases, brought about certain useful reforms. However, with their lack of scope or general applicability they were ill-suited to realise the ambition of the Natural Law School.

For codification to be successful two conditions had to be fulfilled. It had first of all to be the work of an enlightened sovereign, one unhampered by the past and willing—even at the expense of the privileges of an older order—to establish the new principles of justice, freedom and dignity of the individual which, politically,

---

[3] It may be observed here that in the U.S.S.R. and Socialist countries the revolutionary transformation of society through legislation is always presented as being imposed by the "natural law" of historical materialism.

the Natural Law School maintained must be the basis of society. The new compilations also had to be established in a country powerful enough to exercise an inescapable influence over others. In other words, codification could hardly have succeeded, and renew as it did the existing elements of the system, except under the very conditions in which it was in fact realised: that is, in France, immediately after the Revolution and in association with the new ideas of 1789 and the prestige of Napoleonic expansion. The Prussian *Allgemeines Landrecht* of 1794 failed for lack of the first condition; the Austrian Civil Code of 1811 had only a limited influence by reason of the failure of the second.

48. Merits of codification

Codification is often said to have caused a division of European law, and to have fragmented the European legal community and Romano-Germanic family. This observation requires some comment.

The critics of codification argue as though the law taught in the universities prior to codification was the law as practised, and as though a uniform European common law had in fact existed. This had never been true. Codification, when the process was finished, reduced European laws to a certain number of national systems. This regrouping helped to reinforce the European community rather than fragment it. The adoption outside France of the Napoleonic Code in particular, which has often been described,[4] had a considerable influence in this sense.

In itself, therefore, codification has in no way broken the unity of European law. On the contrary, it is the fulfilment of a common trend. Codification moreover constituted an admirable instrument for extending the Romano-Germanic system both in Europe and beyond its borders. This last is an important point, which will be re-examined.

49. Regrettable consequences of codification

But the codification movement was not wholly beneficial even with respect to the cohesion of the system. Its harmful effects were

---

[4] *L'influence du code civil dans le monde* (Travaux de la Semaine internationale de droit, Paris, 1950), 1954. *Adde* the articles published in the *Revue internationale de droit comparé* of 1954, no. 4 (the 150th anniversary of the Civil Code). *Cf.* also Schwartz (B.), *The Code Napoleon and the Common Law World* (1956).

however produced independently of the principle itself, and it now falls in large measure to jurists to correct them. The "perfection of reason" achieved in the form of the civil codes of France (1804), Germany (1896) and Switzerland (1881–1907) obscured the university tradition—that of promoting, through teaching, the search for just laws and the proposal of a model law—in favour of expounding and commenting the practitioners' law of this or that country or region. After the appearance of national civil codes these two functions seemed to coincide; the role of the universities was seen as limited to carrying out a mere exegesis of the new texts. Gone were the practical spirit of the post-glossators, the advanced thinking of the pandectists; in their stead, law professors returned to the spirit and approach of the glossators' school and merely glossed the new texts. Contrary to the very ideas which had inspired them, the codes engendered an attitude of legal positivism which was further aggravated by nationalistic sentiment.[5] Jurists now considered their national law to be *the Law*. They took refuge in their codes, abandoning the idea that law, as a norm of social conduct, was in essence supranational.

50. Legislative positivism and legal nationalism

The purpose of codification was to enunciate the principles of a rejuvenated *ius commune*, adapted to the circumstances and needs of the nineteenth century. As successors to the *usus modernus*, the codes were to have been a *usus modernissimus Pandectarum*. But the decline of the universalist spirit and the rise of 19th century nationalism made something else of codification—at least for a time. Under these conditions the codes were treated, not as new expositions of the "common law of Europe," but as mere generalisations or new editions of "particular customs" raised to a national level. Instead of seeing them as their promoters had envisaged, as a new expression of the *ius commune*, they were regarded as instruments of a "nationalisation of law." This led to the virtual disappearance in Europe of the very idea of a *ius commune*. The dramatic event in Europe was not codification itself,

---

[5] However it is interesting to note that in 1827 Zachariae wrote that there must "exist in all Europe, at least among the interpreters of the civil law, as among those who study nature, a union which no difference of a political nature should upset" (*Handbuch des französischen Rechts*, 3rd ed., 1827 p. viii). It is known that the work of Zachariae was used as a model by Aubry and Rau for their famous *Cours de droit civil français*.

but the German rejection of French codification.[6] And, as success-ive European states adopted codes, not one university continued to follow the admirable instructions of the Marquis de Pombal embodied in the new statutes of the Portuguese University of Coimbra (1772) which prescribed that the quest for law be carried out, not among the subtleties of Roman law, but in the principles of law common to all civilised nations.

Codification, and the whole subsequent legislative movement, led therefore to an attitude of legislative positivism. At the same time, it brought about a legal nationalism, in which the existence of a European (but also an increasingly extra-European) legal community of nations and the idea of a Romano-Germanic family of law seemed to founder. Law ceased to be identified with justice and was now associated with the legislative sovereignty of each nation. All European countries but especially France and Germany were drawn to adopt this point of view which is that of Marxism. The countries least affected were the smallest and, para-doxically, those without universities or which exhibited greater national modesty. It was, of course, only after codification in each country that this change in attitude became evident. Paradoxically, it should be remembered that the codes themselves were often constructed on the basis of comparative law, or that the model for one code was sought in one country and that for another in some other country.[7] This double practice really does attest to the kin-ship of all the laws in the Romano-Germanic family and should be taken as a condemnation of that view which believes it possible to concentrate solely upon any one national law. The progress of legal science and the improvement of law cannot advance on that basis.

51. New tendencies

Today the crisis seems to have abated. The passage of time since codification, the ageing of the codes, have at least diminished if not eliminated nineteenth century legal positivism. The essential

---

[6] The fortunes of continental law might have been different if the French code, received in Belgium, the Netherlands, the Rhenish provinces, Luxembourg, Baden, Poland and Italy, had been accepted throughout Germany as well.

[7] *Cf.* for Greece, Zepos (P. J.), "The Historical and Comparative Background of the Greek Civil Code," *Inter-American Law Review*, (1961), Vol. III, pp. 285–316. The same thing occurred in Japan, Rumania and Turkey.

role of doctrinal writing and judicial decisions in forming and evolving the law is more openly acknowledged. Positivism has taken on a new meaning; no jurist in France or Germany would now think that legislative texts alone suffice for a knowledge of the law. Even in criminal law, where the principle *nulla poena sine lege* (no penalty without prior legal authority) might seem to support such a belief, the ever greater powers given either to judges or administrative officials to fix a penalty and regulate its execution put the law, as a matter of fact, very much in a state of dependence upon the professed ideal of those who administer it. With the proliferation of international conventions and the development of comparative law, judges are increasingly obliged, or at least encouraged, to take into account foreign concepts and legal interpretation. Legal nationalism is thus on the decline, and it is to be hoped that the crisis provoked by the European codification movement in the nineteenth and twentieth centuries has been no more than temporary. The present revival of interest in natural law may well lead to the renaissance of the idea of a *ius commune*—to a renewal of the feeling that law should not be identified with legislation and should not therefore be imprinted with any special national characteristic.

It is clear, however, that law is now passing through another crisis. Formerly the main concern was with the idea of corrective justice; today the main preoccupation is with notions of a distributive or social justice. The consequence is that emphasis is no longer placed upon private law and how the state and government can bring about a new justice in a renewed society. The notions and techniques that served in earlier times are ill-adapted to this new vision. It was relatively easy to ascertain how justice could be satisfied in the relations of buyer and seller, landlord and tenant, publisher and author. In all these cases there were sufficiently precise rules to settle the matter. It is much more difficult to monitor and regulate the government when it comes to such matters as whether a building permit should issue, what land should be expropriated for a work of public interest, whether some business enterprise should receive a grant, or whether foreigners should be given entry into the country. Our traditional legal techniques leave us poorly equipped to solve such problems to the point where some people even question whether they really involve law at all. The answer should be that they clearly do because the role of law and that of jurists is to implement and make tangible the concepts of justice prevailing in society. And it is no less evident that to achieve this new law demanded by these new ideas, it is especially relevant to observe the practices in other countries and to appeal to comparative law.

Nineteenth-century French doctrinal writers had no interest in foreign writings. About 1900, however, this attitude changed; French authors increasingly turned their backs on the nationalism of the last century which, in our modern world, is nothing less than provincialism. The work of François Gény (1861–1959) marks the turning point.[8] Today, modern thinkers are prepared to return to the original idea of codification and, like such thinkers as Pombal, Jhering, Edouard Lambert (1866–1947) and R. Saleilles, are ready to regard comparative law as the successor to Roman law and as the means of discovering and developing a European *ius commune*. The same idea is taking hold—perhaps even more firmly—in other European countries. In Germany, K. Zweigert has exposed the "pathological condition" which, in a shrinking world, will result from confining law within national frontiers; in Spain, the president of the Supreme Court, don José Castán Tobeñas,[9] has declared his apostleship of comparative law. In France the reappearance of the teaching of the philosophy and sociology of law indicates a return to universalism on the part of the law faculties. The recent development of public law studies does not contradict this tendency, since it is generally agreed that the *ius commune* of the twentieth century, unlike that of earlier times, must include public as well as private law.

52. Continual change of the system

In the preceding passages some of the main factors contributing to the unity of the Romano-Germanic family of law have been discussed. It is now necessary to complement them by indicating certain movements which, at different times and in different countries, may have appeared to compromise this unity and imply that a portion of the family might break away to become autonomous. Romano-Germanic law is a living law; and this implies

[8] *Méthode d'interprétation et sources en droit privé positif* (1899).
[9] Castán Tobeñas (J.), *Los sistemas juridicos contemporaneous del mundo occidenta* (1956).

continual change which naturally originates more especially in one or another of the countries adhering to the system. The continued life of the system is thus linked to a certain amount of natural diversity; the movements of change originate in one country or group of countries before being generally followed or rejected by others in the family. There is always, therefore, a certain disparity between the different national laws of the system, any one of which may be somewhat out of step in relation to the others. Comparison shows that in some aspect or branch of the law one country may sometimes take the lead, by way of experiment for example, and the question then arises whether the unity of the family is disrupted. The answer depends on whether the change will be adopted in other countries or whether, alternatively, it will be abandoned by its originators in favour of tradition.

When examining the sources and structure of the continental European laws, there will be opportunity to draw attention to this diversity which always tends to obscure the fundamental unity of the Romano-Germanic family. Without anticipating this discussion, it is nevertheless useful to mention here several facts which illustrate this movement, this permanent diversity which characterises and conditions the very life of the system.

53. Historically transient factors of diversity

We have already noted the differences between the various Romanist schools over the centuries in the actual teaching of the universities: the *mos gallicus*, historical in tendency, confronted the *mos italicus* oriented towards an adaptation of the rules of law to practice; the *mos ibericus* was distinguished by its more conservative tendencies; the more daring and innovating *mos germanicus* gave rise to the School of Pandectists. One might think that these regional tendencies would have put the uniformity of continental European law into constant danger; it survived nevertheless because its unity was restored by the triumph of the Natural Law School which, by overtaking these various tendencies, resolved their differences.

Even so, the very success of the concept of codification seemed at a later period to put this unity in question once again. It was problematical whether France would be followed in the experiment of Napoleonic codification, and then whether the codes would bring about a fragmentation of European law. In the end, however, the French formula of codification was adopted by almost all countries. It now seems increasingly clear that the diversity of the codes, similar to that of the customs and laws of earlier times, does not necessarily create a split in the Romano-Germanic family of law.

It is true, however, that the time-lag between the codifications in France and Germany did leave certain traces. During the entire period when French jurists were devoting themselves to the exegesis of their own codes, German jurists continued the work of the universities on the Roman law texts, and in Germany, a new school—that of the Pandectists—was successful in bringing the Romanist principles to a degree of systematisation hitherto unattained. The drafting of the German Civil Code at the end of the nineteenth century was carried out on the basis of this Pandectist scholarship. The result is a difference in both method and style between the French and German Civil Codes. This difference is visibly the product of an historical accident, and it is unlikely to be the source of a permanent opposition between German and French laws; it would certainly be unwarranted to see in it a difference in principle between Latin and Germanic conceptions of law, in the face of their similar historical development and when, indeed, the laws of the "Germanic" countries other than Germany (Austria, the Netherlands, Switzerland, and the Scandinavian countries) have remained closer to French law than they have to German law in their distaste for abstractions.

54. "Latin" and "Germanic" laws

It is possible, then, to speak of a group of "laws of Latin countries" in contrast to German law, which would include in addition to French law those of Italy, Spain and Portugal? Such a proposition does not meet with unanimous approval. The laws of the various Latin countries of Europe certainly are similar if only in the terminology they employ. But they differ in numerous ways, and these differences can be considered just as basic as those existing between French and German or Swedish law. J. Carbonnier, pointing out that Spanish and Italian laws have remained Catholic, concluded that "there is a confessional aspect in what one might call the Latin juridical system, which distinguishes it from present

French law."[10] Other authors stress the greater influence of German legal doctrines in Italy and Spain than in France. But one might just as well emphasise the important differences between Italian law and the laws of the Iberian peninsula in respect, for example, to matrimonial property law or civil procedure, or constitutional and administrative law.

Each law on the European continent—and this is certain—has its originality. No attempt is being made here to deny this originality; nor is it intended to underestimate the significance of these differences. Two things seem clear, nevertheless. The first is the great resemblance which in the last analysis exists among these laws, all elements considered: it is certainly possible to speak of a Romano-Germanic family. The second is that grouping laws within the Romano-Germanic family as Latin or Germanic, attempted by some, is artificial and forced when the sub-group is based on only one or several branches of law. French law, seen as a whole, does not seem closer to Italian or Spanish law than it is to German or Swiss law. Nor do the differences that can be detected among the laws of the Scandinavian countries prevent them from being included in the Romano-Germanic family.[11]

55. The secession of the socialist laws

The diversity of economic structures and political regimes in various countries has posed and still does pose another problem. True, the unity of European continental laws was established and maintained over the centuries, in very different countries, from feudal systems to the socialising democracies of our own time. One must not, however, underestimate the risk implied by the diversity of economic structures and political regimes. Historically this unity was based on the development of the private law. If the unity achieved to date can withstand the present economic and political variations, it is because the private law in each country is largely independent of economics and politics. However, law today is no longer made up of only private law; a public law, of ever increasing importance to private individuals, has been developed since the

---

[10] Carbonnier (J.), *Droit civil*, t. I: *Institutions judiciaires et droit civil* (14th ed., 1982), p. 88. Divorce was however admitted in Italy in 1970.

[11] Sundberg (J. W. F.), "Civil Law, Common Law and the Scandinavians" (1969) 13 *Scandinavian Studies in Law* p. 181–205.

French Revolution, and one cannot ignore the fact that the unity of the Romano-Germanic family will be one-sided, and dangerously little more than a façade, if it is limited to private law and not extended to public law. This is more so today than ever before because the ever increasing intervention of the state gives more and more importance to the public law upon which private law is more and more dependent.

The danger of rupture within the family is particularly great when a regime is established in one country which aspires to being truly revolutionary and which, not content with merely remodelling the country's institutions, may go so far as to repudiate our basic philosophical concept of law. Leaving aside the tragic episode—happily behind us—of Germany's National Socialism, there is today a very serious division among countries which formerly belonged to the Romano-Germanic family: that is, between the U.S.S.R. (and those countries adhering to Marxism-Leninism) on the one hand and the other countries of continental Europe on the other. At the present time, this division is sufficiently marked to be considered a veritable secession. Therefore, and as advocated by socialist thinkers themselves, we have grouped Soviet law and the laws of the people's socialist republics as a distinct family of laws, independent of the Romano-Germanic family.

It is difficult to maintain, however, that the concept of law now held in the U.S.S.R. and the people's republics is completely original. Based principally upon the philosophy of Karl Marx and Vladimir Ilytch Lenin, both of whom received their legal education in a country of Romano-Germanic tradition, the socialist concept of law can be directly traced to the movement of legal positivism. This movement, prevalent in the nineteenth century and still vigorous in the twentieth, sees law as the expression of the will of the legislators, supreme interpreters of justice. Soviet authors have pushed this idea to its extreme limit, whereas Western jurists have reacted against it and, in order to reaffirm the traditional idea of a close link between justice and law, have sought to free themselves from the association established in the nineteenth century between law and the state. Soviet thinking does fundamentally differ from ours, however, in its prediction of the future, in which it purports to see a society without law. For the moment, however, the Soviets retain the notions of a state, of law and of a principle of legality which, even though qualified as socialist, nonetheless are reminiscent of the bourgeois ideas of state and law. At the present time, the law of the states of the socialist bloc appears to adhere more faithfully to the positivist ideas now in decline in the West than to herald a truly new order. This is undoubtedly true of the U.S.S.R.; it is even more so of the people's republics. It is not impossible however that in 50 or 100 years this early unity will be re-established.

CHAPTER III

EXPANSION BEYOND EUROPE

The colonisation of vast territories beyond the seas brought about the expansion of the Romano-Germanic family of law outside Europe. The technique of codification adopted in the nineteenth and twentieth centuries also favoured its establishment in many other countries.

56. The new world

The Spanish, Portuguese, French and Dutch colonies in America, established in practically uninhabited areas or those where the indigenous civilisation was eventually to disappear, accepted the characteristic legal ideas of the Romano-Germanic family quite naturally. Rudimentary law applied in practice, to begin with, outside the towns and a few centres, in view of the lack of established government and in the absence of jurists. As the development of colonies in the new world progressed, the law as practised drew closer to the scholars' or doctrinal law taught in the early American universities[1] and the mother countries, and afterwards as incorporated in codes drafted according to the European example. At no time was there ever any suggestion of rejecting this tradition. The only question is the extent to which the laws of America, which grew to maturity in conditions very different from those prevailing in Europe, have developed original characteristics when compared to the European laws of the Romano-Germanic family. An agrarian system may thus, for example, have survived in various Indian communities of Mexico, Guatemala or Peru in which the ostensible owner of the land, according to custom, is really no more than a representative of the group on whose behalf and in whose interest he works the land. Daily life is carried on in Haiti,

---

[1] The University of San Marcos of Lima was created in 1551, the University of Mexico in 1553.

in many spheres, according to custom that is quite divorced from the formal law of the country.[2]

A further question, moreover, remains with respect to certain areas of North America, formerly subject to Spanish or French domination but which today belong to larger political units where the Common law is preponderant (Louisiana, Quebec) or which are subject to the sovereignty or dominating political influence of a Common law country (Guyana, Puerto Rico, and the Panama Canal Zone).[3] Can the traditional membership in the Romano-Germanic family be maintained in such circumstances? A negative answer must be given in the case of the vast former French possession known as *Louisiane*, with the exception of the present State of Louisiana which, as the former territory of New Orleans at the mouth of the Mississippi, formed only a small part of it. The former Spanish possessions which are now states of the United States (Florida, California, New Mexico, Arizona, Texas, etc.) have preserved certain institutions of the old colonial law, but today they too have become Common law jurisdictions. The same is true of the Panama Canal Zone and Guyana. The State of Louisiana, St. Lucia, the Province of Quebec and Puerto Rico have, on the contrary, successfully maintained their private law tradition up to the present time. They are "mixed" jurisdictions, borrowing certain elements from the Common law and only to some extent retaining their membership in the Romano-Germanic family.

57. Africa and Malagasy (Madagascar)

An expansion of the Romano-Germanic family has also taken place through the effects of colonisation in Black Africa and Madagascar. No truly established system of law existed in these countries where generally very fragmented tribal structures paralysed any legal evolution. The very idea of law was imported, along with order and peace, by the colonial powers. The states emerging from the former French colonial empire, the former Belgian Congo, Rwanda and Burundi, and the Spanish and Portuguese possessions have become members of the Romano-Germanic family. Mauritius and the Seychelles, despite their place in the

---

[2] Montalvo-Despeignes (J.), *Le droit informel haïtien* (1976).
[3] Cuba has now passed into the family of Socialst laws.

British Commonwealth, also belong to the same group for historical reasons. Ethiopia, apart from any European colonisation, adopted codes in 1957 and 1960 (criminal, civil and commercial) of French inspiration.[4] Elements provided by tradition and custom have, of course, been retained, especially in the private law. Civil and criminal procedure are, however, contained in codes of English inspiration. Only evolution will show whether Ethiopian law and the other laws of Black Africa are to be considered as one or several autonomous groups within the Romano-Germanic family.

Before their annexation by England, the countries which make up the Union of South Africa belonged to the Romano-Germanic family by reason of their Dutch colonisation. The Roman-Dutch law applied there was endangered by English rule. Under the latter influence changes were made which suggest that today the laws of South Africa, Zimbabwe (Rhodesia), Botswana, Lesotho and Ngwane are "mixed laws."

North Africa, as well, belongs to the Romano-Germanic family, because the different countries into which it is divided received French or Italian laws through the effects of colonisation or under the political or cultural influence of France. However, Muslim law has continued to play an important role in these countries; their laws, which today combine ideas from both systems, must also be considered "mixed."

58. Asia and Indonesia

The Romano-Germanic family of law has gained adherents at the two extremities of Asia. Turkey, since the beginning of the *Tanzimāt* era in 1839, has looked to continental codes for the models to modernise its law. It remained faithful to its Muslim tradition until World War I, but has since endeavoured to bring about change by rejecting this tradition and removing all Muslim elements from its law; by reason of its legislation it has, since that time, become a full member of the Romano-Germanic family.

The Arab states, formed in the Near East following the breakup of the Ottoman Empire in 1918, have been less revolutionary. Their evolution has been similar to that of Egypt. Since 1918 they have retained and emphasised legal ties with France, bequeathed

---

[4] David (R.), "Le Code civil éthiopien de 1960" (1961) 26 *Rabels Z.* 668.

by the Ottoman Empire and corresponding moreover to their own inclinations. However, they have not completely secularised their law as Turkey did, and some matters remained governed by Muslim law for citizens of that faith. Israel is a special case; because of the British mandate, the influence of the Common law has largely supplanted that of the Franco-Ottoman law formerly in force.[5] The same thing occurred in Iraq and Jordan but the disappearance of the British mandate in these countries was followed by a return to the concepts of Romano-Germanic law.

The Arabian peninsula has undergone little Romano-Germanic influence up to the present time. How it will modernise still remains something of a puzzle. It cannot now be said whether the English and American economic influence, powerful in Saudi Arabia, South Yemen and the different emirates of the Persian Gulf, will prevail or whether closer links with the Egyptian and Arab worlds will orient the laws of these countries towards at least a partial adherence to the Romano-Germanic family. The People's Socialist Republic of Yemen has drawn close to countries of the Socialist family.

Iran, with a codification on the French model, is in a situation comparable to that of Egypt, Syria or Iraq. Here again there is a mixed law, partly Romano-Germanic and partly founded on Islamic ideas. Afghanistan has indicated its desire to move towards the Romano-Germanic family but this evolution is only beginning. The situation in these two countries is therefore not clear. It is difficult to say whether the preponderant influence will be Romano-Germanic or Socialist and the extent to which one or the other will be countered by a return to the Muslim tradition.

At the other end of Asia, the Romano-Germanic family had only a transient success in China; the preponderant position of continental European laws was destroyed by the success of the Communist Party. The same thing occurred in Vietnam and North Korea. However links with the Romano-Germanic family remain in the case of Japan, Formosa (Taiwan), Siam and South Korea whereas in the states replacing French Indo-China (South Vietnam, Cambodia, Laos) the situation is more complex. Here, as in Africa, colonisation and spontaneous reception explain this connection.

---

[5] Shaley (G.) & Herman (S.), "A Source Study of Israel's Contract Codification" 35 Louisiana L.Rev. 1091–1115 (1975).

Spanish colonisation brought the Philippines into the Romano-Germanic legal family. Fifty years of occupation by the United States of America have nevertheless introduced new elements, making Philippine law a mixed system.

Finally, the law of Sri Lanka (Ceylon) has undergone an evolution similar to that of South Afirica; it too must be considered a mixed law.

To a certain extent Indonesia, colonised by the Dutch, belongs to the Romano-Germanic family. Here, however, Romano-Germanic concepts combine with Muslim and customary law (*adat* law) in such a way that it is appropriate to consider this system as mixed also.

TITLE II

STRUCTURE OF THE LAW

59. Outline

The laws of the Romano-Germanic family differ considerably in their substantive rules. This is especially true of public law, which varies according to each country's political options and the degree of centralisation it has attained. It is also true of private law, which in its various branches has reached different stages of development and comprises in some countries concepts unknown to others. But apart from the substantive rules, the laws of the Romano-Germanic family can be considered together because of their structural similarity.

This last statement must, however, be verified from two points of view. First, what are the categories within which the legal rules themselves are arranged and classified? Secondly, is the concept of the legal rule—the primary element of any legal system—the same in these various laws? Each of these aspects will be discussed in a separate chapter.

CHAPTER I

DIVISIONS AND CONCEPTS

60. Public law and private law

In all the countries of the Romano-Germanic family, legal science places the rules of law in the same principal categories. Everywhere the same great basic division between public and private law is found.[1] The distinction is based upon an idea which is taken as fundamental by jurists of this family: the sphere of relations between those who govern and those who are governed raises special problems and calls for a different approach when compared with that of relations between private persons. The reason is, simply, that the public interest and the interest of private individuals cannot be weighed in the same balance.

History supports this observation. It has always been easier to impose respect for the law upon private persons, as between whom the state can act as an arbitrator, than it is to impose it upon the state itself. A distinction between "public law" and "private law" has therefore traditionally been drawn, in response to the idea that law derives from a natural order of things which is both earlier than and superior to any notion of "state." But in fact only private law was the object of any serious scholarly attention for many centuries; public law appeared to be a vain, even a dangerous subject. Rome had no constitutional or administrative law, as we would understand it. Criminal law developed only in the shadow of private law because it too appeared, more often than not, to be a matter involving private individuals (the wrong-doer and his victim or their families); it never really became part of "public law" and never attained the degree of development that private law did.[2]

Some early writers, placing themselves at the confines of law

---

[1] In general *cf.* Szladits (C.), *International Encyclopaedia of Comparative Law* (1974), Vol. 2, Chap. 2.
[2] *Cf.* Kunkel (W.), *Roman Legal and Constitutional History* (1973).

and political science, sought to systematise public law rules in several areas. The subject matter was, however, too closely bound up with politics and governmental mechanisms for them to have had any really practical significance. Critical descriptions of various institutions and practices then followed might be compiled easily enough, but these efforts at clarification and reflection were very different from the work accomplished in respect of private law by the universities. In the nineteenth century new perspectives in the development of public law were opened up when doctrines advocating the primacy of reason and the existence of the "natural rights" of man were accepted in a number of European countries and ushered in democratic political regimes. This brought with it the desire to transform into a reality what had hitherto been only an ideal—that the state, no longer ruled by the divine right of kings, would be organised in conformity with reason and with a view to guaranteeing the natural rights of citizens against abuses of power. In the twentieth century these two aims have become even more pressing because the policeman-state of the past has given way to a welfare-state charged with many more functions affecting private individuals.[3]

The problem has thus been how to superintend and discipline the state in the many activities which, in the nature of things, necessarily imply the exercise of its discretionary power. The government directs the country's social and economic development, it imposes restraints upon the exercise of ownership, it regulates the professions, grants permits, licences and special favours,—how are these various activities to be reconciled, as they must be, with the cherished principles of freedom and equality? And how can the government, without a paralysis of its own operation, be required to take into account a range of private interests that the constitution itself may enshrine? There is therefore a range of new problems to be faced for which one might well ask whether some new administrative science, rather than law, is not more appropriate. And these new problems exist alongside those that have been ever present and have taken on new importance— how can the courts created by the state and called to judge in its name be guaranteed at the same time a role sufficiently independent of it? How, moreover, can the state's agencies be brought to

---

[3] Cortinas Pelaez (L.), *Perspectivas del derecho publico en la segundad mitad del siglo XX. Homenaje a Enrique Sayaguès-Laso* (1969) 5 vols.

submit to the courts' jurisdiction and to execute their judgments? An effective public law calls for a highly developed civic sense in both administrators and in the public at large. It is not, in short, workable unless the feeling is widely shared that all government bodies must bow to judicial control. It supposes, in addition, that government officials view the people as citizens rather than as subjects. Past experience has demonstrated how great the difficulties can be when an effort is made to prompt the state to carry through with some act of elementary justice or to renounce some unreasonable project.[4]

61. Weakness of public law

The realisation of all these conditions is difficult; it has been very slow and, in some countries, very incomplete, In the Romano-Germanic family, public law has attained a degree of development and perfection certainly inferior to that of the private law.

Consider the example of France. France is without doubt the country, or at least one of the countries of the Romano-Germanic family, where administrative law (*le droit administratif*) has attained the highest degree of development. The work accomplished by the French Council of State (*Conseil d'Etat*) in this area is justly admired; it has been used as a model in numerous other states, and even English jurists have paid tribute to it.[5] But when this much-praised administrative law is compared to the civil law, what insufficiencies, what weaknesses! The care taken not to intervene unduly in matters relating to the courts leads the Council of State to refuse to exercise any control over judicial police authorities; but very great powers, on the other hand, are conceded to the police authorities for detaining individuals suspected of activities which are sometimes very poorly and very inadequately defined.[6] Unlike the sanctions which the government may impose, many of the favours which it can confer are not subject to any judicial control. Thus a taxpayer, even in the absence of any textually established right or some error actually committed in his

---

[4] Peyrefitte (A.), *Le mal français* (1977), chaps. xxiv, xxv.
[5] Hamson (C. J.), *Executive Discretion and Judicial Control* (1954).
[6] Burdeau (G.), *Les libertés publiques* (4th ed., 1972), Colliard (C. A.), *Libertés publiques* (6th ed., 1982).

case, can bargain with the tax authorities or obtain a release in view of his "special circumstances."[7]

French administrative tribunals do not see themselves as having the power to address orders to administrative agencies[8]; they restrict themselves to quashing illegal actions or decisions and recognising that private persons involved are owed compensation. The delays and difficulties involved in enforcing judgments of administrative tribunals have, moreover, too often weakened what would otherwise be a truly effective administrative law.[9]

Scandals are relatively rare and mild in France, but one must not have any illusions. Their number and scope are limited by the sense of duty and the conscientiousness of an administration which is generally excellent; but administrative law, with its controls and sanctions, would by itself be insufficient to prevent them. If this is so in France, the country renowned for its administrative law, what must be the situation in a number of other countries where there is neither the liberal French tradition nor a government, like that of France, devoted to the service of the state and the law?

62. Different branches of law

In public as well as in private law, the same fundamental branches are found in all countries of the Romano-Germanic family: constitutional law, administrative law, public international law, criminal law, the law of procedure, civil and commercial law, labour law, etc. And this same correspondence of established categories, found again at a lower level in their institutions and concepts, accounts for the fact that, as a general rule, no major difficulty is experienced in the translation of legal vocabulary within the French, German, Spanish, Italian, Dutch, Greek or Portuguese languages.

This conceptual similarity gives anyone familiar with one such law great facility in understanding the others. The substantive

---

[7] According to the French Ministère de l'économie et des finances, about 200,000 taxpayers each year obtain some reduction in or release from taxes upon an appeal to the *bienveillance* of the administration. *Le Monde*, August 9, 1968.

[8] This principle, which has an historical justification, is now widely criticised. The power to address orders to the government has been recognised to some extent in the administrative tribunals of the Federal Republic of Germany by a law of 1960. *Cf.* Fromont (1972) Rev. dr. public 135, 154.

[9] Rivero (Jean), "Sanction juridictionnelle et règle de droit" (1964), *Etudes juridiques offertes à L. Julliot de la Morandière* 457–469.

rules enacted in one or another may indeed differ, but one immediately knows what they are about; the question asked or discussed is understood; its context and nature are grasped without the subject being explained and without having to adapt to a foreign way of thinking.

The reason for this community of thought has already been examined. It derives from the fact that for centuries the science of law throughout continental Europe was based on the same teachings rooted in Roman and Canon law. The methods of imparting this knowledge and of accommodating it to practical needs may have differed with the period or the country, but the vocabulary employed was always the same and it expressed the same ideas.

But this explanation itself raises a question. If it is true that the similarity of laws in the Romano-Germanic family is explained by the fact that historically the same legal knowledge flourished in the universities, does it not also follow that the connection between them only exists in the subjects taught? In other words, does the Romano-Germanic family exist only with respect to the private law developed on the basis of the Roman law? Is it still possible to speak of a Romano-Germanic family in public law, criminal law or procedure? To define the degree of affinity between the laws of the Romano-Germanic system, private and public law must be considered successively.

63. Private law

To what extent, first of all, does the private law of the different countries of the Romano-Germanic family have a uniform structure?

Among the actual subject matters regulated by the civil codes some are not of Roman origin. The French Civil Code, for example, has adopted some institutions from Canon law (marriage, filiation) and others from customary law (matrimonial property regimes). It has, on the other hand, profoundly changed certain other subjects (property and inheritance) by affirming the ideas of the Revolution of 1789. What, then, in the end, remains of the legal scholarship as developed in the universities? It is not in fact to be doubted that each national law has an originality, manifested by its particular institutions, in its own private law. Nonetheless, a definite affinity between them does exist.

In the first place, this resemblance is evident in the case of subjects developed on the basis of Roman law. The similarities, however, do not stop there. In the subjects based on Canon law there is the same close community, at least in so far as the laws of Christian countries are concerned. In those subjects deriving from customary law, however, a distinction must be made. The codes may have been drafted on the basis of national or regional customs and in such cases their originality must be acknowledged even though the national or regional customs are, in the end, linked to a limited number of definite types. But in other cases the rules of the code may have been drawn up on the basis of a customary law which, even before codification, was international in character, and in this case the affinity between the different laws reappears. This observation is of considerable practical significance, because it applies to the whole of commercial law, inland as well as maritime. The commercial customs formed in the Middle Ages were fictitiously linked to Roman law in the work of the post-glossators; accepted in the whole of Europe, where they originated, they were received with the Civil law in those countries of the East and Far East that wanted to join the Romano-Germanic family. They constitute, with the pure "Civil law of obligations," a bloc which provides a structural unity for all that relates to business and commercial law.

64. Law of obligations

The "law of obligations," to which reference was made above, is a fundamental category in all laws of the Romano-Germanic family. Those trained in this tradition have great difficulty in understanding that this legal category does not, as such, exist in other legal systems and, in particular, the Common law; their surprise is even greater at the fact that the very concept of "obligation," so basic to the Romano-Germanic philosophy, is unknown in English legal thought and not even susceptible of accurate translation in English legal vocabulary.

An "obligation" in the Romano-Germanic system is the duty of one person, the debtor, to transfer the ownership of property or create a right over it, to do or not to do something to the benefit of another person, the creditor. The obligation may derive from the law alone, as in the case of the "alimentary obligation" between certain close relations; or it may arise by contract (whether nominate or innominate) or even, in some cases, by reason of a uni-lateral undertaking of one person. The obligation may also arise because of a *delict* or *quasi delict*, which language refers to the fact that a person has committed a fault or must compensate for the damage caused by a thing under his care or by a person for whom he must answer. An obligation may, finally, arise from the fact that a person is, by reason of a number of various circumstances, unjustly enriched at the expense of another person who has suf-fered an impoverishment. The "law of obligations" has been developed over the centuries, on the basis of Roman law elements, into the central and fundamental part of the civil law, which itself is the principal subject of legal scholarship in the Romano-Germanic family of laws. This part of the law establishes when and in what circumstances an obligation arises, the particular rules to which it is subject, the consequences of its non-performance, and how it may be modified, performed or extinguished. Its practical importance is obvious, and it has thus been a major doctrinal study over many centuries to the point where it has attained a very high degree of technical perfection. The law of obligations, as a unify-ing factor in the Romano-Germanic family, has an importance equal to, and to the same effect as, the trust in Common law coun-tries or property law in socialist legal systems.

65. Public law

Is the same unity to be found in the system outside the private law and in the jural concepts of procedural, criminal, labour or public law? The answer is of primary interest because of the importance of these branches of law in the contemporary world.

Even though these subjects were not formerly taught in the uni-versities and most of them are inspired by entirely new principles developed in the nineteenth and twentieth centuries, there are great similarities between the various laws of the Romano-Germanic family here as well. Two factors explain these resemb-lances.

The first, an extra-juridical factor, is that a community of thought, especially in philosophy and political science, has devel-oped between these countries. Law very often only gives effect to ideas and tendencies first evident in other spheres. Montesquieu (1689–1755) and Rousseau (1712–1778), for example, had a considerable influence on the development of public law on the whole European continent. In criminal law, the Italian Becarría (1738–1794)[10] laid the modern bases; the theories leading to the individualisation of penalties or admitting the idea of rehabilitation of the offender have, as well, spread to the whole of the western world and from there to other parts of the globe.[11]

The second factor which explains the existence of a Romano-Germanic family of laws, even outside the private law where it originated, is the common *formation* of jurists. In order to translate new philosophical and political ideas into legal terms and develop new branches of law, recourse was had to jurists educated in the civil law. Very naturally, the new rules were established by taking as a model, or at least as a point of departure, the concepts of the Civil law. In various legal orders, therefore, the Civil law has played the role of a "common law" which other branches of law (such as administrative law) have either emulated or attempted to perfect (as in labour law).

The need to consider foreign experience was, on the other hand, greater in those subject matters requiring new development than it was in the Civil law which, on the basis of the Roman law model, had already arrived at a high degree of perfection. There are many examples in constitutional and criminal law showing how legal knowledge has remained international. In administrative law, the work of the French Council of State has placed France, of all the countries of the European continent, at the head of the free democracies, even though the organisation of administrative tribunals is everywhere very different.[12] It is remarkable that the first treatise on administrative law written in Germany was a treatise on *French* administrative law; it was only after this first treatise that its author, Otto Mayer (1846–1924), considered himself ready to write, on his own model,[13] a treatise on German administrative

[10] Cesare Beccaria-Bonesana, *Del delitti e delle pene* (1764), translated by Farrer (J. A.), *Crimes and Punishments* (1880).
[11] On the comparative evolution of criminal law, *cf.* the introduction of M. Ancel to the collection *Les codes pénaux européens* (1957) Vol. 1—published in English as *The Collection of European Penal Codes and the Study of Comparative Law* 106 U. of Pa L.R. 334–384 (1958).
[12] Sayaguès-Laso (E.), *Tratado de derecho administrative* (2 vols. 1953) translated into French as *Traité de droit administratif* (1964).
[13] Mayer (Otto), *Theorie des französischen Verwaltungsrechts* (1886). The *Deutsches Verwaltungsrecht* by the same author was only published in 1895–1896 (French translation: *Le droit administratif allemand*, 4 vols., 1903–1906). For the difference between the French and German concepts of administrative law, *cf.* however, Fromont (M.), *La répartition des compétences entre les tribunaux civils et administratifs en droit allemand* (1960).

law. It is true that France has gone further than other countries in developing the autonomy of administrative law. But the difference between them is one of degree rather than of principle, and it constitutes an interest rather than an obstacle to the comparison of continental European laws.

There is of course no more similarity in the public law structure of the different laws than there is in the more traditional subjects of civil or commercial law. Nevertheless, despite the total renovation of public and criminal law in the past one hundred years—and in spite of the fact that it occurred in subjects where there was no Roman law tradition—the similarities between European or extra-European laws of the Romano-Germanic family are hardly less than in more traditional subjects. Here, as elsewhere, there exists a family of Romano-Germanic law.

66. Originality of certain concepts

The structural similarity of the laws of the Romano-Germanic family is not complete. Different categories or ideas found in one law are not known to others. Numerous examples of this can be given. Spain, for instance, has not completely unified its Civil law; even if the rules of the Spanish Civil Code of 1889 have instituted a "common law" (*derecho común*), there subsist nevertheless special regional laws (*derecho foral*) in different parts of Spain. These two concepts, *derecho común* and *derecho foral*, must be explained to jurists of other countries where the distinction is unknown. Elsewhere, as in Germany, Mexico or Switzerland, a federal law may be distinguished from that of states or cantons. In the realm of concepts Germany may admit a form of forfeiture called *Verwirkung*, Argentina a new form of *sociedad de habilitación*, Switzerland a notion of *charge foncière*, Mexico a particular system of land holding known as *ejido*, and Sweden and other Nordic countries with the *ombudsman* a special institution designed to be a watchdog of the administration. For jurists familiar with any one law of the Romano-Germanic system all these notions are relatively easy to understand because it can be immediately grasped to what end the new institution corresponds and the place it holds in the law. Nevertheless these different concepts do diminish the unity of the system. One of the tasks of those whose concern is the maintenance of this unity is to determine whether the new institution should be integrated into the system because of its general usefulness, or whether its use corresponds to conditions peculiar only to the country experimenting with it. Fortunately, legal science has not failed in this task and a certain parallelism is still to be observed in the development of laws belonging to the Romano-Germanic family since—and despite—the national codifications.

When a new concept appears the problem is clear, but there is greater difficulty when a known institution is deformed. There is then the danger that the similarity of a term, which is retained, may hide a difference in content which this same name tries to express. There is some difficulty in recognising that words and terms such as movables (*meubles*) and immovables (*immeubles*), good faith (*bonne foi*), impossibility of performance (*impossibilité d'exécution*) and unjust enrichment (*enrichissement sans cause*) may have a different content and are, therefore, to some extent different concepts. It suffices here that the difficulty be simply mentioned and note taken of the danger which, because of the difference in the substantive rules, hangs over the structural identity of the laws in the system.

67. Unification of civil and commercial law

Comparative law lawyers have given special attention to two particular developments in the private law. The first is the new technique of the German Civil Code (BGB) which contains a "General Part" (*Allgemeiner Teil*), and the second is the fusion of Civil and commercial law.

In truth, the second development appears to be little more than a mere change in form and therefore of minor importance. The Civil law has been commercialised to such a degree in all economically developed nations that there are hardly any rules left in which commercial obligations are treated differently from civil obligations. Moreover, as a result of the national codifications, the international character of commercial law which formerly distinguished it from the Civil law has now been lost. Whether it is expedient to regulate certain matters in a special code—negotiable instruments, partnership, industrial property, bankruptcy—of particular interest to commerce or businessmen, no longer seems to be a major problem.[14]

As early as 1866, the Province of Quebec had placed a number of commercial subjects in its Civil Code and forsaken any idea of duplicating the French *Code de commerce.*[15] In 1881, Switzerland, for constitutional reasons, enacted a Code of Obligations, rather than a Civil Code, containing the rules of the *civil* law of obligations and commercial law, and this code remained in place when the Civil Code of 1907 was enacted at the federal level for other civil law subjects.[16] In the Netherlands, as early as 1934, the substantive unification of Civil law and commercial law was brought about by means of a provision to the effect that commercial law would apply to everyone, traders and non-traders alike, and to all transactions, as was the case prior to 1807. Italy, in 1942, placed Civil law and commercial law subjects in a single code.

Does this mean that the traditional distinction should be condemned? In Quebec, Switzerland, Italy and the Netherlands Civil law and commercial law remain distinct subjects in university curricula and are taught by specialists in each area. The legislative unification of Civil and commercial law has in these circumstances no more than a purely formal significance. More important today, no doubt, is the transformation of traditional commercial law into "law and economics" and the need to give fresh consideration to political and social factors involved and the interpenetration of public law and private law. Works on commercial law today give a one-sided view of the law of importance to commercial dealings when they are restricted to the traditional framework of commercial law and neglect a whole series of measures (taxation, regulation of exports, credit control, wage policies, etc.) which are of primary importance to trade and commerce.

68. The "general part" of the civil law

The "General Part" (*Allgemeiner Teil*) of the BGB raises quite another problem. It modifies the Civil law system in a way which

---

[14] Rotondi (M.) ed., *L'unité du droit des obligations* (1974). The work comprises 45 articles most of which are in French or English.

[15] Brierley (J. E. C.), "Quebec's Civil Law Codification" (1968), 14 McGill L.J. 521 at pp. 561–562.

[16] In theory the Swiss federal Code of Obligations constitutes Book V of the Civil Code.

may, in the view of some, seriously compromise the unity of the Romano-Germanic family.

The German Civil Code (BGB), promulgated in 1896, has, unlike codes that came into force earlier, a "general part." Here are found various provisions relevant to different branches of Civil law, such as rules on the capacity of persons, the calculation of delays, prescriptive periods, etc. in a first "book" which is then followed by four books dealing with the law of obligations, property, the family and inheritance. This feature of the BGB is the result of the highly dogmatic teaching of German universities in the nineteenth century which, dominated by the philosophy of the Pandectist school of thought, had completely changed (while purporting merely to systematise) the German *ius commune*.[17]

Has this systematisation, given the level of its abstraction, been pushed too far? Jurists everywhere, including those in Germany, have asked this question. New codes promulgated since the German Code have sometimes followed its example and sometimes not. In codes adopted since 1900, it has been incorporated by Brazil, Greece, a number of Soviet Socialist Republics, Poland and Czechoslovakia, but was rejected by Switzerland, Mexico, Italy and Hungary. In the Netherlands an intermediate position was adopted—a general part (Book III of the Civil Code) relating only to property rights was inserted.[18]

The existence of a general part in some codes and not in others does at first sight appear to compromise the unity of the Romano-Germanic family. But the distinction between those accepting and those rejecting it really lies more in the intellectual approach of each group to the technique of systematisation and in its propensity to indulge in abstractions rather than in a fundamental structural difference of their respective laws. The idea advanced by some thinkers who believe that one can distinguish between a Germanic style and a Romanist style in this connection is really, in our view, no more than a difference in individual attitudes—some

---

[17] The idea of a "general part" was presented in legislative form for the first time in 1858 in Brazil in the *Consolidação das leis civis* of Augusto Teixeira de Freitas. The Brazilian Civil Code of 1916 may well have incorporated it for this reason rather than by way of imitation of the BGB.

[18] Hartkamp (A. S.), "Civil Code Revision in the Netherlands" 35 Louisiana L.Rev. p. 1059–1090 (1975). Langemeier (G. F.), "La réforme du code civil néerlandais" (1965) Rev. int. dr. comparé 55–72. Zajtay (I.), Rechtsvergleichende Bemerkungen über den Code civil und das Bürgerliche Gesetzbuch (1959) 157 *Archiv für die civilistische Praxis* 479–494.

tending to a general and abstract approach, others having a preference for a more empirical approach. There have been, and there are, in France, those who advocate the inclusion of a general part and those in Germany who are opposed to it. The existence of a "general part" in itself does not in our view undermine the structural unity of the Romano-Germanic family.

CHAPTER II

CONCEPT OF THE LEGAL RULE

69. Unity of the system

The similarities or differences of structure, however, must be observed from a viewpoint other than that of the principal conceptual and organisational classifications—more concretely, how is the legal rule itself conceived? What are its recognised scope, nature and characteristics? A most important element is brought out by this new point of view—an element which once again accounts for the unity of the Romano-Germanic family of law throughout its geographical area as described in this work.

In countries of the Romano-Germanic family, the legal rule is formulated, characterised and analysed in the same way. In this family, in which doctrinal writing is held in high esteem, the legal rule is not considered as merely a rule appropriate to the solution of a concrete case. Through the systematising efforts of the doctrinal authors, the legal rule has risen to a higher level of abstraction: it is viewed as a rule of conduct, endowed with a certain generality, and situated above the specific application which courts or practitioners may make of it in any concrete case. It is fashionable to view with a certain disdain, and as casuistic, the opposite view which places the rule of law at the level of concrete cases only. Digests of decided cases, form books and legal dictionaries are certainly useful working instruments for practitioners, and they provide much of the raw material for jurists in their work. But these compilations do not enjoy the high prestige associated with legal scholarship. The function of the jurist is to draw from this disorganised mass first the rules and then the principles which will clarify and purge the subject of impure elements, and thus provide both the practice and the courts with a guide for the solution of particular cases in the future.

70. Formulation of the legal rule

Such is the attitude prevailing in the countries of the Romano-Germanic family. But it would be wrong to conclude that the laws of the family were drawn up by theoreticians who neglected the realities of life in favour of constructing nothing other than a perfectly logical system. Some theoretical thinkers, in various countries over the years did, it is true, adopt such an attitude, but while their influence was felt in law teaching, it had little effect upon the practice of law.[1]

It was on the basis of specific cases that the jurisconsults of Rome formulated their opinions and it was on the basis of decisions rendered by the *Parlements* of France that the older French authors wrote their treatises; similarly, it is by considering judicial and extra-judicial practices that modern authors have broken fresh ground to meet the new needs in administrative, labour and business law. The doctrinal writers, however, do not limit themselves merely to organising and presenting the materials offered by legal practice and judicial decisions. From this mass, formed day to day through the chance of events and under urgent pressure and without very clear guiding principles, they extract the rules of law which will guide judges and practitioners in the future. The formulation of the legal rule is not left to be enunciated by the judges; they do not have the time to reflect upon it, equitable considerations relevant to the particular case may disturb their judgment, and it is not part of their function to lay down general rules of conduct.[2] Since it cannot, and indeed must not, be the work of the judge, at the level of his individual decision, the legal rule only appears at a second stage; it is the product of reflection founded partly on an observation of judicial practice but also on considerations of justice, morality, policy and consonance of the system, all of which may have escaped the judge. This work of reflection leads to the formation of a *rule* which implies a certain generalisation: the rule must be general enough to provide a principle for the decision of concrete cases in the future.

The legal rule decants and purifies judicial practice by rejecting

---

[1] The French codes were drawn up by practitioners rather than university professors. *Cf.* Dawson (J.), *The Oracles of the Law* (1968), p. 387.

[2] According to art. 5 of the French *Code civil:* "Il est défendue aux juges de prononcer par voie de disposition générale et réglementaire sur les causes qui leur sont soumises." (Judges, in deciding the cases before them, are prohibited from laying down general or regulatory rules).

what is discordant or superfluous. It simplifies the study of law by reducing the mass of material which would otherwise have to be considered. It renders these elements more meaningful by showing how they help to assure better social justice or a more stable economic or moral order. It allows public opinion and the legislators to intervene more efficiently in order to correct various forms of behaviour and even to orient society towards certain goals. That such is a function of law conforms to the tradition according to which law is held up as a model of social organisation. This policy-directing and not purely litigious aspect of law is today confirmed and reinforced because we now expect the law to assist in the creation of a society very different from that of the past.

This concept of the legal rule in the Romano-Germanic family is the fundamental basis of codification such as it is conceived in continental Europe. A code would be no more than a mere compilation, and more or less successful as such, if one were to see a legal rule in every judicial decision and only at the level of such decisions. According to the Romano-Germanic notion, a code should not attempt to provide rules that are immediately applicable to every conceivable concrete case, but rather an organised system of general rules from which a solution for any given problem may be easily deduced by as simple a process as possible.

71. Optimum generality of the rule

The Romano-Germanic legal rule is situated midway between the judicial decision in a dispute, which is seen as a concrete application of the rule, and the more general principle of which the rule itself may be considered the application. In Romano-Germanic countries, the art of the jurist consists in finding and formulating the rule at this point of equilibrium. It must not be too general, for then it would no longer be a sufficiently reliable practical guide; on the other hand, the rule must be general enough to cover a series of cases rather than merely apply to some particular situation as does the judicial decision. It must also be added that this point of balance is neither necessarily nor in fact the same in all branches of law; a more concrete and specific rule may be desirable in such fields as fiscal or criminal law where it is intended that discretion be reduced as much as possible. Greater generalisation, on the contrary, may be preferable in certain other and more fluid areas where it is thought that the full rigour of legal solutions should be less strictly observed.

One might think that as the idea of the legal rule may be differently conceived according to the branch of law, so too it might be differently conceived in the various countries of the Romano-Germanic family. As a matter of historical fact, there have been compilations of a highly casuistic character adopting a case-by-case approach: such was the style of the Prussian Code of 1794[3] and, even more so, of the Russian compilation of 1832 (*Svod Zakonov*). At the present time, however, a fairly similar degree of abstraction has been achieved in most countries because of the general tendency to use the Napoleonic codes as a model,[4] except perhaps for the more casuistic tendency of Scandinavian legislation.

In this respect, the opposition exists perhaps more within each of the countries, and between traditional subject matters and new legislation, than it does between such countries themselves. The criticism, encountered in various countries, that new laws are the result of poor legislative technique largely results from the fact that legislators when dealing with new subjects do not fix the legal rule at the right level of abstraction. Sometimes they give way to an exaggerated case-by-case approach and this defect becomes especially obvious in the many amendments later made to the original text; on other occasions, however, they express themselves in terms too general, and the meaning of the law is not understood until it is "interpreted." Criticisms levelled at poor legislative techniques certainly have some basis; however, it must be remembered that the legislative task is technically very difficult and that it has required centuries of doctrinal effort to arrive at the style of expression of the French Civil Code, for example, which today seems so simple and obvious.

72. Legal interpretation and the technique of "distinguishing"

The common concept of the legal rule and of its relation to both the principles and the solution of concrete cases is one of the fun-

---

[3] *Allgemeinese Landrecht für die preussischen Staaten von 1794*. The code has been translated into English, von Winiwarter (J. R.) and Baeck (P. L.), *General Civil Code of Austria* (1972) (1st ed., 1966).
[4] The "Napoleonic" codes were the *Code civil* (1804), *Code de procédure civil* (1807), *Code de commerce* (1808), *Code d'instruction criminelle* (1811) and *Code pénal* (1811).

damental—and insufficiently emphasised—points creating a close community of outlook and reasoning among jurists in countries adhering to the Romano-Germanic family. It is one of the clearest and most important practical indications of this kinship. This same concept is, in fact, also at the origin of the present theory of the sources of law in the Romano-Germanic family. The generality of the legal rule explains why the task of lawyers in these countries is conceived as essentially one of *interpreting* legislative provisions, and is thus unlike that of Common law countries where legal technique is characterised by the process of *distinguishing* judicial decisions. The "right" legal rule itself is not thought of in the same manner: in Common law countries it is expected that the rule which provides a solution to the dispute will be framed as precisely as possible; in the Romano-Germanic countries on the contrary, because its function is simply to establish the *framework* of the law and to furnish the judge with *guidelines* for decision-making, it is considered desirable that the legal rule leave him a certain margin of discretion. No further attempt to spell out the detail of the legal rule must be made, because its author, be he jurist or legislator, is quite unable to foresee the variety of concrete cases which may arise in practice.

73. Predictability and certainty of the law

The concept of the legal rule in the Romano-Germanic system means that there are far fewer actual rules of law than in those countries where the legal rule, because it is less abstract, enters into the greater detail of specific situations.

From this it follows—or so it would seem at first sight—that it is much easier to acquire a knowledge of French law, or some other law belonging to the same system, than of some law in the Common law system. The French, Egyptian or Japanese practitioner will have less trouble than his English, American or Canadian confrère in telling his client what legal rule, or rules, will be applicable to his problem. This apparent advantage of the Romano-Germanic family must not, however, delude us. It is largely illusory.

The concept of the legal rule prevailing in such countries does not mean that it is easier to forecast the actual solution to any particular dispute. The less specialised the legal rule, the greater will be the work of judicial interpretation. To formulate the legal rule in the most general terms means that it is less precise; it means that the judge is given greater discretion in its application. Thus although the applicable legal rule may have been easier to find, the certainty of legal relationships is not thereby increased; indeed, the reverse is true.[5]

A further observation must be made. The legal rules, as formulated by the legislators and the doctrinal writers, do not give an exact idea of the complete content of the law. Everything below the level at which the legislators have fixed the legal rules cannot, in effect, be treated as simply *facts of the case.* In striving both to assure greater security in legal relations and to avoid arbitrariness, the highest courts have made those rules formulated in too general a manner more specific by exercising a control, not only over the *fact* that the rule has been applied, but also over the *manner* in which it was interpreted and applied by the judges of the substantive question. The legal rule as formulated by the legislators, in these circumstances, is thus only the kernel around which "secondary" rules are built up.

It is difficult to determine both the extent of this control and that to which "secondary" legal rules have, in fact, been thus elaborated by the body of decided cases. It varies according to country and the branch of law, and is related to the manner in which rules are legislatively framed, judicial organisation, the judicial tradition and many other factors. Although only more or less widespread and conspicuous, the phenomenon is nonetheless of general significance. The frontiers of law and of fact are everywhere largely artificial, and it is difficult to see to what extent the solution of a dispute brings into play either its particular facts or the interpretation of a legal rule.

The most one can say is that when a factual situation appears to be sufficiently *typical,* and therefore likely to arise frequently, there is the assurance that by one technique or another it will be covered by the same legal rule, so that those concerned may know their position and how they are expected to behave. In such cases the French Supreme Court (*Cour de Cassation*) will "supervise" the manner in which the "judges of the facts" (*juges du fait*) apply

[5] Sereni (A. P.), "The Code and the Case Law," in *The Code Napoléon and the Common Law World* (1956), pp. 55–79.

a legal rule; it will, in effect, then impose its own "interpretation" of the rule. In other and less typical cases however it will refuse to exercise this control and restrict itself to stating that the lower judges alone may appreciate the facts giving rise to the dispute.[6]

74. Real importance of secondary rules

In countries of the Romano-Germanic family, therefore, the law is found not only in the legal rules formulated by the legislators but also in their judicial interpretation. It is appropriate to ask whether this last observation does not in fact destroy the previous affirmation that the legal rule is conceived in a relatively abstract and general manner. Does one not return, indirectly by means of such "secondary legal rules" formulated in the cases, to a concept very close—if not identical—to that which places the legal rule at the level of individual cases submitted to the judge?

It is clear that many jurists in the Romano-Germanic countries have, more or less consciously, become more casuistic, more orientated towards merely describing the contents of individual judicial decisions and less inclined to the work of general critical reflection. If this attitude were to prevail, and if every judicial decision were to be seen as embodying a rule of law, the Romano-Germanic system would be fundamentally changed and approximate that of the Common law. This has not happened however, and the existence of such "secondary" rules of law has not yet transformed the Romano-Germanic laws into a case-law system, nor permeated the Romano-Germanic concept of the legal rule with a case-by-case approach foreign to its essential tradition.

Whatever in fact may be the number and importance of these "secondary legal rules," as the judicial interpretation of legislative legal rules may be termed, it is certain that they are of a greater generality than the rule at which the judge arrives when he is not guided by the legislators at all. As a result, in countries of the Romano-Germanic family, there is still much "less law" than in those where the rule is of direct judicial formation. The laws of the Romano-Germanic family are still founded on principles, as the

---

[6] Marty (G.), *La distinction du fait et du droit* (1929), pp. 365–366: "Every time a decision of the *Cour de Cassation* may have, by reason of its character, a general effect and serve as a guide for the solution of difficulties in the future, the court must take up one side or another." As to the distinction between law and fact in England, *cf.* Devlin (Sir P), *Trial by Jury* (1956), p. 61; Cornish (W. R.), *The Jury* (1968), p. 105.

system implies; they are not oriented to specific cases, and because of this fact it appears that they have the advantages of simplicity and clarity.

It is very clear, however, that the legal rules in these countries, such as their jurists and legislators traditionally deem appropriate to formulate, do not suffice alone; to be complete and precise, they require secondary rules. Nonetheless, and this is not without benefit, they give the law a solid and unquestioned framework. In countries where the law is judicially created, there is sometimes hesitation about abolishing or changing a rule because the consequences in relation to the whole of the law are not clear. In countries of the Romano-Germanic system, such reforms are more easily accepted because it is more evident which rules will be affected and which left unchanged. In particular, changes may take place more easily in the "secondary rules" of the law. Because they do not reach to the very foundations of the system, changes in the pattern of the decided cases do not present the same danger nor create the same uncertainties as they may in countries which do not admit the Romano-Germanic concept of the legal rule.

TITLE III

SOURCES OF LAW

75. Difficulties of the subject

It is difficult to present the theory of the sources of law as practised in the Romano-Germanic family. The original Roman law ideas on the subject are no longer observed and Roman law does not provide the common basis of approach. There are many laws within this family and each of them, when compared with the others, has its own originality. Moreover, even within each system of national law, the subject is complex and often provokes discussion. The way in which the solution to a given question is found may differ according to the branch of law considered, and may further depend to some extent on the mentality and personal views of each jurist. In addition, the theory of sources varies from one historical period to another, because it is related to the preponderant philosophical tendencies of the time to which people adhere consciously or unconsciously.

76. Theory and reality

Enacted law or legislation, considered *lato sensu*, is apparently the primary, almost exclusive, source of law today in countries of the Romano-Germanic family. They are, to borrow the terminology of an earlier period, *countries of written law*. In the search for legal rules and solutions jurists look first of all to the legislative or regulatory texts emanating from the principal legislative body or governmental or administrative authorities. Their task seems to be essentially one of discovering, by means of varied methods of interpretation, the solution which in each case corresponds to the intention of the legislators. *Jurisconsulta sine lege loquens erubescit*, as was formerly said in Germany. According to this analysis, other possible elements occupy a place subordinate to and of lesser importance than legislation, the source of law *par excellence*.

No matter how current this analysis may be, it is, in fact, very far removed from reality. Such a doctrine, as summed up by the above description, may well have been the ideal of a certain school of thought dominant in nineteenth century France, but it has never been fully accepted as a matter of legal practice. Even in theory it is now increasingly admitted that the absolute sovereignty of legislation is a fiction in the Romano-Germanic family and that there is room for other and very important sources of law.

To confuse law and legislation, and to see in legislation the exclusive source of the law, is in fact contrary to the whole Romano-Germanic tradition. The universities, through whose teachings its legal concepts were moulded, may have based themselves on Roman legislative texts, but we know to what extent they distorted them; and the courts, especially the French *parlements*, which had such a considerable influence upon the evolution of national legal systems, made little, indeed only exceptional, use of legislation as we understand it. Moreover, until the nineteen century, the universities were not interested in what were to become the national legislations. It is true that from the seventeenth century the School of Natural Law demanded that legislative authority sanction those rules which had been doctrinally elaborated on postulates derived from nature and reason, but in recommending the new technique of codification it never intended to say that law and legislation were to be identified, or that the study of legislation alone might lead to an understanding of law. Only later was there confusion on this point; it suffices to read the admirable *Discours préliminaire du Code civil*[1] by Portalis (1746–1807), one of the principal architects of French codification, to dispel it.

77. Persistence of the tradition

A thorough revolution would have been necessary to reject the traditional concept that law is something other than legislation. Law, the quest of all men of good will and more especially of jurists, cannot be sought exclusively in written texts; its definition and very nature would change if it were no longer regarded as the expression of what is just, but simply as the will of those who gov-

---

[1] Fenet (P. A.), *Travaux préparatoires du Code civil* (1827), t. I, p. 463, also published in *Discours, rapports et travaux inédits sur le Code civil* (1844).

ern. Such a revolution did take place in the Soviet Union and the people's democracies; in other countries this has not occurred.

Following codification, a positivist theory which held that legislation was henceforth the exclusive source of the law certainly appeared to triumph generally in different countries of the Romano-Germanic world. Specialists in various branches of the law too often continue to present this absolutist doctrine to students as still being the received view. As a result, in many countries, and especially in those of the Common law tradition, this explanation is often taken as an accurate description of the state of things in the Romano-Germanic family. In truth, a position much less dogmatic has been adopted by most jurists. The doctrine of Natural Law is today enjoying a revival.[2] The adherents of positivism have themselves abandoned the myth of legislation, such as it was entertained in the nineteenth century; they now recognise the creative role of the judge; no one thinks any longer that legislation is the sole source of law or that a purely logical process of interpretation of legislation can, in all cases, lead to the required legal solution.[3]

The countries of the Romano-Germanic family now have constitutions, codes and much enacted or statute law, whereas formerly the legal rules had to be sought in less systematised series of documents which more often than not had no official character. This change in legal technique is unquestionably of the utmost importance; the law has been accommodated to the needs of modern society through the removal of much of the useless variations and dangerous uncertainty which too often destroyed the authority of the former law in the era prior to codification. At a time when our ideas about justice were being re-examined because of profound changes in economics and technology, legislators came to play a greater part in the enunciation of the law. It is a long way from this admission, however, to a complete repudiation of our traditional idea of law, such as would be implied by an acceptance of a dogma of absolute state sovereignty.

The French jurists of the nineteenth century may have thought that their codes were, as Coke said of the Common law, "the per-

---

[2] *Archives de philosophie du droit*, No. 6, "La réforme des études de droit. Le Droit naturel." (1961) *Adde* Héraud (G.), "Regards sur la philosophie du droit française contemporaine," in *Le droit français*, vol. II, pp. 517–554. Brimo (A.), *Les grands courants de la philosophie du droit et de l'Etat* (2nd ed., 1968).

[3] Bobbio (N.), "Sur le positivisme juridique" in *Mélanges Paul Roubier* (1961), pp. 53–73.

fect of reason" and that henceforth the surest means of arriving at a just solution, or of knowing the law, was simply to perform the exegesis of these codes. Jurists of other countries may have had the same feeling when they in turn adopted codes. This supposed coincidence between law, which is justice, and legislation, which is the will of the legislators, did indeed enjoy acceptance at one time. Comparative law helps to rectify this error. We see Soviet jurists, for example, who advocate that law be identified with the omnipotence of the state, denouncing jurists of the Romano-Germanic tradition for the hypocrisy with which the latter purport to apply legislation whereas, in reality, they often deform it to serve the political interests of the bourgeois class in power. Again, comparative law shows how American or English jurists are surprised to discover that continental legislative provisions are not the capricious commands of a sovereign which must be executed to the letter and that codes, closely related to doctrinal works, are very often the simple framework within which a creative activity in the search for just solutions is carried on.

78. Technique and policy of decided cases

It is still true today that the courts and jurists of the Romano-Germanic family are not at ease unless they can invoke one or more texts of enacted law to justify or support the legal solution which they recommend. It may sometimes even be necessary to demonstrate that a legislative provision has been violated for the court to be seized at all or for there to be recourse to a higher court. This attitude and such provisions may create the impressions that the law and statutory texts are still considered to be one and the same in the Romano-Germanic world.

However, to have an exact view of things, consideration must be given to the way in which these legislative texts are interpreted, solicited and, sometimes, neutralised. The French courts, even after the Napoleonic codification, never restricted themselves merely to applying legislative texts, but their contribution to the development of the law throughout the nineteenth century remained in obscurity. The new social conditions at the beginning of this century required a bolder, more open approach. The centennial celebration of the *Code civil* gave an opportunity to the highest French judicial magistrate of the time, Ballot-Beaupré

(1836–1917), first president of the *Cour de cassation*, to proclaim, even before there was doctrinal acceptance of the idea, that decided cases (*jurisprudence*) had advanced "by the Civil Code, beyond the Civil Code" just as, at an earlier period, the law had progressed "by Roman law, beyond Roman law."[4] The whole of administrative law as constructed by the French *Conseil d'Etat* is another example of the creative role of judicial decisions.

The idea of law such as it was understood for centuries in European universities has not been abandoned. The legislators certainly can, and indeed must, aid in defining the law, but law itself is something more than legislation. It is not to be confused with the will of legislators; it can only be discovered by the combined efforts of all jurists and especially of those involved in judicial administration. Today, the relative place of legislative and doctrinal sources, compared to what it was under the French *ancien droit*, may be reversed; nonetheless, in conformity with tradition, Romano-Germanic laws remain a system that can be described as a jurist's law (*Juristenrecht*). Legislation has become the principal though certainly not the only means of knowing the law, but it only has meaning when taken in conjunction with other elements. In France, Germany and Italy today, as in the past, the law can only be known through a search in which the legislators and all jurists participate. Even though the fact may be hidden by legal technique, the law is made up of other important sources in addition to enacted law.

79. Unity of western law

In the final analysis, a similar attitude exists in countries of both the Romano-Germanic family and those of the Common law, because in all of them the idea of law is linked to the search for what is just. As will be seen, the principal difference between them is that whereas in the Romano-Germanic family these solutions are sought by a technique which considers first of all legislation, in the Common law family the same results are sought by a technique which first considers judicial decisions. Consequently, a different analysis of the *legal rule* results. It is conceived as legislative and doctrinal in Romano-Germanic family and as judicial in Common

---

[4] *Le Centenaire du Code civil* 1804–1904 (1904).

law countries. With such a difference in approach, however, it does not follow that there is a difference in the nature of law itself as understood in each—for law, in a vast "western" family called "bourgeois" by Soviet authors, is conceived in the same way and is, precisely, to be opposed to the idea of law as prevailing in the "socialist" family.

It must now be determined how the legislators and administrative authorities by enacting and prescribing general provisions, and how judges and jurists by interpreting the law and appealing to other sources, specifically shape solutions in the Romano-Germanic family. The following subjects[5] will be successively examined: the role of legislation, custom, decided cases, doctrinal or legal writing and certain general or super-eminent principles.

[5] *Cf.* David (R.) and Kindred (M.), *French Law* (1972) where all these questions are examined more particularly in the context of French law. For German law, Fromont (M.) and Rieg (A.): *Introduction au droit allemand*, t. I: *Les fondements* (1977).

CHAPTER I

LEGISLATION

80. Present primacy of legislation

Under modern conditions, and for philosophical and political reasons, it is generally thought in countries of the Romano-Germanic family that the best means for achieving justice, the mission of law, is for jurists to rely upon the provisions of enacted law. This tendency predominated in the nineteenth century when nearly all the member-states of the Romano-Germanic family accepted codes and drew up written constitutions. It has been reinforced in our own time with the triumph of the idea of planned economies and the increased role of the state in all areas. The struggle for progress and the reign of law remains the task of all jurists, but in this work the role of legislators is preponderant at the present time. This attitude is in agreement with democratic principles; it is also justified by the fact that state and administrative bodies are, without doubt, best placed to coordinate the different sectors of social activity and to determine where the common interest lies. Finally, legislation, because of the rigours of drafting involved, appears to be the best means of enunciating the rules needed at a time when the complexity of social relations demands that precision and clarity be paramount.

In countries of the Romano-Germanic world, the provisions of law issuing from legislative or administrative bodies, which jurists are to interpret and apply in order to discover the solution to a problem, exist in the form of a hierarchy.

81. Constitutional rules

At the summit of this hierarchy are constitutions or constitutional laws. All countries of the Romano-Germanic family have written constitutions, the provisions of which are acknowledged to enjoy a special prestige. In some countries this prestige is above all a political one; the constitutional provisions may have been adopted or may only properly be modified according to special procedures, but in law they have no more authority than ordinarily enacted laws. In other countries, however, the constitutional provisions are legally something more than that; their special authority is revealed by the fact that a means of controlling the constitutionality of other laws is established, although the manner and character of such control may vary.[1]

There is, at the present time, a distinct tendency to heighten the value of constitutional rules by giving them a status in fact greater than that enjoyed by ordinary legislation. The Constitution of the Federal Republic of Germany declares that "The Legislative Branch is bound to respect legislation and the law. If no other means are available, every German has the right to resist the efforts of any person attempting to subvert this order."[2] New efforts have been made generally throughout the family to find ways to guarantee the constitution and, as in the United States, to establish the principle of a judicial control of the constitutionality of ordinary legislation. The most noticeable developments have occurred in Germany and Italy, in response to the fact that in both countries earlier governments had made a mockery of democratic principles and fundamental human rights. In both countries the courts have on numerous occasions set aside laws that violated fundamental rights (*Grundrechte*, *diritti fundamentali*) laid down in the declaration of rights included in the constitution.

Judicial control of the constitutionality of legislation while less far reaching has been accepted in many other countries as well. The authority exercising this control, and the means of doing so, vary from one country to another. In Japan and some countries of Latin America[3] it is open to the judge, as in the United States, to find that a statute is unconstitutional and to refuse, therefore, under the control of the Supreme Court, to apply it. In European

---

[1] Max-Planck-Institut für ausländisches öffentliches Recht und Völkerrecht: *La juridiction constitutionnelle à l'époque contemporaine. Exposé de la situation en différents pays et étude comparée* (articles in German, English and French) (1963). Cappelletti (M.), *Il controllo giudiziario della constituzionalità delle leggi nel diritto comparato* (1968).

[2] Fundamental Law (*Grundgestz*) of the F.R.G., art. 20, paras. 3 & 4.

[3] Argentina, Bolivia, Brazil, Columbia, Mexico, Venezuela. But judicial review in Chile, Cuba, Haiti, Panama and Uruguay is exercised only by their supreme courts. Only Equador, Peru and possibly the Dominican Republic (whose constitution is silent on the subject) deny the possibility of judicial review.

and African countries, on the other hand, the power to declare legislation unconstitutional is attributed to a specially created court. Such is the case in Germany, Austria, Italy, Monaco, Turkey and Cyprus. Here the ordinary courts, if they entertain a doubt about the constitutionality of some statute can only adjourn the proceedings and transmit the matter to the constitutional court. In some countries (Germany, Columbia, Cuba, Panama, Venezuela), it is also open to certain authorities, or even private persons, to test the constitutionality of some law independently of any actual litigation. This avenue is not available in the United States.

In assessing the importance in practice of the judicial control of constitutionality, one must be mindful of the circumstances in which it operates. Its significance is limited if the constitution it is intended to protect can be easily amended or if its application can be suspended by executive authority. These factors considerably reduce the real thrust of judicial control in many African, Latin and South American countries; it is worth noting that even in Germany the "fundamental law" has been amended 27 times since its enactment in 1949 and 1970. Account must also be taken of the psychology of judges and the hesitation they may feel before exercising their power of declaring a law constitutionally invalid. This is the reason why, in Japan, judicial control is used less than it is in the United States even though, on this point, in theory at least, there is no difference between the two legal systems. In Sweden, Denmark and Norway, legal writers agree that in theory the courts can refuse to apply a law found unconstitutional but no example of this having happened can be cited.

In other countries of the family it is not open at all to the courts to strike down a statute as unconstitutional. This is the case in the Netherlands and in France. The French courts were deterred from doing so for largely historical reasons. A change in approach seems, however, discernible in the decisions of the *Conseil constitutionnel* since it was created in 1958.[4] The *Conseil* can only be seized in such matters however by a number of high state officials (or a group of 60 members of the legislature), outside any actual

---

[4] Favoreu (L.) & Philip (L.), *Les grandes décisions du Conseil constitutionnel* (2nd ed., 1979). On the subject of the refusal of the ordinary courts to exercise judicial control, *cf.* Cass. civ. December 20, 1956, Bull. civ. 1956, II, no. 714.

litigation, and before the statute comes into force. It is not at all therefore the equivalent of the constitutional courts found in Germany or Italy. In Switzerland the control exercised by the federal court bears only upon the conformity of laws of the cantons to federal law and does not extend to the constitutionality of federal law itself.

82. Treaties

A place similar to constitutional law is attributed to international treaties and conventions, although here again the practice varies from one country to another. Some constitutions declare that international treaties enjoy an authority superior to any enacted law, and this is the case in France and in the Netherlands. Here the question arises whether a law enacted after the coming into force of the treaty and incompatible with it will be applied. The *Conseil constitutionnel* in France decided that it had no jurisdiction to prevent such a law from coming into force; the *Conseil d'Etat* declined to exercise judicial control in such a case. The *Cour de Cassation*, on the other hand, did not pronounce upon the precise point because it was able to find, upon an interpretation of the texts, that the new law did not conflict with the treaty.[5] The same attitude is found in the German courts where treaties as such are assimilated to ordinary statutes even though the Fundamental Law states that "the general principles of international law" have an authority superior to ordinary legislation. The interpretation of a particular treaty may of course fall within the purview of a supranational body, in which case the national courts may be required to divest themselves of the question of their interpretation. This is the case for example when a question of construction arises in connection with the treaties of Paris (1951) and Rome (1957) which created the various European "communities."

83. Codes

Within the class of ordinary legislation, some laws are called *codes*.[6] Originally, in an historical context, the term designated a

---

[5] The case dealt with the European Convention on Human Rights which proclaims a number of principles similar to those in the American Constitution.
[6] Vanderlinden (J.), *Le concept du code en Europe occidentale du XIIIe au XIXe siècle. Essai de définition* (1967).

collection of distinct enactments—the codes of Theodosius and Justinian were no more than this. In the nineteenth century, this name was given to compilations which sought to lay down the principles of a modern *ius commune* and which, though formally declared to apply in only one state, aspired to have universal application. This type of compilation was thus distinguished from those rules, inspired by considerations of convenience rather than justice, which would continue to exist within each nation.[7] The terminology is, however, not as precise today as it once was; the word *code* is now used to refer to compilations which attempt to gather together and systematically organise the regulation on any special subject.

First of all, then, it must be observed that nearly all countries of the Romano-Germanic family, throughout the nineteenth and twentieth centuries, have adopted the formula of codification; and further that these codifications have all adopted the same organisational framework as that established in France, between 1804 and 1811, by the five Napoleonic Codes.[8]

The only exception to this general pattern to note, in Europe, is made up of the Nordic countries. A single code was promulgated in each of them: in Denmark in 1683, in Norway in 1687, and in 1734 for both Sweden and Finland. These codes, very much earlier than the Napoleonic Codes, deal with the whole of the law, as did the later Prussian *Allgemeines Landrecht* (1794) and the Russian *Svod Zakonov* (1832). A divergent evolution has taken place since in the two groups of Nordic countries. In Denmark, Norway and Iceland the codes no longer exist; their different parts have been abrogated and replaced by statutes that have not been integrated into the former codes. In Sweden and Finland, on the contrary, the Code of 1734, the nine parts of which in Sweden are curiously called "beams" (*Balk*), continues to be cited as such. Draft codes, especially a civil code and a commercial code, have been considered at different times for some of these countries or for all of

---

[7] The idea that a code is a body of permanent law is best illustrated by the case of Portugal where the enactment of a constitutional law is required in order to authorise an amendment to the code.

[8] However, the word code (*Gesetzbuch*) is not used in German-speaking countries with respect to the "Ordinances of Procedure" (*Zivilprozessordnung, Strafprozessordnung*). Procedure is a subject too linked to matters of judicial administration, too imprinted with national peculiarities, to be regulated by "codes." The same scruple was felt in Spain (where there exists only a *ley de enjuiciamiento civil*), but not in the countries of Latin America.

them together but, whether arising from private or official initiatives, they have until now never been completed, nor is it likely they will be in the near future. The collaboration which has taken place between Nordic countries will indeed be much more difficult to bring about with respect to complete and comprehensive codes than in the case of more specialised statutes.[9]

The recent tendency, referred to above, to draw up "codes" in respect of subjects in which no attempt is made to articulate the principles of a "common law," has created a new diversity within the Romano-Germanic family. The "administrative codes," promulgated in France since 1945, for example, their subject matter being wholly regulatory in character, exhibit a very pronounced *national* character. It may well be, however, that a number of systematic reforms accomplished in some countries may serve as models for others which will adopt, as Italy did, a code on maritime shipping or, as in the case of Belgium, a judicial code. Perhaps the real question to ask at the present time is whether the moment is not now near when *European* codes should be adopted within the framework of the European Economic Community (or even perhaps in a larger context) in order to defeat a new but nonetheless observable European provincialism.

84. Codes and statutes

The existence of codes in the Romano-Germanic family of law raises a further question. Do the generality of subjects which they cover, the anticipated permanence of their application and, above all, their mission of universal application, not require that they be considered differently from ordinary statutes with which they coexist in any given country? Does it not have to be acknowledged that they possess a special authority and that they therefore must be made subject to principles of interpretation other than those applicable to "ordinary" legislation? It is in fact common for legal writers to deprecate new laws and to seek to restrain their application by qualifying them as "special" statutes or exceptional legislation.

This attitude and this distinction can find some historical justification if it be true, as it has been suggested here, that codes were

---

[9] *Cf.* Eek (Hilding), "Evolution et structure du droit scandinave", *Revue hellénique de droit international*, 1961, 33–51.

laws which endeavoured to express a European common law transcending any particular national characteristics. However, national laws or customs, whatever their fortuitous character, have never been considered, in respect of their application and inter-pretation, as inferior to the principles of this common law. And it is proper that this tradition be maintained. Apart from cases where the legislators may have enacted expressly to the contrary, codes do not enjoy any special pre-eminence over those laws or statutes that have not been incorporated therein. When interpreted by jur-ists, codes and statutes are treated on exactly the same basis. This is especially the case today since the original idea of the code—that is, a repository expressing the European *ius commune*—has been largely forgotten: many statutes are called codes which in no way purport to be the expression of universal and abiding principles of justice. However, in the case of the older and most prestigious codes, it may very well be that their value is in practice superior to that of other laws: there is a natural tendency to attach a greater respect to their established principles because they have been, for many years, the object of a more detailed study and for this reason they are generally taken to have been more wisely framed than ordinary statutes are.

85. Regulations and decrees

Besides statutes in the strict sense, the "written law" of the countries of the Romano-Germanic family today includes a multi-tude of different rules and regulations emanating from authorities other than the legislative organ. These can be separated into two major categories.

First, there are those regulations promulgated for the imple-mentation of statutes. Their existence, and even their multiplica-tion, have raised no problems of a policy nature. It is evident that in a modern state, the "legislators" themselves cannot provide all the necessary regulations which are, in their detail, increasingly complex. All that can be expected of them, at least in many areas, is a statement of principle and more or less general rules. For the more detailed regulations required, it is necessary to depend upon the activity of administrative authorities. This is done by providing for the implementation of regulations and by delegating the power to make such regulations to administrative authorities. For some time the principal problem appeared to be the control of these administrative authorities and in particular what form of control would guarantee the supremacy of statutory law and the conformity of regulatory provisions made by such administrative bodies in its application. Was this control to be exercised by all the courts (as in Germany) or reserved to special administrative tribunals (as in France)? Under what conditions was it to operate?

At the present time, there is some tendency to formulate a new relationship between legislative provisions and regulatory acts, and this by means of a new interpretation of the basic principle of the separation of powers. The feeling had arisen in some countries that the principle had been incorrectly applied and that the balance of powers which the principle attempts to put into operation had not been fully realised—the legislative branch, in appearance at least, had become all-powerful. In reality it would be more accurate to say that it had simply become overburdened and was discharging its legislative tasks unsatisfactorily. The executive branch, entrusted with the direction of administrative agencies, has enjoyed very considerable autonomy, and has often been called upon to initiate measures, by way of decree, that escape any control by the legislative branch. The French Constitution of 1958, apart from any political factors,[10] can be considered as having given effect, in law, to the idea that the French *Parlement* was only to have those powers it was in fact able to exercise. Consequently, it restricted the scope of statute to certain areas; the legislators can only draw up fundamental principles in certain specific fields. Alongside the legislative power, exercised by the *Parlement*, the new French Constitution thus recognised the existence of a regulatory power not subordinate to the executive power but which, by its nature, was to be autonomous. The new principle put by the French Constitution has now raised a number of important questions relating to the distinctions to be drawn between the spheres of statute and regulation which the *Conseil constitutionnel* has been called upon to resolve. In return it has had the advantage of assuring the submission to a high court, the *Conseil d'Etat*, of a whole series of rules which, formerly, when enacted by the French legislature, escaped any such surveillance.

---

[10] Friedrich (C. J.), "The New French Constitution in Political and Historical Perspective," 72 Harv. L. Rev. 801–837 (1959).

This development has not occurred in other countries. In Federal Germany, the Fundamental Law prohibits the establishment of a regulatory power distinct from that of the executive branch and forbids the use of decrees. In Germany therefore regulations can only be adopted within the scope of and in furthering the purpose of regular legislation. It should be noted however that the Federal Constitutional Court has steadfastly upheld the validity of legislation that confers considerable power on the government.

86. Administrative directives

A clear distinction of principle is made in countries of the Romano-Germanic tradition between regulations which establish legal rules and mere administrative directives which indicate the manner in which the government understands the law and intends to apply it. In truth, the distinction in many cases tends to be more theoretical than real. Often civil servants know the law only by means of the departmental instructions received by way of directive; and, even if it were otherwise, they most often prefer to observe these instructions rather than expose themselves to difficulties with their administrative superiors. Private individuals often have no means of obliging the government to respect the law, especially when irregular administrative practices unduly benefit certain individuals but do not directly harm anyone else. Moreover the citizen often hesitates to act when faced with all the risks and inconveniences involved in an action taken against the administration. In order to know how far the government in different countries is effectively subject to legislation, it does not suffice to proclaim as a matter of principle that it is bound by the law. Suitable structures, procedures and political conditions must also exist in order to impose on government a conduct conforming to the law and to redress the illegalities it commits. As in private law relations, the existence of good rules and the affirmation that they must be observed do not suffice; these principles are only valid if people generally are knowledgeable about their rights and can in fact assert them, all of which supposes that there are easily accessible courts, upright judges and a government that is disposed to consider itself bound by judicial decisions.

In all these respects there certainly do exist differences between the various countries of the Romano-Germanic family. But it is characteristic that jurists of this tradition pay little attention to such matters which they consider as belonging to the science of governmental administration rather than to that of law. Studies in legal sociology have an important part to play here. They must not be conceived from only a general cultural or philosophical standpoint; by demonstrating the realities of life, they can help to bring jurists back to earth and to check their tendency to indulge in speculation and theoretical systematisation.

87. Legislative style

With respect to legislative style, there are two different tendencies in the various countries of the Romano-Germanic tradition: one is for a style as comprehensible as possible for the layman and the other, inversely, and adopted at the risk of turning law into a somewhat esoteric science, is to give expression to the legal rules in as precise a technical language as possible. In fact jurists in all countries are divided between these two contradictory tendencies. The opposition between the BGB on the one hand and the French and Swiss Codes on the other clearly indicates the obstacles to mutual understanding which may arise because of differences in legislative technique. It is remarkable that with respect to judicial decisions the positions are reversed; it is the French holdings which, by reason of their concision, tend to be esoteric, whereas German judgments, more expansive, are easier to read.

88. Interpretation of legislation

To enact statute law or regulations is the business of the appropriate authority. However, the practical value of enacted law depends on the way in which it is applied. The application of law supposes a process of interpretation, the importance of which is now more emphasised by legal writers. The most varied methods have been recommended in different countries of the Romano-Germanic family: from a strictly exegetical interpretation to the theories of the School of Free Law (*Freis Recht*), and including the *Interessenjurisprudenz* of Jhering and Heck in Germany and the plea for a free scientific research by Gény in France.[11]

[11] Gény (F.), *Méthode d'interprétation et sources en droit privé positif* (2nd ed., 1919 reprinted 1954), translated into English in 1954 by the Louisiana State Law Institute.

It is difficult to assess the practical influence of these theories in different countries. Legislators, with praisworthy wisdom, have never been under the illusion that they might impose particular methods of interpretation; the rules established on the subject in each country leave a wide latitude to interpreters. Consequently, in this matter everything depends on the psychology of those concerned and the current thinking by which they are more or less consciously guided. Judges in all countries, naturally anxious to avoid any charge of arbitrariness, in principle prefer an interpretation that follows the letter of the law and thus respects the legislative intention of a text. In most cases therefore they adopt a logical, if not a purely grammatical, construction which can be completed or corrected when necessary by reference to the legislative history of the text. Where, however, justice demands it, judges are able to find ways of freeing themselves from the strict letter of the texts, and different methods have been adopted for doing so.

89. Facts and their appreciation

When the legislator, deliberately or not, uses terms or expressions which are not absolutely precise, a considerable scope for interpretation is open to the judge who can still maintain the full respect owed to the text itself. The judge, when confronted with terms such as "good faith," "public order and good morals,"[12] "fault," "grievous injury," "impossibility of performance" must, in each case, decide whether the particular facts of the case require the application of the law to which such expressions refer. Through his restrictive or liberal interpretation of the facts, as the case may be, he is thus able to control to a very large extent the circumstances in which the law will apply—by extending the notion of grievous injury, by enlarging or restricting the concept of "good faith," by admitting or denying certain types of compensation, and so on. In the Romano-Germanic system, the judges are not bound to follow precedents and may, therefore, in their differing appreciations of the facts, considerably change the conditions in which the law is applied. Nothing, moreover, could be more

---

[12] Thus, for example, the Dutch Supreme Court has held that to take advantage of circumstances in order to obtain a favourable contract is a violation of public order and good morals: H.R. January 11, 1957, N. J. 1959, no. 37.

legitimate in the Romano-Germanic family. Indeed, because the legislators employ terms the precise significance of which has not been articulated, they may be taken as having authorised a complementary "free research *intra legem*," and this free research invites judges to make independent value judgments which cannot be deduced from positive law.[13]

Nevertheless, in some instances this avenue has been found insufficient; the courts, in order to render just decisions, have had to take greater liberty with texts in order to free themselves of the strict rules found unsuitable to new social conditions. Two techniques have been used.

90. New textual meaning

A first technique is to detach the text from its historical context. The words of the text are interpreted without considering either their historical origins or the original intention of the draftsmen, and with a view to giving them a meaning which, at the time, satisfies the then current sense of justice.

A number of excellent reasons have been advanced in order to justify this method of interpretation, the "teleological method."[14] The laws in force in a country, in order to make up a coherent system, must all be interpreted in the same spirit, that of the time when they are to apply, without paying heed to the earlier conditions and circumstances in which they were originally enacted. Ascertaining the original intention of the legislators is, more often than not, largely guesswork in any event. And it is especially difficult in contemporary democracies when legislation is so often the product of complex processes and of a collective will.

Judges in many countries have been open to these arguments; they do, however, continue to attach importance to the legislative intention of a text, even though they do not consider themselves absolutely bound by it. If this intention must be sought outside the text itself they will turn to its legislative history. This approach has been adopted even in those countries such as Austria and Italy where a provision requires that judges interpret legislation strictly, according to its expressed intention.

---

[13] Germann (O. A.), *Probleme und Methoden der Rechtsfindung* (2nd ed., 1967), pp. 388 *et seq.*
[14] Germann (O. A.), *op. cit.* pp. 66–78.

91. French approach

In a famous speech in 1904, on the occasion of the centenary celebrations of the French *Code civil*, Ballot-Beaupré (1836–1917), the president of the French Supreme Court (*Cour de cassation*), rejected the historical method of interpretation which had been faithfully observed up to that time. "When a text expressed in imperative language is clear, precise, unambiguous, the judge must apply its literal meaning. . . . But when the text is ambiguous, when there are doubts as to its meaning and intent, when it can be either restrained or extended or even contradicted by some other text, then, in my opinion, the judge has the widest power of interpretation; he must not then stubbornly attempt to ascertain what the original thought of the draftsmen of the Civil Code was 100 years ago; he must rather ask himself what their intention would be were that provision to be drafted by them today—in the face of all the changes which have come about in the last century in ideas, social manners, institutions, the economic and social condition of France, he must say to himself that justice and reason require that the text be liberally and humanely adapted to the realities and requirements of modern life."[15] The no less than spectacular development since 1900 in the law of liability for civil (as opposed to criminal) wrongs, *i.e.* the law of "civil responsibility," corresponds to the emergence of this new approach. Several words of the text of article 1384 of the French Civil Code—words to which the original draftsmen undoubtedly attached no particular significance[16]—have been given a new meaning by the courts in order to develop a law on the delictual liability for things under one's care quite apart from the principle of fault. The French *jurisprudence* thus filled a gap created by the inactivity of the legislature which had not faced up to the problems created by the development of machines and, more especially, the modern phenomenon of automobile accidents.

---

[15] *Livre du Centenaire du Code civil 1804–1904* (1904), p. 27. *Cf.* also, Saleilles (R.), "Le Code civil et la méthode historique," *ibid.* p. 95.

[16] Art. 1384, para. 1: "A person is responsible not only for the damage caused by his own actions, but also for that which is caused by the actions of persons for whom he must answer *or that caused by things under his care.*" This phrase, in the thought of the original draftsmen, merely served to introduce the provisions which followed on the subject of the vicarious liability of parents and employers (art. 1384, para. 2) and the liability of the owners of animals (art. 1385) and buildings (art. 1386).

But this particularly dramatic example of judicial law making must not lead us into error. It is, all things considered, unique and in no way characteristic of the usual technique of interpretation by French courts. When the legislative intention is clear, and when circumstances have not raised an entirely new problem since the time of its enactment, French judges normally take legislative history into account in their interpretation, as do their fellow judges in other Romano-Germanic countries.

92. German approach

Another method used to adapt the law to modern conditions not anticipated by its draftsmen, and without changing the meaning of the text, involves applying general provisions of law in order to neutralise more specific provisions. German practice offers the best examples to illustrate this technique.

Since the coming into force of the German Civil Code (BGB) (January 1, 1900), Germany has been shaken by a number of serious crises which rendered even more necessary there than elsewhere an adaptation of the law to meet new social and economic conditions. The courts had to assume the task of the legislature, which was too often slow to react. But because the German Code was of recent date, the courts were hesitant to give any of its special provisions a forced interpretation manifestly contrary to the originally intended meaning. They therefore respected the intended meaning but, when the need arose, neutralised these detailed provisions by bringing into play the general articles or provisions (*Generalklauseln*) in the BGB itself.

This technique was used even before the 1914 War. The requirement that respect be paid to good morals (*Gute Sitten*) specified at § 826[17] has been used by the German Supreme Court (*Reichsgericht*) to modify the system laid down elsewhere in the BGB in respect of delictual responsibility. It has awarded damages to compensate for loss of future and prospective profits without paying heed to § 823[18] which appears to intend to exclude them. It has restrained private persons from certain future conduct by way of

---

[17] § 826 BGB: "Whoever intentionally causes injury to another in a manner violating good morals is bound to repair the injury."

[18] § 823 BGB speaks of repairing injuries which result from intentional or negligent actions.

injunctive relief (*Unterlassungsklage*) in hypotheses where the Code envisages nothing more than reparation (*Ersatz*). It has penalised persons whose conduct has contributed to the breach of contractual obligations of others without applying the rule laid down in the Code that contracts have effect only between the contracting parties.

It was however after World War I, and in the special circumstances brought about by extreme inflation—the mark in 1923 had fallen to a mere fraction of its value—that this tendency became more pronounced. It was to § 242 BGB, which sets up the obligation to act loyally and in good faith (*Treu und Glauben*)[19] rather than § 826 BGB, that the courts turned. The Supreme Court recognised the need to intervene in order to prevent intolerable injustices produced by the classical methods of interpretation. As early as 1920 it accepted the principle of impossibility of performance which had been repudiated earlier. The specific instance concerned the lease of a building whose owner had contracted to heat it; in two years the heating costs equalled the rent payable over 10 years.[20] In 1923 another decisive step was taken. The *Reichsgericht* rejected the principle of monetary nominalism ("one mark equals one mark," *Mark gleich Mark*) and refused to admit that a debtor might discharge his debt by paying his creditor the nominal amount of the debt in marks which were then without value.[21] The general requirement that loyalty and good faith characterise payment, as specified at § 242 BGB, prevailed over the special provision in other pre-war legislation that the obligation to pay a sum of money is discharged by the repayment of the number of monetary units equal to that which was received, *i.e.* that the paper mark was legal tender at its nominal par. In effect, therefore, the *Reichsgericht* held that a general provision of the 1900 Civil Code could render nugatory a provision of a statute subsequently enacted.

---

[19] § 242 BGB: "The debtor of the obligation is bound to perform it in the manner required by good faith and with regard to prevailing business usage."

[20] *Entscheidungen des Reichsgerichts in Zivilsachen*: 100 R.G.Z. 129 (September 21, 1920). Translated by von Mehren (A.), *The Civil Law System* (1957), p. 733. Dawson (J. P.), "Effects of Inflation on Private Contracts," 33 Mich. L. Rev. 171 (1934); Hay (P.), "Frustration and its Solution in German Law," (1961) 10 Am. J. Comp. L. 345.

[21] 107 R.G.Z. 78 (November 28, 1923). Translated by von Mehren, *op. cit.* p. 743. Specific legislation (*Aufwertungsgesetze*) was later enacted to establish a revalorisation of money debts. Some specific classes of such debts were expressly dealt with in it and the balance were referred to the courts for decision according to "general principles of law." The position taken up by the *Reichsgericht* was thus subsequently legitimised by legislation.

93. Nordic countries

The idea that general provisions can prevail over special provisions seems, at first sight, to be established in Sweden and Finland as well. The official edition of Swedish laws (*Sveriges Rikes
lag*), published annually, is preceded by "rules for judges"
(*Domareglerna*) following a very old tradition encountered as
early as the law of the Westrogoths of the thirteenth century.[22]
These rules for judges, 43 in number, were drafted about 1550 by
a well-known advocate of the Reformation, Olaus Petri
(1493–1552). These same rules are included in the publications of
Finnish legislation. Even though they never had the force of law,
the fact that they have been inserted in the official editions of
Swedish laws for over three centuries makes them worthy of mention—especially since some of them prescribe surprising methods
for judges: "The law which proves mischievous is no longer law";
"the conscience of an honest man is the supreme law"; "the good
judge always knows how to decide according to the circumstances"; "one will consider as law that which proves to be most in
conformity with the good of Man, even when the letter of the written law would seem to provide differently." But it would be an
error to assume that such principles free the judge from a strict
interpretation of the law. The "rules for judges," even though
referred to by the doctrine, decisions and even sometimes by the
legislators, are no more than the expression of popular wisdom.
As often happens in such cases, the most contradictory precepts
are to be found side by side. Apart from those just cited one finds
for example the maxim *Summum ius summa iniuria* (*högsta rätt är
högsta orätt*) or, again, the affirmation that "he shall not judge
who does not know what the law contains or what is the reason and
meaning of the law." There is hardly a judgment which might not
be justified by invoking one or another of the maxims contained in
the rules for judges. With the establishment of democratic
regimes, the judges in Nordic countries, as on the Continent, have
come to consider that their power to decide in equity is restricted

---

[22] The National-Socialist *Volksgesetzbuch* of 1942 which, it was intended, would replace the
German Civil Code, also began with "fundamental rules" (*Grundregeln*) inspired by the
Swedish example; it is however from the Roman law and the Old Testament that Olaus Petri
took most of his maxims. Only these "rules" and the first part of the *Volksgesetzbuch* were
drafted and the code itself was never promulgated.

and that, whatever their personal preferences, they must apply the rules formulated by the legislators. The interpretation of enacted law in Nordic countries is ruled by the same principles, save for several nuances, applicable in other countries of continental Europe.[23]

94. Critical assessment

The technique of allowing a Code's general principles to prevail over specific provisions has been used in France as well, but it has been roundly criticised and even suggested that the interpretation of article 1382 C.civ. in connection with delictual liability may in the end only serve to subvert the legal order created by the French *Code civil*.

In appearances of course this method does respect expressed legislative intention: it is never *said* that a text has taken on a new meaning. And the technique employed is, indeed, a purely logical one—in the face of two texts, each of which appears to dictate opposite results, that one is made to prevail which permits the best solution for the day. It should hardly be necessary to state that this is no more than an artifice. The draftsmen of the German Civil Code certainly never imagined that their special provisions would, one day, appear unjust; and it was not to eliminate them, but only to interpret and if necessary to complement them, that they laid down a number of general principles. To apply such general provisions as against the Code's special provisions is thus certainly to fly in the face of the established rule of interpretation that a special provision is a derogation from a more general one as expressed in the maxim *specialia generalibus derogant*, and to run the risk of subverting the legal system. It means in effect that one opts for a legal system in which judicial decisions are based on equity rather than upon a true interpretation of the law.[24] Would it not be preferable to recognise, frankly, that texts of law, like clauses of a contract, are necessarily linked to their own time and place and, in the event that an entirely new set of circumstances unforeseen at

[23] Folke Schmidt, "Construction of Statutes" (1957) 6 *Scandinavian Studies* 157–198. Von Eyren (W. E.), "The Attitude Towards Judicial Precedent in Danish and Norwegian Courts" (1959) 3 *Scandinavian Studies* 53–86.
[24] The well known essay in the German literature dealing with the dangers of a "flight into the general clauses" is that of Hedemann (J. W.), *Die Flucht in die Generalklauseln. Eine Gefahr für Recht und Staat* (1933).

the time the law was enacted supervenes, that judges can, if the ends of justice require it, depart from the formal texts?[25] It is, after all, part of tradition to admit this *nobile officium* of judges. The excessive respect paid to enacted law which dominated nineteenth century doctrinal thinking has stimulated a number of artificial stratagems designed to maintain that attitude rather than eliminate it. But as T. Ascarelli has written: "The interpreter must exhibit wisdom rather than learning; and it is to wisdom rather than to learning that law must be drawn."[26]

95. Common principles of interpretation

In the final analysis, despite all the various doctrines, the practice in all countries of the Romano-Germanic family is to follow a middle course characterised by its empiricism but varying according to the judge, the times and the branch of law in question. The legislative texts are often treated as guides in finding the just solution rather than as commands which impose a strictly predetermined solution upon the interpreter. In all countries, a logical and grammatical interpretation is definitely preferred, and when respect for the intention of the legislators leads to a just solution this approach is willingly acknowleged. Logical interpretation nevertheless does give rise to a choice, either between reasoning by analogy or *a contrario*, or by the combination one can establish between various principles. An historical interpretation, clarifying present texts in the light of previous circumstances and taking into account the legislators' intention, may help to correct such a logical approach.[27] The same result may sometimes be obtained by considering the *ratio legis*, on the principle that this is related to all kinds of fact-situations and that the meaning of the enacted texts may therefore vary with the times.

In countries of the Romano-Germanic family, the starting point for all legal reasoning is found in various forms of "written law." Today these textual materials consist mainly of codes, statutes and regulations whereas formerly they were made up of Roman law

---

[25] Rüthers (B.), *Die unbegrenzte Auslegung. Zum Wandel der Privatrechtsordnung im Nationalsozialismus* (1968).

[26] Ascarelli (T.), "Norma giuridica e realtà sociale" *Il diritto dell'economia*, (1955), Vol. I, p. 6. Marcic (R.), *Vom Gesetzesstaat zum Richterstaat* (1957).

[27] But as to the English tradition, *cf.* Kilgour (D. G.): "The Rule Against the Use of Legislative History," 30 Can. Bar Rev. 767 (1952).

texts or other compilations, official or private. But these documents are only the basic materials. Rather than seeing such texts
as having established a system of norms, they are considered to be
a more or less well-defined juridical framework which the work of
interpretation will complete.

The interpreter which is, in fact, sovereign—a supreme court,
from the decisions of which there is no appeal—has a certain latitude. But it prefers to dissimulate its creative role and to give the
impression that it merely applies rules drawn up by someone else.
The extent to which its work is in fact creative, and the care taken
to hide this creativity, vary according to the time, country,
branches of law and the courts considered. It is difficult here to
make comparisons with any certainty, because the practice on this
point is poorly described by doctrinal writers who are themselves
often fairly unconscious of the way in which it operates. It happens
not infrequently, moreover, that authors endeavour to make one
particular interpretation prevail rather than to analyse effectively
the methods of construction used. French judges, while upsetting
the principles of delictual liability established by the Civil Code,
believe in good faith that they are applying articles 1382 to 1386 of
that Code. Some of them acknowledge that they first of all "sense"
the just solution and then look for its justification in law; others
indignantly repudiate this process as being against their conscience
as judges.[28]

The same holds true for the other countries of the Romano-
Germanic family.[29] However, for historical or sociological
reasons, it may be that a given country is intent on preserving the
appearance that statutory law is the only source in the rendering of
some particular decision—and it may be, too, that at certain times
or in certain branches of law this appearance does indeed correspond to reality, because the law is satisfactory and requires no
adjustment.

Among the historical or sociological considerations which can
play a part there must be noted those differences between the traditions of French and German jurists which P. Koschaker
(1879–1951) thought possible to detect.[30] German judges and jur-

---

[28] *Travaux de l'Association Henri Capitant*, Vol. V, for the year 1949, p. 74.
[29] Itoh (H.), "How Judges Think in Japan" 18 Am. J. Comp. L. 775 (1970).
[30] *Europa und das römische Recht* (3rd ed., 1958).

ists never constituted as independent a social group as the French
judges who were protected, under the monarchical regime, by the
proprietary and hereditary character of judicial positions. Also, in
Germany a greater influence was exercised at one time on legal
practice by professorial and philosophical doctrines. German law,
according to Koschaker, was traditionally a *Professorenrecht* or
"professors' law" compared to French law which he saw as a "jurists' law" or *Juristenrecht*. One must be careful, however, about
attributing such labels today even though they may once have been
historically justified. It now seems that German law has overtaken
French law in this regard; and as much if not more so than in
France, legal developments in Germany are directed, at least in
some areas, by judicial decisions. Italy, in which a markedly dogmatic tendency prevails, is probably more removed at the present
time than Germany from the extremely flexible methods of interpretation practised in France. The dissociation between School
and Courts which persists in Italy makes it difficult for a foreigner
to discover how Italian judges and practitioners interpret their
laws.[31] Even the way in which Italian decisions are written and
published is misleading: they are in general incompletely reported
and it is often the part omitted (the *omissis*) which contains the
true explanation of the decision—always supposing that the
judges, wishes to indicate their respect for the legal texts, are bold
enough to give such an explanation.[32]

Similar observations might be made concerning Spanish and
Portuguese laws and the laws of Latin American countries. Traditional methods have not lost their place in these countries either.
But the theorists appear to have been won over to that political
philosophy—to which Marxism is linked—which exalts the role of
enacted law, and this may have led judges to be extremely cautious
in revealing the extent of their own contribution. In Argentina,
however, exegetical interpretation has given way to a progressive
construction of statutes to the point where a legislative reform of
the whole Civil Code now appears uncalled for.[33] The Soviet

---

[31] Cappelletti (M.), Merryman (J. H.), Perillo (J. M.), *The Italian Legal System* (1967).

[32] *Cf.* the studies published since 1967 by G. Gorla and M. Lupoi in the Quaderni del Foro
italiano *in Raccolta di saggi sulla giurisprudenza*. Gorla (G.), "Lo studio interno e comparativo
della giurisprudenza e i suoi presupposti: le raccolte e le technice per la interpretazione delle
sentenze" *Il Foro italiano* (1964), Vol. 87, p. 1–31.

[33] Garrido (R.) and Andorno (L.), *Reformas al Código civil* (2nd ed., 1971).

authors clamour with indignation about bourgeois hypocrisy[34]; they see evidence of it in the independence which judges of the capitalist countries show with respect to enacted law. One may question their interpretation of this fact, but not, we believe, the fact itself. In Romano-Germanic countries, because the law and enacted law are not the same thing, the judges do indeed enjoy a certain independence with respect to legislation. The very existence of a *judicial power* and, consequently, the very principle of the separation of powers with all the advantages which we attribute to it, are linked to this independence. This has the effect, in our western tradition, of placing law above politics. Is this good or bad? The reply to such a question goes hand in hand with the choice made between the two concepts of the social order which stand face to face in the contemporary world.

96. Conclusion

The countries of the Romano-Germanic family are united today by the same view that a primordial role must be attributed to legislation. Certain differences may of course be noticed in this respect. Some of these, the judicial review of the constitutionality of statutes, codification, the distinction between statute and regulation and the interpretation of enacted law, have been mentioned. These differences have very definite importance. However none of them places any one law outside the Romano-Germanic family; in fact, it is difficult to find any element which would lead to distinguishing an autonomous Latin, Germanic, Graeco-Italian or even Scandinavian group.

More important than these differences are the noticeable similarities between the various laws—similarities bearing mainly on the important place given to legislation. In the whole of the Romano-Germanic family, legislation appears to encompass the whole of the legal order; jurists, and even the law itself, certainly admit in theory that the legislative order may have gaps, but in practice it seems that these gaps are insignificant. The reality of the situation, however, which this view obscures is very different and may well surprise those who believe in purely doctrinal formulations. Legislation forms no more than the skeleton of the legal

---

[34] Zivs (S. L.), *Razvitie formy prava v sovremennyh imperialističeskih gosudarstvah* (1960).

order, and flesh is given to this skeleton largely by other factors. Legislation must not be considered in its texts alone and independently of its often very extensive interpretation which reveals the creative power of judicial decisions and doctrinal writings. The codes are only looked upon by jurists as a starting point, not as the end; for this reason they are clearly distinguishable from the compilations (consolidations or codes of the American type) found in Common law countries, just as they are to be distinguished from the written customs or codes antedating the French Revolution. They are in fact the successors not of the customs or older codes but of Roman law and the works of Romanist scholarship. This will become more apparent upon an examination of the present role of the sources of law other than legislation.

CHAPTER II

CUSTOM

97. The idea of custom

According to a sociological concept of the sources of law, custom plays a preponderant role in all legal systems[1]; and in developing or applying the law, legislators, judges and authors are, as a matter of fact, more or less consciously guided by the opinion and custom of the community. According to this notion, the role of custom as a source of law is analogous to that attributed by Marxist thinking to the material conditions of production; they are both an infrastructure upon which the law is built. The positivist school, on the contrary, has attempted to dismiss the role of custom altogether; according to this view, custom now occupies only a minimal place in a codified system in which the law is to be exclusively identified with the will of the legislators. While this position is not realistic, that of the sociological school, which gives the expression "source of law" an unusual sense, exaggerates the role of custom in the other direction. Custom is not the fundamental and primal element of law that the sociological school would like it to be; it is but one of the elements involved in establishing acceptable solutions. In modern societies, this element is far from having the primordial importance of legislation. But it is also far from being as insignificant as the doctrine of legislative positivism would have it.

In theory, French and German jurists have different attitudes to custom. French jurists are tempted to see in it a somewhat outdated source of law which, since the recognition of the undisputed predominance of legislation, is insignificant. They would subscribe to the legislative provisions which, in Italy and Austria, only anticipate the application of custom when the law itself expressly says

[1] Levy-Bruhl (H.), *Sociologie du droit* (4th ed., 1971).

130

so. In Germany, Switzerland and Greece, on the other hand, one is inclined to represent legislation and custom as two sources of law on the same level.[2] This view derives from the Historical School which, in the nineteenth century, saw law as a product of popular consciousness. This theoretical difference is however of no practical consequence. The fact is that in France and Germany one behaves as though legislation had become almost the exclusive source of law; but in both, the reality is something else. Custom has a much more important place than appearances would seem to allow.

98. The practical role of custom

Legislation itself, in order to be understood, often has to appeal to custom for the necessary clarification of the ideas of the legislators. Without such a reference it cannot be said for example when a person has committed a fault, whether a certain mark constitutes a signature, whether the person committing an infraction may plead attenuating circumstances, whether an object is a family keepsake, whether a person has acted within a "reasonable" delay, or whether there is the moral impossibility of procuring written proof of an obligation. Any effort made to eliminate the role of custom in these respects will result in a conceptualism or in a case-by-case approach contrary to the spirit of the law of Romano-Germanic countries; an attempt to suppress the enormous role which custom, *secundum legem*, has thus acquired seems futile.

On the other hand, the role of custom *praeter legem* has greatly diminished with the progress of codification and the acknowledged primacy of legislation in the democratic regimes of modern political societies. Today, jurists of the Romano-Germanic family seek at any price to cite legislative texts in support of their reasoning. Under these conditions, custom *praeter legem* is relegated to a very secondary role.

In the same way the role of custom *adversus legem* is very restrained, in appearance at least, even though it is not denied in

---

[2] Zepos (P. J.), "Quinze années d'application du Code civil hellénique," Rev. int. dr. comparé, 1962, pp. 281–308. Beguelin (M.), *Das Gewohnheitsrecht in der Praxis des Bundesgerichts* (1968).

principle by legal authors. The courts, it is clear, do not like to set themselves up against the legislative power.

Any analysis of custom's role is, in truth, distorted because of the long-standing primary importance attributed to "written law," whether in the form of the Roman texts of an earlier time or the national codifications of the present day. Custom has certainly exerted an important influence upon the development of law in Romano-Germanic countries but it has appeared necessary to seek a justification for this. In the Middle Ages it was found in texts of the Digest.[3] Even today it is not easy for lawyers to free themselves of this Romanist canonical view; justification for the recognition of custom is nowadays sought *within* a legislative framework, even if, in doing so, custom must be falsely presented as being in harmony with legislation when really it is either filling in the gaps of a text or is even contrary thereto. Apart from some very rare exceptions, custom has thus lost its place as an autonomous source of law; it almost seems as though it were best forgotten, the only real problem for contemporary jurists being the interpretation of construction of legislation.

A more exact view of custom—a view, moreoever, enabling one to understand the traditional laws of Africa—can only be grasped if one ceases to confuse law and legislation. If legislation is not identified with law, but thought of simply as a means—the main one today—of arriving at a knowledge of law, there is nothing to prevent acknowledgement of the usefulness of sources other than legislative texts. Among these other sources, custom will figure very largely so natural and, one may say, so inevitable is it to consider men's behaviour in order to establish, objectively, what is considered socially just. Custom, however, has no intrinsic value; it is only worth retaining to the extent that it serves to indicate the just solution. The jurist must not therefore apply it automatically; he must bring his criticism to bear on it and, in particular, ask whether it is reasonable.

---

[3] In particular, a fragment drawn from Julian, D.1.3.32. *Cf.* Dawson (J. P.), *The Oracles of the Law* (1968), pp. 128 *et seq.*

CHAPTER III

DECIDED CASES

The place given to judicial decisions as a source of law distinguishes the laws of the Romano-Germanic family from the Common law and from Socialist laws. It is by comparison with the concepts in these other families that a definition of the position of Romano-Germanic laws will be attempted. Among these latter laws, there once again appear to be more differences in detail than in principle.

99. Criterion for evaluating the role of decided cases

In order to judge the importance of judicial decisions in formulating the law, one must again be wary of those ready-made formulae which, with the aim of underscoring the exclusivity of enacted law, flatly exlude decided cases as a source of law. These statements are somewhat ridiculous when used in countries such as France or Germany, where cases have been of primary importance in the evolution of some branches of the law and where doctrinal works very often do no more than provide an exegesis of judicial decisions.[1] They are equally false, despite appearances, in countries where the doctrine is seemingly little if at all concerned with decided cases.[2] Most often this attitude is simply a sign of the dissociation of the academic milieu from that of the practitioner; it in

---

[1] Enneccerus (L.) and Nipperdey (H.), *Lehrbuch des bürgerlichen Rechts, Allgemeiner Teil* (15th ed., 1959) Vol. I, p. 275, still nevertheless assert that judicial decisions as such do not constitute a source of law and this view appears to be that most commonly accepted in Germany even today. Zweigert (K.) and Puttfarken (H. J.), "Statutory Interpretation: Civilian Style" 44 Tulane L.R. 718 (1970). But *cf.* Esser (J.), *Grundsatz und Norm in der richterlichen Fortbildung des Privatrechts* (1956) and Larenz (K.), *Methodenlehre der Rechtswissenschaft* (2nd ed., 1969), pp. 291, 341.

[2] In order to clarify the influence of judicial decisions as a factor in the evolution of Italian law, an enquiry was carried out under the auspices of the Consiglio nazionale delle Ricerche: Gorla (G.), "Giurisprudenza" in *Enciclopedia del diritto* (1969).

no way signifies that judicial decisions are not a source of law. To have a correct idea of the matter, one must investigate the existence and development of collections or digests of judicial decisions, rather than the doctrinal works or the formal statements of legal writers. These collections or digests are not compiled for the use of legal historians or sociologists, nor for the pleasure of their readers; they are designed to be used by lawyers in practice, and their existence can only be explained if judicial decisions are a source of law in the true sense of the term; their quantity and quality will give some indication of the importance of judicial decisions as a source of law in the Romano-Germanic family.

The process of evaluation just stated requires some qualification. In certain countries, especially small, new or under-developed nations, the importance of judicial decisions must not be measured only in terms of their published collections. It may be, as a matter of fact, that some use (with the necessary reservations) is made of collections published in other countries with the law of which there are particular affinities. The importance of French reported cases is thus for example in no way limited to French frontiers. The decisions of the French Supreme Court (*Cour de Cassation*) and those of the Council of State (*Conseil d'Etat*) are studied in and exercise an influence upon various neighbouring or distant French-speaking countries, and even in other European or extra-European countries of the Romano-Germanic family where particular importance is attached to French practice in certain domains.

100. Obedience of judges to statute law

The role of judicial decisions in countries of the Romano-Germanic family can only be determined by considering its relationship to statutory or enacted law. Given the present unfailing tendency of jurists in all countries to look for support in a text of law, the creative role of judicial decisions is always, or nearly always, hidden behind the screen of an "interpretation" of legislation. It is exceptional for jurists to abandon this habit or for judges to admit frankly that they have the power of creating rules of law. They persist in their attitude of obedience to enacted law, even when the legislature itself has recognised that there may be gaps in the legislation. In such cases the judge must nonetheless of course render a decision.[3] He cannot, like the judge in Roman times, refuse to adjudicate when the law is uncertain. The Swiss Civil Code (art. 1, para. 2) has an express rule for such cases: the judge must decide as though he were the legislator and, in the process, may look to usage and decided cases. This provision of the Swiss Code has not been a dead letter; it has even happened that Swiss judges have somewhat artificially discovered legislative gaps in order to invoke the article and avail themselves of the power it confers. In general however it has not been used extensively.[4] It would seek that this provision, which aroused such interest among theoretical thinkers, has in the end very little changed the practical face of Swiss law. The "free scientific research" (*libre recherche scientifique*) advocated by F. Gény, to the extent that it is employed, is practised without denying the dogma according to which the legislative order is all-sufficient. It is easier, in other words, to maintain the fiction.

If we wish, therefore to analyse the role of judicial decisions in the evolution of the law, we must resign ourselves to looking behind the process of interpretation of legislative texts, be it real or fictitious. In each country, judicial decisions play a creative part in this process to the extent that judges depart from simple exegesis. An attempt has already been made to outline the situation in countries of the Romano-Germanic family in this respect.

Whatever the contribution of the courts to the evolution of the law, it certainly differs, therefore, from that of the legislators in countries of the Romano-Germanic family. Legislators, who nowadays are called upon to establish the framework of the legal order, do so by formulating commands and creating rules of law. Very rarely are courts authorised to use this method: the provision of the French Civil Code[5] which prohibits judges from laying down general and regulatory rules has its equivalent in all the laws of the Romano-Germanic family. The few possible exceptions which may exist, while undoubtedly interesting, leave the principle nevertheless intact.

---

[3] C. civ. 4 (France). Most other civilian codes have comparable provisions.
[4] Du Pasquier (C.), *Les lacunes de la loi et la jurisprudence du Tribunal fédéral suisse sur l'art, 1er du Code civil suisse* (1951); Meier-Hayoz (A.), *Der Richter als Gesetzgeber* (1951); Germann (O. A.), *Probleme und Methoden der Rechtsfindung* (2nd ed., 1967), pp. 111–227.
[5] C. civ. Art. 5. *Cf.* para. 70, note 2.

101. Significance of judicial precedents

Judicial decisions do not create rules of law because this task, so say the judges, belongs exclusively to the legislators and the governmental or administrative authorities called upon to complete their work. Despite this self-effacing position, are rules of law in fact created by judges? Between the supposed judge-made rules of law and the rules of law articulated by the legislators there are, in any case, two important differences.

The first concerns the relative importance of one or the other in any given system. Judicial decisions develop within the legal framework established by legislation, whereas the task of the legislators is specifically to create this framework. For this reason, the scope of judicial law-making is limited, and the situation in countries of the Romano-Germanic family is, in this respect, exactly the reverse of that of those in the Common law system.

In the second place, the "legal rules" laid down by the courts do not have the same authority as enacted legal rules. They are fragile and may be rejected or modified, at any time, upon examination of a new case. *La jurisprudence* in France, *i.e.* the body of cases on a given topic, is not bound by the rules it has made; it cannot even generally cite them to support the decision to be rendered. If, in a new decision, the judge applies a rule which was previously applied, it is not because this rule has acquired any special authority through such previous application; in effect, this rule has no obligatory character. A reversal in the trend or pattern of judicial decisions (*revirement de jurisprudence*) is always possible without the judges being obliged to justify it. Such changes are of little importance: they do not threaten either the framework or the principles of the law. The judicially created legal rule only exists and is only applied so long as the judges—that is, each judge—consider it a good rule. Under these conditions it is understandable that one hesitates to speak of a truly *legal rule*.

The rejection of the doctrine of binding precedent, whereby judges must abide by the rules previously applied in an earlier decision, is no accident. The doctrine of precedent has been contrary to the tradition of the Romano-Germanic system since the Middle Ages when, instead of confiding the creation of a new system of law to judges, the ready-made model of Roman law was accepted. Since then it has always been considered necessary that the legal rule be doctrinal or legislative in origin; it must be thought out in advance so as to cover a series of typical cases reaching beyond the limits of and free from the contingencies of a particular trial. As a matter of principle, it is important that the judge should not make of himself a legislator. This is the philosophy of the Romano-Germanic family. Thus, the statement that the body of decided cases is not a source of *law* is not quite exact, but it does express a truth if it is understood to mean that judicial decisions are not a source of legal *rules*. *Non exemplis, sed legibus, iudicandum est.*[6]

102. Organisation of the courts

Apart from technical rules which may differ on matters of detail, this common concept of the role of judicial decisions demonstrates the unity of the Romano-Germanic family. This concept, as already stated, is bound to tradition and is also linked to the organisation of the courts and especially to the way in which judges are trained and appointed.

The organisation of the courts varies enormously, of course, from one country to another. There are nonetheless certain common characteristics which, saving exceptions, do stand out. The courts in the first place are established in a hierarchy. Courts of first instance, established throughout the territory of the country in question, are a first level. Above them, and fewer in number, are courts of appeal, and a supreme court heads the whole structure. There are important differences however in the implementation of this scheme. Courts of first instance are especially varied, and in one and the same country they may be of several different types according to the nature of the dispute and the amount involved. In some, but not all countries, there are special courts or divisions for commercial law matters, family law, labour law, etc.[7] The variations in the organisation of appeal courts correspond to those in the organisation of the courts of first instance and the conditions

---

[6] Constitution of 529; Codes 7.45.13: "Things are to be judged not by examples but by law." In other words, disputed matters are to be determined according to the applicable principle of law rather than by previous decisions or precedents. It should be noted however that in Portugal the legal rules confirmed by the full Supreme Court have the same authority as those created by the legislators. *Cf.* Fragitas (C. N.), "Les précédents judiciaires en Europe continentale" in *Mélanges Maury* (1960), p. 139.

[7] The "commercial courts" of Italy, the Netherlands, Portugal and Brazil have however been abolished.

and grounds upon which an appeal may be lodged. In some jurisdictions the supreme court acts as a court of final appeal, whereas
in others it cannot substitute its own decision on the merits and
may only annul or quash the decision of the lower court.

In some countries, moreover, there are other courts outside this
hierarchy. Many countries have an autonomous structure of
administrative tribunals. Such is the case in France, where the final
court in administrative law matters it the *Conseil d'Etat*, and in
federal Germany, Austria, the Netherlands, Finland, Italy, Lich-
tenstein, Luxembourg, Monaco, Sweden and several Latin American countries (Colombia, Mexico, Panama, Uruguay). These
administrative tribunals may, on the other hand, be subject to the
control of the ordinary supreme court, a separate division of which
specialises in administrative law litigation; such is the system in
Belgium, Spain, Switzerland, and in most French-speaking African countries. Finally in yet other countries there are no administrative tribunals at all (Denmark, Norway, Japan, Argentina,
Brazil, Chile, Peru, Venezuela) and recourse to the ordinary
courts is often restricted when the matter involves the governmental administration. In countries where specialised administrative law courts do exist, the principles establishing the respective
jurisdictions of the administrative tribunals and the regular courts
naturally vary as well. Whereas in France, for example, there is
the principle that the ordinary courts cannot be seized of cases
involving administrative acts,[8] other countries (Belgium, the Netherlands, Switzerland) have organised their administrative tribunals
as bodies having jurisdiction only in those specific instances where
it is expressly provided.[9]

Apart from administrative tribunals many countries have yet
other independent court systems. Germany has a series of
supreme federal courts for labour law, social security matters and
tax law. In Switzerland there are autonomous federal courts in
social insurance law, military law and customs and excise.

In countries with a federal structure, a further factor complicates the above picture: the administration of justice is most often
a matter within the competence of the federated units themselves

---

[8] The origin is in the *Loi des 16–24 août 1790* and that of *16 fructidor an III*. Rivero (J.), *Droit administratif* (5th ed., 1977), no. 132.

[9] Sayaguès-Laso (E.), *Traité de droit administratif* (1964), t. II, nos. 942 *et seq.*

(states, provinces, cantons) and, at the head, there will be only one or several federal courts. This is the situation in Germany, Switzerland and, since 1937, Brazil. In Venezuela, on the other hand, the courts are all federal. In Argentina and Mexico, as in the United States, there are two parallel hierarchies: the courts of provinces or states exist alongside the federal courts. The analogy with the United States is however no more than apparent because the principles which determine the jurisdiction of the two orders of courts are not the same, and the scope of the federal laws which the federal courts apply is not the same in these several countries.[10]

103. Judges

In Romano-Germanic countries judges are, in general, persons who have had a formal legal education and assume a full-time appointment. The Roman law tradition in which neither judges nor praetors had any legal training has not survived.[11]

There are, however, some exceptions to this general principle. Sometimes there are judges elected for a limited period who have no legal training (rural Swiss cantons, French commercial courts). Assessors or a jury may sit with the judge in criminal matters (French *Cour d'assises*) or even in civil matters (Swedish *nämnd*). As a general rule, however, judges are appointed for life and are irremoveable, and their independence is thus guaranteed. A contrary principle applies however in Switzerland to judges of the Federal Court[12] and in some other European countries (Germany, Italy) in the case of judges sitting on the constitutional court. In South America, supreme court judges are named fo life only in Argentina, Brazil and Chile; elsewhere they are appointed for terms varying from three to ten years. This factor has, on occasion, put into some doubt the integrity of the judicial process in such countries.

In Romano-Germanic countries, the judicial function is, gener-

---

[10] The civil and commercial codes of Argentina are federal codes. In Mexico there is a federal commercial code but there are civil codes in each of the 29 states and the federal civil code is only in force in the federal district and territories.

[11] *Cf.* Dawson (J. P.), *The Oracles of the Law* (1968), pp. 100–123 who explains the importance of the "prudents."

[12] They are elected for a term of six years by the federal assembly but may stand again and are very generally re-elected.

ally speaking, a career entered at the beginning of one's professional life. It is rare that judges be appointed from among practising advocates at the height of their reputation, according to the practice in Common law countries.[13] Their attitude is therefore distinctive from that of a Common law judge—because of their training, in university and as judges, they are prepared to envisage the matters submitted to their adjudication in a large or general manner and beyond the confines of the instant case; their view of the law is less technical, less insular perhaps. This attitude is, moreover, reinforced by the presence of a further category of judicial personnel with whom they work closely, the advocates of the *ministère public* whose function it is to argue the public interest dimensions raised in a case. Indeed, the existence of this branch of judicial administration appears to be a characteristic feature of the Romano-Germanic system itself.

The general characteristics traced above do not, of course, exclude variations from one country to another. The body of judges in each country does not have the same organisation and traditions. In France, for example, the hereditary and venal character of the judicial function, and the political role which the *parlements* attempted to arrogate, made French judges in the *ancien régime* a kind of autonomous caste. But the same conditions were not encountered in all countries and the independence of the judiciary has elsewhere therefore been traditionally less pronounced. These differences, historically very important, are however no longer significant. The status of French magistrates today is not dissimilar to that of civil servants and any notion of a truly "judicial power" in France has completely disappeared. On the other hand, in other countries, there is a newly developed sense of the distinctive nature of the judicial function. The feeling runs deep among judges that they must not in any sense be the servants of, or take orders from, the government which itself has more and more been made subject to judicial review and control.

Finally the very large number of professional judges in the Romano-Germanic countries, as contrasted with the figures in Common law countries, should be noted. There are in all almost 15,000 judges in the Federal Republic of Germany and approxima

---

[13] This is the case in some Latin American countries at least in respect of appointments to the supreme courts.

tely 5,000 (in the judicial as opposed to administrative courts) in France.

104. Reports of judicial decisions

The role played by judicial decisions in various countries is affected by a number of different factors. Among these, mention must now be made of the existence and varying quality of published reports of judicial decisions, as well as their official character in certain countries. On this point it is interesting to note that the changes within the last century have increasingly tended to improve the quality of such collections; these changes reflect the now greater importance attributed to judicial decisions.

Official collections of decided cases exist today in many countries of the Romano-Germanic family—France, Germany, Spain, Italy, Switzerland, and Turkey. On occasion, these official reports enable a distinction to be drawn (although this is not usually admitted) between decisions of "jurisprudential" value and those which are best forgotten. This is the case in Turkey, where the reporting of selected decisions should help jurists to understand the new law. It is also, although more discreetly so, the case in France, where the *Cour de cassation* will only attribute authority to those decisions which the court itself has decided to publish; in Germany, where only "decisions of principle" (*Verwaltungsgerichtshof*) are published by the Court of Administrative Justice; and in Switzerland, where it is clearly intended from the choice of decisions and from their manner of presentation (and particularly the summary which precedes them) that the doctrine of observing only reported decisions is to be followed. In Spain, on the other hand, the distinction between decisions published and unpublished in the official collection is ruled by another criterion: only those decisions concerning the jurisdiction of the supreme court, or the admissibility of suits instituted before it, are included.

105. Style of judicial decisions

Another element to consider is the style of judicial decisions.[14] Today they must always contain the reasons for judgment,

---

[14] Dawson (J. P.), *The Oracles of the Law* (1968), pp. 376, 433. Sauvel (T.), "Histoire du jugement motivé" (1955) Rev. dr. public et sc. pol. 5–53. Gorla (G.), "Civilian Judicial Decisions. An Historical Account of Italian Style" 44 Tulane L. R. 740 (1970).

although this requirement is relatively recent. Over a long period it was thought that judgments were prerogative acts and, as such, did not call for any justification. The practice of supplying reasons grew gradually in Italy from the sixteenth century and in Germany from the eighteenth century, but as an obligation imposed on all judges it was only laid down in France in 1790 and in Germany in 1879. Today it is firmly established—and in Italy it is guaranteed by the Constitution itself—because it is viewed as one means of guarding against arbitrary judgments and providing some assurance that the decision will be well thought out.

Although judicial decisions in all Romano-Germanic countries must furnish written reasons, the style in which the judgment is drafted will follow one of two main types.[15] In certain countries there is the French technique of "whereas-es" (*attendus*), a feature apparently deriving from the style of solicitors' conclusions; the judgment, formulated in a single sentence, is considered all the more perfect for its concise and concentrated style, so that only experienced jurists are able to understand and admire it. In Europe, outside of France, this practice is followed in Belgium, Luxembourg, the Netherlands, Spain, Portugal and the Nordic countries with the exception of Sweden which recently abandoned it. In other countries however the judicial decision is presented in the form of a dissertation, which varies in length and in its organisation. This is the case in Germany, Greece, Italy, Switzerland and Sweden. Decisions in these countries very often include references to previous decisions or to works of legal doctrine, something not generally found in those of the first group.[16]

106. Dissenting judicial opinions

A further element to consider is the existence, or the absence, of judgments expressing the dissenting views of judges who have

[15] See especially the study by Gillis Wetter, *The Style of Appellate Judicial Decisions* (1960) and the historical studies of G. Gorla, "Lo stile delle sentenze: ricerca storico-comparativa e testi commentati" *Quaderni del Foro italiano* (1967–1968), pp. 351, 367; *I grandi tribunali italiani fra i secoli XVI a XIX*, *Quaderni del Foro italiano* (1969), p. 629; Die Präzedenzentscheidungen der Senate von Piedmont und Savoyen im 18 Jahrhundert *Ius privatum gentium*, *Festschrift für Max Rheinstein* (1969), Vol. I, p. 103.

[16] The mode of citation of judicial decisions varies from country to country within the Romano-Germanic family and even within any one country (such as France for example where it varies according to the court in question); *cf.* Szladits (C.), *Guide to Foreign Legal Materials* (*French, German, Swiss*) (1959), pp. 70–72 (France); pp. 245–246 (German); pp. 468–469 (Swiss).

taken up a minority position.[17] It should not be thought that minority judgments, looked upon with extreme hostility in France, are peculiar to countries of the Common law. Many countries of the Romano-Germanic family accept them, especially in Latin America (*discordias, votos vencidos*). In Europe, they may derive from the fact that the proceedings are entirely written (Portugal) or it may be that they are admitted to ease the conscience of judges whose minority votes will be noted in the record but not made public (Germany,[18] Spain: *votos secretos*). Even when a collective decision is to be rendered, the idea that a judge's vote should be secret is not necessarily accepted everywhere; the procedure of oral deliberation observed by the Swiss federal court enables each judge to express his opinion. In France itself a similar procedure has been adopted in the *Cour de cassation*. Nevertheless even in Romano-Germanic countries where it is admitted the influence of minority votes seems fairly weak at most.

107. Uniformity of judicial decisions

Particularly interesting are the different processes used to achieve legal certainty by assuring that there is some consistency among judicial decisions. This concern, found in many countries, points out the true authority of judicial decisions even though many legal writers persist in denying that they are a source of law.

The very principles governing the judicial organisation bear witness to this. In general the judicial organisation is headed by a supreme court whose mission, while it theoretically consists of watching over the strict application of legislation, is often in fact to assure a uniformity of judicial interpretation. The existence of this supreme court may well threaten rather than guarantee the supremacy of enacted law. The legislators would hardly need to fear any competition from a series of scattered local courts whose decisions could only with difficulty constitute any kind of coherent or firm patterns of decision-making. The supreme court, on the other

---

[17] Nadelmann (K.), "The Judicial Dissent. Publication v. Secrecy," 8 Am. J. Comp. L. pp. 415–432 (1959). Heyde (W.), *Das Minderheitsvotum des überstimmten Richters* (1966) and discussions of the 47th Juristentag (Nuremberg, September 1968).

[18] German legislation of December 21, 1970 has however expressly authorised judges of the federal constitutional court to make known their dissenting opinions once the decision is rendered.

hand, endowed with greater prestige and inclined to see questions from a more general angle (especially when, as in France, it is not allowed to review the facts) is inevitably tempted to become a complementary, if not a rival, authority of the legislators. In England, the concentration of judicial power was the prerequisite for and cause of the development of the case-law which is the Common law. In France, the concentration of administrative law litigation in the *Conseil d'Etat* had the same effect respecting the formulation of administrative law. By avoiding conflicts between judicial decisions through the action of a supreme court, the authority of decided cases is guaranteed much more than a "right application" of the law.

However, the existence of a supreme court has often been judged insufficient, and steps have been taken to assure a uniformity of decisions among the divisions or chambers of this court. In France, in the *Cour de Cassation*, this function has been assured by the procedure of "mixed chambers" (*chambres mixtes*) employed since 1967 and, at a higher level, by the procedure of a "full bench" (*assemblée plénière*) of the court in order to resolve conflicting decisions between the chambers of that court and inferior courts. So too in Federal Germany, the federal Supreme Court (*Bundesgerichtshof*) has provision for special panels (*Grosse Senate, Vereinigte Grosse Senate*), if one chamber wishes to reject the jurisprudence established in another. Similarly, the full bench (*Vollversammlung*) of the court of administrative justice must meet if one of its divisions wishes to break away from the accepted doctrine of a reported decision of this court. It should also be noted that in Germany the court's leave to appeal, which may be legally necessary for an appeal to lie, must obligatorily be granted when the criticised decision has deviated from supreme court practice.

108. Binding precedents

Contrary to general principle, it may on occasion happen in some countries that a judge must observe a judicial precedent or a line of previously decided cases.

The authority of binding precedent is attributed in Federal Germany to the decisions of the federal Constitutional Court, the decisions of which for this reason are published in the official

Federal Journal (*Bundesgesetzblatt*). In Argentina and Columbia the same authority is attributed to decisions in their Supreme Courts in constitutional law; the canton courts in Switzerland are similarly bound by the decision of the Federal Court when it has declared a law to be unconstitutional. In Portugal, the decisions (*assentos*) of the full bench of the *Tribunal supremo de justiça* are binding when they are reported in the official government publication, *Diario de Governo*, and in the publication of the Ministry of Justice; in Argentina, those of the Supreme Court are binding when it has been seized of a case by way of special appeal; in Turkey, certain leading decisions of the Supreme Court and Council of State are binding upon lower courts.[19]

The creative role of decided cases is officially recognised in Spanish law by the concept of *doctrina legal*.[20] Appeal to the Supreme Court from a judicial decision is permitted by law if this decision has violated a *doctrina legal* admitted by this court; by *doctrina legal* is understood a judicial practice based on several decisions of the Supreme Court. It should be noted in this connection that in Spain the word *jurisprudencia* is reserved to decisions rendered by the Supreme Court or by other superior courts (*Dirección general de registro, Tribunal de la Rota*) to the exclusion of those rendered by the courts of appeal (*Audiencias*) or lower courts. Moreover, the Spanish Civil Code has no provision corresponding to article 5 of the French Civil Code. A concept analogous to the Spanish *doctrina legal* is admitted in Mexico and Honduras in matters pertaining to civil liberties (*amparo*). In Germany, similarly, it is admitted that when a rule has been applied by a fixed line of cases (*ständige Rechtsprechung*) it becomes a rule of customary law and must, as such, henceforth be judicially applied. This position is not adopted in Switzerland but there it is exremely rare for the federal court to reverse itself.[21]

---

[19] "Unification decisions" were very frequent at one time: more than 460 were rendered between 1926 and 1966 in civil and criminal matters whereas 100 were handed down by the Council of State. Since 1960 they are much rarer. There is only one instance where the Supreme Court has not followed the position taken up in a "unification decision." *Cf.* Bilge (N.), "Autorité de la jurisprudence en droit turc" *Receuil de travaux de la 3e rencontre turco-suisse* (1966), pp. 191–211. Postačioglu (I. E.), "L'autorité de la jurisprudence en droit privé" *ibid.* pp. 213–228.

[20] Herzog (J. B.), *Le droit jurisprudentiel et le Tribunal suprême en Espagne* (1942); Puig Brutau (J.), *La jurisprudencia como fuente del derecho* (1953).

[21] Meyer-Hayoz (A.), "Zur Frage der normativen Kraft der Rechtsprechung" *Recueil de travaux de la 3e rencontre turco-suisse* (1966), p. 229.

109. Administrative practice

In addition to court decisions, mention must be made of administrative practices. The difference between them may be slight when one considers the actual decisions handed down by certain administrative agencies, even though the latter may not be "courts" in the technical sense. Administrative disputes of one kind or another may in fact be confided either to the ordinary courts or to special (administrative) courts, or even to non-judicial bodies. The practice of these special courts or bodies may be very close to the judicial practice of the regular courts, but it may also vary considerably according to the relative development, in different countries, of its administrative law, which is in any case everywhere of recent date and has nowhere attained a sufficient degree of maturity and stability to warrant codification.[22]

When referring to administrative practice, however, further consideration must also be given to the internal regulations and instructions which various administrative departments distribute to their officers and agents. In themselves, these administrative instructions have only a "doctrinal" value. Even though issued by administrative bodies, they are not normative in character and, consequently, are not considered as sources of law by those who support the principle of legislative positivism. The authors of the sociological school, on the other hand, will consider them to be sources of law *par excellence*, because in the immense majority of cases it is certain that civil servants will observe the instructions received as these are their only means of knowing the law. It is no less certain that in most cases private persons will accept the application of the law as laid down in such administrative directives. The fact that the attention of jurists, in countries of the Romano-Germanic family, has traditionally been given to problems of private law explains the scant study of these administrative regulations and instructions, the practical importance of which today in the modern welfare state is primordial in many areas.

---

[22] Some special subjects may, on the other hand, be ready for immediate codification in administrative law; the law of government contracts has, in this connection, been codified within the general Civil Code in Ethiopia and in a special code in Senegal.

CHAPTER IV

LEGAL WRITING

110. Fundamental importance of "doctrine"

Works of legal scholarship were for a long time the fundamental source of law in the Romano-Germanic family. It was essentially in the universities that the principles of law emerged between the thirteenth and nineteenth centuries. Only recently has the primacy of doctrinal writing given way to that of enacted law, with the establishment of democratic ideas and the advent of codification.

The recentness of this change and an understanding of the real rather than theoretical nature of enacted law reveal the true importance of doctrinal writing as distinguished from the over-simplified view, sometimes expressed, according to which it is not a source of law. Such an attitude is evidently only meaningful if one admits, along with most nineteenth century French opinion, that all law is to be found in the *legal rules* issuing from the estab-lished public authorities. However; this opinion, contrary to the whole Romano-Germanic tradition, is hardly acceptable. Today, there is a growing tendency to recognise the autonomous nature of that process of interpretation which no longer attempts to deter-mine only the grammatical or logical sense of legal terms or legisla-tive intention.[1]

One may, of course, define law as only enacted rules. Neverthe-less, for the person who takes a realistic approach and has a more comprehensive—and to our mind, more exact—view, *doctrine* is now, as in the past, a very important, living source of law. This is shown by the fact that it creates the legal vocabulary and ideas which legislators subsequently use; it is even more evident from the fact that doctrinal writing establishes the methods by which law will be understood and statutes interpreted. There is, further, the

[1] Arnaud (A. J.), *Les juristes face à la société. Du XIXe siècle à nos jours* (1975).

influence that legal scholarship can exercise on the legislators themselves; often the latter merely give expression and effect to tendencies that have developed doctrinally, or enact laws which have been conceived by legal writers. There is no suggestion whatsoever of underestimating the role of the legislators. In our era this role is of prime importance; that it remain so is, assuredly, a step forward and an absolute necessity in present conditions. But the recognition of the role belonging to and played by legislators must not blind us to the real relationship between legislation and doctrinal commentary, or lead us to believe in a "dictatorship" of enacted law. In reality, the matter is much more complex, much more delicate. Legal writing stimulates the legislators to action; here, then, it is only a mediate source of law. But it also plays a role in the application of enacted law; in this respect, unless reality is distorted, it is difficult to contest its status as a source of law.

111. French and German law

Legal scholarship is thus of fundamental importance because it creates in different countries the various working tools of jurists. In many cases, the differences in the tools so created and used may very well be a source of difficulty for the foreign jurist; they may even create the impression that two laws, in reality very close to one other, are separated by basic differences. That, it seems, is what has happened in the case of French and German law; it is one of the reasons for the opposition, albeit very superficial and artificial to our mind, so often made between the "Latin" and "German" legal groups.

What troubles the French jurist when he studies German law is the difference in form, rather than of substantive law, between the legal works of French and German jurists. The latter, as well as the Swiss, prefer a form of annotated codes (*Kommentare*) which certainly exist in France but which are only used by practitioners. The preferred instrument of the French jurist is the more systematic treatise (*traité*) or manual; in the absence of such treatises, contemporary jurists prefer to consult an alphabetical digest rather than an annotated code. Penal law is the only subject in which the French have retained the annotated code, probably because of the preponderant role assured—in reality and not in virtue of a mere fiction—to enacted law in this field. It will be interesting to see if with time the Germans and Swiss move away from this still popular form of *Kommentare*, as did the French.

112. Latin countries

The styles of doctrinal writing in France and Germany are, it would seem, more approximate now than at one time. The annotated codes (*Kommentare*) are now more often discursive and critical in approach, and German manuals or treatises (*Lehrbücher*) deal more with decided cases and aspects of actual practice than they once did. The works produced in Italy and in Spanish and Portuguese countries, on the other hand, are in yet another tradition.

In general, the works published in these countries are characterised by an extreme dogmatism—a dogmatism which causes some astonishment when it is learned that the same people who write these works, and who systematically neglect the study of judicial decisions are also very often, in their own country, the most pragmatic of lawyers and legal counsellors and the owners of libraries largely made up of reports of judicial decisions of their own courts. Once again it is history which explains this curious dissociation, one linked to the pre-code dualism of the law of the universities and the law of the practice. There has been in these countries a closer observance of the Pandectist tradition than in France or Germany itself. Law teaching is directed principally to the exposition of the basic principles and concepts of the legal system rather than to explaining to students how a problem is solved in practice. The immediate solutions to problems are of less importance, in this way of thinking, than the system itself; and the law, in this approach, is treated as though it were a wholly autonomous science, detached from any historical perspective—the *Corpus iuris civilis*, after all, retained across the centuries its place as law despite the total transformation of society. The jurist reared in this tradition therefore need not concern himself with social and economic problems and their effect upon the law—these matters belong to the political sphere from which legal science must remain distinct as much as possible.[2]

---

[2] Cappelletti (M.), Merryman (J. H.) and Perillo (J. M.), *The Italian Legal System. An Introduction* (1966), *passim*, and especially at pp. 165 *et seq*. For a critical view, *cf.* the preface of M. Cappelletti to *Processo e ideologie* (1969).

CHAPTER V

SUPER-EMINENT PRINCIPLES

113. General principles of legislation

The collaboration of jurists in the formulation of the law, and not only in its application, is seen in the use made of certain "super-eminent principles" (*Generalklauseln, principes généraux*).[1] These are found sometimes in the enacted law and also, if need be, outside it. The recourse to these principles and the use made of them are difficult for theorists of legislative positivism to explain; they bring to light the fact that in the Romano-Germanic family there is a subordination of law to the commands of justice, such as it is conceived at a given moment in a given period, and that this legal family is a *jurists' law*, not merely a system of legislative norms.

Mention has already been made of the way in which the legislators may sometimes renounce their function and, as among other choices open, expressly appeal to the co-operation of jurists in order to find the right solution to a problem. The limitations of enacted law are obvious when the legislators intentionally adopt general language, confer power to judge in equity or refer to usage or even to natural law,[2] or permit the application of statutory provisions to be set aside or modified in the interests of public order or good morals. No legislative system can do without such correctives or loop-holes; in their absence there would be the impermissible risk of creating a divorce between law and justice. The strict enforcement of rights to the point of creating injustice (*summum ius summa iniuria*) was never the ideal of the Romano-Germanic laws, nor is it acquiesced in by them today.[3] Some injustice in par-

---

[1] The French term *principes généraux* (or sometimes *supérieurs*) rendered by H. C. Gutteridge (1876–1953) as "super-eminent principles" in his *Comparative Law* (2nd ed., 1949), pp. 94 *et seq.* has been adopted here.

[2] *Cf.* art. 7 of the Austrian Civil Code.

[3] Esser (J.) ed., *Summum ius summa iniuria* (1963). *Cf.* in particular his own essay, *loc. cit.* p. 22, "Wandlungen von Billigkeit und Billigkeitrechtsprechung im modernen Privatrecht."

ticular cases may be the necessary price for a just social order; but the jurists of this family are not prepared to accept a legal rule which would be *socially* unjust. It is characteristic of the flexibility of legal ideas in the Romano-Germanic family that the concept of equity (*équité*) has at all times been part of the law, and that there has never been any necessity of correcting legal solutions by means of autonomous rules or courts of equity.[4]

Legislative positivism and attacks on natural law lose most of their weight when one considers the extensive use made, in periods of crisis or socially ill-suited legislation, of such general formulae (*Generalklauseln, Blankettnormen*) found in constitutions or enacted law. The decline of positivism in the contemporary world becomes apparent when the legislators themselves, expressly and by their own authority, ordain such new precepts as that of article 2 of the Swiss Civil Code which prohibits the abuse of rights.[5] Article 281 of the Greek Civil Code similarly provides that the exercise of a right is prohibited if it manifestly exceeds the limits imposed by good faith or good morals or by the social or economic purpose of that right.[6]

Mention must also be made of the freedom of action which the courts possess when they are called upon to examine whether legislation has respected certain "fundamental human rights." In Federal Germany, article 117 of the Fundamental Law has rendered nugatory all legislative provisions which the courts consider contrary to the principle prohibiting discrimination based on sex, with the result that for some time it fell to the courts to reform the law of property relations between married persons. More recently, the Constitutional Court laid down a specific delay within which the legislature might act and beyond which it would be for the courts themselves to give effect to the principle of equality as between legitimate and natural children. A further stage in this development occurred in 1971 when the German Constitutional

---

[4] Newman (R. A.) ed., *Equity in the World's Legal Systems. A Comparative Study* (1973). Yntema (H. E.), 'Equity in the Civil Law and the Common Law" 55 Am. J. Comp. L. 60 (1966–1967).

[5] Art. 2 is often invoked at the bar but rarely applied by the courts which are suspicious, quite rightly, of the all too easy solution which this provision would sometimes seem to offer: Grossen (J. M.), "Le projet de réforme du Code civil français et le droit suisse," in 76 Revue de droit suisse, Nouvelle série, pp. 21–51 (1957).

[6] On the interpretation given to this provision, *cf.* Zepos (P. J.), "Quinze années d'application du Code civil hellénique," Rev. int. dr. comparé, 1962, pp. 291–292.

Court refused to apply certain rules of German private international law because, in their reference to the national law of the husband, these rules violated the principle of equality between the sexes or because they led to the application of some foreign law under which the freedom of marriage was insufficiently guaranteed in the eyes of German law.[7]

114. Super-eminent principles not provided for by legislation

In cases where these super-eminent principles are provided for by law, it may be said that judges act in virtue of a kind of delegation of powers from the legislators. But even when such powers have not been expressly conferred, jurists have nevertheless considered themselves entitled to act in the same way *by reason of the very function* they are called upon to exercise. This power has been sparingly used, because it is thought that the best way to bring about justice in our society is to conform to the order established by the legal rules themselves. Nevertheless, there has been no hesitation about making use of it on occasion.

French law, particularly, illustrates this attitude—whether in private law, for example, in the theory of the abuse of rights (*l'abus des droits*), or in public law with the appeal to the *principes généraux du droit administratif*. The theory of the abuse of rights was originally developed from that useful tool, article 1382 of the Civil Code.[8] It has now become clear, however, thanks to the Swiss example in particular, that this principle is not merely one of civil liability for fault; it involves a general principle dominating the whole law which, if legislators were to formulate it, would come at the beginning of the Code—the "general part" of the whole national law.[9] Similarly, the development of the general principles of administrative law[10] since the Second World War has revealed the insufficiency of the legislative order and shown, with

---

[7] Labrusse-Riou (C.), *L'égalité des époux en droit allemand* (1965); "Droit constitutionnel et droit international privé en Allemagne fédérale" (1974) Rev. crit. dr. int. privé 1–75; Fromont (M.), "Les droits fondamentaux dans l'ordre juridique de la R.F.A." *Mélanges Charles Eisenmann* (1974), pp. 49–64.

[8] "Any act by which a person causes damage to another binds the person by whose fault the damage occurred to repair such damage."

[9] Swiss Civil Code art. 2: "Every person is bound to exercise his rights and discharge his obligations in good faith."

[10] Jeanneau (B.), *Les principes généraux du droit dans la jurisprudence administrative* (1954); Chapus (R.), "De la soumission au droit des règlements autonomes" *1960 Chronique*, XXII, p. 119–126.

renewed clarity, that a distinction is to be drawn in French law between law (*droit*) and enacted law (*loi*). This doctrine, initially used to construe, in a somewhat leading manner, legislation passed during the German occupation that was contrary to democratic principles, received a fresh application when the French Constitution of 1958 drew its distinction between legislation and regulation. "Independent regulations"—those drawn up in a sphere where statute cannot enter—are measures which, by hypothesis, are not open to any judicial review. The Council of State nevertheless held that it was empowered to review such regulations in order to annul those contrary to "general legal principles," the existence of which principles is affirmed in the preamble of the French Constitution itself.

Because of its history, France is probably the country where it was most natural for jurists to make their contribution to the evolution of law by reacting against the tenets of legislative positivism. Since they were the first to be attracted by these arguments, it was only natural that they should be the first to break away from them. It is interesting to note, however, that today the same tendency is being established in Germany and as a healthy reaction to the doctrine which, in the National-Socialist era, tended to sacrifice justice to politics and the racial myth, or to see in law only that which is useful to the state (*Recht ist, was dem Staate nützt*). The value and sharpness of the German reaction become particularly clear when it is considered that it touches even the highest form of legislation. The Supreme Court and even the Court of Constitutional Justice of the German Federal Republic have not hesitated to confirm this in a series of judgments: constitutional law is not limited to fundamental legislative texts but is also made up of "certain general principles which the legislators have not rendered in the form of positive rules"; there exists, moreover, a supra-positive law which binds even the constituent legislators. "The adoption of the idea according to which the constituent power could provide for everything at will would indicate a return to an outmoded positivism; one can imagine 'extreme circumstances' in which the *idea* of law itself should prevail over positive constitutional law; the Federal Court of Constitutional Justice might then . . . be led to appraise such 'unconstitutionality'."[11] Norwegian legal doctrine

---

[11] Buerstedde (W.), "La Cour constitutionnelle de la République fédérale allemande" Rev. int. dr. comparé, 1957, pp. 56–72.

admits, for its part, the idea of "emergency constitutional law" which serves to legitimise irregular constitutional acts (the secession of Sweden, or the events of 1940–1945) which are, however, consonant with the fundamental principles and values of the Norwegian Constitution.

In other countries, too, jurists have not hesitated on occasion to apply principles of a moral nature—principles such as *fraus omnia corrumpit* (fraud taints everything) and *nemo contra factum proprium venire potest* (no one can contradict his own deed)—which have not been expressly articulated in legislation.[12] In Spain, furthermore, recourse to such principles has a legal basis: article 6 of the Spanish Civil Code enumerates, among the possible sources of law, the general principles deduced from the Spanish codes and legislation.[13]

Finally, the theory of the sources of law in all countries of the Romano-Germanic family seems both destined to realise and capable of fulfilling the traditional concept to which the reign of law in these countries lays claim: that law cannot be laid down *a priori*, nor can it reside exclusively in the rules of only enacted law. The quest for law is a task to be accomplished by all jurists in common, each acting in a given sphere and using his own techniques, but always inspired by a common ideal—that of arriving, in each instance, at the solution which best conforms to the general sense of justice—a justice founded upon a reconciliation of all kinds of interests of private individuals and those of the community at large.

---

[12] As to French law, *cf.* Roland (H.) & Boyer (L.): *Locutions Latines et adages du droit français contemporain* (1977–1979), 2 vols.

[13] Puig Brutau (J.), *Estudios de derecho comparado. La doctrine de los actos propios* (1951).

PART TWO

SOCIALIST LAWS

115. Originality of socialist laws

In 1917 Russia began to build a new type of society. The society to be created is communist, under the aegis of fraternity, where there will be no more State and no more Law. These will have been made superfluous by a new feeling of social solidarity developed upon the disappearance of the capitalist world's antagonisms: the need for coercion will have disappeared, and social relations, to be ruled primarily by communist morality, will only be subject to simple rules of economic organisation and necessity.

This ideal of a communist society has not yet been achieved in the U.S.S.R., where in our time only a socialist state has been created, one characterised economically by the collectivisation of the means of production and politically by the omnipotence of the Communist Party. The socialist state's objective is to prepare for the advent of communist society, but that society is still very much in the future. Coercion, far from being banished, is more prevalent now than ever before because of the need for protection against attacks by enemies of the regime and the further requirement that citizens be strictly disciplined in order to create the conditions which will make communism possible. The state, before it can wither away, thus has enlarged spheres of activity and intervention, and is stronger than ever; until its decline becomes possible, it rules every aspect of society with an unprecedented rigour. The same holds true for law. The Soviets are today very conscious of the importance attaching to the place of law in their country. The building of a planned economy has ushered in a vast body of regulations and the existence of the principle of socialist legality is witness to the real authority of the law.

Is the present law of the U.S.S.R. to be considered an original system when compared with those of the Romano-Germanic

155

family? It is clear that the promised communist society, once it is realised, will be entirely different from society as we know it. For the moment, however, it has not been achieved, and the present law in the U.S.S.R. has an undoubted affinity with Romanist laws; it has to a large extent retained the terminology of these laws and, in appearances at least, their structure; it has a concept of the legal rule which seems no different from that of French or German jurists. Various authors, therefore, especially English and American, are inclined to deny Soviet law the originality that it claims, and to classify this law in the family of Romanist laws.

Jurists of socialist countries unanimously maintain the opposite thesis. In their view, law is nothing more than a superstructure, the reflection of a certain economic structure; it is unscientific and contrary to all reason to ignore the bond of fundamental importance uniting the law and the economy and to fasten on resemblances or differences which, in the last analysis, are purely formal. To the two types of different economies, two entirely different types of law necessarily correspond: laws of socialist countries and laws of non-socialist countries evidently belong to two different families so long as the play of economic forces in the latter is directed by private interests whereas, in the former, the means of production are exploited in conformity with a plan established in the collective interest.

It would be inappropriate here to deal at length with the question whether or not the opposition thus expressed is fundamental. By putting into effect new social—if not socialist—ideas, the free democracies have profoundly changed in the twentieth century, and their legal institutions are a far cry from those which Marx and Engels justly criticised. Whatever such transformations may have been, it must nevertheless be admitted that, at the present time, fundamental differences persist between the structures, institutions, and ways of life and thought of socialist and other countries. Perhaps, when the present lack of understanding and suspicion are dissipated by a recognised need for participation in common tasks, these differences will one day become less marked. For the moment, one passes into a new world by crossing the frontier of a country of the socialist camp; the problems are different to those in the non-socialist countries and words themselves often have a different sense. The terms "democracy," "election," "parliament," "federalism," "trade-union," and "collective agreement,"

for example, take on very different meaning because of the existence of an all-powerful Communist Party; the words "property,"
"contract," "civil service," and "arbitration" denote different
realities because of the collectivisation of the means of production
and state planning. For these reasons Soviet law must be classed in
a different "family" from the Romano-Germanic. The jurist wanting to study Soviet law may indeed benefit from his training in a
Romanist country, compared to his American or English colleagues but he is nevertheless far less at ease in the study of this
law than he would be with another continental European law.

A major challenge today is to assure the co-existence of socialist
and non-socialist countries. It is thus important that we in the West
understand the socialist countries' attitude to their law. But an
understanding of their efforts to create a new social organisation
according to ideas and using techniques different from our own is
also of interest in its own right—the study of socialist law enables
us to adopt a new critical stance in regard to our own law. It may
also frequently happen that, without rallying to the theoretical
positions of Marxist doctrine, experiments attempted in socialist
countries can be put to good use as well in the West.

116. Geographical area

The word "socialist" is not precise in meaning. Political parties
of various hues have made use of it because of its connotations.
The terms "socialist countries" and "socialist laws" suffer from the
same imprecision. No attempt will be made here to dissipate such
ambiguity; no debate on the appropriateness of Sweden, Syria or
Tanzania, for example, claiming that they adhere to "socialist"
doctrine, will be taken up. The study of socialist law presented
here is centred around that of the Soviet Union rather than all
"socialist" countries. Some attention will however be given to the
laws of a number of European countries[1] which, like the U.S.S.R.,
aspire to create communist societies. As between the law of the
U.S.S.R. and these other nations there are, however, many differences which must be underscored in order to destroy the fairly current myth that together they make up, without any differentiation,

---

[1] Rumania, Czechoslovakia and Yugoslavia are today classed as Socialist Republics; four
countries (Albania, Bulgaria, Hungary and Poland) are termed People's Republics; East Germany is the Democratic Republic of Germany (D.D.R.).

a monolithic bloc of countries devoted to an unvarying totalitarian ideology. Indeed, these differences are such that, despite their similarities and common adhesion to a number of fundamental principles, some authors have explored whether it is really even appropriate to group these laws within only one socialist family.[2] In our view, however, the many similarities between them and their adherence to common leading principles, justify their grouping within a single family.

In this part of the work, we have omitted the laws of the non-European socialist countries. The law of China, which is the issue of a different tradition and civilisation, must be dealt with apart and in the context of our treatment of the laws of the Far East. The laws of countries on other continents which claim to belong to the socialist camp also depart in some important respects from the basic position of the Soviet Union,[3] with the possible exception of Cuba. Whatever may be the sympathy expressed for their political regimes, these countries are not considered, at least in the Soviet Union, to belong to the family of socialist laws, and we, for our part, have adopted the same attitude.

The historical evolution, the sources and the structure of socialist law, using Soviet law as the prototype, will be examined in the three principal divisions of this Part.

---

[2] Hazard (J. N.), *Communists and their Law. A Search for the Common Core of the Legal Systems of the Marxian Socialist States* (1969). The "Socialist Commonwealth of Nations" studied in this work includes the European countries just listed and China, Outer Mongolia, Korea, North Vietnam, and Cuba. Chapter 18 of the work is devoted to Mali prior to the *coup* of November 1968.

[3] Hazard (J. N.), "Marxist Models for West African Law," *Ius privatum gentium, Festschrift für Max Rheinstein* (1969), Vol. I, pp. 285–297.

TITLE I

HISTORICAL EVOLUTION

117. Outline

This Title is divided into three chapters. The first is devoted to an examination of the legal tradition in the period preceding the assumption of power by the Communists. The second chapter explains the basic principles of Marxism-Leninism upon which the Communists intend to transform the whole of society. The final chapter traces the legal developments that have occurred from the time when that doctrine triumphed and a new order was established in the various countries to be examined.

CHAPTER I

THE LEGAL TRADITION

118. Importance of subject

The will to transform the whole of society has inspired socialist leaders ever since they took up the task of building a communist society in their respective countries. But to understand how they view this challenge, one must be familiar with the position from which they began. History alone explains why, quite apart from the adoption of new political principles, certain techniques have been used and why the law exhibits a particular organisational style. It is history as well which explains certain psychological attitudes that sometimes help and sometimes hinder, or orient in special ways, such developments.[1] The notable differences between the various socialist countries are, of course, the result of the different circumstances in which their laws developed—in other words, their common adherence to one doctrine on the subject of the society of the future, Marxism–Leninism, has left undisturbed their several conceptions of the best manner in which to achieve it. The Russian legal tradition[2] and that of other socialist countries can therefore be examined with profit.

SECTION I—RUSSIAN LAW BEFORE 1917

119. The Russia of Kiev: Russkaïa Pravda and Byzantine law

The historical period in Russia only begins at the end of the ninth century, when a tribe called the Varangians under the leadership of Riurik, apparently from Scandinavia, established its

---

[1] Berdiaev (N.), *Les sources et le sens du communisme russe* (1936).
[2] Russian words have been rendered according to their pronunciation in English (Lenin, Russkaïa Pravda, Khrushchev). The transcription according to the Czech alphabet has however been retained in the notes (Lenin, Russkaja Pravda, Hruščev), except of course where reference is made to texts written in other languages.

domination over the Russia of Kiev in 862. The state then created lasted until 1236, when it was destroyed by the Mongols. The most important event in its history was the conversion of the tribe to Christianity under the reign of Saint Vladimir (*d.* 1015) in 989. The first landmark in Russian law—excluding certain early treaties concluded with Byzantium[3]—appears immediately after this conversion. As in the West, the need to reduce the customs to writing was felt at this moment, principally with the aim of extending the influence of the Church through the magic power of the written word. The Russian customs of the Kiev region were drafted in the first half of the eleventh century; the collections, containing numerous variants explaining the custom, date from this time to the fourteenth century, and have the generic name *Russkaïa Pravda* (Russian law).[4] Drafted in Slavonic, they reflect a more generally evolved society than that of the Germanic or Scandinavian tribes at the time of the redaction of the "barbarian laws in the West." The law described is territorial not tribal in nature and, on many points, its provisions presage the feudal regime.

In addition to the indigenous customary law set forth in the *Russkaïa Pravda*, Byzantine law had an important place in the Russia of Kiev. Whereas in the West the Church observed Roman law, in Russia it observed Byzantine law as represented by the *Nomocanons*, the content of which united private law (that is, of secular society) and canon law.[5] Byzantine law is of extreme importance in the Russia of Kiev: the Church applied it directly to clerics, as well as with respect to its extensive land holdings in which its jurisdiction was exercised. It extended its use, moreover, by means of arbitration and by various interpolations in the drafted customs.

120. The Mongol domination

With the establishment of the Mongol domination (the Golden Horde) in 1236 the second period in Russian history begins. This

---

[3] Sorlin (I.), "Les traités de Byzance avec la Russie au Xe siécle," *Cahiers du monde russe et soviétique*, t. II (1961), pp. 313, 447.

[4] On the Russkaïa Pravda, *cf.* Goetz (L. K.), "Das russische Recht," *Zeitschrift für vergleichende Rechtswissenschaft* (1911), Vol. 26, pp. 161–426. Portions of it have been translated into English in Vernadsky (G.), *Medieval Russian Laws* (1947) no. XLI of the *Records of Civilization. Sources and Studies* series of Columbia University.

[5] The nomocanons, translated into Slavonic in the 13th century, were called, generically, *Kormchaïa,* (*Kormčaja*) (Guide). On the subject of the Byzantine nomocanons, *cf.* Mortreuil (J.), *Histoire du droit byzantin ou du droit romain dans l'Empire d'Orient, depuis la mort de Justinien jusqu'à la prise de Constantinople en 1453* (3 vols., 1843–1846).

domination was only brought to an end under Ivan III in 1480, after a war of liberation lasting 100 years. Its political consequences are still felt today. One of them was the new prominence given to Moscow, rather than Kiev. But its most important effect was to isolate Russia from the West; nor did this isolation end when Russia regained its independence, since it was still separated from its western neighbours by its Orthodox faith. From 1056 the schism with Rome was complete. The Byzantine Empire had ceased to exist. Russia, with its new independence, was isolated and considered itself to be "the third Rome," heir to Byzantium in the crusade for the true faith.

From the purely juridical viewpoint, the Mongol domination had a negative rather than positive influence. Mongol custom (*yassak*) had never been imposed on the Russians and therefore had little influence on Russian law which merely stagnated as a result of Mongol domination. This Mongol presence explains the rise in the influence of the clergy and, because of the regrouping of the faithful around their clergy, the development of Byzantine law.

121. The code of 1649

A third period in the history of Russia and Russian law runs from the end of the Mongol domination to the accession of Peter I (the Great) (1672–1725) in 1689. During this period Russia had no windows open to Europe. It submitted to the despotic rule of the Tsars in order to avoid anarchy and preserve its independence against aggression from the West. In 1591 serfdom was established. The Church itself, deprived of any outside assistance, was subordinated to the Tsar. The sentiment took root that those who governed, and whose whim was law, were all-powerful. The distinctions between police, justice and governmental administration were poorly defined in this regime dominated by a routine adherence to custom, except for the occasional exercise of the arbitrary discretion of the Tsar, the local nobility or other administrators. The Tsars made no systematic attempt to reform society, although an effort to achieve some judicial reorganisation is shown in the *Codes of Law* (*Sudebnik*) of 1497 and 1550. The most interesting landmarks in the history of law during this period were the compilations establishing new, up-to-date editions of the *Russkaïa Pravda* and the *Kormchaïa*. Particularly important in this connection was the work done under the second Tsar of the Romanov dynasty, Alexis Mikhaïlovich (1629–1676) through whose initiative a work of consolidation was carried out in both Russian secular and canon law. The first was compiled in the Code of Alexis II (*Sorbornoé Ulojenié*) of 1649, comprising 25 chapters and 963 articles. The second was set forth in the official 1653 edition of the *Kormchaïa*, which replaced an earlier work known as the *Hundred Chapters* (*Stoglav*) of Ivan the Terrible (1551).

122. Peter the Great and his successors

The fourth period in the history of Russian law covers the time between the accession of Peter the Great in 1689 and the Bolshevik revolution of 1917, during which Russia renewed her contact with the West. Although Peter the Great and his successors endowed Russia with a modern administration, their efforts did not extend to private law and they therefore had no long lasting influence. The Russian people continued to live according to their customs, but under a more efficient administration to which they were generally submissive. Both great Russian sovereigns of the eighteenth century, Peter I and Catherine II (1729–1796), failed in their aim to revise the Code of Alexis II—Peter by favouring the adoption of a code based on the Swedish model, Catherine by adopting a code inspired by the doctrines of the Natural Law School.

123. The Svod Zakonov (1832)

A first step towards modernising Russian law, inspired by the French example, was taken at the beginning of the nineteenth century by Speranski, a Minister of Alexander I (1777–1825). But the rupture with Napoléon and the subsequent reaction were such that only a new "consolidation" rather than codification and modernisation of the Russian law was accomplished under Nicholas I (1796–1855). The body of Russian laws so established in 1832 is known as *Svod Zakonov*. It contained some 42,000 articles (later enlarged to 100,000 articles) arranged in eight sections over 15 volumes. About two-thirds of it was devoted to public law subjects. Because of its eclectic contents, casuistic method and approach, it is more closely related to the Prussian *Allgemeines Landrecht* of 1794 than to the Napoleonic codifications. Nicholas I had given instructions that Russian laws be systematically arranged and presented without, however, any of the content being changed. These instructions were doubtless not followed literally by Count Speranski to whom credit is owed for the compilation. Nevertheless, it may be said in general that from the *Russkaïa Pravda* to the Code of 1649, and from the Code of 1649 to the *Svod Zakonov* of 1832, the work accomplished was always one of consolidation and exposition, and never one of complete reform and modernisation.

It was only in the second half of the nineteenth century, and under the reign of Alexander II (1818–1881), that a liberal reform movement developed. This movement, marked principally by the abolition of serfdom (1861) and by a reform of the judicial organisation (1864), also provided Russia with a penal code (1855, revised in 1903); but it never produced a Civil Code, although a draft was prepared.

When the Bolshevik regime came to power in 1917, such was the situation. The general character of the legal system as it then existed can now be briefly sketched.

124. Russian law in the Romano-Germanic family

To begin with, the science of law as it existed in Russia took its models from Byzantine law—that is to say, from Roman law—and from the countries of continental Europe belonging to the Romanist system. Original Russian customs certainly existed, as did original French or German customs; but, as in eighteenth century France and Germany, the only science of law to be found in Russia was that of the Romanists. Consequently, the categories of Russian law and the concept of law in the universities and among jurists were those of the Romanist laws. Although Russian law was collected in publications adopting the case-by-case approach, the Russian jurist did not conceive of law as "case-made" by nature. For him, as for the French or German jurist, the legal rule was, essentially, a rule of conduct to be formulated by doctrinal writers or legislators, not the judge. Russia was not as completely supplied with codes as the other countries of continental Europe, but it was ready for them.

125. Weakness of the Russian legal tradition

Another point worth emphasising was the weakness of the legal tradition and the very idea of law in Russia.[6] The serious matter here was not the technical backwardness of Russian law, nor the fact that it was incompletely codified; it was more a matter of the difference in the Russian people's attitude to law engendered by a different history, as compared with that of other European peoples.

Throughout continental Europe, as well as in England, law is considered a natural complement to morality and one of the fundamental bases of society. This idea did not take root in Russia. Until relatively recently, there were no trained jurists in Russia; the first Russian university, the University of Moscow, was only created in 1755, and the University of Petersburg in 1802. A Russian legal literature only appeared in the second half of the nineteenth century, and it was only with the judicial reform of 1864 that a professional bar was organised and the career pattern of a judge established as distinct from that of an administrative official. Until then no distinction was made between police power, justice and the civil service. Written law moreover was altogether foreign to the popular Russian mentality. What written law existed was essentially administrative and without roots in the private law. The portion of private law it did touch upon was not of interest to the vast majority of the population. It was a "law of the cities" and made for merchants and a small middle class, while the peasant masses continued to live according to their customs. For example, only family ownership (*dvor*) or communal ownership (*mir*), to the exclusion of the individual ownership which was anticipated by legislation, existed for the peasants. For them, too, justice meant equity as administered by the court of the *volost'*, made up of elected judges who were not jurists; and the court of the *volost'* came under the Minister of the Interior, not the Minister of Justice. The law in general was not based on the social consciousness of the people, as in the other countries of Europe, nor on tradition. Established only by legislative provisions, it was very largely the arbitrary work of an autocratic sovereign or a privilege

---

[6] Kucherov (S.), *Courts, Lawyers and Trials under the last Three Tsars* (1953); Berman (H.), *Justice in Russia, An Interpretation of Soviet Law* (1950).

of the bourgeoisie. It was, therefore, taken for granted that the sovereign was above the law which in itself was identified with his good pleasure: *princeps legibus solutus.* Jurists were the servants of the Tsar and the state rather than of the law; they had no *esprit de corps* of an independent professional group.

The unity of the Russian people is not founded upon a developed common sentiment about the law. Western authors may well mock justice and men of law, and scoff at their failings; yet no one imagines that society could exist without courts and without law. *Ubi societas ibi ius.* The opposite attitude is by no means shocking in Russia. Like Saint Augustine, Leo Tolstoy wished for the disappearance of law and the advent of a society founded on Christian brotherhood and love. The Marxist ideal of a communist and fraternal society does find deep roots therefore in the moral and religions sentiments of the Russian people.

SECTION II—OTHER SOCIALIST COUNTRIES

126. General characteristics

A number of important differences exist in the history of the former law of each of these countries. On this point, as in the case of Russian law, only general observations will be made here and emphasis will be placed on those characteristics which appear to have retained some importance for the explanation of the present law or which point out the differences between the development of a particular law in a people's democracy and that of the law of the U.S.S.R. Those characteristics which may have given any one of these laws some particular originality within the framework of the family of Romano-Germanic laws before the establishment of a people's democracy—however interesting they may be in fact—will not be discussed.

All the European states in which a people's democratic regime has been established were, before such event, members of the Romano-Germanic family of laws. Apart from this essential characteristic and considering only very generally their legal history, they can be divided into two groups. Those in the first, linked for religious reasons to Rome, were associated with the movement of ideas and the development of institutions of western Europe with which they always had very close links. On the other hand, those in the other group, of orthodox Christian persuasion, were very much affected by the decline of the Byzantine Empire and for centuries were cut off from the West by the Turkish occupation.

127. Countries of western tradition

The development of Hungarian, Polish, Czechoslovakian and Slovenian and Croatian law was consistent with that in Germany, Austria and France.[7] The conditions affecting the laws of the countries of this first group were the same as those in the Germanic and Latin countries of Europe as opposed to those in Russia. A strong legal tradition existed; the civil law at least was in harmony with the feelings and habits of the population. Law was considered to be one of the bases of society; a large and respected body of jurists assured its administration and collaborated in its development.

128. The Balkan states

In the Balkan states which make up the second group, Albania, Bulgaria, Rumania, Serbia, the course of history was completely different. Like Russia these countries were at first subjected to a Byzantine rather than a western European influence. As in the case of the Mongolian occupation of Russia, the Turkish occupation in these other countries paralysed the evolution of law for centuries but, which was worse, it lasted much longer than in Russia, and only ended in the nineteenth or even twentieth century. Because of this, it is not surprising that conditions similar to those in Russia, only worse, existed in these countries. The attachment to the principles of law was weaker, because for centuries law did not appear to be an essential, or even important, part of national consciousness.

When compared to Russia however an important distinction attenuates, even if it does not altogether remove, the difference between these two groups of states. Russia freed itself from the Mongolian domination through its own efforts and, immediately

---

[7] On the development of Hungarian law, *cf.* Zajtay (I.), *Introduction à l'étude du droit hongrois* (1953). More generally, Csizmadia (A.) and Kovacs (K.), eds., *Die Entwicklung des Zivilrechts in Mitteleuropa 1848–1944* (1970). Wagner (W. J.), ed., *Polish Law throughout the Ages* (1970).

after this liberation, it created a state the breadth and power of which assured its complete independence and enabled it to consider itself as the successor to the Byzantine empire. The Balkan states, on the contrary, only gained their independence with outside help and afterwards were only small nations obliged to seek external support. In order to recover from the Turkish occupation and resume what were thought to be essential ties, they voluntarily submitted themselves to the cultural influence of central or western European states.

129. Conclusion

In these parts of the world the law had, in fact, a much greater prestige and the ties with the West were incomparably closer than was the case with Russia, and these conditions did not immediately change when a government dominated by the Communist Party came to power. It was indeed with some reluctance that the citizens of these countries saw their contacts with France, Germany, Austria and Italy fall away. Proud of their legal tradition they attempted to retain it as much as possible in the building of the new form of government. For them, therefore, it was not deemed necessary to accept, along with the development of the socialist state, the rules or institutions which, in Russia, are explained more by the weakness in their legal tradition and the absence of jurists than as a necessary consequence of an adherence to Marxist teachings.

CHAPTER II

MARXISM-LENINISM

130. Marxism: basic doctrine of Soviet society

A change of the utmost importance came about in the countries under study once the Communists assumed power. Attitudes and institutions were systematically examined, and more often than not rejected or transformed, in the light of Marxism-Leninism, a doctrine accepted as an indisputable truth. In order to understand the policy basis of the new law and institutions of socialist countries, it is therefore appropriate to review at least the major principles of that doctrine.[1]

Marxism-Leninism in the socialist countries represents something quite different from any philosophical doctrine in Western countries. It is, in fact, the official ideology, and every other doctrine appears to be not only erroneous but to constitute a subversive threat to the social order. Marxism-Leninism has discovered the laws which rule the development of society, and the ultimate formula which will make possible the advent of a society founded on peace and harmony, victorious over misery and free from crime. Those who do not adhere to this doctrine and who reject, or even put in doubt, the postulates of Marxism are, whether consciously or not, the enemies of mankind whose false ideas must be eliminated. Marxism-Leninism is at once an explanation of the world and a guide for action, indicating the path to follow in order to create a supposed better world. All citizens are obliged to know

---

[1] The fundamentals of the doctrine were put forward in the *Communist Manifesto* of 1848. The bibliography on Marxism-Leninism is immense. An excellent and easily readable work, presenting the views considered orthodox at the present time in the U.S.S.R., was published by the Foreign Languages Publishing House, Moscow, in 1961, *Fundamentals of Marxism-Leninism*. The *Collected Works of Lenin* have also been published in 40 vols. (1960–1966) by the same organisation. An excellent résumé of the doctrine, especially for that part concerning jurists, has been made by Stoyanovitch (K.), "La conception de l'Etat en Yougoslavie," *Revue du droit public et de la science politique* (1959), pp. 214–239; *La pensée marxiste* (1974).

the principles of Marxism-Leninism and this knowledge must be all the more complete on the part of those assuming greater responsibilities. "Practice is blind and can only grope," said Stalin, "if it is not enlightened by revolutionary theory." It is essential that those who govern belong to the circle of enlightened persons who best understand this doctrine and fully support it. It is no less essential that administrators, judges and citizens be familiar with it as well, in order that they may make an informed contribution to the implementation of a policy destined to guide society on the now revealed path of progress.

131. Evolution and progress: historical materialism

The Marxist doctrine, founded by Karl Marx (1818–1883) and Freidrich Engels (1820–1895), takes as its starting point the philosophical doctrine of materialism and the idea of evolution. The doctrine of materialism, simply stated, is as follows: the material principle, Nature, is the primary given factor; thought and intellect are simply properties of matter; consciousness is no more than a reflection of the material world. The idea of evolution is expressed thus: "Motion is the mode of existence of matter" (Engels); there are no permanent, immutable things in the world, fixed once and for all; there are only processes and things undergoing change. Nature and its different phenomena are therefore in perpetual evolution. The laws of this development are not established by God, nor do they depend on human will; they are peculiar to Nature itself, discoverable and entirely comprehensible.

In 1859, Darwin, in his *Origin of the Species*, had put forward an explanation of the principles governing biological evolution. Marx and Engels thought that in the social as well as in the natural sciences it was possible in similar fashion to discover the *laws* ruling the development of humanity. They believed they had discovered these laws, and were thus able to propose a *scientific socialism* in place of the dreams of the earlier *utopian socialism*. They took up the Hegelian thesis of the mechanics of evolution (the historical dialectic), but rejected Hegel's idealistic analysis of the causes which explain this evolution of society as based on advances made by human intellect. They, on the contrary, applied materialism to social life (historical materialism): it is Matter which commands the intellect, and Reality which give birth to ideas. Man is *homo faber* before he is *homo sapiens*. "It is not the consciousness of men that determines their being," wrote Marx. " . . . The material productive forces of society condition the progress of social, political and spiritual life. . . . For me, ideas are merely the material world transposed and translated in the mind of Man. . . . The anatomy of civil society must be found in political economy . . . ."[2]

132. Infrastructure and superstructure

Marxist doctrine is in no way fatalistic. Man plays an important part in the accomplishment of historical laws. But the possibilities open to him are limited: "It is men who are the makers of their own history," writes Engels, "but in established surroundings which condition them on the basis of inherited objective material conditions."

What is truly decisive in a society is its economic basis or *infrastructure* and the conditions in which the means of production are exploited. As with Saint-Simon (1760–1825), the superiority of the principles of political economy over those of private law is admitted. All else is *superstructure*, closely dependent on the economic infrastructure, whether one envisages ideas, social habits, morality or religion.

Law, in particular, is only a superstructure; in reality it only translates the interests of those who hold the reins of command in any given society; it is an instrument in the service of those who exercise their "dictatorship" in this society because they have the instruments of production within their control. Law is a means of oppressing the exploited class; it is, of necessity, unjust—or, in other words, it is only just from the subjective point of view of the ruling class. To speak of a "just" law is to appeal to an ideology—that is to say, a false representation of reality; justice is no more than an historical idea conditioned by circumstances of class. The law of a capitalist state, which neglects the interests of the workers is, from their point of view, really the negation of justice.

The way in which Marxists consider law is thus entirely opposed to our traditional views. To grasp it and understand how the Soviet

---

[2] Marx (K.), Preface to *A Contribution to the Critique of Political Economy* (1859). This materialism differentiates Marxism from the "African socialism" of L. S. Senghor and that applied in India.

rulers conceive the communist society of the future, it is first necessary to be familiar with the Marxist theory of the origins and meaning of law and the state, as explained by F. Engels in his book *The Origin of the Family, Private Property and the State* (1884). In the following summary of this work, every effort is made to be consistent with Soviet orthodoxy.

133. Marxist concept of state and law

In the beginning, according to Engels, there existed a classless society in which all persons enjoyed the same position with respect to the means of production; individuals were equal and independent of each other, because the means of production were free and at the disposal of all. They respected rules of *conduct* but these rules, being founded simply on habits and corresponding to current behaviour, neither imposed nor sanctioned through the use of force, were not *legal rules*.

Later, primitive society became socially divided through the division of labour and split into classes. One of these classes appropriated the means of production for itself, dispossessing the others which it then began to exploit. It was at this moment in time that Law and the State were born. For the Marxists, there is a close bond between these two ideas. Law is a rule of human conduct which differs from other rules of conduct because it involves coercion, that is the intervention of the state. The State is a social authority which, either by the threat or the use of force, assures that this rule is respected. There is no law without a state, and there is no state without law; state and law are two different words designating the same thing.

Not every human society has a state organisation and law. The state and the law are the results of a specific economic structure of society. They are only to be found in a certain form of society at a particular stage of its evolution. Law and the state only appear when society is divided into social classes, one of which economically exploits the other or others. In such a situation, the ruling class has recourse to law and the state in order to strengthen and perpetuate its domination.

The law is the instrument which, in the class struggle, safeguards the interests of the ruling class and maintains social inequality for its own profit. It can be defined as that series of social norms which regulate the dominating relationship of the ruling class to the sub-jugated class, in those areas of this relationship which cannot be maintained without recourse to the oppression wielded by a solidly organised state. And in itself the state is the organisation of the ruling class which assures its continued oppression of the exploited class for the purpose of safeguarding its own class interests.

Law and the state have not always existed. The moment at which they appeared represents a "dialectical leap" in society's development; the greatest social revolution humanity has ever known was the transition of a society without either law or state to a society possessing these institutions. All the later changes which have resulted from advances in the methods and means of produc-tion have been merely "quantitative" changes of lesser imortance. They may have brought about changes in the existing law and state, but they left intact the characteristics of a class society, rooted in private ownership of the means of production. These may have changed hands and altered in nature, but—whether one considers the periods of slavery, feudalism or capitalism—there is one observably permanent phenomenon: the exploitation by the "haves" of the "have-nots."

The history of humanity is essentially the history of class strug-gle: in other words, it is the incessant struggle engaged in by one class or another in order to seize the means of production and thus establish its own dictatorship. The turning points of history are marked by the victories of the exploited class which in turn becomes the exploiting class. The advent of a new social class rep-resents a step forward, because it corresponds to a type of produc-tion which is more advanced and more in line with technological progress and the general aspirations of society. Society will con-tinue to suffer from a fundamental defect, however, so long as the means of production remain the property of only some and so long, therefore, as there are those exploit and those who are exploited.

134. Prediction of a society without law

Class war and the misery of the exploited will end when this analysis is accepted. The way in which to solve society's problem will then be obvious; the merit of the Marxist ideology is to have revealed this solution to humanity. Since private ownership of the means of production is the origin of social inequality and class struggle, such ownership must be abolished. The means of production must be made the property of the collectivity; they must no longer be exploited in the interests of only a few profiteers but for the benefit of the entire community. Such a transformation of the economic system will lead to a transformation of man himself, because his present evil propensities only result from the now defective organisation of society.

The essence of the Marxist doctrine, therefore, lies in this belief that the root of all social evil is class antagonism; social classes can, and must, be suppressed by prohibiting the private appropriation of productive forces and by putting them at the disposal of the collectivity which will exploit them in the common interest. Purged of the "antagonistic contradictions" of present society, a fraternal society will then emerge; a communist society in which the exploitation of man by man will have ceased, and in which harmony will reign; each will then work for the community according to his ability, and each will receive from the community according to his needs. In this communist society all coercion will be needless: state and law, the aim of which is to assure the compulsion necessary in other societies, will become useless and so disappear. In theory, this doctrine is the antithesis of fascism which sacrifices any interest of the individual in order to exalt the role of the state.

The transition to the new society, which will have neither state nor law, represents a new dialectical leap in the history of humanity—the inverse of that noted earlier. All exploitation having disappeared, there will be no further need for force. Man will once again be free. He will be his own master, and will be himself because he will no longer have to sell his labour-power to the profit of a ruling class exploiter. The rules of conduct in the future society will have the same character as those of primitive society; they will be moral rules, customs, technical precepts and forms of habitual behaviour. Individuals will observe them spontaneously since they will be freely accepted by everyone as emanations of a truly general interest and thus seen as a true expression of justice. Public services, such as health, education, transportation, communication and policing will be assured by all citizens in turn. This society will be one of complete equality and economic and social liberty. Its members will be equal because they will be provided for, not according to their capacities, but according to their needs;

they will be free because they will not be subject to any compulsion. Society wll no longer be democratic because it will not be subject to the rule of anyone, not even that of the people as a whole. With the disappearance of law and the state, democracy will also vanish: there will be a reign over things, not persons.

135. The Marxist doctrine of action

Marxist doctrine, broadly outlined in 1848 in the *Manifesto of the Communist Party*, was developed by Marx and Engels as a teaching, defended against its enemies and refined for the use of its adherents during the authors' lifetime. The Socialist International adopted it as its platform. As members of the Communist Party and philosophers, Marx and Engels frequently analysed the situation of society and the events of their time and decided what, according to them, was the line to follow in order to move forward and ensure ultimate success for those who supported their doctrine. Marxism, therefore, is not simly an explanation of history; it is at the same time a guide, based on the dialectical method, to political action and a blueprint for revolution.

136. Marxism-Leninism

In the eyes of the adherents of this doctrine, the historical and philosophical parts of Marxism retain their full value; and all the studies undertaken in this connection since the time of Marx merely aspire to confirm his theses by analysing the developments of ancient, modern or contemporary history in their light. On the other hand, the political part of the doctrine required up-dating and adapting to new circumstances, especially when a Marxist party—the Bolshevik party—succeeded in gaining power in Russia in 1917. The leaders of this party, principally Lenin (1870–1924), played such an important role in this respect that it has now become current in the U.S.S.R. and elsewhere to speak of *Marxism-Leninism* instead of simply *Marxism*.[3]

The contribution of Leninism was necessary in order to fix the line of action in the special period running from the assumption of power by a Marxist party to the achievement of a communist society. Marx and Engels were not able to forecast in which

---

[3] Chambre (H.), *Le marxisme dans l'Union soviétique: idéologie et institutions* (1955).

country a Marxist party would gain power for the first time, or the state of the world at the time of, or after, such an event. Marx's works contain at most only an indication that the advent of communism would necessarily be preceded by an intermediate phase—that of a socialist state, in which the dictatorship of the proletariat would be assured. "Between capitalist and communist society," he wrote, "lies the period of the revolutionary transformation of the one into the other, to which there corresponds a period of political transition in which the State will be nothing other than the revolutionary dictatorship of the proletariat."[4] It had to be specified how the structure and tasks of the socialist state were to be defined and understood in the country the communist party had to govern. Leninism, as a political doctrine, added on many points to the inevitably abstract work of Marx, but it nevertheless complements and does not refute Marxism; it reinforces Marxism, and by adopting the dialectical method and the materialistic philosophy of the world as set forth in Marxist doctrine is wholly consistent with it.

137. The importance of Marxism-Leninism

Before studying different aspects of Soviet law, the importance of this philosophy and the concept of law deriving from it in the U.S.S.R. should once more be stressed. Soviet society at the present time is considered imperfect by its own leaders, even though, of course, it is far superior to capitalist societies. The present organisation of social relationships, that of a socialist state, corresponds to a necessary stage in the construction of a communist society. Soviet Russia, therefore, has not yet completed its revolution; it is, and wishes to be, a revolutionary state. This point of view must constantly be borne in mind, and it follows from it that law in the U.S.S.R. is considered in a special way and plays a new role compared to its function in the West.[5]

Essentially, Soviet law is not meant to establish a rule of order by providing a principle for the solution of disputes. First and foremost it is a means of transforming, and thus guiding, society towards the communist ideal apart from which no true liberty, equality or morality can exist. The law is essentially an instrument

---

[4] Marx (K.), *Critique of the Gotha Programme* (1875).
[5] Toumanov (V. A.), *Pensée juridique bougeoise contemporaine (1974)*.

in the service of the ruling class. There are no scruples about freely admitting this, since Soviet policy is in itself different from that of bourgeois states. Enlightened by Marxist doctrine, Soviet leaders know what goal to strive for according to the scientific laws governing the development of society. To endow society with the economic organisation which conforms to these scientific laws is the aim of Soviet law and policy; their further aim is to educate the people by showing them the now deviant nature of behaviour which was comprehensible and in fact normal in the capitalist era.

Soviet law is thus characterised by its essentially economic pre-occupation and didactic approach, as opposed to "bourgeois law" which blindly tries to establish order and morality, both of which are unobtainable in a world organised on the basis of a defective economic system. To the Soviet people, capitalist politicians and jurists appear to be tossed about on the sea of events, navigating conflicting currents at random without any compass to guide them. The leaders and jurists of the Soviet Union, on the other hand, have found their compass in the ideology of Marxism-Leninism; judges, administrators and citizens alike possess a sure guide for the interpretation of law. Soviet law, therefore, is not a law like other laws; obviously, its study cannot be dissociated from Marxist-Leninist doctrines which fix its objectives and guide its evolution, interpretation and application.

The Soviet regime only makes sense if one is convinced of the truth of the Marxist-Leninist doctrine, if one considers as scientifi-cally exact its explanation of history and accepts as inevitable the solution it constructs for eliminating social conflicts and ushering humanity into a new era. In the U.S.S.R. everything takes on new meaning in the light of this doctrine. Communist morality, the only humane and true morality, makes of man "a fighter capable of transforming life according to the objective laws of nature and history in the interest of all humanity. . . . " To be a moral being, means dedicating all one's strength and energy to the struggle for communist society.[6] Freedom, far from being destroyed, takes on its full meaning under the regime of the Soviet dictatorship; and, in agreement with the ideas held in western Europe before the

---

[6] Prokofiev (V. I.), Antigumanističeskij harakter religioznoj morali, *Voprosy Filosofii*, 1959, no. 9, p. 42. A code of Communist morality was made part of the programme of the Commu-nist Party of the U.S.S.R. in 1961: Hazard (J. N.), *Communists and their Law* (1969), p. 11.

eighteenth century, it is conceived as a neutral force which must be educated before it can be turned to good use. Before the eighteenth century, there was never any idea that private enterprise, left to itself, could orient production in the general interest.[7] "Liberty," wrote Montesquieu, "is not independence; it by no means consists in doing what one wishes, but in being able to do what one ought to wish to do."[8] Marxism creates the conditions of true freedom for man by teaching him, in the light of a scientific theory, what he should want.

Soviet society is not only a new but also a superior type of social organisation founded on scientific principles, and one more advanced on the road of progress than bourgeois societies. Whatever the efforts made to create greater social justice in these societies, such attempts are doomed to certain failure. Their aim is to perpetuate an essentially evil state of things, a social structure which carries with it an inadmissible and odious inequality. This becomes apparent once one penetrates the motives or subconscious mind of those who make such attempts.[9] There is no truly lasting solution, no salvation apart from the Marxist doctrine and the collectivisation of all means of production which it postulates. In the international sphere, the non-socialist states represent a permanent threat to humanity because of the basic internal contradictions inherent in their structure; there is always the danger that they will seek to escape these contradictions and prolong their existence by enslaving other peoples (colonialism), or by resorting to war (imperialism). Coexistence with non-socialist states is possible only on condition that the U.S.S.R. is stronger than they are.

138. Relations between Soviet and foreign jurists

Adherence to Marxism-Leninism imposes certain limits on the possibilities of a comparison between Soviet and bourgeois laws. Soviet writers do, certainly, define law in the same way in each case. "Your law," said Lenin, "is nothing more than the will of your class made into laws applicable to all." But the differences in the economic structures of socialist and capitalist countries result

---

[7] Piettre (A.), *Les trois âges de l'économie* (2nd ed., 1965).

[8] *Esprit des lois*, XI, III.

[9] Zivs (S. L.), *Razvitie formy prava v sovremennyh imperialističeskih gosudarstvah* (1960). Krutogolov (M. A.), *Antidemokratičeskaja suščnost' buržuaznyh vyborov* (1963).

in Soviet law being fundamentally good and bourgeois laws being fundamentally bad. According to the Marxist analysis, therefore, bourgeois jurists, who cannot be anything other than the instruments of bourgeois class interests, whether consciously or not, are suspect.[10] All steps taken in the bourgeois countries are interpreted in the light of Marxism-Leninism as being for the purpose of consolidating the dictatorship of the propertied classes. Some of these measures, it is true, may have been extorted from bourgeois leaders through fear of the proletariat. But a just social organisation and just law can never be hoped for so long as the fundamental defect of society has not been remedied by suppressing the possibility that private persons usurp the forces of economic production. The exploitation of man by man is the inevitable consequence of the private ownership of such property.

It would indeed be vain to try to persuade Soviet jurists that they are mistaken, and that a just law may be sought by jurists committed to the principle of private ownership. For a Soviet jurist to make this concession would amount to denying Marxist doctrine and undermine the very foundations upon which the Soviet regime is built. Western jurists have some difficulty in imagining that anyone might see an incontrovertible truth in an ideology that does not purport to be a *revealed* truth, one which makes no attempt to give meaning to life and the universe and which so obviously belongs in the context of nineteenth century thought and is, in their eyes, already outdated in the second half of the twentieth century. But we must accept their point of view as inevitable. In the U.S.S.R. everything does take place as though the Marxist-Leninist doctrine were a revealed dogma; it does not occur to Soviet jurists to question its merits; for them it is beyond any possible discussion.

Soviet and bourgeois jurists cannot, for these reasons, ever come to an agreement on fundamental principles; and a worthwhile comparison between the Soviet and bourgeois laws can only take place on the technical level.[11] In spite of different political

---

[10] Toumanov (V. A.), *Pensée juridique bourgeoise contemporaine* (1974).

[11] Constantinesco (L. J.), *La comparabilité des ordres juridiques ayant une idéologie et une structure politico-économique différente et la théorie des éléments déterminants*, Rev. int. dr. comparé (1973), p. 5. Loeber, *Rechtsvergleichung zwischen Länder mit verscheidener Wirtschaftsordung*, Rabels Z. (1962), p. 206. *The Comparability of Socialist and Non-socialist Systems of Law*, Tel Aviv University Studies in Law (1977), p. 45. "Droit comparé et systèmes socio-politiques" *in Livres du Centenaire de la Société de législation comparée*, Vol. II (1971), p. 145. 15 *Acta juridica Academiae Scientiarum Hungaricae* (1973).

regimes, the problems in the U.S.S.R. and the West are often nonetheless the same because each, in its own way, is concerned with moral, social and economic development. The fact that one side considers economics to be subordinate to morality, while the opposite opinion is held by the other; the fact that these concerns are inspired by the desire to perpetuate the rule of the middle class in the one and in the other to create the conditions for the transition to communism—these differences, however essential they may be in principle, are seldom perceptible when one is dealing with technical rules or practical matters. It then becomes apparent that on many points the West has a great deal to learn from the experiments which have been and are being carried out in the U.S.S.R. The idea, for example, that an active participation by citizens in the various aspects of public administration is necessary for them to be efficient in their operation and in order that a true democracy be established is more and more accepted today, even outside Marxist countries.

CHAPTER III

THE NEW ORDER

139. Soviet Union and other countries

Russia and the other countries which, in its track, have embarked upon the road to communism have all had different legal traditions. The circumstances in which communists came to power in each case were also different. The leaders of the people's republics have moreover been able to profit from various experiments attempted in the U.S.S.R. It is thus appropriate to examine separately the situation of the U.S.S.R. and these other countries. The first two sections of this chapter will outline their differences; the final section will explain how, at the present time, apart from such differences, a common principle, that of "socialist legality," unites them all.

SECTION I—SOVIET LAW SINCE 1917

140. The Bolshevik revolution

On November 7, 1917 (October 25, according to the Julian calendar then in force in Russia), a victorious revolution brought the Bolsheviks to power. From this date a new epoch began in the history of Russia.

The Bolshevik Party was resolutely determined to build the communist society announced by Engels and Marx as quickly as possible. Many points remained obscure, however, and now that a communist party had come to power the Marxist doctrine had to be perfected. Marx and Engels had enunciated the laws governing social evolution; they had described the final phase when happiness and peace would be found; and they had specified the technique for gaining power. But the Marxist doctrine was deficient on such questions as what was to be done after the seizure of power? and how was society to be organised at this particular moment and during the waiting-period before the communist society was established throughout the world?

Marx anticipated that the revolution would first succeed in a highly industrialised country; yet it had just taken place in the most rural of nations. He thought that the revolution would spread rapidly through the entire world or, at least, the whole of Europe; instead, Russia remained the only country in which the Communists came to power. How, in such circumstances, was the intermediate stage of the socialist state which he predicted to be conceived? Their disciples did not clarify this question any more than Marx or Engels did. The attention of the Marxists had focused on the contradictions of capitalism, on how to secure power, and on the description of communist society in order to provide directives for the acting forces of the Party and an ideal for the proletariat. The study of the intermediate, socialist stage had been neglected, especially at the level of its institutions and of law. It was agreed that a dictatorship of the proletariat would rule. But should industrial workers alone be counted as the proletariat, after the revolution had triumphed in a country where that class was so small? Above all, how was the proletariat going to exercise this dictatorship? What measures should be taken, and what kind of institutions should be set up? While it was rich in philosophical, historical, economic and political studies, Marxist doctrine was poor in legal thought. To the extent that they existed, works on "socialist law" were open to suspicion because they had generally been written by authors who were not orthodox communists and who viewed the building of socialism as a process of evolution outside the dictatorship of the proletariat.

In these circumstances, it was necessary to establish some kind of working doctrine by fairly experimental means; jurists would, of course, be called upon to collaborate, but it was mainly to be done on the impetus of, and in conformity with, the principles laid down by political leaders—and, most importantly, by Lenin (notably in his pamphlet *The State and Revolution*, 1917).

The development of Soviet law since 1917 falls within two main phases. The first runs from the October Revolution to the U.S.S.R. Constitution of 1936; this is the period of the construction of socialism. The second, begun in 1936, continues still, and includes the strengthening of the socialist state and the march towards communism.[1]

§ 1. From Bourgeois to Socialist State

The first phase of the history of Soviet law is itself divided into three periods: that of so-called revolutionary communism (1917–1921), · that of the New Economic Policy (N.E.P., 1921–1928) and, thirdly, that of the collectivisation of agriculture and the five-year plans (1928–1936).

141. Period of revolutionary communism, 1917–1921

The period of revolutionary or militant communism extends from the October Revolution to the end of the civil war and the final triumph of the Communist (Bolshevik) Party in Russia in 1921.

The very important work carried out in this period is distinguished by the exceptional circumstances in which it was accomplished. Russia was prey to civil and foreign wars and in a state of total disorganisation. The Bolsheviks were by no means sure of remaining in power. For them, the essential thing was not to establish practical working arrangements adapted to the possibilities of the moment but rather to defeat their enemies, remain in power, re-establish peace and, if they were to be eliminated, to have at least heroically proclaimed the principles for which they fought. "It is of no importance," declared Lenin in 1917, "that many of the provisions of our decrees may never be enforced. Their aim is to teach the masses how truly to progress. . . . We do not consider them as absolute rules applicable in all circumstances." Trotsky (1879–1940) too said: "The early decrees were more important as articles of propaganda than as administrative texts."[2]

The work accomplished in the period of revolutionary communism outwardly lacked realism. It seems that there was a desire to construct the communist society then and there by skipping the socialist stage forecast by Marx. The first Russian constitution of

---

[1] On the development of the different branches of Soviet law during the course of each of these phases, *cf. Istoria gosudarstva i prava* (2 vols. 1967). *Cf.* also, the excellent summaries of the historical evolution given in the various chapters of Hazard (J. N.), Butler (W. E.) and Maggs (P. B.), *The Soviet Legal System* (3rd ed., 1977).

[2] Trotsky (L.), *My Life* (1930), Ch. XXIX.

1918 avoids use of the word "state" (*gosudarstvo*). The right of peoples to self-determination (Declaration of the Rights of the Peoples of Russia) and a Declaration of the Rights of the Toiling and Exploited People were proclaimed; a message was addressed to all the Muslim workers of Russia and the East. The Church was separated from the State and a marriage code promulgated. Land, mines, industrial establishments of any importance and banks were all nationalised, and private enterprise was forbidden. It seemed as though money itself would disappear and that a system of sharing would be substituted for contractual bargaining. Inheritance was suppressed. The old courts and judicial procedures were abolished; jurists, a suspect class, were distrusted. Everything promised an immediate leap forward to the communist society without any transitional period. The newly established courts were asked to judge, with no formal procedures, according to revolutionary conscience, the socialist feeling of justice and the interests of the workers' and peasants' government.[3]

These measures are very interesting because, with a view to propagandising, they reveal the final objective of communism and the Russian leaders' views of the future. The desire to achieve this programme by a stroke of the pen, however, was not only unrealistic but also contrary to Marxist doctrine. Some dreamers in the U.S.S.R. retained a nostalgic view of the deeds of those early years, and endeavoured to hasten a return to the ideas proclaimed at that time. The more realistic leaders sought to delay the realisation of communist society until some later time and to work for the building, and then the consolidation, of a socialist state in the U.S.S.R. which differed greatly from this ideal.

The return to realism and a concern for practical considerations came with the end of the civil war and foreign interventions, when the communists, as the unchallenged masters, were faced with the gigantic task that awaited them: the reconstruction of the country and the building of socialism.

142. New Economic Policy (N.E.P.), 1921–1928

Putting the war-devastated country back on its feet was the most pressing task. In the seven years devoted to this, the building of

---

[3] Hazard (J. N.), *Settling Disputes in Soviet Society. The Formative Years of Legal Institutions* (1960).

socialism passed into the background—at least to all appearances. These seven years from the summer of 1921 to 1928 are the period of the N.E.P.[4]

Compared to the positions taken up in the preceding period, the N.E.P. is characterised by a certain withdrawal. Concessions were made, which sometimes affected matters of principle, in order to encourage the peasants to work and attract foreign capital. The impression was given that the excesses of the preceding period were repudiated; that the regime was "settling down," and no longer revolutionary; that it was going to become "liberal" by recognising the traditional values represented by private initiative and private ownership and by renouncing the chimera of a society not founded on law. In fact, the concessions made on the economic level were only of limited significance. The State retained control of industry and commerce. Violation of principle was admitted only in agriculture where the regime accommodated itself to the existence of a well-to-do peasant class, the kulaks, who employed hired labour.

On the other hand, the quite erroneous impression that the Bolsheviks were reverting to the thinking of the bourgeois world was given by what was, precisely, a return to true Marxist doctrine. The leaders of the U.S.S.R. abandoned the illusion—if, indeed, they had ever entertained it—that communism could be established immediately, and embarked on the building of socialism by putting the state in order and recognising the importance of law.

143. Return to legality

The period of the N.E.P. left its mark in several respects. The most apparent, and that which seemed reassuring to foreign countries, was the promulgation of codes; a civil code, a code of civil procedure, a criminal code, a code of criminal procedure, a family code and a new agrarian code. For the time being the regime renounced the ideal of a society founded on simple equity and on the natural feeling for justice of a fraternal community. At the same time the judicial system was re-organised, a new principle of socialist legality was laid down and a new institution, the *Prokuratura*, was created in order to ensure its strict observation by both

---

[4] "Novaja Ekonomičeskaja Politika."

the administration and citizens. The government itself was brought under control; henceforth state enterprises were to be managed not by a workers' committee but by a single person—the director responsible. They were, moreover, recognised as financially autonomous and were subject to the "principle of economic accounting," as well as obliged to keep within the limits of a balance-sheet and to take an interest in good management.

144. Abandonment of the N.E.P.

The N.E.P. had the success hoped for. It gave the Russian economy, disorganised by the war, a fresh start, and order was established on U.S.S.R. territory. These results were gained in the space of seven years, after which the Soviet leaders abandoned the N.E.P. This was not done with a view to establishing communism immediately—that was still premature.

To the minds of Soviet leaders—and in fact they have stated as much—the N.E.P. was no more than a strategic withdrawal, a necessary pause before the effort required for the building of socialism. It went without saying that this pause would not last long; the programme of the Communist Party was neither abandoned nor modified; it still required the total collectivisation of the economy, the complete elimination of man's exploitation by man. But once the leaders had embarked on economic planning as a means of developing Russian economic power, the abandonment of the N.E.P. was patently necessary from a practical point of view. It soon became clear that in such a plan of economic development everything was interwoven; in particular the industrialisation of the country demanded an increase in agricultural production which in turn could only be made possible by the mechanisation and, therefore, the collectivisation of the rural economy. On the other hand, the class of kulaks, in whom foreign "bourgeois" powers might have found an almost natural ally for the realisation of designs hostile to the U.S.S.R., appeared to be a danger in view of the growing international tension of the time.

145. Total collectivisation of the economy

When the first five-year plan for the nation's economic development, covering the years 1928–1932, was put into application, the N.E.P. was therefore abandoned. This was marked first of all by the total collectivisation of industry and commerce, and by the suppression of concessions made to private individuals for carrying on certain industries. From 1930 on, however, it was mainly characterised by the pitiless liquidation of the kulaks and by the complete collectivisation of agriculture, the peasants being "invited"— and in fact obliged—to regroup their lands in agricultural co-operatives known as *kolkhozi*. This movement was completed in 1937; at that time 243,000 *kolkhozi*, representing 93 per cent. of Soviet soil under cultivation, had replaced 18,500,000 family farms.[5]

By this collectivisation of agriculture, the U.S.S.R. attained the economic infrastructure required by Marxist doctrine. Doubtless not all property and means of production were nationalised in the strict sense of the word; in addition to that belonging to the nation or the state, other property continued, and still does continue, to belong to co-operatives of production. However property and means of production in the U.S.S.R. are indeed "collectivised" in the sense that they are exploited according to a plan of economic development drawn up by the leaders and approved by the Soviet Parliament. The admitted exceptions to this principle are of limited significance; these are related to certain artisanal activities,[6] and particularly the complementary economy of the enclosures in which members of the *kolkhozi* may cultivate a few vegetables and rear some animals within limits strictly controlled by law.[7] Since 1935, commerce in the cities has become state-controlled; in the country it is carried on principally by co-operatives.[8] Private individuals are prohibited from carrying on any business; to do so constitutes the crime of speculation and profiteering. To the extent that it is admitted, private ownership of goods has been renamed "personal ownership" in order to underline the idea that it must serve to satisfy the personal needs of the owner and cannot be used as a means of producing income.

---

[5] *Cf.* below, para. 150, note 12.

[6] On these activities, *cf.* Hazard (J. N.), Butler (W. E.) and Maggs (P. B.), *The Soviet Legal System* (1977), p. 187. The artisanal co-operatives became state-controlled in 1960.

[7] The importance of this complementary economy must not be under-estimated although it has considerably diminished since the war. Today about 30 per cent. of consumer foodstuffs are produced on these family holdings according to official statistics. Nove (A.), *The Soviet Economy* (1966); Kerblay (B. H.), *Les marchés paysans en U.S.S.R.* (1968).

[8] 16,000 consumer co-operatives controlled 335,000 retail stores in 1963; they are the rural branch of the state's retail business. *Adde* Hazard, Butler and Maggs, *op. cit.*, Pt. 2, p. 181. Chambre (M.), Wronski (H.) and Lasserre (G.), *Les coopératives de consommation en U.R.S.S.* (1969).

146. Maintenance of the law

The abandonment of the N.E.P. was characterised by the collectivisation of the Soviet economy, but it did not involve a return to the communism of the preceding period. On the contrary, the period of the five-year plans is marked by the strengthening of the state, whose functions grew through the development of authority, discipline and compulsion in all forms, and through an increasingly clear affirmation of the principle of socialist legality. The codes promulgated in the period of the N.E.P. were left in force for another thirty years. A multitude of provisions of various kinds did gradually modify and perfect them, mainly by regulating new aspects of Soviet life. The partial desuetude of these N.E.P. codes was by no means a sign that Soviet law was on the wane; in fact, it became increasingly rich and perfected. According to the Marxist dialectic, the predicted disappearance of state and law during the era of communism was prepared for by an unprecedented development and exaltation of these two institutions. "Engels said that after the victory of the socialist revolution the State was to wither away. . . . The Soviet Marxists have arrived at the conclusion that, given the capitalist encirclement, the country of the victorious revolution should not weaken but strengthen the mechanism of the State in every way."[9]

The results of 20 years of effort were clear in December 1936, when a new Constitution was victoriously presented; the exploitation of man by man in the U.S.S.R. had ceased; the forces of production had been placed at the disposal of the collectivity and were exploited in the interest of all; a multi-national state had resolved the conflicts between nationalities; the world's first socialist state and law had been built; and the road to future progress and the realisation of communism seemed open.

§ 2. From Socialist State to Communist Society

147. Prolongation of the socialist state

More than 40 years have passed since the promulgation of the Soviet Constitution of 1936 and the firm establishment of the economic infrastructure on which communist society can be built.

[9] Stalin (J. V.), *Concerning Marxism in Linguistics* (1950).

Where, then, is the U.S.S.R. in the "march towards communism"?

One point is certain: a communist society has not yet been achieved in the U.S.S.R. where "power will be exercised by the Soviets, the unions, the co-operatives and other people's organisations." The stage of the dictatorship of the proletariat has now been surpassed and since 1961 the Soviet Union is described as "a state of all the people."[10] This term is revealing. The state, far from withering away, is stronger and more powerful than ever; nor is Soviet law being eclipsed; it is more abundant and just as imperative as it ever was.

The second point to be noted is that no turning back has taken place. The Soviet state has remained a socialist state, founded on an economic infrastructure that conforms to Marxist doctrine and it differs profoundly in its structure from the "bourgeois" states. A communist society has not yet been achieved, but it remains the proclaimed, and desired, ideal to which the U.S.S.R. must one day come.

A third and final observation is necessary: from 1936 to the present day there has been no stagnation. Despite the cruel war that caused its citizens untold misery and subjected its economy to large scale losses, the Soviet Union is today more powerful than ever on both the national and international levels. If it be true that the possibility of realising a communist society can only come with an unprecedented exaltation of the power of the state, we are now closer than ever to the conditions necessary for the advent of communism in the U.S.S.R.

148. Obstacles to the realisation of communism

What, according to Soviet doctrine, are these conditions, and how is it that communism still appears to be a distant ideal, forty years after the erection of the socialist state?

There are several reasons. The first of these is the "capitalist

---

[10] *Report on the Program of the Communist Party of the Soviet Union*, published as Vol. 2 of *Documents of the 2nd Congress of the C.P.S.U.* (1961) as approved in August 1961. Collignon (J. G.), *La théorie de l'Etat du peuple tout entier en Union Soviétique* (1967). The Chinese Communist Party was critical of this rejection of the proletarian dictatorship. *Cf.* Hazard (J. N.), "Socialisme et humanisme," in *Annales Africaines*, 1965, pp. 71–94. It was, however, vigorously defended in an article published in a Polish review: Zawadski (S.), "Controverses au sujet de l'essence de la dictature du prolétariat," *Pańtswo i Prawo* (November 1963).

encirclement." The Soviet Union succeeded in building a socialist state within this encirclement, and yet it is clear to Soviet leaders that in the present state of international relations, it would be suicidal to attempt to bring about the withering away of the state and to want to achieve communism now. This explanation alone suffices to justify the policy followed. The U.S.S.R. may very well try certain experiments intended to move closer to communism, but as long as it feels threatened by the existence of powerful non-socialist states, it will not be able to bring about completely a communist society.

The "capitalist encirclement" is not, however, the only explanation for the limited progress made towards communism. Another must be taken into account, namely the "survival of the habits of the capitalist era in the minds of citizens." Centuries of bad social organisation cannot be simply abolished; men have become accustomed to certain faulty ways of thinking and have come to regard as natural certain forms of behaviour which are, in reality, selfish and anti-social. It is not enough, although it is required by Marxist doctrine, to have remedied the fundamental defect of society and put its economic infrastructure on a sound footing by collectivising the means of production. Another task is involved: men must be re-educated and made to understand that the anti-social attitudes formerly excusable and even justified are so no longer in today's socialist state.[11] This task is to be accomplished by taking a person in hand from his childhood, and it is with this in mind that the new Soviet teaching programmes are conceived. This re-education is to be pursued during a man's entire life, and the Communist Party assumes a special responsibility in this connection.

The maintenance of state and law is all the more necessary at the present stage because, while social classes in the strict sense have disappeared, social groups—whether city dwellers or those of rural areas, intellectuals or manual workers, officials or the people at large—remain whose ways of life are still different. The differences between them are no longer "antagonistic" (in Marxist language), but there still is the danger that one of these groups may be tempted to appropriate the increased value of the work of

---

[11] A reading of the decisions rendered by Soviet courts shows how deep-seated this malady is, and what a long road is still to be covered in this respect. *Cf.* the many cases reported in the different chapters of Hazard, Butler and Maggs, *op. cit.*

the others, in order to become an exploiting class; the state must continue in order to prevent anyone from so harming socialist institutions. All feelings of opposition between these groups must be removed by equalising their living standards and bringing their various ways of life closer together before the disappearance of coercion, which will characterise a communist society, can be achieved.

To obtain of citizens this desired social behaviour and thus to allow the realisation of a communist society, the fulfilment of another preliminary condition, that of abundance, is also required. "From each according to his ability, to each according to his needs." This motto of communist society cannot become a reality if production is not pushed to the extreme, providing sufficient consumer goods for everyone. The maintenance of the machinery of the socialist state and the coercion it implies are necessary to achieve this.

149. The three tasks of Soviet law

The tasks of the Soviet state and law, during the present period of transition from socialism to communism, are thus threefold. The first, which need not detain us here, is one of national security: the power of the state must be consolidated and increased in order to discourage the enemies of socialism from attacking the Soviet regime and to assure peaceful co-existence between nations. Soviet law has, in addition, the economic task of developing production on the basis of socialist principles so as to create the abundance which alone will enable everyone to be supplied "according to his needs." The third task of Soviet law is one of education: that is, to destroy in Man those tendencies to selfish and anti-social behaviour that are the heritage of centuries of poor economic organisation.

150. Economic power: organisation of production

The economic task of Soviet law is in itself immense. The socialist regime puts far greater problems to its leaders in this respect than those facing leaders in capitalist countries. Law in the "bourgeois" countries can certainly come to the aid of the economy and is doing so more and more. Its basis remains, nevertheless, essentially a moral one. Observe the rules of justice and morality, it is thought, and order will reign even on the level of the economy. With the Marxist doctrine the positions are reversed: guarantee a certain economic organisation of the collectivity, place the means of production at the disposal of the collectivity, and morality will be satisfied and justice realised besides.

Law in bourgeois countries may well have an economic function but, to the large extent that there is a private sector, it is individual initiative that assumes the task of organising production and seeking commercial outlets. The state provides the incentives, the means of co-operation and a measure of control, but it has not taken unto itself the direct exploitation of property. In the U.S.S.R., on the other hand, "economic power" has been consciously taken out of private hands and the instruments of production have been collectivised in order that they be exploited in the general interest rather than to show a profit. It is for the nation's rulers to define the terms of this exploitation, to specify how the means of production are to be developed and how the products thereof will be distributed in function of the general interest as they define it. The state has become the great overlord of industry, agriculture and commerce. To provide the leadership, to organise the development of productive forces and the sharing of economic wealth on the scale of a nation such as the U.S.S.R. is obviously an extremely difficult task. Soviet leaders do not pretend to have found the perfect solution to this problem. If the guiding principles established by Marxist-Leninist doctrine are clear, namely that "economic power" be taken away from private interests, it does not specify how this power is to be exercised anew by the representatives of all the people. It has proved necessary therefore to indulge in a continual process of experimentation and adaptation. And it is doubtful that final solutions will ever be found.

Agreement was reached early on to develop the economic resources of the country according to a plan. But views differed, and methods were altered, on how such planning was to be carried out—was it best to begin in the production sector (metallurgy, construction, industrial chemistry) or within a functional framework (labour, supply, financing); should economic management be centralised or de-centralised; what duration should the different plans have; which sectors were to be priorities (heavy industry or consumer goods, industrial chemistry or space exploration);

how was the management of state enterprises to be organised and controlled, and so on. In agriculture, a choice had to be made between state farms (*sovkhozi*) and co-operatives (*kolkhozi*), their maximum size determined, and the status of the workers established in each.[12] Bureaucratic tendencies in industry had to be put into check and a stimulus to production found. Constant critical re-appraisal of all these aspects of organisation is still seen as necessary in order to prevent the development of abusive practices whether in the form of a too-powerful bureaucracy, the slackening-off in production, the favouritism of special interests or the degeneration of the collectivisation of property into mere state capitalism and to ensure that the need to build for communism is not forgotten.[13]

In the history of the exercise of this economic power and the organisation of the means of production, some serious errors were committed and some unfortunate decisions made. Stalin (1879–1953) may very well have said that "the aim of production is [not] profit, but man and his needs, in other words the satisfaction of his material and cultural needs."[14] His own style of government did not however respect that policy: man, during his time, was in effect sacrificed to production and to the state. Although the Stalinist era was a painful one, the Soviet people today are reaping its advantages: the economy has been completely collectivised and the danger of National-Socialism eliminated. Since then it has been possible to condemn the excesses of the Stalinist era and to return to true Marxist teaching, which aspires to be a humanism. Marxist doctrine teaches that power and wealth are not sought for their own sakes but rather in order to liberate man and to promote his complete fulfilment in a society in which he is no longer oppressed.

---

[12] Between 1959 and 1963, one-fifth of the *kolkhozi* were transformed into *sovkhozi* and the *kolkhozi* themselves organised into larger units. In 1978 there were about 27,500 *kolkhozi* providing employment for 13 million peasants. Each *kolkhoz* worked, on average, 6,000 hectares. In 1976, there were 19,639 *sovkhozi* employing 11 million people in the working of almost 50 per cent. of the land under cultivation. Since 1966 an equalisation of the status of the members of *kolkhozi* and *sovkozi* has been achieved: the members of the former now have a minimum wage and enjoy social security benefits.

[13] Chambre (H.), *Le pouvoir dans l'Union soviétique* (2nd ed., 1960). Nove (A.), *L'économie soviétique* (1963). Hazard (J. N.), Butler (W. E.) and Maggs (P. B.), *The Soviet Legal System* (1977). Mayer (M.), *L'entreprise industrielle d'Etat en Union soviétique* (1966). Dumont (R.), *Sovkhoz, Kolkhoz ou le problématique communiste* (1964). Hazard (J. N.), *The Soviet System of Government* (1980).

[14] Stalin (J. V.), *Economic Problems of Socialism in the U.S.S.R.* (1952).

151. The re-education of man

Soviet law has an educational as well as an economic role. To make communism possible, and to remove the mechanisms of force which the state represents, it does not suffice that the means of production be collectivised and that they be reorganised in the interest of all. It is also necessary to change man, to rid him of reactions, attitudes and feelings engendered by millennia of defective social organisation. "The socialist state," wrote the First President of the U.S.S.R. Supreme Court, I. T. Goliakov, "must totally re-shape the conscience of the people; that is its most important task."[15] More than ever before this aspect of socialist law and policy is of the first importance.

Remarkable results have already been achieved: for a Soviet citizen it has become inconceivable that a private person or company might own a factory or exploit any natural resources whatsoever in his own interest or that of share-holders; peasants, it would seem, voluntarily accept the transformation of their *kolkhozi* into *sovkhozi*. Much more, however, remains to be done. The task of re-educating citizens, a work in which jurists are invited to co-operate, must be carried on with indefatigable patience. The Soviet Communist Party numbered only 17,480,768 members in 1980, or about 9 per cent. of the population. It is up to this *élite* to convert a disciplined population, but one which lacks a profound faith. Citizens must be inculcated with a new sense that work has become a matter of honour, as much as of necessity. They must be imbued with a sense that socialist ownership, which is an ownership of all,[15] is one they have the sacred duty to protect. They must be shown that law at the present time is just because it fully reconciles private and general interests. Citizens must obey the law not, as in the time of defective social organisation, through fear of a policeman, but because they feel in conscience bound to observe, without coercion of any kind, the natural principles upon which the newly reformed society is based. Law today in the U.S.S.R. is reason and true justice. It is important that everyone assent to the rules of socialist law, that the law be "popular."

Considerable and repeated efforts are made to familiarise citizens with the Soviet Constitution, institutions and laws. The local

---

[15] Goljakov (I. T.), *Vospitaltel' noe znavčenie sovetskogo suda* (1947).

Soviets, guided by the preparatory deliberations of the Communists among their members, are there to learn and, in turn, to explain to the population the sound basis and wisdom of decisions prepared by the Party.

All citizens are called upon to participate in drawing up important laws by suggesting appropriate amendments to the established drafts. The number of meetings at which the draft of the constitution of the U.S.S.R. or that of a law on the re-organisation of agriculture or on pensions has been discussed, and the number of amendments proposed, is cited with pride.[16] The citizens must feel that the law voted by their representatives is truly their own—a law desired by them, the strict observation of which they must support and safeguard. The Soviet court is thought of as a school. It admonishes, encourages, and gives advice as the law itself often does. Its composition, rules of procedure and very existence are explained by the educative role of Soviet law. A failure has occurred if the condemned party does not approve of his sentence, and if opposing parties do not leave the court reconciled by recognising the just character of the decision made in application of socialist law. This work of persuasion is gradually to render all coercion unnecessary, and in this way law can finally lose its sanctionist aspect in order to assume a merely directing role. According to the saying of Engels, "the government of men will give way to the administration of things;" everyone will spontaneously observe the rules laid down by the administrators of collectivised property, so evident will the usefulness of these rules be to all. Society will then function without any coercion; there will be no more Law in the sense that the Marxists understand this term.

152. Interest of Soviet law for non-socialist countries

The ideal of a communist society has not been fulfilled up to the present time, but this ideal, which the system of government applies itself to bring about, has nonetheless led Soviet leaders to try out new ideas in which social relationships are no longer, as in the past, regulated essentially, or even normally, by law. The transfer of functions presently carried out by the state to more

---

[16] Tchikvadze (V. M.), *Le concept de la légalité dans les pays socialistes* (1961), pp. 211–214. When the Fundamental Principles of Family Law were under consideration, 7,000 suggestions were made and 8,000 letters sent by citizens to *Izvestija* and *Literaturnaya Gazeta*.

flexible bodies, and the use of techniques other than law to regulate certain aspects of social life in the U.S.S.R. merit our attention.

In a number of capitalist countries even criminal law, for example, tends to become diluted or to take on new characteristics when there arises a new concept of social defence, dominated by a cluster of criminological sciences in which psychology, medicine and sociology are associated. In other areas (such as commercial and labour law) the techniques of arbitration and mediation also tend to be substituted for strict rules of law. In the U.S.S.R. the desire to see law vanish applies to all domains as a matter of principle. This stand may lead it to try experiments which, even in non-socialist countries, are of interest and value.[17]

Section II—Other Socialist Countries

153. General characteristics

Ever since communist regimes assumed power in other European socialist countries their general pattern of development has been the same as that of the Soviet Union. It could not really have been otherwise: adhesion to the Marxist doctrine carries with it the same understanding of social history and of law, the same need to collectivise the means of production and to install the dictatorship of the proletariat. The Marxist governors of the European people's democracies very naturally looked for guidance to the Soviet Union which had been on the road to communism since 1917; its political power, moreover, afforded them protection in this early period.

But the conditions of the U.S.S.R. and the European socialist countries are, nevertheless, from many points of view, very different. No European country has either the continental dimensions or the world power and responsibilities of the U.S.S.R., and this geo-political factor alone necessarily implies much variation in the way in which problems are put and resolved. Then, too, the circumstances in which the communists came to power were different

---

[17] David (R.), "Le dépassement du droit et les systèmes de droit contemporains," *Archives de philosophie du droit*, no. 8 (1963), pp. 3–20. Jampol'skaja (T. S.), *Les organisations sociales et le développement de la socialisation de l'Etat* (1968).

in Russia and elsewhere. Economic and social conditions and traditions in these countries never were, nor are they now, those of Soviet Russia. Their several policies, while oriented towards a common goal, necessarily involve some adaptation to these conditions and circumstances. In other words, the model provided by the U.S.S.R. could not simply be adopted in these several states whose traditions, degree of industrialisation, social structure and culture were different.

For all these reasons, it is admitted in the Soviet Union that there can be differences between the laws of the U.S.S.R. and the people's democracies. It is seen as natural that there be departures from the Soviet model, although the deviations must have some limits if the state in question intends to remain within the socialist camp. The desire on the part of some countries to build "a new model of socialist society" is not, however, looked upon favourably by the U.S.S.R. There is a real fear that, under the cover of such a formula, there will be a new interpretation given to the fundamental doctrine of Marxism-Leninism and thus an abandonment of a number of its basic principles.

154. Respect for law

The Russian people, for the most part ruled only by their customs, did not consider law to be the basis of the social order before the Bolshevik revolution. For them legislation was associated with the whims of the sovereign and represented an essentially administrative technique. Marxism forecast the withering away of law and this so little shocked the Russians that they thought it possible, immediately after the Revolution, to look to the total and immediate disappearance of all law. There was also a lack of jurists in whom confidence could be placed for the administration of a new law. Lenin's affirmation of the principle of socialist legality at the time of the N.E.P. appeared to many as a backward step on the road to socialism; it was expected that this principle would be abandoned as soon as possible, along with the N.E.P. itself, if the principles of the revolution and Marxism were to be faithfully maintained.

On all those points the situation was different in the people's republics. Prior to 1945 in all these states, although to differing degrees, there was, or it was at least proposed that there should be, the ideal of a state founded on law.[18] When the political regimes dominated by the Communist Party were established, it would have been possible to reject the idea of law held in the Romano-Germanic family and to deny, according to Marxist-Leninist doctrine, the continuity between the old and the new law. Not one of the people's democracies however passed through the stage of revolutionary communism known to Russia. And profiting from the Russian experience, it was unhesitatingly admitted in the people's republics that a transitional period between capitalism and communism was necessary; the principle of socialist legality was easily acknowledged. The traditionally respectful attitude for law very naturally remained, especially since in these countries, unlike Russia in 1917, there were both old and new jurists who were willing to serve the regime.

155. Survival of former law

Moreover, in none of the people's republics was it judged necessary, as it had been in Russia, to make a clean break with and to abolish *in toto* the existing law. Existing codes and legislation were left in force to the extent that they were not contrary to the principles of the newly created public order. Economic and political structures were, of course, thrown into confusion but an effort was made to retain in the sphere of law anything of the former system that might be salvaged. Techniques known from experience to be valuable and which were in no way incompatible with a renewal of the law were preserved. Substantively, legal provisions in which class characteristics were evident were abrogated; but the whole of the law was not rejected since it contained a portion of the national cultural heritage that was worthy of admiration and confidence.

Consider the case of Yugoslavia. A decision of February 3, 1945 by the praesidium of the Yugoslav Anti-fascist Council of National Liberation abolished the whole of the former law of the country, but it allowed judges to continue to apply those provisions that were not "opposed to the victories of the struggle for national liberation, the declarations and decisions of the different anti-fascist councils and the committees of national liberation." The Yugoslav Supreme Court in 1951 clearly indicated the value of the

---

[18] Wagner (W. J.) ed., *Polish Law Throughout the Ages* (1970).

former law by demanding of a lower court, when the latter refused to apply a rule of this law, that it specify "the rule, the institution or the political principle which the application of this rule would violate. It cannot simply reject a rule of the former law by saying that it no longer has force of law, without any further amplification."[19] This decision censures the opinion formerly held by Yugoslav authors that judges should no longer be allowed to give reasons for their judgments by referring to the articles of the old codes on the ground that these no longer had any value save as general legal principles. This legal point is now out of date but it is an example of a willingness to be original. Much legislation has been enacted since then, a recent example of which is the law of October 1, 1978 on the subject of obligations.

156. Renewal of the law

Not everything therefore in the former law was necessarily condemned; some of its provisions were only the result of the dictatorship of the bourgeois class, whereas others, corresponding to the customs of the people, could very well be in agreement with true justice. However the importance of the maintenance of the former legal system must not be over-estimated. Even though much old legislation has been preserved, it has often been interpreted in a new manner reflecting the political revolution that has occurred. A considerable amount of codification and new enactment has intervened which renders more and more theoretical the maintenance of the earlier legislation.

With regimes whose aim it was to create socialist societies completely different from old societies, it is obvious that the law had to change and that a vast work of revision of the codes and, in some countries, the unification of the law, had to be accomplished. But two methods of doing so were possible. It might, in the first place, have been tempting to copy the Soviet model; on the other hand, however, it was also possible to try to make use of existing institutions, by infusing them with a new spirit so that they could be put to the service of the socialist state.[20]

The first method was employed in the beginning but in a manner

---

[19] Stoyanovitch (K.), *Le régime socialiste yougoslave* (1961), pp. 169, 359–360.
[20] On the influence of Soviet law upon the law of the people's democracies, *cf. Izv. Inst. pravi nauki* (Sofia, 1968), Vol. 22 and especially the article by L. Vasilev.

which today is considered to have been excessive. The second is more and more gaining in importance. Was it not Lenin himself who stated that "When the national character is neglected in the building of socialism, the very meaning of socialism is distorted"?[21] Most jurists of the people's republics have welcomed the readjustment of Marxist-Leninist teaching which took place in March 1956 at the XX Congress of the Soviet Communist Party and the new, less strictly dogmatic and authoritarian current which has seemed to prevail since that time. "The mechanical opposition of the law, legislation and judicial practice of the socialist state to the corresponding institutions of the capitalist state," wrote the Polish Minister of Justice, "has been one of the negative factors exerting an influence on our legal development. The fact that these institutions were the product of a centuries long heritage has been underestimated; in the interests of socialism it would be better to perfect rather than to suppress them." It is regrettable, she continues, that "the traditions of progressive Polish scholarship" have been abandoned "in favour of a mechanical importation into Poland of the legal institutions of other states working for socialism."[22]

157. Collectivisation

The work of reform was directed, first of all, to bringing about the collectivisation of the means of production. Complete success was achieved in respect of industry.

Vast industrial development plans in the various people's republics required the complete annexation of industrial enterprises by the state; it was unthinkable that the proletarian working class, the members of which make up the ranks of the Communist Party, should remain subject to and be exploited by private employers. Moreover, the nationalisation of industry was easy and popular because the enterprises themselves often belonged to foreign interests or to capitalists whose position was compromised by reason of their association with the previous political regimes.

Although it was not pushed as far in the new democracies as it

---

[21] Cited by Maneli (M.), "Les idées de la Révolution d'octobre," *Państwo i Prawo*, November 1957.

[22] Wasilkowska (Z.), "Les tâches de la commission de codification," *Państwo i Prawo*, January 1957.

was in the U.S.S.R., private commerce was also forbidden. There are however privately owned stores in Bulgaria and Hungary, especially in the food-stuff trades. Elsewhere, in Poland for example, an accommodation was reached whereby the state conceded to private enterprises the right to operate various commercial concerns.

As in Soviet Russia, however, the more delicate matter was the nationalisation of land and the collectivisation of farming. The difficulties were overcome in most of the people's democracies and the resulting situation is very comparable if not identical to that in the U.S.S.R. Two states, however, Poland and Yugoslavia, only followed the movement to a very limited extent.

In Poland the land was not nationalised and the greater part of agricultural production is still carried out by individual farmers. The latter possess 86·3 per cent. of the cultivated land whereas 8,300 state-farms cultivate only 12 per cent. of the land; since 1956 the *kolkhozi*, which were never very extensive, have almost completely disappeared. The law only prohibits individual farms of more than fifteen to twenty hectares; in 1957 the free disposal of land was re-established subject to various conditions. Polish leaders and jurists are striving to create new means whereby the idea of co-operation can be re-enforced to prepare the peasants for collectivisation without provoking their resistance.

The collectivisation of agriculture is no more developed in Yugoslavia than in Poland. A first Yugoslav reform, carried out in 1945, limited to 25 or 35 hectares, depending on their nature, the superficial area of individual or family farms. This measure, however, only amounted to a confiscation of the lands belonging to the church and other large landowners; it did not achieve the collectivisation of agriculture because the confiscated lands were distributed to poor peasants who then cultivated them on an individual or family basis. Progress in collectivisation was only made after the break with Moscow in 1949. The association of peasants on *kolkhozi* was then actively encouraged, but because of its unpopularity this reform had to be dropped in 1951. Only in 1953 was the movement resumed by a further reform limiting individual farms to 10 hectares and family farms (*zadruga*) to 25 hectares. To the extent that land is collectivised in Yugoslavia the *sovkhoz*, and not the *kolkhoz*, has been employed. But even this measure has been minimal: 90 per cent. of the cultivated agricultural land remains in the form of 2,300,000 small individual or family farms, 30 per cent. of which have a superficial area of less than two hectares. The largest part of agricultural production, quite apart from any institutional collectivisation, is still carried on by a generally poor peasantry that trades its produce as it chooses at the current market prices.

Agricultural collectivisation, in Yugoslavia as in Poland, remains a more or less unsolved problem. As an ideal, however, it has not been abandoned, but the efforts to establish co-operatives of various sorts take the form of trying to attract the peasants through education and persuasion and the prospect of material advantages rather than through dangerously authoritarian measures.

158. Planning

Like the economy of the Soviet Union, that of the people's republics is developed by means of a series of economic plans geared to create gradually the conditions necessary for the passage to the stage of communism. But the modalities of the plan are substantially different in each country. There is nothing surprising in such varied economic planning; it is the very principle itself of planning, and not its modalities, that Marxist-Leninist doctrine imposes; even in the U.S.S.R. successive phases of centralisation and decentralisation occurred with a rigour or a suppleness which varied according to current thinking about the best means to promote the development of the means of production. For reasons of a social or geographical nature, problems in planning often arise differently than they do in the U.S.S.R. The desire to work out suitable solutions in each country has however raised two types of suspicion. On the one hand it is feared that there may be a return to capitalistic methods; on the other, it has been observed that the new orientations may seem to imply a criticism of Soviet policies.

159. Yugoslav criticism of the Stalinist policy

The communist leaders of Yugoslavia were at first very closely linked to the U.S.S.R. but since 1948 there has been conflict with Soviet leaders on these matters. Considered to be "revisionists" or "deviationists" by the latter as well as other communist parties, Yugoslav leaders insist upon their loyalty to Marxism-Leninism but claim the right to interpret the doctrine and to pursue communism in their own way. Moreover they severely criticise the mistaken ideas, especially those of the Stalinist period, entertained in the U.S.S.R.[23] The Yugoslavs consider that the U.S.S.R. is far from being a socialist state and has departed from the path indicated by Marxist doctrine in order to build a new kind of capitalist state. For them, the Soviet regime is a form of "state capitalism" in the service of a new class of bureaucrats; the riches of the nation are not exploited in the interests of all the people but in those of this new class of leaders despite the current terminology which is, in effect, worth little more than the hypocritical talk of the leaders of bourgeois countries.

Marxist-Leninist teaching, as seen by the Yugoslavs, requires that the means of production *in fact*—and not simply as a form of legislative fiction—be placed at the people's disposal. It therefore requires that the power of the state immediately disappear in all those areas where this can be carried out without endangering the victory of socialism. The ideal of the Russian and Yugoslav communists is the same. The Russians, however, think that the best means of achieving this ideal is to delay provisionally its realisation; the Yugoslavs, on the contrary, maintain that such a delay constitutes a repudiation. The new and wished for society must be set up gradually but *immediately* by means of new methods which are not simply a transfer to the state, dominated by a communist oligarchy of bureaucrats, of the wide powers formerly held by capitalist exploiters.

The abolition of the commercial classes in the U.S.S.R. ought normally to have led to the beginning of the withering away of the state; the different groups of the new social order are not, in fact, as bitterly opposed to each other as were the former social classes; there is therefore no more justification for the maintenance of the former functions and authority of the state and law. In the U.S.S.R., however, as Stalin himself proclaimed, exactly the opposite has occurred: the Soviet state has been more and more re-enforced by its taking into hand not only industrial relations,

---

[23] Stoyanovitch (K.), "La conception de l'Etat en Yougoslavie," *Revue du droit public et de la science politique*, 1959, pp. 214–239. *Adde* Djilas (M.), *The New Class. An Analysis of the Communist System* (1957). Garaudy (R.), *Le grand tournant du socialisme* (1969). Another break occurred in 1961 with Albania, which has turned towards the Chinese Maoist model.

which alone form the true competence of a state, but the whole of social life as well.

The reason for this state of affairs is that the corps of Soviet leaders, which at one time came from the heart of the proletariat, has now become detached and separated from it; they have made of themselves an autonomous group with its own interests, and these are different and sometimes even opposed to those of the proletariat. This group, now an extremely powerful bureaucracy, has brought the whole Soviet state under official control rather than democratising it; instead of creating a state that would waste away, it has created a totalitarian state the like of which history offers no peer. And the Soviet bureaucracy has not been content with the role of domination confided to it by the proletariat; it has, in turn, taken on the role of an exploiting class like that enjoyed by the middle class before the revolution. In the U.S.S.R. a simple system of state capitalism has been substituted for the intended socialist system.[24]

160. Yugoslav constitutions

The essential difference between the dictatorship of the working class and all other forms of dictatorship is not the fact that it brings about a dictatorship by the vast majority of workers over the minority of now dispossessed exploiters. It means rather that the proletarian state is not a state in the traditional sense but a transition between the state and the "non-state." To avoid the greatest danger for the proletariat—the bureaucratisation of the socialist state—it must be democratised—that is to say, the masses must participate in public administration as well as the management of the national economy. This is accomplished by removing from the *state* its former functions, one by one, for the benefit of *society*. Only in this way will the socialist state, so long as it does exist, remain a proletarian state and then wane, one day completely and finally to disappear.

This, it is declared, has been accomplished in Yugoslavia, where the regime led by Marshall Tito (1892–1980) has made a faithful and consistent application of Marxism-Leninism. The Yugoslav

---

[24] From quite another quarter, the Soviet regime has been criticised for the same reasons; the Chinese "dogmatists" accuse the Soviet leaders of having lost contact with the masses and any sense of revolutionary action.

Constitution of 1946 laid the basis for a centralised state similar to that of the Soviet Union. But with the collectivisation of the means of production and the disappearance of the capitalist bourgeoisie, its historical task, was completed and it was replaced in 1953, 1963 and then again in 1974 by new constitutions the role of which was to re-organise the state on a new foundation more in agreement with the newly developed conditions. The organisation of public authorities and the economic system were both reformed. The former were decentralised through the introduction of as large a measure of local autonomy as possible and the economic system was democratised by means of a participation by workers and salaried employees in the economic management of the country.

The economic policy of the proletarian state must tend to create and favour not a *state* but rather a *social* ownership which will be transferred without delay to the working people by removing it from the state and its bureaucracy. The economic functions of the state, therefore, are the first that should be transferred to society or, in other words, to the "free associations of producers." As a parallel to their participation in political power the Yugoslav people participate actively in the direction of economic power because, in each republic, as a federal unit, there is a chamber of producers which is also a chamber of the National Assembly. In each commune committee, in the same way, there is a chamber of "associated workers."

161. Self-management of enterprises

In addition, each economic enterprise has a workers' council, the highest managerial body of the enterprise. This is the famous industrial self-management of which Yugoslav leaders are so proud: economic management and administration of society, as required by Marxist-Leninist teaching (or at least as it is interpreted in Yugoslavia) are thus assured by the producers themselves.[25] The director of the enterprise is named by the workers' council upon an open competition. Before making its selection the council takes advice from the enterprise itself and from the commune in which it is located. The director, among other things, has the job of supervising the legality of the work of the enterprise in

---

[25] On self-management, *cf.* Stoyanovitch (K.), *Le régime socialiste yougoslave* (1961), pp. 312 *et seq.*; Hazard (J. N.), "Le régime juridique de l'administration des entreprises dans les pays communistes," *Liber amicorum baron L. Frédéricq* (1965) t. I, p. 539.

order to prevent it, under workers' management, from becoming a private enterprise in their hands and assures that its operation sufficiently observes the "social plan" and interests of the socialist economy of the whole country. A further, but temporary limitation of the workers' self-management can also occur with the "taking in hand" of the enterprise if this is necessary for the protection of social interests threatened by an insufficient social consciousness on the part of the producers.[26]

162. Withering away of the state

In Yugoslavia the state retains those functions, presupposing the exercise of force, that are necessary for the maintenance of order and social peace. These functions are the last to be exercised by society directly; their transfer will only occur when all the persisting inegalities to which, precisely, all violations of peace and the social order are due, have disappeared from society.

The state also continues to assure the defence of its frontiers. But that does not prevent it from withering away in all other respects. It has just been seen how the withering away of the state was conceived and organised in economic matters. The state and its bureaucracy must also immediately lose other functions, especially those relating to intellectual life, public health, education and social planning. For this reason attempts have been made in Yugoslavia to create a system without political parties. In 1952 the Communist Party became the Yugoslav Communist League in order to make it understood that it had become simply an organisation for the diffusion of communist ideas. The right to make actual decisions and to militate for their adoption as acts of state has been transferred to the Socialist Alliance of Working People which is, properly speaking, not a political party but rather a diversified organisation intended to include almost all citizens participating in the exercise of power in order to teach them how best to discharge this task.

163. Influence of Yugoslav revisionism

The Yugoslav criticism of the Soviet regime and institutions was considered in the U.S.S.R. in 1948 as a betrayal of the socialist

---

[26] Apart from the Constitution, the regulation of self-management is principally found in legislation of November 25, 1976.

bloc. But with the disappearance of Stalin in 1953 and the denunciation of the Stalinist dictatorship by Khrushchev in February 1956, it was at last asked whether in fact there was not some truth in these criticisms and whether, in any case, the Yugoslav Republic, being in a special situation, different from that of the U.S.S.R., could not legitimately adopt a course of action distinct from that of the U.S.S.R. Since that time considerable efforts have been made in the U.S.S.R. and in other Marxist-Leninist countries to eliminate those traits which gave weight to the Yugoslav criticisms. The "deviations" brought about in certain areas by the domination of a bureaucratic centralisation, the delays in official business, the excessive formalism and plethora of personnel have all been denounced. The down-grading of the elective bodies, which were unable to exercise any effective control, was recognised as having resulted in a separation of state and Party machinery from society and to have brought about violations of legality and encouraged oligarchical tendencies. "At the heart of socialist society there are contradictions that must be eradicated if its development is to continue."[27]

Since 1956 other countries of the socialist camp, and even the U.S.S.R. itself, have thought it necessary to undertake a "regeneration of socialist democracy;" the reforms introduced to "rectify the bureaucratic deviations of socialism" do, in their principle, recall the changes advocated in Yugoslavia.[28]

164. Cohesion of the Marxist-Leninist countries

The crisis that occurred in the relations between Soviet and Yugoslav Marxists is much less acute, now that experience has shown that even though it went its own way Yugoslavia has no intention of joining the capitalist camp. Other crises have occurred, or been threatened, between the Soviet Union and other countries which, in turn, have also wanted to depart from the Soviet model. It is difficult for those living in the Soviet context not to have some doubts about them in such circumstances; and this,

---

[27] Ehrlich (St.), "Notion et garanties de la légalité socialiste dans les pays de l'Europe de l'Est," *Politique, Revue internationale des doctrines et des institutions*, 1958, pp. 311, 324–325.
[28] On the similarities in the U.S.S.R. and Yugoslavia respecting the administrative regime of state enterprises, *cf.* the article, already cited, of J. N. Hazard in *Liber Amicorum Frédéricq* t. I.

in all probability, will always be, so long as the capitalist encircle-ment subsists and is looked upon as a menace in the U.S.S.R.

The picture of the Marxist-Leninist countries in the contempor-ary world is thus one of considerable variety. An American author has endeavoured to identify that factor which unites them all in respect of their law.[29] No great difficulty is encountered in finding many similarities, but in no domain—whether in public or private law—has he been able to state that there is uniformity. Variations are, however, natural in these societies which, from so many points of view, are different and fully intend to remain so. That voice which, at the creation of the Soviet Union in 1922, exclaimed to the constituent assembly "Long live the Soviet Socialist Repub-lics of the whole world!" has ever since been without echo. The Soviet Union has not taken over any country which has come under the control of a communist party since 1945.

Each such country has its own originality and enjoys its own institutions and law. And the cohesion of the socialist bloc does not, moreover, imply that they renounce thereto—it merely sup-poses that they all adhere to a number of basic principles, a certain idea of what the social order should be and to some sense of soli-darity with the Soviet Union. It cannot be forgotten that the Soviet Union itself has not yet achieved that form of society heralded by Marxist theory. Different paths can, then, be followed to advance towards this goal which itself legitimises the present day vari-ations.

Section III—The Principle of Socialist Legality

165. Position of the problem

The Marxist prediction of the disappearance of law in commu-nist society, and the policy followed by Soviet leaders during the period of revolutionary communism, troubled many jurists of bourgeois countries who wondered if any Soviet law existed at all and whether the socialist state, aspiring to bring about its own dis-appearance, still recognised a principle of legality.

---

[29] Hazard (J. N.), *Communists and their Law. A Search for the Common Core of the Legal Systems of the Marxian Socialist States* (1969). See also Eörsi (G.) and Harmaty (R.) ed., *Law and Economic Reform in Socialist Countries* (1971). Martinet (G.), *Les cinq communismes* (1971).

It would be as well to remove all doubt on this subject—the question may well once have existed in the case of China, but not in that of the U.S.S.R. and other European socialist countries where a principle of socialist legality is emphatically stated and where, at the same time, there are real guarantees to make this principle effective.[30] The principle and its guarantees will now be examined.

§ 1. Meaning of the Principle

166. Existence of a socialist law

The utopian position taken up at the time of revolutionary communism, when it was thought possible to abolish immediately the principle of legality and to replace all law by revolutionary conscience, has long been a thing of the past. With the affirmation of the principle of socialist legality, law has been given the character and authority that it has in capitalist countries.

The U.S.S.R. is not yet a communist society in which social relationships are exclusively governed by spontaneous feelings of solidarity and social duty. At present, discipline is the keynote in all fields: labour discipline, planning discipline—and coercion and law both play a role, far from exclusive but incontestable nonetheless and therefore not to be underestimated, in assuring this strict discipline. Law and state are necessary at the present stage. By conforming strictly to the law, the various parts of the administration, state enterprises, co-operatives and citizens work for the accomplishment of government policy and make way for the advent of communism. Strict compliance with the principle of socialist legality, in other words strict conformity to the Soviet legal order, is absolutely imperative.

167. Meaning of the word "socialist"

What does the epithet "socialist" add to the term "socialist legality"? It is far from meaningless. Indeed, in the eyes of Soviet jurists it is this adjective that legitimises the obligation to obey the law and makes the principle of legality meaningful.

---

[30] "Le concept de la légalité dans les pays socialistes," *Cahiers de l'Académie polonaise des sciences, XXI*, 1961. Alekseev (S. S.), *Social "naja cennost" prava v sovetskom obščestve* (1970).

Socialist Laws

Soviet citizens must obey Soviet laws because they are just; and they are just because the state is a socialist state which exists in the interest of all and not that of a privileged class. In all countries the Marxists have fought and still fight against the law, because to them it appears that law, in the non-socialist countries, serves only to defend and perpetuate a fundamentally unjust social order. When they demand on the contrary that citizens in the U.S.S.R. conform strictly to the legal order, they must therefore justify this change of attitude.

"The economic structure of society and the material conditions of the ruling class determine the social consciousness, the will and the interests that find their expression in law. To dissociate law and legality from the economy, to analyse the legal system independently of the existing economic relations is therefore incompatible with the basic principles of Soviet legal science."[31] The law is of value only in relation to the order which it serves to establish and the content of the legal rules it contains. The epithet "socialist" supplies, therefore, an indispensable justification; it underscores the idea that the principle of legality is only meaningful in a socialist economy and when it is subordinate to the interests of this economy. A "fetish" must not be made of law. Law only has value because it serves the interests of a socialist state. Law is important and indispensable, but it is, after all, merely a superstructure; its authority can only be based on a sound infrastructure, that of an economy in which the means of production are collectivised and exploited in the interests of all. The epithet "socialist" thus recalls this fundamental principle of Marxist thought.

168. Affirmation of the principle of socialist legality

But the principle, once admitted, was not accepted without some difficulty to which the present terminology still bears witness. Apart from any basic doctrinal position, the principle of socialist legality simply could not be recognised during the period of revolutionary communism. To be meaningful, the principle presupposes the existence of sufficiently detailed legal rules, and these did not exist at the time. It was only during the period of the

---

[31] Tchikvadze (V. M.), "Socialist Legality in the U.S.S.R.," *in Le concept de légalité dans les pays socialistes* (1961), p. 206. *Adde* Jaroszyński (M.): "Les éléments populaires dans le concept de la légalité socialiste," *ibid.* pp. 327–336.

N.E.P. that the principle of legality was first asserted in the U.S.S.R. This was, however, a period of compromise, when there was real fear that the capitalist elements (private industrial enterprises or *kulaks*) subsisting in society would attempt to use the existing laws for their own ends and to the detriment of socialism. Many jurists were not enthusiastic about these laws because of their suspicion of such capitalist elements, for whose benefit it might seem that the codes had been drafted in order to win them over and give them some reassurance. The full adherence of Soviet jurists to the principle of socialist legality, and the complete victory of the principle, only came about after the abandonment of the N.E.P., when the U.S.S.R. became a completely socialist state.

169. State enterprises

At this particular moment, there was some question whether a distinction—recalling that between public and private law—should not be made between state agencies or enterprises and citizens, the latter alone being fully subject to the principle of legality. Under current Soviet law, litigation of any importance involving such enterprises is not resolved by the ordinary courts established under the Soviet Constitution, but submitted to distinct arbitration organs ("state arbitration" or "administrative (department) arbitration"). As employed here, the word arbitration is equivocal. It suggests that in dealings between state enterprises a strict application of the law is not made or that such application may be tempered by other considerations. It is quite likely that in 1931, when the system of state or "administrative" arbitration was put into effect, the choice of this term was influenced by some such idea.[32] Whatever the situation may have been originally, it is now quite clear that state enterprises, like citizens, are strictly subject to the principle of socialist legality, and that dealings among them are rigorously governed by law; the arbitration organs must apply rules of law in the solution of disputes among these enterprises, to the exclusion of any considerations based on equity or some other non-juridical consideration.

---

[32] Hazard (J. N.), "Flexibility of Law in Soviet State Arbitration" *International Arbitration, Liber amicorum for Martin Domke* (1967), p. 120.

170. Imperative nature of Soviet law

The regime established in the U.S.S.R., however, changes the fundamentals of every problem, and the principle of socialist legality proclaimed in this country differs from the principle of the supremacy of law, *i.e.* "the rule of law," such as it is found in the bourgeois countries. It is now appropriate to consider some of the differences demonstrating the originality of the Soviet system in the present phase of socialism.

The first difference lies in the new functions that the law is called upon to fulfil in the Soviet Union. The Soviet government is revolutionary and its aim is to bring about a radical change in present conditions so as to establish a communist society. The primary function of Soviet law is not, as in the bourgeois countries, to express a certain concept of justice based upon tradition but to organise the nation's economic forces and to transform the behaviour and attitudes of its citizens. The dynamic nature of these functions distinguishes Soviet from bourgeois laws. To avoid or disobey the law in the U.S.S.R. does not merely constitute an infringement on the interests of private persons or an insult to the code of morality; it is a threat to the success of the policy of the leaders and involves the risk of delaying the advent of communism, if indeed not definitively compromising it. In bourgeois countries, the way in which a contract is negotiated, interpreted and executed concerns mainly private interests; in the U.S.S.R. the success of the plan and the economic development of the nation depend upon it. These new functions assigned to law in society and the revolutionary character of the government make respect for the law much more imperative in the Soviet Union than in capitalist countries in which, after all, the matter is often of more interest to private persons than it is to society in general.

Jhering vainly exhorted citizens of bourgeois countries to fight for law.[33] The feeling persists, however, in these countries that a poor settlement is worth more than a good trial, and society adapts itself to this feeling and practice. The same point of view would be inadmissible in the Soviet Union, where respect for law as the policy instrument of the leaders is a major social concern. "We have no more private law," wrote Lenin, "for with us all has

---

[33] Jhering (R. von), *Der Kampfum's Recht* (1872) translated as *The Struggle for Law* (1915) by A. Kocourek.

become public law." This statement must be understood to mean that all of Soviet law is intended to construct a new social order; any violation of the law is of concern to the public authorities and the state, quite apart from whoever is the immediate victim.

In the U.S.S.R. the principle of legality is more necessary and more demanding than in bourgeois countries, where the law attempts to promote justice mainly between private persons and where, to a very great extent therefore, law is only obligatory in so far as interested citizens are disposed to act in order to protect their rights. The differing functions given to law in the Soviet Union result in a stricter conception of the principle of legality and a more efficient guarantee that it will be respected, because there, unlike the bourgeois countries, both society and the powers that govern have a greater concern for its respect. The role of law and the importance of training good jurists were particularly emphasised by Party leaders in 1960 when it was decided to increase significantly the number of lawyers especially with a view to their employment in state enterprises.

171. Socialist laws and natural law

A second difference distinguishing socialist laws from other laws lies in their respective attitudes to natural law. Marxism has often been explained as a purely positivist doctrine and as one rejecting natural law. The reality of the matter is, however, more complex.[34]

Marxists will only qualify as law and as legal rules those rules of conduct laid down and sanctioned by the state, and in this sense they may be called positivists. But Marxists do not refuse to look behind the formal or exterior aspect of law; for them the law must not be divorced from its social context. Beginning with this idea, therefore, Marxism corrects the positivist view by recognising that there is a "given factor" in law—the social or natural context in which law, unfolding in an historical perspective, operates the "construction" of law. The legislature is not omnipotent; it cannot create law arbitrarily because it is limited in its actions by certain material considerations and prevailing ideals. The work of the

---

[34] Naschitz (A. M.), "Le problème du droit naturel à la lumière de la philosophie marxist du droit", *Revue roumaine des sciences sociales* (Série des sciences juridiques), t. X (1966), p. 19. Toumanov (V. A.), *Pensée juridique bourgeoise contemporaine* (1974).

legislature is thus conditioned and to some extent predetermined, by many varied social relationships prevailing among men.

Marxism, in this way, as a global philosophy, is different from positivism becuase it is willing to encompass in its conception and definition of law the fact that there are real limits to legislative power. The legislature is not completely free in its work of creating law; it is restricted by a number of exterior or anterior factors. And, therefore, because it recognises that its work is not wholly free and arbitrary, Marxism is close to the idea of natural law, even though it attaches a new meaning to this term (which is already attributed so many meanings). For the Marxist, natural law does not refer to the natural order of things, an abstract nature, or to some concept of an immanent and universal justice. The essential thing, that which in the end dictates any action by the legislature, is, for the Marxist, the material condition of life, the way in which the means of production are exploited and the productive relationships are arranged, rather than, as it would be for the Natural Law school, the factors of an idealised nature.

The Marxist position on this matter in no sense implies the negation of the basis, or the ethical finality, of law. The fact that a state has become socialist does not free it from constantly seeking out a better concordance of law and morality. The socialist state, indeed, takes up the challenge even more readily than others because it sees its morality—that of a classless society—as superior to that of other non-socialist states which are based upon the exploitation of the workers by the privileged classes. It can come as no surprise, therefore, to learn that those societies professing materialism also exalt the value of law and emphasise its moral or just character. And there is no objection to the use of the word "sacred" to describe a variety of legal institutions of Soviet law, whether it be the family, socialist ownership or the obligation to work.

172. The provisional character of socialist law

The principle of socialist legality has been proclaimed and today reigns uncontested in the U.S.S.R. and other socialist countries. However it must not be forgotten that this principle, like the structure of the socialist state itself, simply meets the necessities of a transitional period. The present law of socialist countries, writes the Czech professor V. Knapp, is, generally speaking, just from the point of view of a socialist society but unjust, on the contrary, from the point of view of the later phase of communism. The dialectic contradiction between the just character of socialist law and its unjust character in a communist society will only disappear with the withering away of law upon the advent of communism itself.[35] The end in view is the construction of a communist society in which law and the state, and therefore the principle of legality, will no longer exist. For this reason there are insitutions in Soviet law which, within the framework of the principle of legality, presage and prepare for the non-juridical forms of tomorrow's society. And there are also institutions which do not appear to be fully in agreement with the principle of legality itself. Each of these observations is an opportune reminder that Soviet society does not want to be, and is not, "a society like others," and that its whole structure is dominated by Marxist-Leninist ideology.

§ 2. Guarantees of the Principle

173. Soviet conception of the problem

How is respect for socialist legality on the part of administrators, as well as people in general, to be guaranteed? In the broad sense it is assured by the entire range of institutions set up in the socialist state and by the consensus of the people who must be convinced of the excellence of their regime and its laws. This point of view, valid for all societies, is particularly true of the Soviet Union and other socialist countries.[36] There the advent of a society in which all coercion will be banished is predicted; henceforth, it is emphasised, the social order is to be assured by extremely varied techniques, in which state bodies, unions, the press and all citizens will fully and freely participate.

According to Soviet authors, the most fundamental guarantee of socialist legality lies in the fact that individual interests and the general social interest are in complete accord—an accord which, in a socialist regime, is assured by the collectivisation of the means of

---

[35] Knapp (V.), *Filosofické problémy socialistického práva* (1967).
[36] *Cf.* the different articles in the work previously cited, *Le concept de la légalité dans les pays socialistes* (1961), especially the report at pp. 327–336 and the article at pp. 91–115 of Professor M. Jaroszyński.

production which brings about the disappearance of any exploitation of man by man. Only within the framework of such a regime is it possible to expect—from both administrators and citizens— civic spirit and virtue which cannot exist in a country of socially antagonistic classes.

And so the guarantees of socialist legality in the U.S.S.R. are manifold.[37] A Soviet professor, G. I. Pietrov, mentions the activity of local soviets at many different levels of government and administration, that of the Control Commission of the Council of Ministers of the U.S.S.R., the varied inspections taking place within the administration, as well as the activity of the *Prokuratura* and the courts, the surveillance of social organisations and especially the unions, and the widely recognised right to lodge complaints and claims which administrative bodies are obliged to investigate.

In this work it is not possible to study all such guarantees and therefore examine all the institutions of Soviet law. Having placed them in a fairly general context by showing that the principle of socialist legality is guaranteed in many ways, our examination here will be limited to three particular institutions designed for this purpose. These institutions are the *Prokuratura* or Procurator's Office, the People's Control Commission and the *Advokatura* or College of Advocates.

174. The Prokuratura

In order to guarantee the principle of socialist legality a special institution, known as the Prokuratura, has been organised in the U.S.S.R.[38]

The creation of the Prokuratura in the Soviet Union dates from 1922, but it recalls to mind an ancient Russian institution created by Peter the Great in 1722—"the eyes of the monarch"—by means of which agents of the central power were posted in the provinces to watch over the legality of the acts carried out by administrative authorities. It was suppressed in 1864 in favour of a department of

---

[37] Pietrov (G. I.), *Le concept de la légalité dans les pays socialistes* (1961), pp. 375–376. Akademija Nauk SSSR, Institut Gosudarstva i Prava, *Pravovye garantii zakonnosti v SSSR* (under the direction of S. Strogovič, 1962).

[38] *Cf.* Timasheff (N. S.), "The Procurator's Office in the U.S.S.R." in *Law in Eastern Europe* (1958), p. 8. Collignon (J. G.), *Les juristes en Union Soviétique* (Paris thesis) (1974), p. 339.

state attorneys of the French type (*ministère public*). This department, associated in the mind of the public with the autocratic regime of the tsars, was abolished on November 24, 1918, along with the courts, and local authorities were therefore left with complete discretion. Although the present Prokuratura was re-established at the time of the N.E.P. in 1922, it is a return to the pre-1864 tradition. The 1936 Constitution confirmed the principle, and it is at present regulated by an ordinance of November 30, 1979.

The Prokuratura, since 1936, has been a completely autonomous body; its sole head is the procurator-general of the U.S.S.R. It is an indication of the Prokuratura's full independence that this official, enjoying the rank of a minister, is appointed for a period of five years (an altogether exceptional term in the U.S.S.R.) by the Supreme Soviet to which he reports directly and exclusively. He therefore appears as a kind of symbol of the permanence and authority of the law.

The Prokuratura is a highly developed part of the administration with numerous branches. Under the procurator-general, and appointed by him for a period of five years and strictly subject to his orders, are the procurators of the Soviet Socialist Republics, who in turn appoint the procurators of the provinces, districts or departments and towns. There are also special sections of the Prokuratura in the armed forces, work camps and a special division to watch over state security agencies. Its double function, in general supervision and collaboration with the courts, will now be examined.

175. The role of general supervision

The main function of the Soviet Prokuratura is to safeguard the respect for socialist legality. It is a body set up for purposes of surveillance rather than administration. It never renders a decision itself, but is limited to exercising a supervisory control and bringing illegalities or irregularities to the attention of the administrative, judicial or governmental bodies whose function it is to take the appropriate action.

The main role of the Prokuratura is one of "general supervision." One of its members attends meetings of the executive committees of local soviets and can therefore prevent illegal decisions or the passage of illegal resolutions. The Prokuratura moreover undertakes a systematic examination of all administrative acts, some of which must in law be obligatorily communicated to it before becoming executory. It may also be seized, by way of complaint or petition from interested persons, of any case in which there has been a violation of the law. It thus exercises a general control over the whole administration.

If the Prokuratura does uncover an irregularity, its agents are bound to raise the appropriate objection on pain of their own disciplinary or penal liability. In some cases a time-limit is provided. The law also determines to whom the objection must be addressed—either to the authority that has made the questionable decisions, to a higher authority or, if necessary, to the judicial authorities. If the authority, once notified of an illegal measure, does not then annul or modify it within a specified delay (generally ten days), the Prokuratura is bound to seize a superior authority of the matter. In principle the objection of the Prokuratura does not have the effect of suspending the act complained of, but there are many exceptions to this general rule. If the act infringes upon the rights of citizens or legally protected freedoms, the act is suspended in its effects upon the lodging of the objection until such time as the competent authority has decided the matter.

Practice has shown that the Prokuratura effectively exercises this supervisory role. In all the cases reported[39] it appears that the objections raised by the Prokuratura were found to have been justified. It is worth noting however that the review in which they are reported (*Socialist Legality*[40]) is published by the Prokuratura itself. Its interventions appear to have occurred principally in labour law matters and in relation to the measures taken by local authorities. The decrees of more highly placed organs are less exposed to its criticisms because such bodies have in their own right greater administrative expertise and a greater ability to study matters in depth.[41] There is no lack of examples, however, of a decision of a ministry, or of the council or ministers of an autonomous republic or even of a Soviet Socialist Republic, being

---

[39] *Cf.* Morgan (G. G.), "The Protests and Representations lodged by the Soviet Procuracy against the Legality of Government Enactments, 1937–1964," *Legal Controls in the Soviet Union, Law in Eastern Europe* (1966), No. 13, pp. 103–286. The author analyses 242 cases. This study is carried forward by Boim (L.), "Protests of the Procuracy in the U.S.S.R., 1965–1973" *Law in Eastern Europe*, Vol. 20.

[40] *Sotsialistitcheskaya Zakonnost'*.

[41] Berezovskaja (S. G.), *Ohrana prav graždan sovetskoj prokuratoroj* (1964), p. 137.

annulled. In 1960, for example, the procurator-general of the U.S.S.R. obtained the quashing of a decree of the Lithuanian S.S.R. Council of Ministers which had prohibited the sale of cattle by citizens and *kolkhozi* outside the country.

But the role of general supervision of the Prokuratura is not limited to seeking to strike down acts violating socialist legality. It may also intervene directly by way of "representations" (*predstav-lenie*) if it is of the view that some state agency or organ is, in a general sense, in violation of legality by refraining, for example, from decisions or actions that fall within its function. The bodies to which such representations are directed must report back, within a delay fixed by law, how they intend to rectify the situation. If the Prokuratura is not satisfied with the response, it will then carry the matter to the appropriate administrative or judicial authority for penal or other disciplinary action.

176. The role of collaboration with the courts

The Prokuratura also has a role of collaboration with the courts. It is charged with instituting actions in criminal matters[42] and may take the initiative in a civil action, as well as filing memoranda and conclusions in the court. It is charged with the surveillance of prisons. No person may be detained without an order from the judicial authority or the consent of the Prokuratura, and the latter may order the release of any person illegally detained; this is one of the rare instances where the Prokuratura itself is authorised to intervene directly.

In civil as well as criminal matters, therefore, the Prokuratura assumes the functions which in the West devolve to the department of a *ministère public* or to an attorney-general. Its role is much more extensive, however, because of the increased intervention of public authorities in all areas, as well, perhaps, because of its great power and extensive personnel,[43] and the further fact that judges are not necessarily legally trained in the Soviet judicial organisation. All these factors, and the desire to convince the population that it henceforth lives in a wholly just society, encourage the Prokuratura to participate actively in many cases—either

---

[42] In political matters the role of prosecutor falls to the K.G.B. (the State Security Committee).

[43] It was estimated that in 1971 it had 18,000 employees.

by instituting actions itself, intervening in trials already begun, exercising remedies against a decision which in its opinion is incorrect or supervising the execution of judicial decisions. A provision of 1955 even allows it to take action against a decision of the *plenum* of the Supreme Court of the U.S.S.R. and to take cases decided there to the Praesidium of the Supreme Soviet. This provision is a good indication of the great concern of present Soviet leaders that the principle of legality be exalted and given full effect.

177. Other socialist countries

As an institution, the Prokuratura has been adopted in other European socialist nations. It has, however, been criticised in various countries on the ground that it was ineffective in preventing many serious violations of socialist legality during the Stalinist era. In those countries in which it was adopted, the Prokuratura is understaffed and working with out of date structures, and its action has been limited to the traditional role of superintending the administration of justice rather than exercising, as much as would be desirable, a more general administrative supervision. In many of these countries, before they became socialist, there were administrative courts that held the government to respect for the law and which were much esteemed by the public. It is now therefore sometimes asked whether it was a good idea to have abolished them in favour of the Soviet system.

There is no obstacle in principle to the re-establishment of the former administrative courts. But other paths have nevertheless been pursued. A reform of the Prokuratura itself, first of all, was undertaken in Czechoslovakia in 1956 in an attempt to render it more efficient. Its function of surveillance has, elsewhere, been enhanced by regulating more precisely the procedures by which the administration must act; thus codes of administrative (non-contentious) procedure have been enacted in Czechoslovakia (1955), Hungary (1957), Yugoslavia (1957) and Poland (1960). There is moreover no objection to creating other forms of control in addition to that exercised by the Prokuratura and, in particular, by enlarging the jurisdiction of the ordinary courts so as to allow interested persons to contest the legality of administrative acts. The Rumanian Constitution of 1965 has anticipated this possibility and a 1967 law permits private persons to take legal action against individual administrative acts, saving those decided upon by the Council of Ministers. In Yugoslavia administrative decisions are subject to judicial review in the ordinary courts. Further improvement can be sought, finally, by having the people participate more fully in the public administration. This last technique, especially, has attracted attention, so certain does it seem that the work of civic education drawing on popular feelings will always be, in the final analysis, and in all countries, the best guarantee of the principle of socialist legality.[44]

178. People's Control Commission

The control of legality is a formidable task in a country the size of the U.S.S.R. where the whole economy is collectivised. The Prokuratura, which specialises in the field of law and administration, therefore, has its parallel in the realm of the economy and finance. This body is the People's Control Commission, formerly the Party and State Control Commission, reporting to the Supreme Soviet of the U.S.S.R., its Praesidium and to the Council of Ministers of the U.S.S.R. and now regulated by a decree of November 30, 1979. But the role of the Commission goes beyond a mere control. It must ensure that important decisions taken in the economic field are effectively observed; it must defeat the tendency of any body or person to approach problems from the point of view of one branch of the administration only or with only local interests in mind. It must fight against bureaucracy and delays, and devise measures which might improve the functioning of the Soviets or administrative bodies of one kind or another in the Soviet Union.

179. Advocates: the Advokatura in the U.S.S.R.

The institution of advocates in the U.S.S.R. was originally viewed with some mistrust. The bar was suppressed after the October Revolution, at a time when it was thought possible to attain the communist era immediately; there was to be no need for courts or auxiliaries of justice in a regime where there would be no

---

[44] Wasilkowska (Z.), "Les taches de la commission de codification" *Państwo i Prawo* (January, 1957).

more law. These illusions were short-lived, but it took some time for the restoration of a professional bar to be allowed. Since that time a consistent effort has been made to see in the advocate—who also fulfils the function of solicitor, according to Russian tradition—a true auxiliary of justice striving for socialist legality, rather than a legal representative or defender concerned only with the interests of his client. For this reason in the U.S.S.R. at one time there were simply lists of legal experts who might either be employed as defending or prosecuting attorneys, and who received a salary from the state whenever the court called upon them to exercise such functions. This experiment and the one following, in which lawyers practised without fees and in addition to another often more principal activity, were abandoned in 1922. Since that date a professional bar has existed in the U.S.S.R. and today it is mainly regulated by a law of November 30, 1979, on the *Advokatura*[45] or College of Advocates.

There are important differences between the ways in which the legal profession is conceived and organised in Western countries and the U.S.S.R. According to the Soviet idea, the advocate must be thought of as a member of a team, made up of the judge, the prosecutor and himself. All three collaborate by attempting to examine the matter before the court in all its aspects; the advocate must not think of himself principally as an adversary of the public official with whom he appears before a judge who alone has the duty to discover the truth. Thus, if the advocate is convinced of the guilt of his client, he must not attempt to hide it from the court,[46] nor make the crime appear less serious than it really is. He must call attention to whatever may attenuate the responsibility of his client; but he must never lose sight of the interests of society and always keep in mind the impression his pleading might have on those attending the hearing. If, during interviews with his client, he gathers information affecting the security of the state, he is bound—more than any other citizen—to bring it to the attention

---

[45] On the whole of this evolution, *cf.* Hazard (J. N.), *Settling Disputes in Soviet Society. The Formative Years of Legal Institutions* (1960). Poltorak (A.) and Zaitsev (E.), *Le Barreau soviétique* (1963). Friedman (L. M.) and Ziles (Z. L.), "Soviet Legal Profession. Recent Developments in Law and Practice" Wisconsin L. R. 32–77 (1964). Hazard (J. N.), *Managing Change in the U.S.S.R. The Politico-Legal Role of the Soviet Jurist* (1983).

[46] Before 1958 the advocate in such a situation was advised to abandon the defence of his client, but the Fundamental Principles of criminal procedure of 1958 now forbid him this course.

of the competent authorities. It is evident that the Soviet lawyer is first and foremost an auxiliary of justice and a servant of socialist legality. To a certain extent this conception deviates from the prevailing practice in bourgeois countries, where the judge is called upon to play the role of an arbiter between the prosecution, represented by the public prosecutor or some other person, and the defence, to which the advocate devotes himself without the restrictions imposed in the U.S.S.R.

The Soviet idea of the advocate's role is reinforced in practice by the collective organisation of the U.S.S.R. bar. Interested persons may certainly indicate their preference for a particular lawyer, but they must always apply to a group of lawyers (*Kollegija*) to designate the advocate who will plead their case. It is the director of the "collective" who determines the fees payable by the client according to a fixed tariff. The client pays these sums to the group which then divides its revenue each month on a scheduled basis. This depersonalisation of the relationship between client and lawyer prevents any danger of collusion and, in the minds of Soviet jurists, should serve to impress upon the advocate the idea that he serves the interests of society as much, if not more, than those of his client. The notions entertained immediately after the Revolution have, moreover, been abandoned in the interests of socialist legality, and it is increasingly emphasised that advocates must be qualified jurists; in principle, only those who have completed university studies in law can be admitted to the practice of law.

The professional lawyer in the U.S.S.R. today is free from the suspicion and low esteem in which he was held shortly after the Revolution. The end of the Stalinist era favoured a return to the humanist outlook and a greater effort was made to defend accused persons, in order to give effect to the fundamental principles of justice set forth in the Constitution.[47] Among lawyers at the present time there are many members of the Communist Party, and articles have been published aimed at rehabilitating the profession by emphasising that Lenin was a lawyer. However, the legal profession at present offers only a mediocre income to practitioners; most of the activities which make it profitable in the West have in effect now disappeared in the U.S.S.R. with the suppression of

---

[47] On the practice in this respect, *cf.* Hazard (J. N.), Butler (W. E.) and Maggs (P. B.), *The Soviet Legal System* (1977), pp. 77–81.

private commerce, and the organisation of legal departments in public enterprises has removed the need for consulting lawyers. A Soviet lawyer's work is thus principally in the criminal law field; his services in civil cases are called for in only 5 per cent. or 6 per cent. of cases. Thus there are relatively few lawyers in the U.S.S.R.— 19,000 in 1980 for the entire country, 96 per cent. of whom have done graduate work and 60 per cent. of whom are members of the Communist Party.

180. Other socialist countries

Several additional observations may be made which indicate a number of differences between the various people's republics and the U.S.S.R. In Czechoslovakia, the professional organisation of advocates is based on that of the U.S.S.R.; they are grouped into "colleges." Legislation of December 1963 has made the same system obligatory in Poland. In Yugoslavia, on the other hand, they exercise their profession on an individual basis and sometimes in association with others. Lawyers enjoy full independence in their work. They are registered in the bar of the republic in which they practise and the bars of the various republics are grouped within a federal bar.

TITLE II

SOURCES OF SOCIALIST LAW

181. Introduction

By sources of law, Soviet jurists mean first and foremost the economic infrastructure which, according to Marxist teaching, both conditions and determines the legal system of any country. In this sense, then, the fundamental source of Soviet law is composed of two factors: the collectivisation of the means of production and the establishment in the U.S.S.R. of the proletarian dictatorship. The techniques by which legal rules are developed or defined in any given place or at any time are, in Soviet doctrine, sources of law in only a secondary sense. While taking into account the country's economic and political structure, it is the study of these technical matters that will be undertaken here, with a view to determining the role played by legislation, decided cases and other factors in the development of law in the U.S.S.R.

CHAPTER I

LEGISLATION

182. Pre-eminence of legislation

Legislation in the broad sense is evidently and without doubt the main source of Soviet law. This fact may create the impression that, on this point at least, there is a similarity between Soviet and Romano-Germanic laws. The similarity, however is no more than superficial. The importance of legislation in Romano-Germanic countries derives from the belief that it is the clearest, and therefore the most satisfactory, way of *expressing* legal rules. In socialist countries, on the other hand, the primacy of legislation derives from the attitude that enacted law is the most natural way of *creating* law because law is seen as the will of the country's rulers. Legislation, moreover, in socialist countries, is pre-eminent because rapid and revolutionary social change is wanted in short order. The dynamism of Soviet law itself naturaly leads to an exaltation of the role of legislation when contrasted to the slower evolution that takes place through judicial decisions and the development of custom.

On the purely technical level as well, legislative texts are very different in Romano-Germanic and socialist countries. Marxist-Leninist doctrine views the political and economic organisation of power very differently from what they are in the western democracies.

SECTION I—THE SOVIET UNION

183. Rejection of the separation of powers

To begin with, there is a difference in policy outlook. In continental European countries, a distinction is often drawn between law in the formal and material senses. Law in the formal sense is

226

the statute voted by parliament and promulgated by the executive power; in the material sense it is any act which, though not necessarily emanating from the legislative power, contains provisions of a general nature prescribing compliance with certain rules of conduct.

This distinction is not simply descriptive. In the liberal democracies it is considered legitimate. According to the principle known as the separation of powers, an effort is made in these countries to achieve a balance of power. It is normal in these circumstances that rules of conduct prescribed by law should come from different sources and that the privilege of creating them not be exclusive to one of those powers.

Marxist-Leninist doctrine rejects the principle of the separation of powers. It has had ample opportunity to demonstrate how, in the reality of the modern world, this principle has increasingly weakened the role of real law—that is to say, the statutes enacted by the legislature—to the benefit of other "powers," especially the executive or administrative.[1] The development of the practice of legislating by way of decree, the new distinction between the province of legislation and that of regulation made in France by the Constitution of 1958, and the independence of the judiciary in Common law countries, are all denounced as ingenious tricks geared to undermine the principle of the people's sovereignty. In the U.S.S.R. these practices, being contrary to a true democracy, are not tolerated; all power is concentrated in the hands of the Supreme Soviet, under the Constitution; and, in each S.S.R., all power is concentrated in the Supreme Soviet of the Republic. The Councils of Ministers of the U.S.S.R. and the S.S.R. and all branches of the administration and all judges are subordinate to these Supreme Soviets. There is no question of a separation or a balance of powers; at most there is a sharing of functions among different bodies of the state administration, courts and the Prokuratura; but it is inadmissible that administrative agencies or courts should set themselves up as the equals of the Supreme Soviet in which, as the highest organ of the state, all powers are vested according to the principle of unified power held in the Soviet Union.

---

[1] Zivs (S. L.), *Razvitie formy prava v sovremennyh imperialističeskih gosudarstvah* (1960); Burdeau (G.), "Le déclin de la loi," *Archives de philosophie du droit*, no. 8: *Le Dépassement du droit*, 1963, pp. 35–54.

Legislative power is exercised by the Supreme Soviet of the U.S.S.R. or those of the S.S.R.[2]; and no one in the U.S.S.R. is disposed to weaken or deflect this principle by recognising a distinction between laws in a formal and material sense. It is thought that law in a material sense must also be law in the formal sense, unless the Constitution is to be rendered meaningless.

184. Application of the principle

There is one difficulty, however. How is it possible to apply this principle in practice so that all the laws of a society as complex as the U.S.S.R. are to be the work of the legislature? Soviet doctrine considers the practice of legislating by way of decree and the recognition and extension of an autonomous regulatory power, both of which are observable in bourgeois countries, to be the results of a conspiracy against the sovereignty of the people. But jurists of bourgeois countries explain this evolution differently—simply as a result of the increased number of tasks assumed by the state and imposed by the necessities of efficient administration. How, in the U.S.S.R., has it been possible to reconcile the respect for popular sovereignty with this need for efficient administration?

One method might have been to increase the sphere of competence and the powers of the local soviets which, like the supreme soviets, express the popular will. This communalisation of power has not been, however, the means generally followed up to the present time, even though the competence of local soviets has been enlarged in recent years.

Another means has been in fact adopted. The practice of decree-laws is unknown in the U.S.S.R. and legislative power is never delegated to state administrative organs such as the Council of Ministers. But the needs of efficiency are satisfied, without affecting principles, by the practice of the Supreme Soviet authorising a permanent delegation of power between sessions to its *Praesidium*. Legislation thus remains the exclusive production of the legislative authority, although in fact it is most often the creation of the Praesidium, the decisions of which are merely ratified by the Supreme Soviet. The number and the length of these

---

[2] The ability to propose legislation, on the other hand, also lies with the U.S.S.R. Supreme Court, the Procurator-General of the U.S.S.R. and the people's organisations, under article 113 of the 1977 Constitution.

sessions of the Supreme Soviet make this clear—the U.S.S.R. Supreme Soviet in general holds only two sessions each year and these last no more than two or three days each.[3] The Supreme Soviet itself is only called upon to vote directly the more important legislation (the Constitution, approval of the social and economic development plans, codes or fundamental principles of legislation). On these occasions it is seen as important that the representatives of the people themselves, after a debate that will have exalted the progress which the measure represents in the construction of socialism, actually vote the law, which will be passed unanimously. All other legislation is adopted by orders or decrees of the Praesidium of the Supreme Soviet or by orders or ordinances of the Council of Ministers. It should also be noted that the Supreme Soviet can freely amend the U.S.S.R. Constitution and that in these circumstances there is no judicial control whatsoever over the constitutionality of legislation.

The Council of Ministers is authorised under the Constitution to issue decrees and make regulations but this can only be done "on the basis of and for the furtherance of statutes in force." There is no autonomous regulatory power recognised in the Soviet Union. In fact, however, the broad language used in the texts of statutes and ordinances leaves to the administrative authorities a very considerable latitude, and most of the measures which regulate life in the Soviet Union have been decided upon by the Council of Ministers or its subordinate authorities.[4]

Moreover, whether one considers the activities of the Praesidium or of the Council of Ministers, it must be borne in mind, in order to have a realistic view of the situation, that there are close ties between these two organs and the U.S.S.R. Communist Party. Under the 1977 Constitution, article 6, the Party directs and orients Soviet society; it is the central element of the political system and of all state and social organs. The Secretary-General of the Party has become the chief of state, a function before 1977 carried out by the *Praesidium*. In fact, the new Constitution has

---

[3] There is a tendency today to increase the role of the Supreme Soviet by developing the number and activities of the standing committees of this Soviet. Lesage (M.), *Les régimes politiques de l'U.R.S.S. et de l'Europe de l'Est* (1971).

[4] Gélard (P.), "La loi, le décret et l'arrêté en Union soviétique" *L'actualité en U.R.S.S.* (*Droit et science politique*), 1967, pp. 81–107 and, by the same author, *L'activité et le fonctionnement du Soviet Suprême de l'U.R.S.S.* (1965–1972), *Ann. de l'U.R.S.S. et des pay socialistes européens* (1972–1973).

merely enshrined previous practice. Before 1977 the Communist Party had full direction of all national business. While decisions are theoretically made by the Party's Central Committee they are, in reality, the work of the *Politburo* or policy office assisted by the Secretariat.[5]

185. Soviet federalism

The U.S.S.R., made up of fifteen Soviet Socialist Republics (S.S.R), is a federal state. The size of the country and the many nationalities co-existing within it make necessary this federal structure which the tsarist regime had never managed to set up.[6] The Supreme Soviet is made up of two chambers. Since the Constitution of 1977 (art. 110), there is an equal number of members in each chamber. Alongside the *Soviet of the Union* to which members are elected in proportion to the number of inhabitants without reference to the division into republics, the U.S.S.R. Supreme Soviet also has a *Soviet of Nationalities* within which that division is operative, as well as the existence of the autonomous republics, regions or districts within each S.S.R. Soviet federalism is however tempered by reason of the fact that the Communist Party is centrally organised, without any reference to the federal structure, and the various S.S.R. governments are in fact dominated by the Party.

Since the U.S.S.R. is a federal state, there is a division of power between federal authorities and those of the federated republics. The development of the relationship between federal legislative competence and that of the S.S.R. which has taken place since the death of Stalin must be noted. The 1936 Constitution had made provision for the working out of legislation or federal codes for numerous branches of the law: judicial organisation and procedure, criminal law and private law. In fact, however, no federal law other than that of 1938 relative to judicial organisation, had been promulgated in execution of this constitutional provision. The preparatory work on federal codes only went as far as first drafts which remained unpublished. After 1953 there was a reac-

---

[5] The Central Committee at the present time has 319 regular members and 151 alternate members, to which are added the 75 members of the Central Examination Committee. The Politburo has 14 regular and eight alternate members. The Secretariat has a secretary-general and nine assistant secretary-generals. The Central Committee generally holds two very short meetings each year.

[6] Lalcharrière (G. de), *L'idée fédérale en Russie de Riourik à Staline 862–1945*, (1945).

tion against the excessive centralisation of the Stalinist period. The 1936 Constitution was amended and the newly admitted principle was re-affirmed in the 1977 Constitution (art. 73): apart from a customs code (1964), a commercial navigation code (1968) and a code of air law (1961), the Supreme Soviet charged with the task of ensuring the uniformity of legislation throughout the whole country, has enacted "fundamental principles of legislation," on the basis of which each S.S.R. then enacts its own legislation and codes.

186. Fundamental principles of law and recent codes

The drafting of these "fundamental principles" has been actively pursued since the constitutional reform just mentioned. Fundamental principles were promulgated on December 25, 1958 respecting judicial organisation, criminal law and criminal procedure; the fundamental principles of civil law and civil procedure were promulgated December 8, 1961. Those relating to family and agrarian law came into force in 1968, those on corrective labour and public health in 1969, those relating to work and water legislation in 1970 and those on national education in 1973. The principles relating to administrative infractions and to housing were enacted in 1980 and 1981. The work of codification, undertaken on the basis of these principles, has been carried out assiduously in the different republics. The largest of the Soviet Socialist Republics, the Russian Soviet Federated Socialist Republic (R.S.F.S.R.), promulgated its new law on judicial organisation, as well as its new criminal code and code of criminal procedure, in 1960; in 1964 it adopted its new civil code and code of civil procedure, its marriage and family code in 1969 and its agrarian code in 1970.

The provisions enacted in the "fundamental principles" are generally reproduced *verbatim* in the codes, except for necessary adaptations. The laws or codes established on the basis of these principles are nevertheless much more detailed: the law on the judicial organisation of the Republic mentioned above, for example, contains 64 articles compared to 39 in the fundamental principles; the number of articles for the criminal code is 269 (principles: 47), and for the code of criminal procedure 413 (principles: 54); the civil code has 569 articles based on 106 articles in the principles. These figures are interesting because they given an idea of the margin of autonomy left to each S.S.R. In general this autonomy is only very moderately exercised. There is no organisation attempting to coordinate the codes and to assure their uniformity, but a practice of communicating a draft code to other S.S.R. does exist, and there is, in fact, some attempt made to have the codes as similar as possible.

187. Ordinances of the Praesidium

The conditions under which the Supreme Soviets of the U.S.S.R. and the S.S.R. meet and function are such that the number of actual laws (*zakoni*) passed by them is very small. This procedure is only used when a law is to be given special solemnity. In practice, laws are most often replaced by ordinances (*ukazi*) drawn up by the Praesidium of the Supreme Soviet; this practice seems so natural that it has been used in some cases to change the Constitution. The Supreme Soviets restrict themselves to approving *en bloc*, in each session, the *ukazi* drawn up by their Praesidium during the interval between sessions and without discussing their provisions.[7]

Laws and ordinances form the basis of the Soviet legal order. Both are easily accessible and are in fact published in the various official journals of the U.S.S.R. and the S.S.R. Chronological and special subject editions have recently been published for the laws of both the U.S.S.R. and the various S.S.R.

188. Other types of regulation

The measures decided upon by the Council of Ministers and the various ministries of the U.S.S.R. and the S.S.R., on the basis and in the execution of laws, vary in nature and form. These may be decrees of the Council of Ministers or an individual ministry, sometimes endorsed by the Central Committee of the Communist Party; ministerial decisions, collective agreements, or general terms of delivery or transport approved by one or several of the interested ministries; model statutes for *kolkhozi*, *sovkhozi* or artisanal enterprises, or statutes for a particular group of enterprises or combines; instructions addressed to a branch of the

---

[7] The Supreme Soviet adopts only a few laws each year (less than ten) whereas the Praesidium will issue several times more that many decrees.

administration or to a category of industries. The complexity of this regulation is considerable and surpasses that already deplored in bourgeois countries. One of the reasons lies in the second factor mentioned earlier—the national collectivisation of the economy—which considerably changes the role of legislation in socialist countries.

189. Role of government administration in Soviet economy

Because of the collectivisation of the means of production, and the authoritarian state planning which governs national economic development, the government administration in socialist countries has to assume tasks in the economic field which are not comparable to those of governments in the liberal democracies. The difference is not merely quantitative but also, so to speak, qualitative. Since the industries of the economic sector are collectivised and have the appearance of so many "public bodies," it becomes rather arbitrary, despite their admitted managerial and accounting autonomy, to attempt to distinguish clearly between different forms of "administrative" acts on one hand and "contractual" acts concluded by enterprises or groups of enterprises on the other.

In free enterprise democracies—but because these are becoming less and less free—there is a host of regulations, decrees and orders which put into actual application the laws passed by the legislature. In these countries there does nevertheless exist a vast area where the free play of private enterprise is possible. Business, industrial or agricultural ventures are increasingly subject to a framework of regulations within which they must organise their activity; they nonetheless retain a large measure of freedom respecting their direction of development, the degree of expansion they hope to carry out, the location of their branch offices, the choice of clients with whom they will deal and so on. The scope for action by the head of the enterprise and the principle of contractual freedom are subject to increasing restrictions; they are nonetheless still the rule and this, despite all these restrictions, enables us to speak of free democracies.

The opposite is true of the U.S.S.R., a socialist democracy. There the *raison d'être* and the mission of all enterprises is to carry out the plan for national economic development. Their activity is both defined and limited by the statutes handed down to them by the state and by the provisions of the plan. They must accomplish what is imposed upon them by the plan and cannot exceed the sphere of action allotted to them according to their particular status. From this double rule derives the unprecedented importance of administrative regulation in the U.S.S.R. Apart from the functions which appertain to it in the free nations, the socialist government administration, through its regulations and decrees and other instruments, must fulfil the greater part of the economic role which in other countries is undertaken on the initiative of private enterprise. There is, therefore, a countless mass of different measures, with various names, flowing from the several ministries; a western author has estimated that in the first fifty years of the Soviet regime there were no less than 390,000 ministerial orders of which about 15,000 remained in force in 1967.

Legal writers in free democracies make a very clear distinction between the decree or regulation and the departmental administrative memorandum on one hand, and the administrative act and the contract on the other. In Soviet law these distinctions are blurred, if not altogether inexistent.

190. Regulations and departmental instructions

The essential difference between the regulation and the departmental instruction is that the first lays down obligatory rules for all, whereas the second is restricted to giving administrative directives which do not establish rules of law. In fact, however, the governmental administrative agencies in the free democracies are hardly ever concerned with the legality of the departmental instructions received; they apply them just as they would true rules of law. This attitude and identification cannot but be reinforced in the U.S.S.R., because there all important acts of economic life are carried out by public establishments. These may very well be autonomous, but they are nonetheless subject to a ministry. That they make any distinction therefore between regulations and departmental instructions is unlikely.[8]

---

[8] What is true of the economic sector is equally so of others. Art. 58(1)(*c*) of the former code of criminal procedure provided, in certain cases, for the punishment of members of the family of a delinquent (in cases of desertion or treason). This article fell into disuse even before it was removed from Soviet legislation by the introduction of the new codes because the organs of the Prokuratura received instructions not to institute suits to ensure its application.

191. Administrative acts and contracts

In the same way, the distinction between the administrative act and the contract becomes blurred in the conditions created by the Soviet economic structure. Contracts between public establishments have their origin in the requirements of the national plan for economic development. Their basic role is to put into concrete form the elements of the plan to which they constitute a sort of appendix. Only in appearance are they equivalent to the freely— anarchically, say the Marxists—concluded contracts of the capitalist economies. In the U.S.S.R. it seemed advantageous to retain the technique of contracts in the collectivised sector; but this is explained more by a desire for good administrative management than to allow for a sphere of free action to industrial leaders. It is perfectly conceivable that contracts could be wholly suppressed in the relations between establishments or organisations of the collectivised sector. It would suffice to articulate the plan in greater detail and to have the appropriate administrative organs intervene, and in this way contracts would become unnecessary. This is inconceivable in free economies, but it is by no means so in socialist economies where, apart from matters of principle, the problem of the inter-play between administrative acts of planning and contracts only brings up the question of the respective advantages of centralisation and decentralisation in administrative and economic life. Unlike the capitalist democracies, there is no question of finding the best balance between the contradictory demands of authority and freedom.

192. Difficulties of documentation

Relative to the above passage and keeping in mind the absence of distinctions between regulations, departmental instructions and even contracts, it is very difficult to gather satisfactory legal documentation on any point whatsoever of Soviet administrative or economic life. In the U.S.S.R. the dividing line between what concerns the public in general and what concerns only one or more industries—and, therefore, between what must normally be published and what need not be—is not clearly drawn by means of a distinction in principle. More subtle criteria may be used or, what is even more likely, the choice may be based altogether on practical considerations. This empiricism is traditional. Before ministries were introduced in Russia, each of the old bureaux (*prikaz*) built up for its own use collections of administrative acts affecting the activities of its agents—and these collections were accessible only to such agents. In modern terms the situation would be described as follows: there were no rules of public law, properly speaking, only administrative practices or customs; there were no regulations, only departmental orders. The tradition of the old Russian *prikaz* has been revived in present Soviet practice.[9] Each ministry compiles one or more collections of administrative provisions affecting its own agents or establishments whose activity it directs and controls. These collections are intended for internal use and are only distributed to subordinate services or establishments. They are not for sale and they are not usually to be found even in Soviet public libraries. Official journals only publish those measures which for some reason are to be given wide publicity. All other acts are seen as having a somewhat confidential nature, like the internal departmental instructions in most branches of a western government administration. Fear of economic espionage has thus revived an old Russian practice in the U.S.S.R. This by no means facilitates the task of anyone wishing, in good faith, to study the workings of Soviet institutions. Even Soviet writers complain of the difficulties of obtaining primary source materials. In this respect the situation of Soviet law is far from satisfactory for legal scholarship. It is only fair to say, however, that even in the free democracies the study of law is often reduced to mere theory, since the actual practices of the *milieu* in question are not always readily known and are often considered by those belonging to it to be confidential and of no concern to outsiders.

It has already been observed that in the respective domains of administrative acts and contracts, there is a swing of the pendulum between advance and retreat, centralisation and decentralisation; there is a similar swing, depending on the period, in the amount of publicity given to administrative measures. The value of codifying the substantive rules of administrative law, such as has been attempted in France since 1945, is under discussion but in general the idea is still rejected. On the other hand, the possibility of a code regulating non-contentious administrative procedures is more favourably regarded.

---

[9] Loeber (D. A.), "Legal Rules for Internal Use Only" (1970) 19 Int. & Comp. L.Q. 70.

193. Interpretation and application of the law

The Soviet regime, guided by the Communist Party, is attempting to create an entirely new social order through legislation. The leaders' will is expressed and their policies enforced by promulgated laws and subordinate administrative regulations. Like any new body of law, it is highly imperative in nature and its interpretation must conform strictly to the intention of its draftsmen. Soviet jurists and judges are expected to interpret the law so as to ensure its application in the manner envisaged by its authors.[10] The imperative rather than the rational side of a new body of law is, naturally enough, always emphasised.

It does not necessarily follow however that legal interpretation in the U.S.S.R. is always a purely literal one. The Romano-Germanic tradition persists on this point in the Soviet Union, and Marxist doctrine in no way implies that legislation must be literally applied according to a wholly grammatical interpretation. Such an attitude would result in making a "fetish" of the law as an end in itself, independent of its underlying policy and therefore in direct opposition to Marxist doctrine.

Consequently the interpretation of legislation by the Soviet judge is not grammatical but logical; it tends to interpret the real meaning of legislative texts, taking into account the whole of the system and principles by which the Soviet rulers' policy is unquestionably guided.[11] The Soviet attitude towards interpretation of legislation cannot be properly understood unless one takes into account Marxist-Leninist teaching. The laws, ordinances and decrees of Soviet law have been made by legislators imbued with these teachings. To give them full effect, their intention must be interpreted in the light of these doctrines. But this involves no risk of legislative subversion. Any comparison with the situation as it exists in capitalist countries would be false. There the judge has no sure guide; in fact, when the bourgeois judge purports to be taking the needs of society into consideration, it is his own personal ideol-

[10] It has however happened, although the instance is rare, that judicial decisions and legal authors have "interpreted" legislation in a spirit contrary to its original intention in order to arrive at a result considered desirable: Eorsi (G.), *Comparative Civil (Private) Law* (1979), no. 329.

[11] *Cf.* Ordinance No. 3 of the plenum of the U.S.S.R. Supreme Court of May 26, 1960, reproduced in Hazard (J. N.) and Shapiro (I.), *The Soviet Legal System* (1962), Pt. 2, p. 138. The Supreme Court declares that one of its ordinances rendered on May 5, 1950 has largely ceased to be applicable, because of new developments.

ogy that prevails. He thus falsifies the meaning of the law in a way
which naturally favours the interests of the ruling class. On the
other hand, by resorting to the principles of Marxist-Leninist
teaching, Soviet jurists clarify the meaning of the law which is in
complete harmony with this doctrine.

Although it was paramount for a considerable time, the present
role of Marxist doctrine in the Soviet Union as a guide for judges is
less important than it was. Formerly, since there was little legislation, the judge often had to look for the solution to a dispute in
the principles of Marxism-Leninism. The regime's first laws dealt
with this need by directing judges to be guided by the political
principles of the government of the Soviets, or to decide according
to their socialist sense of justice. Nowadays this vague kind of formula seems incompatible with the desired stringency of the principle of socialist legality and the strict discipline needed in society.
Soviet laws are numerous and detailed; it is by applying them that
the Soviet judge satisfies the socialist sense of justice to which he
need no longer refer as though it were an autonomous source of
law. The tendency now is to exclude from legislation such general
formulae as were found in the N.E.P. codes and simply to state in
detail their various possible applications. At the time of the
N.E.P., formulae of this type were indispensable since the legislators had not yet been able to draw up and perfect detailed provisions. Moreover, it was then necessary to keep close watch over
the capitalist elements allowed to remain in society. The usefulness of these formulae is however very much reduced at the present time, as there is not the slightest worry now in the U.S.S.R.
that the provisions of the law will be eluded in the name of vague
considerations of equity.

The elaboration of Fundamental Principles, promulgated in
1958 and 1961, has given us some idea of the different currents
which divide Soviet doctrine on this point. In the drafts of Fundamental Principles, as originally published, all general formulae had
disappeared. Only article 4 of the Fundamental Principles of Civil
Law specified that rights and obligations could arise outside those
cases provided for by law, "by virtue of general principles and
according to the spirit of the civil laws." On the other hand, the
famous provision of the 1922 Civil Code (art. 1), excluding legal
protection of civil rights when exercised contrary to the general
interest, was omitted. It is interesting however to note that a pro-

vision reproducing the substance of this article was finally re-intro-
duced into the Fundamental Principles of Civil Law: "Civil rights
are protected by the law, except in cases where they are exercised
contrary to the purpose of such rights in a socialist society during
the period of the building of communism" (art. 5, para. 1). The
Fundamental Principles of Civil Procedure also contain a provision
which was not in the draft: "In the absence of a law regulating the
dispute, the court is to be guided by the law regulating analogous
relationships; in the absence of such law, the court is to be guided
by the general principles and spirit of Soviet legislation" (art. 12,
para. 3). On the other hand, the possibility that criminal charges
could be admitted by means of analogy, included originally in
article 16 of the 1922 Criminal Code of the R.S.F.S.R. (in accordance, moreover, with the precedent established by the previous
Code of 1855 and retained until the revision of 1903), was dropped
in 1958.

In fact—as the discussion which took place on this subject indicates—there is a division in the U.S.S.R. between two contradictory tendencies. One tendency favours maximum rigour in
applying the law; the other advocates that equity be taken into
account and favours the exclusion of all formalism and making a
'fetish" of the law. The existence of two such tendencies is not
peculiar to the U.S.S.R. However it does have a particular aspect
in this country: that of being linked to a political option. The problem is not simply whether the law should be flexible or supple; it is
a question of knowing to what extent one can and must envisage,
as of now, and in relation to Marxist doctrine, the possibility of law
withering away and being superseded. The respect for socialist
legality is of course still obligatory; but it is difficult for a Marxist
to resign himself to injustice in the law. He tends to favour a legislative statement which provides some loophole when necessary,
just as he supports the many provisions of the law which free the
judge from formalism.[12]

194. Authentic interpretation of the law

A feature of Soviet law which should be mentioned in relation to
legal interpretation is the existence of institutions set up to provide

---

[12] *Cf.* especially art. 47 of the Fundamental Principles of Civil Procedure (1961): "No court
decision can be set aside for a matter of pure form when it is correct in substance." Bellon (J.),
Le Droit soviétique (1963), p. 106.

an "authentic" legal interpretation and to issue instructions concerning such interpretation to the organs responsible for administering justice. These are, aside from the Praesidium of the Supreme Soviet, the Supreme Court and the Chief Arbitrator of the U.S.S.R.

The present role of the U.S.S.R. Supreme Court, as we shall see, is more to give such instructions to judges than to revise decisions rendered in particular cases. Its mission is generally to watch over the way in which laws are interpreted and justice administered by the various existing courts. If, in the course of this surveillance, it notices any diversity in the interpretation of a particular law, it intervenes by issuing directives for the use of such courts.[13] Judges are obliged to abide by them, and it is up to the *Prokuratura* to intervene should the directives falsify the meaning of any particular legislation or be contrary to the law. It would seem however that this latter problem has never arisen.

What has been said concerning the authentic interpretation of Soviet Codes or laws by the Supreme Court also holds true for the Chief Arbitrator of the U.S.S.R. He examines the decisions of public arbitral bodies just as the Supreme Court examines those of the Soviet courts; and, in the same way, he formulates directives for their guidance.

Section II—Other Socialist Countries

195. Place of legislation

In the European socialist or people's republics, as in the U.S.S.R., legislation is the principal source of law. And, as in that country, state power is concentrated in the legislature which alone can establish national policy and enact law. The Rumanian Constitution of 1965, for example, specifically states that there is no autonomous power to make regulations.

But while the principles may be the same, there are numerous differences to be noted between the various socialist countries and

---

[13] For example, it intervened in December 1971 to instruct the courts on the interpretation of art. 7 of the Fundamental Principles of Civil Law relating to the honour and dignity of Soviet citizens when it appeared that there was a difference in application by the lower courts—some repressing any criticisms at all, others refusing to levy any sanction when the defendant had acted in good faith.

the U.S.S.R. Yugoslavia created a Court of Constitutional Justice in 1963 and it is empowered to request that the legislature re-examine a statute judged to be contrary to the Constitution. The law lapses if, within six months, the parliament has not amended it. Various statutes, and in particular legislation on social security, have been referred to the court in the course of litigation between citizens. A Constitutional Court was also set up in Czechoslovakia to watch over the division of legislative competence as between the federal authority and the federal units. Rumania in 1965 also insti-tuted a form of review of the constitutionality of legislation, but there it is undertaken by a committee drawn from the legislature itself.

Only Yugoslavia and, since 1968, Czechoslovakia are federal states; the division of legislative competence between the federal authority and the republics is not however the same as in the U.S.S.R.

In countries smaller and less populated than the U.S.S.R., and having a stronger parliamentary tradition, the legislative bodies meet more easily and are less prone than the Supreme Soviet to delegate their functions. The Polish Diet, for example, in which several political parties have representatives, plays an active part. It is altogether rare for its executive branch, the Council of State, to legislate in its place between sessions. Most draft laws prepared by the government are amended when presented to the Diet.

196. Codification

Extensive codification has been carried out since the commu-nists came to power, especially in countries such as Poland, Czechoslovakia and Yugoslavia where the unification of laws on a national scale was never accomplished earlier.[14] These codes, compiled in some haste, have in some instances been more recently replaced by others in which the progress towards socia-lism is more fully reflected. Poland adopted new codes in civil law, family law and procedure in 1964. Since then codes in penal law, criminal procedure, private international law, labour law and mar-itime law and administrative procedure have been promulgated; work is progressing on the codification of administrative law and

---

[14] "Codification in the Communist World." Symposium in memory of Zsolt Szirmoi, organ-ised by D. D. Barry, F. J. M. Feldbrugge and D. Lasok, *Law in Eastern Europe* no. 19, (1975).

international commercial relations, in which subjects, however, the number of organisms involved in some aspect of the law-making function has brought about a degree of confusion. Czechoslovakia completely reformed its codes with the adoption in 1963 of codes in family law, civil procedure, international commerce and private international law; its economic and civil codes were adopted in 1964 and its labour code in 1965. The German Democratic Republic adopted a new code on family law in 1965, new codes in civil law and civil procedure in 1975 and legislation on the application of law and on private international law and, in 1976, a statute on international economic contracts. In Albania, Bulgaria and Yugoslavia, major statutes have replaced the former law in a number of areas. Hungary in 1959 promulgated a civil code which it had not been able to achieve earlier.

197. Interpretation of legislation

Legislation is interpreted in the people's democracies much as it is in the Soviet Union. Jurists have submitted to the strict principle of interpretation imposed by Marxism-Leninism. "In socialist law," writes Professor Szabo, "the purpose of legislation is not to camouflage the will of the ruling class. It follows that the idea and the role of legislative interpretation are necessarily limited, since the will of the legislators does not allow, either at the time of promulgation or later on, that the substance of the legal rules be changed under the pretext of interpretation, or that there be introduced into the law by means of a so-called intepretation according to its spirit any element foreign to it . . . In bourgeois laws, the judge has become the pivot of the legal system. Socialist evolution has not made this error. Any remedial 'interpretation' is contrary to the principles of Marxism-Leninism."[15] These principles, however, are only valid with respect to the legislation or other legislative enactments adopted since the coming to power of the Marxist governments. The interpretation of such of the old laws as may have remained in force must be made according to other criteria. The rule used in Yugoslavia puts it very clearly: the application of

---

[15] Szabo (I.), *A jogszabályok értelmezése* (1960), cited from the French summary of the work, analysed by R. Lievens, *Revue de droit international et de droit comparé*, 1961, pp. 172–183.

such laws may be excluded if they appear to be contrary to the dominant principles of the new legal order.

With the gradual disappearance of these former laws and their replacement by legislation of Marxist inspiration, the advisability of preserving general legislative prescriptions has been discussed by jurists of the people's republics. And, just as in the U.S.S.R., it has finally been decided to adopt provisions which introduce a certain flexibility in legal interpretation and re-enforce the necessary link between law and society. The Czech Constitution of 1960, in article 102, allows judges to interpret legislation according to socialist legal conscience; a preamble of eight articles at the beginning of the civil code of 1964 gives more detail on this point. Article 5 of the Polish civil code states that acts contrary to "the rules of social life" or to the social and economic purpose of individual rights are not considered to be within the exercise of the right and are thus refused any legal protection. This provision has been applied with particular reference to acts leading to a deterioration of the environment.

198. Publicity of the law

The different and stronger legal tradition of the people's republics is indicated by the better publicity given to all kinds of regulatory texts. The typically Russian practice of somewhat confidential collections, designed only for the use of a ministry and not circulated to the public, is not followed. Because of this it is often somewhat easier to study the socialist law of these countries than that of the U.S.S.R., although for texts to be known it does not suffice, of course, that they may be published. And the jurists of the people's republics, like their colleagues in other countries, complain of the excessive proliferation and detail of such materials.

CHAPTER II

DECIDED CASES

199. The Soviet concept

The U.S.S.R. sees the role of judicial decisions quite differently from the capitalist democracies. If one asks a Soviet jurist what place they do have in the U.S.S.R., he will reply, in all good faith, that is an important one. If, on the other hand, the question is whether judicial decisions are a source of law, he will not hesitate to reply emphatically in the negative. What, then, is the real status of judicial decisions in the U.S.S.R.? An understanding of this point requires some familiarity with the Soviet judicial organisation as well as with certain other institutions created for the resolution of disputes by extra-judicial, but contentious, procedures.

§ 1. Judicial Organisation[1]

200. The hierarchy of courts

The principles governing Soviet judicial organisation are determined by Chapter XX of the U.S.S.R. Constitution. There are also Fundamental Principles of December 1958 respecting judicial organisation which replaced a federal law of 1938. These were supplemented and put into operation in the R.S.F.S.R. by a law of October 27, 1960.

Leaving aside special courts for the moment, it will noted that the Soviet judicial hierarchy has four levels: from the people's

---

[1] Kucherov (S.), *The Organs of Soviet Administration of Justice: Their History and Operation* (1970).

courts at the bottom to the U.S.S.R. Supreme Court at the top, through the provincial and S.S.R supreme courts. Depending on their nature and importance, civil or criminal actions may be instituted at any one of these levels. The general rule is in favour of the competence at first instance of the district people's court. If the case involves over 100 roubles in value, the court of first instance is the provincial court or even a higher court: the accusation lodged against a minister, for example, would be heard at first instance by the supreme court of an S.S.R. or the U.S.S.R., and the same holds true of certain trials of a political nature or involving high treason. Remedies, to the extent allowed, never omit a level; if there is an appeal, the judgments of the people's court are referred to the provincial court, those of a provincial court to the S.S.R. Supreme Court, and those of the latter to the U.S.S.R. Supreme Court. It should be mentioned, however, that since a decree of 1954 remedies against judgments may even be available within a given court; the decisions handed down by the various chambers, civil or criminal, of a provincial court or an S.S.R. Supreme Court can, under certain conditions, be annulled or revised by the Praesidium or *plenum* of that court.[2]

None of this will trouble a jurist familiar with the judicial organisation of a Romano-Germanic country. However, very great differences will be noted with respect to the manner in which Soviet courts are constituted and the way in which the range of remedies against judgments is organised.

201. Judicial personnel

The staffing of Soviet law courts is altogether different from that of bourgeois courts. In all courts of first instance, there are two classes of personnel: people's assessors and one or more judges. At higher levels there are only judges. A brief consideration of the judges and the role played by the people's assessors is called for here.

---

[2] The Praesidium is made up of the court president, vice-presidents and a number of judges fixed by the executive committee of the Soviet of the province or republic. The praesidium may also be directly competent in the case of appeal instituted against decisions of a lower court. The Praesidium in an S.S.R. Supreme Court is also called upon to decide cases referred to it by the U.S.S.R. Supreme Court (Law on judicial organisation of the R.S.F.S.R., arts. 36–38 and 52).

202. System for the election of judges

The characteristics of the Soviet judge are, first, that he is elected and, second, that he has not necessarily had any legal training.

Without exception, all Soviet judges are elected, by direct and universal suffrage in the case of judges of the people's courts and by the Soviets (of the U.S.S.R., S.S.R. or the provinces) in the case of other judges. All are elected for a period of five years, unless the electoral body exercises its right to revoke its choice. This right of revocation is only employed in exceptional cases, but it has been used even in the case of judges of the U.S.S.R. Supreme Court and, in the 1970 elections, 17 per cent. of retiring judges did not stand for re-election. The electoral system, provided for in the Communist Party programme as early as 1903, was adopted in the U.S.S.R. because of its democratic nature; this seems natural in a country where so much emphasis is placed on the dogma of popular sovereignty and where the law is defined as an instrument of policy. According to the democratic ideal both the creation of rules of law and their application must revert to the people's elected representatives. It hardly need be said that the election of judges, like other elections, is dominated by the all-powerful Communist Party. The voting by citizens or their representatives in the different Soviets is scarcely more than a ratification of the chosen candidates of the Party; there is thus eliminated much of the inconvenience which results from the election of judges in other countries. The candidates standing for election are most often members of the Communist Party. In May 1977, in an election in the R.S.F.S.R., 95 per cent. of the judges elected were Party members and women made up 35 per cent.

The Soviet judge has no need to be a jurist: no qualifying conditions of special aptitude, training or apprenticeship must limit the electors' freedom of choice. Apart from this, a matter of principle, an historical reason for the rule is found in the "trial and error" period of revolutionary communism. It was thought at that time that the law would be immediately replaced by a socialist sense of justice; moreover it was impossible to find politically safe judges among jurists immediately after the revolution. Today, the increasingly strong affirmation of the principle of socialist legality has led to a change of attitude. The Communist Party puts forward more and more only those candidates whose university degrees or practical experience substantiate their legal capacities. It would seem, however, that much remains to be done in this respect concerning the judges of the people's courts. The remuneration paid judges is no greater than that of other workers; judges of the people's courts receive much the same salary as that of an ordinarily qualified workman.

203. The collegial principle

The prevailing principle in the U.S.S.R. is that of the collegiality of judges. Several judges hear each case in the higher courts and even at first instance, except in the people's courts.[3] When a case is heard in first instance, however, the judge is never alone except in those minor cases specified by law; whether there be one or several judges, the court is in effect completed by the presence of assessors in accordance with the U.S.S.R. Constitution.

204. The people's assessors

Like jurors, people's assessors are citizens who, for civil as well as criminal cases, complete the court for the purpose of hearing and judgment. The lists from which the assessors are selected are established by an elective process: either by universal suffrage in the general assemblies of workers, employees and peasants (lists for the people's courts), or by the Soviets of different levels (other lists). Election is for two and a half years (art. 152 of the Constitution). Two assessors join the judge in the people's court, and a varying number in the other courts, so that the assessors will always form the majority. During the time they fill this post, the assessors are relieved of the employment which they normally hold; they cannot be asked to take on this legal duty for more than two weeks each year. When they are called to hear a case they are, for purposes of hearing and judgment, placed on an equal footing with the judge; their voice has the same weight as that of the judge, whether in matters of fact or law. In reality, however, the judge—at least when he has had legal training—appears to have a

---

[3] A re-organisation of people's courts took place between 1959 and 1967 in which the number of courts in the R.S.F.S.R. was reduced from 4,500 to 2,375 and the new courts given as many or more than 15 judges. However, today, as formerly, a judge sitting alone hears the case.

great ascendancy over the people's assessors, and it is exceptional for him to be outvoted by them, although this has occurred.[4]

What is the purpose of people's assessors? At first glance it is rather difficult to see its usefulness. The juries or aldermen found in bourgois countries, and with which one is inevitably tempted to compare the Soviet people's assessors, play a useful role by making their technical knowledge available to the court, as in the case of aldermen, or else as in the case of jurors by bringing the voice of popular sentiment to the court and helping to correct the professional bias of the judge who is a professional jurist. These considerations do not apply in the Soviet Union where both the judge and the people's assessors are elected without reference to any particular qualifications in either case.

To understand this institution one must, once again, refer to Marxist ideology. The basis of the institution is connected to the Marxist idea of the withering away of the law in a communist society; its ideal is a society without law or courts, in which individual behaviour will be controlled only by the opinion of the community. The people's assessors' participation in trials presages and anticipates tomorrow's non-juridical forms. In the meantime it serves to educate the community by reinforcing the link between the court and the Soviet people; it calls upon a very large number of citizens[5] in the work of the law and these people will later return to their homes, factories or *kolkhozi* having seen the inside workings of a Soviet court and been convinced of the eminently just nature of Soviet law. The institution is therefore linked to the desire to educate and transform Soviet man—one of the principal tasks of Soviet law.

205. Special courts

A word should be said about the "special courts" of the U.S.S.R. A reform of 1957 did away with all these courts, except the military tribunals. The latter are specialised courts subject to the rules of the criminal codes and codes of criminal procedure of the different S.S.R. Since 1956 their jurisdiction has been limited to penal infractions committed by enlisted men and certain crimes (espionage, treason) affecting state security. Like other courts,

---

[4] Feifer (G.), *Justice in Moscow* (1965).
[5] More than 600,000 people were on the lists of elected people's assessors in 1970.

however, they are subject to the control of the U.S.S.R. Supreme Court which has a military chamber in addition to civil and criminal chambers.

Apart from the public arbitration bodies, which have a very special role and are to be discussed later, it should be noted that there are no "administrative" courts in the U.S.S.R. Where contentious administrative procedures are allowed, they are judged by the ordinary courts. One can therefore go before a people's court for example if a local Soviet has not respected the law in establishing electoral lists. One can also go before the regular courts to bring into play the civil liability of the government. But in the U.S.S.R. there is no contentious procedure open to individuals that can result in the annulation of some administrative action.

206. Remedies against judgments

The organisation of the system of remedies against judgments in the Soviet Union must now be examined. Once again differences with respect to bourgeois laws will be noted because of both the manner in which the Soviet court is constituted and the tasks incumbent upon Soviet law and the emphasis placed on the principle of socialist legality.

The way in which the Soviet court is constituted excludes any possibility of an appeal by way of a rehearing. That a higher court could reverse the decision of judges in a court of first instance on questions of fact is easily seen to be anti-democratic, since the judge is elected and the case has been heard with the aid of people's assessors. Only remedies against judgments based on an error of law committed by the judges are allowed. Thus the desire and the need to guarantee respect for the principle of socialist legality as fully as possible in a socialist country easily leads to the revision of judgments and sentences when it appears that an error of law may have occurred.

Soviet law admits two types of remedies: the appeal for an error of law (*Kassatsia*) and the petition for revision (*nadzor*). The parties and certain established authorities such as the *Prokuratura* have the right to lodge an appeal and they may, in the brief delay allowed by law, institute it against any decision rendered in first instance—but against these decisions only. The appeal is heard by the next highest court which can confirm the decision, set it aside and return the case to the court of first instance or, which is most often the practice, pronounce upon the merits without, generally, referring the case back.

The petition in revision (*nadzor*), probably corresponding to an ancient Russian tradition,[6] is however an interesting feature of Soviet law. It is not a remedy available to the parties but only to the various authorities empowered to supervise the administration of justice in the Soviet Union. The *Prokuratura* and the presidents of the regional or Supreme Courts exercise a control over the decisions rendered within their respective jurisdictions either on their own initiative or in response to petitions received. If considered appropriate, they refer these decisions to a higher court for revision. The parties themselves cannot directly institute a request for revision; they, like all persons and particularly social organisations, can only request the competent authorities to act by way of petition. Contrary to the French practice in cases of an appeal in the interest of the law (*pourvoi dans l'intérêt de la loi*), the success of the petition in revision may benefit the parties; it does not merely serve to affirm some principle of law.

In the absence of statistics it is difficult to know the extent and significance of this type of remedy in practice. From reading Soviet legal works and collections of judicial decisions, one has the impression that it is far from exceptional and that numerous judgments and sentences are submitted to the criticism of higher courts in this way. In private law matters the grounds for lodging a petition in revision are those relating to some serious defect or irregularity in the procedures followed or judgment rendered. In criminal matters the grounds are broader and the remedy is open to correct a procedure or decision that is simply unfounded in law. The remedy is not subject to any special delays and it has the effect of suspending the execution of the judgment that it seeks to set aside.

207. Multiplicity of judicial levels

With a view to assuring a strict application of Soviet laws, the possibility of an appeal or a revision has been quite freely admitted. The western jurist is surprised by the number of levels through which, in theory at least, a trial may pass before final judg-

---

[6] Rudzinski (A. W.), "Soviet-type Audit Proceedings and their Western Counterparts" *Legal Controls in the Soviet Union, Law in Eastern Europe* (1966), Vol. 13, p. 287–399.

ment. The levels are not limited to the four mentioned in the Constitution. Within each of these possible instances, two kinds of examination can take place: first, by requesting a new hearing of the matter by the Praesidium of the regional court that decided the case and secondly, by submitting the decision rendered by a particular chamber of the Supreme Court of an S.S.R. to its full court.

208. The role of the U.S.S.R. Supreme Court

On the other hand a limit was placed in 1957 on the multiplication of remedies by reducing the role of the U.S.S.R. Supreme Court. The origin of this reform seems to have been the decentralising tendency evident at this period rather than any idea of stemming an excessive number of remedies. It was considered desirable for the Supreme Court of the S.S.R. to render final judgment in a large number of cases, without any appeal to the U.S.S.R. Supreme Court. The significance of this reform becomes clear when one realises the extent to which the personnel of the U.S.S.R. Supreme Court was reduced as a result of the new provisions. Before the reform of 1972 it had a president and 78 members. It now has only a president, two vice-presidents and 16 judges, to which number are added the presidents of the S.S.R. Supreme Courts (in the case of appeals instituted against a decisiosn of the Supreme Court of their own S.S.R.). The number of assessors was also reduced from 70 to 45. The reform has reduced the work of the Court by 70 per cent. The U.S.S.R. Supreme Court has other functions too, which were very important during the period (1963–1971) when there was no U.S.S.R. Ministry of Justice. Since then, however, they have been cut down. The Court retains nonetheless its right respecting the initiation of legislation and publishes its directives which deal with the application of laws and decrees and the administration of justice in general.

§ 2. Extra-Judicial Contentious Procedures

209. Importance of extra-judicial contentious procedures

In any country, a great many disputes are settled by extra-judicial methods. In western countries, for example, many disputes are resolved within a jurisdictional framework by various administrative courts which do not figure in the judicial organisation itself. A great many contestations especially in commercial matters can also be resolved by means of arbitration which, while taking place under the control of regular courts, is not in fact carried out by them. It is the same in the Soviet Union: the courts contemplated by both the Fundamental Principles of Judicial Organisation and the laws governing that subject in the various S.S.R., are far from being the only means of settling differences.

Extra-judicial contentious procedures in the Soviet Union have an even greater importance than they do in non-socialist countries. This is so principally for two reasons. The first is related to the economic structure of the U.S.S.R. It is natural that disputes between state enterprises be submitted to bodies other than the regular courts and that disputes arising out of international commerce be removed from the purview of these same courts. The second reason is related to Marxist teaching and its prognostication of the withering away of law. Like law itself, the settling of disputes by courts is only a last resort. As far as possible, ways are now sought to avoid this by resorting to non-judicial techniques. This notion is important in the solution of certain types of dispute, especially labour problems which are generally heard before "people's organisations" that are distinct from the ordinary courts.

A.—Arbitration

210. Various forms of arbitration

There are two very different forms of arbitration in the U.S.S.R. The first is public arbitration which, according to law, is used to decide disputes between nationalised enterprises or, as the case may be, between different ministries. The second is contractual arbitration which, while it is in principle excluded as a technique for disputes between Soviet citizens, plays an essential part in those arising out of international commerce.

211. Public arbitration[7]

To the mind of a western jurist, Soviet public arbitration bodies suggest a hierarchy of administrative tribunals existing alongside

---

[7] Abova (T. E.) and Tadevosjan (V. S.), Razrešenie hozjaistvennyh sporov (1968). Knapp (V.), "State Arbitration in Socialist Countries" *International Encyclopedia of Comparative Law* (1973), Vol. 16 Chap. 13. Lavigne (P.), "La spécificité organique et fonctionnelle de l'arbitrage d'Etat" (1969) Ann. de l'U.R.S.S. 175–196.

those of the judicial order. This comparison is useful because it helps to explain the existence of organisations whose function it is to resolve contentious questions, but which are not considered to be courts in the full sense since the word "court" suggests a "judicial" body. Comparison with French or other western administrative tribunals is otherwise misleading, however because the *raison d'être* and duties of Soviet public arbitration bodies are different. French administrative tribunals for example are mainly called upon to elaborate and apply a special law—*le droit administratif*—concerning principally relations between the government and citizens. The exclusive task of Soviet public arbitration bodies is, on the other hand, to apply rules which are considered part of the *civil* or ordinary law. Most important of all, their competence relates exclusively to disputes between the various public or state-owned enterprises through which the Soviet economy is for the most part directed. In no event does it cover disputes between government and citizens. This type of dispute is anticipated by the 1977 Constitution (art. 58, para. 2) and the regular courts have jurisdiction. Doctrinal writers see this as one of the fundamental guarantees of the principle of socialist legality.

The existence of administrative tribunals in France is linked to the distinction between public and private law. In the Soviet Union, on the other hand, public arbitration bodies owe their existence to quite a different consideration—the fact that the various publicly-owned industrial or commercial enterprises which help to implement the national economic plans are merely organs or extensions of the state. Conflicts arising between them on the interpretation or the non-performance of mutual obligations are not antagonistic and do not put into conflict two entirely distinct persons requiring an appeal to constitutionally established courts. They amount to conflicts between two or more branches of the same enterprise; it is only normal that they be resolved, without recourse to courts of law, by the arbitration of a common superior.

212. Practical necessity of this institution

In view of the way in which the regular Soviet courts are constituted, it is even more understandable that these types of dispute be removed from their jurisdiction. Elected judges with general qualifications may judge fairly and apply the law effectively in matters relating to the everyday life of the citizens. In such circumstances, it may be beneficial both to contemplate and guide the popular idea of justice. But the disputes between state economic enterprises are altogether different. They bring into play rules of technical organisation rather than considerations of morality and justice, and the political aspect of such disputes is thus less pronounced. In these matters the judge must often have the qualifications of a technician rather than those of a jurist. Alongside the ordinary courts the public arbitration bodies thus provide for a justice applied by technicians. Their particular merit is speed; in 75 per cent. of cases a solution is handed down within fifteen days after the arbitral body is seized of the affair.[8]

213. Different types of public arbitration

Soviet arbitral bodies were created and have functioned for some time without having been mentioned in the Constitution which laid down rules only in respect of the courts. They are now expressly governed by the Constitution of 1977 (at Chap. XX entitled "Courts and Arbitration"). Article 163 puts the principle that "the resolution of economic disputes between enterprises, institutions and organisations is carried out by state arbitral bodies within the limits of their respective jurisdictions.

Soviet doctrine divides public arbitration into two large types: departmental arbitration[9] for the resolution of disputes between enterprises responsible to the same authority and state arbitration *stricto sensu* for the resolution of differences arising between enterprises reporting to different authorities.

214. State arbitration

State arbitration, which originated in a decree of 1918, was organised in 1931 and reformed in 1960. An ordinance of 1974 brought about further considerable changes in the system and the matter is now governed by legislation of November 30, 1979.

State arbitration is organised as a unitary and centralised system with a number of commissions: arbitration commission of the

---

[8] Bellon (J.), *Le droit soviétique* (1963), p. 109.
[9] The literal translation from the Russian (*vedomstvennij arbitraž*) would be "administrative arbitration." In Russian state arbitration is *Gosarbitraž* ((*gosudarstvennij arbitraž*).

U.S.S.R., of the S.S.R., of autonomous republics of the territory of a province, of cities, and of autonomous provinces and regions. The sharing of jurisdiction between the different arbitration commissions depends upon the nature of the parties and the importance of the litigation.

215. Departmental arbitration

Not very much is known about this form of arbitration and its organisation is more complex. It varies according to the different ministries and institutions concerned, and can only be studied by those having access to the internal documentation of such bodies. A decree of July 10, 1967 does no more than lay down a number of uniform rules in respect of the U.S.S.R. ministries; similar provisions have been drawn up for the S.S.R. ministries.

216. Arbitration commissions

The various public arbitration commissions are directed by a chief arbitrator, assisted by a number of deputies. When a case is referred to a commission, an arbitrator is designated. He hears the case, assisted by experts if need be, with the representatives of the parties (such as the director of the enterprise or some other authorised officer).

The procedure laid down for the hearing of economic disputes by state arbitration is distinct from that found in the codes of civil procedure of the various S.S.R. The commission can only proceed after an effort has been made by the parties to come to a solution. Once it is seized of the dispute, moreover, the arbitrator and the parties must as a preliminary procedure attempt to come to a settlement by means of a common search for the legally correct solution. Many disputes end at this stage because the parties are able to find a solution acceptable to the arbitrator. If they are unsuccessful, they then enter upon a quasi-judicial phase of the procedure although it rarely happens that lawyers will then be called in.

The decision of the state arbitration commission may, at the request of the parties, be sent for a re-hearing to other branches of the commission or other state bodies. This re-hearing must be requested within a year of the decision. The decision is verified by the state arbitration commission at the next highest level or by the

chief arbitrator or his deputy. Proceeding against the decision in
this way may have the effect of suspending all further action in the
case if the arbitrator so decides. The procedures are not private
and many of the decisions rendered in public arbitration are published in specialised reviews.

217. Consultations and directives

Public arbitration commissions are not limited to resolving disputes referred to them by state enterprises or branches of the
administration. They have other activities, such as being charged
with a number of administrative and regulatory functions, which
make them resemble administrative organisms as much if not more
than judicial bodies.

They may, for example, in their own right, take up questions
touching upon the proper operation of state enterprises, require
the latter to supply information on the steps taken to correct deficiencies, submit reports to the appropriate authorities and suggest
disciplinary action. They may also occasionally set the terms and
conditions of a contract which parties must conclude or in respect
of which the parties have agreed upon an arbitration. It also sometimes happens that they will give advice by way of consultations to
enterprises, which may ask, for example, whether they are within
their rights in inserting a particular clause in a contract or what
their rights and obligations are in some specified circumstances.

The U.S.S.R. State Arbitration Commission publishes directives and issues instructions on matters within its competence to all
state arbitration bodies. It also participated in the drafting of the
General Conditions governing the delivery of products and supplies among Soviet state enterprises. A collection of instructions
on state arbitration in connection with the U.S.S.R. Council of
Ministers has been published, although irregularly, since 1955; it
also reports the decisions of arbitration bodies. This collection is a
source of documentation of primary importance in the legal problems of the Soviet economy.

218. The extent of public arbitration

The activity of the arbitration commissions is considerable. An
ordinance of the Praesidium of the U.S.S.R. Supreme Soviet, pro-

mulgated on July 26, 1959, decreed that as of January 1, 1960 all disputes between state organisations would be submitted without exception to arbitral bodies. As previously recommended by various Soviet authors, the role of the courts in such disputes has been completely eliminated. According to one author, close to 700,000 cases are now submitted to state arbitration each year.[10]

219. Private arbitration

Public arbitration is compulsory. The disputing parties are obliged to submit to it by virtue of law even though, in practice, efforts are made to have an arbitration agreement signed. Arbitration resulting from an agreement freely concluded by the parties is quite different. By common accord they decide to submit their differences to arbitration.

This type of arbitration, insofar as disputes between Soviet citizens are concerned, is only of minor importance at the present time.[11] It is not to be ruled out, however, that as a means of resolving disputes it might be more developed in the future communist society, since it encourages conciliation and harmony. The law of August 17, 1960 on state arbitration has provided for the possibility that public enterprises submit their disputes to a mutually agreeable arbitrator. The role of the judge, moreover, is often seen as that of a conciliator; many suits instituted by private persons are resolved, prior to any public hearing, in chambers and upon the advice of the judge.

220. International commercial arbitration

If, at the present time, contractual arbitration is not much used in relations between Soviet citizens, it occupies on the other hand in international commercial relations, an understandably important place. Foreign businessmen and merchants dealing with the Soviet Union have no desire to go before the Soviet courts described above. Soviet jurists are the first to admit that because of their composition, operating rules and system of remedies, these

---

[10] *Cf.* Loeber (D. A.), *Der hoheitlich gestaltete Vertrag* (1969), p. 68.
[11] Loeber (D. A.), "Plan and Contract Performance in Soviet Law" (1964) U. of Illinois Law Forum 128–179.

courts are not suited to foreigners contracting with the Soviet Union. On the other hand, they are obviously disinclined to submit possible future disputes with foreigners to the jurisdiction of foreign state courts. For this reason the U.S.S.R. now favours arbitration in international commercial matters and it has actively participated in the efforts of the United Nations and its European Economic Commission by signing and ratifying both the New York Convention of May 1958 and the European Arbitration Convention of April 1961. It has further shown its inclination to settle international commercial disputes by arbitration by concluding numerous bilateral treaties. Of course, like other countries, it hopes that this arbitration will be carried out as much as possible on its own territory and through the offices of a Soviet institution.

The institution in question is the Arbitration Court of the U.S.S.R. Chamber of Foreign Commerce,[12] regulated by a decree of 1932. Soviet bodies authorised to conclude foreign commercial contracts endeavour to include clauses giving this court jurisdiction in the event of a dispute since it can only be seized on the basis of an agreement between the parties.[13] The Court of Arbitration fixes its own procedure; it decides according to the terms of the agreement of the parties and, subsidiarily, according to commercial custom and the national law recognised as applicable. In the U.S.S.R. its awards cannot be appealed. It may be surprising to find such significance attached to the principle of the freedom of contract but it must not be forgotten that in this case one of the contracting parties is the state itself. In view of the Soviet monopoly of foreign trade, the U.S.S.R. has no more reason to take exception to the principle of the freedom of contract than the capitalist monopolies; it is powerful enough to turn it to its own advantage.

---

[12] Ramzaitsev (D. F.), "La jurisprudence en matière de droit international privé de la Commission arbitrale soviétique pour le commerce extérieur," Rev. crit. dr. int. privé, 1958, pp. 459–478;—*Aspects juridiques du commerce avec les pays d'économie planifiée* (1961), a collection of articles published by the International Association of Legal Science. Pisar (S.), *Coexistence and Commerce: Guidelines for Transactions between East and West* (1970). Giffen (J. H.), *The Legal and Practical Aspects of Trade with the Soviet Union* (1969).

[13] No express stipulation is however necessary in connection with the commercial dealings between the U.S.S.R. and other European socialist countries (except Yugoslavia) or Outer Mongolia. Commercial relations with these countries are regulated by an international agreement concluded in 1972 at Moscow which refers to different *General Conditions* drawn up by the "Council of Mutual Economic Assistance" and specifies the details of the arbitral procedures applicable. Caillot (J.), *Le C.A.E.M. Aspects juridiques et formes de co-opération économique entre les pays socialistes* (1971).

B.—*Appeals to People's Organisations*

221. Reason for these procedures

In the courts and public arbitration commissions, justice is rendered according to law and in the name of the Soviet state. However the law and the state must disappear in the superior form of social organisation that communism represents. Disputes will not disappear in communist society, but such conflicts will no longer be "antagonistic," requiring the use of law and force for their resolution; a process of persuasion, undertaken by members of the community to which the parties belong, will resolve them. Even now it is possible in the socialist society already established to experiment—but with care and to a limited extent—with those forms of social organisation to be developed in this new society.

Thus many matters of concern to only the interior life of the *kolkhoz* will not fall within the jurisdiction of the courts. They are finally decided by the general meetings of the *kolkhoz* itself. As a general rule the courts must refuse to intervene if the criticised decision concerns the allocation or boundary lines of individual plots of land; in such cases the executive committee of the local soviet is the organ exercising control over the legality of the decision. On the other hand, the courts can be seized by the *kolkhozian* who maintains that he has not received his due in respect of his work.[14]

In labour relations, the role of the trade unions has been developed in the same way. These people's organisations, called upon to play a role of the very greatest importance in communist society, can henceforth be given many of the tasks of the state organisations destined to disappear.[15] Particularly with respect to labour problems, they have quite naturally been entrusted with the task of bringing about conciliation and compromise; a decree of January 31, 1957 initiated this development. Labour relations commissions, made up of an equal number of representatives from

[14] *Cf.* the article by Ju. Naumov, in Hazard (J. N.) and Shapiro (I.), *The Soviet Legal System* (1962), Pt. 2, pp. 26–28.

[15] Gélard (P.), *Les organisations de masse en U.R.S.S.: syndicats et Komsomol*, 1966. On the varying importance, according to the period, given to the unions in relation to collective labour agreements, *cf.* Greyfié de Bellecombe (L.), *Les conventions collectives de travail en Union soviétique* (1958). Lowit (T.), *Le syndicalisme de type soviétique. L'U.R.S.S. et le pays de l'Est européen* (1971).

the management and the local union committee, operate in all industries; if the solutions proposed by the commissions are not agreed to by the parties, a new effort is made by the local union committee; only if this second attempt fails can the people's court be seized. To what extent in fact are there judicial proceedings after the exhaustion of these conciliation procedures? Statistics would be necessary on this point; it may be that the pressure of public opinion, represented by the two successive conciliation organs, reduces very considerably the amount of such litigation. Certain important questions, however, can be submitted by the interested parties directly to the people's courts; and this is true especially with respect to the dismissal of workers.[16]

This type of extra-judicial settlement of disputes does not surprise a western observer. In the capitalist countries there are similar conciliation procedures; the difference lies in the conditions under which such procedures are called upon to play a role and to be effective in a country such as the U.S.S.R. Certain recent developments since 1957, however, have no parallel in countries of the West and should be mentioned: in particular, the Comrades' Court and the Community Meetings.

222. Comrades' courts and community meetings[17]

The Comrades' Courts are intended to sanction certain forms of anti-social behaviour of minor importance which do not merit the attention of regular courts. The Community Meetings, instituted in 1961, are designed to reprove certain anti-social acts. They deal with those who evade their social obligation to work or lead a parasitic way of life, and may pronounce penalties of banishment within the S.S.R. for a period of two to five years and impose the obligation to work and the confiscation of profits unduly received.

Community Meetings were not considered to be true courts by Soviet jurists; if they had been, their activity and even their exis-

---

[16] Bellon (J.), *Le droit soviétique* (1963), p. 72. For an example of a non-judicial proceeding in disputes relating to copyright and trade mark, *cf.* the same work, pp. 74–79. The Councils of the bar associations may also adjudicate respecting the discipline of their members: Tchikvadze (V. M.), *Le concept de la légalité dans les pays socialistes* (1961), p. 101.

[17] The Comrades' Courts are regulated in the R.S.F.S.R. by a law of July 3, 1961, modified on October 23, 1963. An English translation of these documents is given in Hazard (J. N.), Butler (W. E.) and Maggs (P. B.), *The Soviet Legal System* (1977), pp. 22–30. On the Comrades' courts and community meetings *cf.* also Hazard (J. N.), *Communists and Their Law* (1969), pp. 117–126.

tence would have been rather difficult to justify in the face of article 4 of the Fundamental Principles of Criminal Procedure of 1958 to the effect that a penalty cannot be inflicted save by judgment of a court according to the criminal law. Soviet authors, however, considered the institution as an experiment of limited significance, *on the fringe of the law*, carried on as a preparation for the advent of communist society through the participation of the masses in the maintenance of social discipline and in observation of the rules of community life. The arguments mentioned above, however, carried the day, and the institution was abolished in 1965. Today only the Comrades' Courts remain, but their modest role and powers do not excite the same criticisms. Now the role of these bodies is to exert a social influence and through education and persuasion to prevent behaviour harmful to society.

They are made up of members elected for two years by the collective of the workers' general meetings and may hear cases of petty theft, public drunkenness and tenants' disputes. They are empowered to levy fines in small amounts, issue reprimands and make findings of public censure. They may also recommend to the management of an enterprise that a guilty person be temporarily downgraded or transferred.

§ 3. Role of Judicial Decisions[18]

223. Soviet concept

When the concept of law and the organisation of the courts and other institutions for settling disputes in the U.S.S.R. are understood, the role allotted to judicial decisions becomes clear. In a country where the law is closely linked to ruling state policies and where there is professed concern that there be an effective sovereignty of the people through its representative legislative body, it is obvious that decided cases must be confined as much a possible to a role of strict *interpretation* of enacted law rather than the *creation* of legal rules. This fundamental position is reinforced by the absence of a body of judges or judicial class which might be tempted to make itself a fully independent—if not a rival—power to that of the legislators. In Russia where the judges until 1864

---

[18] Bratus (S. N.), ed., *Sudebnaja Praktika v sovetskoj pravovoj sisteme* (1973).

were considered to be simply civil servants and where, in the period 1864–1917, there was insufficient time for a judicial corps to develop a sense of autonomy, such a class has never existed.

"Judges," says the Soviet Constitution "are independent and subject only to the law." The independence referred to in this article is with respect to the local soviets, the various branches of government administration and the *Prokuratura*: judges are not subject to the orders of the administration or local soviets,[19] and they are in no sense obliged to conform to the conclusions of the *Prokuratura* in any particular case submitted to them. But the judges are subject to enacted law and they are not allowed to be indifferent to the policies of the government: "The court is an instrument of the governing class; it assures the domination of this class and protects its interests." This notion, as expressed by Vyshinsky (1883–1954) in 1937 is still true today. In a country proclaiming the principle of the concentration of state power in the Supreme Soviet, the independence of judges has nothing whatever to do with an attempt to strike a balance between the judicial and the legislative powers. Judges, while applying the law, must be sensitive to the directives given by the Communist Party and the government.[20]

224. Supremacy of enacted law

There is no review of the constitutionality of legislation in the U.S.S.R. Such control cannot be confided to the courts, nor can it be carried out by the *Prokuratura* whose only function is to exercise "the highest supervision over the strict execution of the laws," not their constitutionality. The only provision touching on the constitutionality of laws is article 74 of the Constitution by virtue of which, in case of contradiction, a law of an S.S.R. gives way to a federal (all-union) law.

Soviet tribunals might, without violation of any principles, be

---

[19] In order to avoid any interference by the government in the machinery of justice, the U.S.S.R. federal Ministry of Justice was abolished in 1956 as were, sometime later, the Ministries of Justice of the S.S.R.; their right to inspect the courts and tribunals was attributed to the Supreme Courts. This reform was itself abolished, however, in 1970. In China, on the other hand, it is still considered desirable that local soviets exercise a surveillance over the judges. *Cf.* Hazard (J. N.), "Socialisme et humanisme" in *Annales africaines* (1965) pp. 71–94.

[20] Feifer (G.), *Justice in Moscow* (1964), p. 275 shows how at times a policy of leniency and at others a policy of severity has been applied in the field of criminal law as a result of campaigns led by the Communist Party of the S.S.S.R.

authorised to judge the simple legality of all acts of different branches of the state administration, such as the Council of Ministers, individual ministries or other parts of the administration. As a matter of fact however they do not exercise this power. Only very exceptionally are Soviet citizens permitted to complain before the courts of some government act which they esteem illegal and prejudicial. Reliance is placed rather upon the *Prokuratura* to assure respect for socialist legality on the part of the administration or the local soviets.

The courts, therefore, apart from any review of constitutionality or legality, simply apply the laws, ordinances, decrees, regulations, orders and instructions made in execution of the legislation in force. Their sole function is to interpret in order to apply Soviet law which they neither create nor develop by means of adapting it to particular circumstances. Soviet law itself does confer, when it is deemed appropriate, a certain latitude upon the judges in specific instances. But apart from such cases the judges cannot, either out of equity or for any other reason, stray from the terms of enacted legislation. The legislators, not the courts, create the law. "The court," declared Lenin, "is an organ of state power. The liberals sometimes forget this. For a Marxist it is a sin to do so." In our free democracies we are prone to admire the creative work carried on through judicial decisions and the judicial preoccupation for social justice and equity. The Soviet regime intends that judges be kept in their place—which is that they apply and not create the law. *Aequitas legislatori, ius iudici magis convenit.*

What has just been said will surely convey the impression that the role of judicial decisions is considerably less than it is in many bourgeois countries. This impression is confirmed when the place occupied by judicial decisions in Soviet legal literature is considered. For a long time the only collection of reported cases was the "Practice of the Courts"[21]; but this collection has not appeared since 1957 when it was replaced by a Bulletin of the Supreme Court of the U.S.S.R.[22] Since that time the Supreme Courts of the S.S.R. have also published collections of their judicial holdings but there is still no systematic organisation of the publication. Legal writings make very few references to judgments. These publi-

---

[21] *Sudebnaja Praktika.*
[22] *Bjulleten' Verhovnogo Suda S.S.S.R.*

cations were in effect established for the use of other courts to which they are sent, and not for general distribution outside the judicial system.

225. Real importance of decided cases

The conclusion naturally drawn from all these observations must not, however, be made without some reservations. In reality, decided cases play a very important role, quite apart from the essential matter of simply restoring peace and order by resolving disputes. But to understand their creative and political role, it is necessary to appreciate the Soviet milieu and not expect to find the equivalent of what we are accustomed to in western countries.

The concern for discipline and the preoccupation for legality in the U.S.S.R. do not permit either a formation or an evolution of the law through the anarchical initiative of judges. On the other hand, however, a realist must recognise that the legislative order necessarily has gaps. Laws are sometimes incomplete or insufficient and an examination of judicial decisions brings these *lacunae* to light. Consequently, the Soviet constitution itself provides that a control over all judicial activity will be exercised by the highest judicial organ, the Supreme Court of the U.S.S.R. and, in turn, that an analogous control will be exercised by the Chief Arbitrator of the U.S.S.R. over the activity of the organs of public arbitration.

The Supreme Court of the U.S.S.R. and the Chief Arbitrator are not limited to a review of cases already judged by inferior courts or bodies. One of their functions—the principal one, probably, in the case of the Supreme Court since 1957— is to publish instructions or issue orders with a view to guiding Soviet courts or the organs of public arbitration in their application of enacted law. It is possible of course to say that in the exercise of this activity the Supreme Court and the Chief Arbitrator are transformed into administrative organs and no longer have a properly judicial function. A Soviet author for his part would reply that by creating rules of law a French or an English judge is changed into a legislative organ and departs from his judicial role. In the U.S.S.R., it is important to observe, the experience of the courts is not neglected. Judgments and decisions are not perhaps cited as such in order to know what the law is; but in the light of judgments and decisions rendered, judicial authority co-operates in the development of Soviet law by publishing instructions and orders relative to the application of the law. As with the organs of state administration, it is well understood that the instructions issuing from the Supreme Court, like those of the Chief Arbitrator of the U.S.S.R., must intervene on the basis of and in execution of "the laws in force." In practice, however, this only means that they cannot be contrary to enacted law; in fact their object will sometimes be to specify the manner in which the application of a particular law must be conceived and sometimes to fill a gap in the legislation. By way of example of the first type, there is an instruction relating to the application of the Family Code which provides judges with directives concerning the possible grounds for divorce (which the law does not specify); of the second type, there is the example of an instruction (ante-dating the coming into force of the new Fundamental Principles of Civil Law) ruling matters of conflicts of law. The U.S.S.R. Supreme Court has had, moreover, ever since 1958, and this is confirmed by the 1977 Constitution, the right to submit legislative proposals to the Supreme Soviet, and, we are told, much use is made of this prerogative.

It has also been realised in the U.S.S.R. that it may be very useful to refer to the holdings of the courts in order to explain the provisions of the law in a more lively and concrete manner. Doctrinal works seek more and more to illustrate the rules by means of actual cases which are approved or criticised for their interpretation of the law. And in recent years even works devoted especially to the study of questions considered by the courts in particular branches of the law have been published. For some time a summary of judicial decisions has appeared quite regularly in the official review *Soviet State and Law* (*Sovetskoe Gosudarstvo i Pravo*).[23] Nor are decided cases ignored by the legislators; the Fundamental Principles of Civil Law, adopted in 1961, embody many of the solutions previously admitted by the courts.

226. Educational role of decided cases

The study of court decisions in Soviet law would not be complete without asking what place is given them by Soviet legal doc-

---

[23] This review has been published since 1938 under this title.

trine itself. The matter is treated in a completely different way to that to which we are accustomed in western countries. Since the starting-point is the premise that the law is an aspect of policy, legal doctrine insists that the role of the courts must be to co-operate in bringing about the success of the state policy. To this end the courts do not exist simply to interpret and apply Soviet laws in the manner described above. They must also help to assure the success of government policies and prepare for the withering away of law by means of an active participation in the work of educating the Soviet people. Of this they are capable. In each case to be resolved, the court must bring to light, and especially in the minds of the popular assessors, that the solution founded on an application of Soviet law is both reasonable and just, and one that every honest citizen would be happy to accept. The party who loses his case, and even the condemned man himself, must approve the judgment rendered; public opinion must support it and be in agreement with the law on the basis of which it was rendered. The Soviet court must not be a show; it must be a school.[24] It is important to demonstrate that, in achieving a socialist state, one enters into the kingdom of justice.

Section II—Other Socialist Countries

227. Comparison with U.S.S.R.

The judicial systems of the people's republics are patterned on the same principles as those applying in the U.S.S.R. They organise a corps of judges entirely devoted to the programme of social change set up by the government rather than a caste of jurists. "Judges must not be animated by an *esprit de corps* which will

---

[24] The Fundamental Principles of Judicial Organisation, promulgated in 1958, specify in art. 3, entitled *The Tasks of the Court:* "In all its activities, the court educates the citizens of the Soviet Union in a spirit of devotion to the country and to the cause of Communism, in a spirit of exactitude and firmness in the execution of Soviet laws, of honesty in behaviour towards socialist property, observation of discipline in work, of sincere attachment to the duties owed to the State and society, of respect for the law, of honour and dignity of citizens and the rules of the socialist community. When it provides measures for the repression of crime, the court does not limit itself to punishing the delinquent, but devotes itself to his reform and re-education." Art. 2 of the Fundamental Principles of Civil Procedure (1961) also underlines the role that procedure must have in the education of the citizen. *Cf.* also the most vivid description of cases by Feifer (G.), *Justice in Moscow* (1964).

make more difficult their understanding of State policy, the directives of which are laid down by the Workers' Party."[25] There is thus
a natural subordination of the judicial authorities to the organs of
state power and the lower courts are obliged to give an account of
their activity to the people's councils.[26]

Despite this basic similarity as to principle, the judicial organisation of the people's republics is not a simple duplication of that in
the U.S.S.R. No serious reason was seen for upsetting a system
which had proved its worth; the Soviet organisation, so it
appeared, was due in part at least to conditions particular to the
U.S.S.R. and to which no heed had to be paid in countries where
similar conditions did not prevail. The decisive consideration for
the leaders of the people's republics is the need to devise the best
means of bringing about socialism in their own countries rather
than to follow in all respects the model provided by the U.S.S.R.
The principle of socialist legality may be more surely respected by
means different than those used in the U.S.S.R.; and no feelings
of vassalage therefore force adoption of Soviet solutions.

228. Hierarchy of courts

A number of remarks should be made respecting the existing
hierarchy of courts. Some differences are explained by the fact
that the people's republics, with the exception of Yugoslavia and
Czechoslovakia, are not federal states; they therefore have no
court comparable to the Supreme Court of the U.S.S.R. and the
interpretative role given to this court in the Soviet Union is attributed to other judicial or non-judicial organs. There are also other
differences respecting the jurisdiction of the courts. The Czech
and Rumanian regional courts, for example, unlike the provincial
courts of the U.S.S.R., are always at the second degree; it is
altogether exceptional, and in effect only by virtue of specific legislative texts, that they can be seized as courts of first instance.

Further differences also exist in the case of the special courts
and quasi-judicial organs of both groups of countries. It has

---

[25] Ehrlich (St.), "Notion et garanties de la légalité socialiste dans les pays de l'Europe de
l'Est," *Politique, Rev. int. des doctrines et des institutions*, 1958, p. 327.
[26] Polish law on judicial organisation, art. 13. The *People's Council* in Poland (*rady naro-
dowe*) is the equivalent of the Russian *Soviet*.

already been noted that Yugoslavia now has a court of constitutional justice. The Polish judicial organisation comprises courts of social security alongside military courts; both, since 1962, are subject to the control of the Supreme Court. On the other hand, minor infractions or misdemeanours, which, since 1961 have not been included in the penal code, are within the competence of penal administrative commissions, the decisions of which are subject to appeal to the praesidium of the People's Councils of each province (*voivodie*). These special bodies are sometimes provided for by the constitution as in the case of Yugoslavia and the German Democratic Republic.

The Soviet Comrades' Courts have their Hungarian equivalent. They were created in Hungary in 1957—prior to their establishment in the U.S.S.R. therefore—and have a considerable workload. The Czech experiment with "local people's courts" appears, on the other hand, to have been a failure and legislation of 1969 abolished them. A first attempt along the same lines was a failure in Poland, but the idea was taken up again in a new law of 1965 which, in the perspective of the new society, created "social conciliation commissions" and "social enterprise courts."[27]

229. Public arbitration

Like the U.S.S.R., the other European socialist countries, as well as North Korea, Outer Mongolia, and Cuba—but not China—confide litigation arising in the collectivised sector to specialised bodies, independent of the regular courts, which are called either "economic arbitration commissions" or "state arbitration commissions" (*Staatliches Vertragsgericht* in the German Democratic Republic). These systems have always been somewhat different from that prevailing in the Soviet Union and such differences have been accentuated in the last few years as the economic organisation of these countries has developed along separate lines.[28]

---

[27] Rybicki (M.), "La participation des citoyens à l'administration de la justice en Pologne et dans les pays socialistes" (1971) Rev. int. dr. comparé 553–565.
[28] Knapp (V.), "State Arbitration in Socialist Countries" (1973) *International Encyclopedia of Comparative Law*, Vol. 16, Chap. 13.

The public arbitration commissions in general only exist at two levels, central and regional, and may sometimes be attached to various different authorities such as the President of the Council of Ministers in Poland or the Committee for Economic Co-ordination in Bulgaria. Sometimes their jurisdiction is greater than it is in the U.S.S.R., as for example in Bulgaria, Poland and Czechoslovakia where it includes litigation arising between agricultural co-operatives and state enterprises. Public arbitration procedures may also differ. In the German Democratic Republic, for instance, the sessions are private. In Bulgaria and Poland the decisions of the regional commissions may be appealed to the central commission; in Czechoslovakia the decisions of the central commission may be taken on appeal to its *praesidium* (constituted by the chief arbitrator and his first assistant). In East Germany some decisions of the arbitration commission may be treated as binding precedents (*Grundsatzverfahren*). The extent to which administrative functions are confided to these bodies also varies considerably; it is very limited in Bulgaria and Poland compared to the practice in the U.S.S.R.

Apart from these matters of detail, a most remarkable development has occurred in three countries, Yugoslavia, Albania and Hungary. Public arbitration commissions were abolished in Yugoslavia in 1955, in Albania in 1969 and in Hungary in 1972. In Yugoslavia they were replaced by an autonomous hierarchy of economic courts, in which people's assessors collaborate, whose jurisdiction extends to litigation with foreigners as well as between organisms of the collectivised sector. In Albania litigation arising in the collectivised sector has simply been placed within the jurisdiction of the ordinary courts. In Hungary yet a third technique has been adopted for this type of litigation: special chambers have been instituted within the Provincial Courts with an appeal lying to the economic division of the Supreme Court.

In addition to its adjudicative functions, the *plenum* of the Supreme Economic Court in Yugoslavia, like the State Court of Arbitration it replaced and the Federal Supreme Court, also has a regulatory function; it thus promulgated a statement of "general usage respecting merchandise exchanges" on January 18, 1954, published in the Official Journal; this regulation is a summary of the rules of civil and commercial law rather than a true collection of commercial usages, and it remedied in part the absence of a federal code of obligations in Yugoslavia.

230. Election of judges

The principle of electing judges applies in all European socialist countries but the details of the implementation of this principle are often very different from those in the U.S.S.R.

All judges—even those at the base of the court system—are picked by elected assemblies, such as the different levels of the people's councils in Czechoslovakia and Yugoslavia, or of the office of the National Assembly (Diet) in Hungary and Poland. And whereas in the U.S.S.R. any citizen may be elected judge, the law in Bulgaria, Hungary, Poland, Czechoslovakia and Yugoslavia requires that judges have some legal training. In Bulgaria, courses of instruction are even organised for the people's assessors in order that they have some introduction to legal principles. The term of office for judges varies as well from country to country: three or five years in Bulgaria (according to the court), eight years in Yugoslavia, 10 years in Czechoslovakia. In Poland, the Supreme Court judges hold office for five years and others "for an indefinite period," which really means for life because in Poland judges at all levels can only be removed for the grounds specified by law.

231. People's assessors

The participation of people's assessors in the judgment of disputes has been adopted in Poland, as in the U.S.S.R., but with a difference: the Polish assessors are elected by people's councils rather than by universal suffrage. It is thought that this innovation has generally produced good results because it allows for a continuous exposure of the professional judge to public opinion. However, it is now apparent that the principle of such participation has perhaps been over-extended; and it has been limited therefore by different means and, in particular, by providing in certain cases for a simplified procedure according to which a professional judge sits alone. Such, for example, is the general rule in criminal matters when the maximum penalty to which the accused may be liable is less than two years' imprisonment. In civil matters, with certain exceptions, the president of the district court may decide that the case will be judged by a single or by three professional judges.

There is also provision for people's assessors in the Czech Constitution of 1960. In order to indicate the equality of assessors and professional judges, it mentions (in section 100) judges who practise their functions as a profession and people's judges who exercise such functions but not as a profession. These judges are elected for a four year term by district national committees; their role is now limited in civil matters because the principle of the judge sitting alone was admitted in 1969 except in family and labour law matters. Similar rules apply in Hungary.

In Yugoslavia the institution has been adopted as well. People's assessors sit with the judge in all courts of first instance except in those cases where the law authorises the judge to decide alone. Unlike the other people's republics, such assessors are also to be found in the Yugoslav economic tribunals, which are treated as real courts.

232. System of remedies

The system of remedies against judgments in the people's republics also differs on certain points from the system in the Soviet Union. In Czechoslovakia and Yugoslavia, for instance, the principle of an appeal by way of rehearing is still retained whereas it is not admitted in Russia. In Poland it has not been retained although the exercise of other types of remedies is more available to private citizens than in Russia. The recourse by way of special revision is in particular different from that in Soviet Russia; it is taken directly to the Supreme Court but it does not result in the quashing of the judgment or decision unless it is lodged within a delay of six months from the time such judgment or decision became final; after this delay, it may be decided in the interests of legal principle that the decision or judgment was poorly decided, but it nevertheless retains the authority of *res judicata*. It is also necessary to remember that in practice the Polish public prosecutor fulfils a much less important role than the Soviet *Prokuratura*; his control is exercised primarily with respect to the application of criminal law; the recourse by way of a petition in revision, which can only be taken by the minister of justice, the attorney-general and the first president of the Supreme Court, is in such circum-

stances therefore if not theoretical at least very rare in civil matters.[29]

233. Role of decided cases

The different rules discussed above respecting the existing court
structure of the U.S.S.R. and certain of the people's republics may
have some influence upon the role of decided cases. There is no
doubt at all that in both the U.S.S.R. and the people's republics
decided cases are strictly subordinate to enacted law: Marxist-
Leninist teaching requires that this be so. A different relationship
can however exist between the courts and the legislators according
to another tradition. The distinction as to what is a matter of principle, and which must, therefore, be determined by the legislators,
and what is simple application or development of the principle,
which can then be left to government administration or judges, is
not always very precise. And so, while strict compliance with doctrinal requirements is everywhere observed, the working out of
relationships between state and administrative or judicial authorities may therefore vary from one country to another.

A Polish law of March 28, 1958, modifying the code of civil procedure, increased the jurisdiction of the district tribunals and diminished correspondingly that of the *voïvodie* tribunals; the purpose
was to lessen the burden of the Supreme Court, a court of second
instance, and to allow it to be devoted, more than in the past, to its
general duty of supervisory control over judicial decisions. This
reform provoked certain objections. Some Polish jurists think that
the Supreme Court would work more effectively for the success of
socialist legality by exercising its control, as it did in the past, over
specific decisions which it would revise or quash, rather than by
developing a more abstract method consisting of instructing judges
on the ways in which the law should be understood and applied in
the light of a whole series of judicial decisions which it will have
reviewed *ex officio* in the discharge of its administrative duties.[30]

In Hungary, Poland, Czechoslovakia and Yugoslavia, the

---

[29] In 1958, 378 petitions in civil matters are recorded, of which 282 were held to be founded
and 35 rejected. After October 1956, the procedure of special revision was used to reverse a
large number of unjust condemnations from which no appeal lay, after having been handed
down during the oppressive regime which was later repudiated.

[30] Woner (T.), "Rola jurysdykcyina sadu Najwyszczego," *Nowe Prawo*, 1959, Vol. 2,
pp. 148–153, analysed in *L'U.R.S.S. et les pays de l'Est*, 1960, Vols. 2–3, p. 38.

administration of justice is entrusted to judges who qualify, by their education and national traditions, as jurists much more than Soviet judges. This factor is not without its significance. Although it would be contrary to official doctrine to claim this to be so, it is altogether likely that decided cases will have a more important place in fact in these countries than in the U.S.S.R. A comparison of the collections of reported cases published in the U.S.S.R. and the people's democracies supports this supposition. In Yugoslavia the law gives the Federal Supreme Court the task of supervising the regular publication of its own important decisions and those of the different supreme courts. Three annual volumes of the decisions of the supreme courts have been published every year since 1956 in the federal Official Journal. A similar legal provision respecting economic courts obliges the Yugoslav Supreme Economic Court to ensure the regular publication of judgments within its jurisdiction. In Poland, as well, an official collection of decisions of the Supreme Court in civil and criminal matters, and an official collection of the arbitral awards of the General Arbitration Commission, are published regularly.

The series of reported cases published in the people's democracies are official; only selected decisions are included and in this respect Soviet practice is observed. Decisions are chosen for publication because of their usefulness to judges or jurists and because they are considered to agree with official policy. They are not, therefore, as in bourgeois countries, used to shape legal development independently of the will of the legislators.

CHAPTER III

CUSTOM AND RULES OF SOCIALIST COMMUNITY LIFE

234. Custom

The preceding discussion of Marxist-Leninist doctrine and the role of legislation in Soviet law may convey the impression that custom has a very restricted role in this legal system. The total transformation of society—and even of man—which will be brought about in order to establish a truly communist regime implies a revolutionary upheaval, one in which no further dependence can be placed on the customs of what appears to be a bygone era.

Custom only remains important in the U.S.S.R. to the extent that it is useful or necessary for the interpretation or in the application of enacted law (*consuetudo secundum legem*), or in those very few instances where the law itself refers to custom or usage and allows them some scope of application.

This secondary place to which custom is relegated in the Soviet legal system is not at all surprising. Particular mention should nonetheless be made of it because it constitutes a complete rejection of what was Russian tradition. But the rejection of custom by Soviet law has nothing to do with the phenomenon which, in countries of the Romano-Germanic system, during the nineteenth and twentieth centuries, brought about the substitution of an essentially enacted law, founded on codes, to the previous customary law. This latter transformation was essentially one explained by a change in techniques and not, as a general rule, in either its object or its result, a change in the substantive principles of customary law. In the U.S.S.R., on the other hand, a complete change in the substance of the law accompanied the change in technique; it was intended, in a truly *social* revolution, that citizens become accus-

:omed to living in a completely different manner and according to
าew rules.

235. The rules of socialist community life

The decline of custom in the U.S.S.R. is however only temporary. The ideal of Marxism-Leninism is to build a society in which
there is no longer any law and where social relations will be ruled
by custom alone. Custom, therefore, although rejected today, is
called upon to play a future role of the very greatest importance
when the communist goal has been attained and law will be needed
no longer. This future held out for custom is already apparent in
certain expressions of Soviet law or doctrine which make reference
to rules of community life in the socialist society. Article 59 of the
Soviet Constitution states: "It is the duty of every citizen of the
U.S.S.R. to observe the Constitution of the U.S.S.R., to respect
the law and the rules of socialist community life and to bear with
dignity the high calling of citizen of the U.S.S.R."

Writers, both in the U.S.S.R. and outside, have wondered what
significance should be attached to the analogous terms found in the
1936 Constitution and what consequences should be drawn from
it. For some the reference to the rules of socialist community life
appeared to constitute a principle susceptible of replacing the
bourgeois legal notion of public policy or public order and good
morals. Others have seen in it the basis for a kind of custom
praeter legem through which certain obligations might be imposed
on citizens (such as that of bringing help or assistance to one's fellow citizens in certain circumstances) apart from those instances
where such obligations result from a legislative text. Thought of in
either of these ways, the words of the Constitution have received
little application outside of those cases where further consequences have been specified more concretely by other legal texts.[1]

In fact however the principle has quite another meaning; and it
is deformed when any attempt is made to charge it with juridical
content and therefore to attribute to it some precise significance

---

[1] It has a place, *e.g.* in the definition of the civil offence of "hooliganism": *cf.* Marie (N.),
"Le houliganisme en Union soviétique" (1970), Rev. de l'est 143–166. Similarly, in Poland a
Supreme Court directive of March 18, 1968 states that divorces must not be granted if it
appears to be contrary to the rules of social life: Gorecki (J.), "Les directives de la Cour
suprême en matière de divorce" *Państwo i prawo*, August–September 1968.

within the framework of the legal order. The "rules of socialist community life" to which the Constitution refers are not—and are not intended to be—law. The expression can only be really understood by considering the future era of communist society: law will disappear and only precepts of living in a communist society will remain to govern men's behaviour. At the present time the words of article 59 of the Constitution have only a very limited significance; they are however the basis for certain experiments in new social structures in the U.S.S.R. The rules of socialist community life in a socialist society are the basis for all the administrative activities of the country in which citizens can, right now, voluntarily co-operate, by enrolling in the militia or in various social services for example. These activities presage the full reality of life among men in the communist society of tomorrow.

CHAPTER IV

DOCTRINAL WRITING

Doctrinal writing, like the other sources of law, requires several comments. On this point as well the Soviet legal system is original.[1]

236. Marxism-Leninism

When speaking of doctrinal writing and its role in Soviet law, it is impossible to consider only those published works which are strictly legal in nature. Even before making any reference to them, consideration must be given to the materials in which the doctrine of Marxism-Leninism itself is authoritatively expressed. In the U.S.S.R. the law is nothing other than the putting into practice of this doctrine; it is the very basis of the policy of the Soviet leaders.

Soviet authors are wholly convinced of this. They find as much if indeed not more support for their affirmations in citations from or references to the writings of the "doctrinal fathers" of Marxism than in the published works or articles of jurists; the writings of Marx, Engels and Lenin whose complete works are the basis of any law library have first place. Appeal is also made to writings or speeches of Soviet political leaders and to the programmes and other resolutions of the Communist Party itself. These last materials are not, strictly speaking, legal sources but their doctrinal authority is uncontested: there one finds the currently authorised explanation of the Marxist-Leninist doctrine in the U.S.S.R. with respect to any number of matters. A Soviet jurist or anyone wanting to study Soviet law must refer to them constantly.

237. Doctrinal writing properly speaking

Alongside these basic documents indicating the spirit of Soviet law

[1] Tchkhikvadze (V. M.), "L'évolution de la science juridique soviétique" (1968) Rev. int. dr. comparé 19–34.

and providing general guidelines for Soviet judges, what we in the bourgeois countries understand by legal writing or *doctrine* also presents certain special characteristics in the Soviet Union. In fact the organisation of things in this respect forces an almost complete distinction to be made between the teaching of law and legal research.

Professors of law do not criticise the law; they are only expected to simplify its teaching and application, by clarifying the intention of the legislators; and, like judges, they must also seek to ensure the success of government policy by convincing citizens of the eminently wise and just character of Soviet law. The works written for this purpose therefore make no attempt to be original. Moreover they are very often the work of a group (*kollektiv*) of authors headed by an editorial chief who supervises their collaboration. Before the work is published it is generally submitted to the criticism of a committee which examines it in detail for its conformity to law and to the orthodoxy of the regime.

The tasks of those who have opted for a career in research is quite different. They are not professors nor do they teach law; they are scholarly associates in some institute of the U.S.S.R. or one of the S.S.R. The most eminent of these is the Institute of State and Law of the Academy of Sciences of the U.S.S.R. which employs about 400 associates divided into a number of sections.[2] At the federal level, the Institute of Soviet Legislation, reporting to the U.S.S.R. Ministry of Justice, and the Institute specialising in criminal matters attached to the *Prokuratura* are also important. Research in these different institutes is organised according to a plan, but this plan is to a very great extent established on the basis of suggestions made by the various sections themselves and their own researchers; the authorities who finally decide upon the plan do little more than make sure that the many different paths of research on the same subject are carried on with all possible coordination and control the desire to expand, or on the other hand to relax, the research of any particular section. Before being printed the work prepared by researchers is the object of detailed

---

[2] These sections are devoted to the following purposes: problems of constitutional law; administrative sciences; general theory of law and the state; administration of agriculture; economic law; general problems of socialist legality; history of the state and of law; private law; contemporary bourgeois states and laws; international (and cosmic) law; laws of newly independent countries. The official journal of the Institute is the publication *Sovetskoe Gosudarstvo i Pravo*.

discussions within each section or at a higher level, but it is finally published under the name of the individual researchers who prepared it. The institutes—or at least the most important of them—possess excellent libraries and facilities for this work and a very high calibre of scholarship is the result of their organised research. For some years the efforts of the institutes were hampered by various factors, but at the present time, and in an atmosphere of greater freedom, they have been successful in their reaction against excessively conformist attitudes. It has been realised that legal scholarship should not merely be a matter of explaining Soviet law and exposing its merits. Research in new areas has been taken up; an increasingly important place is given to sociology, especially by those working in criminal, family and labour law. There is also new interest in comparative law, especially in the laws of the other socialist countries.[3]

238. Other socialist countries

The role of doctrine in other socialist countries, especially in Poland, is closer to the Romano-Germanic system than to that of the Soviet Union. It is not limited to explaining the rules of positive law, but also to co-operating, actively and in the national interest, in improving the law. Polish leaders freely admit the legitimacy of this position; and they show it by consulting the Polish Association of Jurists before enacting new legislation. But this very full co-operation in the work of legislation and codification somewhat monopolises the attention of legal authors so that their publications are in the form of articles or commentaries on individual laws rather than general, less fragmentary, works.

The legal writers in the people's republics are less doctrinaire than their Soviet counterparts because they have a greater attachment to the western tradition of intellectual freedom and have retained a closer connection with western Europe. They know, and have no hesitation about writing to this effect, that the capital-

---

[3] Szabo (I.), "La science comparative du droit," *Annales universitatis Budapestinensis. Sectio juridica*, Vol. 5, 1964, pp. 91–134. Eorsi (G.), *Comparative Civil (Private) Law* (1979), "Comparative Analysis of Socialist and Capitalist law," *Coexistence* (1964), pp. 130–151. Dutoit (B.), "Die sowjetische Rechtswergleichung gestern und heute" *Jahrbüch für Ostrecht* (1975) p. 49–71. Tille (A. A.) & Svekov (G. V.), *Sravnitel' nÿ metod v juridiceskih disciplinah* (1973). Tille (A. A.), *Sotsialisticeskoe sravnitel' noe pravovedenie* (published also in English as *Socialist Comparative Law*) (1975). Tumanov (V. A.), ed., *Sravnitel' noe Pravovedenie* (1978).

ist regimes have undergone great changes since the time of Marx and Engels. It would seem that they want to co-operate in bringing about a greater understanding between the two camps rather than condemn the bourgeois laws outright. They do not systematically interpret the preoccupation of capitalist states with social justice as the inevitably suspicious and hateful reaction of a threatened bourgeois class.[4] They believe that western legal science continues to provide them with models and that the experiments of Western states, despite the differences in their political systems, are worthy of study and may, sometimes, even inspire their own socialist leaders. "Many bourgeois legal ideas and opinions," writes a Polish author, "are not acceptable, but that does not mean . . . as it once was thought, and wrongly . . . that certain ideas, statements and theories advanced by their legal science are *a priori* to be rejected as erroneous or sterile. Our task is not to refute *a priori* all intellectual attainments of bourgeois scholarship but rather to examine critically such attainments."[5] Today's generally accepted point of view is very well expressed by an Hungarian author was writes: "While socialist legality reveals itself to be historically the antithesis of capitalist legality, it is also its continuation and historical successor. The socialist principle retains all the progressive principles included in the capitalist notion of legality; it maintains and uses every method and technique susceptible of bringing about the goals pursued by socialist legality . . . We study the legal institutions of the West in order to draw lessons from their legal method and technique so that socialist legality can be strengthened and developed."[6]

The prevailing attitude in the people's democracies is, therefore, in the end, in substantial agreement with that of the jurists of bourgeois countries who, although they may consider that the Soviet regime is oppressive and based on a highly doubtful doctrine, do not for this reason think that they must inevitably condemn everything done in the U.S.S.R.

---

[4] Zawadski (Z.), "Contribution à l'origine de la conception du "welfare-state," *Państwo i Prawo* (August–September, 1960).

[5] Auscaler (G.), "Les buts idéologiques actuels de la science du droit," *Państwo i Prawo* (July 1956).

[6] Szabo (I.), in *Le concept de la légalité dans les pays socialistes* (1961), p. 402.

TITLE III

STRUCTURE OF THE LAW

239. Originality of socialist laws

The structure of a law can be considered from three different points of view: by investigating its principal divisions and categories, by examining its jural concepts and by studying the manner in which the legal rule itself is conceived.

Soviet law, as the successor to the former Russian law, inherited the concept of the legal rule shared by the countries of the Romano-Germanic family; no particular remarks are required in this respect.

On the other hand, Soviet law is certainly original with respect to its categories and concepts, for while the *form* of the categories and concepts of the Romano-Germanic family has been retained a total renewal of their *substance* has been achieved. In a new type of society founded on a completely different economic organisation and professed ideal, the problems are not the same. The names of former categories and concepts may thus have been retained, but for the most part they have been changed in their real nature and are not, save in a formal sense, the categories and concepts of the pre-Soviet period familiar to jurists of the Romano-Germanic family.

CHAPTER I

DIVISIONS OF SOCIALIST LAW

240. Formal resemblance to bourgeois laws

In appearances the divisions of Soviet law have remained, with some exceptions, those of the Romano-Germanic laws. There are, of course, some differences: family law is distinct from civil law, the classification known as commercial law has disappeared and a *kolkhoze* law and a law of habitation have been created. However variations also exist among the different laws of the Romano-Germanic family and those to be noted in Soviet law do not, simply in themselves, justify the classifying of this law as a special family.

Soviet authors do not admit however that only such formal differences can be considered and argue that one must take into account the actual content of each branch of law.[1] They stress that the resemblance between Soviet law and non-socialist laws of continental European countries with respect to principal legal divisions is wholly one of form, and therefore superficial; in reality, they maintain, the difference in economic structures of the two groups of countries means that the substance of private, constitutional, administrative and criminal law is very different. The law in general may very well be divided into a certain number of branches having the same name, but the analogy can be carried no further because substantially different problems exist in socialist and non-socialist states. Moreover, the Marxist-Leninist doctrine leads to a new non-individualist way of envisaging these various problems.

241. Constitutional law

There is hardly any need to insist upon the fact that Soviet constitutional law is very different from the constitutional law of capitalist countries.

---

[1] *Cf.* especially the observations of P. S. Romachkin, in *Le concept de la légalité dans les pays socialistes* (1961), pp. 364–371.

There are two principal features which characterise the constitutional system of socialist countries.[2] The first is the very great importance of the Communist Party at the political level. The second is the fact that the soviets of different levels exercise real political and administrative powers. The events of 1968 in Czechoslovakia, and that country's policy of appearing to admit criticism too freely and thus endangering the primacy of the Party itself, show the importance attached to the first point. The events in Poland in 1981 confirm the same point. The very name, *Soviet Union*, shows the fundamental character of the second. It is the acceptance of these two principles that makes of a country a member of the socialist family of laws. A political regime in which the Communist Party would share power with other parties, or in which there were no people's councils modelled along the lines of the soviets of the U.S.S.R., would not be looked upon as a socialist country, at least in the sense that it is understood in the U.S.S.R. itself.

The Soviet state structure did not figure in the original platform of the Communist Party; it was articulated immediately after the 1917 Revolution as a way of showing that, even with the small number of actual Party members, power really did henceforth belong to the people. In fact however real power has always resided within the Party itself. It is the Party that selects candidates for election to the soviets of different levels and controls the training and assignment of personnel to all posts included in the lists (*nomenklatura*) established by its own executive authorities.

242. Other branches of law

The completely original character of the institutions of Soviet constitutional law can hardly be questioned, but its originality in other branches is no less marked when they too are compared to those of bourgeois countries. The transition to the socialist state, on the basis of Marxism-Leninism, has given rise to an almost complete transformation of attitudes and structures. This is so

---

[2] Hazard (J. N.), *The Soviet System of Government* (5th ed., 1980), *Communists and their Law* (1969). Mouskhély (M.) and Jedryka (A.), *Le gouvernement de l'U.R.S.S.* (1961). Chambre (H.), *L'Union soviétique. Introduction à l'étude de ses institutions* (2nd ed., 1966).

whether one examines private law or administrative law, or again such fields as labour relations, social security or criminal law.[3]

243. Private law

Consider the private law. The fundamental issue facing jurists in capitalist legal systems is the preservation of individualist interests and therefore private ownership, the economic basis of a capitalist society; the essential concern is to recognise the *meum* and the *teum* in the law of property, contract or succession. In the Soviet Union, on the contrary, the regulation of what is called "personal ownership"—and not *private* ownership, in order to show that even here a change has come about—is only of secondary importance. Soviet civil law is centred around the notion of *socialist ownership*, the various forms, the legal regime and the guarantees of which are studied in the U.S.S.R.[4] A reading of the Soviet Constitution makes the primordial importance of this new type of ownership apparent; it is also evident from a reading of the Fundamental Principles of Civil Law (1961) which contain an enumeration of the things which are the property either of the state (art. 21), the *kolkhozi* (art. 23) or co-operatives (art. 24) on the one hand and, on the other, those which may be owned personally (art. 25) or by the family of the *dvor* or collective farm household (art. 27). The protection of socialist ownership raises problems quite different from those of individual private ownership. It is much more difficult to protect adequately and effectively. Private individuals are always ready to fight for their own rights and interests and can be counted upon to defend their own private property; but the protection of socialist ownership must be organised by means of special institutions for the defense of general interests. To the extent then that Soviet law has socialist ownership as one of its objects—and it is on this point that the Soviet jurist faces his greatest problems—it is very different in content from the private law of non-socialist countries where there is not much, or sometimes any, preoccupation with such problems.

---

[3] Hazard (J. N.), Butler (W. E.) and Maggs (P. B.) *The Soviet Legal System* (1977). Bellon (J.), *Droit pénal soviétique et droit pénal occidental* (1961). Ancel (M.), *Introduction au système de droit pénal soviétique* (1962). Lowit (T.), *Le syndicalisme de type soviétique. L'U.R.S.S. et les pays de l'Est européen* (1971).
[4] Stoyanovitch (K.), *Le régime de la propriété en U.R.S.S.* (1962).

244. Administrative law

In administrative law as well there has been considerable change in the types of questions raised and the kind of emphasis they receive.[5] To a jurist of the capitalist world the essential challenge is once again to protect the individual and affirm his rights against a government administration whose abuses must be curtailed or punished. The Soviet jurist is not indifferent to these problems either, but he does not approach them from the same point of view.[6] For him it is vain to want to assure a protection of the individual outside of the complete social change which Marxist-Leninist doctrine has brought about through the collectivisation of the means of production. Moreover, this collectivisation suffices, as a general rule, for solving the problems which concern jurists of the capitalist world; from the Soviet point of view, individual rights and interests are automatically protected and guaranteed once society is founded on the wise principles of Marxism respecting economic organisation; complete agreement between the interests of the individual and those of society is in fact brought about, it is argued, in a socialist regime.

The administrative law problems of primary interest to jurists of the socialist countries are thus largely new ones. Here, once more, the notion of socialist ownership is very important. The instruments of production, in the U.S.S.R., have all passed into socialist ownership. Socialist laws endeavour to multiply methods of control which will assure an ordered exploitation of such property and its protection from all kinds of wastefulness and encroachments. For reasons already mentioned, reliance cannot be placed, as in capitalist countries, on the initiative of private persons; many different kinds of compulsory controls must be set up, and new institutions created, if the collectivisation of the means of production is to amount to more than a moral gesture—the suppression of man's exploitation by man—and really benefit all citizens.

The discussions at the conference of the International Association of Legal Science held at Warsaw since 1958 showed this to be so. Jurists from socialist and non-socialist countries had a great

---

[5] *Cf.* the report of the Polish professor Jaroszyński, in *Le concept de la légalité dans les pays socialistes* (1961), pp. 91–115. *Cf.* also the reports and discussions at the end of the same volume. The remarks respecting Polish law apply with equal force to Soviet law save in the case of several of the examples provided.

[6] Hazard, Butler and Maggs, *op. cit.* pp. 181 *et seq.*

deal of difficulty in understanding each other. The non-socialist jurists had trouble in understanding an administrative law which is not centred around the protection of individuals, nor dominated by some kind of judicial control over the administration. But the jurists of socialist countries were concerned with something else; for them it is essential that the government's policy for building communism be successful; and they have replaced judicial control with a new type of control exercised by the people's representatives and organisations. But the 1977 Constitution has somewhat drawn together these different approaches. Article 58 (para. 2) of the Constitution provides in effect that "the actions of officials in violation of the law, in excess of their powers, or infringing the rights of citizens may be the basis for proceedings in the courts according to the conditions established by law." This text is significant because it enlarges considerably the scope of judicial review.[7] Soviet administrative law nonetheless remains distinct from its counterpart in bourgeois countries in this respect. Marxism-Leninism leads socialist jurists to seek solutions to problems by means of principles quite different from those admitted in capitalist countries.

245. Rejection of the public law—private law distinction

The originality of Soviet law is further shown by the doctrinal rejection of the *summa divisio* of law as understood in the Romano-Germanic family.

The distinction between public law and private law is both fundamental and traditional in the countries of the Romano-Germanic family. It dates from Roman law and is fundamental in the sense that these countries have always considered private law to be the heart of law. Public law, very closely linked to politics and distinguished only with difficulty from the "science of governing," was, for many centuries, wisely left aside by jurists; even today in many respects public law remains uncertain and unstable compared to private law.

Marxist-Leninist doctrine is on quite a different footing. In a letter to Kursky, Lenin used an expression which has since become famous: "We do not recognise anything 'private,' and regard

---

[7] Lesage (M.), "Judicial Review of Administration in the U.S.S.R." (1980) 4 Rev. soc. Law, 465.

everything . . . as falling under *public* and not *private* law." The idea has been taken up by all Soviet jurists. It should not be understood as meaning that public law has absorbed private law; it merely signifies that in the economic field the dualism of public law and private law as two autonomous bodies of rules is not admitted. To deny the distinction between public law and private law is therefore to affirm the unity of law; and this unity results from the fact that law, in all of its branches, is essentially a reflection of the economic organisation of society.

There is, too, a further consideration. Marxism-Leninism identifies law with coercion. It does not consider rules conforming to justice or inspired by morality, and which men spontaneously follow in their mutual relations, to be rules of law at all. According to this doctrine, only those rules imposed more or less openly or hypocritically by the ruling class and in order to protect its economic interests and perpetuate its own "dictatorship" are *legal* rules. Law is only an application of policy, an instrument in the service of the ruling class. There is therefore, in this view, no more place for a private law which, independently of any political character or preoccupations—and that, after all, is the essence of the idea of private as opposed to public law—purports to give expression to ideas of good organisation and social justice.

The negation of private law is imposed by the new concept of law affirmed by Marxism. To say, as Lenin did, that all law has become public law is simply to state, in another form, the idea that all legal relationships are ruled by a political idea and that rules of law are in no sense the expression of an immanent justice. Law is policy and reciprocally what is not policy is not law.

There are several practically important consequences which flow from this rejection of the distinction between public and private law.

246. Mandatory character of law

Because all law, and not simply what we would call public law, is an aspect of policy, and in order that that policy be successful, an imperative or mandatory character is inevitably given to the largest possible number of laws; and the imprint of public policy is given to the largest possible number of rules. This is especially desirable because the Soviet regime is not satisfied with society in its present form. It aspires to bring about its total transformation in order to create a new kind of society.

All kinds of relationships and behaviour must therefore be changed in order to create the conditions in which it will be possible to renounce force and law, and so that citizens will henceforth behave with respect to each other with automatic mutual understanding and fraternity. Suppletive legal rules which may mean the perpetuation of past mistakes must disappear to make room for imperative rules—these alone will be able to create, and impose, the new society.

But it will not be enough to affirm that civil law is in reality public law and to say that its rules must all be mandatory. In many cases this imperative character must be reinforced, in order to guarantee better the success of the policy of Soviet leaders, by applying penal sanctions for the violation of private law rules. The non-performance of contracts in the collectivised sector of the Soviet economy thus carries penal sanctions; the member of a *kolkhoz* who does not accomplish the minimum amount of work due to the *kolkhoz*, and purchases made for the purpose of resale, are both punishable under criminal law; the creation of a private business under the simulated form of a co-operative is also a criminal offence.

247. Search for new systematics

Soviet authors, imbued with the desire to break away completely from the capitalist societies they consider so unjust, sometimes seem ill at ease for having retained, even though only in a formal sense, the legal categories of bourgeois laws. The entire renewal of the concept and the very substance of Soviet law also requires, in their eyes, that the law repose on a new systematic classification rejecting that of the past. These efforts up to the present time have not, however, met with much success; they must nevertheless be mentioned because they are linked to some of the crises through which Soviet law has passed and they give some indication of the way in which the evolution of law and its eventual disappearance are understood in the Soviet Union.

Doctrinal quarrels on this point have twice centred around the question whether or not it would be suitable to recognise a special branch of law to be called "economic law" within the legal system.

Briefly put, the idea of "economic law" was that law in the true sense (*i.e.* containing definite rules) was really only suitable for private relations and that when the state (or some public body or organism) was concerned such rules should give way to considerations of what is simply opportune and suitable in the public interest. Such a conception would obviously clothe public authorities with very great discretionary power.[8] No attempt will be made here to retrace the often heated discussions which took place on this point. Today the quarrel seems to have subsided. As long as a socialist state and law subsist in the U.S.S.R. there is every likelihood that the present categories of Soviet law and its reliance upon "rules" will be retained. In the U.S.S.R. and most socialist countries, therefore, no concerted legislative attempt is being made to enshrine the idea of such a distinct branch of law.[9] But it has prevailed in Czechoslovakia and in East Germany and, in the former, great efforts have been made to present the law in a new organisational framework that reflects its socialist structure. Apart from the distinction between the civil and economic codes, a new terminology has been developed for use in the civil code itself: in the place of the traditional notion of "contract," for example, there has been substituted the notion of "services" owed by bodies of the collectivised sector to citizens. And with the promulgation of a code on international commerce it has been recognised that for a socialist country at least there is a considerable difference between internal governance and international commercial activity.

[8] Hazard (J. N.), "Le droit soviétique et le dépérissement du droit," in *Université de Bruxelles, Faculté de droit, Travaux et conférences*, VIII (1960); *adde* Bilinsky (A.), "Ringen um das Zivilrecht im Ostblock," *Europa Recht*, 1961, pp. 174–190. Kučera (J.), "La théorie du droit économique socialiste. Son application en Tchécoslovaquie" *Ann. Univ. sciences sociales de Toulouse*, t. XXI, 1973, p. 337.

[9] On the present state of the question, *cf.* Mateesco-Matte (M.), "Le droit économique socialiste dix ans après sa 'codification' dans la législation civile soviétique" *Annuaire de l'U.R.S.S. 1970–1971*, p. 35.

CHAPTER II

SOCIALIST LEGAL CONCEPTS

248. Domination of Marxist doctrine

The people's dictatorship and the collectivisation of the national economy bring about a distortion of a whole series of traditional concepts; in the new conditions in which they are used, they mean something quite new. Although they employ a vocabulary inherited from Russian law, Soviet jurists deal with different problems and they examine them from a quite different point of view. In these circumstances familiar words have taken on vastly different connotations. In studying Soviet law, therefore, it is necessary to rid oneself of our established conceptual philosophy and to realise that these concepts have a variable, not an absolute, value. Adversaries of the Soviet regime deny that a democracy exists or that there are any real freedoms in the U.S.S.R. It would be fairer to say that these concepts have changed meaning in Soviet society. For the sake of clarity, it may be regretted that a new terminology, clearly specifying these changes, has not been created. However, we must adjust ourselves to Soviet terminology and realise that the concepts of Soviet law, whatever the vocabulary employed, are not really those of the bourgeois laws. A study of the Soviet substantive law itself is necessary in order to appreciate the breadth of the change that has taken place. So much, however, cannot be attempted here.

Observations on ownership and contracts in Soviet law, and on the "most-favoured nation" clause in commercial relations with the Soviet Union, must suffice by way of characteristic examples.

Section I—Ownership

249. Bourgeois and socialist concepts

The central notion of Soviet law—that which Soviet jurists proudly state they have completely changed—is the notion of ownership. The western jurist is at first somewhat surprised that so much emphasis is placed on a notion which, in French law at least, is not of primary concern.

It is however altogether natural that the regulation of ownership be placed in the forefront by Soviet jurists. Marxist doctrine holds that law is conditioned above all by the economic structure of society; of essential importance to society, then, is the manner in which property is appropriated. The law ruling ownership and property is therefore crucial. And with respect to the law of property and ownership Marxism requires a complete change of ideas—a revolution, the effects of which will consequently be felt in all other branches of law and even in men's consciences.

The apparent simplicity moreover of the regime of ownership even in the capitalist countries is in itself a pit-fall. The usual description given in continental civilian systems, for example, of the substance of the law of property is undoubtedly far from exhaustive and gives an entirely false idea of this part of the law. The many restrictions on the rights of owners are often omitted and little mention is made of municipal law or environmental law or the status of the tenant farmer; these matters are studied elsewhere.[1] Even the autonomy of the law of contract as distinguished from the law of property is only a consequence of the extreme individualism, and therefore of the primary role attributed to the individual will, admitted in western societies; in the absence of this attitude, the contracts of sale, lease and hire and others similar might very well be regarded as forming part of the law of property in a large sense.

Soviet law rejects such a narrow concept of the law of property. In the U.S.S.R. property law consists of the whole body of rules dealing not only with the appropriation of things and the transfer of the right of ownership, but also with its administration and management and the legal operations in which it is involved.

250. Difficulties of comparison

The law of property in the Soviet Union therefore differs from that in the capitalist countries from many points of view.

---

[1] Compare the comprehensive approach given to the presentation of property law in English law, for example, in the work of Lawson (F. H.), *Introduction to the Law of Property* (1958).

The distinction considered fundamental to the Common law, that of "real" and "personal" property, or to the laws of the Romano-Germanic family, that of "movable" and "immovable" property, is of no interest to the Soviet jurists. The distinction they make, and for them one no less fundamental in Marxist doctrine, is between means of production and goods for consumption.[2] Compared to the unity—apparent at least—of the ownership regime of the Romanist countries, there are three regimes in Soviet law: personal ownership, collective ownership and, most important and newest of all, the regime of socialist or state ownership.

It must be added that Soviet law also rejects the traditional Western notion of real rights. According to Soviet jurists rights are created to regulate relations between men; only a capitalist mentality could conceive of a right linking a person and a thing, the owner and the object of his ownership.

For all these reasons it appears to Soviet jurists that the socialist regime has made something new of ownership compared to what it is in a capitalist regime; this is so much the case that they say it is difficult to see how a truly meaningful comparison between the property laws of each society can be made. When Soviet jurists express themselves in this way, they have in mind above all the capitalist law as it existed in their own country before the socialist revolution. Their point of view is less justified if one considers the present property laws of non-socialist European countries with all their present complexities. But even so, the Soviet point of view is still largely justified; there are, it will be seen, very considerable differences between the capitalist and Soviet laws because of the different principles upon which the society of each is based.

251. Personal ownership

The differences are not too marked however with respect to the first type of ownership in the U.S.S.R., *personal ownership*. Private ownership has been so re-named in order to show that it must only be used for the satisfaction of the personal needs of the individual enjoying such right, and for the purpose for which such

---

[2] The notion of "goods for consumption" is in no way comparable—need it hardly be mentioned—to that of *choses consomptibles* or "fungible" property known to Romanist laws.

property is intended, and not in order to draw profit from it or to use it for speculative ends.

With this important reserve, personal property deriving from money earned through employment is otherwise subject to the same general rules as private property in capitalist countries: the owner may use his thing, dispose of it for value or gratuitously, or bequeath it by testament.

The only really special characteristic of this kind of ownership is, apart from the prohibition to employ it for purposes of gain, that only consumer goods in the Marxist sense, as opposed to goods of production, enter the restricted category of things which can be owned in this way. Article 13 of the 1977 Soviet Constitution specifies that "Personal property consists of articles of everyday use, for personal consumption and convenience, things used in subsidiary household husbandry, a dwelling house, savings derived from employment . . . ." In some socialist countries, such as Yugoslavia, small artisanal enterprises (employing no more than 5 salaried persons) forming part of the "small economy" may also be personal property.

252. Collective ownership

Soviet law, however, is entirely original with respect to "socialist" ownership and its two forms: collective ownership and state ownership.

The typical form of *collective ownership* is the ownership of the *kolkhozi*. Land, of course, has been nationalised; it does not, therefore, belong to the *kolkhozi*. The latter have over it only a perpetual right of use and enjoyment. It would be gratuitous to remark that this form of perpetual enjoyment is in no way similar to the notion of *usufructus* known to Roman law or its modern derivative of *usufruit* found in continental civil law: the adjective *perpetual* suffices to indicate this since, in such laws, *usufruct* is essentially a temporary right. Further, and corresponding to this right to the land conceded to the *kolkhozi*, there exists a whole series of obligations which so distinguishes this Soviet right of use and enjoyment from the Romano-Germanic concept of *usufructus* that it is quite impossible to conceive of the Soviet form of the right as a fragmentation of the right of ownership or a true real right.

The *kolkhoz* is obliged to cultivate or exploit the soil granted to it in a definite way; it may be obliged to make certain payments or render certain services to the state; and it must also be organised and carry out its management according to the rules of the law of *kolkhozi*.[3] The collective ownership of the *kolkhozi* involves for those so invested a whole series of obligations over and above the prerogatives it confers. It is difficult, if not impossible, to compare it to the ownership found in laws on co-operatives in capitalist countries or to see in it the notion of an *estate* known to the Common law.

253. State ownership

Even more different is the regime of *state ownership* (or "of the whole people") prevailing in the industrial sector and in the state agricultural farms (*sovkhozi*). This form of ownership bears on two types of property the regimes of which are themselves very distinct: fixed capital and circulating capital or, to be more concrete, the soil, buildings, installations and machines on the one hand and, on the other, the raw materials and products. The reason for the differences in the legal regime of these categories is that the first is intended for exploitation (and cannot normally therefore be alienated), whereas it is intended that the second category, on the contrary, be disposed of.

For both types, however, a similar preliminary question may be asked: who in fact *owns* them? This question excited long doctrinal discussions which in themselves indicate the originality of this particular Soviet institution. But the discussions led to the following conclusion: in a socialist regime the important thing is not so much to know *who* is the owner but rather to know *by whom*, and *how*, such property will be exploited. In the face of this kind of conclusion we are far removed indeed from the capitalist point of view according to which the owner is, in principle, sovereign and the manner in which he chooses to exploit his property is not, as a general rule, even a question taken into account by the law.

The holder of the state right of ownership is the state, or rather

---

[3] A new regime was adopted in respect of *kolkhozi* in 1969 by the National Council of Kolkhozi and approved by the Central Committee of the Communist Party and the U.S.S.R. Council of Ministers.[3]

all the people or the nation of which the state is the provisional representative. The theory of socialist ownership thus evokes the theory of *domaine* of French *droit administratif* rather than the civilian or Romanist theory of ownership. However any comparison on this point with the doctrine of the capitalist countries is not very satisfactory for a number of reasons.

The property belonging to the state, and therefore handled by state industries, is of many different kinds. That property forming capital assets has been gratuitously affected by the state to certain enterprises by virtue of a kind of concession, the terms of which can always be unilaterally modified by the state authorities; with respect to such assets, therefore, the enterprise has, properly speaking, no right which can prevail over that of the state itself. Other kinds of property, on the other hand, are produced by those working for such enterprises; and this factor, as well as the consideration that such products are destined to be disposed of (to the benefit of another enterprise or a consumer), means that they are subject to a distinct legal regime.

In both cases, however, the essence of the socialist regime of state ownership results from the affectation of property to the needs of production and consumption. It is not really important to specify to whom the property belongs or how such property (or its enjoyment) can be transferred. It is much more fundamental to know how it is to be "operationally managed' or exploited and in what way such property will be disposed of according to the established provisions of the national economic plan. The existence of such a plan in the U.S.S.R. makes the law of property a matter subject to a completely different regulation from what it is in non-socialist countries. It is true of course that even in the latter countries the state plays an important role in today's economy. But the "flexible" economic planning that may exist in capitalist countries is quite distinct from the U.S.S.R. "strict" planning, which is not limited to setting general objectives but strives to establish a specific task for each enterprise. The quantitative difference between state intervention in socialist and capitalist countries becomes, by virtue of its dimension in the U.S.S.R., a qualitative difference as well. Socialist ownership, therefore, has now very little to do with ownership as understood in the capitalist countries, even though the word *ownership* has been retained and even if state or public property in the capitalist countries is taken into account.

254. Different function of contract: economic contracts

Soviet law defines contract in the same way as the laws of the Romano-Germanic family; but a contract nevertheless represents something different in Soviet law from what it is in bourgeois laws because in Soviet economic conditions the contract fulfils an often very different function. Jurists of the Romano-Germanic family and Soviet jurists are frequently speaking of two distinct things, therefore, when they consider even the idea of contract.[4]

The difference between the contract of Soviet law and that of the western laws is at once apparent when the "economic contracts"—that is to say those occurring in the collectivised sector of Soviet economy—are considered. This sector is managed, according to the directions of the organs of economic planning, by state enterprises, monopolies or *sovkhozi*, collectives or *kolkhozi*. An examination will be made here of the manner in which these state monopolies or enterprises, which are responsible for the whole of industrial production in the U.S.S.R., carry on their activities.

In the Soviet Union, this whole subject is dominated by the principle of economic planning. State enterprises exist solely in order to execute the plan of national development (both economic and social) approved by the Supreme Soviet.[5] They must do whatever is necessary to accomplish the plan and they are not permitted to undertake activities or duties which are not connected to such plan. The particular enterprise which, according to the plan, must produce x kilometres of railway track is bound to perform this planned task; it cannot manufacture in the place of or in addition to such rails, metallic tubing or steel girders, on the pretext that it is better suited to such an activity or that it would be more profitable. A *sovkhoz* which has been granted land for the purposes of agricultural exploitation cannot then begin to mine or draw

---

[4] Halfina (R. O.), *Značenie i suščnost' dogovora v sovetskom socialističeskom graždanskom prave* (1954). Pfuhl (E.), *Der Wirtschaftsvertrag im sowjetischen Recht* (1958). Halfina (R. O.), *Pravovoe regulirovanie postavki produkcii v narodnom hozjajstve* (1963). Loeber (D. A.), *Der hoheitlich gestaltete Vertrag* (1969). Loeber (D. A.) and Rossi (G.) "Autonomia contrattuale delle imprese di Stato soggette al piano" (1969) Rev. dir. comm. 62–94. *Adde* Tunc (A.), "La possibilité de comparer le contrat dans les systèmes juridiques à structures économiques différentes" (1962) *Rabels Zeitschrift*, 478.

[5] Mayer (M.), *L'entreprise industrielle d'Etat en Union Soviétique* (1966). Crespi Reghizzi (G.), *L'impresa nel diritto sovietico* (1969).

materials from the sub-soil or exploit a peat-bog.[6] Each must remain within the limits of the task assigned to it.

255. Socialist economic planning and capitalist financial direction

The "strict" economic planning of a socialist country is not at all similar to the "flexible" financial planning of a non-socialist country. In western European countries or other capitalist nations there may very well be a plan for national development which involves a certain amount of state control. But such a plan is no more than a statement of desirable objectives which the government wishes to achieve; and if it really hopes to reach these goals, the government will take various steps such as credit arrangements, granting of aid, customs and labour regulation and so on. It is hoped thereby that the outlined goals will be attained by making it advantageous for private industries to take the plan into account. But the plan itself imposes no specific duties on such industries; they are not obliged to carry on a specific activity or assure a fixed amount of production. It is altogether different in the U.S.S.R. because there all the means of production have become the property of the nation and all industrial enterprises are now state enterprises. Because of these facts planning has of course a quite different character. Concrete steps are taken in the form of administrative acts; each state enterprise is assigned a particular job within the framework of the plan and, when these various enterprises have completed their work, the goals of the plan will then have been attained.

256. Planned and unplanned contracts

In order, therefore, to understand the idea of contract in the collectivised sector of Soviet economy, it is important to bear in mind this principal idea—that the task of each enterprise is determined by an administrative planning decision before there is any question at all of a contract. This decision is, in a way, a kind of reason or *causa* (in the Romanist sense) for the contract that will come about.

The role of contract cannot therefore be understood except in connection with the directives of the plan. The latter may have

[6] Kazancev (N. D.), *Zemel'noe pravo* (1958), pp. 89–92.

been more or less mandatory and more or less detailed according
to the period or the branches of the economy considered. The role
of contract, to put it simply, has varied, and continues to vary,
according to the character and specifications of the administrative
decisions upon which it is based.

Sometimes, therefore, these administrative planning decisions
go into considerable detail, specifying the products to be
delivered, their price, the dates of such delivery and between
which enterprises such contract will occur. Psychologically, as well
as economically, the interest of the contract in such circumstances
is the assurance that the obligations resulting from the administrative acts of planning have in fact been understood by those upon
whom they are imposed; the latter, by signing the contract anticipated by the plan, indicate that they consider themselves capable
of discharging these obligations and they engage their personal
liability by placing their signatures on a document reproducing the
details of the administrative decision.

That the contract however fulfil only this role alone is exceptional. Most often the administrative planning decisions do not
enter into any great amount of detail; they leave room for the
initiative of the enterprises themselves, and the contract, economically, is thus called upon to play an even more important role. Two
hypotheses must therefore be distinguished: that, according to the
Soviet terminology, of the planned contract and that of the
unplanned contract.[7]

257. The legally imposed contract

In the first hypothesis, that of the planned contract, the administrative decisions have already specifically enumerated the enterprises between which the contract must occur. It is simply laid
down that enterprise *A* will contract with enterprise *B*. This was
the case mentioned previously, but up to this point it has also been
assumed that every aspect of the future contract will have been
specified by the administrative decision. In the vast majority of
cases, however, this is not so; it is expected that the parties will
make more concrete in the contract the duties imposed upon them
by the plan. The quantity of products and their price, of course,

---

[7] Ioffe (O. S.), *Graždanskoe pravo* (1958), p. 390.

will as a general rule be fixed by the plan. There also exist, for a whole series of items, "general conditions of delivery," established by administrative authorities which specify many of the clauses of the future contract in a generally mandatory fashion. There remains, nevertheless, a certain number of practically important points with respect to which experience has shown that there is nothing better than a direct agreement between the interested parties. The contract will deal with these points: the quality and various kinds of commodities, the packaging, the timing of deliveries and so on. A retail enterprise, for example, is in a better position than the administrative authorities to know the needs and tastes of the public: the size of shoes required, the preferences for material of a certain colour and so on. A construction enterprise is in turn more qualified than the administration to know the exact dimensions of the boards, tubes, sheet metal or other materials needed. In most cases it is the contract that serves this function: it translates into concrete details the general scheme of the plan in the interests of an improved quality of work to be performed or of goods to be delivered.

258. The economically necessary contract

The second hypothesis is where the administrative decisions made by virtue of the plan do not specify that enterprise *A* or enterprise *B* has any obligation to enter into a contract. The only duty imposed on either of them is the performance of a certain task, but they are left with the choice of the methods to do it. The obligation to enter into contracts in the vast majority of instances results therefore, but indirectly, from the need to perform the tasks set out by the administrative decisions of the plan. But the latter do not state between what parties the contract must be made: this choice is left to the individual enterprises even though it is, in fact, limited. Unless the contrary has been specified, one Soviet enterprise can only deal with another Soviet enterprise and what it requires to be done by such other enterprise must be within the scope of the latter's activities according to the plan. In this second hypothesis, however, there is some resemblance to the notion of freedom of contract such as understood in bourgeois countries. Important differences do nonetheless subsist. Many aspects of the contract to be drawn up will have been established in advance by a whole series of measures that govern the Soviet economy (such as general conditions relating to the delivery and naming of products, decrees setting the deadlines for the conclusion of contracts, pricing policies and so on). An essential difference lies above all in the fact that the specific task to be performed is fixed *for each enterprise* by the plan's administrative decisions; the plan, therefore, is not restricted to indicating in a general way and for a limited period what the economic policy of the government will be.

The present tendency in the U.S.S.R. is to develop the practice described above and to allow different enterprises, to the maximum extent possible, to choose their contracting parties. Administrative designation of the contracting parties is becoming more exceptional, but is still employed in special instances, as for example when one of the parties enjoys a position of monopoly in the furnishing of raw materials like coal, iron, petroleum and so on. But by generally leaving the choice of the contracting party to the enterprise in question, it is hoped, generally, that those involved will be favourably stimulated, that poorly managed enterprises will be detected and the quality of production improved. In granting this freedom it is in particular hoped that state enterprises will find it possible to establish long-term production schedules, and that then the contract will be part of the drafting of the plan and not merely the instrument for carrying it out. This would help to eliminate a poor matching of production to needs. Too often massive stocks of items that will not sell have been produced when the needs of consumers have nonetheless remained unsatisfied. It is, of course, difficult to attribute such a double function to contracts and to return, to some extent, to a market economy while at the same time retaining the principle of centralised planning which is the very basis of a socialist economy. It is still not clear how, and in what sectors and to what extent, it will be possible to reconcile these two different principles in the U.S.S.R. of the future.

259. Role of contract

The preceding remarks indicate the role played by contract in Soviet economy and law. It is clearly very different from that of the countries of free enterprise even when the latter have moved in the direction of a more planned economy. In the U.S.S.R. the contract exists only in order to assure the execution of the plan, with respect to which it is no more than a subordinate instrument. In non-socialist countries, on the other hand, the contract is a fully autonomous instrument upon which the very dynamic of the economy rests; and even when economic planning does exist in such countries it is only a statement of a generally political nature, devoid of that truly legal character so fundamental to the way in which the organisation of relations between enterprises is conceived in the Soviet Union. From this difference in the role of contract, and the relations existing between the plan and the idea of contracts, there flows a completely different legal technique for its regulation. It will now be useful to examine these differences with respect to the formation, the effects and the performance of contracts and the consequences of their non-performance.

260. Formation of contracts

First of all, with regard to the formation of contracts, a further distinction must be made in connection with the two hypotheses described above. If the administrative decisions of the plan have anticipated that a contract will be concluded between enterprises *A* and *B*, then this contract is obligatory. If they do not agree on the terms of the contract upon those conditions (often very detailed) laid down in the administrative texts, they will then be forced to do so by the decision of an arbitral organ; these organs of public arbitration therefore deal in many cases with a *pre-contractual dispute*. At the present time, however, such disputes are less frequent than they once were because of the fact, already mentioned, that planning is now more flexible and enterprises are more often given the choice of their contracting party.[8] Thus when one enterprise refuses to contract with another, the organs of public arbitration cannot be seized of the question.

261. Performance of contracts

Soviet legislation also departs from the capitalist position respecting the effects of contracts and the consequences of their non-

---

[8] In Hungary in 1967 and in Rumania in 1969, legislation withdrew from the purview of public arbitration organs any such pre-contract dispute. Litigation arising in the context of negotiations preliminary to contracts which the plan made mandatory have, since then, been resolved by purely administrative action.

performance. Bourgeois laws, since they see the contract as only a pecuniary matter or an opportunity to turn a profit, are satisfied by its performance in the form of an equivalent value: the party who has not discharged his contractual obligations is condemned to pay damages—that is, an equivalent sum of money—to the benefit of the other party.

Such is not the case in the law of the U.S.S.R. The performance of contractual obligations by the payment of damages cannot satisfy Soviet enterprises because their aim is not to make a profit. For them it is essential that the plan be actually carried out. There thus must be specific performance of a contract because the execution of the plan depends upon it; this is all the more important in the U.S.S.R. because of the country's economic structure and the impossibility of one enterprise being "replaced" and demanding that another be substituted for the defaulting enterprise unable to perform its contractual obligations.

The principle of specific performance is therefore—not in theory, as in the Romanist laws, but in actual fact—the ruling principle of the U.S.S.R. And since it involves the guaranteeing of a basically important objective, the execution of the plan, the enforcement of contractual obligations is strictly conceived. The non-performance of a planned contract will be severely sanctioned: the contract itself must necessarily specify penalties which, especially in the case of delay, will be added to the specific performance. The penal clause of Soviet law is not a contractual evaluation of the damages resulting from non-performance; it is a private penalty *in addition to performance*.[9] One party does not even have the right to free the other of the penalty; such a collusive agreement, contrary to the interests involved in the strict performance of the plan, cannot be admitted in Soviet law. Apart from this, disciplinary and even penal sanctions may sometimes be imposed in the case of non-performance of contractual obligations assumed.[10] In the U.S.S.R., the performance of contracts within the framework of the execution of the plan is thus a matter of public order.

---

[9] Benjamin (P.), "Penalties, Liquidated Damages and Penal Clauses in Commercial Contracts: A Comparative Study of English and Continental Law," (1960) 9 Int. and Comp. L.Q. 600–627.

[10] *Cf.* examples given in Hazard (J. N.), Butler (W. E.) and Maggs (P. B.), *The Soviet Legal System* (1977), pp. 247 *et seq.* and pp. 263 *et seq.*

262. Conclusion

Is there, then, anything in common between the contract of Soviet and bourgeois laws? The word itself has been retained and it may, sometimes, refer to the same reality: the contracts which occur "outside" the plan—contracts between commercial state enterprises and consumers and those between citizens—are very similar to the contracts known in western countries. As important as these may be—for it is to them ultimately that the whole dynamic of the economy is aimed—such contracts are not of great practical interest to the jurist because, for the most part, they are the simple contracts of everyday life and do not raise many legal problems.[11] Jurists' attention is directed rather to contracts of the planned sector: their regulation, and indeed the very concept of contract in this context, has completely changed because of the new connection linking them to a type of economic planning unknown in western countries. However tempting, it would nonetheless be inexact to speak of them as "administrative contracts." It is certainly true that they have more kinship with our administrative contracts than with our civil or commercial contracts, but essential differences—arising from the collectivisation of the means of production, the existence and modalities of the Soviet plan, and the absence of an opposition of interests between the contracting parties—distinguish them from all the various contracts known to non-socialist countries. In this respect, therefore, the complete originality of Soviet law must be frankly admitted.[12]

Section III—Most-Favoured Nation Clause

263. New aspect of the question

Integrated into an administrative system of economic planning, the contract of Soviet law is no longer called upon to play the role expected of it in the countries of free enterprise. The change which

[11] On these contracts, *cf.* Hazard, Butler and Maggs, *op. cit.*, p. 269. It should be noted that labour relations are not based on "contract" in the Soviet context.
[12] The possibilities but also the limitations of a comparison appear upon a reading of Loeber (D. A.), *Der hoheitlich gestaltete Vertrag. Eine rechtsvergleichende Untersuchung über den Planertrag im Sowjetrecht und den "diktierten Vertrag" im Recht der Bundesrepublik Deutschland* (1969).

has occurred in its function dissociates the Soviet contract from the idea of freedom of contract which to our eyes is fundamental; a profound transformation of the very idea, as well as the role, of contract is the inevitable result. Soviet law speaks of contract in the same way as bourgeois laws, but something very different is actually meant. To understand what a Soviet jurist considers to be a contract and what problems confront him in this area, the Soviet economic structure must be constantly borne in mind.

By examining the most-favoured nation clause, the highly practical importance for the bourgeois countries of understanding the changes that have occurred in the Soviet economy can be illustrated. The most-favoured nation clause in itself has not become something distinct in the Soviet Union, but since it still has a place in what is now an entirely changed legal and economic system, it loses, more or less entirely, the meaning it has in relations between countries of free enterprise.[13]

An analysis of the clause without reference to the function it fulfils would be a hollow exercise; in order to understand any institution, the purpose it serves must also be considered. From this point of view, the very idea of the most-favoured nation clause has been modified in the Soviet system.

264. Meaning of the clause in a socialist economy

The purpose of the clause in relations between countries of free enterprise is to establish an equality between the businessmen of different foreign countries with which the national commercial interests have dealings so as to obtain either the goods or services required. The operation of the clause presupposes a milieu of free enterprise in which national business interests plan their own development and obtain their own supplies, by taking into account essentially commercial considerations, because they have primarily in mind the realisation of a profit. In the Soviet system, the role of the clause is completely altered.

Soviet enterprises cannot, any more than Soviet citizens, contract directly with foreign parties. Foreign trade in the Soviet Union is the monopoly of about fifty bodies which specialise in dif-

---

[13] Domke (M.) and Hazard (J. N.), "State Trading and the Most-Favoured Nation Clause" (1958) 22 Am. J. Int'l. L. 55–68.

ferent branches of the economy, such as *Eksportles* which deals in wood, *Sovnafteksport* trading in mineral oils, and so on. The decision by these bodies to export or import some product is made in the light of considerations different than those taken into account by profit-seeking enterprises in capitalist countries of free competition. No real effort is made in the Soviet Union to develop exports; prices are not competitive, the products themselves are often poorly presented, and there is never any servicing of the customer after the sale. Little heed is given to the fact that an item may be purchased cheaply in a foreign country and then sold at a profit in the Soviet Union. And the conditions in which something may be bought or sold are only taken into consideration once it has been decided that it is necessary, or at least opportune within the framework of the plan, to get in a supply or sell. Even at this stage the decision to buy from or sell to foreign parties is not necessarily based on price alone. The choice of dealing with one country rather than another may be based on political considerations, such as the desire to be of assistance to that country or because it is disposed to buy certain Soviet products and that this will assist in the general balance of payments. The U.S.S.R. only imports products in order to carry out its plan of national economic development and the plan is not profit-oriented. It is as though the whole country were an immense monopoly in which the decisions to buy or sell were never based exclusively on the price of the product but taken rather in the general context of political or economic relations, existing or anticipated, between the Soviet Union and the foreign country. Considerations other than price may very well therefore prompt the choice of the foreign contracting party in the first place. It is characteristic, and significant, that it has never been thought necessary to set up a preferential tariff system within the bloc of European socialist trading countries,[14] whereas the creation of a customs union was one of the very first objectives of the European Economic Community.

What meaning, moreover, could custom duties really have in a socialist country? The state, which collects them, is also in the end bound to pay them when a nationalised enterprise imports pro-

---

[14] That is, within the Council of Mutual Economic Assistance (COMECON) created between socialist countries in 1948. Caillot (J.), *Le C.A.E.M. Aspects juridiques et formes de co-opération économique entre les pays socialistes* (1971). Lavigne (M.), *Le Comecon (Le programme du Comecon et l'intégration socialiste)* (1974).

ducts upon which they are owing. The "equality" of foreign traders in the scheme of the customs tariff is thus no more than an enticement in a country whose economic system is one where imports are the monopoly of state enterprises and the latter may receive compensatory payments from the state itself.

It should also be noted that the terms of the contracts of trade in the trading relations between socialist countries themselves are largely unknown. The whole subject is treated as a state secret. In these circumstances it is therefore very difficult for an outside nation to urge that its nationals have not been treated as they ought to have been under the most-favoured nation clause.

265. Possible solutions

In the end the most-favoured nation clause, conceived originally for market economies based on the profit motive, has no meaning when it is inserted in trade agreements with socialist countries; and it provides no guarantees at all for those trading with them. The socialist countries may well insist upon it, because it serves them in avoiding any discrimination directed against them in their trade with the free enterprise countries. But the reciprocity of the clause is illusory. Nothing guarantees to the foreign trader that exports will be facilitated. And so trading countries with free economic systems are endeavouring to find other means for promoting their trade with socialist countries. The European Economic Commission of the United Nations has, in particular, taken up the study of the problem. Since the nationalisation of trade has changed the conditions of normal competition, attention has now turned to the actual results of these trading exchanges and socialist countries are now being asked to enter into purchase agreements for specified amounts. The General Agreement on Tariffs and Trade (GATT) has encountered difficulties in its attempts to settle trading relations with countries whose economy is completely planned and whose foreign trade is a state monopoly. But preference and discrimination can in fact be achieved in respect of these countries by methods other than those employed in countries of free competition. Special agreements have thus been created for those socialist countries that have adhered to GATT (Czechoslovakia, Poland, Yugoslavia, Rumania, as well as Egypt and Cuba).

PART THREE

THE COMMON LAW

266. Basic importance of English law

The Common law system came into being, historically, in England largely as the result of the activity of the royal courts of justice after the Norman Conquest. Apart from English law, its originator, the Common law family includes all the laws of English-speaking countries with a few exceptions. Apart from the English-speaking countries themselves, the influence of the Common law has been considerable in most, if not all, countries that have been or still are politically linked with England.[1] These countries may well have retained, in certain areas, their own traditions and concepts, but in all cases the English influence on the manner in which jurists think has nonetheless been great—principally because the judicial system and administrative organisation and the laws of evidence and procedure, civil and criminal, have everywhere been established and set out along English lines.

A study of the Common law must therefore begin with a study of English law. The Common law has been profoundly shaped by its history and this history is exclusively, at least until the eighteenth century, the history of the law of England. This is an essential factor even though it must be put into perspective by the further observation that certain laws—such as that of the United States, for example—are very different today from English law, whereas others—such as the law of India or that of the Sudan—have received only part of its structure and have in matters of "personal status" remained faithful to their own legal traditions.

As the scope of this work is necessarily restricted, only English law and the law of the United States of America will be studied in this Part; the laws of India and Pakistan will be examined in the fourth Part.

[1] The Commonwealth today comprises 36 member states and 30 dependencies.

TITLE I

ENGLISH LAW

267. Geographical area

Technically, the area of application of English law is limited to England and Wales. English law is neither the law of the United Kingdom, nor that of Great Britain because Northern Ireland, Scotland, the Channel Isles and the Isle of Man are not ruled by "English" law. The contrast, however, between this strict concept of English law, taken as a body of rules legally in force in England and the universality of this same law, considered as a model for a large part of the world, will soon be seen.[1] English law occupies in effect a pre-eminent place within the family of the Common law. This is so not only because it was in England that the Common law was historically developed; today as well English law continues to be, for many countries, a model law which may not, of course, on different points and in all respects, be actually followed but which nonetheless is still generally respected and taken into consideration. The history, structure and sources of English law will be considered.

---

[1] Goodhart (A. L.), "The Migration of the Common Law" (1960) 76 L.Q.R. 39.

CHAPTER I

HISTORY OF ENGLISH LAW

268. Historical character of English law

Even more than in the case of French law, a knowledge of history is indispensable for an understanding of English law. The law of England did not experience a "renewal" through Roman law nor was it transformed by means of codification—the two principal characteristics of French and other laws of the Romano-Germanic family. It developed autonomously and only in a very limited way was it influenced by contacts with the European continent. The English jurist—who sometimes underestimates the continuity of continental laws because he believes, incorrectly, that the codification of these was a break with tradition—likes to emphasise the historical continuity of his own legal system; to him it appears to be the result of a long tradition untroubled by revolution and he is proud of this fact because he sees in it, and with good reason, evidence of the great wisdom of the Common law, its ability to adapt, its lasting value and those other qualities that correspond to the nature of English jurists and the character of English people generally.

However, the "historical" character of English law must not be exaggerated. The truth is that the English like to emphasise the traditional character of their law, whereas Frenchmen are rather more prone to emphasise the logical and rational character of French law. In reality the part played in both laws by tradition and rationality is probably not very different since both French and English law have had to adapt to new circumstances and meet new social needs which have always been, and still are on the whole, very similar. The revolutions in France were really no more, so to speak, than accidents along the way of the long historical evolution of French law.

There are four principal periods in the history of English law.

The first is that before the Norman Conquest in 1066; the second, stretching from 1066 to the accession of the Tudors (1485), is that of the formation of the Common law, the period during which this new legal system was developed at the expense of local custom. The third period, running from 1485 to 1832, is that during which a complementary, and occasionally rival, system in the form of "rules of equity" developed alongside the Common law. The fourth period, beginning in 1832 and continuing up to the present time, is the modern period in which the Common law faces an unprecedented development in legislation and has to adapt itself to a society directed more and more by the intervention of governmental and administrative authorities.

Section I—Anglo-Saxon Period

269. Germanic laws

The year 1066, when England was conquered by the Normans, is as fundamental to the history of English law as it is to the general history of England and Europe. The period in England preceding this date is that of Anglo-Saxon[2] law. Although the Roman occupation of Britain lasted four centuries—from the Emperor Claudius (A.D. 41–54) to the start of the 5th century—no more traces of it were left in England than that of the Celtic period in France or the Iberian period in Spain. For English legal historians the beginning of the history of English law dates from the end of the Roman occupation when the different tribes of Germanic origins—Saxons, Jutes, Danes and Angles—divided up England. It was, further, at this time that England was converted to Christianity by the mission of St. Augustine of Canterbury in 596.

Little is known about the law of the Anglo-Saxon period.[3] Just as in continental Europe, laws were reduced to writing (not in Latin, as on the continent, but in Anglo-Saxon) shortly after the

[2] The common continental use of the term *Anglo-Saxon* to designate the law of the English or American people of today is quite rightly considered, at least outside the European continent, to be absurd.

[3] Collections of Anglo-Saxon laws include Liebermann (F.), *Die Gesetze der Angelsachsen*, 2 vols. (1898–1912); Attenborough (F. L.), *Laws of the Earliest English Kings* (1922); Robertson (A. J.), *Laws of the Kings of England from Edmund to Henry I* (1925). *Cf.* in general, Richardson (H. G.), *Law and Legislation from Aethelbert to Magna Carta* (1966). Simpson (A. W. B.) and Arnold (M. S.) (eds.), *On the Laws and Customs of England* (1982).

conversion to Christianity; and, again like these other countries, these laws regulated only very limited aspects of those social relationships to which our present idea of law now extends. The laws of Aethelbert (Ethelbert) King of Kent (*circa* 540–616), drafted in Anglo-Saxon about the year 600, comprise only 90 brief sentences; those of the Danish King Canute (1016–1035), four centuries later, are much more developed and suggest a transition from the tribal era to the feudal period. The principle of the personality of laws gave way to that of territoriality, as in France, but even though the country was ruled by a single monarch, the law in force was still made up of strictly local customs; there was no law common to the whole of England at any time before the Norman Conquest.

SECTION II—FORMATION OF THE COMMON LAW (1066–1485)

270. Norman conquest (1066)

The Norman Conquest did not in itself alter the state of things. William I (1028–1087) is perhaps incorrectly named the "Conqueror" for he maintained that he ruled England by virtue of hereditary titles derived from Edward the Confessor and not by reason of the conquest. He expressly proclaimed the maintenance in force of Anglo-Saxon law; and even now it is sometimes possible for English lawyers and judges to invoke, and even apply, a rule of law dating from the Anglo-Saxon period.

The Norman Conquest, however, is an event of the utmost importance in English legal history because it brought to England, in addition to the foreign occupation, a strong and centralised administrative organisation, rich in experience, that had shown its worth in the Duchy of Normandy. With the Norman Conquest the period of tribal rule is finished and feudalism is installed.

271. Feudalism in England

The English form of feudalism was very different from that existing in France, Germany or Italy at the same period. The *seigneurs* of Normandy who accompanied William to England were in a conquered country, they did not speak the language of the inhabitants and they were scornful of local habits and manners. They felt the need to band around their sovereign in order to maintain the conquest and defend their lands. The Conqueror, for his part, knew how to ward off the danger of over-powerful vassals; in the distribution of land made to his supporters, no very large fief was constituted and thus no baron was able to challenge his power. The statute *Quia Emptores* (1290) prohibited moreover any sub-infeudation so that all the nobles were directly subordinate to the king.

It was rather as though an army were encamped in England; that there was a sense of discipline and organisation was shown by the drafting, as early as 1086, of the *Domesday Book*, a document in which 15,000 manor estates and 200,000 homes were inventoried.[4] This military and highly organised character of English feudalism, so unlike that of the European continent, prepared the way for the development of the Common law.

272. Definition of common law

What was this Common law—at the time called *comune ley* in "law French" which, from the reign of Edward I (1272–1307) to the seventeenth century, was the spoken language of law[5] while the written language, as in the rest of Europe, was Latin?

Comune ley or Common law, as distinct from local customs, is the law common to all England but in 1066 it did not exist. The assemblies of free men, called County or Hundred Courts,[6] applied only local custom; in other words they only decided, according to custom, which of the parties had to establish his claim by submitting to a system of proof that had no pretentions to rationality. Although they remained competent in principle even after the Conquest, the Hundred or County Courts were gradually replaced by new feudal courts (Courts Baron, Court Leet, Manor-

---

[4] *Seu Liber Censualis Wilhelmi Primi Regis Angliae*, Farley (A.), ed.; 1783, vols. I and II; Ellis (Sir H.), ed., 1816, vols. III and IV (Public Record Commission); Maitland (F. W.), *Domesday Book and Beyond* (1897); Hoyt (R. S.), *The Royal Demesne in English Constitutional History 1066–1272* (1950).

[5] French was the language of the royal court until the Tudors came to the throne at the end of the fifteenth century, and was therefore naturally used in the royal courts of justice. Use of English declined as the jurisdiction of the royal courts was extended. French, however, was *spoken* less and was also gradually abandoned from the sixteenth century by legal writers who preferred English. Unsuccessful attempts in 1362 and by Cromwell in 1650 were made to establish English officially to the exclusion of French and Latin; this was only achieved in 1731. On the subject of "law French," *cf.* Maitland's Introduction to Volume 17 of the *Selden Society*, pp. xxiii–lxxxix. Baker (J. A.), *Manual of Law French* (1979).

[6] The *Hundred* was a subdivision of the County.

ial Courts), but these also decided disputes by applying the local customary law. Ecclesiastical courts set up after the Conquest applied Canon law, common to all Christianity. The creation of the *comune ley*, an English law truly common to the whole of England, was to be the exclusive work of the royal courts of justice, commonly called the Courts of Westminster, and so named after the place where they sat from the thirteenth century.

273. Jurisdiction of royal courts

After the Norman Conquest, disputes were normally brought before the various courts just enumerated. The king only exercised "high justice"; he did not consider himself authorised to hear contestations except in very exceptional cases, such as when the peace of the kingdom was threatened and circumstances made it impossible for justice to be rendered in the usual forum. The *Curia Regis*, from which the king dispensed justice assisted by his closest officials and the persons of highest rank in the kingdom, was a court for only the most important personalities and disputes; it was not an ordinary court open to all and sundry.

But from the thirteenth century certain parts of the *Curia Regis* gradually became—as did parliament itself—autonomous bodies; certain commissions of a judicial character ceased to accompany the King in his progresses about the country and established their seat at Westminster. But these royal courts of justice by no means had general jurisdiction. The royal courts of Westminster had to treat with some consideration the sensibilities of the feudal barons who wanted to be their own masters and were not, therefore, very willing to submit to the justice of these new courts. The royal intervention in matters of concern to them and their subjects was undoubtedly as intolerable and contrary to what they considered the natural order of things as are certain measures of state intervention or nationalisation to property holders of today who regard ownership as a sacred right. The royal courts, furthermore, were not really equipped to render justice, even on appeal, in all the different kinds of contestation that arose in the kingdom. Their intervention was thus at first limited essentially to three main types of cases where it did appear more or less natural: royal finances,[7]

---

[7] Fiscal immunity was not so extensive in England as in France. *Cf.* Joüon des Longrais (F.), *L'Est et l'Ouest. Institutions du Japon et de l'Occident comparées* (1958), p. 31.

matters respecting the ownership and possession of land[8] and
serious criminal matters affecting the peace of the kingdom. Three
different courts—Court of Exchequer, Court of Common Pleas,
Court of King's Bench—heard matters coming within each of
these categories at the beginning, but very soon this division of jurisdiction disappeared and each of the three courts at Westminster
could hear any dispute brought before the royal courts.

Apart from these three categories, all other disputes were
settled by the Hundred or County Courts, feudal courts, ecclesiastical courts—and later, as well, when this became necessary, by
different commercial or municipal courts. The privilege of rendering justice was granted for certain types of cases to the latter and
they applied the international customary law of commerce, the *lex
mercatoria* or *ley merchant*, or municipal regulations.

274. Extension of royal jurisdiction

The powers of the king grew as sovereign justiciar. It was, moreover, in the interests of the chancellor and the royal judges that
they hear more and more cases because of the fees accruing from
the administration of justice. The courts were also prompted to
increase their jurisdiction upon the solicitation of the people in
whose eyes royal justice appeared superior to that of any other
court. It was only the royal courts that had the means to summon
witnesses and to enforce judgments; and only the king, apart from
the church, could require the swearing of an oath. The royal
courts, therefore, employed more modern procedures and submitted the judgment of cases to the verdict of a jury,[9] whereas
other courts perpetuated their out-moded procedures and archaic
system of making proof.

The royal courts thus gradually enlarged their jurisdiction and,
by the end of the middle ages, had become in fact the only courts
of justice. The feudal courts were eclipsed, as the Hundred Courts
had been; municipal and commercial courts handled matters of

---

[8] An owner is master in his own house, but who is an owner? To decide this it was natural to resort to the royal courts. Questions of rights to possession of land concerned the public order and peace of the kingdom.

[9] For the conditions in which the jury appeared and developed in England, and its consider-able influence upon English procedure right up to the present time, *cf.* Hamson (C. J.) and Plucknett (T. F. T.), *The English Trial and Comparative Law* (1952).

only minor importance; and the ecclesiastical courts only heard cases in relation to marriage and the discipline of clergy.

275. Writs

The royal courts, however, only became the ordinary courts of general jurisdiction in the nineteenth century. Until 1875 they remained, at least in theory, special courts to which the citizen had no automatic access.

Historically, then, to press a claim before the king's courts was not a right but a favour which the royal authority might or might not grant. The person who solicited this privilege had first of all to address his request to an important royal official, the Chancellor, asking him to deliver a writ (*breve*), the effect of which was to enable the royal courts to be seized of the matter upon the payment of fees to the Chancery. Apart from this procedure the judges could only be seized directly upon a complaint or petition (*querela*, *billa*). Some of the writs appear to have been the crystallisation of judicial practice established on the basis of such complaints.[10]

It was not automatic that a writ would issue from the royal Chancery or that the judges would be convinced that they should take up a matter upon which a complaint was lodged. Royal authority in the thirteenth century was not such that the chancellor might issue a writ or the judges consent to render judgment in all cases. For some considerable time, each instance had to be individually examined to determine whether it was expedient that the writ should issue, and the list of established situations where writs were granted automatically (*brevia de cursu*) was slow to grow. A first list of writs, drawn up in 1227, reveals that there were 56, and there were only 76 in 1832 when the system was considerably modified.

The extension of the jurisdiction of the royal courts is not, however, to be measured by the increase in the list of the *brevia de cursu*, nor is it to be explained (contrary to what was believed and taught for many years) by the passage of the *Statute of Westminster II* of 1285[11] which authorised the chancellor to deliver writs *in con-*

---

[10] Milsom (S. F. C.), *Historical Foundations of the Common Law* (1969).
[11] Plucknett (T. F. T.), "Case and the Statute of Westminster II" 31 Col. L. Rev. (1931) 778–799.

simili casu, that is to say in instances having great similarity to others for which the delivery of the writ was already established. The technique adopted was rather as follows: the plaintiff, in his "declaration," the initial step in the procedure, explained the details of the facts of the case and prayed the royal judges to hear the case and render judgment. The new instances in which they did admit their jurisdiction were for this reason called "actions on the case" (actions *super casum*). In time these actions multiplied and were given special titles in the light of the facts which justified them—actions of assumpsit, deceit, trover, negligence and so on.

276. "Remedies precede rights"

The procedure observed before the royal courts at Westminster varied according to the manner in which the suit was begun. To each writ there corresponded in effect a fixed procedure which laid down the others steps to be followed, the handling of incidental questions, the admissibility of evidence, and the means of enforcing the decision. In any given procedure the plaintiff and defendant had to be styled by specific wording; their inappropriate use in another procedure would be fatal to the proceeding. In one type of action the jury would be employed; in another, the evidence was adduced by "wager of law" (the action would fail if the defendant were able to produce the required number of witnesses who attested under oath to his credibility). In some actions judgment could be rendered against the defendant after his default to appear; in others not. The features of this system applied to the procedures of whichever writ was seen as most appropriate in the circumstances. A procedure very generally followed was that of the writ of "trespass," which was regarded as the most modern and most satisfactory.[12]

Procedural considerations, therefore, had a primary importance in the development of English law. While jurists on the continent turned their attention principally to the determination of the individual's rights and duties (*i.e.* substantive legal rules), English jurists concentrated on matters of form and questions of procedure. If the historical background of English law is to be grasped, the importance of procedure must always be borne in mind.

---

[12] Maitland (F. W.), *The Forms of Action at Common Law* (2nd ed., 1948), p. 52.

Remedies precede rights. The Common law, in its origins, was made up of a number of procedures—"forms of action"—upon the completion of which a judgment would be rendered, although the substantive principle serving as the basis for the decision might itself be uncertain. The first and foremost consideration for the litigant was to select the correct form of action or writ by which the court could be seized, and thereby convince the court that it had jurisdiction in the matter, and then to carry through with the formalistic procedure laid down. What would the judgment be? That question had no certain answer—the Common law was only gradually evolving substantive principles defining individual rights and duties.

277. Contemporary interest of this history

These circumstances in which the Common law developed are not of merely historical interest. From at least four points of view they have left their mark upon English law and even today their influence can be detected. English jurists have, in the first place, traditionally emphasised matters of procedure. Secondly, many of the categories and concepts of English law have been shaped by these historical circumstances; they have, in the third place, led to the rejection in English law of the distinction between public and private law. Finally the early development of the Common law was an obstacle to the reception of Roman law categories and concepts. Each of these points will now be discussed.

278. Emphasis upon procedure

The principal concern of English jurists until the nineteenth century was directed to the various formalistic procedures put into operation by the writs, rather than to the elaboration of those principles upon which just solutions to disputes would be based. *Remedies precede rights*. Attention was focused on procedures because the procedures had a single purpose: the formulation of questions of fact to be put to the jury. It must not be lost from view that even as late as 1856 actions instituted in the Common law courts involved submissions to a jury and that the other more archaic procedures that did not rely upon this institution had only gradually been abandoned. English law was thus deeply marked by a preeminence given to matters of procedure.

It was, therefore, within the framework of these various procedures available to litigants that the development of English law
was—indeed, had to be—organised. The law, to adopt the striking
phrase of Sir Henry Maine (1822–1888), appears to have been
"secreted in the interstices of procedure."[13] The Common law did
not appear to be so much a system attempting to bring justice as a
conglomeration of procedures designed, in more and more cases,
to achieve solutions to disputes. The twelfth century author Glanvill (d. *circa* 1190),[14] and the thirteenth century author Bracton
(*circa* 1210–1268),[15] describing the whole of English law by means
of an explanation (in Latin) of its principles, gave analyses of the
various writs available in the courts of Westminster. The chronicles known as the *Year Books*, written in Law French, which
inform us of the state of the law between 1290 and 1536, concentrate principally on relating matters of procedure and often omit
altogether whatever solutions were given in the disputes themselves which they recorded.[16]

279. Example drawn from law of contract

In order to illustrate the artificiality in the development of English law, an example may be drawn from the history of the law of
contract.

In the thirteenth century, at the time of the *Statute of Westminster II*, contract fell within the jurisdiction of various courts—
ecclesiastical, municipal or commercial. The courts of Westminster did not hear cases on contract. Glanvill, at the end of the
twelfth century, states with simplicity: "Private covenants are not
generally protected in the courts of our lord the king." There were
no writs or any procedures for contractual matters through which,
in fact, the royal courts could be seized. What was to be done? In
some cases the notion of ownership sufficed. The lessee, the borrower, the person who had possession of property for another or

---

[13] Maine (Sir Henry S.), *Early Law and Custom* (1861), p. 389.
[14] *The Treatise on the Laws and Customs of England commonly called Glanvill.*
[15] *De legibus et consuetudinibus Anglie* (On the Laws and Customs of England) written in the
1250s.
[16] The *Year Books* appear to have been used as student texts. Some were printed as early as
1482, and a further selection was published in 1679 by Sergeant Maynard: *Reports del Cases en
Ley*. A critical edition was undertaken at the beginning of this century under the auspices of the
Selden Society. *Adde* Lambert (J.), *Les Year Books de langue française* (1928).

transported it for him—these persons were bound because they detained, without title to it, the property of another rather than because of any agreement, and the *writ of detinue* was sufficient to sanction those situations. In other instances the obligation to perform a promise was linked to the *form* in which it was entered into, and the defendant was bound upon the *writ of debt* because he had described himself as a debtor in a formal document without, however, any enquiry being made as to whether he really did consent.

But the *writ of detinue* and the *writ of debt* did not cover all possible cases and the procedures involved in each were not entirely satisfactory. For these two reasons an effort was made to find other means for developing the law of contracts, and the form of action known as *trespass* was used. The object of the writ of trespass was to sanction an act of a wrongful nature committed by the defendant, such as an unjust blow or attack on the person, or some harm to land or goods. As such, it had nothing to do with contracts, but the pleaders endeavoured to persuade the court in cases where a promise was made but not fulfilled that the facts of the case justified that it be treated like those which had been previously considered matters of *trespass*. Gradually the royal courts accepted this line of reasoning. First they sanctioned contractual engagements in cases of *misfeasance*, that is to say an act committed in the performance of the contract by one of the parties causing damage to the person or goods of the other party. More than a century elapsed however before the courts accepted to sanction in addition to *misfeasance* the case of *non-feasance*: where a person who has entered into an agreement simply did not perform it at all. It was a particularly delicate matter to admit an action *on the case* when the plaintiff could still act by using the action of *debt*; it was accepted where an express promise to perform the undertaking (*special assumpsit*) had been made before it was admitted that such an obligation was itself implicit in any promise (*indebitatus assumpsit*); the decision of 1602 which did make this step was considered a victory and it is really only from this date that the English law of contract begins.[17] A long time and much effort were necessary for the action of *assumpsit*, an off-shoot of the delictual action of *trespass on the case*, to be freed from the rules linked to its delictual origin, such as those preventing transmissibility of the action,

---

[17] *Slade's case* (1602), 4 Co. Rep. 92a, 76 E.R. 1073.

requiring proof of fault and establishing the precise amount of damages resulting from non-performance.

280. Categories and concepts of English law

The forms of actions have now been abolished for more than one hundred years, but the rules and categories of English law still bear witness to the obstacles which prevented, because of procedure, a fully rational development of its institutions. "The forms of action we have buried," said Maitland (1850–1906), the great historian of English law, "but they still rule us from their graves."[18] The remark was significant.

Take another example from the law of contracts: the Common law could only allow for the awarding of damages as a sanction for the breach of contracts, because the ancient action of *assumpsit*, a derivative of the action of *trespass*, could only so conclude. Moreover, for English law, the concept of contract only included those agreements which, until the middle of the nineteenth century, were sanctioned by the action of *assumpsit*: it included neither "gratuitous contracts" nor those involving the restoration of a thing of which the plaintiff remained owner (the cases of *bailment* or what in the Romano-Germanic laws are known as "deposit," "loan for use" and the carriage of goods, in which the plaintiff has delivered his property in bailment ("bailed" it) to another), nor certain kinds of agreements in which English law sees a "trust."

The grip of the past is even more evident in the law of *torts*, that is to say the law of liability for civil wrongs (delicts). English law never achieved a general principle linking this liability to a comprehensive idea of fault or to the custody of property, but developed a series of special or nominate civil wrongs: deceit, nuisance, trespass, conversion, libel and slander, the "rule in *Rylands* v. *Fletcher*," and so on. Some of these civil wrongs correspond to the ancient writs; others, having been introduced by actions "on the case," are of more recent date. The important point to note is that an English jurist has difficulty in freeing himself from the way of thinking produced by these ancient procedures. It was only with some effort that a general principle of civil liability was developed

---

[18] Maitland (F. W.), *The Forms of Action at Common Law* (2nd ed., 1948), p. 2.

from a nominate tort (that of *negligence*), and even today, alongside this principle, there remain special regimes for a number of nominate torts.

281. Wasting away of private law

The royal courts enlarged their jurisdiction by developing the basic idea that their intervention was justified in the interests of the crown and kingdom. Other courts in this way of thinking were, therefore, available only if private interests were in question. But these other courts gradually declined, and with them the very idea of private law disappeared in England. All cases submitted to the English royal courts thus had the appearance, as it were, of being public law disputes.

The "public law" aspect of English law emerges from an examination of the special technique of the *writ* by which the action before the royal courts began. The writ was not simply the plaintiff's authorisation to act; technically it was an order given by the king commanding his officers to order the defendant to act according to the law by satisfying the claim of the plaintiff. If the defendant refused to obey the order, the plaintiff could then proceed against him; his action before the royal court would be justified not so much because of the opposition made to his claim but because of the defendant's disobedience of an order of the administration. The English trial is a matter of public not private law. It was essentially a debate as to whether an administrative act, the writ, issuing from the royal chancery, was properly issued and whether the order it embodied to the defendant was to be maintained. The trial was not for the purpose of setting aside an administrative act prejudicial to the person who requested it; on the contrary, he who obtained and meant to take advantage of it instituted an action in order that the procedure, if contested, be confirmed.

282. Substantive law: reception of Roman law impossible

Where did the judges find the substantive rules that would provide solutions to disputes brought before them?

The answer given in England is different from that on the European continent at the same period; and the result has been that for centuries, and indeed right up to the present time, English law has a different appearance from continental laws. The courts of Westminster were in a situation very dissimilar to that of the various traditional European continental courts which, rather than wasting away, continued to function, as they had in the past, with changes only in their composition and their internal rules and an increasing submission to royal authority. It was only natural that they continue to render justice according to the custom of their territory, and changes on this matter came about very slowly. From the beginning these courts had general jurisdiction in all litigation; they were never restricted to only certain kinds of cases made possible through special procedures. And since they were free from such obstacles, the continental courts were able to modernise their procedures generally by turning to the new, written procedures of Canon law. Having general jurisdiction, they were also able to concentrate upon the systematic development of principles of justice and to allow themselves to be guided in this respect by the model offered by Roman law.

In England on the other hand the situation was totally different because the royal courts, the courts of Westminster, were special courts only having jurisdiction in special cases for each of which there was a particular procedure; they had come into existence because of a completely new factor—the development of a centralised royal power. The royal courts, emerging as independent branches of the *curia regis*, were first of all political rather than judicial organs because it was intended that they resolve problems involving the interest of the king and the kingdom—in other words, the general interest—and not principally, in theory at least, the private interests of individuals. For the new kinds of problems that had arisen a new kind of law was therefore required. The courts of Westminster could not apply local customs because these had not evolved with these new kinds of problems in view. And of course the overriding necessity that all questions be handled within the traditional procedural framework was a major obstacle to the reception of the rules and concepts of Roman law.

In these circumstances, the courts of Westminster had to construct a new law. Many of its elements derived from different local English customs, selected and synthesised into a coherent whole. It also took some elements from Roman law; it is established, for instance, that in Bracton's thirteenth century description of legal institutions much was borrowed from the post-glossator, Azo (*d.* 1230).[19] All these elements, however, were re-shaped and melded in the procedural moulds used by the courts. Moreover, their origin was never divulged by the judges; the Common law, constructed decision by decision by the courts, was presented as essentially a work of reason (*resoun*); it expressed the idea of justice and political expediency of the thirteenth century, its great period of development. Later, the so-called *general immemorial custom of the realm*, of which the judges were the oracles, was said to be the basis for this work of reason. But one must not be misled by such language: this general immemorial custom was a pure fiction; the only true customs existing in England in the twelfth and thirteenth centuries were *local* customs. It was in order to provide the Common law with a foundation in agreement with the traditional, canonic and Roman theories of the sources of law that this concept of general immemorial custom was, *a posteriori*, invented. It was not based on any reality.

The rigour of the Common law procedures and the need to conform to a traditional framework were the main reasons preventing the wholesale reception of Roman legal concepts in England, at a time when the courts at Westminster, extending their original jurisdiction, gradually made it complete and most often were deciding purely private law disputes. These procedures, from many points of view archaic and typically English, forced a process of "anglicisation" to take place when substantive elements were borrowed from Roman or Canon law. The complexity and technical nature of these procedures were such that they could only be learned through practice. A university education based on Roman law might very well be of some help for meditating upon the just solution for a dispute; it did not help win a trial. In England, practitioners and judges, right up to the present time, have been trained essentially in the practice of law; for them, unlike their counterparts on the continent, university training has not been either necessary or, for many centuries, even usual.

---

[19] Maitland (F. W.), *Select Passages from the works of Bracton and Azo* (1895); Winfield (P. H.), *Chief Sources of English Legal History* (1925), p. 60.

283. Need for reform of common law

Because it had developed in strict compliance with formalist procedures, the Common law was exposed to two dangers: that of not developing with sufficient freedom to meet the needs of the period and the danger of becoming paralysed because of the conservatism of the legal world of the time. After its remarkable expansion in the thirteenth century, it did not escape either of these dangers and was thus exposed to a very great risk: the formation of a rival system by which, in the course of centuries, it might be supplanted just as the classical civil law of Rome was supplanted by the law of the praetors and the local customs supplanted by the Common law itself. This rival was *Equity*.

The limited jurisdiction of the royal courts may have been tolerable so long as other courts existed alongside them to decide disputes for which Common law offered no remedy. But the decline and disappearance of these other courts made it necessary to find a corrective for the insufficiencies of the Common law.

284. Appeal to royal authority

The obstacles encountered in the administration of justice by the courts of Westminster inevitably meant that in a number of cases no just solution could be, or was in fact, found. In such a case, it came very naturally to the mind of the disappointed party to seek another way of obtaining redress: a direct appeal to the king, the fountain of all justice and favour. If the royal courts were unable to give satisfaction could not the king remedy the malfunctioning of his courts? To the medieval mind, this final appeal to the king was very natural and the royal courts were not offended, at least at the beginning, to see the parties requesting the King to exercise his "prerogative." After all, the royal courts themselves owed their development to the operation of the same principle— that one could, in exceptional cases, appeal to the king to obtain justice.

From the fourteenth century it happened, therefore, that private persons unable to obtain justice from the royal courts or shocked by the solution given, addressed the king asking him to intervene as an act of royal grace "to satisfy conscience and as a work of brotherly love." In such cases the appeal normally passed through the chancellor; as a member of the royal household and the king's confessor, he had the responsibility of guiding his conscience and would, if he thought it appropriate, transmit the request to him for judgment in his council. This recourse to the "prerogative," perfectly justifiable and unopposed so long as it remained exceptional, could not fail to give rise to a conflict when it became institutionalised and developed into a system of legal rules set up in opposition to the Common law.

That precisely is what happened at the time of the Wars of the Roses (1453–1485) when it was difficult for the king himself to sit as judge in his own council. In the fifteenth century the chancellor became a more and more autonomous judge deciding alone in the name of the king and council upon a delegation of their authority. His interventions were, in addition, more and more frequently requested because procedural difficulties and judicial traditionalism stood in the way of the necessary development of the Common law. His decisions, in the beginning made on the basis of "the equity of the case", became increasingly systematised and the application of "equitable" doctrines soon amounted to additions and correctives to the "legal" principles applied by the royal courts.

285. Equity under the Tudors

Tudor absolutism of the sixteenth century was based on an extensive use of the royal prerogative. In criminal law, the famous Court of "Star Chamber" (*camera stellata*), after having been usefully employed to re-establish order following the civil war, was a formidable threat to the liberty of subjects. In civil matters, the equitable jurisdiction of the chancellor, founded as well on royal prerogative, was also considerably broadened. After 1529, the chancellor no longer served as confessor to the sovereign and was not an ecclesiastic but usually a lawyer. The chancellor examined the petitions addressed to him as a real judge, and in observation of a written procedure inspired by Canon law, one entirely different from the principles of procedure observed at Common law. The substantive principles he applied were also largely taken from Roman law and Canon law to whose reception procedure was no obstacle in this case as it was at Common law. These principles, rather than the very often archaic and outmoded Common law rules, generally gave more satisfaction to the Renaissance ideas of social good and justice. And because of their concern for justice and good administration, the English sovereigns of this period favoured the chancellor's jurisdiction.

The play of political considerations was also in its favour. The private, written and inquisitorial procedure of Chancery which never made use of the jury, rather than the oral and public Common law procedure, may also have been preferred by a monarch of authoritarian disposition. There was also probably some idea that if Roman law were to be adopted by the chancellor the law would then be reduced to a simple private law and lawyers' work, as in Rome, would then be limited to private relations, thereby giving greater scope to royal absolutism and executive discretion. *Princeps legibus solutus est.*[20] *Quod principi placuit, legis habet vigorem.*[21] How were such attractive maxims found in the Digest to be resisted? It may also have seemed simpler, in fact, to evolve an entirely new legal system and judicial administration than to attempt to bring about the reforms in the Common law that were so necessary at this time. English law thus narrowly escaped joining the European continental legal family in the sixteenth century because of the success of the chancellor's equitable jurisdiction and the decay of the Common law.[22] There was a risk that disputing parties would abandon the Common law courts and that these would fall into disuse, just as the Hundred Courts were deserted and abandoned three centuries before when the courts of Westminster, then in their full glory, offered a more modern justice administered according to a procedure superior to the traditional methods.

286. Compromise between common law and equity (1616)

Several reasons explain why this did not take place. The resistance of the common lawyers had to be taken into consideration by

---

[20] Digest, 1.3.31. (The prince is above the law.)

[21] Digest, 1.4.1. (That which receives the assent of the prince has force of law.)

[22] Maitland (F. W.), *English Law and the Renaissance* (1901). It was Roman law and Canon law rather than English law to which reference was made when, in the seventeenth century, the courts set up in India were directed to apply the principles of "justice, equity and good conscience." *Cf.* Derrett (J. D. M.), "Justice, Equity and Good Conscience" *in* Anderson (J. N. D.) ed., *Changing Law in Developing Countries* (1963) pp. 114–153.

the monarchy. To defend their position and their work, and to support them against royal absolutism, the Common law courts found an ally in Parliament. The poor organisation of Chancery, its congestion and venality were all weapons in the hands of its enemies. The revolution that might have brought England into the family of Romanist laws did not take place. In the end, a compromise was worked out which left the Common law courts and the court of the chancellor side by side, in a kind of equilibrium of power.

This compromise was not the result of legislation or a formal decision by royal authority or the judges. Very much the contrary. At the end of an extremely violent conflict[23] between Chancery and the Common law courts represented by Chief Justice Coke (1552–1634), who was also leader of the liberal parliamentary opposition, James I pronounced in favour of the former in 1616. The danger, however, had been serious and the chancellors were wise enough not to abuse their victory, and thereby disarmed parliamentary hostility. Parliament was, in truth, more interested in ending another abuse of royal prerogative, the Court of Star Chamber (abolished in 1641), than it was in the disappearance of Equity as such. A tacit understanding was established on the basis of the *status quo*. It was understood that the jurisdiction of the chancellor was to remain but that it would attempt no new encroachments at the expense of the Common law courts; it would also continue to adjudicate according to its precedents and thus escape from the criticism that it was arbitrary. It was further understood that the king would no longer use his prerogative to create new courts independent of the established Common law courts. Even the nature of Equity itself was to change[24]: the chancellor, as a legal or political figure, was no longer seen as judging on the basis of morality alone and tended to act more and more as a true judge. Further, after 1621, the control by the House of Lords over the decisions of the court of Chancery was admitted. In

---

[23] The decisions or decrees of the Court of Chancery were not directly enforceable; their effectiveness, however, was assured by the possibility of imprisoning the contravening party or by the sequestration of his property. The common lawyers declared that they considered a person who opposed such measures, even to the point where he had killed an officer of the Chancery charged to enforce them, as having acted in legitimate self-defence.

[24] Yale (D. E. C.), *Lord Nottingham's Manual of Chancery Practice and Prolegomena of Chancery and Equity* (1965); the introduction describes the transformation of Equity in the seventeenth century.

these new conditions the Common law courts were inclined to admit those interventions of the chancellor which were authorised in virtue of precedents.

287. Dual structure of English law

This is the reason for the dual structure of English law up to the present time. Alongside the Common law rules, the work of the royal courts of Westminster or, as they are also called, the "Common law courts," it also has *rules of Equity* or "equitable remedies" which complement and correct the Common law. Until 1875 the characteristic of Equity was its exclusive application by a special court, the Court of Chancery. However, over the centuries the rules of Equity became as strict and as "legal" as those of the Common law and their approximation to equity in the usual sense as such was not much more than that of the Common law rules themselves. English Equity was originally an expression of natural justice such as it was understood in the fifteenth and sixteenth centuries and to the extent that it was possible for the chancellor to give effect to it. This double reservation is important. English courts are today very reserved about any suggestion that they take up once again the work of the chancellors of the fifteenth and sixteenth centuries for the bold development of new equitable doctrines of natural justice. For them Equity is a body of rules which corrected English law in the course of history and which today is an integral part of English law. The reasons formerly justifying the intervention of the chancellor no longer exist; if English law is in need of remedial measures, there is Parliament. The security of legal relations and the supremacy of the law would be threatened if judges were willing to bring the rules of established law back into question under the pretext of "equity"; the English judiciary has clearly indicated, in striking language, its determination not to do so.[25]

288. Absorption of the ley merchant by the Common law

The thirteenth century was the formative period of Common law and the sixteenth century was the formative period of Equity; these were the two great moments in the development of the

---

[25] Lord Eldon in *Gee* v. *Pritchard & Anderson* (1818) 2 Swans. 403, 414, 36 E.R. 670, 674; Buckley J. in *Re Telescriptor Syndicat Ltd.* (1903) 2 Ch. 174, 195.

essential characteristics of the structure of English law. After the crises between Common law and Equity, the seventeenth and eighteenth centuries are the periods in which English law pursued its work of harmonisation without any notable disruption. The second half of the eighteenth century is of importance for the absorption of the law merchant by the Common law principally through the decisions of Chief Justice Lord Mansfield (1705–1793). Until that time, commercial law in England was considered a distinct and international body of law, the application of which was to be reserved to merchants as such. However the specialised commercial courts of the previous age had lost their autonomy with the passage of time and the evolution was completed in the second half of the eighteenth century, therefore, when the unification of what in the Romano-Germanic family is called "civil" law and commercial law was brought about. Commercial law was integrated into the Common law; its institutions were no longer a matter of privilege for the merchant class.

289. Legal writing and law reports

The most significant works on law of this period are those of Littleton (*circa* 1415–1481) *Of Tenures*, written toward the last quarter of the fifteenth century and of Coke (1552–1634), *Institutes of the Laws of England*, published between 1628 and 1644. Of considerable interest as well is the work of Fortescue (*circa* 1385–1479), *De laudibus legum Angliae*[26] (1470) and the dialogues between a partisan of the Roman law and one of the Common law, published by Saint-Germain (1460–1540), as *Doctor and Student* (1523–1532).[27]

For a knowledge of the Common law, the collections of judicial decisions or reports, which replaced the ancient chronicles of court practice or *Year Books* ending in 1535, are also very important. These collections, reporting the decisions in which the origins of many later English legal developments are found, have even today a practical importance and they have been re-published with excellent tables, in the basic collection *English Reports*.[28]

---

[26] "In Praise of the Laws of England." A translation was published by Chrimes (S. B.), *Sir John Fortescue De Laudibus Legum Angliae* (1942).
[27] The first dialogue in a Latin edition in 1523, the second dialogue in English in 1530 and the whole republished in English in 1532. There have been numerous later editions.
[28] For the period 1220–1865 in 176 volumes.

A classic work, *Commentaries on the Laws of England* by Sir William Blackstone (1723–1780), describes English law in the second half of the eighteenth century and at a time when the Common law was at its zenith. The *Commentaries*, published 1765–1769, constantly re-edited and brought up to date, are comparable to the work of Pothier (1699–1772) in France. The influence of this work in England and in all English-speaking countries has been considerable because it defined the framework of English law and thus facilitated, especially in the United States, its expansion and reception.

SECTION IV—MODERN PERIOD

290. 19th century reforms

After the thirteenth and sixteenth centuries, the nineteenth and twentieth centuries are periods of fundamental transformation in the history of English law.[29] The striking feature of this period, with the triumph of democratic ideas and through the influence of Jeremy Bentham (1748–1832),[30] is the unprecedented development of legislation. A great work of legal reform and modernisation was accomplished. Through the operation of radical reforms in procedure, especially in 1832–1833 and 1852, a veritable revolution took place. Until that time English law had developed within the procedural framework of the different forms of action. Once freed from these fetters, English jurists, like their continental colleagues, paid greater attention to the substantive law and it was on this basis that Common law principles were henceforth systematically re-organised.

Judicial organisation was also greatly changed by the *Judicature Acts* of 1873–1875 which removed the formal distinction between Common law courts and the court of the chancellor; all English courts became empowered to apply the rules of Common law as well as those of Equity, unlike the earlier position when a Common law court could only award a Common law remedy and one

---

[29] On the evolution of English law in the nineteenth century, *cf.* Dicey (A. V.), *Lectures on the Relation Between Law and Public Opinion During the Nineteenth Century* (1905).

[30] Hollond (H. A.), "Jeremy Bentham," (1948) 10 Cambridge L. J., pp. 3–32. Bentham's *An Introduction to the Principles of Morals and Legislation* was first published in 1789.

had to seek a remedy available in Equity from the Chancery Court.

In substantive law, a considerable amount of re-organisation was accomplished through the abrogation of lapsed legislation and the process of statutory consolidation; English law was in this way purged of many archaisms and the systematic presentation of its rules in various areas was thus facilitated. But the law did not lose its traditional aspect because of such important legislative work: there was no codification along French lines and legal development remained, essentially, the work of the courts. Parliament provided the new possibilities and directions for such development rather than creating new law itself. There was no author with the ambition of a Glanvill, Bracton, Coke or a Blackstone attempting to describe the whole of the law that now reflected the complex relationships of modern civilisation. Dating from this period, the essential tools for a knowledge of English law were the *Law Reports*, a new collection of judicial reports, organised in 1865 and, for a general view of English law, the systematic presentation of its principles provided by the encyclopedic collection *Laws of England*, originally published under the direction of Lord Halsbury (1823–1921).[31]

291. Twentieth century: common law in the welfare state

The work of modernisation that began in the nineteenth century continues today but with some new features. The liberalism dominant until 1914 has been replaced by a socialist trend attempting to create a new social order. With this change the Common law is undergoing a serious crisis; the judicial and case by case methods characteristic of its original development are no longer suited to the idea of bringing about rapid and extensive social change. Statutes and regulations now occupy a far more important place than they did in the past. The setting up of many new administrative regimes has brought about much litigation between citizen and government which numerous bodies, alongside the ordinary courts, have been established to handle. Because of the volume of this work and the need for special expertise in many fields which the regular judiciary did not have, it was thought inappropriate to

---

[31] The 4th ed. by Lord Hailsham contains 50 vols. (up to 1984), with cumulative supplements.

place such matters within the jurisdiction of the regular courts. The same thinking that in France and elsewhere prompted the creation of administrative tribunals also occurred in England, and it matters little that England did not follow suit by setting up an independent hierarchy of courts. More important than the question of structure is the fact that a large number of cases—in fact not less than the volume handled in the ordinary courts—is heard before these bodies in which jurists may sit with non-jurists or are altogether absent. This new range of disputes is therefore often handled and resolved through the use of methods that are not those of the traditional Common law.[32]

For many of the new problems of the welfare state it seems that the Romanist system of the European continent, more familiar with a legislative and doctrinal construction of the law, is better prepared than English law. A *rapprochement* may thus come about between English and continental laws and some see signs of it already. Such a movement is encouraged by the needs of international commerce and by a clearer realisation that affinities do exist between all European countries linked as they are to the values of western civilisation; the entry of the United Kingdom into the European Economic Community in 1972 will undoubtedly give it further force. These new characteristics and new tendencies of English law will also be noticed when examining the structure and sources of the Common law.

[32] Street (H.), *Justice in the Welfare State* (2nd ed., 1975). Lord Scarman, *English Law. The New Dimension* (1974).

CHAPTER II

STRUCTURE OF ENGLISH LAW

292. Importance of legal structure

Until recently the theory of the sources of law has been emphasised as the most striking feature of English law. European continental jurists have been educated to believe in the superiority of legislation and are filled with admiration for codes. For them it was strange—almost unseemly—that a highly civilised country and the greatest trading nation on earth should reject codification and remain attached to the philosophy, outdated in their eyes, that decided cases constitute the fundamental source of law.

Legislation and judicial decisions do not, it is true, play the same role in continental and English law. Before, however, dealing with the notable differences existing in this respect, it is important to bring to light another, a difference in the very structure of Romano-Germanic laws and the Common law. Today there is some tendency to admit that this difference is even more fundamental than that to be observed in relation to the sources. It is the most difficult for a jurist of the European continent to understand but it explains, in the last analysis, why English legal thinkers have a different theory of sources of law and why, in particular, English law has not accepted, and indeed could only accept with great difficulty, the Romano-Germanic principle of codification.

These structural differences have been neglected; only very recently has their essential character been noticed, and the reason for this is that for a long time, and under the influence of one prevailing theory, it was thought possible to analyse law as merely a series of legal norms. A better perspective, however, shows that the essential in law is not so much its rules at any given moment but rather the structure of the law, its classifications, the concepts it makes use of and the type of legal rule upon which it is based. No teaching of law could be conceived if this were not so because,

333

in fact, beyond the ever-changing *rules* there is a *framework* of the law which is relatively stable. The essential for a law student is to learn a *vocabulary* and to become familiar with certain constant *concepts* which will equip him to study any question, even though the *rules* he has learned will have very probably changed. The legislators may modify or abolish any particular rule of present law, but they can hardly change the language used or alter the traditional structures within which our legal reasoning takes place. Despite, for example, the many social changes and political revolutions that have occurred in France, the words and concepts of ownership, contract, marriage and *hypothèque* have been maintained. The actual rules on these subjects are not today what they once were, but the new rules are explained within an organisational framework in doctrinal works that has little changed over the centuries.

293. Categories and concepts

It is, precisely, in all these respects that English law is so very different from the French and other laws of the Romano-Germanic family. English legal structure is not the same as that of French law and it poses the greatest difficulty for a continental jurist since it is, in fact, totally different to anything with which he is familiar. There is for example no principal division of law into "public" and "private" law, no divisions such as "civil law" and "commercial law"—all those distinctions so natural to the mind of a French civilian; in their place, however, there are other divisions such as, first and foremost, the distinction between Common law and Equity. At a less abstract level, that of concepts, there is a similar disorientation for the French civilian: he discovers no concept of paternal authority (*puissance paternelle*), acknowledgment of natural children (*reconnaissance des enfants naturels*), usufruct (*usufruit*), moral persons (*personne morale*), *dol* or *force majeure*; instead, there are new concepts such as trust, bailment, estoppel, consideration and trespass which mean nothing to the French mind. And since there is no identity between such different legal ideas and concepts (although there may be some overlapping in the functions they perform within each system), English legal terms cannot be translated simply and effectively into French or some other Latin language. If a translation must be made, whatever the price, the meaning is most often completely distorted; the difficulty is usually no less even when it appears to be possible: the *contract* of English law is no more the equivalent of the *contrat* of French law than English *Equity* is that of French *équité*; *administrative law* does not mean *droit administratif*, nor can civil law be properly rendered as *droit civil*, and *common law* does not mean *droit commun*.[1]

294. The legal rule

The evident structural differences between Romanist laws and English law do not end with their respective categories and legal concepts. Even at the basic level of the definition of the legal rule the continental jurist will not find the sort of rule with which he is familiar. For English law, evolved through judicial decisions, the *legal rule* is something different from the doctrinally systematised or legislatively enunciated *règle de droit* familiar to the French jurist. It is, most obviously, framed in less general terms than the continental legal rule and this has the consequence, as will be seen, that the elementary distinction found in the Romano-Germanic family between imperative rules and suppletive rules (*règles impératives et règles supplétives*) is not made and that a codification of the Romanist type is more or less inconceivable in England.

Section I—Legal Divisions and Concepts

295. Importance of legal categories

When a legal problem is put to a person trained in law, his first reaction is to consider in which legal category the question should be situated. Is it a matter of criminal law, property law, the law of contract, a matter of labour relations or company law? It is of crucial importance that the problem be characterised in this manner since he must decide whether he is qualified to solve it. There has always been specialisation in the different branches of any

---

[1] The French-English or English-French dictionaries of legal terms, despite all the authors' efforts, are inevitably imperfect and often dangerously misleading when they attempt to explain the concept of one legal system by means of a concept employed in another. It is preferable to use one-language dictionaries among which the most recent for English law is *The Dictionary of English law*, published under the direction of Earl Jowitt (2nd ed., 1977), 2 Vols.

country's law. The complexity of modern law has forced upon us an even greater specialisation: no jurist thinks himself capable of advising a client, and ultimately handling a trial, in fields as different as copyright, bankruptcy, criminal, family or tax law. Each branch of law has its specialists and its own literature which really only those concerned with the field know intimately; those outside the area have usually only a very general knowledge, often more or less out of date because of the development of new ideas and the evolution of the law itself in that sector.

296. Originality of categories and concepts of English law

The same considerations hold true, of course, for the English legal system. But for historical reasons its principal divisions are not those found in Romanist laws. There are, therefore, many difficulties for a person trained in a Romano-Germanic system when taking up the study of English law. A bibliography of English law, no matter how inclusive or rich it is, may not provide him with the basic textbook corresponding to the legal category with which he is familiar and within which, in his eyes, the problem should be handled.

The basic works used by an English lawyer have titles like Contract, Torts, Real Property, Personal Property, Trusts, Evidence, Companies, Sale of Goods, Bankruptcy, Master and Servant, Bailment, Quasi-contract, Local Government, Conflict of Laws, Pleading and Practice and so on. French divisions and categories are thus replaced in England by others which may or may not, depending on the case, be capable of translation into French but which are not, at least in general, the same as the elementary divisions and categories of French law.

All these structural differences to be observed at the level of principal legal divisions—the division of Common law and Equity, substantive and adjective law and the rejection or lack of acquaintance with the basic divisions of continental law—are encountered again at the lower, altogether fundamental, level of the legal concepts. Here again the French jurist will rarely find his own familiar notions; such ideas as *personne morale, dol, contravention* and *établissement public* do not exist in English law. To express himself in comprehensible language the French jurist must use the concepts offered by English law such as domicile of origin, memorandum of association, misdemeanour, indictable offence, perpetuity, charity and injunction which have no counterparts in French law.

297. Historical explanation of English legal structure

The reason for these structural differences is obviously to be found in the different histories of the two legal traditions, Romanist laws and Common law.

The Romanist legal system is relatively rational and logical because its substantive rules were organised by the universities and legislators. A number of inconsistencies and anomalies certainly do subsist in their work because of historical and purely practical considerations; the laws of the Romano-Germanic family are far from being pure works of logic. But very great efforts have been made to render them logical and simplify their understanding. English law on the contrary has evolved quite apart from any real concern for logic and within a framework that was *imposed by procedures*; it is only very recently—during the last century in fact—and with the abolition of the former procedural system, that English legal scholarship has been able to rationalise this framework. Much progress of this kind has been made, but in general the ideas and classifications that are the product of a long tradition have of course been retained.

Several examples will serve to show the real strength of this tradition. The most typical instance is perhaps the celebrated definition of Equity of the distinguished historian of English law, F. W. Maitland (1850–1906), its most illustrious exponent, who stated: "Equity is that body of rules administered by our English courts of justice which, were it not for the operation of the *Judicature Acts*, would be administered only by those courts which would be known as Courts of Equity."[2] The English law of property is divided into personal property and real property: and by real property is meant those rights which before the procedural reform of 1833 were guaranteed by the actions called "real actions" and by personal property those rights which, before 1832, were protected by the actions called "personal actions." The English notion of contract only includes those undertakings which formerly were sanctioned by the action of *assumpsit*; it does not apply to gifts,

---

[2] Maitland (F. W.), *Equity* (2nd ed., 1949), p. 1.

nor trust, nor deposit which historically were sanctioned otherwise than by that action. From these few examples it can be understood that the categories and concepts of English law are wholly different from those of Romanist legal science.

298. Role of the universities

At this juncture, an objection might be made: did not the English universities created in the thirteenth century teach Roman and Canon law like their continental counterparts? It was only in 1758 that a course in the law of England was given for the first time at Oxford: and it was even later (1800) that a similar course was given for the first time at Cambridge. These, then, are the facts, but there is a fundamental difference which must be taken into consideration—while the continental practising jurists received their training in universities, this was not the case in England. Because of the law's almost total domination by procedure, a complete divorce took place between law as applied by the courts and that taught in the universities. English procedure, therefore, was not only an obstacle to Roman law influence; its complexity discouraged students from attending universities to learn principles that would be of no use to them in legal practice. It has never been the tradition for English lawyers to be educated in universities; even today when a university degree is mandatory in order to become a barrister or a solicitor, the degree need not be in law.[3] Traditionally, these persons were educated in legal practice in which no mention was ever made of Roman law and in which attention was constantly focused on matters of procedure and evidence upon which the success and indeed even the receivability of the action depended. In these conditions, therefore, it is quite understandable that English law was constructed along procedural lines and on the basis of the different forms of actions admitted before the royal courts. Only since these forms of action were abolished in 1852 has there been a tendency to organise a more rational system; the evolution, however, has been slow, and this is not surprising in view of the fact that the legal framework itself is in question. It is, very naturally, only *within* this framework that the institutions and

---

[3] In recent years,however, many more members of the legal professions do have law degrees, *cf.* Ormond (Hon. Mr. Justice), *Report of the Committee on Legal Education* (1971), p. 16.

rules of English law have been rationally organised to the extent possible; there could never be any question of adopting the categories and concepts of the Romanist tradition.

In a work such as this it is not possible to introduce all the different categories and concepts of English law.[4] It will be useful, however to give certain characteristic examples of some of the fundamental notions of English law. Two have been chosen: the distinction between Common law and Equity and the concept of trust. This section is then concluded by emphasising the importance of some of the rules of judicial administration—the laws of procedure and evidence, classically called *adjective law*, which, in the eyes of the English, is to be distinguished from the rules of *substantive law*.

§ 1. Common Law and Equity

299. A fundamental distinction

In the Romano-Germanic system, the most elementary distinction communicated to a student when he begins the study of law is that between private law and public law. No such distinction is traditionally made in English law, however. Indeed, such a distinction is specifically denied because it was seen as an indication of the idea that the state and government might not be subject to the law.

The fundamental distinction taught to a student of English law, that between Common law and Equity, is completely unknown to the laws of the Romano-Germanic family. It has already been shown that the history of English law provides the explanation: Equity is a series of remedies evolved mainly in the fifteenth and sixteenth centuries and applied by the court of the chancellor in order to complete, and occasionally correct, the Common law which had become insufficient and defective. This understood, the rules of Equity must now be considered in some greater detail and, in particular, further attention must be given to the distinction

---

[4] For the differences between English *administrative law* and French *droit administratif*, *cf.* Lawson (F. H.), "Le droit administratif anglais," Rev. int. droit comparé, 1951, p. 412 and Evans (R. N.), "French and German Administrative Law, with some English Comparisons," 14 Int. & Comp. L.Q. (1965) 1104; and with respect to the English rejection of the French concept of commercial law, *cf.* Burin des Roziers (H.), *La distinction du droit civil et du droit commercial et le droit anglais* (1959).

between Common law and Equity which is still important today despite their "fusion" achieved at the level of judicial organisation by the *Judicature Acts* of 1873 and 1875. In fact, the distinction is still fundamental to English law, and thus comparable to the French distinction drawn between public and private law, in the sense that English jurists are naturally divided into "common lawyers" and "equity lawyers," just as in France they are classed as *privatistes* and *publicistes*.

300. Origin of equity

It is necessary to return briefly to the conditions in which the rules of Equity were developed. When the Common law system functioned poorly—that is to say, when the royal courts were not able to hear a dispute, could not provide an adequate remedy, were unable to bring a procedure to a proper conclusion or rendered an inequitable judgment—then, according to the ideas of the Middle Ages, it was possible for individuals to request the king, by appealing to his conscience, to intervene and to render a decision that would make possible the proper course of justice or provide a just solution. The king, as sovereign justiciar, had the moral duty of assuring that his subjects would receive justice; his intervention was therefore justified in cases where the legal techniques were deficient.

301. "Equity follows the law"

The chancellor never intervened with a view to creating new legal rules which later judges would have to apply. He never purported to change the law, such as it had been established and applied by the Common law courts; quite the contrary—the chancellor professed his respect for the law: "Equity follows the law" was a maxim proclaimed by Chancery. But to "follow" the law did not necessarily mean that considerations of morality were to be put aside and it was in the name of morality that the chancellor intervened without, however, clashing with the law. It could never be admitted in effect that the enforcement of a right might amount to an injustice, that a *summum ius* amounted to a *summa iniuria*. In other countries, the judges themselves could supply the required remedy by prohibiting the abuse of a right or fraud, or by

applying the principle of public order and good morals; such remedies were possible on the European continent within the very
framework of the legal principles. In England, however, the royal
courts did not have the same freedom of action because they had
never had the same general jurisdiction and were bound to
observe rigid procedures. And so it was that, avoiding them and
appealing to a special court created upon the authority of royal
prerogative, solutions drawn from the dictates of conscience and
morality were brought to bear as limitations upon or complements
to the strict Common law. A number of examples will illustrate
how this took place.

302. Applications of equity

In the case of breach of contract, the prejudiced party could
obtain only damages at Common law because the action of
assumpsit for sanctioning contracts, delictual in origin (*trespass*),
could only conclude for a condemnation to pay damages. It might
happen, of course, that this sanction was inadequate and that the
aggrieved party was more interested in obtaining the actual performance of the undertaking. There was, however, no action available before the Common law courts to obtain this result. By
proceeding before the court of Chancery a decree of "specific performance" enjoining performance could be obtained. Common
law was not violated in any way; a remedy was simply granted that
it was not able to provide.

Common law considered the trial as a kind of combat in which
the judge only plays the role of umpire. Each party had to produce
its own proof but neither had the means of obliging the other to
produce a document in his possession. The court of Chancery, in
such case, could also intervene by a "discovery order" to enjoin
the party to produce the document.

Further, the archaic Common law system had a doctrine of
reality of consent (what the French call *vices du consentement*) in
contract that was fairly primitive and under-developed. Its conception of *duress*, for example, covered only physical violence and not
moral coercion. The chancellor intervened therefore against those
who unconscionably took advantage of their position as parent,
guardian, master, confessor or physician to obtain a contract or
some undue advantage from another; such person was prohibited

from invoking the contract or demanding its performance. And in this way the doctrine of *undue influence*, as a moral imperative, was added to the legal rules of *duress*.

A person places property in the hands of another, because of the confidence he has in the latter, so that such property will be administered in the interest of a third person to whom it was inconvenient or even impossible to transfer ownership and to whom the revenues produced by such property must be remitted. At Common law the person who received the property, the *trustee*, became the outright owner; his undertaking to manage it in the interests of and to make over the revenues to a third person was not enforceable. The chancellor however gave effect to this agreement; he did not oppose the Common law rule by denying that the trustee was the owner of the property but complemented the rule by means of the effective sanction he gave to the obligation which, in conscience, the trustee had assumed.

In all these cases, it cannot be said that Common law, strictly speaking, was violated. Its principles were accepted (Equity *follows* the law), but an equitable intervention took place in a number of instances—resulting finally in a number of complementary rules called rules of Equity—so that the legal system applied by the courts was perfected in the interests of morality. It might perhaps have been preferable for the Common law courts to have developed these complementary rules themselves, but for a number of reasons this was not possible and did not, in fact, come about. But this other authority, the Chancery, was able to do so.

Because—in the beginning at least—the Chancery was not considered a court, it did not appear to be deciding "in law"; this would certainly have created a dangerous conflict with the law courts at Westminster which were financially and morally interested in retaining their monopoly over judicial administration. Even the terminology adopted by the Chancellor's court bears witness to this—the procedure before the court is a "suit," not an "action," in certain "causes" or "matters"; one invokes "interests," not "rights"; the Chancellor grants a "decree," not a "judgment"; he may award "compensation," not "damages." The chancellor intervened "in equity" without purporting to modify the legal rules as administered by the courts. In every case it was by virtue of the demands of conscience that the intervention occurred. Conscience was shocked by the solution resulting from an imperfect law. It was contrary to conscience for the person against whom the proceedings were taken to act as he might because of the inadequate state of the law.

303. "Equity acts in personam"

The chancellor always intervened in the same manner: *Equity acts in personam*; by means of orders and injunctions addressed to a person whom he could, in fact, physically coerce, he enjoined or on the contrary forbade such person to act in a certain way and imposed on him, for his own salvation (the chancellor originally being an ecclesiastic), behaviour consistent with the dictates of morality and conscience. The law was not altered but the defendant who disobeyed an order issuing from the Chancery could be either imprisoned to meditate upon the fallacious nature of a strict reliance upon his absolute "rights," that is to say upon the dangers of the adage *summum ius summa iniuria*, or his goods would be seized and sequestrated. The chancellor only intervened when he could in fact apply these sanctions, and therefore the rules establishing his jurisdiction were different from those governing that of the Common law courts.

304. Discretionary character of equitable remedies

The intervention of the chancellor, originally prompted by considerations of conscience, gradually became more systematic; it was accepted that he might intervene in a number of typical recurring cases (just as formerly there were the *brevia de cursu*). A number of institutions (the principal being the trust) and concepts (misrepresentation, undue influence, specific performance, subrogation, *etc.*) were thus developed in the chancellor's equitable jurisdiction. In all these matters, however, the intervention of the chancellor always retained a certain discretionary character; he only intervened if it was considered that the conduct of the defendant was contrary to conscience and if the plaintiff had no cause for reproaching himself: he, on his side, had to have "clean hands" and must have acted without undue delay (*laches*) in asserting his right. From the seventeenth century precedents were established to "guide" the chancellor in the exercise of the discretionary power implied by such principles.

305. Procedure in chancery

Since the chancellor was not bound by Common law rules, he heard cases according to a procedure and in the light of an evidentiary system entirely different from those of the Common law. Proceedings were initiated by a *writ of subpoena* and there were no *forms of action*. The procedure was largely written, inquisitorial and inspired by Canon law; in no case did it involve the participation of a jury and in these circumstances it was possible to attach greater weight to written proofs and to the file on the case. Since the chancellor decided matters in the light of considerations of morality, there were means open to him for discovering the truth that were not available to the Common law judges.

It should be added that Chancery also acts in many instances of a non-contentious nature; it is frequently called upon to give directions to trustees respecting the management of property confided to them, to approve changes in by-laws of an incorporated company and to take steps in the interest of minor persons declared wards of the court and so on.

306. Common law and equity

Until 1875 five basic features distinguished Equity from the Common law. The historical origin of the law of Equity was, as seen above, different, and it was applied in a court outside the regular system of Common law courts. Its procedure, which was written, never involved a jury. The remedies in Equity, that is to say the principles applied by Chancery, were different from those available at Common law; and, finally, the granting of such remedies was discretionary.

But, all these differences having been noted, it nonetheless happened that as of the seventeenth century Equity became a body of truly legal rules administered by the Court of Chancery according to procedures and with a formalism and detail which were in no way less than those of the Common law. In any one dispute, it might have been necessary to institute two actions: one before a Common law court, the other in Chancery; such, for example, was the case if in addition to the specific performance of a contract (a remedy obtained in Equity) damages for the delay in the performance of the contract (a remedy obtained at Common law) were also wanted. This state of affairs was changed in 1873–1875. From this date all English courts were able to order the equitable remedies as well as apply the rules of Common law. The old procedural duality is now avoided: the principles of Common law and the rules of Equity may be invoked and put into application before the same court and in the same action. It is in this sense that it is said that a "fusion" of Common law and Equity was brought about by the *Judicature Acts* of 1873–1875.

307. The Judicature Acts, 1873–1875[5]

In truth, however, the Judicature Acts did not seek to bring about a fusion of the very principles of Common law and Equity. Parliament, in 1875, merely enabled all superior courts to adjudicate according to both systems. The two groups of rules, not in any conflict prior to 1875, were henceforth administered in the same manner as they were applied before 1875. In other words, the Acts did not change the law as it stood before but merely enabled Common law and Equity to be administered concurrently by the same courts.

A question relevant in the early days and still relevant after 1875 was this: of the two very different procedures available at Common law or in Equity, which should be selected in any given matter? Both in fact have been retained. Within the divisions of the High Court of Justice created by the legislation some judges sitting in the Queen's Bench Division decide according to the oral and contradictory procedures of traditional Common law and others, in the Chancery Division, according to the written, inquisitorial procedures derived from the old Equity proceedings. The same barristers do not plead in both divisions; the tradition of being either a "common lawyer" or an "Equity lawyer" persists, and the two callings do not suppose the same tastes, training or even the same kind of ability.

308. Equity since 1875

The distinction between Common law and Equity is still fundamental in English law today, but the character of the distinction is now quite different. Two factors must be considered. In the first place the historical origin of the law to be applied is no longer of any importance in the assigning of subject matters to one or

[5] 1873, 36 & 37 Vict. c.66; 1875, 38 & 39 Vict. c.77.

another of the divisions of the High Court. Much more relevant is the consideration as to which of the two procedures, that of the Common law or that of Equity, is most appropriate in the circumstances. Thus it has happened that Equity has come to comprise certain new subjects, such as company law, which was developed through legislation and has had no historical connection with the Chancery jurisdiction. The Chancery Division may also sometimes now dispose of some kinds of litigation which, historically, fell within the Common law; such is the case, for example, of the law of bankruptcy ever since the legislation on the subject has emphasised the need to organise the liquidation of the debts and assets of the bankrupt rather than his poor management. The distinction between Common law and Equity is not, therefore, what it once was; the difference has, so to speak, been "rationalised." Equity now includes that series of subjects in which it appears appropriate to proceed by way of written procedures, whereas the Common law comprises those in which the oral procedures of the past are retained.

Generally speaking, today, in order to know whether one is within the area of the Common law or that of Equity, it is more important to know which branch of law is involved rather than what sanction is available. Common law thus comprises, besides criminal law, the whole of the law of contract and torts; but the "common lawyers" of today apply, without any difficulty, such doctrines as misrepresentation, undue influence and estoppel, now perfectly integrated into Common law and which, it is perhaps only barely remembered, once had their origins in Equity. On the other hand, Equity includes the law of real property, trusts, partnerships, bankruptcy, the interpretation of wills and the winding up of estates. Historically, some of these subjects belong to Equity but with regard to others, on the contrary, it has simply been deemed more advantageous that they be handled by "equity lawyers" according to their own procedures and methods rather than those of the Common law. Rather than speaking of the Common law system and the rules of Equity—which is usually done in order to show the complementary character of Equity—it is well-founded today to speak of two branches of English law, each made up of a certain number of subject matters and characterised by the use of a definite procedure and marked by its own juristic attitude.

The relationship between Common law and Equity has inevitably been modified, in the second place, ever since the same judges have had to apply both bodies of law. Since there is no longer any rivalry between them, judges have been prompted to enquire whether there is any further justification for declining to develop new equitable doctrines in addition to those recognised at the close of the seventeenth century and, more particularly, whether certain Common law doctrines should not be judicially re-examined in the light of Equity principles.

On the first point, opinion is divided. The efforts of some judges to develop principles of "a new equity" are not favoured by the majority of jurists, according to whom such reform would more properly be carried out by Parliament. The second tendency, on the other hand, does not provoke the same criticism. For example, contemporary English judges may now be inclined to apply more restrictively the traditional Common law doctrine of "error" because they are able to apply as well the complementary Equitable doctrine, more flexible and just, of "innocent misrepresentation" (*i.e.* the error provoked by one contracting party without fraud).

On the other hand, English judges have enlarged the range of circumstances in which specific performance of a contract may be ordered.[6] It has become the usual remedy in the case of a contractual obligation to transfer land, where the goods have a special or unique character for the buyer, for stocks and shares that cannot be freely traded, but not for goods that can be readily obtained or sold in the market.

The history of the distinction between Common law and Equity is an example of the movement that has taken place in favour of a rationalisation of English law, made possible by the nineteenth century reforms on procedure and judicial organisation. But this process has taken place within the traditional framework and in particular without abandoning the deeply rooted legal categories of Common law and Equity.

§ 2. Trusts

309. The trust mechanism

The concept of *trust*, unknown to the Romano-Germanic system, is fundamental to English law and the most important cre-

---

[6] Lawson (F. H.), *Remedies in English law* (2nd ed., 1980), p. 211.

ation of Equity. The trust, in a general way, embodies the following idea: the person who constitutes the trust, the *settlor* of the
trust, provides that property will be administered by one or more
trustees for the benefit of one or more other persons, the *cestuis
que trust* or beneficiaries. This kind of arrangement is very frequent in English law because it fulfils such useful purposes as making provision for incapable persons and married women; the
settling of estates, endowments and charitable institutions also
very often rely upon this technique. The trust is used as well in
company affairs and international commercial transactions.

How is the trust, this fundamental English legal institution, to
be analysed? A continental jurist,[7] seeing it used for the protection
of incapables or the administration of property of what he would
call "moral" persons, is tempted to see the trustee as the *representative* of the incapable or moral persons and the latter as the real
owners of the trust property managed for their benefit. He is
therefore led to think that the trust is an application of a principle
of *representation*, a kind of mandate or agency conferred by the
settlor of the trust, or in some cases by the law, upon the trustee.

310. Analysis of trust

The above analysis is, however, completely incorrect. In reality,
the trust, like the majority of English legal concepts and institutions, can only be explained by history. At Common law, the trustee was not simply an administrator or a representative of the trust
beneficiaries; on the contrary, he was very much the owner of the
property placed in trust. He therefore administered the property
as he wished, he could dispose of it at will and he did not have to
account to any person for his management. This was his position
"at law."

The restriction placed on his right of ownership was of a moral
not a legal nature.[8] It was not according to law but *according to
conscience* that he had to administer the property as a reasonably

---

[7] For further explanation of this institution from the French point of view, see David (R.),
Le droit anglais (4th ed. 1981); Wortley (B. A.), "Le 'trust' et ses applications modernes en
droit anglais," Rev. int. dr. comparé (1962), pp. 699–710. *Adde* de Wulf (C.), *The Trust and
Corresponding Institutions in the Civil Law* (with a foreword by Jean Limpens) Centre Interuni-
versitaire de droit comparé (Bruxelles), 1965. Batiffol (H.), "The Trust Problem as seen by a
French Lawyer" (1951) 33 J. Comp. Leg. 18.

[8] It is to be noted however that the trustee's personal creditors could not seize the property
placed in trust.

prudent man and pay the revenues, and at a later time the capital, to certain persons, the beneficiaries designated by the settlor of the trust. At Common law, however, the beneficiaries had no right of action to enforce their rights; indeed, at Common law they had no rights at all. It must not be forgotten that contractual agreements were not generally enforced at Common law at the period when the trust was emerging.[9]

In the face of this gap in the Common law, and when the trustee, abusing the confidence placed in him and acting contrary to conscience did not manage the property in the interests of the *cestui que trust* and failed to pay over to the latter the profits arising from such property, the chancellor was requested to intervene. In this event the chancellor ordered the trustee to perform whatever act was necessary or to respect his undertakings as set out in the document creating the trust and, more especially, to remit the benefits arising from the trust to the *cestui*. And such order was accompanied by a *personal* sanction: the trustee would be imprisoned or his property seized if he did not obey.

In fact the threat of this sanction was most often effective and the trustee would act in the manner prescribed by the Chancery Court. But he was not for that reason reduced to the role of a representative. "Equity follows the law": and according to the present day English concept, the trustee is still held to be owner; his quality as such is quite apparent upon an examination of the extent of his powers over the trust property. These powers are dispositive and not simply administrative; he may dispose of the property by way of sale or even by gift. In law such acts of disposition are completely valid; the ownership of the property in question is thereby transferred to the acquiring party.

In these cases of alienation of trust property, however, Equity intervenes in two ways. First it gives effect to a principle of real subrogation: if the trustee has alienated the trust property for value received, the property received is subrogated to the original trust property; the trustee will henceforth be considered the trustee of the amounts arising from the sale of the property or such property as may have been acquired through the re-investment of these funds; the beneficiary's interest attaches to this new prop-

---

[9] The concept of trust thus developed quite apart and remained entirely separate from that of contract, even though at the basis of a trust, there may be, in most cases, an agreement which the civilian jurist would consider to be contractual in nature.

erty. In the second place, if a third party has acquired such property gratuitously, that is to say without paying valuable consideration, or is in bad faith (as when he knew or ought to know—has "notice"—that the trustee should not have disposed of the property in such manner) this factor does not prevent the ownership of the trust property from passing into his hands; but the acquirer of the property, considered to have become its legal owner—the owner *at law*—becomes at the same time a *trustee* and he must, in turn, like his author in title, manage it in the interests of the trust beneficiaries.

311. Legal nature of the rights of cestui

What are the rights of the beneficiaries under a trust? In strict law, the answer is that they have no *right*; they only have an *interest*—a "beneficial interest" in the trust property guaranteed, to a certain extent and according to certain rules, by Equity. Now that Equity has been systematised and has become in fact a body of rules complementing those of the Common law, the trust can be interpreted, in substance, differently.[10] But it is still not to be understood as an application of the principle of representation or agency. Such an analysis, in addition to the fact that it is historically false, leaves unexplained a certain number of principles admitted in English law. Rather than being related to such a concept, the trust appears to be a fragmentation of the attributes of ownership—some attributes constitute the *legal ownership* belonging to the trustee, and other attributes make up the *equitable ownership* belonging to the *cestui que trust*.

312. Romanist concept of ownership

The problem for the *civiliste* in this concept is that ownership in the context of the trust is not fragmented according to the familiar Romanist pattern to which the traditional analysis of the content of the right of ownership leads. Civil law ownership is conceived as the sum of three prerogatives vested in an owner: his right to the *usus*, *fructus* and *abusus*. However traditional this analysis may be, the concept of trust forces the civilian to admit how surprisingly rudimentary it is.

---

[10] On this transformation of Equity, *cf.* the introduction by Yale (D. E. C.), *Lord Nottingham's Manual of Chancery Practice and Prolegomena of Chancery and Equity* (1965).

Is it anything less than arbitrary to group under the heading *usus* the right to make use of a thing (live in a house) and that to administer such property (to have repairs made, or to grant the use of it to a third person)? Is it any less strange to group under the heading of *abusus* prerogatives as different as the right to destroy the thing in a material sense and that to alienate and dispose of it? As soon as it is understood how limited the Romanist concept of ownership really is, then one can understand the trust. The trustee is an owner whose prerogatives are determined and may be limited by the instrument constituting the trust and by the rules of Equity developed by the Court of Chancery. Generally, in practice, he has the right to perform acts of administration and, in the course of such management, to dispose of the trust property; on the other hand he has neither the use (in the true sense) or the enjoyment of such property, nor the right to destroy it materially.

313. English concept of estates

The division of the owner's prerogatives, as it occurs in the trust, is not possible in Romanist laws in which only specific, and very limited, fragmentations of ownership are admitted—and the distintegration, so to speak, or dismemberment of ownership along the lines of the trust is not one of those authorised by law. English jurists, in this respect, have trouble understanding the principles in Romanist laws which prevent the recognition of a combination of proprietary interests the practical importance and advantages of which are, in the eyes of jurists of both systems, incontestable. There is even more difficulty in understanding the Romanist rule according to which there is a *numerus clausus* of real rights and that ownership can only be dismembered into a limited number of real rights according to a specific pattern. Such thinking is quite foreign to the mentality of English jurists and English law; the principle that one can freely dismember ownership is as natural to the English as the principle of the freedom of contract is to the jurist of continental Europe.[11]

314. Joint tenancy and tenancy in common

In connection with the institution of trust, the English distinction between two forms of co-ownership, *joint tenancy* and *tenancy in common* should be noted. Tenancy in common is the equivalent

---

[11] Lawson (F. H.), *Introduction to the Law of Property* (1958), pp. 59 *et seq.*

of the civilian concept of co-ownership, although in its detailed regulation it does differ; joint tenancy, on the contrary, is peculiar to English law and, at first sight, is strange to the eyes of a Romanist. In this form of co-ownership, no one is actually called to succeed to the co-owner who dies, but the right belonging in common to several persons at the start is vested in a gradually decreasing number of survivors. To what does this correspond? It is easy to explain in the light of the trust. The *cestuis que trust* will normally be tenants in common; the trustees, on the other hand, will be joint tenants. It is in fact quite common for there to be several trustees and this provides an additional protection for the trust beneficiaries because the administrative acts and dispositions of the trust property must be made jointly by all the trustees. But if one of the trustees dies, it would not be desirable that the administration of the trust fall to the trustee's heirs, who are perhaps incompetent. Such eventuality is avoided by providing for a joint tenancy: with the death of one of the trustees, the trust continues to be validly administered by those surviving, and it is also often provided that the latter may, if need be, complete their number by naming a new trustee in conformity with the provisions of the trust instrument or the orders given by the court—today the Chancery Division.

Many other examples showing the structural differences between the concepts of Romanist and English law might be given. In all these areas, the different legal histories of each have given rise to ways of arranging the rules and working out concepts which basically differ in England and on the European continent. The Romanist legal concepts were thought out essentially in the universities on the basis of Roman law; the English concepts have principally been derived from ancient procedural forms and are still heavily impregnated with ways of thinking which date from the Middle Ages, even though they have to a very large extent since that time been rationalised to satisfy the needs of modern society.

§ 3. Importance of Adjective Law

315. Tendencies of Romanist jurists

Continental jurists have traditionally concentrated on substantive law (*règles de fond, materielles Recht*). They have neglected matters of procedure as well as what relates to evidence or the enforcement of judicial decisions—those rules in the Anglo-American tradition known collectively as *adjective* or *adjectival law* (*formelles Recht*). This hierarchy established between substantive law and procedure is of the greatest antiquity: in Rome a careful distinction was made between the *prudents* who alone were jurisconsults worthy of the name and the advocates (*oratores*) whose dignity and rank were unquestionably lower. The university formation of continental jurists has re-enforced this feeling; for centuries law has appeared to be linked to moral theology and the jurist, who had studied Roman law as a model of reason, was always distinguished from the practitioner who knew procedural forms and local rules but who lacked a general legal culture; those with no university degree, and therefore deemed to be unfamiliar with "the principles," were always somewhat looked down upon.

316. Different character of English law

English law, however, was not a law of the universities, or a law of principles; it is a law shaped by proceduralists and practitioners. The legally trained person of rank in England is the judge who has been elevated to the bench from the profession of barrister, not the university professor. Few practitioners, in former times, would have had university training in law; none of the leading judges of the nineteenth century had a university degree. Legal education was gained in the practice, by listening to judges and by participating in the daily work of a law office. To have studied a body of principles would not have been very useful; in England, until the nineteenth century, it was more essential to determine the form of action that would successfully bring a matter before the royal courts and to avoid the procedural pit-falls existing at every turning in such a formalist system. If the trial were completed, the jury was relied upon to render a reasonable verdict on the merits of the case. The first difficulty however was to complete the trial, and for that it was necessary to pay especial attention to all possible procedural obstacles. Moreover this procedure took place before a jury and therefore strict rules of evidence had to be drawn up if reasonable verdicts were to be given by jurors who were mostly uneducated and easily impressionable.

A concern for procedure was thus primary among the pre-occupations of the practitioners who have been England's jurists. It was, first of all, abundantly clear to the English, imbued with a keen idea of good sense, that it was no use being right if it was not possible for justice to be actually *done*. Further, the substantive law of England, at least until the nineteenth century, was extraordinarily imprecise and under-developed. The English law of contract, for example, really only dates from the nineteenth and twentieth centuries.[12]

317. Present English procedure

English procedure, in the last 100 years, has been simplified a good deal. English substantive law too has been considerably enriched; in rigour it is wholly comparable to that of European continental law. Much of legal training is now acquired in universities where matters of principle, systematised today as much as in the different Romanist systems, are studied. Nevertheless, the state of mind produced by this centuries' long secular tradition is still perpetuated in various institutions and continues to be very much part of present day attitudes.

For example, the procedure followed in the law courts remains largely the same as it was when it was normal to have jury trials even though at the present time the use of the jury, especially in civil matters, has become quite rare. The procedure is nevertheless carefully prepared so that the points of disagreement between the parties will emerge clearly and in such a way that they may be placed in the form of questions to which a "yes" or a "no" answer is possible.[13] There is then a public hearing—"the day in court"—when the points in disagreement will be clarified by a wholly oral system of evidence: Witnesses are heard by means of successive questioning by the barristers of the two parties (the *examination-in-chief* and the *cross-examination*); there is no *dossier* of the case in the French sense, because all steps taken at the hearing must be accomplished orally so that the jury, formerly illiterate, could give

---

[12] Blackstone, in his *Commentaries on the Laws of England*, in the 4 volumes that appeared in 1765–1769, devotes only 26 pages to the law of contract in Book II "Of the Rights of Things," Chap. 30 "Of Title by Gift, Grant and Contract." The first English text on the law of contract—and a mediocre one—was published in 1847. Lawson (F. H.), *The Oxford Law School 1850–1965* (1968), p. 21.

[13] The practice is similar to that in France in the *cour d'assises*, the only court functioning with a jury.

its verdict. Nor can the hearing be interrupted; the judgment in the case must be rendered immediately: the jury, if there were one, had to be liberated as soon as possible. In civil as well as criminal matters certain kinds of evidence are excluded because they might produce an unwarranted effect on the minds of uneducated jurors who are, in theory, still present; the English law of evidence is very rich but also highly—and, in the opinion of some overly—technical.[14] Through the effect of all these rules, English procedure has retained considerably more importance than it has in countries on the European continent, especially in the traditional parts of English law or what has been called *lawyers' law*.[15]

318. Attitude of English jurists

It is moreover necessary to remark upon the persistence in England of a state of mind that places great importance on procedural matters.

The European continental jurist sees law as a series of principles, or perhaps the very principle, of social order, and he attempts to define and improve it through the formulation of such principles. He enunciates the principle of political liberty, that of social rights, that of respect for ownership and contractual freedom, and he leaves to practitioners the work of putting such principles into operation—or, it may be, leaving them without any sanction. The English jurist, as a successor to generations of practitioners, is suspicious of what he easily considers to be empty statements: what, in fact, is it worth to affirm the existence of a right or a principle if, in practice, there is no means of putting it into effect? For centuries the attention of English jurists was focused upon matters of procedure and only slowly did it shift to the principles of substantive law.

Most disputes in England are handled by the lower courts, various administrative boards, tribunals, commissions and private arbitrators. The control exercised by the "superior courts"[16] over

---

[14] Some recent reforms have lessened its rigour somewhat; and the Lord Chancellor himself (Lord Gardiner) declared in March 1968 in the House of Lords " . . . I will go on record as saying that within twenty years we shall have no law of evidence at all. . . . Our existing law of evidence really comes from the time, not long ago, when no judge was ever allowed to decide questions of fact: he could only decide questions of law." H.L. Deb., Vol. 289, cols. 1461–1462 (1968).

[15] Hamson (C. J.): "Le trial anglais," Rev. int. dr. comparé, 1956, pp. 529–537.

[16] On the meaning of this term, *cf.* below, paras. 328, 333.

these bodies may in many instances deal with the manner in which
they have interpreted and applied the law, but very often,
especially in the case of the administrative boards and commissions, rental boards and arbitration,[17] it will only review the
manner in which the procedures were carried out. English law
does not always attempt to verify whether, on the merits, the
decision of an administrative authority is justified or not; it is more
essential to ensure that such authority hands down its decision only
after having observed a fair procedure during which it will have
heard all the interested parties and at the conclusion of which it
will be in possession of all material facts. What will the decision
be? The English jurist is not primarily concerned with that because
he has confidence in the system. These administrative authorities
in England are, however, obliged to give reasons for their
decisions.[18]

The concepts that the accused must have a *fair trial* and that
decisions can only be rendered upon completion of an established
procedure embodying the rules of *natural justice* are central to
English law—a law conceived, essentially, in the light of litigation
and one more concerned with the administration of justice, or so it
often seems to the continental jurist, than with justice itself.[19] The
two things cannot, quite clearly, be dissociated. The English
attitude, however, should be noted: observe a well-regulated procedure, fair in all respects, and you will surely arrive at a just solution. The French jurist, on the contrary, thinks that the judge must
be told what the just solution is and if he knows it already then he
must not be prevented from achieving it by an overly detailed
regulation of procedure and evidence.

These two attitudes have undoubtedly been shaped by history.
The English attitude very naturally took root in a country where
there was no body of law to which to refer and where the judges
were led to construct, empirically, the Common law. The French

---

[17] An arbitral award can only be scrutinised by the court for points of law. But the parties
may agree to exclude such review.
[18] The position of French law on this point is exactly the opposite. There is no general duty
for such authorities to furnish reasons, unless it is expressly provided by law. However, an
important feature of French *droit administratif* is the proceeding termed *recours pour excès de
pouvoir* which is unknown as such in English law. *Cf.* Braibant (G.), Questiaux (N.) and
Weiner (C.), *Le contrôle de l'administration et la protection des citoyens. Etude comparative*
(1973).
[19] "Justice before Truth" appears to be the directing principle of English law: *cf.* the article
by the former Lord Chancellor, Viscount Kilmuir, in (1960) 76 L.Q.R. 41 at p. 43.

attitude, inversely, is explained by the reception or at least by the prestige of Roman law, the heritage of which was accepted.

319. Justice and administration

A final point to note is the importance attached in England to the enforcement of judicial decisions. In this respect two matters should be emphasised.

In the first place, it is considered quite natural in England for the courts to issue orders to the various branches of the government administration in order that the law be respected. English courts do not limit themselves to quashing an illegal administrative act; they will direct by a *mandamus* order that the legally required administrative step be taken; they will also order the police, or any person, through the writ of *habeas corpus*, to put at liberty a person who has been illegally detained or confined. The existence of such *procedures* is characteristic of English law but, on the other hand, it is very little concerned with abstract legal declarations which enunciate principles of justice without giving any heed to their practical enforcement.

It would be inconceivable to an Englishman, in the second place, that the authority of the court be flouted as it sometimes is in Romano-Germanic countries where, for example, a person condemned to pay a sum of money may continue to live in an opulent style without being obliged to reveal where his property is located or from what sources he derives his income[20]; or where again an administrative authority can, without incurring any real responsibility, even refuse to make use of public authority to proceed to the enforcement of judgments.[21] The English lawyer has difficulty in understanding why in certain countries, such as Spain and parts of Latin America, it may even be necessary to institute further judicial proceedings to obtain the enforcement of a final judgment.

The rigour and the effectiveness of English enforcement procedures are impressive. That a private person, and much less an administrative authority, ignore the law is not admitted: if he did

---

[20] Pekelis (A.), "Legal Techniques and Political Ideologies, A Comparative Study," 41 Mich. L. R., pp. 665–692 (1943), also reprinted in *Law and Social Action* (1950), pp. 42–74.
[21] Rivero (J.), "Le Huron au Palais-Royal," *Chronique Dalloz*, 1962, VI, pp. 37–40; Frejaville (M.), "Le déclin de la formule exécutoire et les réactions des tribunaux," *Mélanges Ripert* (1950), t. I, pp. 214–225.

he would be obliged to reflect in prison upon the inconvenience of ignoring court orders. The concept of *contempt of court* is fundamental and expresses the very idea of English law.[22] Legislation of 1970 has however limited imprisonment for debt to instances of debts owing under a maintenance order, income tax or social security contributions.[23]

SECTION II—CONCEPT OF THE LEGAL RULE

320. Concept of judge-made legal rule

Another structural difference between the laws of the Romano-Germanic family and that of the Common law, but at another level, lies in a comparison of the formulation of the mould of thought by which the law is articulated, that is to say the *legal rule*.

The very important difference between continental and English law in this connection will be further emphasised when the respective roles of decided cases and legislation, as sources of law, are examined. English jurists think of their law as essentially a *case law*—a *droit jurisprudentiel*, to borrow the French terminology. The rules of English law are, fundamentally, the rules to be found in the *ratio decidendi* of the decisions rendered by the English superior courts. To the extent that he gives opinions not strictly necessary for the solution of the case before him, the English judge is speaking *obiter*—he is giving an opinion which may be questioned and debated again because it does not constitute a rule of law. The English *legal rule* is situated at the level of the case for which—and only for which—it has in fact been found and enunciated in order to decide it. If it were placed at a higher level, it would make English law "doctrinal" and greatly distort it. The English are very naturally hesitant to bring about such a transformation and, in fact, they only truly adopt the legislative rules, if they are not absolutely clear and obvious, when they have actually been interpreted by the courts. The judicial application of such rules then takes the place, as it were, of the provisions the legislators have enacted.

It is of course quite different in the laws of continental Europe.

<hr>

[22] Fox (Sir John C.), *The History of Contempt of Court* (1927).
[23] Administration of Justice Act 1970.

The web of these laws is not made up of judicial decisions but of principles constructed in the universities by doctrinal writers who systematised and modernised the elements provided by the law of Justinian. The English legal rule is capable of providing the solution to a dispute immediately but it is not really understood and its significance cannot be measured unless one knows all the facts of the case in which it was enunciated. The continental legal rule, linked to moral theology rather than to procedure, is enunciated by the *doctrine* or the legislators and designed to direct the conduct of citizens in a range of cases without any reference necessarily to a particular dispute. The two rules, which from their origins envisage different ends, cannot possess the same degree of generality; the French legal rule is inevitably wider than the English rule. On the other hand, in the eyes of an Englishman, the French *règle de droit* is situated at the level of a *legal principle* (*principe juridique*); to him it appears to be more a moral precept than a truly "legal" rule.[24] The English *legal rule* on the contrary, in the eyes of a French jurist, is situated at the level of a particular *judicial application* made of the rule; it is easy enough for him to understand but to him such a concept gives English law a case-by-case and therefore an organisationally unsatisfactory character. In these circumstances, the translation of *legal rule* by *règle de droit* or vice versa amounts to no more than a rough approximation; in fact it distorts the true sense of both ideas.

321. Examples

The difference in the style of approach can be illustrated by taking as a first example the subject of contracts *inter absentes*. Jurists of the Romano-Germanic family would ask whether it is suitable to accept as the ruling principle the theory of "emission" or that of "reception," in other words is the contract formed when the acceptance is sent or when it is received by the offeror? From the point of view of an English jurist this way of phrasing the question is far too general; he would argue that different rules might well be applicable, according as to whether one wishes to determine the

---

[24] Sereni (A. P.), "The Code and the Case Law," *The Code Napoléon and the Common Law World* (1956), p. 61: "The civil law *règle juridique* may appear at times to an Anglo-American lawyer to be nothing more than an abstract precept or at most a general directive rather than an actual legal provision."

date of, or the place where, the contract was formed, or whether the contract was concluded through an intermediary (the post office, for example) or directly (by telephone or telex).

In respect of civil liability, by way of second example, no thought is given in England to the formulation of those kinds of general principles such as are found in European codes and, especially, the French *Code civil*. Different types of fault or of prejudice suffered, the widely different kinds of circumstances in which the damage might occur, all these appear in English law to call for as many individual rules. Since the law has no abstract concept of fault, English jurists work with notions of different kinds of illicit behaviour, a series of various civil "wrongs" or *torts*, and in the case of the tort of *negligence* would ask whether in the given circumstances there is a duty of care upon the defendant. In the case of the liability of the landed proprietor, there are distinct rules which take into consideration whether the person suffering the damage had the right to be on the land, whether he had been invited there by the defendant, whether an adult or minor person is involved, whether the accident was caused by some special arrangement given to the land, and so on. Again, in connection with the various torts that are recognised, consideration is given to the nature of the damage suffered, and different rules govern the case when the damage was to a person, or to property or the two together, and whether the damage was material or merely moral. It is significant that the French words *faute* and *préjudice* cannot be adequately translated into English and that the key word in the English law of torts is *damages*. The general principles of continental codes thus appear to the English legal mind to be general *moral* precepts rather than true *legal* rules. Conversely the articulation of the English legal rule demands a case-by-case, a casuistic approach which sometimes has become so complicated and so subtle that it has prompted Parliament to intervene in order to simplify the expression of the state of the law.

322. "Open" and "closed" systems

The preceding remarks are fundamental to an understanding of English law and, especially, the method of English legal reasoning. The laws of the Romano-Germanic family are coherent but, one may say, "closed" systems in which any kind of question can, and must at least in theory, be resolved by an "interpretation" of an existing rule of law. On the other hand English law is an "open" system: it has a *method* that can assure the resolution of any kind of question that may arise, not substantive principles which must, in all circumstances, be applied. The technique of English law is not one of interpreting legal rules; it consists, beginning with those *legal rules* already enunciated, of discovering *the legal rule*— perhaps a new legal rule—that must be applied in the instant case. This is accomplished by paying very great attention to the facts of each case and by carefully studying the reasons that may exist for distinguishing the factual situation in the case at hand from that in a previous case. To a new fact situation there corresponds—there *must* correspond in the English legal mentality—a new legal rule. The function of the judge is to render justice, not to formulate in general terms a series of rules the scope of which may well exceed the terms of the dispute before him. The English concept of the legal rule, much narrower than the corresponding continental notion, is historically explained by the fact that the Common law was formed by the judges and that their technique was one of making *distinctions*, rather than one of *interpretation*, and this remains the basic approach of English law today.

323. Abnormal character of legislative rules

There are further important consequences deriving from the different concepts in England and continental Europe of the legal rule. For example, in the eyes of an English jurist, law which is legislative in origin—*statute law*—has traditionally appeared as somewhat abnormal in character. Whatever the care with which the English legislators formulate statutory provisions, so as to make them as concrete and specific as possible,[25] they are not speaking from the same position as the judges (apart from the case of course where they are simply correcting an *erratum* of the Common law). It follows from this that the legislative provisions so formulated are not fully assimilated into the English legal system until they have been taken up and affirmed—and sometimes even

---

[25] In English legislative drafting it is in fact intended that the judges should not be able to make rules of law; thus the English legislators avoid the use of general and comprehensive expressions, contrary to the legislative practice in the Romano-Germanic systems: Sereni (A. P.), *loc. cit.* p. 59; *adde* Gutteridge (H. C.), "Comparative View of the Interpretation of Statute Law" (1933) 8 Tulane L. Rev. 1.

deformed—by the courts in the course of the *normal* working processes of the Common law. This observation is of extreme importance because it means in fact, if not in theory, that it is impossible for a codification *à la française* to be achieved in England. As confirmation of this it should be noted that in different Common law countries where codification along French lines has been attempted—in the United States or in India for example—the promulgated codes have not become the basic legal structures the way the Napoleonic codes have in France.

The traditional analysis of the legal rule in England gave rise to serious difficulties when legislation and administrative regulation became the instruments for transforming the social order. Such legislation was often able to articulate only leading principles, establish standards of behaviour and to delegate considerable discretionary powers to administrative bodies and those called upon to control them. The English courts admitted in these circumstances that statutory interpretation might be carried out otherwise than in the traditional manner and, in effect, in a way that calls to mind European continental techniques. This was achieved by limiting the scope of the control that the courts—alone empowered to pronounce upon the law—exercised over the decisions of bodies handling quasi judicial disputes[26] rather than by admitting some new concept of the legal rule that carried with it new principles of interpretation.

324. "Inflation" of law

The English concept of the legal rule leads, in the second place, to what might be called an "inflation" of the law. In the Romano-Germanic concept, the wish to reduce law to a number of principles, because it is thought that *doctrine* or legislation cannot enter into a detailed appreciation of facts, has perhaps resulted in some areas in leaving too much scope to judicial discretion. French law thus seems to an English legal scholar to be made up of only a framework within which it is often easy for the courts to change the contents of rules in a way hardly propitious for the security of legal relations. English law gives exactly the contrary impression to a continental jurist; he finds it over-burdened with legal defi-

---

[26] Street (H.), *Justice in the Welfare State* (2nd ed., 1975).

nitions[27] and detailed solutions which, he would think, are better left to the discretion of the judge in each individual case rather than chaining him to their observance through the play of the rule of precedent.

English legislation may indeed grant judges a "discretionary power" in certain cases. But this power may mean something very different from what it does in a Romanist system. Such a legal term is in effect only meaningful for an English jurist once a large number of *legal rules*, judicial in origin, have determined in precisely what manner the judge may exercise his discretionary power. For example, a rule of the English Supreme Court of Judicature did provide, in a brief statement, that the judges of that court were to have full discretionary powers with respect to legal costs.[28] This laconic provision was literally drowned in a flood of decisions explaining how, in law, this discretionary power was to be exercised; a new instrument was drafted in 1959 to systematise this line of cases and stated, in the place of the former and overly concise rule, 35 new rules which with their appendices occupied no less than 148 pages of rules of practice compiled by this court.[29]

The French rule providing that a businessman must not practise unfair competition to the prejudice of his competitors would not be regarded in England, in the same way, as a true legal rule. It would be considered a vague principle only intended to provide judges with a general and equitable directive. To locate the true *legal rule* it would be necessary to wait for a court's pronouncement that in the facts of a concrete case there was, or there was not, unfair competition exposing that particular businessman to some form of legal reprimand.[30] The English legal rule cannot therefore be separated from the factual elements of the case, which alone enable its true meaning to be understood. It is not disembodied in a legal statement. Facts permeate the structure of English law and often accede themselves to the rank of legal rules. The use made in England of legal dictionaries in itself attests to the

---

[27] Cf., e.g. Saunders (J. B.) ed., *Words and Phrases Legally Defined* (2nd ed., 1969) in 5 volumes with annual supplements. Stroud (F.), *Judicial Dictionary of Words and Phrases* (1975), 5 vols.

[28] Rules of the Supreme Court, Ord. 65, r. 1, adopted by the Judicature Act 1925, s. 50(1).

[29] The Supreme Court Costs Rules, 1959, now R.S.C. Ord. 62, r. 3, published in the *Supreme Court Practice*, known as the White Book.

[30] As Mr. Justice Holmes said: "General propositions do not decide concrete cases."

resulting excessive growth of English law which various writers have deplored on many occasions.

325. "Imperative" law and "suppletive" rules

The English concept of the legal rule excludes, in the third place, the elementary distinction made in Romanist laws between "imperative" and "suppletive" legal rules (*lois impératives, lois supplétives*), expressions containing ideas which are, really, untranslatable into English. When the difference between the *legal rule* and the *règle de droit* is understood, it is easy to see why the concept of a "suppletive" legal rule is incomprehensible to an English jurist. A "suppletive" legal rule is only conceivable if one takes up a doctrinal or legislative perspective in which one envisages a series of typical cases in which a rule of law is to apply, unless the parties have otherwise agreed or the law itself otherwise provides. The English judge, of course, does not have to concern himself with even the possibility of typical cases; his function is to decide a concrete case by taking certain precedents into consideration. How could he, for example, state that, unless the contrary is provided, a payment will be called for in person by the creditor and not be made payable at the address of the payee (that the debt is *quérable* and not *portable*) or that, saving a stipulation to the contrary, the vendor is held to warrant the object sold against latent defects (*vices cachés*)? Evidently such pronouncements on his part would amount to speaking *obiter*. The qualification of such general statements as rules of law will thus, inevitably, be denied because to English jurists they appear to be of doctrinal nature; situated at a level higher than that of the *ratio decidendi* of any particular judicial decision, they cannot be legal rules.

For an Englishman, it should be added, there is also perhaps something shocking in the suggestion that all laws might not be mandatory or "imperative" to the same degree. When, therefore, English doctrinal writing does in fact enunciate what continental jurists would call "suppletive" legal rules, it is speaking from a different point of view, that of the contracting parties, and it employs the term *implied conditions* of the contract rather than that of suppletive legal rules. Suppletive rules of law can of course, on the other hand, be enacted by the legislature. Legislation suppletive in character has not however gained any real place in English law because it is still seen, as its tradition dictates, as a judge-made law in which the part played by legislation is really secondary in importance.

CHAPTER III

SOURCES OF ENGLISH LAW

326. Justification of the analysis

English law, the Common law fashioned by the Courts of Westminster and Equity by the Court of Chancery, is not a judge-made law only by reason of its historical origins. Since the influence of the universities and of legal writing has been less in England than on the continent and since no complete re-shaping of the law has ever taken place through the technique of codification, English law has retained its original characteristics as much with respect to its sources, to be considered now, as in its structure. It is, typically, a judge-made law, a *case law*, and it is with a study of the place of judicial decisions that an examination of its sources properly begins.

Legislation—*statute law* to employ the English usage—has traditionally occupied only a secondary position in English law and was limited to correcting or complementing the work accomplished by judicial decisions. In truth, however, the position today is reversed to a large extent. In England, statutes and delegated or subordinate legislation can no longer be considered as secondary; their importance is in fact equal to that enjoyed by these same sources on the European continent. However, for historical reasons, the role of legislation in England is still somewhat different; and, because of English law's structure, the work of the English legislators is not fully the equivalent of continental codes and legislation.

Compared to the decisions of the courts and statutes, the other sources of English law—custom, legal writing and reason—do rank as secondary sources. Their importance however is far from negligible and it is, accordingly, important to take them into account as well.

The study of judicial decisions as the principal source of English law presupposes a familiarity with the major features of English judicial organisation. These, therefore, will be explained before examining the *rule of precedent* and the authority attributed to judicial decisions in English law.

§ 1. English Judicial Organisation[1]

327. Classes of courts

English judicial organisation was, for a very long time, extremely complex and even though the reforms of a century ago did much to simplify and rationalise it, it is still found to be so today by continental jurists.

A fundamental distinction, unknown on the continent, is made, first of all, between "superior" courts and all other courts ("lower" or "inferior" courts and "quasi-judicial" bodies). Particular interest attaches to the decisions of the superior courts because it is from them that decisions having value as "precedents" are drawn, and it is through their study that the state of English law on a particular point can be established. Most cases are however decided by the lower courts and quasi-judicial bodies (whose decisions are generally of much less interest) even though they do not enjoy the judicial power or authority of the superior courts.

328. Superior courts: the Supreme Court of Judicature

Throughout English history there have been many superior courts: the Courts of Westminster (Court of King's Bench, Court of Common Pleas, Courts of Exchequer) administering the Common law; the Court of Chancery administering Equity; the Court of Admiralty for most maritime law matters; the Court of Divorce for subjects falling within Canon law; the Court of Probate in respect of wills. A very great simplification of this picture was

---

[1] Jackson (R. M.), *The Machinery of Justice in England* (7th ed., 1977); David (R.), *Le droit anglais* (4th ed., 1981).

achieved upon the enactment of the Judicature Acts of 1873 and 1875 which abolished all these separate courts and grouped them within a single superior court, the Supreme Court of Judicature, over which the Appellate Committee of the House of Lords exercises a final appellate jurisdiction.[2]

The organisation created by the Judicature Acts has been modified several times and in particular by the Administration of Justice Act 1970 and the Courts Act 1971[3] which came into force in 1972. Only this present structure will be described here. The Supreme Court of Judicature is organised in three sections: the High Court of Justice, the Crown Court and the Court of Appeal.

The High Court of Justice is made up of three "divisions," the Queen's Bench Division, the Chancery Division and the Family Division. Cases are assigned to these divisions in the light of available resources and facilities since each, by law, is in principle competent to hear any case that falls within the jurisdiction of the High Court. The fact that within the Queen's Bench Division there is an Admiralty Court or a Commercial Court, or that within the Chancery Division there is a Companies Court or a Bankruptcy Court merely signifies that within the divisions there are judges with a special expertise in such fields and that there are special rules of procedure for these specialised subject matters.

The High Court has, by law, a maximum of 75 *puisné* judges[4] (styled *Justices*) for the three divisions, presided over by the Lord Chief Justice in the Queen's Bench Division, the Vice-Chancellor in the Chancery Division and the President in the Family Division. All judges are appointed from among barristers for whom the nomination as one of Her Majesty's Justices is the pinnacle of professional and social success. At first instance cases are heard by a judge sitting alone. In earlier times the judges were always assisted by a jury where the subject matter of the dispute fell within the Common law; in civil matters today, however, a jury has become altogether exceptional and, in those rare cases in which it is used, there is no longer the requirement that its verdict be unanimous.

---

[2] There are only two other superior courts at the present time: the Restrictive Practices Court created in 1956 and re-organised in 1976 with jurisdiction over certain matters of commercial practices; and the Employment Appeal Tribunal created in 1978.

[3] 19–20 Eliz. 2, c. 23.

[4] In 1800 there were only 15; in 1900 only 29. *Cf.* below, para. 334.

The Crown Court, a new division of the Supreme Court of Judicature, was instituted by the Courts Act 1971 and hears cases in criminal matters. Its personnel is more varied. According to the nature of the charge, the case may be heard either by a justice of the High Court, by a "circuit judge" (also a full-time, professional judge) or by a "recorder" (a barrister who is temporarily serving as judge). If the accused pleads "not guilty," the judge will be assisted by a jury.

The Court of Appeal is the second level of jurisdiction within the Supreme Court of Judicature. It has 16 Lord Justices presided over by the Master of the Rolls. Cases are, in principle, heard by a bench of three judges, each of whom expresses his own opinion separately; the appeal is denied if a majority does not decide in favour of modifying the decision against which it is lodged. The Criminal Division of the Court of Appeal sits as a specialised division in criminal law. Here the case is generally heard by a Lord Justice and two judges from the Queen's Bench Division. It is not customary for a judge in the minority to write a separate opinion.

329. The House of Lords

From the decisions of the Court of Appeal a further appeal may lie to the Appellate Committee of the House of Lords.[5] Leave to appeal must be granted and is only given exceptionally; in fact the House of Lords renders no more than thirty or forty decisions each year. Cases are judged by a varying number of law lords, normally five but never less than three. In the Lords, only the Lord Chancellor (who presides), the 11 Lords of Appeal in Ordinary who have been specially created (non-hereditary) peers for this purpose and certain other lords, who formerly occupied various legal offices enumerated by law, are qualified to sit. Cases are heard usually by a bench of five and not less than three Lords. The appeal is brought in the form of a petition. Each judge expresses, separately, his own opinion technically called a *speech*, and the appeal is rejected if there is no majority in favour of allowing it. At this

---

[5] In 1873 it was decided to abolish the appeal to the House of Lords but it was re-established in 1876—which explains the inappropriateness of the name *Supreme* Court of Judicature. In some cases, since 1969, it is possible to proceed directly from the High Court of Justice to the House of Lords.

level, as well as that of the Court of Appeal, there is no procedure similar to the French practice of *cassation avec renvoi*—a quashing or annulment and re-transfer of the case to a different court of appeal for re-trial. Both the Court of Appeal and the House of Lords adjudicate on the merits of the case.

330. Judicial Committee of the Privy Council

The House of Lords is the court of last resort for the whole of the United Kingdom, although only for civil matters in the case of Scotland. Judges from the Lords also constitute, either alone or with others from overseas, the Judicial Committee of the Privy Council. This body hears appeals from decisions of the Supreme Courts of those British overseas territories or Commonwealth states which have not yet abolished its jurisdiction (Australia in some subjects, New Zealand, Gambia, Sierra Leone, etc.). These judges must therefore often apply laws other than English law. This circumstance is singled out with interest by some authors who see in it a guarantee against an excessive "nationalisation" of the law of the jurisdiction in question. The decisions of the Judicial Committee—which in theory merely gives "advice" to the Sovereign in the exercise of his or her prerogative—have an authority more or less equal to those of the House of Lords in Common law matters. Both are published in the same series of judicial reports, the *Appeal Cases*.

331. Lower courts

The vast majority of cases that arise are heard before a large number of lower courts.

In civil matters the principal court is the County Court, constituted by legislation of 1846. It resembles only in name the ancient County Court of the early Middle Ages. The County Courts of today play a most important role in the administration of civil justice in England because of their very broad jurisdiction. Although the jurisdiction of the High Court of Justice is unlimited in general principle, it does not hear cases involving small sums which thus proceed before a County Court. Actions in divorce are also begun in certain County Courts which can, when the action is uncontested, grant the relief. The number of County Court judges (called new circuit judges) is fixed at 260; and, as in the High Court, they are selected from among experienced practitioners. More minor affairs may also be judged by the judge's auxiliary, the registrar, or, in the light of 1973 legislation, be referred to arbitrators. The reference to arbitration may also occur at the request of the parties. The arbitrator will often be the registrar, or the judge if the case is significant or some other person agreed upon by the parties.

In criminal matters the "petty" or "summary" offences are judged by magistrates, members of the community who enjoy the title "justice of the peace" but receive no remuneration. They are now about 22,000 in number; they have no legal training but are assisted by a legally trained clerk. In London and several other large cities, the justices of the peace are replaced by full-time, paid *stipendiary magistrates.* They are appointed by the Queen upon the recommendation of the Lord Chancellor and must have been a barrister or solicitor for not less than seven years. As a general rule at least two magistrates must hear the case and render judgment, whereas the stipendiary may sit alone.

The magistrates' jurisdiction in criminal matters is not however limited to petty offences. For all major or "indictable" offences it falls to them, within the framework of a preliminary hearing, to decide whether there are sufficient grounds to send the suspected person to trial before the Crown Court. In many cases, however, it is possible for the accused person to opt to be tried before the magistrates and 88 per cent. of indictable offences are in fact so tried. For the accused person the advantage is that, since the magistrates' powers are limited, he cannot be condemned to more than a six months' prison sentence, whereas appearing before the Crown Court he runs the risk of incurring a much more severe penalty. The trial in the Magistrate's Court is however without a jury.

It should be added finally, that Magistrates have a limited jurisdiction in civil matters, such as family law (separations, maintenance orders, child custody) and in some claims for debt (taxes and rates owing to public utility bodies and municipalities).

Appeals, when permitted, from decisions of the County Courts are taken directly to the Court of Appeal. Appeals from decisions of the Magistrates' Courts, when authorised, proceed either before the Crown Court (where the bench is composed of a pro-

fessional judge and two to four magistrates) or before the Queen's
Bench Division (where the bench is of three judges).

332. "Quasi-judicial" disputes

In administrative matters and for problems arising under certain
statutes, different bodies known as Boards or Commissions or Tribunals have a "quasi-judicial" jurisdiction; certain disputes must
be referred to them before they may be submitted to the Supreme
Court of Judicature. There are many such bodies and their scope
of activity is extremely wide. They exist in such varied fields as
economic matters (air and land transport,trade marks, copyright,
broadcasting, company shares and securities); tax law (income and
land taxation, tax fraud); land (expropriation, land development);
social security (social benefits, hospitals, insurance, pensions, discharging of employees); renting practices (in furnished and unfur-
nished premises); military matters (postponement of military duty,
conscientious objectors) etc. A Council on Tribunals, created in
1958 to oversee the operations of some of them, now has authority
over 2,218 tribunals of 41 different types which, in 1978, decided
well over a million cases.

As varied in their composition as in their attributions and
powers, these tribunals are sometimes connected to a branch of
the government administration, but there are some totally independent bodies such as those having jurisdiction in matters opposing property-owners and tenants or employers and employees.
Some are constituted to hear disputes but many are merely authorised to oversee whether the administrative unit in question has
come to its decision in observance of the procedures laid down by
law and whether, in particular, the enquiry undertaken was carried
out in a "quasi-judicial" manner.[6] For these two reasons these
bodies cannot be easily assimilated to the French *tribunaux
administratifs.*

All such bodies do, however, at least in theory, come under the
supervisory jurisdiction of the High Court of Justice. There is, in
England, no hierarchy of administrative courts distinct from the
regular or ordinary courts; and, in particular, there is no *special-*

---

[6] The subject is, in English law, and legal systems derived from it, of very great complexity.
Cf. de Smith, *Judicial Review of Administrative Action*, (4th ed., 1980).

ised superior court for cases in which a branch of the governmental administration is a party.[7] The suggestion has been made to create an "Administrative Division" within the High Court of Justice but this has met with the objection that the way might then be opened up for the development of a "continental-type" administrative law, one operating beyond the confines of the ordinary law. The various bodies created to hear administrative disputes in England really do function as "inferior courts"; and, as such, and being staffed in general by persons without legal training, they appear to be designed to relieve the ordinary courts of what would otherwise be an impossibly large number of cases, rather than to decide according to law by exercising true judicial power and authority.

333. Judicial authority in England

The eminent position of English superior court judges shows that in England, unlike the European continent and in particular France, there is a real *judicial* authority which, in its importance and dignity, is on the same level as the legislative and executive authorities.

The superior courts do in fact constitute a real power. Historically, first of all, they were responsible for the development of Common law and Equity; they have, therefore, created the law of England in its very foundations. The situation has changed somewhat in modern times, but no codification of the whole body of the law has taken place such as would prompt English jurists to think of legislation as the primary source of law. It is not easily forgotten, moreover, that in England the courts themselves were the champions in the struggle for the affirmation and protection of English rights and freedoms. There are many who believe that the courts can continue to play such a role and that the existence of a real judicial authority can be a useful counter-balance to the consummated alliance that now exists between Parliament and government. And the principle that there is no decided case that can escape the supervisory jurisdiction of the superior courts in the exercise of their inherent jurisdiction may now be taken as a rule

---

[7] For a comparison of administrative law in France and England, *cf.* para. 291, and Pepy (D.), 'Justice anglaise et justice administrative francaise" *Etudes et documents* (1956) vol. X pp. 159–175. Mitchell (J. D. B.): "L'absence d'un système de droit adminisratif au Royaume-Uni: ses causes et ses effets" *Etudes et documents* vol. 18 (1964) pp. 211–225. Distel (M.): "La réforme du contröle de l'administration en Grande-Bretagne" Rev. int. dr. comparé 1971, p. 355.

of established constitutional usage. The existence of a fully independent and highly respected judicial authority is seen as indispensable to the proper functioning of English institutions, to the formation and strengthening of which the courts have made such important contributions throughout history.

A number of principles of English law indicate the scope of the power of the superior courts and the importance attaching to their authority. All disputed cases in England may in principle be adjudicated by the Supreme Court of Judicature or at least come under its supervisory authority, whether they be civil, criminal or administrative in nature. The High Court of Justice and the Crown Court can, in all cases, be seized directly by the parties but they may, in the exercise of their discretion, refer cases to some lower court; they can, in the same way, at any time, evoke a case from the cognisance of any inferior court. The High Court of Justice and the Crown Court have a truly complete jurisdiction throughout England under the supervision of the Court of Appeal and the House of Lords.

Masters in the creation of the law, the superior courts are also masters in its administration. The procedural rules for practice before the court (*Rules of the Supreme Court*) are the work not of Parliament but of a commission upon which judges are the dominant influence.

Finally, it should be noted that the superior courts have the effective means for ensuring that their decisions are respected. They may, for example, unlike the situation prevailing in France, address orders ("prerogative orders"[8]) to public officers (but usually not officers of the Crown) and, through contempt of court procedures, imprison those who disturb the course of justice (upon the publication, for example, of comments upon a criminal case which is *sub judice*) or wilfully refuse to comply with certain judicial decisions and orders.[9]

334. Concentration of judicial power

A factor which had an extremely important part in the establishment of this judicial authority in England was its *concentration* within the superior courts themselves. In 1800 there were only 15 judges in the superior courts at Westminster and in 1900 there

---

[8] Formerly known as "prerogative writs" (*mandamus, prohibition, certiorari*).
[9] *Cf.* above para. 319.

were only 29. All of them, moreover, lived and sat in London; decentralisation only occurred during the "assizes" or circuits that the judges of the Court of King's Bench (and, later, the King's Bench Division) periodically made in a certain number of provincial cities. English advocates or barristers have also traditionally been concentrated in London and must necessarily belong to one of four barristers' societies or "Inns of Court" located there (Gray's Inn, Inner Temple, Lincoln's Inn, Middle Temple).[10]

Today, this centralisation appears to be threatened. The number of superior court judges has been considerably increased. The assizes have been abolished and in their place the High Court itself may sit in the provinces as well as in London. The Crown Court now sits in all the principal English urban centres. The Bar itself is becoming decentralised: even though they receive their "call" to the Bar in London, more and more barristers are established outside London in local Bar associations and retain only passing contact with their Inn in the capital.

There are, therefore, signs that an evolution is under way in the traditional organisation of English justice which has created some uneasiness in at least traditional milieux.[11] The addition of many more new judges, the decentralisation of judicial organisation and the administration of justice are thought by some to be fatal to the maintenance of a true judicial power, and the fear is reinforced for those who see a menace in the new importance attaching to the place of legislation as a source of law.

335. Absence of Ministère Public

In England there is no *ministère public*[12] or procurator's office of the Romano-Germanic type connected to the courts. The presence

---

[10] The barristers are about 4,000 in number; they enjoy the exclusive right to plead before the superior courts. In addition, there are about 28,000 solicitors in London and throughout the country who act as legal counsellors and prepare cases for trial for barristers. Solicitors may plead before the inferior courts. Some are styled "notary public" but they are not equivalent to the French *notaire*. A description of the role of the solicitor is given by Cockshutt (H. J. B.), *The Services of a Solicitor* (1961—paperback); *adde* Gutteridge (H. C.), "The Origin and Historical Development of the Profession of Notaries Public in England" in *Cambridge Legal Essays* (1926), p. 123.

[11] Hamson (C. J.), "Les effets de l'accroissement de la criminalité sur l'administration de la justice en Angleterre" Rev. int. dr. comparé pp. 253–261 (1974).

[12] Hazard (J. N.), "The Role of the Ministère Public in Civil Proceedings" in Hazard (J. N.) and Wagner (W. J.), *The Law in the United States in Social and Technological Revolution* (1974), pp. 209–226. Rolland (M.), "Le ministère public in Civil Proceedings" 1956 *Semaine Juridique* 1271.

of such an officer, representative of the executive power and intervening in litigation to advise the court on matters of public interest implied therein, appears to the English to be irreconcilable with the autonomy and dignity of judicial authority. The existence of such an officer would moreover upset the balance that should be maintained between the accused and the prosecutor in criminal matters. In the same way there is no ministry of justice in England, even though learned writers have in fact more than once recommended its establishment. The real power and authority of the judiciary is also demonstrated, historically, in the fact that the education and admission to practice as a barrister was controlled through the Inns of Court rather than through the universities or some other body independent of the courts.

§ 2. Rule of Precedent[13]

336. Differences with continental Europe

In French and other laws of the Romano-Germanic family, legal principles have always been sought in a pre-established body of rules: in the *Corpus iuris civilis* in former times and today in codes. The decisions of the courts in the "countries of written law" (*pays de droit écrit*) were of secondary importance: *non exemplis sed legibus judicandum est* declares the Code of Justinian. Decided cases may very well have some authority, but apart from quite exceptional circumstances they are not considered to contain rules of law. This is, in fact, unnecessary because quite independently of them there is a sufficient legal system.

The situation is quite different in England where the authority of Roman law was never recognised in the same way as it was on the continent. The Common law, created by the royal courts of Westminster, is a "judge-made" law. The role of judicial decisions has not only been to *apply* but also to *define* the legal rules. In such circumstances it is only natural that in England the judicial decision should have gained an authority quite different from

---

[13] The bibliography on the rule of precedent and the way in which it is applied in England is immense; among the most recent works the following should be noted: Cross (R.), *Precedent in English Law* (3rd ed., 1977) and the article by Simpson (A. W. B.), "The *Ratio Decidendi* of a Case and the Doctrine of Binding Precedent" in Guest (A. G.), *Oxford Essays in Jurisprudence* (1963), pp. 148–175. A classical study of the subject was made by Goodhart (A. L.), "Determining the *Ratio Decidenci* of a Case," 40 Yale L.J. 161 (1930–31).

whatever position it may have in Europe. The rules set by decided cases must be followed or else the certainty of the Common law will be destroyed and its very existence compromised.

The duty to observe the rules as stated by the judges (*stare decises*—"let the decision stand"), in other words to respect judicial precedents, is the logic of a "judge-made" legal system. The need for certainty and security of legal relations, however, was formerly not felt so keenly as it is today and in fact it is only since the beginning of the first half of the nineteenth century that the *rule of precedent*, obliging English judges to observe the rules as stated by their predecessors in prior decisions was firmly established. Before this period there was concern for assuring a uniformity in judicial decisions, in order to maintain coherence in the law as a whole, and great consideration was frequently given to what had been previously decided in order to resolve a new dispute, but the principle that it was *strictly obligatory* to observe precedents was not established as such. The legalistic tendency of the nineteenth century, of which the French school of strict grammatical construction (*l'ecole de l'éxégèse*) was one expression, gave rise in England to a strict rule of precedent. The establishment by the *Judicature Acts* of a more systematic judicial hierarchy and the improvements in the quality of the judicial reporting[14] were also important contributing factors.

337. Meaning and scope of the rule

Theoretically, the analysis of the rule of precedent amounts to three simple propositions: (1) the decisions rendered by the House of Lords are binding precedents to be observed by all other courts, including, until very recently, the House of Lords itself; (2) the decisions of the Court of Appeal are binding precedents for all lower courts and the Court of Appeal itself except in criminal matters; (3) the decisions of a judge of the High Court of Justice must be observed by lower courts and, although not strictly obligatory, have great persuasive value and are very generally followed by the different divisions of the High Court of Justice itself and by the Crown Court.

The propositions enunciated in this way considerably simplify

---

[14] On the historical connection, *cf.* Allen (C. K.): *Law in the Making* (7th ed., 1964).

the matter. At the present time, however, a tendency appears to be developing to increase the number of exceptions to these rules, or at least to render them more difficult to fulfil, even though the principles themselves are not put into question. Until 1966 the House of Lords considered itself strictly bound by its own previous decisions[15]; in a formal declaration, the Lord Chancellor, in that year announced however that, in the future, it might consider itself no longer so bound if the circumstances indicated this to be necessary in the interest of justice.[16] The House of Lords since then has only taken limited advantage of the new rule, and considers that the Court of Appeal is still bound by the old rule.[17] It should nonetheless be noted that the only *binding* precedents are the decisions emanating from the *superior* courts, that is to say, the Supreme Court of Judicature and the House of Lords. The decisions rendered by other courts or quasi-judicial bodies and tribunals may indeed have some persuasive value but they are never binding precedents.

338. Form of English judgments

What does the term "binding precedent" really mean? To understand it consideration must be given to the form of English judicial decisions which is very different from French and, to a lesser degree, from German, Italian or Swiss decisions.

Strictly speaking, an English decision is no more than a simple resolution or order making known the judgment in the dispute as decided by the judge: X must pay a certain sum to Y, the contract between X and Y is set aside, the estate of X has devolved upon some specified person. English judges need give no reasons for their decisions; to oblige them to do so might even be considered derogatory to their dignity. They command and need not justify whatever action they decide upon.

But apart from the actual decision, which need not contain reasons, it is nevertheless customary for an English judge to explain why he has decided as he did. This is done not because of any desire to justify the decision in the eyes of the parties but

---

[15] *London Street Tramways Co.* v. *London County Council* [1898] A.C. 375.
[16] *Practice Statement (Judicial Precedent)* [1966] 1 W.L.R. 1234; [1966] 3 All E.R. 77. *Cf.* Kavanagh (P. B.), "Stare decisis in the House of Lords" (1973), 5 N.Z.U.L. Rev. 323.
[17] *Rookes* v. *Barnard* [1964] A.C. 1129; (1964) 1 All E.R. 367. *Cassell & Co. Ltd.* v. *Broome* [1972] A.C. 1027; (1972) 1 All E.R. 801.

because of the need, historically, to instruct law students, the future barristers who traditionally received their legal education through an attendance at court and participation in the practical handling of cases. The English judge, thus placed in the position which in other countries is enjoyed by the professor, readily explains the rules and principles of English law involved in the judgment he has just rendered. The discursive commentary on his own decision often goes beyond the four corners of the trial issues to examine related points; it is quite removed from the rigour and dryness which characterise the exposition of the *motifs*, or reasons, found in a French decision. Often the judge's statements and comments are substantially broader than is strictly necessary for a decision in the instant case. This fact is what has prompted the technique of distinguishing cases.

339. The technique of distinguishing cases

The application of the rule of precedent in English law involves an analysis of these opinions or commentaries accompanying the judicial decisions. Among the *reasons* given by the judge in support of his decision, a distinction must be made between what is a necessary basis to this decision—the *ratio decidendi* of the judgment—and, on the other hand, what was *obiter dictum*, that is to say what the judge has stated without being absolutely obliged to do so to reach his decision. The *ratio decidendi* constitutes the "judge-made" rule which is then part of English law and must be observed in future. Of course, the judge himself does not state what the *ratio decidendi* is in that case; it is for a judge in a later case to do so in order to decide whether the earlier decision applies in the matter he must decide. On the other hand, what is only *obiter dictum* does not have such authority; its value is simply persuasive and therefore depends on the prestige of the judge who made such remarks, the acuteness of his analysis and the circumstances of the case.

340. Example drawn from contracts inter absentes

The operation of the rule of precedent, its limits as well as its flexibility, and the distinction between *ratio decidendi* and *obiter dicta*, will perhaps be better indicated by means of an example. English courts have frequently had to pronounce on the question of contracts by correspondence (concluded between absent persons) and in such cases they have decided that the contract is formed at the time and in the place where the letter of acceptance is placed in the mail by the recipient of the offer. " . . . [A]s soon as the letter of acceptance is delivered to the post office, the contract is made as complete and final and absolutely binding as if the acceptor had put his letter into the hands of a messenger sent by the offeror himself . . . ."[18] Confronted with this decision, a jurist of continental Europe would be tempted to conclude that English law admits the theory known as *la théorie de l'émission*. Such a conclusion, however, would amount to a hasty generalisation and would not take into account the application of the rule of precedent. The decision was rendered in a case in which the letter of acceptance was mailed in England and to an addressee in the same country. It remains doubtful whether the rule, so stated, would be accepted in a different factual situation. The true *ratio decidendi*, in effect, is not likely to be found in such an abstract, almost philosophical, proposition to the effect that consent is established at the moment of the sending of the letter of acceptance. It is more likely that it derives from the consideration that the English post office must in such circumstances be considered the common agent of the two parties and the fact that it has a regulation forbidding the sender of a letter to retake possession of it once it has been placed in the mail. It remains to be decided whether the rule as stated in *Household Fire, etc., Insurance Co. v. Grant* should be extended to the situation where the letter of acceptance is sent either from a place outside the United Kingdom or to a place outside the United Kingdom (where different postal rules may apply). It would be permissible, therefore, in the face of this decision, and while paying complete respect to it as a precedent, to argue that the rule applied therein is not a general but only a *special* rule of English law, peculiar to those acceptances accomplished by mail (or telegraph) within the United Kingdom or when other countries which, in this respect, have an identical postal regulation are involved. Outside these hypotheses, however, it could be argued that the *general* rule of English law to the effect that the contract is formed only at the moment when the acceptance is *received* by its addressee, should apply. And indeed this solution was some time later

---

[18] *Household Fire and Carriage Accident Insurance Co. v. Grant* (1879) 4 Ex. D. 216, *per* Thesiger, L.J., at p. 221.

accepted with respect to contracts formed through the operation of Telex in *Entores Ltd. v. Miles Far East Corporation.*[19]

341. Rule of precedent in Equity

The natural area for the application of the rule of precedent is in the Common law *stricto sensu*. Its admission here was not perhaps surprising, only that it took so long to be acknowledged. In Equity however the situation was different. Here the rule of precedent could not be strictly applied so long as Equity retained its original character as an application of natural justice and, therefore, before it became a body of rules of *law*, complementing or correcting the Common law system. In fact at the present time there is very little difference between the operation of the rule of precedent either at Common law *stricto sensu* or in Equity. In both areas it is applied with the same strictness. The "discretionary" power of English courts in their application of Equity should not delude us; this "discretion," as a matter of fact, must be exercised in the manner specified by a number of precedents.

342. Rule of precedent and statute law

The rule of precedent is also applied in the interpretation of statutes. Here of course it no longer rests on the same justification and its application has been criticised by a number of authors. Its use in this area means, in fact, that English statutory provisions are soon burdened by a mass of precedents the authority of which quickly replaces the text of the statute itself. The general spirit or policy of the law may thus be obscured and the object which it was intended it should attain may be lost in a jungle of decisions each of which, in itself, only decides some particular point of detail. The manner in which statutes are applied by the courts, therefore, as a result of the application of the rule of precedent, has generally disappointed the promoters of new legislation. And so an effort has been made to exclude all judicial control, which has proved possible because a sovereign Parliament can lay down what the limits of judicial control shall be. A statute can thus confer upon an administrative body some absolute discretionary power and the

---

[19] [1955] 2 Q.B. 327 (C.A.).

exercise of it (saving cases of established bad faith) cannot be open to judicial scrutiny.[20] Judicial review is thus effectively excluded.

343. Publication and citation of decisions

Some relaxation in the operation of the rule of precedent results from the conditions in which the decisions themselves are reported. Only selected cases are published: 75 per cent. of the decisions of the House of Lords, 25 per cent. of those of the Court of Appeal and 10 per cent. of those of the High Court of Justice. It is possible therefore to eliminate a large number of decisions considered unsuitable as precedents. This practice also avoids the danger that the English lawyer will be immersed in a mass of precedents which would, in all likelihood, lessen their authority.

English court decisions are not cited in the same manner as French judgments. The correct form of citation is as follows:

Landauer v. *Asser* [1905] 2 K.B. 184

Landauer is the plaintiff; Asser the defendant. When the decision in appeal is reported, the first name is that of the appellant and the second that of the respondent. When spoken, the abbreviation "v." (for *versus*) is rendered as *and* or *against*. The elements following mean that the decision is reported in the series of the *Law Reports* known as the *King's Bench* series in the second volume published for the year 1905, beginning at page 184.

344. Current judicial reports

The series most currently cited at the present time are those included in these *Law Reports* composed of the following series: Appeal Cases, *A.C.*, the decisions of the House of Lords and the Privy Council; Court of Appeal, *K.B.* (or *Q.B.* when the reigning sovereign is a queen); Chancery, *Ch.* and, until 1971 Probate Division, *P.*; since 1972, Family Division, *Fam.* Apart from these quasi-official reports, other frequently used are the *All England Law Reports* (All E.R.) and the *Weekly Law Reports* (W.L.R.).

The letters serving as abbreviations of the titles of English law reports are given in any volume of Halsbury's *Laws of England*.

---

[20] *Liversidge* v. *Anderson* [1942] A.C. 206. *Anisminic Ltd.* v. *Foreign Compensation Commission* [1969] 2 A.C. 147.

Section II—Statute Law

345. Traditional theory

A second source of English law is legislation, that is to say *statutes* or *Acts of Parliament* and the various rules and regulations made in execution of legislation by different authorities which English authors group under the generic term *delegated* or *subordinate legislation*. It is to be noted that there is no written constitution in England as found in continental European countries or in the United States. The "constitution" is composed of a series of rules, sometimes in the form of legislative provisions but most often judicial in origin, which guarantee fundamental rights and freedoms and limit the arbitrary exercise of power by established authorities. Parliament itself however is not limited in its sovereignty save by the force of public opinion.[21] In England tradition and democratic attitudes constitute a powerful political reality. Today the United Kingdom Parliament is however bound to respect the legislation emanating from the European Economic Community.

According to the classical theory, legislation *lato sensu* is only a secondary source of law, a series of *corrigenda* and *addenda* to the main body of English law formed by the decisions of the courts: it only makes corrections and adjunctions to these judicially established principles or renders them more specific. In this same classical view, therefore, one should not expect to find in statutes an affirmation of leading legal principles but only particular solutions to specific problems raised by the decided cases. And because statutes are the work of a sovereign parliament[22] representative of the nation, they are given complete respect and judges will apply them to the letter. But since statutes also constitute exceptions to the Common law they will be restrictively interpreted in conformity with the adage *exceptio est strictissimae interpretationis*. Characteristic examples of this double principle of literal and restrictive interpretation are given by English authors[23]—and the technique

---

[21] A classic description of the English constitution is found in Dicey (A. V.), *Introduction to the Study of the Law of the Constitution* (10th ed. 1965), by E. C. S. Wade.

[22] It is an enactment by the sovereign with the advice and consent of the House of Lords and the House of Commons and by their authority.

[23] *Cf.*, *e.g.* Maxwell *Interpretation of Statutes* (12th ed., 1969).

of English legislative draftsmanship has been very substantially affected by it. Legislative rules have been traditionally formulated in the same style that formerly would have been used by judges in their judgments.

Apart from interpretation in criminal law, however, the essence of the matter is not to be found in these somewhat striking, but exceptional, examples. The essential point is that in traditional English legal thought legislation is not the *normal* means for giving expression to law; it is still something of a *foreign element* in the English legal system. Judges of course apply it but the rule contained in the statute will only be finally accepted and fully incorporated into English law when it has been applied and interpreted by the courts, and then it is accepted only to the extent to which such application and interpretation have taken place. In other words, in England, the decisions applying the provisions of the statute will be cited in preference to the text of the statute itself. Only when the English legal scholar deals with such decisions will he then find the legal rule in a context familiar to him, that of judicially created legal rule.

Such is what may be called the classical theory of legislation according to English tradition. It may very well be, however, that present day circumstances requires that it be re-examined.

346. Present importance of legislation

For the last 100 years, but more especially since the 1939–1945 war, intense legislative activity has taken place in England. Legislation of a dirigent inspiration, very much removed from the liberal spirit of the Common law, increasingly regulates relations between private persons and government administration in wholly new sectors of English public and social life. It may very well still be true to say that the legislation changing in some detail or re-organising the traditional branches of English law—what is sometimes called *lawyers' law*—can still be interpreted and applied according to the traditional canons of construction. On the other hand, legislation directed towards building, economically or socially, a completely new society—creating new forms of social welfare, establishing principles for city planning, organising economic production, co-ordinating means of transport, reforming the educational system and national health schemes—is so foreign to the traditional system that there can be no question whatsoever of such legislation continuing to be interpreted according to traditional English methods. There is no time for these statutes to be digested and assimilated by the usual judicial process; moreover, when parliament votes these laws it requires that they be applied with the same spirit in which they were adopted. The *Law Commission Act 1965* has created a new agency whose task is to study the reform of English law. And one of the subjects under review by the Commission is the construction and interpretation of statutes.[24] But the great challenge is to change the attitude of judges and lawyers towards legislation itself, and this change can hardly wait until the promulgation of new technical rules on the subject.

347. Traditional common law and modern law

There is, therefore, alongside the traditional Common law, a trend to create in certain areas a complementary system of rules, legislative or administrative in nature, not dissimilar to the French *droit administratif*. In England, to be sure, there is no hierarchy of administrative courts, distinct from the regular law courts of the judicial order. A sovereign judicial control is still exercised over the application of new statutes. As previously stated, however, it may happen, and even quite frequently, that this control is restrained and reduced to a mere supervision of the procedures employed in the course of settling disputes with the administration and therefore that it remains distinct from any control over the substantive solutions themselves. This new body of law, administered by a variety of government boards and commissions, may very well constitute, in the end, a *public officers' law* or a law of government administration as distinct from the traditional *lawyers' law*. It is very often this new body of law respecting pensions, social security benefits or the Enlish economy ("economic law"), rather than the law applied entirely at the hands of the traditional courts and lawyers, that most directly touches the interests and concerns of most private citizens.

If this new development, now of primary importance, is ignored, the true role of legislation in England cannot be appreci-

---

[24] Farrar (J. H.), *Law Reform and the Law Commission* (1974). The entry of the U.K. into the EEC in 1972 would itself suggest the need for reform on this matter, at least for the application of the Community's legislation and directives.

ated intelligently. It is reasonably to conclude, therefore, that in present day England statutes do not have a place inferior to that of judge-made law. It is nevertheless still true to say that in contemporary conditions English law still retains its essential character as a judge-made legal system for two reasons: first, because judicial decisions continue to guide legal development in certain areas still of great importance and, secondly, because English jurists, accustomed as they are to a centuries old reign of judge-made law, have not yet freed themselves from this tradition. For English jurists there is no true legal rule except that which is seen through the facts of a case and, therefore, reduced to that principle which is required to resolve that dispute. This traditionalism is a drawback and prevents English statutes from achieving fully a status in the hierarchy of sources equivalent to continental European legislation and codes.

348. Citation of statutes

Ordinary English statutes are generally cited, without any indication of their precise date (as distinct from the *regnal* year of their enactment), by the *short title* specified in every statute. For example: the *Local Government Act 1948*. The *sections* of the statute are indicated by the letter *s.* followed by the number of the section. The enumerated paragraphs within each section are termed *subsections (subs.)*.

The texts of English legislation are published in the *Statutes* series of the Law Reports or in Halsbury's *Statutes of England* and Halsbury's *Statutory Instruments*. More important statutes and parliamentary papers are published individually by Her Majesty's Stationery Office in London. There is no official governmental journal or Gazette comparable to the French *Journal Officiel*.

SECTION III—CUSTOM

349. General immemorial custom

The third source of English law, in addition to court decisions and legislation, is custom but its importance is very inferior to that of the first two.

English law is not a customary law. The "general immemorial

custom of the realm" upon which the Common law is theoretically based was never anything more than a simple fiction employed in order to remove any suspicion of arbitrariness with respect to what the early judges were actually doing. Law in England, before the elaboration of the Common law, was essentially customary, and the Common law borrowed many rules from the varied local customs formerly in force, but the process of building the Common law itself was the fashioning of a judge-made law, based on reason, which replaced the customary law of the Anglo-Saxon period.

350. Local and commercial custom

At the present time the place of custom in English law is very much reduced. It is denied any great importance because of the rule requiring that for it to be obligatory it must have existed from "time whereof the memory of man runneth not to the contrary," that is from time "immemorial"; a statute of 1275, still in force, specified this condition by prescribing that immemorial custom was custom that existed in 1189.[25] Today, proof of such great age—to the time of "legal memory"—is probably not required but in England a custom is not considered to be legally binding if it is established that it could not have existed as early as 1189. Many different customs have also been sanctioned by the courts over the centuries, or been taken up by statutes, and these rules have thus lost their original customary character to become legislative or "judge-made" rules. In these circumstances the sphere in which custom may be considered as a truly living source of the present law is, in England, as in France, very limited.

The requirement, however, that custom be "immemorial" is only demanded of *local* custom and it not a feature of commercial or *mercantile* custom or usage.[26] It is therefore principally in this area, since the absorption of commercial law by the Common law, that legally binding customs are said to exist. Recent practices show that here again customs occasionally do appear, but their importance is limited, especially when a custom is absorbed by statute or by case law; it then loses its customary character, and thus its flexibility and possibilities of development, and becomes

---

[25] Statute of Westminster I, 1295.
[26] Wortley (B. A.), "Mercantile Usage and Custom," 24 *Rabels Z.* (1959), p. 259. In general see Schmitthoff (C. M.), ed., *The Sources of the Law of International Trade* (1964).

The Common Law

instead a judicial or enacted legal rule subject to the operation of the rule of precedent. The phenomenon, already noted with respect to legislation, occurs again here: the customary rule is replaced as soon as possible by the judicial decision that has applied it. The essence of English law is decidedly judge-made.

351. Real importance of custom

Despite what has been said the importance of custom must not be under-estimated. English society is not, any more than any other, ruled exclusively by law in the formal sense. If, in strict legal terms, custom no longer enjoys any great importance, it does in fact play a determinant role in English life. It has a definite effect on the way in which law governs English society.

Constitutionally for example, and as a matter of strict law, England is still in many respects an absolute monarchy. Ministers are the servants of the sovereign and dismissed at pleasure; warships and public buildings are the monarch's property; even the salaries and pensions of civil servants are granted *ex gratia* through royal favour. It would be absurd to describe English constitutional law, however, only in terms of strict law and without taking into account the "conventions of the constitution"—the custom which in theory is denied any *legal* character but which nevertheless dominates English political life.[27]

The same thing is true of criminal matters. For example, the jury is in theory probably an institution which the judge is free or not, as he chooses, to employ in order to render his judgment; nevertheless, in certain cases custom definitely obliges him to make use of it. In the eyes of a continental observer this kind of custom is law; an Englishman, on the other hand, would hesitate before saying so and would prefer to call it a *usual practice*, analogous to constitutional convention which no one would ever think of not observing but which nevertheless is not law strictly speaking. Similarly, the monopoly, held by barristers, of questioning witnesses before the superior courts is no more than a matter of simple practice, founded on custom, and not a strictly binding rule.

---

[27] Dicey (A. V.), *Introduction to the Study of the Law of the Constitution*, 1885 (10th ed., 1965 with an introduction by E. C. S. Wade).

Life in society is dictated by certain traditional ways of behaving which are never questioned. These conventional rules of conduct, and the practices to which they give rise, are not regarded in England as matters either of custom or of law properly speaking so long as they have not "received" the sanction of the courts; and it is often difficult to see how they ever might be so sanctioned.[28] A study of the role of custom would nevertheless be incomplete and misleading if the existence of these rules of social conduct was not mentioned.

SECTION IV—LEGAL WRITING AND REASON

352. Open and closed systems

The Common law was originally founded on reason although this was dissimulated by the fiction of general immemorial custom of the realm. To the extent that further detailed rules of law are still to be defined, so as to give increasing security to social relations, reason remains an inexhaustible source of law to which the courts continue to turn. Reason helps to fill the gaps of the English legal system as well as to guide its evolution.

The principle here is no different in England than in the countries of the Romanist system save for one particular which must be noted. In countries of *droit écrit*, where the law is principally in the form of enactments, the legal rules are formulated with a generality such that the resort to reason generally takes place within the framework of already established legal principles and as an application and interpretation of these rules. The existence of legislative gaps is acknowledged but only with difficulty; reason plays a greater role *in the interpretation of the legislation* rather than in completing the legal order. In a case law system such as that of English law the situation is quite different. It is quite intentional that the case-by-case approach of the law should leave many gaps exposed; and reason is frankly recognised as a subsidiary legal source relied upon for filling such gaps. Instead of a technique of

---

[28] This way of looking at things is comparable to the socialist concept according to which only those rules the observance of which is imposed by state authority really make up law.

legal interpretation, there is, therefore, a technique of drawing *distinctions*—a technique which aspires to create new and increasingly precise rules rather than to apply pre-existing ones. The legal systems of the Romano-Germanic family, as already stated, are *closed* systems whereas the Common law is an *open* system in which a host of new possible rules are constantly being discovered, and when they are these new rules are based on reason.

353. Legal principles

This analytical difference is of greater interest, it is true, to the theory rather than the practice of law. Even in countries of case law, it is usual to place in the foreground the "legal principles" resulting from an analysis of a series of judicial decisions rather than reason itself as a subsidiary legal source. But the use of reason can be seen, essentially, in the identification and articulation of these legal principles which are its most vivid demonstration.

354. Elements of a rational decision

What, in effect is meant by "reason"? To seek the reasonable solution to a dispute—when with respect to its content there is no precedent, no legislative provision and no binding custom—means above all to seek the solution most satisfactory from a number of points of view: one most in agreement with existing legal rules, one not disrupting the security of legal relationships and, tempering that primary consideration, one respecting the idea of justice, the basis of all law. To seek the reasonable solution is by no means an arbitrary process. It implies that certain general principles deriving from already existing rules must be sought out and then applied. To this end attention will be given to works of legal scholarship and, for the most part in England, to the *obiter dicta* of judges and to those judicial decisions that are not strictly binding precedents (those rendered in other Common law countries or those rendered by English courts that do not constitute precedents strictly speaking such as the decisions of the Judicial Committee of the Privy Council). If legally binding precedents were involved, considerations of natural justice and reason could only play a very limited role in the correction of legal principles. But if there are no precedents to be strictly applied, then more importance can be given to these factors in the adjudication process.

The role of reason, therefore, while in theory only subsidiary, is in reality one of primary importance. The merit of the Common law is in fact that it has remained over the centuries the "perfection of reason" (to cite the phrase of the *Year Books*). English jurists, dismissing as dangerous too close an attachment to precedents, have supported, save at certain periods, the truth of Coke's statement that "Reason is the life of the law; nay, the common law is nothing else but reason." But this *reason* is no imprecise or merely current feeling among people as to what justice should be (*gesunder Menschenverstand*); it is reason as understood by judges preoccupied with the essential question of building a coherent legal system. There is, indeed, as Coke said to James I, to prevent the latter from inter-meddling in judicial matters, an "artificial reason of the law."

SECTION V—CONCLUSIONS

There are so many erroneous opinions and misconceptions in circulation in European continental countries concerning the theory of sources of English law that it is not inappropriate to review this subject once again, within a comparative perspective, in order to remove all doubt and misunderstanding.

355. Custom

In the first place the idea—extremely current—that English law is a customary law should be abandoned immediately. This misconception, entertained by many continental European jurists, is derived from the idea that one of two alternatives must be true: *either* the law is "written" and is therefore based on codes, *or* it is "unwritten" and is therefore customary. English law has never been a customary law: it is a judge-made law. The impact of the Common law was to bring about the disappearance of whatever local custom there was. The concept of an obligatory line of court decisions (*jurisprudence constante, ständige Rechtsprechung*), in itself related to that of custom, is unknown in the present operation of the rule of precedent; in England a single decision rendered by a court of a certain degree is enough to constitute a binding precedent.

356. Legislation

Secondly, the idea that legislation in English law is a source of only secondary importance should also be laid to rest. This point of view is no longer acceptable today. It is true that England has no codes of the Napoleonic type, but "written law" is, in practice, and in almost all respects, as important and as developed as it is in continental Europe. Today statutes contain much more than merely corrections to the Common law; there are vast areas of social activity for which the very principles of the legal order are to be looked for in legislation. However it is still true that a similar legislative tradition does not prevail in England and on the continent; the formulation of legislative legal rules of general scope or application is generally badly done in England. And it is also true that English lawyers still have some difficulty in adapting to the techniques of legal rules expressed legislatively. English statutes have a casuistic character or case-by-case approach not found in continental legislation. In England there is never any question that the synthetic statements devised by legal writers will be adopted in legislation in the way that the draftsmen of the French Civil Code adopted those of Pothier. The inevitable generalisation required in the formulation of such statements is regarded with suspicion in England. The English are disconcerted by the continental manner of expressing legal rules; to them, these rules are general principles, expressing moral *desiderata* or establishing programmes of policy rather than creating legal rules. In English legislation an attempt is made to situate legal rules as much as possible at the level of the judge-made rule, still considered its only normal form of expression. The principles expressed in the statute are not, moreover, fully recognised by English jurists, and therefore truly integrated in the Common law, until they have been applied, reformulated and developed by decisions of the courts.

357. Rule of precedent

Finally, and in the third place, the idea that the rule of precedent is applied with a kind of automatism, thereby paralysing the evolution of English law, must also be dismissed. History has shown the falsity that such was ever the meaning of the rule. The operation of the rule is no more an obstacle to the evolution of English law than codification has proved to be to continental European law, despite the forebodings of its opponents in the last century.

The only purpose of the rule of precedent is to provide a framework for English law and this through the conservation of its traditional "judge-made" structure. If it was applied with an apparently great strictness in the nineteenth century the reason is that conditions of the time required this rigour; at exactly the same period, and in analogous circumstances, the exegetical school (*l'école de l'exégèse*) prevailed in France. Present social evolution requires a greater flexibility because of the accelerated rhythm with which these social changes are taking place. On the European continent this need has already been met, even though the codes have been retained, because more supple methods of interpretation have been adopted. In England, the rule of precedent has been maintained but adjustments to the needs of a new society, in those areas where they are required, have been made through the application of new doctrines on the subject and above all by the use of the technique of "distinguishing" judicial decisions. And the evolution has been rapid enough in the traditional areas of Common law that the legislators have only rarely been required to intervene.

358. Technique of distinctions

The technique of "distinguishing" judicial decisions is fundamental in English law. The legal education of an English jurist is largely devoted to mastering this technique and learning its possibilities and limitations. It is analogous to the process of interpretation employed on the European continent. In Romanist systems there are no strict canons of legal interpretation; more important is the development of a certain sensitivity enabling the jurist to know to what extent, and with what hope of success, use can be made of any particular method of interpretation or any change obtained in a line of judicial decisions. It is the same in England. A reversal in the case law (*revirement de jurisprudence*) is, in principle, excluded in England because the affirmation of a rule of precedent is necessary to a judge-made legal system. Analogous results are however achieved in fact through the technique of distinctions, without damage to the legal edifice, and new developments in the law brought about—somewhat as in France when new solutions are found in the apparently unchanged rules of the Codes.

In England, as on the continent, the rules in some parts of the law are more stable than in others. The possibilities of an evolution may for a time be limited, or even stopped altogether, by a particular statute or a new decision on some special point. A great deal also depends upon the judge's frame of mind: some judges are inclined to admit new distinctions without difficulty, thereby facilitating new development; others—the majority—are more hesitant or more conservative: they too, through the use of distinctions, temper the daring—sometimes, it might be said, the extravagances—of their more progressive colleagues.

This technique of distinctions is therefore very closely linked to the analysis of the *legal rule* found in English law. Through suggested distinctions, the English jurist endeavours to limit increasingly the extent and the wording of a rule which inevitably seems to have originally been expressed in too general terms. It is thus not a matter of chance that the English concept of the *legal rule* is much narrower than the continental *règle de droit*. Not only is it natural, it is also necessary in a judge-made law. And the English theory of the sources of the law is a logical result of this point of view.

359. Legal writing

A word must be added respecting legal writing. Its importance has always been underestimated in England (even more than that of *doctrine* has been on the continent). It is generally true that in England the law owes less to professors than it does on the continent and more to judges. Here again however care must be observed. England is a country where certain legal works—written mostly, it is true, by judges—were treated as *books of authority*: the works of Glanvill, Bracton, Littleton and Coke had such prestige that they were considered, in the courts, to be the most authoritative expositions of the law of their time and were endowed with a status that Europeans would only accord to legislation itself.

Since the nineteenth century, the role of legal writing has changed and developed. Today law students are more and more educated in universities. They study law more in the courses, writings of their teachers, treatises and text-books, than in the collections or digests of judicial decisions compiled for legal practitioners; the teaching of law concentrates today on substantive law, and procedure and practice is now only exceptionally taught in English law faculties. A new attitude towards legal writing will inevitably result from these changes.

360. Reason

English law is very clearly a product of English history when one considers particularly its categories and concepts and the prominent role played by the courts. "The life of the law," wrote Holmes, "has not been logic; the life of the law has been experience." We must however be careful not to exaggerate the difference which is sometimes said to exist between French and English law on this point. Romanist laws are in no sense less a product of history than English law. Their history however has been different: it gave a greater place to university teaching, *la doctrine* and legislation, and the result has been that Romanist law appears structurally more systematic and, perhaps, more apparently rational than English law. But is English law really less logical and more practical than the Romanist laws? This is at least doubtful. Between the practical sense dear to the English and the logic dear to the French, there is a middle path, a factor that reconciles them because it is at the heart of each law, and this is *reason* (*la raison*).

It is of course true that English law was fashioned and its legal rules enunciated only as a function of the disputes with which the royal courts chanced to deal. But when the royal courts adjudicated they were not dominated by such a sense of what was practical that they were led to render a simply equitable solution in each case. While constructing the Common law system it was always necessary to seek the solution most in agreement with reason, and a deciding factor in the discovery of this solution was the desire to achieve a consistency in legal decision-making. This, necessarily, supposed a recourse to logic.

In England as in France, even though different paths were followed in the discovery of legal rules, there was always a similar idea of the very basis of law: the concept that law was, before anything else, reason. *Lex est aliquid rationis*. This way of thinking was more or less rejected in nineteenth century continental Europe, with the ascendancy of the doctrine of legislative positivism which held that law and legislation were one and the same thing; today however, on the continent, there is clearly a tendency to return to the pre-nineteenth century position. This same view is also very much alive in England today where the law remains primarily a work of reason and distinct from legislation or statute. It sometimes seems natural to couple the word *law* (*droit*) with some particular nation—French law, Belgian law, Greek law—and many would probably say that there is no law apart from these national laws. In the eyes of the English, on the other hand, there flows from the idea that law is reason, a certain traditional feeling that the law is as well supra-national or, perhaps more accurately, non-national. The words *Common law* are generally used without any other qualification. One does not think of the Common law as a system of "national" law; it is much more "the common heritage of the English-speaking peoples" and, as such, is destined to play a part analogous to that enjoyed by Roman law in continental Europe until the period of codification.[29]

There are of course in practice very real differences in the laws of different Common law countries and this will be seen upon an examination of the law of the United States of America. It is useful however, as part of the concluding thoughts on the study of English law, to emphasise that, because it is founded on reason, the Common law has a non-national dimension. It is, finally, the element creating a unity among the laws of the western world because reason sets them above the arbitrariness of national politics and thus distinguishes them from the Soviet concept of law.

[29] David (R.), "Droit commun et common law" in *Studi in memoria di Tullio Ascarelli* (1968), I. p. 345–363.

TITLE II

LAW OF THE UNITED STATES OF AMERICA

361. Expansion of English law

The law of England, originally and principally the work of the royal courts of justice, has undergone a considerable geographical expansion. The Common law has become one of the world's great legal systems along with the Romanist and, more recently, the Socialist systems.

But this expansion of the Common law has necessarily meant that it has undergone certain changes in the course of its adaptation to the special conditions of the countries where it has been received. These alterations vary in their importance and nature according to the strength of the ties which such countries have maintained with England, the mother country, the variations in geographical conditions of the countries in which the system was implanted, the possible influence of an indigenous civilization and many other factors.

Unfortunately, the scope of the work only allows a study to be made of the law of the United States of America and not the laws of the other Common law countries.[1] Its history, structure and sources are examined in the next three chapters.

---

[1] See the summaries published as "The Migration of the Common Law" (1960) 76 L.Q.R. 39–77; the law of India is however examined *infra* paras. 451–480.

CHAPTER I

HISTORY OF AMERICAN LAW

362. Historical factors: the rule in Calvin's case

The first English settlements in what is now American territory only date from the seventeenth century. Indpendent colonies were created in Virginia in 1607, at Plymouth in 1620, in Massachusetts in 1630 and in Maryland in 1632; the colony of New York, founded by the Dutch, became English in 1664 and the colony of Pennsylvania, originally Swedish, became English in 1681. There were thirteen separate colonies by 1722.

What was the law of these English colonies?[1] If this question were asked in London the answer, in conformity with the holding in *Calvin's Case*,[2] decided in 1608, would have been that in principle the Common law of England was applicable. In effect English subjects carried it with them when they settled new lands which were not under the control of a civilised nation. The American colonies fell within the scope of this rule with the result that in principle the Common law was applicable along with those statutes which, up to the time of the colonisation of America, had completed or modified it. According to the American author James Kent (1763–1847), the date in this respect for all the colonies was 1607, the moment of the founding of the first settlement.[3] This opinion, although certainly debatable in that there was never any link between these colonies before 1776, seems nevertheless to have been generally accepted.

The rule in *Calvin's Case* suffers a restriction, however: the Common law of England was only applicable in the colonies "so far as it was adapted to [local] institutions and circumstances."

---

[1] Pound (R.), *The Formative Era of American Law* (1938); Wengler (W.), "Die Anpassung des englischen Rechts durch die Judikatur in den Vereinigten Staaten," *Festschrift für Ernst Rabel* (1954), t.I., pp. 39–65.

[2] (1608) 7 Co. I, 17b, 77 E.R. 397.

[3] *Commentaries,* vol. I, Lecture XXI.

363. American law in the seventeenth century

In seventeenth century America this restriction counted for much more than the holding in *Calvin's Case*. The English Common law rules were wholly inappropriate to the conditions and circumstances of colonial life.

The Common law was bound to an archaic procedure requiring experienced legal technicians and was therefore largely unsuitable as the law of territories where, for all practical purposes, however varied the population might have been, there were no lawyers and no attempts made to encourage them to settle or to train new ones. Moreover, the substantive Common law rules, to the extent that they did exist, had been made by and for a feudal society as remote as possible from the kind of community found in American settlements. The problems facing the colonists were new, and ones for which the Common law offered no very satisfactory answers. Moreover the Common law itself was distasteful to the colonists because in many cases they had been forced to emigrate to escape persecution in England and they were not at all ready to share the English view that the Common law was the bastion of personal liberties. And finally the Common law was not really known in America; according to Dean Roscoe Pound (1870–1964) "a prime factor in shaping the law . . . was ignorance."[4]

What then was the law applied in America in fact? Apart from certain special regulations issued by local authorities, the law applied in practice must have been fairly primitive—in some colonies it was founded on the Bible and more or less everywhere amounted to little more than the exercise of judicial discretion. As a reaction against such arbitrariness, several colonies undertook a "codification" of the law and primitive codes were thus drafted from 1634 (Massachusetts) to 1682 (Pennsylvania). These of course had no connection whatsoever with the Romanist or modern techniques of codification. Their main interest lies more in the idea that inspired them than in their actual contents. Unlike the English, who at the same period saw the statute as a dangerous weapon and even a threat to their liberties, the American colonists of the seventeenth century looked favourably upon "written law." From this original difference the divergence between American

---

[4] Pound (R.), *The Formative Era of American Law* (1938), p. 11.

and English points of view and the American orientation towards
methods out of favour with English jurists can be traced.

364. The eighteenth century

During the eighteenth century, with improvements in colonial
living conditions and changes in the economy and political ideas,
the need was felt for a more developed law. Gradually the Common law was seen in a different light; it was realised that it could
be used as a bulwark to protect civil liberties against royal absolutism on the one hand and, on another, that it was a link between all
that was English in America in the face of the menace constituted
by Louisiana and French Canada (*Nouvelle France*). The extent to
which the Common law was applicable as a matter of principle and
that to which it was in fact applied is still the subject of some discussion and doubt; there was at this period a continuing lack of
persons trained in law and it was rare even for judges to have had
any professional training. Nevertheless there was a movement in
favour of a more general application of the Common law—American courts showed their intention in this regard by applying certain
English statutes, such as the *Statute of Frauds* of 1677.[5] Later the
Commentaries of Blackstone were published in Philadelphia
(1771).[6]

365. American Independence

American independence proclaimed in 1776 and finally established in 1783 created completely new conditions for these English
ex-colonies, then constituted as the the United States of America.
The French threat, first reduced by the English annexation of
Canada in 1763, was later altogether removed with the American
acquisition of Louisiana in 1803. France had in fact become the
friend and ally of America and hostile feelings were reserved for
England. The increasingly popular idea of an autonomous American law was in complete agreement with the new American political independence. Republican ideals and an enthusiasm for
natural law also naturally encouraged the idea of codification. It

---

[5] 29 Charles II, c. 3.
[6] James (E. R.), "A list of Legal Treatises printed in the British Colonies and the American
States before 1801." *Harvard Legal Essays* (1934).

seemed normal therefore that the Constitution of the United States (approved by the Federal Convention on September 17, 1787) and the Bill of Rights[7] be completed by codes. The territory of New Orleans, detached from the larger area that constituted Louisiana at the time, seemed to provide the necessary example when shortly after its incorporation in the Union it adopted codes of the French type and in particular a Civil Code (1808). Bentham offered his services in 1811 to President Madison for the purpose of providing the United States with a code.[8]

There was some hesitation until the middle of the nineteenth century about the outcome of the struggle taking place in America between the supporters of the Common law and those who championed codification. In Massachusetts in 1836, a law commission requested the drafting of a code; the constitution of the State of New York of 1846 provided for the drafting of a "written and systematic code" which was to include the whole of the law of that state; and in 1856 the English legal historian Sir Henry Maine (1822–1888) predicted the success in America of the Romano-Germanic system. Indeed various events seemed to presage or at least encourage this development. Soon after independence, several states prohibited the citation of English judicial decisions rendered after 1776; a number of territories in which French or Spanish law applied (at least in theory), and where no tradition of Common law existed, were annexed to the Union; America was also populated by a host of new settlers from countries where the Common law was unknown or where, if one thinks of the Irish for example, anything English was disliked. Pothier and Domat were translated into English in the United States[9] and a powerful movement best symbolised in New York by David Dudley Field (1805–1894)[10] advocated the codification of American Law. A

---

[7] 7 *U.S. Statutes at Large* 10.

[8] Bentham (J.), *Works*, (1843) vol. IV, pp. 459–460. Vol. I of *Theory of Legislation*, entitled *Principles of Legislation; Principles of the Civil Code*, was first published in French by E. Dumont (Paris, 1802).

[9] Domat had been translated into English as *The Civil Law in its Natural Order* by W. Strahan in 1722 and re-published in 1737, but the first American edition by L. S. Cushing appeared only in 1850; Pothier's work on *Obligations* was translated by F. X. Martin in 1802 and edited as *On the Law of Obligations or Contracts* by W. D. Evans in Philadelphia in 1826, 1839 and 1853; L. D. Cushing edited *On the Contract of Sale* in 1839; C. Cushing edited *On Maritime Contracts of Letting to Hire* in 1821, and *On Partnership* was edited in London in 1854 by O. D. Tudor followed by an American edition the same year.

[10] Fiero (J. N.), "David Dudley Field and His Work," 18 Rep. N.Y. State Bar Assoc., p. 177, 51 Alb. L.J. 39 (1895).

number of states did in fact enact codes of criminal law and civil
and criminal procedure.

366. Triumph of the Common law

Ultimately however the United States remained within the
Common law family with the exception of the Territory of New
Orleans or, as a portion of it became in 1812, the State of Louisiana. While other territories annexed to the Union might in theory have been subject to French, Spanish or Mexican law as well,
such laws were really unknown for all practical purposes; and so in
Texas in 1840 and in California in 1850, the English Common law
was adopted in principle. Their earlier traditions were only
retained for certain institutions (matrimonial property law, land
law). The legal concepts of the former English colonies were thus
preponderant and these colonies themselves remained fundamentally attached to the Common law, at least such as it was at the
time of independence.

There is hardly any need to ask why the Common law did triumph in the end. It was, very simply, a victory of tradition. A new
regime can easily change or alter the solutions and legal rules of an
abolished regime; it is much more difficult to break away from
familiar concepts, techniques and intellectual or sentimental reactions instinctively employed or experienced. And the use of the
English language was necessarily the vehicle for the Common law
throughout the country. The outstanding works of certain authors,
above all Kent's *Commentaries* (1826–1830) and those of Justice
Joseph Story (1779–1845)[11] were also largely responsible for
America's adhesion to the Common law family. The law schools,
although only fully developed after the Civil War (1861–1865),
also helped to shape legal structures by their teaching of the Common law from the time of independence.

The Common law did then triumph in America. In many states
legislation specified that the Common law as of a particular date
was to be the basis of the law in force, whereas in others it was not
considered necessary to state this specifically. But the "conflict" in
the United States during the half century following the Declar-

---

[11] His *Commentaries* on *Bailments* (1832), *The Constitution of the United States* (1833), *The
Conflict of Laws* (1834), on *Equity Jurisprudence* (1836), *Agency* (1839), *Bills of Exchange*
(1843).

ation of Independence between the Common law tradition and the advocates of the Romano-Germanic system was not unproductive. It influenced American Common law in important respects and explains certain of its peculiarities as compared to English Common law. The United States has remained a Common law country in the sense that it retained the concepts, the methods of legal reasoning and the theory of sources such as these are generally understood in England. American law nonetheless has a special place in the world-wide Common law system because, much more than any other law within the family, it has a number of rather original characteristics; and these same characteristics are those which very often link it to the Romano-Germanic family to which, at one moment in its history, it experienced a certain attraction.

367. Reasons for differences

But the triumph of Common law in American was not won without difficulty, nor was it complete. Many English Common law rules were never introduced because of prevailing American conditions. Other rules were never introduced because of their non-judicial origin; it has in fact always been considered that statutes enacted by the English parliament do not apply outside England unless parliament itself has specially so provided.

The most important point to note however is that the English law received in America was the law in force in England at a time when this country controlled America. There was never of course any question that statutes enacted after 1776 were to apply in the United States; nor were the English Common law developments after that date ever considered as inevitably having to form part of American law. In principle the development of the two laws, American and English, has been independent ever since the declaration of American sovereignty.

This principle cannot be doubted. If suffices to consider first of all the evolution of English law since 1776 and, on the other hand, the transformation of American society since the same date to realise that there is, because of these two factors, a serious threat to, or at least serious limitations upon, the unity of the system as a whole. England and English law are obviously profoundly different from countless points of view from the England and English law of 18th century; and, by the same token, America is no longer

the same country. Even in geographical terms there is no real similarity between the thirteen colonies of 1776 and the America of
today. It is now a country of 220 million inhabitants, highly industrialised and the world's first and richest power, and has nothing in
common with the small string of Atlantic settlements inhabited by
less than three million who proclaimed their independence 200
years ago. The ways of living and thinking and new economic conditions pose quite different kinds of problems to those of the colonial period, or again to those of the European environment to
which England belongs. American law cannot be the same as English law because it is separated by the same distance that now separates American and English life and civilisation.

368. English influence

For a long time however the Americans continued to view English law as a model. English progress, both economically and cul-
turally, and the slow development of the American universities
and legal writing, prompted American judges and lawyers to look
to the English and to adapt the developing American law along
English lines, even when they were no longer obliged to do so.
From this general point of view it can be said that there was a certain parallel development in the two laws, and that as American
social conditions developed to an approximation of European conditions, American law in certain respects was closer to English law
after Independence than it was in the colonial period.

The reforms in the structure of English law in the nineteenth
century had, generally, their equivalent in the United States. In
the individual states, the ancient forms of action were abolished in
favour of much less formalistic procedures in such a way that lawyers' attention was directed much more than in the past to matters
of substantive law rather than to questions of judicial administration. In the same way the relation between Common law and
Equity was revised in most states to bring about the abolition of
the old court duality. In a number of states there was a movement
to rationalise the law; as in England, an effort was made to purge
the system of its archaisms by repealing out-of-date legislation
and, through statutory consolidation, the rules in many areas were
systematically organised so as to facilitate their study.

This evolution began in the nineteenth century continued into the twentieth. And in America, just as in England, the twentieth century has seen a new effort to organise and reform society through law. Law is no longer thought of as simply a means of resolving disputes but more and more, by lawyers and citizens alike, as the proper instrument for creating a new kind of society. An "administrative power," unknown during the earlier period, has developed on both the federal and the state levels alongside the three classical powers, legislative, executive and judicial.

The *general* characteristics therefore of English and American legal development since the time of Independence are substantially very similar.

369. Originality of American law

The two laws have never nonetheless become re-united.[12] The original and essential difference between them from the earliest times has been the impossibility of applying the whole of English law in America. Today the difference, amounting sometimes to an opposition, may be explained (apart from the fact of national sovereignties) by a whole series of complex factors which make the United States a very different state from England and the Americans very different from the English as a people.[13] England is a European island; the United States is a continental mass less dependent upon its immediate neighbours; the English have ancient traditions and respect them whereas Americans, proud of those who threw off the colonial bonds and largely made up of immigrants who found a new home in America, place much less reliance on older ways. England has a constitutional monarchy, its political system is parliamentary; the United States is a republic with a presidential system. England has always been a unitary nation with a highly centralised judicial administration; the United States is a federal state in which national interests and individual state interests must be reconciled. Their economic structures are also very different; and their populations differ in size, ethnic origin, religious affiliations, life styles, feelings and ambitions. "The American way of life" is neither the reality nor the ideal of the

---

[12] Pound (R.), "The Deviation of American Law from English Law" (1951) 67 L.Q.R. 49–66.
[13] Kahn-Freund (A.), "English Law and American Law. Some Comparative Reflections" in *Essays in Jurisprudence in honour of Roscoe Pound* (1962), pp. 362–409.

English; their educational systems differ; and even their languages are increasingly distinctive.

It therefore follows that countries so different will have different problems and their own means of solving them. American law has evolved in the light of its own circumstances. That there be differences in the rules and solutions of the two laws is not at all surprising; the opposition, however, is greater than that and has a deeper significance. The two laws are no longer similar in their structure or their concepts. American lawyers are trained, and professionally organised, quite differently from the English; the theory of the sources of law, as well as its practice, are not the same. The American attitude towards the law is not that of the English.

It may very well be that these differences should not be overstated and it certainly remains true that there is a very important common basis to the two laws. These similarities are sufficient for the Americans themselves to admit unhesitatingly that they form part of the Common law family. It is best to realise however that apart from this community of feeling there are nonetheless very real differences between the two laws. Even though an American may have no very great difficulty in dealing with English law, the opposite is not true. The English jurist is not at ease in American law, and to become familiar with it he requires some kind of initiation.

CHAPTER II

STRUCTURE OF AMERICAN LAW

370. American and English law

Because of its structure, American law is a member of the Common law family. The English and Americans have the same general concept of law and its role; the principal legal divisions and concepts and the conception of the legal rule are the same in each country. Categories such as Common law, Equity, torts, bailment and trusts belong naturally in each system. For both law is thought of as essentially judge-made; legislative rules, no matter how numerous, are viewed with some discomfort because they are not the *normal* expression of the legal rule. They are only truly assimilated into the American legal system once they have been judicially interpreted and applied and when it is possible to refer to the court decisions applying them rather than to the legislative texts themselves. When there are no precedents, the American lawyer will say: "There is no law on the point," even though there may besome legislative provision covering the matter.

The structure of American law is therefore generally analogous to that of English Common law. This, of course, is a very general observation and upon examining any particular problem it is soon seen that between the two laws, as already mentioned, a number of structural differences of true importance do exist and cannot be ignored.

One such particular and fundamental difference must be examined—the distinction made in the United States, but not of course in England, between federal law and the law of the different states. These two related notions will be examined first, and then some other differences respecting the classification, concepts and terminology of English and American law will be studied.

371. Two-fold problem

In England any idea of a federal law is completely unknown because it has a unitary political structure. In the United States, a federal state, the respective attributions of the federal and state authorities is a matter of primary importance.

In legal terms and because of the concept of the legal rule in the Common law countries, this question has two aspects. In the first place it is important to know which authority—federal or state—has legislative jurisdiction or administrative authority to regulate any given subject matter. Similar questions arise in any federal state, and the problem is easy for any jurist to understand. In the United States the answer, at least as to the principles involved, as might be expected, lies in the American Constitution.

But in the United States the question of respective federal and state jurisdictions has another and more difficult aspect, one related to the very concept of law as understood in Common law countries generally. To say that the United States Congress, or some federal administrative authority, has jurisdiction in a particular area, does not exhaust the question in a country where the law is not primarily thought of as legislative in nature. In both England and the United States, as already pointed out, law is essentially conceived as judge-made, that is to say founded above all on judicial precedents and reason rather than the commands of some constituted authority. Enacted law and regulations are traditionally thought of as complements or rectifications to a pre-existing body of law—the *Common law stricto sensu*.

Inevitably therefore this other question will arise: Is the Common law a "federal" or an individual "state" Common law in the American context? In other words, is there an American Common law—a *federal Common law*—or is there a Common law for each individual state and thus as many *Common laws* as there are states in the Union? It is an interesting question because it helps to make more precise the very idea of the Common law, and indeed law itself, and the way these are understood in English-speaking countries.

372. Principle of state legislative competence

What are the respective areas of jurisdiction of the American Congress and federal authorities and the individual state legislatures and their administrative authorities?

Amendment X to the American Constitution, enacted in 1791,[1] is as specific and unambiguous as possible on this matter: "The powers not delegated to the United States by the Constitution, nor prohibited by it to the States, are reserved to the States respectively or to the people." This principle has never been abandoned and the legislative competence vested in the states is, therefore, the rule, whereas the legislative competence of the federal authorities is the exception and must always be based on a specific text of the Constitution itself.[2]

There is nothing surprising in this principle; it was only natural, immediately after Independence, that it be laid down in this way. Until the War of Independence the thirteen colonies had been entirely independent of each other; they had nothing in common either in their origins, colonisation, religious affiliations, political structures or economic interests. There had never been any political ties between them apart from their common link to the mother country; there was no institutional framework bringing them together before the Revolution.

373. Breadth and Diversity of State Law

The operative principle is thus in favour of state rather than federal jurisdiction.

There are, therefore, between the laws of the various states, many and often very important differences arising under their respective statutory rules and judicial interpretations. Court and administrative structures vary from one state to another and so do civil and criminal procedure. Divorce is not granted everywhere upon the same grounds or in the same way; matrimonial property law may be community of property in one state and the principle of separation of property in another. Company law and tax law

---

[1] 1 U.S. *Statutes at large* 21, Art. 10.
[2] The same principle applies in Australia but not in Canada, where the *Constitution Act, 1867* (formerly the *British North America Act, 1867*) 30 & 31 Vict. c.3 (U.K.) was enacted following the American Civil War to emphasize the power of the federal authority in order to counter any possible impulse for secession.

also vary. The list of criminal offences and penalties is established by each state. Whatever importance federal law may have attained, it is nonetheless state law with which, in daily life, most citizens and lawyers have regular contact.

374. Residual state jurisdiction

To understand the importance of state law, it should also be added that even with respect to those matters within the legislative power of Congress, the jurisdiction of the states is not thereby altogether excluded. State authorities have a "residual jurisdiction" in such areas but they are prohibited from enacting measures which will conflict with the provisions of federal law. On the other hand they are not prevented from passing measures which complete the gaps left by the federal law or serve as additions thereto. Thus, alongside federal taxes, there are also taxing statutes in each state.[3]

In respect of many subjects where it has authority, Congress has refrained from intervening. It must be remembered that in Common law countries there is considerable reserve about legislation and codification. While, therefore, it is open to Congress to legislate upon international or inter-state commerce, there are no federal statutes on such subjects as negotiable instruments, the contract of sale, commercial companies or the conflict of laws. In the first three there are state statutes but the last is still governed by the Common law. And, until as late as 1938, there were no special rules of procedure for proceedings before federal courts (other than the Supreme Court itself) and it was therefore admitted that the federal courts should follow the procedures laid down by the several states for their own courts.

This principle of residual state jurisdiction does however have its limits. The workings of the commerce clause is an example: in the absence of relevant federal legislation the states have not been allowed to legislate against the spirit of the Constitution by bringing restrictions to the concept of inter-state commerce. On other occasions it has been decided, in the same way, that state

---

[3] In the international sphere this duality raises a serious problem. International conventions intended to avoid double taxation only have effect with respect to federal taxes, because only federal authorities have agreed to them; the states are not bound by them with respect to whatever taxes they themselves may impose. *Cf.* for example, Lazerov (H.), "The United States— French Income Tax Convention" 39 Fordham L.Rev. 649 (1971).

legislation is unconstitutional, even though not incompatible with federal provisions, because the area in which it attempts to intervene must be considered completely occupied by the federal legislation in force.[4]

375. Is there a "United States Common law"?

The fact that there is a constitutionally established principle that federal laws can only exist in certain subjects or, more concretely, that there are only certain subjects in which federal statutes or regulations do indeed exist, does not fully describe the relationship of federal and state laws. In principle American law like English law is judge-made and its basis is made up, in the eyes of American jurists, of "unwritten" law—the legal rules enunciated by the courts and the principles emerging from them. How is this traditional Common law envisaged in the United States? Is there a national, that is to say single, Common law for all the states of the Union or is there a Common law linked to the sovereignty of each individual state, and thus a distinct Common law for each one?

One might think, at first sight, that this question raises no great difficulty. Since the Constitution lays down a list of subjects falling within the legislative authority of Congress, it would seem to follow that in such areas there would be a federal Common law whereas in respect of other subjects there would be distinct state Common laws. However this view of the matter fails to take into account a number of factors and, as an analysis, it is unsatisfactory.

In the first place it must be noted that, even in those subjects with respect to which it can legislate, Congress has most often refrained from doing so. As just seen, in such cases the states have a residual authority: they can, and they often do, legislate in their regard. Does it not then follow that the power to create an individual state Common law therefore falls to the judiciary of each state in the same way that legislative power falls to the legislature of such state?

---

[4] There then arises the question of "federal preemption": *Cf. Pennsylvania* v. *Nelson,* 350 U.S. 497 (1956): the unconstitutionality of a statute of the state of Pennsylvania dealing with sedition against the government of the United States. The *Smith Act* of 1940, a federal statute, carried provisions which in the opinion of the Supreme Court neither required nor authorised any such complement as that enacted. The law of Pennsylvania however was held valid to the extent that it suppressed sedition against the government of that State.

A second element, relating to the organisation of the American
judicial system, complicates the matter. There is in the Unites
States, as more fully explained below, a dual court system: federal
courts and state courts. But the jurisdiction of each type of court
does not correspond to the legislative jurisdiction of Congress and
the state legislatures. State courts may hear disputes arising under
federal law and federal courts may try cases bearing upon subjects
with respect to which Congress cannot legislate. This may happen
when the parties are residents of different states and when the dispute involves a sufficiently large sum of money. Will federal courts
in such circumstances be free to develop their own case law even
though the dispute raises issues outside the legislative jurisdiction
of the federal authorities?

To these two complicating factors must be added a third—that
of prevailing attitudes. However important an individual state may
be, it is not to be doubted that most Americans consider themselves today as belonging first and foremost to the country as a
whole rather than to any individual state. They are American citizens before seeing themselves as citizens of California or New
York. In such a context, can judges and lawyers accept that the
Common law—the law—is different in each state of the Union?

376. Judiciary Act 1789

A federal statute passed in 1789, the Judiciary Act,[5] seemed to
remove all possible doubt on the question by requiring that federal
courts, in subject matters not covered by federal statute, apply
"the laws" of a specific state, the state designated by the conflict
rules applying in the place where the federal court was located.
This provision seemed to imply therefore that, apart from the
cases where federal statutes had intervened, the state law would
always be applicable. But a doubt arose about the meaning of the
words "the laws" as used in the Act. It was at least clear that they
included the statutes emanating from the state legislature in question. But did they, as well, also contemplate the law as found by
the courts to exist apart from statute? In the absence of any "law"
(*i.e.* statute) it seemed to some that the federal courts had an
unfettered freedom; that as an autonomous order of courts they

---

[5] Act of September 24, 1789, c. 20. 1 Statutes at Large 73.

were not bound by case law of any individual state. It appeared therefore that, as soon as a question fell within their jurisdiction, it was for them to develop a federal Common law upon such topic.

377. Doctrine in Swift *v.* Tyson (1842)

American judicial opinion varied on this question. Naturally enough the traditional view was accepted first through an affirmation of the possibility and, in cases of this kind, the duty of the federal courts to decide according to *general Common law* rather than that of a specific state. The doctrine, advocated by Justice Story, was supported by the famous decision of 1842 of the Supreme Court of the United States in *Swift* v. *Tyson*.[6] But this decision was never considered to be of general application and its even limited meaning has always met strong opposition. And it must be admitted that it did indeed lead to shocking results both constitutionally and in practice. Practically, it created a quite unjustifiable legal duality: a dispute might be decided differently according to which court, federal or state, was seized. It was all the more objectionable since in many cases it could enable the parties to create the conditions in which federal courts could—or could not—be seized. A change of residence, no problem in itself, was sufficient in this respect.[7] Constitutionally it was also clear that in providing for the jurisdiction of federal courts in cases of diversity of citizenship it had been intended to assure an equal justice to litigants of different states but that it had never been intended to authorise the creation of federal law in matters with respect to which Congress was not able to legislate. By accepting the idea of

---

[6] 16 Peters 1 (U.S. 1842). The question in this case was whether the holder of a bill of exchange who had given value might benefit by the principle of the non-opposability of certain defenses. The bill had been endorsed to him by one of its drawers. According to the law of the State of New York it was doubtful whether a consideration could be found in the release of his debt by the holder of the note to his debtor. Justice Story decided that no reference to New York law was to be made since it had no statute on the topic and that there was sufficient consideration in virtue of the *general Common law*.

[7] *Black and White Taxicab Co.* v. *Brown and Yellow Taxicab Co.*, 276 U.S. 518 (1928). A Kentucky railroad company gave a Kentucky taxi and transport concern an exclusive right of entry on its land adjacent to its station to solicit clients, and this monopoly was against public order in the State of Kentucky. In order to avoid the effect of the law, the taxi concern dissolved and set up business again in the state of Tennessee, thus changing its "citizenship"; the federal court, competent to hear the disputes with its competitors in Kentucky, judged that the contract giving the exclusive right, contrary to the public order of Kentucky, was not contrary to the public order of the *general Common law*. Cf. Jerome Frank's amusing account in *Law and the Modern Mind* (1930), Pt. I, chap. V ("Legal Realism").

a federal Common law the spirit of the Constitution was violated. It meant in fact that the supremacy of the federal judicial authorities was recognised in matters for which the Constitution had intended to create an exclusive state competence.

378. Erie Railroad Company *v.* Tompkins (1938)

The decision rendered in 1938 in *Erie Railroad Company* v. *Tompkins*[8] took up position against the concept of a federal Common law in the following circumstances. One night, Tompkins was following a foot-path running alongside a railroad track in the State of Pennsylvania, when a passing freight train, because it seemed of an open door, threw him to the ground and injured him severely. The train was the property of the Erie Railroad Company incorporated in the State of New York. Tompkins sued for damages before the federal court of the southern district of that state. The jurisdiction of the federal court was not in question, nor was it doubted that it had to decide according to "the laws of Pennsylvania" pursuant to section 23 of the 1789 federal Judiciary Act. The Erie Railroad Company argued that in the circumstances and by virtue of earlier decisions of the Supreme Court of Pennsylvania, Tompkins was a trespasser on the private foot-path belonging to the Company and had no right to recover damages. Tompkins contested this reasoning, but of much greater importance was his argument that when the Judiciary Act of 1789 placed a duty on the federal judge to apply "the laws of Pennsylvania," this expression was meant to include only the *statute* law of the State of Pennsylvania; he therefore contended that in the absence of any such statutory texts the federal judge had to apply the Common law which, in the circumstances, meant *the general Common law* of the United States, not the *particular Common law* of the State of Pennsylvania.

The district judge and the Court of Appeals allowed this argument and decided that in the absence of legislation the federal courts were to apply the *general law* and that they were able to disregard the Common law rule of the state of Pennsylvania.

The United States Supreme Court however refused to uphold

---

[8] 304 U.S. 64 (1938). *Cf.* Tunc (A.), "L'application du droit des Etats par les juridictions fédérales des Etats-Unis," Rev. int. dr. comparé, 1951, pp. 5–35.

this decision and sent the case back to the Circuit Court of Appeals ordering it to decide according to the Common law of the State of Pennsylvania[9]: "[e]xcept in matters governed by the Federal Constitution or by Acts of Congress," stated Justice Brandeis, speaking for the majority of the court, "the law to be applied to any case is the law of the State. And whether the law of the State shall be declared by its Legislature in a statute or by its highest court is not a matter of federal concern. There is no federal general common law." Since 1938, the United States Supreme Court has frequently had occasion to re-affirm and to apply the principle formulated in *Erie R. R. Co.* v. *Tompkins* and it is now a well established principle of American law despite a number of difficulties to which it, in turn, has given rise.[10]

379. Real significance of this decision

No federal Common law! To the advocates of the unification of law, this decision was nothing less than catastrophic, the promise of eventual legal chaos if not indeed the political disintegration of the United States. At the least it was seen as a spectacular reversal of the 150 year old tendency to re-enforce the legal cohesion of the United States. With the passing of the years, however, these fears have been assuaged. The truth would appear to be that the real, the practical meaning of *Erie R. R. Co.* v. *Tompkins* was overestimated by observers of the American legal system and especially by jurists of the Romano-Germanic family because at the time they did not fully appreciate the point of view of the Common law context in which it was rendered. The decision, whatever its importance, does not have the significance given to it at the time by European jurists. The decision rejected one way of envisaging the unity of American law, one which had in fact given rise to certain abuses and which was criticised both theoretically and practically.

---

[9] The U.S. Supreme Court could not decide the point itself because there was discussion as to what the Common law rule of Pennsylvania itself was in the circumstances.

[10] *Van Dusen* v. *Barrack*, 376 U.S. 612 (1964). An aviation accident in Boston gave rise to some 150 actions by the victims or their legal representatives; a hundred of them were taken before the federal court sitting in Massachusetts, fifty before the federal court sitting in Pennsylvania. In the interests of justice it was decided that all the actions would be heard by the federal courts of Massachusetts. The U.S. Supreme Court approved this transfer but specified that the court in those cases which were transferred to it had to decide the issues according to the law of Pennsylvania whereas in those actions originally taken in the state of Massachusetts it had to decide according to the law of that State.

It did not however amount to a negation of the fundamental unity of American Common law.

It is probably correct therefore to say that as a matter of principle, and as a result of the *Erie* holding, there are as many Common laws as there are individual states and that there is no federal Common law. But, having said this, it is no less important to realise that there is, beyond all the differences in the laws of the individual states, a deep unity in American law. This unity is established by a number of institutional factors and, above all, by the prevailing attitudes of American lawyers and people generally.

380. Institutional factors

Several institutional factors guarantee that no really fundamental divergences arise between the laws of the various states.

The first of these is the possible intervention of federal law itself. Few changes have in fact occurred in the scheme of shared legislative authority as originally laid down in 1787 in the Constitution. This document, narrowly circumscribing the authority of federal power, has rarely been amended: only 28 amendments have been adopted, of which the first ten (constituting the *Bill of Rights*[11]) enacted in 1789 and the Thirteenth, Fourteenth and Fifteenth, adopted shortly after the Civil War, are of importance for our purposes.These amendments have made the federal courts the defenders of the civil rights and freedoms of the ordinary citizen against federal authorities (Amendments I to X) and against state authorities (Amendments XIII, XIV, XV).

Apart from the amendments themselves, the sharing of legislative jurisdiction between federal and state authorities has above all been changed by the U.S. Supreme Court in its liberal interpretation of certain provisions of the Constitution and its amendments. The respect by states for certain general principles of law, as much in the case law as in legislation, has in effect been imposed by reason of this interpretation. Reference is made again below[12] to this topic when the subject of constitutional interpretation is examined. Other initiatives have been undertaken in order to bring about some uniformity in state legislation and this point is also

---

[11] 7 U.S. Statutes at Large 10.
[12] *Infra*, paras. 406 *et seq.*

examined again below when statutes are discussed in the context
of the sources of American law.[13]

381. Prevailing attitudes of American lawyers

Even more important than such institutional factors is no doubt
the attitude of American lawyers. They may willingly accept that,
subject to the necessary respect owing to a number of principles,
statute law may vary from one state to another, but they are not
prepared to admit that a different interpretation can be given
across the country to the Common law. The proposition to the
effect that there is no federal Common law simply means that the
federal courts are not entitled to construct their own body of law
and that they should always decide, in the absence of federal statute, according to the law of the state. But it does not follow in their
eyes that the laws of the various states are wholly independent and
distinct from one another. One studies problems and one reasons
in the United States on the basis of fundamental unity in American
law to which the different state legislatures bring only limited
derogations. This all important attitude is shown in several significant ways.

The most respected works of legal scholarship in the United
States of America are rarely ever devoted to the law of a single
state. The law reports, encyclopedia, legal treatises and law
reviews generally embrace "American law" in those same subjects
in which, in theory, the law would seem to exist only in the mould
of each individual state.

In many instances the law of one state is unsettled, and it may be
that the Common law of that state provides no precedent in the
matter. In such a case the American lawyer very naturally takes
into account what has been decided in other states of the Union.
And these other decisions provide not only the most reasonable
solution to be found but also indicate to him what that solution
must be unless there are specific considerations justifying an
exception in the matter at hand.

When a particular question of law is studied in American law
schools the decisions rendered in any number of states will be

---

[13] *Infra*, paras. 418, 419.

taken as elements in this study, the point of which is to reconcile these different holdings and to attempt to enunciate the general principles flowing from them. It could never be said that this method was to no good purpose or that it was sufficient merely to say that one decision was rendered according to the Common law of New York, another in virtue of that of Ohio. These two systems may very well be distinct, both in theory and according to the Constitution, but the American lawyer reasons on the basis of their identity. If two decisions conflict and there is no possibility of reconciling them, this dilemma is not resolved by simply saying that there is a difference between the Common laws of these states; it will rather be admitted—at least in the law schools, since the courts are more reticent—that one is *good* law and the other *bad* law and should therefore be rejected in the future, not only in other states but also in the state in which it constitutes the present law.

382. Conclusion

To say, therefore, that in the United States there is no federal Common law may be true but it would be more correct to add that the 50 Common laws of the 50 states, even though theoretically distinct, are considered to be, or ideally should be, identical. This does not amount to re-creating a concept of federal law but, as a matter of fact, there is not much difference between 50 uniformly *conceived* laws and a single law which would be, in the breadth of its application, a federal law.[14]

In the end therefore one may say that *Erie R. R. Co.* v. *Tompkins* only decided that the judicial development necessary to re-establish the harmonious unity of American Common law had to be the work of state and not federal courts. It is for state courts to articulate and evolve American Common law in those areas where Congress has no power to legislate. When Brandeis J. said "There is no general federal common law" he did not intend to say anything more than that. The unity of American law has to be achieved by bringing together the law of 50 states; it is not to be

---

[14] *The Restatement of the Law* (*cf. infra* para. 405) has shown that from 95 per cent. to 98 per cent. of the time there is, in those subjects it has dealt with, substantial agreement among the Common laws of the different states. *Cf.* Goodrich (H. F.), "Restatement and Codification," *Field Centenary Essays* (1949), pp. 241–250.

accomplished by creating a federal law alongside the laws of individual states. The Supreme Court has rejected, and with good reason, any effort to create such a dualism.

383. Legislative authority of Congress

There is no federal Common law. The expression itself, however, as used by Justice Brandeis, must be further clarified. To render its meaning clear, the words *in the matters with respect to which Congress cannot legislate* should be added. After, just as much as before *Erie R. R. Co.* v. *Tompkins,* it is admitted that there may be a federal Common law respecting the matters on which Congress can legislate and has in effect done so. There are for example, and this in agreement with the Constitution, federal laws on the subject of patents and trademarks. It has been decided that federal law has completely occupied the field in respect of such subjects and that any state autonomy in their regard has been taken away. The existence of a federal Common law is thus admitted outside the strict application of legislative enactment and it is even conceded that it may also extend to cover related subjects such as, for example, unfair competition.

But the matter is much more delicate in respect of subjects where the federal power, even though it has the authority to legislate, has not done so in fact. In such cases, it really is exceptional to hold to the view that judges may decide in the light of a federal Common law. And yet this too has occurred in some fields, in particular in admiralty law (probably because of its special character deriving from the fact that, historically, it was neither created nor applied by the regular courts).To admit it otherwise than exceptionally would in fact destroy the *Erie* doctrine and subvert the legal system.

384. Conflict of laws

The American system of conflict of laws is not organised at the federal level; each state in fact has its own body of conflict of laws rules. It is probably nevertheless true to say that in this area, as in so many others, there is a very great degree of similarity in the solutions arrived at in the different state laws. This is less true, however, since a doctrinal movement, taken up by the case law of some states but not by others, has rejected the traditional analysis of conflict rules in favour of a new method of interpretation that seeks out in each case that law having the most meaningful connection or link with the question in dispute in light of the factual situation and the policies of the laws in conflict.[15] The U.S. Supreme Court, despite the possibility of doing so by virtue of a number of provisions of the Constitution, has never appeared anxious to intervene in the realm of the conflict of laws in order to encourage greater uniformity. The "due process" clause of the Fourteenth Amendment has been interpreted as requiring that a case offer a sufficient connection with the state of the forum in order that its law be applied to the merits of the dispute, but the Supreme Court not long ago overturned a decision on this point.[16]

It should also be mentioned that the notion of *public policy* may be differently conceived in the several states and be invoked against a statute of another state. This question had an especial acuity in the case of the celebrated Reno divorces, awarded in the State of Nevada under conditions particularly—and according to some, scandalously—accommodating. Some states have refused to consider them valid on the ground that they violate their own public policy.[17] Similarly a Massachusetts statute limiting the amount of indemnity that might be claimed by a victim, or his heirs or legal representatives, in the case of air transport accidents has been judged contrary to the public policy of the State of New York.[18] But this is rare, and the new method of interpretation allows for the non-application of an undesirable statute in a manner less brutal than that of invoking public policy.

Another remark respecting the conflict of laws, and one illustrating once more the American attitude to the Common law and

---

[15] *Restatement (Second), Conflict of Laws,* 1970 (Par. 6). vonMehren (A.), "Une esquisse de l'évolution du droit international privé aux Etata-Unis" Journ. dr. int. (1973), 116. Audit (B.), "Le second Restatement du conflit de lois aux Etats-Unis" Trav. Comm. fr. dr. int. privé 1977–79, p. 29. Hanotiau (B.), *Le droit international privé américain,* Paris-Bruxelles, 1979.

[16] The same does not hold true of conflicts of jurisdictions where the same requirement for a sufficient connection between the forum and the dispute is admitted, *Shaffer* v. *Heitner* 433 U.S. 186 (1977).

[17] This has in fact been admitted even though the Constitution obliges each state to recognise fully the judgements rendered in another state in virtue of the "full faith and credit clause." A kind of compromise was ultimately achieved whereby Reno divorces are considered "divisible"—recognised in some respects but not in others. *Cf.* "Divisible Divorces," 76 Harv. L. Rev. 1233–1252 (1963).

[18] *Kilberg* v. *Northeast Airlines,* 9 N.Y. 2d 34; 172 N.E. 2d 526; 211 N.Y.S. 2d 133 (1961).

statutory texts, must also be made. Is the Common law of one state to be applied in another? Judges of this other state are deemed to know it and there is, therefore, no need to establish formally the content of any particular Common law rule. But does the same hold true of the state's statutes? Here the distinction between the states reappears. Judges are only deemed to know the statutes of their own state (as well, of course, as federal legislation), and the party requiring the application of another state statute must satisfy the judge as to its existence and content. There is no *ex officio* application of the legislation of another state. A legislative movement has now changed this situation, so that judges may take judicial notice of the other state's statutes. But this development involves principles going beyond the scope of the questions dealt with here. In many states the judge is authorised in effect to apply *ex officio* the statutes of other jurisdictions, even those not part of the United States.

Section II—Other Structural Differences

385. The other differences as to structure between American and English law are of less importance when compared with those just examined. They are not however negligible because they may sometimes be a source of difficulty for a mutual understanding between English and American jurists.

386. Equity in the United States

In this context special mention must be made of the very original American development in the jurisdiction attributed to the courts of Equity. In the absence of courts specialising in Canon law, the American courts of Equity simply annexed the matters which had fallen to the ecclesiastical courts in England. The jurisdiction of courts of Equity, the Americans reasoned, should be admitted in all cases when the Common law provided no remedy. For example, since the Common law considered husband and wife to be one person, and therefore incapable of legal proceedings against each other, there was in this instance no available remedy. American Equity was in this way developed to include, before it became statutory in character, the annulment of marriages and divorce, over and above matters relating to wills and estates, which is somewhat surprising to the English.[19]

387. Constitutional and administrative law

Constitutional law and administrative law are in the same way very different branches of law compared to the corresponding English legal branches. The very great differences in constitutional principles and political institutions create quite distinct problems, or substantially alter the elements of what are otherwise related problems. The judicial control or review of the constitutionality of legislation admitted in the United States is not, of course, as already mentioned, known in England. And American administrative law necessarily implies a study of the organisation and the functioning of a large number of commissions, whether federal or state, that have no equivalents in England.[20]

388. Other Subjects

American and English labour law are also substantially different. American unions are not similar to English trade unions and the judicial approaches to labour conflicts are fundamentally distinct. Banking and company law in the United States have been profoundly shaped by the agency known as the Securities and Exchange Commission which has no equivalent in England. The American procedural reforms of the nineteenth and twentieth centuries have, in the same way, taken English and American law along quite distinct paths.

The American Attorney-General is, for all practical purposes, a minister of justice and shares therefore no more than the same title with his English counterpart who is simply the chief law officer of the crown. The U.S. Attorney-General, on the other hand, is the head of a large government department. Each federal court has a "U.S. Attorney" who can intervene as *amicus curiae* in all cases in which the constitutionality of a federal statute is invoked.[21]

[19] Sereni (A. P.), 'L'equity negli Stati Uniti," in *Studi di diritto comparato. Il diritto degli Stati Uniti* (1958) pp. 65–147. See also the study of the Chancery in the Colonies in the collection *Selected Essays in American Legal History*, Vol. II, p. 779.

[20] Compare the two works of Schwartz (B.), *Le droit administratif américain* (1952) and *Law and the Executive in Britain* (1949). Also, Schwartz (B.) and Wade (H. W. R.), *Administrative Law in Britain and in the U.S.* (1972). Davis (K. D.), *Administrative Law Treatise* (2nd ed., 1979–80).

[21] Kramer (R.) and Siegel (N.), *The Attorney-General of England and the Attorney-General of the United States* (1960) Duke L.J. 524. Hazard (J. N.), "The Role of the Ministère Public in Civil Proceedings" in Hazard (J. N.) and Wagner (W. J.), *Law in the United States of America in Social and Technological Revolution* (1974), pp. 209–226.

389. Legal vocabulary

The legal vocabulary employed in the two countries makes the diversity of the two laws very apparent—or, in some cases, may be apt to hide it. The same concept is sometimes expressed by two quite different words, whereas in other cases the same word expresses concepts differently understood in each country. The non-Anglo-American jurist must know this and thus avoid the use of English legal dictionaries when he undertakes the study of some question of American law.[22]

---

[22] The principal American legal dictionaries are Black's *Law Dictionary* (4th ed., 1968) and Ballentine's *Law Dictionary* (1948) and supplement (1954).

CHAPTER III

SOURCES OF AMERICAN LAW

390. Originality of American law

Like English law, American law is essentially "judge-made." Although this is certainly true of the legal structure and the concept of the legal rule, some qualification is required concerning the respective importance of legislation and court decisions in the modern social context, the two principal sources of American law to be considered in this chapter. The development in the United States, as in England, of various kinds of state intervention evidently tends to increase the importance of enacted law; in many sectors legal development is now wholly directed by legislation. But, whereas this phenomenon may be fairly recent in England, it is no novelty in the United States. A whole series of factors has contributed to making enacted law particularly important in the United States ever since the Declaration of Independence, and the most important of these is the existence of a federal Constitution and its Bill of Rights, the very basis of many American institutions and civil rights.

SECTION I—DECISIONS OF THE COURTS

391. English and American law

If one looks at things only superficially, it may seem that judicial decisions play precisely the same role in England as in the United States. This impression would be correct if nothing but the legal structures of the two countries were considered: English and American judges and lawyers do agree in their attitude that the only really *normal* legal rule is judge-made and articulated at the level of a specific case and is thus capable, quite apart from any work of interpretation, of providing the solution to the dispute. If on the other hand consideration is given to the role of court decisions as an actual source of law, then there are very important differences between the two legal systems.

With respect first of all to strict legal techniques, and in particular the rule of precedent or, as it is called in the United States, the rule of *stare decisis* ("let the decision stand"), there are significant differences. The American supreme courts (the supreme courts of each state and the U.S. Supreme Court) have never considered themselves bound by their own previous decisions. To understand the rule of *stare decisis,* in other words the role played by court decisions as well as their relation to other sources of law and in particular legal writing, it is also necessary to take into account, over and above any question of technique, a number of other factors which make the English and American legal worlds very distinctive. American judicial organisation and the American legal profession will be examined from this point of view; and to conclude this section some attention will be given to the *Restatement of the Law,* an effort of legal writers to present and explain systematically the body of American case law.

§ 1. Judicial Organisation

392. Federal and state courts

In the American judicial organisation there are federal courts and state courts. Unlike many federal states in which the federal courts exists only at the apex of the court hierarchy, the United States has adopted a quite different system: in many cases the federal courts may be seized as courts of first instance. There is, therefore, a double hierarchy of courts, each of the components of which must be separately examined before enquiring into their relationship.

393. Federal courts

The many different federal courts may be divided into two groups. There are first of all the traditional courts or *ordinary* federal courts of general jurisdiction. At the base of the hierarchy there are the U.S. District Courts and from these an appeal lies to the U.S. Courts of Appeal; from these there is also a further appeal to the United States Supreme Court. There are about 100 of these District Courts staffed with about 400 judges, and some of them are also divided into several "divisions" each of which may include up to as many as 20 judges. These district judges generally sit alone although on occasion a bench of three may hear certain cases (such as in anti-trust matters). In the most populous centres they are assisted in their work by "commissioners" who may sometimes judge in their place. Each district judge has a clerk, usually a young lawyer who has just completed his university training, who assists him in his research. At least one sitting of the court must be held annually in each subdivision of the district and so the judges are itinerant. About 80 judges sit on the 11 U.S. Courts of Appeal—formerly called the U.S. Circuit Courts of Appeal—one of which is located in the federal District of Columbia. Decisions in this court are generally rendered by three judges who hear cases in all the principal cities of the court's jurisdiction. The U.S. Supreme Court is composed of a Chief Justice and eight Associate Justices, all of whom hear all cases. Different means are employed in order that the court not be overburdened; if the court is to be seized of a case in order to render a decision with reasons, it is first of all necessary in about 90 per cent. of the cases to obtain a writ of *certiorari* indicating the "special and important reasons" for doing so. The court only adjudicates in about 12 per cent. of the cases brought to it and fully written decisions are only given in about 150 cases annually. The court most often considers that the question in dispute is not sufficiently important to justify the hearing and it will state this to be the case.[1]

Apart from this court structure, there are also special federal courts established by federal statutes: for fiscal or excise matters, patents, courts of claims when the liability of the state is involved, and courts in federal districts or territories filling the place of what comparably would be state courts. These courts sometimes have exclusive jurisdiction and in other cases the plaintiff may proceed either in the special court or before the district court. Thus, for example, in tax matters, the taxpayer may sue either in the district court, or before the Court of Claims or before the Tax Court. The numerous administrative agencies, and the important federal com-

---

[1] McCloskey (R. G.), *The American Supreme Court* (1964), first published 1960; the work contains an excellent "Bibliographical Essay" on literature pertaining to the U.S. Supreme Court. Griswold (E. N.), "La Cour suprême des Etats-Unis" in *La Cour judiciare suprême, enquête comparative*, Rev. int. dr. comparé (1978), p. 97.

mittees connected to the U.S. Congress, are also attributed juris-diction by virtue of federal statutes. From all these "legislative" courts and tribunals an appeal is always possible to one of the "traditional" federal courts whether to a district court, directly to a court of appeal, or even directly to the U.S. Supreme Court. It is as inconceivable in America as it is in England that there be no control, at least in theory, exercised by the regular courts over the decisions rendered by such agencies.

394. State courts

Each state has its own particular judicial organisation and it is therefore difficult to make valid generalisations about the whole of the state court system; the size, population and traditions of each state differ widely and different court structures have resulted. Sometimes it will have only two degrees, whereas in about two-thirds of the states there are three levels, a supreme court, a court of appeal and a court of first instance. In thirty-nine states the court at the summit of the hierarchy is called the "Supreme Court," whereas in others some other name is used (as, for example, in Connecticut where it is designated the Court of Errors). There are special courts of various kinds as well in both civil and criminal matters; in a small number of states there are still special courts of Equity.

The court structure of the State of New York, reformed in 1962, is as follows.[2] The court of general jurisdiction at first instance is the Supreme Court and a division of it is situated in each county. Its decisions may be appealed to one of four Supreme Court Appellate Divisions and from there an appeal may lie to the Court of Appeals sitting in Albany, the state capital. In most cases the appeal to the Court of Appeals lies only if that court exercises its discretion in favour of the appeal or if the Appellate Division itself consents. In addition to these regular courts there is a vast network of various inferior courts: Surrogate Courts for matters involving wills and successions, Court of Claims when damages are claimed of the state itself, Family Courts dealing with juvenile delinquency and different family law problems and special courts for small claims or minor disputes (Civil Court and Criminal Court of the

---

[2] Herzog (P.), 'Réforme de l'organisation judiciaire, de la procédure civile et du droit commercial dans l'Etat de New York," Rev. int. dr. comparé (1964), pp. 579–601.

City of New York, County Courts, Justices of the Peace Courts
and Village Police Justices). Appeals from the decisions of these
courts generally lie before the Court of Appeals.

395. The jury

The jury has remained much more relevant in the United States
than in England because, as far as federal courts are concerned,
the Seventh Amendment to the American Constitution guarantees
its retention. Any citizen may require that his dispute be decided
by a jury when the sum involved is greater than twenty dollars,
provided it is not a proceeding in Equity. It has not been possible
to circumvent this constitutional rule directly but it has been found
possible by indirect means to restrict its use. It is now settled, however, that there is no right to a trial by jury before the state courts,
although this was once thought to be so by virtue of the Fourteenth
Amendment. The option to have a trial by jury is nonetheless
widely admitted in numerous states. More than 100,000 cases a
year are decided by jury trials.

396. Relationship of the two court structures

In the relationship between the federal and state courts, a principle similar to that applicable in the relationship of federal and
state laws applies: the general rule is in favour of the jurisdiction of
the state courts.

Federal courts can only be seized in cases where the American
Constitution, or some statute of Congress based on constitutional
provisions, has recognised their jurisdiction, and such recognition
is based on two main ideas: the federal courts are sometimes competent by virtue of the nature of the dispute (when it involves, for
example, some provision of the Constitution itself or some federal
statute) and they are also sometimes competent on account of one
of the parties involved (when the United States itself, a foreign
diplomat or the citizens of two different states of the union are
involved). In cases involving citizens from different states, the sum
involved must be at least $10,000. In practice these principles have
given rise to many difficulties.

When federal courts can be seized in some such matter, their
jurisdiction is rarely exclusive. The parties can frequently still
resort to the state rather than the federal courts. In this eventuality

an appeal may be possible to the United States Supreme Court from the final decision rendered by the state court but only when the case raises some fundamental issue under the Constitution or a federal statute. However, when a case involves a matter which could not, in first instance, be taken to a federal court, it necessarily follows that the decision of the highest state court is final and binding. The United States Supreme Court does not therefore have at all the same role as the French Supreme Court (*Cour de Cassation*).[3]

Ninety-five per cent. (or thereabouts) of cases are exclusively handled by state courts. But this statistic, impressive in itself, is only meaningful if another, and qualitative, factor is taken into account as well: the disputes of the greatest public and political interest—those concerning civil rights, racial integration, the application of anti-trust laws and the constitutionality of laws—these cases are generally judged by federal courts and may lead, in any case, to a judgment by the United States Supreme Court. It is well known that this Court has played and continues to play at the present time a determinant role—and one, it should be added, that has at times been variously appreciated—in the history of the United States.

397. Decentralisation of judicial power

By way of comparison to the English system, it is worth noting that in the United States there is considerably less centralisation of judicial power. English justice is centred in London; the superior courts, with very few exceptions, were until recently found only in London. For quite obvious reasons, both historical and geographical, there has been no analogous development in America. This is so, therefore, not only because there are separate state courts but also because the multiplicity of federal courts runs throughout the union; they are not located just in the federal capital. The concentration of judicial power in London was a decisive factor in the development of the Common law, and thus the dispersion—the inevitable dispersion—of American justice has created a series of problems that never even arose in England. These same problems have tended to encourage the adoption of a more flexible view

---

[3] The operation of the French *Cour de cassation* is discussed above, paras. 102 and 107.

respecting the authority of decided cases, notably because of the introduction, alongside the normal and essential preoccupaton for the security of legal relations, of the further concern for legal uniformity, a matter that does not arise in England.

§ 2. American Legal Profession[4]

398. The legal profession

In the United States, as in England, there is a general concept of the "legal profession." Counted within it are lawyers, salaried legal counsellors of companies, government and public bodies, law professors and judges. Lawyers and judges practise their professions under the supervision of the Supreme Court of the state in which they are located. Law professors and salaried legal counsellors are not subject to judicial control but they are nearly always members of some state bar association although it need not be in the state where they earn a living. This analogy, although limited, should be noted because in every other respect—in legal training and professional organisation—there are completely different systems in England and America.

The conditions of admission to the legal profession differ in each state. Those who are lawyers, that is to say admitted to the practice of law according to the rules of the individual state, may exercise their profession only before the courts of that state and before the federal courts located in that state. Any lawyer admitted to the practice in one state may, upon the payment of a small sum, be admitted to appear before the United States Supreme Court. All the states permit a lawyer from another state to appear in individual cases in its courts and most states admit to the profession those lawyers who have practised in another state for a given period (usually five years).

At the present time the admission to the practice of law in any one state is conditional upon the successful completion of law examinations organised under the control of the courts. A university degree is never in itself sufficient even though, unlike England, it is now required in about three-quarters of the states.

---

[4] Hurst (J. W.), *The Growth of American Law: The Law Makers* (1950); Griswold (E. N.), *Law and Lawyers in the United States* (1964). Rheinstein (M.), *Die Rechtshonoratioren und ihr Einfluss auf Charakter und Funktion der Rechtsordnungen* (1970) 34 *Rabels Z.* 1–18.

399. American law schools[5]

American law schools generally admit only students intending to take up the practice of law; for the most part they are very little concerned with the general cultural development of students because this formation—"pre-legal education"—is normally supposed to have been acquired through a general university education in the years preceding those spent in the law school. The American student comes to the law school for an essentially professional practical training. When he leaves he counts upon the fact that his law training will equip him to practise law. The American law school, in its efforts to provide a professional training, is thus more closely akin to the various French institutes or technical schools than it is to French law faculties.[6]

The teaching method used in the American law schools, generally in the form of Socratic dialogue between teacher and student on the basis of "case-books" or collections of materials prepared by the professor, is very different from that used in France or even England. Before the class, the student must read a certain number of judicial decisions or extracts from legal writings or other materials; he then explains to the group the meaning of what he has read, the problems encountered or recognised, and the interest of these decisions; a general discussion, directed by the professor, then takes place. He questions the students and tries to lead them to the discovery of the relationship between the question studied and connected problems, and he may modify the facts, or other considerations involved, in order to test their developing skill in legal reasoning and the application of legal principles. All members of the group are expected to take part in these discussions and each is encouraged to ask questions and express his own opinion. The classic—and usually formal—lecture method (what in France are called *les cours magistraux*) is only used exceptionally. In the American context the "case-method" undoubtedly produces good results because the student is usually in no way embarrassed to exchange views with his professor and the law

---

[5] The *Journal of Legal Education,* published by the Association of American Law Schools since 1948, is devoted almost exclusively to questions of legal education in the U.S. Stevens (R.)., *Law School. Legal Education in America from the 1850s to the 1980s* (1983).

[6] In France these professionally oriented schools are the *Ecole des Impôts* (for tax officers), *Ecole polytechnique du notariat* (for notaries), *Institut de droit des affaires* (business law), *Centre national d'études judiciaires* (training of judges), *etc.*

school generally has the atmosphere of a professional training school. The method has however been criticised for placing too great an emphasis on litigation and, in particular, upon appellate level decisions. Today, more and more, the "clinical method" is adopted, in which the student advises and even represents real clients within a legal aid organisation and under the supervision of a lawyer who also serves as professor.

400. American lawyers

The American who has successfully passed the professional examinations then becomes a member of the legal bar; he is a *lawyer*.[7] The word does not really have its equivalent in French or even in English (as opposed to American) usage, because the organisation of the profession in France and in England is very different. Meaningful comparisons are difficult.

Most lawyers (70 per cent.) practise law alone or in association with one other (15 per cent.). In the major cities, however, he very often practises law in a large firm of lawyers (anywhere from 10 to 200 lawyers) which has recruited him and there he will specialise, sometimes within very narrow limits, in one subject. A small number, the *trial lawyers*, will specialise in either civil or criminal trials. Others may specialise in the handling of claims (roughly in the same way as the French *avoué*[8]), but most are concerned with non-contentious matters (and therefore with matters similar to those of the French *notaire*[9]) or act as general legal advisers or tax counsellors—with this difference, however, that recourse to lawyers for advice is much more frequent in the United States than it is in France. Large numbers are also employed outside these law firms in different branches of government service and in public or private enterprises. The "notary public" in the United States is not a lawyer and is in no way similar to the French "notaire" or the English notary public. In America he is a person who has merely been confided the right to authenticate (for a fee) signatures of those requiring this service for some reason.

[7] Hurst (J. W.), *The Growth of American Law. The Law Makers* (1950).
[8] The *avoué* is entrusted with all preliminary steps leading to the day in court when arguments will be orally developed by the *avocat*.
[9] The *notaire* in France is not involved with litigation. He is a quasi–public legal adviser for the public in a number of matters (conveyances, transfer of property *mortis causa*, drafting of wills, formation of companies); he records deeds and authenticates them, but he is not a tax counsellor.

In number American lawyers far exceed French or English legal professionals. There are about 350,000 of which some 30,000 are employed by private enterprises and 30,000 by government. Generally, they belong to their own state professional or bar associations. In some states (28 at least) membership in such association is obligatory and the state bar is then said to be *integrated*. The American Bar Association is the federation of these state bar associations but not all lawyers belong to an association and even when they do the general control of the association is far less than that exercised over barristers by the Inns of Court or the Law Society over solicitors in England. As a matter of general practice it is admitted that lawyers may be remunerated in proportion to what has been earned for the client; such a *quota litis* agreement—or contingent fee, as it is called in the United States—is, on the other hand, anathema in England.

Large sums of public money are today devoted to the payment of a variety of "public defenders," *i.e.* lawyers practising independently who specialise in representing those from low income groups. Legal aid or neighbourhood law clinics have, moreover, grown enormously in recent years to the point where about 2,000 lawyers provide about a million free legal consultations annually.

401. American judges

There are in the United States, as a consequence of the court system, two types of American judges, federal and state court judges.

Federal judges are very much like English judges. They are named, as in England, for life by the president of the United States upon the ratification of the Senate, usually from among lawyers who have had considerable practical experience and gained a high reputation. It should also be mentioned that a certain number of the justices of the United States Supreme Court have been appointed from among law professors of the great American universities. This point is important because it indicates the great prestige of the American university professor and suggests that, as compared to England, there is a different relationship between the work of the courts and the role of legal writing in the United States.

Respecting state judges, on the other hand, it is difficult to make any general observations, although a number of the points mentioned respecting federal judges are equally applicable. For the most part, however, the situation is different. Forty of the states, since the time of President Jackson (1767–1845) and his election to the presidency in 1828, carried their preoccupation with democracy to the point where the selection of judges by universal suffrage was adopted. At the start this system was not very satisfactory; at one time the performance of the judges was very much criticised. Such criticisms are today much more rare and are tempered by a number of reforms which have raised the standard of these judges and, to a point, re-instated their independent status. These reforms have included the prolongation of the period during which they hold this elected office, a procedure of simple ratification by the electorate of appointments made first of all by the state governor, and the preliminary approval of the candidates for office by the state bar association. Although these American judges do not enjoy a prestige analogous to that of English judges, they are normally esteemed by the public and their independence, morality and competence are generally admitted. A few exceptions are found in a small number of states and with respect to judges who, usually in criminal matters, have only a very limited jurisdiction. It is therefore no longer possible to accept the descriptions provided on this point of American legal *mores* by works published before 1914.[10]

§ 3. The Rule of Stare Decisis

402. Stare decisis and American federal structure

In England, since the nineteenth century, there has been a rule of precedent which, in circumstances already examined,[11] obliges judges to follow the legal rules already enunciated in individual cases by other judges. In the United States there is a similar rule, but the American *stare decisis* ("let the decision stand") does not operate in quite the same way, nor is it so rigorous, as the present English rule.

---

[10] Dillon (J. F.), *The Laws and Jurisprudence of England and America* (1894); Nerincx (A.), *L'organisation judiciaire aux Etats-Unis* (1909), "Le recrutement de la magistrature aux Etats-Unis" (1898), 30 Rev. dr. int. légis compainée.

[11] Paras. 336 *et seq. Adde* Goodhart (A. L.), *Essays in Jurisprudence and the Common Law* (1931, reprinted 1972). *Cf.* in particular Chap. 3 of the work *Case Law in England and in the United States*, pp. 50–74.

This subject is complicated by the fact that the American federal structure introduces a new element. It is of course desirable that the law ensure security in legal relationships, and from this point of view a rigorous rule of precedent may indeed have much to recommend it. But it is also important that the law of different states should not become hopelessly or needlessly differentiated, and to this end a suppleness in the rule of precedent is also equally desirable. In the face of such competing and even contradictory values it is understandable that American jurists avoid taking up too precise a position. According to circumstances one therefore finds that emphasis is sometimes placed on the need for flexibility, sometimes on the need for security and stability.

403. Repudiation of precedent

All that can really be said with certainty about the American rule of *stare decisis* is that, as compared to the corresponding rule in England, it has an important limitation: the United States Supreme Court and the supreme courts of the different states are not bound to observe their own decisions and may, therefore, operate a reversal of previously established judicial practice. It should of course be recalled that an individual state is sovereign and that the rule of *stare decisis* only comes into operation within that state's own court structure and with respect to the subjects within its legislative competence. The federal courts, when they apply the law of a particular state, have been in a similar position since *Erie R. R. Co. v. Tompkins.*

Such changes in previous judicial trends are not at all rare in the history of the United States Supreme Court, because of the supple manner in which this Court conceives the interpretation of the United States Constitution. For state courts, however, there is another explanation: the repudiation of precedent by these courts is, for the most part, probably due to the pressure exerted by the lawyers themselves and the real desire to align the law of one state with the dominant current prevailing in other states. All of these factors, of course, contribute to bringing about the unity of American Common law.

That it is in fact possible for the United States Supreme Court to overrule previous decisions has proved to be fundamentally important. In this way the Court has been able to adapt the Constitution to modern social thinking and economic necessities; and it has also assured the stability of American political institutions by enabling the United States to continue living under the rule of a Constitution that can only be amended with very great difficulty. The Supreme Court has been able to disarm the hostility directed against it before 1936 because of its exaggerated conservatism and attachment to the principles of an outmoded liberalism.[12] Its present role as a progressive force in national development would have been unpredictable only 65 years ago.

A celebrated example will help to show how the United States Supreme Court brings about such changes. The American Constitution guarantees each citizen that he or she will be treated equally under the laws. How is this "equal protection of the law" of Amendment XIV to be understood? At first the Court admitted a "separate but equal" principle and held to the view that constitutional requirements were fulfilled if, in education, social services and transport, a similar status were given to whites and blacks even though their schools, hospitals and buses would remain separate or segregated.[13] This principle of segregation however has since been rejected: equality under the law, as it is now understood, requires that the law be *colour-blind*—in other words, that it refuse to take into account in any way whatsoever the colour or race of citizens, just as it is unable to take any account of their religion. The enforcing of this new principle gave rise to many difficult problems and, particularly with respect to education, the United States Supreme Court itself admitted that the change must be brought about gradually.[14]

404. Real meaning of stare decisis

In order to assure the security of legal relations (and apart from the two exceptions mentioned above), the state supreme courts

[12] In the famous *Dredd Scott Case,* at the origin of the Civil War, the Supreme Court decided that Congress did not have the authority to prohibit states from admitting slavery. In *Lochner* v. *New York,* 198 U.S. 45 (1905), it ruled unconstitutional a New York statute creating a 60 hours work week in the bakery trade. In 1910, in *Hammer* v. *Dagenhart,* 247 U.S. 251 (1918), it held unconstitutional a statute of Congress prohibiting night work and creating a forty hours work week for children aged 14 to 16 years.

[13] *Plessy* v. *Ferguson,* 163 U.S. 537 (1896).

[14] *Brown* v. *Board of Education,* 347 U.S. 483 (1954); on the racial problem in the U.S.A., *cf.* Lassale (J. P.), "Le développement du problème noir aux Etats-Unis," Rev. int. droit comparé, 1964, pp. 515–544; Griswold (E. N.), *Law and Lawyers in the United States* (1964), pp. 105–150.

will only overrule previous judicial decisions with very great caution. Their attitude may be likened to that of English courts before they openly enunciated the strict necessity of adhering to judicial precedents in the nineteenth century. A strict rule of precedent is not an absolute necessity in the Common law. The difference may in fact however be very slight between the juridical recognition of this rule and the voluntary adhesion by judges to some rule or doctrine stated by their predecessors by virtue of arguments based on reason. The whole question is really much more a matter of legal psychology than of law and this is precisely the reason why American legal writers, at least those advocating a more accelerated evolution of law, have stated that the rule of *stare decisis* is not obligatory; others, more reticent respecting such changes, have stated it to be an essential part of the present day system.[15]

But the important consideration is not to be found in these perhaps too clear-cut statements. The essential factor lies much more in the willingness, or hesitation, of judges to admit that distinctions may be drawn; whether or not they consider themselves bound by an ageing principle; whether they are indeed aware of the need that the law evolve and whether they are to be guided by progressive or conservative ideas. Important too is the considerable number—and still increasing (by about 350 volumes annually)—of published judicial reports in which every shade of opinion can find supporting precedents. The United States, with its great variety and a less cohesive corps of legal professionals, undoubtedly provides a milieu in which the range of possible distinctions, nuances and differences is much greater than in England. In practice, however, it is not always very obvious that there is any real difference between the two countries in this respect. In each, as in France, a kind of balance is finally established between the necessarily contradictory claims of security and progress which are the constant elements in the life of any legal system.

405. A systematic statement of the Common law

To conclude this study of American courts and judicial decisions, mention must be made of a private publication which

---

[15] In order to understand how American law evolves without hindrance from the rule of *stare decisis,* consult the work of Stone (F. F.), *Institutions fondamentales du droit des Etats Unis* (1965).

has attempted to explain in a systematic manner the rules of American Common law. This endeavour, the *Restatement of the Law,* was undertaken by a private association, the American Law Institute. Nineteen volumes appeared in the original edition of the collection:

Contracts	2 volumes	1932
Agency	2 volumes	1933
Conflicts of laws		1934
Torts	4 volumes	1934–1939
Property	5 volumes	1936–1944
Security		1941
Restitution		1957
Trusts	2 volumes	1935
Judgments		1942

The *Restatement* attempts to organise and explain as precisely as possible the subjects within the legislative authority of the states in branches of the law where legislative interventions have not been too numerous and it then indicates which solutions are most in agreement with the American Common law system and which should be accepted by American courts. The *Restatement* itself is completed by two other series: the *Restatement in the Courts,* indicating the judicial decisions of different courts in which an article of the *Restatement* has been cited (either adopting, rejecting or distinguishing it); and the series entitled *State Annotations* indicating to what extent, in actual fact, the rules found in the *Restatement* are followed in different states. The *Supplements* to the *Restatement,* appearing periodically, contain corrections to and clarifications of the systematisation provided in the principal series. A new edition of the *Restatement,* called the *Second Restatement,* was undertaken in 1952 and at the present time volumes dealing with the same nine subjects listed above have been published.

The *Restatement of the Law* was very favourably looked upon by jurists of countries with codified systems, because for them it was seen as a precious tool providing a systematic exposition of American law in a form not dissimilar to their own codes. One must not forget the basic differences however between the codes of the Romano-Germanic family and the *Restatement* which is no more than a private compilation. Whatever authority it may have is no greater than that attributed to its compilers and, in particular, the editor of each individual volume. The respect it commands, therefore, quite naturally varies. The *Restatement* in the United States is not used as a continental code would be. It frequently happens that it is cited in court decisions, but it is not by using the *Restatement* that American lawyers and judges normally seek—or find— the legal solution to their problems. The *Restatement* is no more than a kind of systematic digest in which one only finds the judicial decisions on point.

SECTION II—STATUTE LAW

As indicated above, American legislation is made up of federal statutes and state statutes.

406. American constitution

Within the body of federal legislation, a special place is quite naturally occupied by the fundamental national law, the Constitution of the United States of America enacted in 1787. For Americans it represents a good deal more than the French Constitution does for Frenchmen. It is not only a political charter but the nation's founding document, inspired by the ideas of the Natural Law School and one which put into operation the concept of *social contract*. The American Constitution does not merely spell out the organisation of the country's political institutions; it solemnly traces the limits of the powers of the federal authorities in their relationships with individual states and citizens. These same relationships have been even more specifically enunciated by the first 10 amendments to the Constitution, voted in 1789, which make up what is known as the "Bill of Rights" of the American citizen. And the Thirteenth, Fourteenth and Fifteenth Amendments to the Constitution, voted at the time of the Civil War, also guarantee that certain "natural rights" of citizens will not be violated or frustrated by state authorities.

This written Constitution, containing a declaration of rights, is thus one of the factors distinguishing American and English law. It differs further from English constitutional law by reason of the principle of judicial review of the constitutionality of legislation, unknown in England.

407. Marbury *v*. Madison (1803)[16]

Although no text confers the power expressly, the United States Supreme Court established the principle of judicial review of the constitutionality of legislation, even in the case of federal statutes, in the famous decision of *Marbury* v. *Madison* rendered in 1803.[17] The colourful circumstances in which this principle emerged merit some account. After the "federalist" president (that is to say one who advocated a strong central power) John Adams (1738–1826), the country elected Thomas Jefferson (1743–1826), a member of the rival Democratic-Republican party, as his successor. Before the latter was installed in office, John Adams appointed his Secretary of State, John Marshall (1755–1835), as Chief Justice of the Supreme Court and he made another member of his party, William Marbury, a justice of the peace in the federal district, a really very minor post. Marbury's commission of appointment was approved by the Senate, made out in proper form with the Great Seal of the United States but it was not sent to him by the time Jefferson was sworn into office. James Madison, the new Secretary of State in the Jefferson administration, did not deliver the commission to Marbury who thereupon petitioned the Supreme Court for the issuance of a writ of *mandamus* commanding Madison to perform his official duty and send him his commission. The Judiciary Act of 1789 was clear on the point—the Supreme Court had the power to deliver the writ in such circumstances.

The Chief Justice, John Marshall, wrote the unanimous decision of the court which was made up of a majority of federalists like himself. He recognised that Marbury had been appointed to a judicial office in conformity with the law, that he was legally entitled to receive the commission of appointment and that its delivery was not a matter of discretion for the President and his Secretary of State. He also held that a writ of *mandamus* could issue, in other words, that there was a remedy commanding the Secretary of State to deliver it to Marbury. Marshall also held, however, that the Supreme Court itself was not competent to issue the order because the Constitution provided that, apart from cer-

---

[16] 1 Cranch 137.
[17] On this subject in English speaking countries, generally, *cf.* McWhinney (E.), *Judicial Review in the English-speaking World* (4th ed., 1969).

tain very exceptional cases, this court was only a court of appeal.
The Judiciary Act of 1789, in providing that the Supreme Court
could be seized directly for the purpose of issuing such a writ
addressed to the government, was in conflict with the Constitution
itself. The provision of the Act (s. 13) was therefore *unconstitutional*, and the Supreme Court had to refuse to give it effect.[18]

The judicial review of the constitutionality of legislation was
thus established, with no particular difficulty, in the United States
in a case where, far from asserting its authority, the Court declared
unconstitutional a law which had in fact extended its own original
jurisdiction. The decision in *Marbury* v. *Madison,* moreover,
clearly pleased the executive power; it is easy enough to understand why the executive did not protest the decision and the principle it contained, even though it subsequently proved to have
other implications. During the nineteenth century, however, such
very modest use was made of this principle that its basis was never
again seriously discussed. Today it constitutes one of the principle-
differences between American constitutional structure on the one
hand and the English and French positions on the other. The
American Constitution from the legal as well as the political point
of view is clearly of fundamental importance.

408. Constitutionality of judicial decisions

Judicial review by the Supreme Court (and, under its control, all
other federal or state courts) is exercised not only over federal and
state statutes but also over the manner in which all other courts
interpret the Common law. Any judicial decision may thus be set
aside if it is found to violate a provision of the American Constitution. This power of constitutional review is of immense importance
because, through it, courts and legislatures are held to respect a
number of fundamental principles. It assures, moreover, to the
extent necessary, the uniformity of law within the country. It is
appropriate therefore to examine the manner in which the Constitution is interpreted in the United States. It is a rather unusual
development to occur within a Common law country.

---

[18] For a technical analysis of the decision: Mr. Justice H. Burton, "The Cornerstone of Constitutional Law: The Extraordinary case of *Marbury* v. *Madison,*" 36 Amer. Bar Assoc. J., 805
(1950).

409. The idea of fundamental law

The United States Supreme Court recognised, and very early on, that the Constitution was not "like other statutes." Statute in Common law countries is generally considered an element foreign to the Common law system and only able to make additions to and corrections of individual points of this "ordinary" law. Obviously the American Constitution cannot be treated in the same way. It is the fundamental statute of the country and sometimes it even seems that the force of the Common law itself is derived from its authority, just as the Natural Law School, whose ideas were current in 1787, maintained. The Constitution is considered to be the authorised expression of the social contract uniting the citizens and legitimising the established authorities. It is seen to be the fundamental law (*Grundgesetz, loi fondamentale*), establishing the very bases of society. It could not therefore be treated like other statutes which, by formulating certain detailed rules, simply brought additions or corrections to the usual judge-made law. The Constitution, therefore, dominating the structure of the Common law, is legislation in the Romanist tradition; its primary purpose is not to resolve disputes but to establish general rules of organisation and conduct for those in power and for government administrators. "[W]e must never forget," said Chief Justice Marshall, "that it is a Constitution we are expounding . . . a constitution intended to endure for ages to come, and, consequently, to be adapted to the various crises of human affairs."[19]

410. Interpretation of the United States Constitution

The Constitution for this reason has been interpreted, as a matter of principle, with great flexibility. In their methods of interpretation Supreme Court judges were about 100 years in advance of the "teleological" methods advocated in France by Josserand. As Chief Justice Hughes once said, without equivocation, the Constitution is what the judges say it is. The whole development of American law, the distinction between federal law and the laws of

---

[19] *M'Culloch* v. *Maryland*, 17 U.S. 4 Wheat. 316, at pp. 407, 415 (1819). It was held in this case that the creation of a national bank was authorised under Art. I, s. 8 allowing Congress to take all "necessary and convenient" steps needed to implement the powers expressly attributed to it in the Constitution.

the states, and even American history itself, were influenced by the Court's interpretation of certain of its provisions. As especially good examples of this development mention should be made of Article I, section 8, which empowers Congress to establish taxes for "the general welfare" of the country and "to regulate commerce with foreign nations, and among the several States" of the union (inter-state commerce); the Fifth Amendment[20] which specifies that no person can be "deprived of life, liberty, or property, without due process of law" and the same principle which is again affirmed in the Fourteenth Amendment[21] dealing with restrictions on the powers of the states. The same amendment also prohibits states from refusing any person subject to their jurisdiction "the equal protection of the laws." The Fifteenth amendment[22] declares that neither the United States nor any state can deny or abridge the right of citizens "on account of race, colour, or previous condition of servitude" (*viz.* status as former slaves). Article I, section 9 denies Congress the power to enact statutes with retrospective operation (*ex post facto* laws); and section 10 of this same Article denies the states the power to pass any law "impairing the obligation of contracts."

These different principles have allowed a supple interpretation of the Constitution to take place. The simple reading of legislative texts does not always enable one to appreciate whether some particular statute or action of the federal authorities is, or is not, constitutional and where, therefore, the limit between federal law and state law is to be drawn. One must be familiar with the decisions of the Court to come to some opinion in the matter.

The interpretation of the American Constitution is full of interest because it is an example of the operation of some of the more advanced Romano-Germanic theories of interpretation being adopted and used in a Common law country. There was no hesitation in the United States about rejecting, with respect to the Constitution, the classical maxim according to which statutes, a series of *errata* and *addenda* to the Common law, were to be restrictively interpreted. A number of examples will illustrate the Court's method of interpretation.

---

[20] 1 U.S. *Statutes at Large* 21 (1791).
[21] 14 U.S. *Statutes at Large* 358 (1868).
[22] 15 U.S. *Statutes at Large* 346 (1870).

411. The commerce clause

Among the general statements of the Constitution which have been liberally interpreted, and have thus led to a considerable enlargement of federal authority, the "commerce clause" is among the most important. This provision, at section 8 of Article I of the Constitution, gives Congress the power "to regulate commerce with foreign nations, and among the several States, and with the Indian tribes." At the time of the Constitution, whatever commerce did exist was essentially local. Today, of course, it has to a very large extent become inter-state and international; its modern dimension ignores state frontiers, and it is clearly desirable that it be subject to a uniform regulation throughout the United States.

A two-fold evolution has taken place respecting the interpretation of the commerce clause. In the first place, it has been said to contain, although not in express terms, the principle that a state law will be held unconstitutional, and therefore inapplicable, if it restricts in some way inter-state or international commerce.[23] More recently a very great extension to the notion of inter-state commerce was achieved by holding that the idea of commerce includes that of industry,[24] and by recognising as constitutionally valid federal legislation intending to improve labour conditions or the national economy.[25] Very considerable powers in the economic sector and respecting various kinds of social legislation have in this way been recognised as vesting in Congress and other federal authorities. There is, one might almost say, no kind of undertaking which lies beyond the purview of the clause regulating inter-state commerce as now interpreted.

Despite the great progress made along these lines, no uniform regulation of commercial matters generally has been achieved in the United States. A number of questions, of general commercial interest, and which might very well be suitably included in a uniform federal regulation, are still ruled by individual state laws. The law of "commercial contracts" (sale, agency, carriage of

---

[23] *Gibbons* v. *Ogden,* 9 Wheat. 1 (U.S. 1824): the unconstitutionality of a law of the State of New York restricting navigation between the banks of the Hudson River forming the boundary between the States of New York and New Jersey.

[24] *National Labor Relations Board* v. *Jones & Laughlin Steel Co.,* 301 U.S. 1 (1937): the constitutionality of the National Labor Relations Act which established a series of rules relating to labor law in all industries of a commerical nature.

[25] *Cf.* the preceding note and compare the decisions (which to us today seem scandalous) cited above, para. 403.

goods and security), negotiable instruments and companies are almost wholly covered by individual state statutes and case-law at the present time. The adoption now by all the states (except Louisiana) of the *Uniform Commercial Code*,[26] even though it is no more than a model law proposed to the state legislatures, is a step toward harmonising some important parts of American commercial law.

412. Due process of law

Another general principle which has permitted a control over both the case and statutory law of both the state and the federal governments, arises by virtue of the Fifth and Fourteenth Amendments. According to them, no one may be deprived of his life, liberty or property "without due process of law."[27] In the minds of its draftsmen this provision probably had no particular significance—it very likely merely meant that the deprivation of personal liberty or expropriation of property should only take place in conformity with the ordinary rules of law. The United States Supreme Court has, however, made use of it in order to exercise a control over federal or state legislation and decisions by requiring that interference with persons or property be, in its estimation, *reasonable*. State autonomy has thus been considerably reduced, in many areas, by the broad interpretation given by the Court to the principle.

Two examples will illustrate this development. In the decision of *Gideon* v. *Wainwright*,[28] rendered in 1963, the United States Supreme Court held that a Florida statute violated the principle of due process because it did not recognise the right to free legal advice of an indigent person, charged with an offence making him liable to a five year term of imprisonment. In another case, *Roe* v. *Wade*,[29] handed down in 1973, the Court held unconstitutional the provision of a state statute which rendered liable to imprisonment any woman who procured for herself an abortion. The right enshrined by the two Amendments involved, according to the Court, a right of privacy, which in particular included the right to terminate a pregnancy in the first three months.

[26] *Cf. infra*, para. 419.
[27] The phrase "due process of law" comes from article 39 of the Magna Carta.
[28] 372 U.S. 335 (1963). Lewis (A.), *Gideon's Trumpet* (1967).
[29] 410 U.S. 959 (1973).

These decisions illustrate that it has been and remains possible to speak of a "rule by judges" in the United States. As with any decision however each must be viewed in its context in order that its real meaning be understood, and the particular facts in each of the above cases may well go some way towards explaining the decisions rendered.

413. Equal protection of the laws

A third principle may be cited which shows the variations possible in the decisions of the United States Supreme Court and their relation to public opinion. The American Constitution guarantees each citizen that he or she will be treated equally under the law in all the states. How is this "equal protection of the law" of the Fourteenth Amendment understood? A number of developments here indicate how the principle has evolved. One has already been mentioned earlier in connection with the Court's attitude to precedent.[30]

The principle that citizens are to be treated equally under the Constitution has led to spectacular judicial developments in other fields. The Court has held unconstitutional those statutes which in certain states have artificially delimited electoral districts and thereby failed to assure equal representation to all citizens.[31] Decisions have also struck down legislation which has created unjustifiable discrimination based on sex. More recently, there has been a tendency to require an equality between legitimate and illegitimate children with regard to their legal status and the possibility of establishing their filiation.[32]

414. Cruel and unusual punishments

The Eighth Amendment proscribing cruel and unusual punishments has gained as well a new actuality with the United States Supreme Court decision of 1972, declaring unconstitutional a state law which had provided for capital punishment for the reason that the statute itself did not lay down sufficiently precise rules for determining in which cases the guilty person could be condemned

---

[30] *Cf. supra*, para. 403 *in fine*.
[31] *Baker* v. *Carr* 369 U.S. 186 (1962).
[32] Krause (H. D.), *Illegitimacy: Law and Social Policy* (1971). Buch (M.), Foriers (P.) and Perelman (C.), *L'égalité* (1971).

to death or merely to a prison term.[33] The press in most countries greeted this decision as abolishing the death penalty. But while the decision assuredly reinforced that opinion which was agitating for abolition, it was severely criticised in various quarters and the California electorate shortly thereafter, by a large majority, declared itself in favour of the re-establishment of the death penalty. Since then, the Supreme Court has itself reconsidered the question. A decision handed down in 1976 recognised (seven against two) the constitutionality of the death penalty legislation in a number of states (Florida, Georgia, Texas) on the ground that the legislation was sufficiently precise in its criteria of application. But the Supreme Court never decided in either 1972 or 1976 that capital punishment was constitutional or unconstitutional in itself because it constituted a cruel and unusual punishment.

415. Ordinary statutory interpretation

The supple methods of interpretation used for the federal Constitution have not been extended to the interpretation of state constitutions. It is true of course that these do not have the same fundamental political importance—very often they are no more than a conglomeration of heteroclite provisions and the justification for their inclusion in a constitution is often difficult.

The respect for the federal Constitution, the bastion of American freedoms, and the American habit of dealing with "written law" in the form of federal statutes, might have contributed to the development of a different attitude towards statute in the United States from what it is in England. But this has not taken place. Apart from the American Constitution, what was said about the interpretation of English statutes is equally applicable to American legislation in general.[34]

As in England, the American statute is not fully integrated into the framework of the legal system until its meaning has been explained by judicial decisions. The attitude of the Supreme Court is typical in this regard: the Court refuses to examine the constitutionality of a state law until the state courts have specified, through

---

[33] *Furman* v. *Georgia* 408 U.S. 238 (1972). No capital punishment was carried out in the U.S. for some years following the decision although more recently it has been employed in a number of states.

[34] *Supra*, paras. 345 *et seq.*

interpretation, what its real meaning is. When federal courts are called upon to apply state statutes they have also shown some hesitation to do so unless these have received some interpretation by the state courts themselves.

The traditional canons of legal interpretation continue to be respected even when the constitutions, codes or statutes themselves expressly authorise a departure from them.[35] An explanation for the failure of the movement towards codification in the second half of the nineteenth century lies in this attitude of resistance.

416. Administrative law

The American methods of interpretation have contributed to the development, as in England, of a large variety of boards, agencies, commissions and administrative tribunals within the framework of a new administrative law. The intention has not simply been to relieve the ordinary courts of their burden of work, but rather to assure that new legislation, especially in economic and social matters, and by excluding the methods normally used in the regular courts, will operate in the spirit intended. This development has occurred at both the federal and state levels, but it has been particularly extensive in the case of federal administrative law.

According to American legal theory a "regulating power" was not connected to the exercise of executive power. Modern doctrine maintains that an *administrative power* has in fact developed which constitutes a fourth power distinct from the three traditional powers. Like the executive power this new administrative power ultimately resides in the United States President; however, it is exercised, unlike the executive power, in collaboration with, and under the control of, a number of important commissions set up by Congress. The first of these, the Interstate Commerce Commission, was created in 1887 for the purpose of controlling the railways and to supervise generally inter-state transport. Since that time many other important administrative commissions have been created among which the most significant are the Federal Trade Commission, the Securities and Exchange Commission and the

---

[35] *Cf.* the article by Van Alstyne, "The California Civil Code" in West's *Annotated California Code, Civil Code I* (1954), pp. 29–35, reprinted in Von Mehren (A.), *The Civil Law System* (1957), pp. 70–74.

National Labor Relations Board. These permanent federal agencies are empowered to make regulations and settle disputes. In many areas therefore American law cannot be understood unless the work of these commissions, which in some fields may be thought of as creating a new kind of "Equity," is studied. The substance of this new *administrative law* is partly administrative and partly judicial, like the ancient Equity of England, but it is formulated and administered by bodies subject to the control of the ordinary courts of law.

417. American codes

In the United States there has been, in modern times, a proliferation of statutes. And, as in other countries, measures have been taken to maintain some kind of order within the enacted law and to simplify the business of consulting it. For both federal and state legislation, consolidations of statute law, whether public or private in character, have been made and are brought out in new periodic editions or kept up to date by means of periodic supplements.

These collections or compilations are commonly known as *Revised Laws* or *Consolidated Laws*, but sometimes they are also called *Codes*. There is, for example, the U.S.C.A. (United States Code Annotated) for federal law. But no mistake should be made because of this title. These collections are not codes in the European sense of the term. The organisation of such compilations (subjects arranged in alphabetical order) alone suffices to distinguish them from the traditional European codes. Their aim too is, above all, something quite different: to classify American statutes, whether federal or state, without any reference to the Common law. They are therefore, as to content, more similar to the French *codes administratifs* now being compiled rather than in the tradition of the *codes napoléoniens*.

Codification along the lines of the Romano-Germanic type, explaining in a systematic fashion the rules of law by means of general statements, rather than simply stating the legislative rules in force, was contemplated at one time in the United States and did in a number of American states come to fruition: there are *civil codes* in California,[36] North Dakota, South Dakota, Georgia and

---

[36] Harrison (M. E.), "The First Half-Century of the California Civil Code," 10 Cal. L.Rev., 185 (1922).

Montana; in 25 states there are codes of civil procedure; and whereas only some have codes of criminal procedure, in all states there are codes of criminal law. But here once again no mistake must be made. Even these codes are in no way the equivalent of French codes; they are interpreted altogether differently. In a Common law country legal rules which are not of judge-made origin are never considered entirely "normal"; the codes are thus treated much more like simple consolidations, sometimes successful and sometimes not, rather than as the starting-point for the elaboration and formulation of a new law as they have been in Romano-Germanic countries. In American or other Common law systems, the legislator promulgating a "code" is presumed to have intended to reproduce the old, judge-made legal rule. The text of the law does not really have any true meanaing until it has been judicially interpreted. It is thus altogether exceptional for a court to render a decision only by means of a straightforward application of the text of the law and without invoking some kind of judicial precedent.

The only state constituting an exception is Louisiana where the Romano-Germanic system has been preserved. Louisiana is therefore different because of the *way* in which it conceives of its codes, not *because* it has codes. In short, at least in its private law, it does not form part of the Common law family.[37]

418. Desire for uniformity of America law

The proliferation of enacted law poses a problem for all legal systems, but in the United States it is particular in one respect. There is some fear that the unity of the Common law will be endangered because of differences in the statutory provisions enacted by each state to correct or supplement the Common law. This danger—that legislation may destroy the uniformity of American law—did not arise in the nineteenth century when feelings of independence were still strong in each state and when the reforms enacted had more bearing on procedure than on substantive law. In the twentieth century, on the other hand, there is a much

---

[37] On the law of Louisiana, *cf.* the scholarly introduction by Dainow (J.) to his edition of the Civil Code of Louisiana (1947); *adde* Tucker (J.), "Tradition and Technique of Codification in the Modern World: the Louisiana Experience" 25 Louisiana L.Rev., 698–719 (1965).

greater awareness of this threat. Two methods have been concurrently used to combat it.

419. Uniform state laws

The first method has taken the form of proposing to the different states that they individually adopt uniform or model-laws on certain subjects where it is generally recognised to be eminently desirable from the practical point of view that there be legislative intervention. This work is carried on particularly by the National Conference of Commissioners for Uniform State Laws, a private organisation to which official representatives of each state are mandated[38] and, for the last 30 years, by another private institution working in co-operation with the first, the American Law Institute. A draft commercial code, containing 400 articles, was compiled in this way in 1952 and revised in 1958 and 1962,[39] as well as a code of consumer law. Model codes on criminal law and criminal procedure and the law of evidence have also been drawn up. These efforts have produced important results especially with respect to bills of exchange and the sale of goods. But progress is difficult and slow. First of all the uniform law is not always enacted and there is, of course, no guarantee that the uniform text will be interpreted in the same way in each of the enacting states. There is also some hesitation about modifying a text that may already be open to criticism for fear that the uniformity so laboriously achieved will be endangered. Quite obviously this first method cannot be relied upon to any great extent.

420. Development of federal law

In these circumstances therefore another possibility offers itself: that federal laws be enacted, or that there be an increased inter-

---

[38] Day (J. W.), "The National Conference of Commissioners on Uniform State Laws," 8 Fla. L.Rev. 276 *et seq.* (1955). The Conference met for the first time in 1892 on the suggestion of the American Bar Association; it took its present name in 1912 and since that date all states have been officially represented. The Conference only makes recommendations to the states. The series entitled *Uniform Laws Annotated* (15 vols.) indicates the texts that have in fact come into force in at least one state and the variants of such text such as enacted in others.

[39] On this code, see Farnsworth (E. A.), "Le droit commercial aux Etats-Unis," Rev. int. dr comparé (1962), p. 309; at the present time the code has been adopted in all the states and territories except Louisiana and Porto-Rico. On the whole, the individual states have little changed the code except for the 9th part, dealing with security, which calls for considerable alteration. A permanent Committee of Revision was established in 1961.

vention of the federal administration, in all those areas where uniformity of law is necessary. The general statements of the American Constitution, such as they have been interpreted by the United States Supreme Court, would provide the legitimate basis for such interventions where this may appear necessary. In modern times a considerable change in the respective jurisdictions of the state and the federal authorities has taken place, quite apart from any formal amendment to the Constitution. And it is principally by this means—the extension of the power of the federal authorities—that some success will finally be achieved in the realm of the uniformity of laws when this need is felt in the United States.

PART FOUR

OTHER CONCEPTIONS OF LAW AND
THE SOCIAL ORDER

421. Their significance

The three most important families of law in the modern world are unquestionably the Romano-Germanic, the Socialist and the Common law. They extend over the whole of Europe and the Americas, thus grouping together the most powerful and, economically, the most highly developed nations on earth. They have also had an enormous influence in Africa and Asia. There is virtually no country which has not received the principles of a European law in some measure, whether English, Romanist or Socialist.

However, these three families of law are closely linked to the development of European civilisation. They reflect a way of thinking and living which is western; they express ideas and embody institutions which have been formed in the European cultural and historical context. Their adoption in America offered almost no difficulties because no indigenous civilisation could rival them. The only problem was their adaptation to a different geographical milieu.

It has been altogether different in Asia and Africa, as well as Indonesia. Here European penetration did not take place in uninhabited areas as in America, or where the existing population was ready to accept the European way of life as superior. In Asia, particularly, there were vast populations already established with forms of civilisation which could not be considered inferior to those of the West. In a large part of Africa and Asia the indigenous civilisations also had religious beliefs which could to a certain extent block the reception of western laws and legal concepts. How have traditional conceptions of law in these countries and European conceptions been harmonised, and with what success?

The object of Part Four is to draw attention to problems, fundamental at the present time, which have not been sufficiently studied in this connection. The time has passed when it can be thought that the only valid way of thinking is that known to the West.

Muslim law and the laws of India, the Far East, Africa and the Malagasy Republic (Madagascar) will be considered in four separate titles. These laws, it should hardly be necessary to emphasise, do not in themselves make up a *family* of laws. Not one of them bears any relation to any of the others. The sole justification for grouping them together in the fourth part of this work is the fact that all of them are based upon conceptions of law and the social order which are altogether different from those prevailing in the West. A study of them shows us that western modes of thought have neither universial application nor an uncontested sway in the modern world.

TITLE I

MUSLIM LAW

422. The close link between law and religion

Unlike the laws studied earlier, Muslim law is not an independent branch of knowledge or learning. It is only one of the facets of Islamic religion itself. This religion includes first of all a theology which establishes dogma and states exactly what a Muslim must believe, and it also includes the *shar'* (or *sharī'a*)[1] which lays down rules of behaviour for believers. The shar' or sharī'a—literally "the way to follow"—constitutes what can be called Muslim law. It specifies how the Muslim should conduct himself in accordance with his religion, without making any distinction in principle between duties towards others (civil obligations, alms-giving) and those towards God (prayers, fasting, etc.).[2] It is therefore centred on the idea of man's obligations or duties rather than on any rights he might have.[3] The real sanction for these obligations is the state of sin into which the believer neglecting them will fall. For this reason, Muslim law often shows very little interest in civil sanctions attached to the violation of its prescribed rules. For the same reason, the law is only applicable to dealings between Muslims. The religious principle upon which it is based gives way when non-Muslims are involved.

The fundamental principle of Islam is that of an essentially theocratic society, in which the state is only of value as the servant of revealed religion. Instead of simply proclaiming moral principles or articles of dogma to which Muslim communities would

---

[1] The transliteration of Arabic words in general observes that employed by Schacht (J.), *An Introduction to Islamic Law* (1964) and Coulson (N.J.), *A History of Islamic Law* (1964).
[2] Compare Ulpian's definition (D.I. 1, 10.2, *De justitia et jure*): *Jurisprudentia est divinarum atque humanarum rerum notitia: justi atque injusti scientia.*
[3] The laws of the Far East, Hindu and Jewish law are all based on the same fundamental idea. *Cf.* Silberg (M.), "Law and Morals in Jewish Jurisprudence." 75 Harv. L. Rev., p. 306 (1961).

455

have to make their laws conform, Muslim jurists and theologians have built up a complete and detailed law on the basis of divine revelation—the law of an ideal society which one day will be established in a world entirely subject to Islamic religion.[4] Muslim law can only be really understood by someone with a minimum general knowledge of Islamic religion and the civilisation to which it is so closely connected. At the same time, no student of Islam can afford to ignore Muslim law. Like Judaism, Islam is essentially a religion of the law. "Islamic Law," writes H. A. R. Gibb, "was the most far-reaching and effective agent in moulding the social order and the community life of the Muslim peoples . . . [t]he moral authority of the Law . . . held the social fabric of Islam compact and secure through all the fluctuations of political fortune."[5] Its influence has been felt in almost all aspects of social and economic life as well as in all branches of literature. And according to Bergsträsser, it is "the epitome of the true Muslim spirit, the most decisive expression of Islamic thought, the nucleus of Islam."[6]

423. The law's structure

The science of Muslim law, *fikh* (or *fiqh*), is generally divided into two major parts. One is the "roots," the doctrine of the sources (*usūl*) which explains by what methodology or procedure and on what basis the body of rules making up the *shar'* or Divine Law was established. The other is the doctrine of the "branches" (*furū*), containing the systematic elaboration of the basic categories and rules of Muslim law. In its organisation, classifications and ideas Muslim law is altogether original compared to the systems of law studied so far. These differences in organisation, however, will not be emphasised here and we shall limit ourselves to presenting a brief survey of the theory of the sources of Muslim law. It will then be seen just how adaptable to the conditions of the modern world, in spite of its apparent inflexibility, Muslim law really is. Finally, a general description of the laws of various contemporary Muslim nations will be given.

---

[4] On the conditions in which this law was developed, *cf.* Schacht (J.), *An Introduction to Islamic Law* (1964), pp. 6–111.

[5] Gibb (H. A. R.), *Mohammedanism. An Historical Survey* (1953), pp. 9–11.

[6] Bergsträsser (G.), *Grundzüge des Islamischen Rechts* (edited by J. Schacht, 1935), p. 1.

CHAPTER I

IMMUTABLE BASIS OF MUSLIM LAW

424. Various sources of law

There are four sources of Muslim law: the Koran (*Qur'ān*), the sacred book of Islam; the *Sunna*, the traditional or model behaviour of the Prophet, God's Messenger; the *ijmā'* or consensus of scholars of the Muslim community; and the *kiyās* (or *qiyās*), juristic reasoning by analogy.

425. The Koran and the Sunna

Muslim civilisation, and therefore its law, are based on the Koran, the sacred book of Islam, which is the collection of Allah's revelations to the last of his prophets and messengers, Muhammad (570–632). The Koran is unquestionably the primary source of Muslim law. It is clear however that its juridical provisions are inadequate as a statement of Muslim personal relations and some of the basic institutions of Islam are not even mentioned in it.

The *Sunna* contains the way of life and conduct of the Prophet, whose example serves as a guide for believers. It is made up of the collected traditions, or *hadith*, of the acts and statements of Muhammad handed down through an uninterrupted chain of intermediaries. In the ninth century A.D., two great doctors of Islam, Al-Bukārī (810–870) and the Muslim (820–875), undertook detailed research and verification of the traditions in order to establish the authentic *hadith* of the Prophet. Their work and that of others in the same period laid the solid foundation of the Muslim faith, even though it is now admitted that some of the *hadith* collected are of questionable authenticity in so far as their connection with Muhammad is concerned.

426. The ijmā'

The third source of Muslim law is the *ijmā'*, the unanimous agreement of legal scholars. Neither the Koran nor the *Sunna*—

and in spite of the latter's extended form—could answer all questions. To remedy this, and to explain some apparent discrepancies in their teachings, the doctrine of the infallibility of the Muslim community, when it is in unanimous agreement, was developed. "My community," says one *hādith*, "will never agree upon an error." And according to another "What Muslims find to be just is just in God also." *Ijmā'*, based on these two maxims, has permitted recognition of the authority of solutions which are not derived directly from the Koran or the *Sunna*.

In order that a rule of law be admitted by *ijmā'*, it is not necessary that the mass of the faithful support it, nor need it represent the unanimous feeling of all members of the community. *Ijmā'* has nothing to do with the "custom" of our western laws. The unanimity required is that of competent persons—those whose special role is to discover and reveal the law, that is, the legal scholars of Islam (*fukahā'*). "The scholars are the heirs of the prophets." By amalgamating tradition, custom and practice to form either a rule of law, a principle or an institution, the agreement of Islamic doctors and legal scholars gives the legal solution, thus unanimously accepted, the real force of juridical truth.

427. Muslim rites

It should be noted that the unanimity required of the exponents of *fikh* in order that a solution be accepted as part of Muslim law is not an unblemished unanimity. "The differences of opinion existing in my community," according to one *hādith*, "are a manifestation of the grace of God." In Islam the rule of unanimity makes allowances for certain differences, although these are really of secondary importance compared to what is universally accepted. Within the Muslim community different schools (*madhhab*) are admitted. They are most commonly called "rites," and each maintains a particular interpretation of Muslim law.

These rites came into existence in the second century of the Hijra.[1] Some are considered orthodox and others heretical, just as within the Christian world there are some Christian rites accepted and others condemned by Rome.

There are four orthodox rites or "*sunnites*" named after those

---

[1] Or *Hegira*; the flight of Muhammad from Mecca to Medina in A.D. 622, from which date the Muhammadan era is calculated.

on whose teachings they are founded: the *Hanafī* rite founded by Imām Abū Hanīfa of Kufa (696–767); the *Malīkī* rite founded by Imām Mālik of Medina (715–795); the *Shāfi'ī* rite founded by Imām Al Shāfi'ī (767–820), and the *Hanbalī* rite founded by Imām Ibn Hanbal (780–855). The *Hanafī* rite has the greatest number of followers and has spread into Turkey, the U.S.S.R., Afghanistan, Jordan, Syria, Pakistan and India. The *Malīkī* rite is that of the Muslims of North and West Africa. The *Shāfi' ī* rite prevails in Malaysia, Indonesia and on the eastern coast of Africa, and has also spread to Pakistan. In Arabia the *Hanbalī* rite is dominant.

Apart from the orthodox rites, the principal rite is the *Shī'ite*,[2] predominating in Iran and Irak. The Shī'ites differ from the Sunnites in their concept of constitutional law or the caliphate, in which they would seem to perpetuate the previous monarchical traditions of Persia. In addition, the *Wahhābī* rite is followed in Saudi Arabia, and the *Abadī* (*Ibādī*) or *Harigite* rite in M'zab, in Djerba on the eastern coast of Africa and in Zanzibar.

Differences between these rites exist on many points of detail. On matters of principle, however, their resemblance is most striking. Thus, on the occasion of some specific act it is permitted to place oneself under the authority of a rite other than that usually adhered to. One may also change rites and a sovereign can order judges to adjudicate, either in general or in respect of a specific question according to a particular rite not that of the majority of the population. The administration of justice in Egypt, for example, is carried on under the Hanafī rite even though most of the population adheres to the Malīkī rite.[3]

428. Practical significance of ijmā'

The three principal sources of Muslim law are the Koran, the *Sunna* and *ijmā'*, but they are not of equal importance. The Koran and the *Sunna* are fundamental sources, since the rules of the *sharī'a*, drawn up by the doctors, are based on them.[4] Today, how-

---

[2] The arab word *shī'a* means "partisan." The Shī'ites are so called because they are partisans of Aly, the son-in-law of the Prophet.

[3] Linant de Bellefonds (Y.), "Immutabilité du droit musulman et réformes législatives en Egypte," Rev. int. dr. comparé (1955), p. 5 at p. 17.

[4] On the historical formation of Muslim law, *cf.* Schacht (J.), *An Introduction to Islamic Law* (1964) and his *The Origins of Muhammadan Jurisprudence* (1950) and Coulson (N.J.), *A History of Islamic Law* (1964).

ever, they are simply historical sources; the judge no longer has to consult the Koran and the *Sunna* directly because they have been infallibly and definitively interpreted by the *ijmā'*. Nowadays, as a result, one has only to consult the book of *fikh* approved by *ijmā'* in order to study Muslim law. "As C. Snouck-Hurgronje has so aptly said," writes Edouard Lambert, "the *ijmā'* is at the present time the only dogmatic basis of Muslim law. The Koran and the *Sunna* are nothing more than historical bases. The contemporary judge does not seek reasons for his decision in the Koran or in collections of tradition, but in the books containing the solutions ratified by *ijmā'*. Any Kādī (*i.e.* Islamic judge) who would have the temerity to interpret passages of the Koran or evaluate the authority of the hadīths on his own initiative would be acting disrespectfully towards orthodox belief, in the same way as a Roman Catholic would who took it upon himself to interpret the meaning of texts cited by the Church in support of its dogmas . . . This third sources of Muslim law, the *ijmā'*, is of exceptional practical significance. Whatever the origin of *fikh*, it owes its present applicability to its ratification by the *ijmā'*."[5]

429. The taklid

This was not always the case. Until the fourth century of the Hijra (622 A.D.) a great effort (*ijtihād*) was made to interpret the sources of Divine Law and to state in detail the rules applicable to Muslims. In fact, Muslim law owes little to its scriptural sources; it is primarily based on doctrine that began to develop only after the establishment of the Abbasid caliphate (750 A.D.).[6] However, the possibilities of interpreting the sources gradually diminished until finally in the fourth century of the Hijra, the legitimacy of further research was denied. At this period in the general history of Islam, when political divisions occurred in the previously united Muslim world, the "door of endeavour" (*bāb-al-ijtihād*) was finally shut. The development of Divine Law was complete. It was thenceforth the duty of Muslims to observe the *taklid*: that is, they were to "recognise the authority" of doctors of past generations; the per-

---

[5] Lambert (E.), *Fonction du droit civil comparé* (1903), p. 328.
[6] Chehata (Ch.), *Etudes de droit musulman* (1970). It is difficult, however, to agree with this author when he draws the conclusion from this observation that Muslim law is neither a religious nor a canonical law (p. 48).

sonal interpretation of sources was forbidden. As a result, the same works have been used to teach Muslim law for centuries. Even the most recent authors are adding nothing new to the system. The entire work of legal science consists wholly of expounding the recognised classics. An author today is only permitted to collect, compare, clarify and explain solutions proposed by the great doctors of the past without changing or developing them in any way. How could it be otherwise? The authors' opinions are not deducted from reason as those of western authors are meant to be. They are based on revelation. In such circumstances it is natural that they be unchangeable, and this immutability is equally respected by both the Sunni community and the Shī'ites, although the latter do not theoreticaly recognise the *taklid*.

The *fikh* is a doctrinal system, based on the authority of sources which are either revealed or of recognised infallibility. Muslim law, established according to a tenth century teaching, is immutable; Islam recognises no authority as having the power to modify it. The rulers of Muslim states cannot create law or legislate; they may only make administrative regulations within limits defined by Muslim law and covering subjects which do not overlap or conflict with it.

430. Analogical reasoning

No matter how resourceful the legal doctors' casuistry may have been, it is obvious that they could not provide for all the possible situations of everyday life. Since Muslim law is intended to be complete—a system supplying the answers to all questions—some means had to be found whereby any future situation could be dealt with should the book of *fikh* offer no ready-made answer.

It was agreed that analogical argument or reasoning (*kiyās*) should be admitted, and although this represented a simply *logical* process the Muslim community made it a source of law. Some sects reject, on fundamentalist grounds, this method, but however vehement opposition to it may be in theory, such rejection has almost no practically important results in fact. It merely leads to the conclusion that solutions contained in the interpreted texts are "implicitly understood" by some, while others look upon them as being "deduced by analogy."

Analogical reasoning can only be considered as a means of interpreting and applying the law. Muslim law is based on the principle of authority. If, by admitting analogical argument, room has been made for a rational means of interpretation, it is nonetheless obvious that it cannot be used to create basic rules of absolute value which would be comparable to the traditional rules established in the tenth century. Muslim and Common law jurists therefore differ, in that the latter can develop new rules through the technique of making distinctions.[7] The Muslim jurist's position and psychological outlook differ even more from those of the Romanist jurist. He is accustomed, writes Milliot, "to think that law is made up of individual solutions to particular cases, handed down from day to day in relation to the special needs of the moment, rather than of general principles set forth *a priori* from which the appropriate inference will be drawn for each fresh situation. The Muslim jurist resists abstraction, systematization and codification. He will avoid generalization and even definition."[8]

With the help of analogical reasoning, it is usually possible to discover from the rules of the *fikh* the required solution in any particular case. On the other hand, one cannot hope to adapt Muslim law by this means to the needs of a modern society. The doctors of Islam are not however concerned with this. "The *fikh* is not intended to reflect realilty; rather, it is like a beacon guiding the faithful towards the religious ideal, and often this is in a direction in which they are not progressing. The idea of adapting the *fikh* to contemporary conditions is completely foreign to the system."[9]

431. Rejection of other sources

For this reason Islam regards with suspicion, and generally condemns, forms of reasoning which enable the law to evolve. In particular, Muslim law has refused to admit that a legal solution might be based on a believer's personal opinion or individual reasoning (*ra'y*). Because Muslim law is based on religious tenets, is divinely inspired and essentially non-rational, the support which derives from reason or equity would be insufficient to make such individual reasoning authoritative.

---

[7] For the Muslim jurist there can only be interpretation—and never creation—of law: *Recht-sauslegung*, not *Rechtsfindung*.

[8] Milliot (L.), "La pensée juridique de l'Islam," Rev. int. dr. comparé, 1954, pp. 441, 448.

[9] Bousquet (G. H.), *Précis de droit musulman* (3rd ed., 1954).

Nor has the possibility of departing in special cases from a general rule of the *fikh*, in the name of public order or justice, ever been admitted.[10] There is, too, no agreement about recognising that certain solutions in the *fikh* should be linked to the continued existence of the circumstances in which they were originally established, although the Shāfiʿī and Hanafī have sometimes followed this line of reasoning.

432. Characteristics of Muslim law

A few additional observations must be made about the theory of sources of Muslim law described above.

Certain characteristics of Muslim law are explained by the fact that as a science it was formed and stablised during the Middle Ages: thus the archaic nature of some of its institutions, its case-by-case outlook, and its lack of systematisation.[11] This is not however the most important factor. The essential point is the complete originality of Muslim law, by its vary nature, in the light of the other legal systems in general and of Canon law in particular.

Its originality derives generally from the fact that the Muslim legal system is based on the Koran, a book of revelation, and as a system it must therefore be considered entirely independent of all others which do not have the same source. Any particular resemblance to solutions in other systems can be no more than pure coincidence according to the orthodox Muslim view, because there can never be any question of Muslim law having borrowed from a foreign system of thought.[12] On the other hand, the influence of Muslim law on the laws of Europe appears to have been almost neglible.

433. Comparison with Canon law

Muslim law is also original when compared with the Canon law of Christianity. Like Canon law, it is the law of a church in the original sense (*ecclesia*): that of a community of faithful. But apart

---

[10] *Cf.*, however, Chehata (Ch.), "L'équité en tant que source du droit hanafite," *Studia islamica* (1966), Vol. 25, pp. 123–138.
[11] Chehata (Ch.), "Logique juridique en droit musulman," *Studia islamica* (1965), Vol. 23, pp. 5–25.
[12] On the influence of the law of conquered countries on the formation of Islamic law, in its first century, according to a non-Muslim author, *cf.* Schacht (J.), *An Introduction to Islamic Law* (1964), pp. 20 *et seq.*

from this similarity there are very fundamental differences. Muslim law, down to its finest detail, is an integral part of Islamic religion and of the revelation that it represents. Consequently, no authority in the world is qualified to change it. Not to obey Muslim law is a sin leading to punishment in another world; he who disputes a solution of Muslim law is a heretic and thereby excludes himself from the community of Islam. Finally, a Muslim's life in society is only governed by the rules of his religion, of which Muslim law is an integral part. In all these ways Muslim law differs from the Canon law of Christian society. The spread of Christianity originally took place in a highly civilised society where law enjoyed great prestige. It proclaimed new dogmas and moral principles, but it was not interested in the actual organisation of society. "My kingdom is not of this world," said Christ. And the Gospels confirmed the validity of secular principles: "Render unto Caesar the things which are Caesar's" (Matt. XXII, 21). Not only did the Catholic Church feel it unnecessary to develop a Christian law to take the place of Roman law; it did not consider itself authorised to do so. Neither Saint Paul (*d.* 67 A.D.) nor Saint Augustine (354–430) attempted to develop a Christina law; in fact they advocated the decline of law through the use of arbitration and the observance of brotherly love.[13] Canon law was not a complete legal system designed to replace Roman law. It complemented Roman law or other "private" laws, never anything more, and regulated subjects not covered by these laws such as Church organisation, the sacraments, and canonical procedure.[14] In addition, Canon law is in no sense a revealed law. Although it is most certainly based on the revealed principles of Christian faith and morality, it is the work of man and not the Word of God. The Christian who violates its rules is not necessarily subject to punishment in the next world. As long as the immutable principles of dogma are respected, ecclesiastical authorities are allowed to make changes to improve or adapt it to particular circumstances of time and place. The Church of Rome itself has different Canon

[13] Similarly, the Koran repeatedly emphasises the merits of forgiveness and the remittance or abandonment of claims. However, a more realistic attitude finally prevailed in the Islamic, as in the Christian, world. Schacht (J.), *Esquisse d'une histoire du droit musulman* (1952), p. 13.

[14] Before the Church States disappeared in 1870, there had always been a private law distinct from Canon law. The same holds true today in the Vatican City State.

law codes for adherents to the Latin or Eastern rites. Christian Canon laws have developed enormously over the centuries and continue to do so at the present time.

Under these conditions, Roman law was able to spread throughout the West without conflicting with the Christian religion. Roman law was taught in most of the universities approved by papal bulls. The situation, quite obviously, is totally different in Muslim countries where the law is part of the revealed Islamic religion. The establishment of a purely secular law in these countries is inconceivable. Here the orthodox view excludes any law which does not strictly conform to the rules of the *shari'a*.

434. Inadaptability of fikh to modern society

Since its development was arrested in the tenth century, the *fikh* as a body of law is manifestly incapable of adapting to modern societies. It does not anticipate certain institutions seemingly necessary in these societies. While many of its rules were probably quite adequate in their own time, today they seem outmoded and sometimes even shocking. The inability of the *fikh* to adapt to modern ideas and conditions has thus created a problem, particularly in those countries with a Muslim majority which have abandoned their passive attitude and have looked since the last century to western nations as a model, attracted not only by their material prosperity but by their political ideas and moral concepts as well. Can Muslim countries modernise themselves without rejecting tradition? And what role can the *fikh* continue to play in these new societies?

CHAPTER II

ADAPTATION OF MUSLIM LAW TO THE
MODERN WORLD

435. Permanent authority of Muslim law

What has just been said may give the impression that Muslim law belongs to a distant past. This is not so, however, Muslim law remains one of the great legal systems of the modern world, dealing with human affairs of a total Muslim population in various countries of over 500 million people.

Many states of Muslim population continue to affirm in their laws, and often in their constitutions, their adherence to the principles of Islam. The state's submission to these principles is explicitly stated in the constitutions of Morocco, Tunisia, Syria, the Islamic Republic of Mauritania, Iran, Afghanistan, Yemen, and Pakistan. The civil codes of Egypt (1948), Syria (1949) and Iraq (1951) instruct judges to fill any gaps in the law according to the principles of Muslim law; the constitution of Iran and the laws of Indonesia provide for a procedure intended to assure the conformity of institutions to the principles of Muslim law. And most of these countries wish to modernise, and are rapidly doing so. How can the apparent passivity of Muslim law be reconciled with the development which includes the establishment of new types of political systems and progressive reforms in the field of private law?

436. Possibilities of adapting to the modern world

The immutable nature of Muslim law cannot be denied, but it must also be realised that it is a very resourceful system. Its flexibility should be emphasised just as much as its immutability. The two characteristics are in no way compatible. It is too easily forgotten that in western countries the law for a long time was considered unchangeable, even though it was not sacrosanct. Civil authorities, such as, for example, the kings of France even at the height of their power, had no legal right to alter its content. In western countries, however, means were found for incorporating new solutions when the need was felt without undermining the law. The interventions of the Roman praetor and the English chancellor are the most obvious examples. *Lettres de rescision* and the exercise of prerogative were also employed without altering the theoretical basis of fundamental legal principles.

The same is true of Muslim law. It is immutable, but it leaves sufficient room for the operation of custom, the right of parties to contract and administrative regulation, such that it is possible to arrive at arrangements which will enable a modern society to be developed without prejudice to the law. Only in exceptional cases will the archaic nature of certain institutions or rules in Muslim law constitute obstacles.

437. Recourse to custom

For centuries many Muslim societies have been, and still are, living mainly according to custom while recognising the merit and authority of Muslim law as an article of faith. Custom is not incorporated in the *fikh*, nor has it ever been a part of Muslim law itself. This could only have resulted had one of the basic merits of Muslim law itself been abandoned—its uniform application to the whole community of believers. But while custom is not part of the *fikh*, this does not mean that the law condemns it in any way. It looks upon custom very much as some western laws regard the clause of *amiable composition* in an arbitration agreement[1] or upon the powers of conciliation or equity sometimes exercised by a judge. Parties are often allowed to arrange their dealings and settle their differences without recourse to strict law. The spread of Islam could not have taken place without this liberal attitude which did not require believers to give up a way of life embodied in custom. It goes without saying of course that some customs can be "irregular" from the viewpoint of Muslim law. But a great many are not, and such is the case of those which simply complement Muslim law in matters not covered by it—for example, customs dealing with the amount and forms of payment of dowries, those on the use of running water shared by landowners, and a number

---

[1] In virtue of which arbitrators are not bound to base their decision on strict rules of law.

of commercial usages.[2] It should also be remembered that Muslim law divides all of man's actions into five categories: obligatory, recommended, indifferent, blame-worthy and forbidden. Custom cannot order behaviour which is forbidden by law or prohibit that which the law makes obligatory; but it can deal with conduct which is merely recommended or permitted by law, and it may also forbid something which is blame-worthy or simply permitted by law.

438. The use of contract

Muslim law has very few binding provisions and it thus leaves wide scope to individual initiative and personal freedom. If so desired, it is therefore possible to modernise the rules of social life by using the concept of contract without being unfaithful to Islam. "There is no crime in drawing up agreements apart from those forbidden by law," says a *hadīth*. Through the use of contract very considerable changes can be made in the rules suggested, but not imposed, by Muslim law.

By virtue of this principle, Muslim countries allow husbands and wives to stipulate at marriage that the wife will be allowed to exercise her husband's prerogative and, therefore, will be at liberty to repudiate herself, or that she will be able to do so if the husband does not remain monogamous. The law on marriage and the family has undergone considerable change as a result of such contracts, particularly in Syria. The possible impact of such derogations is in some cases subject to doubt. Unlike the Muslims of the Shī'ite rite, the Sunnites have not, for example, admitted the possibility of stipulating some conditions such as the merely temporary nature of marriage or the establishment of a community of property between husband and wife. The possibilities for developing Muslim law through private contract are nonetheless considerable. It is an easy and classic method to assume contractual intent on the part of individuals, even though in reality this may be a pure fiction. Muslim judicial decisions have sometimes resorted to such stratagems. In Java, for instance, the religious judge can assume

---

[2] Rives (G.), "Le problèmes fondamentaux du droit rural afghan," Rev. int. droit comparé (1963), pp. 63–84. It is also noted that Muslim practice is the basis of certain institutions of commercial law, such as endorsement on a bill of exchange (*aval* in French law, from the Arabic *hawāla*) and cheques (from the Arabic *sakk*, "written document"): Schacht (J.), *An Introduction to Islamic Law* (1964), p. 78.

the existence of a commercial partnership between husband and wife in order to exclude the matrimonial regime of separation of property provided by the Koran and to apply the customary system.[3]

439. Legal stratagems and fictions

Aside from custom and contract, there is another possible means of avoiding archaic solutions: the use of legal devices or stratagems (*hiyal*) and fictions.[4] The *sharī'a*, highly formalist, requires that the letter of the law rather than its spirit be respected. Many formal rules of Muslim law can thus be rendered ineffectual provided they are not directly violated. Thus, polygamy and the husband's repudiation of his wife are permitted. One can, however, without changing such rules, discourage such practices—by awarding the wife substantial damages if she is unjustly repudiated by her husband, or, when the latter, having entered into a polygamous union, does not treat her equally with his other wives. Loans bearing interest are forbidden by Muslim law; but this prohibition can be evaded by means of a double sale, or by giving the creditor as security the enjoyment of some revenue producing property. It is also possible to hold that the ban on interest loans applies only to physical persons; banks, savings societies and companies will therefore be exempt from this rule. Renting land is also prohibited; but this problem is circumvented by substituting a concept of association to that of lease. Again, contracts dependent on uncertain contingencies and insurance contracts in particular are forbidden; but only the person who collects the premium commits a sin. One may, therefore, take out insurance with an insurance company or with a non-Muslim. The actual prohibition on insurance disappears in the case of mutual insurance; here the emphasis is laid on the pledge of solidarity implicit in this operation, making the contract charitable in nature—a quality which, far from being forbidden, is recommended.

---

[3] Bousquet (G. H.), *Précis de droit musulman* (3rd ed., 1954), no. 22.
[4] Schacht (J.), *An Introduction to Islamic Law* (1964), pp. 78 *et seq.* refers to them as the use of legal means for extra-legal ends that could not be achieved directly through use of the *sharī'a*; Roussier (J.), "L'immutabilité du droit musulman et le développement économique," *Annales africaines* (1962), pp. 229–233. *Cf.*, as to Canon law, LeBras (G.), *Histoire du droit et des Institutions de l'Eglise en Occident. I: Prolégomènes* (1955), p. 70.

440. Intervention of authority

A technique continually used to adapt Muslim law to modern conditions is the intervention of the ruling person or body. At first glance such intervention would seem excluded by Muslim legal theory. The sovereign power—whether it be a monarch or a parliamentary body—is not the master but the servant of law, according to the Islamic concept. He therefore cannot legislate. However, while he may have no legislative power, the sovereign can shape state policy (*siyāsa*) and has the special responsibility of watching over judicial administration. Muslim law admits the legitimacy of regulatory measures taken by the authorities in this respect and wide use has always been made of it.

Even operating within the stricter orthodoxy, absolute rulers have thus been able to exert an influence. They have ordered Muslim judges (*kādīs*) to apply, for example, the rules of one or another rite in some subject matter such that, in many countries, it has been possible for women to obtain judicial divorces within the framework of the various cases allowed for in a range of rites. They have made access to the courts subject to certain conditions and thus, in Turkey, for example, a concept of extinctive prescription, otherwise unknown to Muslim law, has been introduced by way of prohibiting judges from hearing cases where the title to property has existed for fifteen years. More recently, the Egyptian legislature declared that the courts should not deal with matrimonial litigation where the marriage had not been civilly recorded or where one of the spouses had not attained marriageable age. The police can also turn a blind eye to the practice of consuming alcohol beverages in Algeria, even though the law prohibits it in respect of Muslims.

In other cases, strict orthodoxy is however abandoned. In addition, therefore, to measures which are irreproachable from the point of view of religious precepts (*nizām*), sovereigns have prescribed others (*kānūm*)[5] which have exceeded the competence allowed them by these same principles. Although theologians are traditionally vehement about the impiety of civil society, their vehemence is mitigated as long as there is continued theoretical admission of Muslim law's superiority and excellence.

---

[5] The technical term for secular laws of the Islamic countries in the Near East, Schacht (J.), *op. cit.*, p. 87.

441. Modernist tendency

The development of Muslim law was arrested in the tenth century with the closing of the "door of endeavour." This was the result of fortuitous circumstances, and came about in an effort to overcome a crisis which threatened the Muslim world with a schism. The eclipse of the Abbasid caliphate upon the Mogul capture of Bagdad in 1258 reinforced this conservative tendency. There are those in Islam today who doubt whether the restrictions placed on the development of the *fikh* at that time should be fully maintained. They contend that Islamic orthodoxy does not require it. They point out that, in fact, very few rules of Muslim law are based on divine revelation which, moreover, is only indicative of orthodox social behaviour of the seventh century and not that of today. For the most part, Muslim law is the work of medieval jurists whose reasoning processes are now out of date. Referring to the practice of the first few centuries of Islam, they point out that those who founded the rites always took special circumstances into account, and made a place in their system for such notions as the purpose of the law, the public good and necessity. They see no risk involved in returning to these principles today, on condition that strict rules and methods of interpretation are imposed for developing solutions necessary to the public good and which will be suitable from the orthodox point of view. They consider the danger now threatening Muslim law is not so much the splitting of the Islamic world, as in the past, but the risk that the *fikh* because of its inflexibility might become a completely idealistic theory of duties. Its significance would then be merely theological and only of use to a few pious scholars, while everyday life would be governed by laws which would be increasingly removed from truly Muslim concepts.

The present-day tendency to reopen the "door of endeavour" has occurred in several countries. This trend is quite obviously attractive to those who are accustomed to rationalist thought and who find it difficult to accept the traditional argument of authority. Most Muslims, however, do not appear to be ready to come over to such a way of thinking. The centuries old approach cannot, in their eyes, be abandoned; departures from orthodoxy must be minimised and only undertaken with great caution. There is a visible danger in any attempt to rationalise and modernise Muslim law by reopening the "door of endeavour." If this trend gains ground, it is difficult to see how Muslim unity can be preserved in a world where the community of believers is spread throughout a variety of independent nations. For this reason it will probably be considered preferable to make use of the many other possibilities for adapting Muslim societies to modern life. These methods are perhaps outside Muslim law in the strict sense (such as custom, contracts, regulations), but they do not contradict it. They offer the advantage of not putting into question the traditionally accepted principles in which the unity of the community of the faithful is rooted.

CHAPTER III

LAW OF MUSLIM COUNTRIES

442. Muslim law is not applied on an integral basis

From Morocco to Indonesia, from the Soviet Socialist Republics of Central Asia and from Albania to Zanzibar and Guinea, over 500 million Muslims make up the majority of the population in some thirty countries, and they constitute large minorities in others. None of these countries is exclusively governed by Muslim law. Although its authority is proclaimed in principle, custom and legislation have everywhere added to or derogated from it.

Muslim law, a religous law, should not be confused with the positive laws of Muslim countries. To avoid misunderstanding, the latter should not even be referred to as Muslim law. Secular societies in Islam have never been identified with the religious society any more than they have in Christian countries. They have always lived according to customs or laws which, while probably generally based on principles of Muslim law and giving it an important place, have also deviated from strict orthodoxy and contradicted the principles and rules of Muslim canon law, in ways which varied according to the period, country and subject matter. Even at the time when the *fikh* enjoyed its greatest authority, not all its elements had the same practical value. In this *mélange* of legal provisions, moral and religious precepts, distinctions must always be made between "reality and Utopia, the genuine products of juridical life and the chimeras of theological imagination." It is partly because of this that the *fikh* only gradually took on the nature of a legal rule. During the period of conquest, the Umayyads (the first dynasty in Islam, 41–132 of the Hijra or A.D. 661–750) did not pay much attention to it, and the reception of the *fikh* as law in Islamic countries only took place under the theocratically-minded Abbasid caliphs.

443. Statut personnel and other subjects

Even then complete reception did not take place. Although in theory all branches of Muslim law are linked to Islamic religion with equal force, a distinction has been made in practice. The law of the family and persons, along with rules of ritual and religious behaviour, have always been considered the most important in the *shāri'a*. To the Muslim mind there is a particularly close connection between religion and these parts of the law making up the *statut personnel*. In fact, most of the Koran itself deals with this subejct.

The secularisation of other subjects, or at least some secularisation of them, was more easily admitted however. As understood by Muslim law, constitutional law has never been anything more than a pious hope. At an early stage both criminal and fiscal law ceased to be orthodox.[1] In the eyes of the theologians, however, those who govern are at fault if they deviate from the rules of the *shari'a* when dealing with these subjects. But no blame can be attached to the faithful who submit to rules prescribed by the authorities, because the Koran itself prescribes obedience to recognised civil authority. In any case, the faithful are dispensed from strict observance of the rules of law in cases of necessity.

444. Judicial organisation

The Muslim ideal, that the community of believers coincides exactly with secular society, has therefore never been achieved. And one factor in particular, the visible duality in the judicial system, offers significant proof of this.[2]

One or more types of court have always existed side by side with the court of the *kādī* established under the Umayyads, the only legitimate court according to Muslim law. These other courts apply the secular customs of the locality and regulations issued by the authorities, and their decisions deviate to some degree from the strict rules of Muslim law in matters such as police, market inspection, and the "equity" of the caliph or his deputies. Traditionally, these courts were seen as courts of exceptional jurisdiction. That

---

[1] Anderson (J. N. D.), *Islamic Law in the Modern World* (1959), pp. 15, 20; Schacht (J.), *An Introduction to Islamic Law* (1964), p. 76.

[2] Tyan (E.), *Histoire de l'organisation judiciaire en pays d'Islam*, 2 vols. (2nd ed., 1961); Schacht (J.), *op. cit.*, pp. 48 *et seq.*

situation changed in the last century. New state courts have been set up and their jurisdiction, at one time limited to the application of modern legislation, has, in the end, often been extended to the whole of the law. The jurisdiction of *kādīs* has diminished correspondingly.

445. Characteristics of contemporary development

Three noteworthy phenomena have occurred in the law of Muslim countries during the nineteenth and twentieth centuries. The first was the westernisation of the law in many subject matters. The second was the codification of subjects which had not undergone that westernisation. The third and most recent is the elimination by some countries of special courts that were previously responsible for the application of Muslim law.

446. Westernisation of law

Muslim law has always held that civil authorities have the power to regulate society for purposes of public order. For centuries this power was exercised with moderation, and in no way offended Islamic theologians. This has not been the case in a number of Muslim countries during the past 100 years, however. Intensive use has been made of this regulatory power, resulting in the development of entirely new branches of law. It matters little that this was brought about in some countries by the promulgation of codes[3] or, in others, upon the enactment of fundamental laws or through the work of the courts. The result was everywhere the same: in subjects which did not involve aspects of *statut personnel* (that range of topics including the law of persons, of family relations, and inheritance falling within the notion of a (personal law) or charitable or public benefactions, Muslim law was no longer applied. Rules taken from the Romano-Germanic or Common law families were preferred. Constitutional law, administrative law, private and commercial law, procedure, criminal law and labour law—all were westernised in many Muslim countries. In these sub-

---

[3] Velidedeoğlu (H. ▾.), "Le mouvement de codification dans les pays musulmans. Ses rapports avec les systèmes juridiques occidentaux," *Rapports généraux au Vᵉ Congrès international de droit comparé* (Brussels, August 4–9, 1958), t.I., pp. 131–178.

jects there are now few provisions still showing traces of Muslim law itself.[4]

447. Codification of statut personnel

The codification of subjects falling within this category has raised a much more delicate problem. That the ruling authority has no power to modify the rules on these topics of Muslim law is a principle so well established that it is beyond discussion. But was it open to them, on the other hand, to expound such rules systematically—without altering them—by carrying out a process of "consolidation?" Many doubted even that as a possibility.

There was a keen desire to undertake such work since it would have done away with the need to refer to the numerous and often obscure works published in Arabic, a language not understood in all Muslim countries. Traditionalists were quite aware, however, of the inherent danger of rationalising the law, and it was only very recently that the authorities have been allowed to legislate on questions of *statut personnel* and public benefactions, even though they aspired to nothing more than setting down rules which had already been admitted. Codes on *statut personnel* prepared by Muhammad Kadry Pasha in Egypt, by D. Santillana in Tunisia and by M. Morand in Algeria are still no more than private works, although their scholarship and strict conformity to the orthodox point of view have generally been recognised.[5] Even in Turkey the Ottoman Civil Code and Code of Civil Procedure, published from 1869–1876 under the title of *Mecelle* or *Mejelle*,[6] omitted the law of persons, the family and inheritance despite enormous inconvenience for the Turks who were obliged to consult sources written in Arabic for a knowledge of these subjects. In 1927 King Ibn Saud

---

[4] Chehata (Ch.), "Les survivances musulmanes dans la codification du droit civil égyptien," Rev. int. dr. comp. (1965), pp. 839–853. Mousseron (J. M.), "La réception au Proche-Orient du droit français des obligations," Rev. int. dr. comp. (1968), pp. 37–78. Tyan (M. E.), "Les rapports entre droit musulman et droit européen occidental en matière de droit civil," *Zeitschrift für vergleichends Rechtswissenschaft* (1963), pp. 18–28.

[5] *Code du statut personnel musulman et des successions d'après le rite hanéfite* (1875). *Avant-projet d'un code de droit musulman algérien* (1916).

[6] Onar (S. S.), "La codification d'une partie du droit musulman dans l'Empire ottoman, *Le Medjellé*," *Annales de la Faculté de droit d'Istanbul* (1954), Vol. 4, pp. 90–128. The Mecelle was translated into French by G. Young, in the sixth volume of his *Corps de droit ottoman* (1906). The spelling *Mecelle* is that of modern Turkish; the rendering *Medjelle* (or in French *Medjellé*) was current before Turkish began to be written in Latinised form. The Mecelle is still the basis of law in part of Jordan, and is applicable to a certain extent in Lebanon. Tedeschi (G.), "Le centenaire de la Mecelle," Rev. int. dr. comparé (1969), pp. 125–133.

of Saudi Arabia (1880–1953) announced his intention of establishing a code of Muslim law based on the teachings of Ibn Taymiyya (1263–1328), but in the face of opposition this project was abandoned.

Although the idea of codification was met with much hesitation, it finally did prevail in several countries. The first Muslim codification to be enacted for family law and the law of inheritance was the Iranian Civil Code promulgated between 1927 and 1935.[7] This example has since been followed by numerous countries. Codes on *statut personnel* have been promulgated in Syria, Tunisia,[8] Morocco[9] and Iraq[10] and in South Yemen; a similar code is also contemplated in the Constitution (art. 44) of the Islamic Republic of Mauritania.

Major reforms have taken place in Egyptian law on the subjects of *ab intestat* successions and public benefications, although not in the form of codes. The regimes of tutorship and *absentia* have been reformed by legislation in Algeria, that of family law in Jordan, and in Pakistan a complete reform of family law and inheritance was carried through.[11] In Iran, in 1979, divorce was reformed. Judicial intervention is required in cases of divorce otherwise than on the ground of mutual consent. As can be seen, the tendency once rejected is now gaining ground in many Muslim countries. But the earlier hesitation about codifying the law of "personal status" was perhaps not altogether unjustified. In spite of the great care taken to preserve appearances by insisting on the irreproachable character of these new compilations and obtaining the concurrence of religious authorities, there is not much doubt that in certain countries they have brought about major innovations which can scarcely be reconciled with orthodox Muslim law.

---

[7] For a French translation, see Aghababian (R.), *Législation iranienne actuelle* (2 vols., 1951). The Code's rules on the subject of personal status for non-Muslim Iranians are replaced by a series of appendices.

[8] Anderson (J. N. D.), "The Tunisian Law of Personal Status" 7 Int. & Comp. L.Q. 262 (1958).

[9] Anderson (J. N. D.), "Reforms on Family Law in Morocco" 2 *Journal of African Law* 146 (1958).

[10] Jwaideh (Z. E.), "The New Civil Code of Iraq" Geo. Wash. L.R., pp. 1–39, 127–186 at p. 176 (1953) (*Symposium on Muslim Law*).

[11] Coulson (N. J.), "Islamic Family Law: Progress in Pakistan" in Anderson (J. N. D.) ed., *Changing Law in Developing Countries* (1963), p. 240–257; Schacht (J.), "Problems of Modern Islamic Legislation" *Studia Islamica XII* (1960), pp. 99–129.

448. Decline of traditional courts

Whatever traditionalist critics may have to say about these compilations, they are evidently based on the fundamental concepts of
Muslim law. The same is not true, however, of the codes introduced within the last hundred years into many Muslim countries
regulating matters other than *statut personnel* and public benefactions. One need only look at the codes introduced in criminal law
and procedure, the law of civil obligations, commercial law and
civil procedure, as well as the development in administrative and
labour law. It is quite clear that they have been instrumental in
introducing western concepts into a number of countries.

The dualism so established was apparently viable as long as
there were distinct courts applying the two systems, which, by
their very nature, were opposed both in principle and method—
one based on comparative law and human reason and contiually
subject to change, while the other is based on premises of authority and faith and is by definition unchangeable. Today however
even the last bulwark has also finally given way. In an increasing
number of countries the same judges are called upon to apply both
"modern" law and Muslim law. The traditional Muslim courts
were done away with in British India in 1772 and in Turkey in
1924; nor do they exist any longer in Egypt, Tunisia, Bengal,
Algeria, Morocco, Guinea or Mali. Their jurisdiction has been
very much reduced in Indonesia.[12]

In some Arab countries the court of the *Kādī* was retained in
appearance but changed. It has become a state court able to hear
cases between Muslim as well as non-Muslims in matters of personal status. This change was made easier by reason of the fact
that non-Muslims in such countries generally apply the rules of
Muslim law in matter of inheritance. From now on, both the
sharī'a and modern codes will be applied in these countries, by jurists trained according to the rational and logical methods of western law. In Iran, after the Islamic revolution, the jurisdiction of
the traditional Muslim courts has been extended; the special civil
courts and the revolutionary courts (in criminal matters) set up are
both religious in character.

This new development is probably a greater threat to Muslim

[12] Leyser (J.), "Legal Developments in Indonesia" 3 Am. J. Comp. L. 399–411 (1954).

law than the promulgation of codes ever was. This observation certainly applies to India. Muslim law, administered by judges trained in the Common law tradition, has there become an independent legal system substantially different from pure Muslim law and now appropriately designated as Anglo-Muhammadan law.[13]

449. Diversity of existing laws

The positive laws of Muslim countries in their present form differ greatly among themselves because their social conditions and traditions are extremely varied. Numerous basic differences distinguish Egypt, Mali, Pakistan and Indonesia. Persia is proud of a tradition that it has not forgotten[14] despite the Islamisation by conquerors of another race. For these reasons it is difficult to have an over-all picture of the laws of Muslim countries.[15] Nevertheless there are some general characteristics worth noting, and three groups of countries can be distinguished.

The first group consists of countries with a majority Muslim population which have become socialist republics: Albania and the socialist republics of central Asia (Kazak S.S.R., Turkmen S.S.R., Uzbek S.S.R., Tadzhek S.S.R. and Kirgiz S.S.R.). In these states, founded on the principles of historical materialism of the Marxist-Leninist doctrine, Islamic religion is considered an error by the established authorities. There is absolutely no attempt made to preserve Muslim law, since it is looked upon as evidence of an obscurantism designed to safeguard an outmoded class structure. These republics now have a secular law that is designed to promote a new type of society based on principles quite different from those of Islam. There are now no courts to apply Muslim law, although it is still observed—almost clandestinely—outside the law by portions of the population which official policy would like to see separated from Islam.[16]

---

[13] Schacht (J.), *Problems of Modern Islamic Legislation, Studia Islamica XII* (1960), pp. 99–129. Husain (A.), *The History of Development of Muslim Law in British India* (1934).
[14] On ancient Persia law, cf. Von Thos (L.), "Das persische Rechtssystem," *Zeitschrift für vergleichende Rechtswissenschaft* (1909), Vol. 22, pp. 348–429; Nasr (T.), *Essai sur l'histoire du droit persan à l'éoque des Sassanides* (thesis, Paris, 1932).
[15] Bousquet (G. H.), *Du droit musulman et de son application effective dans le monde* (1949); Anderson (J. N. D.), *Islamic Law in Africa* (1954), and Islamic Law in the Modern World (1959); Schacht (J.), "Islamic Law in Contemporary States" 8 Am. J. Comp. L. 133–147 (1959).
[16] Bennigsen (A.), Lemercier-Quelquejay (Ch.), *L'Islam en Union soviétique* (1968).

Unlike this first group, the second is made up of countries the least influenced by modern ideas. The most typical examples are the countries of the Arabian peninsula (Saudi Arabia, Arab Republic of Yemen, The People's Socialist Republic of Yemen, the Persian Gulf emirates),[17] Afghanistan and Pakistan. These countries are theoretically governed by Muslim law, but in fact are under customary law which, while admitting the superiority and excellence of Muslim law, sometimes differs greatly from it.

The third group consists of states in which Muslim law has, as in the previous groups, been more or less amalgamated with custom, but applies in its preserved state to matters of *statut personnel*, public benefactions and, occasionally, land law. Otherwise "modern" law has been adopted to govern new social relationships.

The last group can again be divided into two sub-groups, according to whether the modern law in point is based on the Common law (Pakistan, India, Bengal, Malaya, Northern Nigeria), the French System (French-language African states, Arab-speaking states other than the Sudan, and Iran), or the Dutch model (Indonesia). The Sudan is a special case. In this country an ordinance on civil justice of 1900 stated that the courts were to turn to "justice, equity and good conscience" to fill gaps in the law. Through this device many rules of English law were in fact received.[18] But, in order to be more in line with other Arab-speaking countries, the Sudan adopted codes on the Egyptian model in 1971 and 1972 and thus appeared to have repudiated its early English influence. This reform has not, however, been wholly successful and is, at the present time, under reconsideration.[19]

Among countries of Muslim population, Turkey most certainly occupies a special position because it is a non-Arab country which has close political and economic ties with western Europe. From the strict legal point of view, however, Turkey probably differs less from other Muslim countries now than it seemed 50 years ago. The

---

[17] Except in Kuweit, where a code of commercial law containing a chapter on the law of contract was published in 1963, and the idea of promulgating a full code of private law was abandoned.

[18] Guttman (E.), "The Reception of the Common Law in the Sudan" (1967) 6 Int. & Comp. L.Q. 401–417.

[19] Zaki (M.), "Opting-out of the Common Law: Recent Developments in the Legal System of the Sudan" (1973) 17 J. dr. africain, 138–148. Akolawin (N.), "Personal Law in the Sudan: Trends and Developments" (1973) 17 J. dr. africain, 149–195.

"Kemalist" revolution of Mustafa Kemal Atatürk (1881–1938), which introduced the Swiss Civil Code in 1926,[20] did not constitute so brutal a rupture with the past as has sometimes been suggested. It completed and clarified—certainly in a spectacular way—a development which began as long ago as 1839, when the sacred Charter of Gülhane initiated the so-called *Tanzīmāt* (organisation) era. More shocking, however, was Turkey's adoption in 1926 of a law of persons, family and inheritance based on the western model which did break with traditional Muslim concepts. At this time the Turks rejected polygamy, the unilateral repudiation of wife by husband and unequal sharing of inheritances among sons and daughters. Since then, however, these same reforms have been, or are about to be, carried out in many other Muslim countries and, in the final analysis, Turkey was simply the precursor of change.

In many countries with Muslim populations (especially in Somaliland), there is a will to usher in socialism. The problem is to know what type of socialism is best suited and also how the socialist state to be erected may be made compatible with Islamic civilisation and legal principles.[21]

450. Muslim law and westernisation

It might be asked whether all traces of traditional Muslim law have disappeared from Muslim countries where, in the broad picture, the law appears to be increasingly westernised, and whether Muslim law should therefore be dropped from the list of the great contemporary legal systems. Great care, however, should be observed in drawing any such conclusion, whatever the gains in westernising the law in Muslim countries may have been. There are, moreover, countries today, such as Iran and Pakistan, where a

---

[20] On the law of Turkey, *cf.* especially the *Annales de la Faculté de droit d'Istanbul*, Nos. 4 (1954) and 6 (1956). *Adde* Pritsch (E.), "Das Schweizerische Zivilgesetzbuch in der Türkei (Seine Rezeption und die Frage seiner Bewährung)" *Zeitschrift für vergleichende Rechtswissenschaft*, Vol. 59 (1957), pp. 123–180. Some significant changes were brought to the Swiss Code on the occasion of its introduction into Turkey: the grounds for divorce were broadened; the matrimonial regime of separation of property replaced that of the union of property as the regime of suppletive law; delays were prolonged to take into account the special circumstances of the country, etc. Turkey adopted moreover an autonomous commercial code and therefore did not enact the third part of the Swiss Federal Code of Obligations. The Turkish Commercial Code of 1926 was replaced by a new one in 1956.
[21] Crespi-Reghizzi (G.), *Il dizitto socialista nei paesi islamici*, l'Est 1975, no. 2, p. 1–76. Rodinson (M.), *Marxisme et monde musulman* (1972).

return to Islamisation and a strict observation of the Koran are strongly advocated. Noted scholars of Islam remind us of the strength of the Islamic tradition. L. Milliot has said, "The final outcome of the discussion on the adoption of western institutions will probably be . . . their Islamisation."[22] J.N.D. Anderson is also of the opinion that to date Muslim countries have been able to amalgamate the various parts of their present law, whether of traditional or western origin, in a manner consistent with their tradition and mentality.[23]

It is worth recalling here what has happened in the U.S.S.R. and other socialist countries. A systematic attempt was made to repudiate tradition in order to build an entirely new social order and legal system. But experience has shown that the past cannot be obliterated with the stroke of a pen. The substance of the law may have been profoundly changed, but legal structures and, to a large extent, legal methods have remained the same. The experience in Muslim countries will no doubt be similar. A new branch of law based on modern precepts may very well be accepted with the adoption of western concepts; there may be a more or less significant deviation from the basic orthodox rules, even to the point of secularising and repudiating the fundamental concepts of Muslim law. Nevertheless, the law of Muslim countries will still not be completely assimilated into the Romanist family—or at least not for a great many years to come. Apart from any purely legal consideration, jurists in Muslim countries will cling to their traditional ways of arguing and thinking for a long time to come; these are the ways of the society in which they live. If all trace of Muslim legal tradition is to be wiped out, not only the law but the whole of society will have to be altered. In fact, the entire Islamic civilisation would have to be rejected. The will to do so exists in Muslim states which have become socialist republics, but not in other Muslim countries. Even Turkey, although it wishes to become a secular state, does not intend to carry out its revolution to the point of proscribing all things Muslim. In such circumstances it appears

---

[22] Milliot (L.), *La conception musulmane du droit*, a course of lectures at the Faculté internationale de droit comparé de Luxembourg (1958).

[23] Anderson (J. N. D.), *Islamic Law in the Modern World* (1959), p. 18. *Cf.* also the most interesting discussion among Turkish jurists as to whether Turkey in 1926 adopted Swiss *droit civil* or merely the Swiss *Code civil*: *cf.* David (R.), "Réflexions sur le colloque d'Istanbul" *Annales de la Faculté de droit d'Istanbul* (1956), No. 6, pp. 239, 244 *et seq.*

improbable that these countries will adhere fully to either the Common law or Romanist systems. It is more likely that the categories and concepts borrowed from western laws will be synthesised, in some way relatively acceptable to the orthodox point of view, with methods of reasoning and an outlook moulded by the tradition of Muslim law.[24] For this reason, the study of Muslim law from the international and comparative standpoint is, and will continue to be, worthwhile for a long time to come.

[24] Various French doctoral theses reveal how jurists of the Arab nations, Turkey and Iran, when working with texts similar to those of European codes, have more or less consciously perpetuated Muslim tradition in relation to, for example, the notion of causation (*causalité*) or the evaluation of damages and the principle of contractual freedom, all of which concepts are for them different from those found in European law. The Tunisian *Cour de cassation* has seen no contradiction in holding that, even though Muslim law is only a subsidiary source of law in Tunisia, a Muslim cannot inherit from a non-Muslim spouse when the law of inheritance does not specify the disparity of faith as a ground for exclusion. Cass. civ. 31 janvier 1966, *Rev. tun. droit* 1968, 114; Note E. de Lagrange.

TITLE II

LAW OF INDIA

451. Definition of Hindu law

Hindu law constitutes a second system of traditional law recognised and revered by a vast community. It is not, however, the law of India any more than Muslim law is the law of national states of Muslim population. It is the law of a community which, in India and other south east Asian countries and parts of Africa, observes the Hindu religion—that is to say Hinduism. As with Islam, Hinduism propounds a concept of this world which has spiritual and moral implications, with considerable latitude, however, in respect of dogma. This concept implies a special social structure (the caste system) and a particular way of life, with the result that religious precepts in large part assume the role which, in other societies, falls to the legal system. The large majority[1] of the inhabitants of India adhere to this doctrine which, therefore, has an especially important role in relationships arising out of their *statut personnel*. A large sector of social affairs is, however, governed today by legislation national in scope and rooted in English ideas. This traditional law of the Hindu community and the national law of India will both be examined.

---

[1] The population of India in 1977 was 623 million, of which the great majority (about 85%) belongs to the Hindu religion. There are many believers as well in Pakistan, Bengal, Burma, Malaysia, South Yemen and eastern Africa; it is the basis of the legal system in Nepal.

CHAPTER I

LAW OF THE HINDU COMMUNITY

452. Sastras

Indian civilisation rests upon a basis quite different from that of either Christianity or Islam.[1] Christians, Muslims and Jews look to holy scripture for the fundamental idea that men, endowed with souls, are equal before God, in whose image they are created. Hinduism rejects this basic idea. For the Hindu "man" is no more than an abstraction; there are only "men," each marked by the social category to which he belongs. The different categories of men are both complementary and hierarchical, such that distinct rights, duties and even moralities are attached to each.

The rules governing the behaviour of men are explained in texts known as *Sastras*, of which there are three types corresponding to the motives which dictate man's behaviour: virtue, interest and pleasure. Some *Sastras* teach men how they must behave to be righteous: this is the science of *Dharma*[2]; that showing men how to enrich themselves and instructing princes in the art of governing is *Artha*, the science of what is expedient and of politics.[3] Others deal with the science of pleasure, or *Kama*.

Dharma, Artha, Kama are legitimate sciences; the natural order of things requires that men take them into account. Each individual, however, in doing so, will act in a manner consistent with the social category to which he belongs. The Brahmin will attempt to live as much as possible according to *Dharma*; merchants and

---

[1] Biardeau (M.), *Clefs pour la pensée hindoue* (1972). Dumont (L.), *Homo hierarchicus. Essai sur le système des castes* (1966).
[2] Kane (P. V.), *History of Dharmasastra* (*Ancient and Medieval Religious and Civil Law in India*) (1930–1932), 5 vols.
[3] Kautilya, *L'Arthasastra. Le traité politique de l'Inde*. Selected extracts, with an Introduction by M. Rivière (1971).

those who govern will seek out what is expedient by observing *Artha*; women, who have no special destiny after death, will emphasise *Kama*.

A superior place is certainly recognised for *Dharma* in Hindu philosophy, but it does not follow that *Artha* or *Kama* must necessarily give way to its precepts. *Dharma* does not express the totality of Hindu morality; it is thus very different from the *fikh*, which pervades all Muslim society, and is even less of a "law" than the latter, in the proper sense of the term. *Dharma* is rather more a model than a law, and one which can accommodate exceptions and calls for flexibility within the realism and tolerance which are the distinctive traits of Hinduism.

453. Dharma

Dharma is founded on the belief that there exists a universal order inherent in the nature of things, necessary to the preservation of the world, and of which the gods themselves are merely the custodians. That being so, *Dharma* embraces the whole of man's behaviour. It does not distinguish between religious duties and legal obligations. It indicates the penitence to be observed when Hindus have sinned and the occasions when sacrifices must be offered; it lays down precepts in respect of charitable giving and hospitality; it instructs rulers how to assure public safety and when to visit the temples. Any idea of "rights" (*droits subjectifs*) is quite foreign to the *Dharma* and Hindu thought. The main purpose of *Dharma* is to set forth the duties which each man must fulfil if he wishes to be a good man or has any concern for the afterworld. These duties vary according to the status of each person and his age; they are especially demanding for those of superior social caste.[4] They exist without any reference to methods for assuring their sanction.

The authority of *Dharma* is not rooted in custom. Its prestige is linked to the veneration which is felt for those who have given expression to its commandments, the sages of bygone eras who

---

[4] On these fundamental distinctions (caste and age), *cf.* Lingat (R.), *Les sources du droit dans le système traditionnel de l'Inde* (1967), pp. 42 *et seq.* (translated by J.D.M. Derrett as *The Classical Law of India*, 1973).

discovered "good custom" and who had clear visions of the divine order.

454. Dharmasastras and Nibandhas

There are a great many treatises (*dharmasastras*) on the *Dharma*. The best known were written in verse, and include the laws of *Manu, Yajnavalkya* and *Narada*, which are believed to have been written between 100 B.C. and A.D. 300 or 400.

Authoritative works on *Dharma* have been established by tradition. The *dharmasastras*, recognised as such, form a whole, despite their different dates of redaction; all of them must be taken into consideration to acquire knowledge of *Dharma*—no single work, however prestigious it may be, is sufficient. The *sastras* complement and explain each other. Recourse must therefore be made in India to a further category of works, the *nibandhas*. Their purpose is to clarify the often obscure meaning of the *dharmasastras*, to interpret them and resolve the apparent contraditions between them. Some *nibandhas* encompass the whole *Dharma*, others treat only of some particular aspect or institution. Their authors are sometimes known, sometimes not. They date from the eleventh to the end of the seventeenth centuries.

Since *Dharma* is a single whole, it can only be studied by examining the body of *dharmasastras*. But these, as well as the *nibandhas*, are very numerous. It thus happens that one of them may be specially known, or preferred, in one region or another; social groups may come to live under the authority of one particular *nibandha*. There are thus two main schools in Hindu law: the *Mitakshara* school and that of *Dayabhaga*. These schools, with their various distinctions and sub-groups, have in fact, like the Muslim rites, geographical areas of application, even though they are *statuts personnels* and thus apply to the individual wherever he may happen to be. The school of *Dayabhaga* prevails in Bengal and Assam, whereas that of *Mitakshara* applies in the rest of India and Pakistan.

455. Dharma and custom

The life of this world is not and cannot be regulated only by *Dharma*. Although it alone expresses eternal truth, there are other things to be considered in determining human behaviour—that is, expediency (*artha*) and pleasure (*kama*). The wise man reconciles in his own conduct virtue, self-interest and pleasure. In the decadent period in which we now unfortunately live (*kali*), one cannot expect that people wholly conform to *Dharma*.[5]

For this reason *Dharma*, itself, recognises custom both *contra legem* and *praeter legem*. According to the laws of both *Yajnavalkya* and *Manu*, one must forego observance of a rule of conduct consecrated by the texts in cases where it is reproved or spurned by the world.[6] Customary rules, the product of the chances of time and place, nevertheless have no connection with the divine behest which is the basis of *Dharma*. Custom is no more than a simple fact, and as such is not an appropriate object of study or the basis of any real science. In reality, therefore, people live in India according to customs more or less dominated by Hindu doctrine which lays down rules of conduct and according to which the customs have, to varying degrees, been altered, oriented or interpreted.

The customs are very diversified. Each caste or sub-caste follows its own customary rules. Meetings of elders (*panchayat*), at the local level, settle difficulties and disputes on the basis of community opinion. These assemblies, which render unanimous decisions, have powerful means of enforcement available—the most formidable sanction is excommunication, which isolates the individual in a society where life is only conceived in terms of membership in a group

Reason and equity are other elements which can supplement custom in the regulation of Hindu conduct. The *dharmasastras* call upon the individual to act, and the judge to decide, according to his good conscience, justice and equity in cases where strict rules of law do not apply. The laws of *Manu*, for example, recommend that, in doubtful cases, resort be made to one's "inner sense of right."

456. Legislation and judicial decisions

Legislation and judicial decisions are not considered to be sources of law by either *Dharma* or Hindu doctrine. The prince

---

[5] The world is subject to regressive evolution, divided into four periods. We are living in the last, and therefore the most barbarous.
[6] Lingat (R.), *Les sources de droit dans le système traditionnel de l'Inde* (1967), pp. 198 *et seq.*, 212–218. *cf.* above, note 4.

can legislate,[7] but the art of governing and the institutions of public law fall within *Artha*, not *Dharma*. The latter requires that the
legitimate commands of the prince be obeyed but he himself, by
his very nature, remains outside its scope. Legislation and the
orders of the prince have no effect on *Dharma*; they are measures
prompted by the times and are temporary. Since they are justified
only by considerations of the moment, they will be changed when
circumstaces themselves change. When confronted with a law,
therefore, judges do not apply it strictly; they are afforded great
discretion in order that they reconcile, as much as possible, justice
and government.

Judicial decisions are no more a source of law than is legislation.
The organisation of justice, like legislation, is a subject falling
within *Artha*. Judicial decisions may be justified by the circumstances of the case in many instances. *Dharma* is a guide and no
more; it is wholly natural for judges to depart from it, if there are
good reasons for doing so, and provided only they do not violate a
fundamental principle of *Dharma*. Given this empiricism the
judge's decision must never be regarded as an obligatory precedent. Its authority is limited to the dispute submitted to the
judge; it has no justification other than in connection with the
special circumstances which gave rise to his decision.

457. Modern doctrine

Dharma organises and expresses legal rules in a manner foreign
to either western or Muslim laws. Rules of law and rules of a ritual
nature are indiscriminately found in the *dharmasastras*. A large
number of rules dealing specially with legal matters, therefore,
had to be sought out, formerly, in "books" which, by reason of
their titles, appeared to deal with religion rather than law. The
book entitled *Vyavahara*, especially devoted to law in the western
sense, covered the administration of justice and procedure and set
out eighteen classifications of disputes in private and criminal law.[8]
Rules of public law were sometimes found in the *dharmasastras*

---

[7] On the Hindu notion of the royal function, *cf.* Lingat, *op. cit.* p. 231, and on the royal legislative power, pp. 249 *et seq.*
[8] Lingat, *op. cit.*, p. 99. Derrett (J. D. M.) and Krishnamurthy Iyer (T. K.), *Structure and
Divisions of the Law* (VI. Hindu Law) in *International Encyclopedia of Comparative Law*, Vol.
II, Chap. II. (1972).

but the science of government was otherwise treated as a separeate body of rules and explained in the *arthasastras*.

The modern authors on Hindu law, influenced by western thinking, no longer attempt to explain *Dharma* but turn their attention to the rules that are really applicable to contemporary Hindu life. They eliminate from their works whatever appears, according to the western conception, to belong to religion, as well as those matters that are regulated by a territorial law applying to all Indians irrespective of their religious affiliation. Hindu law, in this new context, is composed of the following principal topics: filiation, incapables, adoption, marriage and divorce, joint family property, intestate succession, wills, religious foundations, *damdupat, benami* agreement,[9] perpetual indivision. These divisions in themselves do not reveal the true originality of Hindu law; but upon opening any book on Hindu law, it is soon realised that there are numerous terms and expressions that cannot be translated because there are no corresponding notions for them in western law. There are, for example, in Hindu law, eight types of marriage. And the regulation of joint family property appears very complex to western eyes. One must in fact be familiar with Hindu thought and social structures to be able to understand any book on Hindu law.

458. Muslim domination

The Muslim domination of northern and central India during the sixteenth century hindered the development of Hindu law. The courts of the Mogol applied only Muslim law in fact. The Hindu customary law was still applied by the caste *panchayats* but it was unable to develop or increase its authority through state judicial or administrative institutions. It therefore remained much more a matter of religion, propriety and social habit than the affirmation of a legal system.

459. English rule

Such was the situation in the eighteenth century, when the English replaced the rule of the Grand Mogol—at first only in fact but later in law—and established their own domination.

---

[9] *Damdupat* and *benami* agreements are the principal remaining vestiges of Hindu thought in the modern anglicised law of contract. *Damdupat* is the rule limiting the amount of interest payable in loans; the *benami* agreement is similar to *fiducia* and trusts.

According to the principle which always directed their policies, the English conquest of India did not mean the imposition of English law.[10] It was intended that the rules familiar to the Indian population would continue to apply, principally in private law matters. The establishment of English rule in India did however have a considerable influence on the evolution of Hindu law in two major ways.[11]

As a first and positive influence, it brought Hindu law out of the shadows by officially recognising its authority and value, which had not occurred during the Muslim domination. When English judges were called upon to decide disputes other than those in which Englishmen were involved, Hindu law and Muslim law were put on the same level[12] and applied with the help of native experts ("law officers").

But while the English domination was favourable to the rise of Hindu law in that respect, it was, from another point of view, fatal to traditional Hindu law. As will subsequently be seen, the English completely transformed it. The most important consequence was to isolate the application of Hindu law to a limited number of relationships whereas increasingly important aspects of the newly emerging society were ruled by a new territorial law applicable to all inhabitants of India irrespective of religious affiliations.

460. Recourse to the pandits

The desire of the English to respect the rules of Hindu law was hampered, at least in the beginning, by their own ignorance of its nature. Quite incorrectly, it was originally thought that Hindu law, like Muslim law, was immutable and sacred, and that the *Dharma* constituted Indian positive law. The works on the *Dharma*, the *dharmasastras* and *nibandhas*, were of course in a foreign language and their complexity bewildered the new rulers. To avoid these

---

[10] *Supra* para. 363.
[11] Derrett (J. D. M.). "The Administration of Hindu law by the British" *Comparative Studies in Society and History* Vol. IV (1961), pp. 10–52.
[12] The "plan" drawn up by Warren Hastings (1732–1818), the first governor-general in Bengal) in 1772 contemplated the application of the law of the Koran for the Muslims and the law of the *Sastras* for Hindus, whereas Regulation IV of 1793 refers more exactly to Muslim law and Hindu law. A *Code of Gentoo Laws* was produced in English in 1776 by N. B. Halhed.

difficulties codification was, at different periods, envisaged.[13]
While waiting for codes to be completed an expedient solution was
hit upon. It was decided that English judges would appeal to
learned experts, the *pandits*, who would provide the proper solution to be given on the basis of the *dharmasastras* and *nibandhas*.
Thus until 1864 the role of English judges was really no more than
one of adding executory force to the decisions expounded by the
pandits.

Some authors have vehemently criticised the pandits, accusing
them of venality, poor interpretation of the legal texts, of having
made mistakes, and even forging spurious texts for the sake of a
client; others have however defended them. The pandits were men
instructed primarily in religion—they were moralists rather than
jurists. They were not prepared for the role they were called upon
to play, nor were they subject to any kind of over-all supervision.
Even the very basis for the application of Hindu law and the
recourse to the pandits was incorrect; it was impossible to solve
disputes on the basis of only the sacred books because, according
to Hindu law itself, the rules they contained were more the
expression of an ideal than rules of law and their application had to
be flexible enough to take custom and equity into account.[14]

461. Appeal to other methods

English judges however were never very happy with their role of
providing the executory stamp for the decisions of the pandits. As
soon as a sufficient number of books of the *Dharma* had been
translated and there were books on the law, especially series of
judicial reports in the English language, the former system seemed
outmoded. The old practices were all the more criticised once

---

[13] A codification of Hindu law on contracts and successions, on the model of the "inesti-
mable Pandects of Justinian," was proposed by Sir William Jones (1746–1794) to Lord Cornwallis in 1788. This Digest, completed by the pandit Jagannatha in 1797 was translated into
English by Henry Thomas Colebrooke (1765–1837), in 1798, as a *Digest of Hindu Law*. The
idea of codification was again taken up by the first Law Commission set up in 1833. *Cf. infra*
paras.464, 473.

[14] In 1831 Thomas Babington Macaulay (1800–1859) said that the first thing a civil servant
must learn, when called upon to apply Hindu law, is the hopelessness of thinking that one could
find certitudes in the books of the jurists. However as early as 1819 Elphinstone in Bombay had
named a commission to study the legal customs because, as he pointed out, a study of the
ancient texts was insufficient for a knowledge of the actual law.

scholarship revealed, and condemned, the error made respecting the character and authority of the *Dharma* itself.[15]

Where did the remedy lie? The same solution was not adopted in all parts of India. The provinces and the courts were at this time largely independent of each other. In the north and the centre of the country the popular customs were collected and applied. On the other hand, in the south, in the territorial jurisdiction of the Court of Madras, the former mistaken methods were still followed because, it was thought, the people appeared to be more or less accustomed to it and the security of legal transactions required that the precedents be respected.[16]

462. Deformation of Hindu law

The application made of Hindu law was in either case subject to criticism. If indeed the English judges wanted to observe the rules of the *Dharma*, they were very poorly equipped to do so. About a third, or at the very most one-half, of the *dharmasastras* had been translated into English and thus the judges could only have had a very limited knowledge of this system which, to be correctly applied, required consideration of all its sources. The result was, therefore, that many rules that had never been generally recognised or those that had fallen into desuetude were still sanctioned. If, on the other hand, they wanted to apply custom, the judges accepted too easily, as faithful statements of the law, the interpretations of Europeans who had not always seen or understood, Hindu customs and concepts in all their complexity.[17] The infinite variety and different role of these customs could not be under-

[15] J. H. Nelson, in 1881, spoke of "that monster called Hindu law" (v. *Prospectus of the Scientific Study of the Hindu Law*); John D. Mayne remarked that things were functioning as though one were administering law in England by making reference only to the works of Glanvill, "Fleta," Bracton and Coke (*Hindu Law and Usage*, 6th ed., 1900, p. 44).

[16] It was considered a grotesque absurdity, by a judge of this court, however, to apply the tenets of Hindu law to the Maravans; however it was too late for him to act according to his own conscience in this matter‘ *Katamma Nachiar* v. *Dorasinga Tevar* (1868) 6 M.H.C.R. 310, *per* Holloway J. It must be noted further that the *Madras Civil Court Act* of 1873 gave effect to "any custom having force of law" applicable to persons or property in dispute; but the High Court of Madras only took account of this provision for matters originating in the western portion of the province (Malabar).

[17] An author as well informed as Sir Henry Maine is, for example, now recognised as having over-systematised his explanation of land tenure in Hindu law; his influence on the courts largely accounts for the deformation of this portion of the law; *cf.* Derrett (J. D. M.), "The Development of the Concept of Property in India *circa* A.D. 800–1800." *Zeitschrift für vergleichende Rechtswissenschaft* (1962), pp. 15–130.

stood by lawyers and judges accustomed to the idea of a *comune ley*. English judges, on the other hand, applying their own usual methods, attributed to judicial precedents an authority quite unrecognised in the Hindu tradition. Sometimes, and quite consciously, they changed Hindu law because they were shocked by its solutions, and without realising that they would not be just in the conditions of Hindu society. And the need to employ English vocabulary, quite ill-suited to express concepts of Hindu law, was a further cause of its distortion. In view of these different factors Hindu law was, in fact, considerably deformed during the English rule.

The imported English law of evidence also modified the application of Hindu law.[18] Certain concepts drawn from the English law of Equity were, in the same way, applied in order to regulate the Hindu institution of joint family property and the status of the Hindu charitable foundations; in the first instance the deformation of the Hindu concept of *benami* resulted, and, in the second, the Hindu concept of charitable purpose was distorted and conditions were required of the Hindu liberality known as *dharman* which regular Hindu law did not anticipate.[19]

All these deformations cannot, however, be condemned. They did help to reduce the great diversity of local customs which, even to Hindus, was considered a drawback. Moreover, they contributed to an evolution which many consider beneficial in so far as it modernised Hindu law while respecting its spirit. Hindu jurists thus approve of certain contributions made by judicial decisions in the subject of joint family property or again, respecting the principle of Hindu law obliging the son to pay the debts of his father. In these areas the courts were wise enough to respect the fundamental ideas of Hindu law while at the same time rendering them more supple by introducing ideas of good faith and equity when the traditional law was too absolute or outdated. It was right, and it was necessary, in such areas that an evolution of Hindu law take place. Sometimes, too, the courts merely recognised the validity of new customs in conditions perfectly acceptable to Hindu law; it

---

[18] Venkataram (S.), "Influence of the Common Law and Equity on the Personal Law of the Hindus" *Revista del Instituto de derecho comparado*, nos. 8–9 (1957), pp. 156–179.

[19] Venkata Subbarao (G. C.), "Influence of Western Law on the Indian Law of Trusts" *Revista del Instituto de derecho comparado*, nos. 8–9 (1957), pp. 108–117. On the *benami* see Derrett (J. D. M.): *Introduction to Modern Hindu Law* (1963), pp. 524–528, and on the joint family property Chadha, *Principles of Hindu Law* (1962), pp. 121, 153.

was in this way, for example, that the drawing of a will by a Hindu, completely unknown in the ancient law, was recognised as valid when the practice became widespread.[20]

463. Containment of Hindu law

The British conquest of India not only deformed Hindu law in those instances where it was found applicable; it also had the effect of containing its very application to certain subjects.

Hinduism, which attributes a spiritual value to man's every action is called upon to rule all aspects of life in society; potentially it can formulate rules of conduct for any conceivable situation. In fact, however, only some of these relationships—principally those touching an essentially rural and agricultural society—had been highly developed at the time of the British occupation. While, therefore a body of rules existed on such subjects as the family and the organisation of the caste system, land tenure and inheritance, Hindu law was in other respects underdeveloped. The non-payment of debts, for example, was simply regarded as a sin and the law itself provided no sanction for the defaulting debtor.

English rule cut short the possibility of any further original development of Hindu law which might have evolved in response to newly emerged social conditions. The courts only applied Hindu law in certain defined areas: marriage, inheritance, the caste system, religious usage and institutions. Apart from them another legal system was developed and applied in India, as we shall see shortly.

Might things have turned out otherwise? It is not likely. The principle according to which Hindu law was only to apply in respect of certain subjects was in fact only received in the presidencies of Bombay, Calcutta and Madras. In these districts it was admitted that the Hindu law of contract should apply when the defendant was Hindu. But this principle had little effect in practice. Parties most often preferred to submit their dealings to English law, which was more settled. The interpretation of Hindu law itself was often carried out in English style by judges ignorant of Indian civilisation.[21]

---

[20] *Soorjeemoney Dossey* v. *Denobundoo Mallick* (1862) 9 Moo. Ind. App. 128, 136. There was no word in Sanskrit vocabulary to express the idea of a last will.
[21] Jain (M. S.), "The Law of Contract before the Codification" (1972) J. of the Indian Law Institute 178–204.

464. British legislation in India

The Hindus themselves came to the point where they wished for a reform of a law which corresponded so imperfectly to their customs.[22] The normal way to operate such reforms appeared to be through legislation. British legislative intervention in subjects where Hindu law applied was however undertaken only with considerable hesitation. Laws of only limited scope were adopted during British rule. Thus for example a number of rules of the caste system or those setting up the incapacity of women were abolished because they offended numerous enlightened sectors of Indian society. Hindu wills were also regulated in the Hindu Wills Act 1870. But a general codification, explaining and modernising Hindu law, while contemplated in 1833, was abandoned in 1861.

While a more vigorous legislative intervention was carried out by the English in those subjects where Hindu law no longer applied,[23] there were some subjects in respect of which it was still possible to take account of the original concepts of Hindu law. The Courts of Bombay and Calcutta, for example, continued to apply, even after the Indian Contract Act 1872, the *damdupat* rule according to which interest due could never amount to a sum greater than the capital sum owing. The Madras Court did hold, it is true, that this rule was to be considered abrogated, but legislation of 1938 reintroduced it in Madras in respect of debts connected with agricultural undertakings.[24]

465. Independence

Indian independence, gained in 1947, changed the situation and ushered in new developments in Hindu law.

In judicial organisation, the new Supreme Court is at the apex of the hierarchy of courts established throughout the country. Previously the courts of the princely states (Baroda, Travancore, Cochin, Mysore, Hyderabad) were fully sovereign and removed from the control of even the Judicial Committee of the Privy Council sitting in London to which, however, there was an appeal

---

[22] Derrett (J. D. M.), *Hindu Law Past and Present* (1957), pp. 24 *et seq.*

[23] The development of this Anglo-Indian law is studied *infra*, para. 469.

[24] Rajaraman (C.), "The Law of Contracts in India," *Revista del Instituto de derecho comparado* (1957), Nos. 8–9, pp. 180–185. As to the present position, *cf.* Derrett (J. D. M.), *Introduction to Modern Hindu Law* (1963), p. 521.

from the various High Courts established in British India. This new Supreme Court has been able to confirm and sometimes rectify the decisions rendered during British rule; a re-alignment and unification of Hindu law may well be accomplished in this way.

In legislative matters, a law commission was set up to make a general study of possible legislative reforms on Indian law in general including those that might be suitable to the Hindu community itself. Through its efforts, spectacular results have been achieved. It can almost be said that there is not one important principle of the old law that has not been altered or reformed in someway by statutes or codes.[25]

The 1950 Constitution itself rejects the caste system. Article 15 prohibits any form of discrimination based on reasons of caste. The whole subject of marriage and divorce has been basically changed and unified by the Hindu Marriage Act of 1955 (amended in 1964). Marriage, regarded as a sacrament by the Hindu religion, was traditionally analysed in Hindu law as a gift of the wife by her parents to the husband; the wife, being the object of the contract, did not have to consent. Marriage was indissoluble and polygamy was authorised. All these rules have been rejected by the new Hindu law: polygamy is forbidden; divorce and even the possiblity of alimentary support for the divorced consort are now admitted; the consent of each consort is required because marriage is now analysed as a contract; minimum ages for both consorts have been established and the number of possible impediments to marriage has been reduced. A complete change has thus taken place in Hindu law. The new legislation is nevertheless still a Hindu statute because it is only applicable to Hindus rather than to all Indian citizens, and it retains a number of traditional rules of Hindu law. Three other parts of a *Hindu Code*, of which the law on marriage is the first part, have been voted by parliament: the Hindu Minority and Guardianship Act 1956, the Hindu Adoptions and Maintenance Act 1956 and the Hindu Succession Act 1956.

The last statute on successions, the final step in the reform movement, endeavours to assure that the devolution of successions will occur according to the order of the presumed affec-

---

[25] Derrett (J. D. M.), "Statutory Amendments of the Personal Law of Hindus since Indian Independence" *Rapports généraux au Ve Congrès international de droit comparé* (Brussels, August 4–9, 1958), pp. 101–124. By the same author: *Introduction to Modern Hindu Law* (1963).

tions of the deceased, and women have some place. According to ancient Hindu law the succession could only pass to those who would, in accordance with religious tenets, be able to obtain certain spiritual favours for the deceased. This principal idea excluded shares devolving to women. It should be noted however that the Hindu law of succession had only very limited importance during the period when most property was owned by the family; with the decline in importance of joint family property, in modern times, the reform was necessary.

Very significant reforms have also taken place in the field of Hindu joint family property. As early as 1930, it was established that salaries earned by individuals constituted their own private propery; since 1936, the share in joint family property devolves as private or separate property to heirs or legatees, amongst whom the deceased's widow now ranks. Finally since 1950, agrarian reforms in the Indian States have been pursued in an attempt to reduce the size of large estates, without at the same time excessively fragmenting landed property.

466. Nature of this evolution

Hindu law is only applicable to the Hindu portion of the population in India. It has undergone, however, great reform; many of the local customs which were obstacles to its uniformity have been abolished. This is a first and important change. The reforms have, moreover, brought about many alterations to the substance of the law. Orthodox religion does not condemn them for all of that. *Dharma* was formulated for the use of social groups that had reached very different stages of civilisation; it never purported to be more than a body of ideal rules intended to guide men in their dealings. Because of its very nature, therefore, it has always been admitted that there can be all kinds of provisional derogations or accommodations allowed, whether these arise from custom or legislation; the position is thus very different from that prevailing in Muslim law. While, therefore, contemporary Indian governments have to a great extent departed from this model law, they do not fail to affirm, whenever the occasion presents itself, their attachment to the principles of Hindu civilisation which continues to condition their attitude. The desire to remain faithful to tradition subsists throughout all these changes. Hindu law itself, therefore, retains its place as one of the fundamental notions of the social order in the modern world.

467. Hindu law or law of India?

When the law is examined in the geographical context of India rather than in that of the Hindu community, its radical transformation is however more clearly perceived. This change, examined below, has occurred in many areas in which it is now more appropriate to speak of "Indian" or "Anglo-Indian" rather than "Hindu" law.

Article 44 of the Constitution anticipates the generalisation of such a system by means of a Civil Code applicable to all Indian citizens. To date, it is true, that has not been accomplished because the main effort has been devoted to the work of modernising and unifying Hindu law itself. It is not impossible however that the promise of the Constitution will gradually be carried out by means of reforms which, on particular points, will either remove or amend the laws of *statut personnel* and substitute a common system.

A number of statutes suggests that this movement is already under way in so far as they envisage and regulate relations between Indians of different religions which the religion of either one group or the other may not authorise. The Special Marriages Act 1954, for example, declares legally valid marriages between Hindus and Muslims or other non-Hindus. The enactment of this statute is a very good indication of the change in ideas over the last 100 years. Sir Henry Maine, in effect, had the idea of such a law a century ago but it was abandoned in the face of unanimous opposition—"bishops, pundits, rabbis, mobeds, and mullahs found themselves for once in complete agreement."[26] It is not impossible therefore that an "inter-personal" law might develop to form a new kind of *ius gentium* applicable in areas until now reserved to distinct *statuts personnels*.

Whatever may be its future evolution, Hindu law, for the immense majority of Indians, is, at the present time, still the basis of the only law of any concern to them. Hindu law regulates their

---

[26] Vesey-Fitzgerald (S. G.), "The Projected Codification of Hindu Law" 29 J. Comp. L. 19–32 (1947).

statut personnel, and this *statut* is understood in the widest sense. The personal law does not include only family relations but also certain very important property matters as well, whether in the law of succession or joint family property. And through these means Hindu law penetrates the whole law of trading and commerce. If, for example, some commercial concern is operated by all the members of one family (and this often occurs), and there are no non-family associates, the rules of Indian commercial law in Indian Partnership Act will not apply. The dealings of the partners will come under Hindu law because they form part of their *statut* rather than part of a contract between them. Nor should it be necessary to insist upon the importance of the concept of joint family property in matters of credit in a country where only the family can in principle own property, although this form of property holding is becoming rare.

468. New law and traditional mores

But far and away the most important question is the extent to which the new state law takes into account present Indian sociological realities. The legislature can, with the stroke of a pen, abolish the whole caste system, authorise inter-caste marriages and substitute village *panchayats* to the place of the traditional caste *panchayats*. But this work, even if it is necessary to the country's development, cannot, from one day to the next, change the habits and outlooks of centuries linked as they are to religious beliefs. Eighty per cent. of Hindus, living in rural areas, will continue to live as their ancestors did; they are governed by the institutions they have always known and are judged through means outside the official organs. Legislation is not in itself sufficient: a patient process of re-education is also needed. And the success of this work is intimately linked to the development of a modern Indian economy. The evident difficulty here is to escape from a vicious circle: economic development itself is considerably retarded by the country's structures, the people's religious beliefs and behaviour, all of which have been created by an ancient and venerated tradition.

CHAPTER II

NATIONAL LAW OF INDIA

469. Definition of Indian law

Hindu law is the law of a community organised around its attachment to a religion. Today, this law is being replaced by a national law, the application of which will be independent of the religious beliefs of those concerned. The modern tendency in India is to replace the traditional religious law (Hindu law, Parsee law, Muslim law, Canon law) with the western concept of a secular law, independent of religion. This new national law of India must therefore be referred to as an *Indian* rather than a *Hindu* law. It includes all the laws of India which are, in principle at any rate, of some general application even though some parts of these laws may be inapplicable to certain categories of citizens. The Indian Succession Act, for example, is considered part of Indian law even though it expressly provides that, with some few exceptions, it will not apply to Hindus, Muslims, Buddhists or Parsees—with the result that the vast majority of Indians do not fall within its purview in respect of intestate succession.

470. Notion of lex loci

The idea of a territorial law (*lex loci*), in which the law is considered an autonomous body of rules existing independently of religious or tribal affiliations, is a western and modern concept altogether foreign to Indian tradition.[1] It was quite unknown in India before the English rule. It is true that at that time Muslim law was the only system applied by the courts and enforced by public authorities, but it was not for all of that a territorial law. Muslim law was linked to Islam, and by its very nature was inappli-

---

[1] In the same way, the *ius civile* only applied to citizens of Rome and it was necessary to develop another system, the *ius gentium* for those dealings in which a non-citizen was involved.

cable to all non-Muslims whether Christians, Jews or gentiles (or *gentoos* as Hindus were called at that time). Before the English it was only in criminal matters that Muslim law applied to Hindus throughout most of India,[2] whereas in other subjects they were allowed to follow their own customs. There was no territorial law.

The creation of a national law only came about during the British rule. This seemed to be the best solution for the regulation of affairs of people belonging to many different communities. Further, both Muslim and Hindu laws were inapplicable to important portions of the Indian population[3] made up of Christians, Jews, Parsees and persons whose religious affiliations were doubtful. With respect to all these persons, who were increasing in numbers, some form of national law was essential, particularly from about 1833 when India was opened to all European. Moreover, Muslim and Hindu law, even though in theory apt to regulate the totality of human relationships, had, as a matter of fact, many gaps; it was realised that Indian development would be encouraged if a new territorial law were to be created, applicable to Hindus and Muslims and those of other religious persuasions, to deal with the host of new problems.

471. Lex loci in the "Presidency Towns"

What was this territorial law to be? How was it to be created? The answers have varied according to the complexity of the political and constitutional developments of India.[4]

A first and principal distinction was made between the Presidency Towns of Bombay,[5] Calcutta and Madras on the one hand and the rest of India (known as the *mofussil* or *mofussel*) on the

---

[2] Bombay Province however did not come under this rule.

[3] It may be observed that there are few countries where so many people would not be subject to any law at all if there were no *lex loci*. In these circumstances some judges applied Canon law to Christians: *Lopez* v. *Lopez* (1885) I.L.R. 12, Calc. 706, whereas on other occasions some made appeal to their own idea of what was just, or simply applied English law. Maine described India as "a country singularly empty of law." He advocated codification in order to prevent the judiciary from adopting certain rules of English law which could only be explained by the very special historical context in which they had been formed.

[4] Setalvad (M. C.), *The Role of English Law in India* (1966).

[5] The Island of Bombay was ceded to the English by the Portuguese in 1661 at the time of the marriage of Charles II; the latter granted it to the East India Company in 1668 and ordered it to establish laws in agreement with reason and as close as possible to English law. In the execution of this charter the court set up in Bombay in 1672 was instructed to apply English law and Portuguese law was formally abolished. *Cf.*, in general, Fawcett (Sir C.), *First Century of British Justice in India* (1934).

other. English courts operated in the Presidencies and in principle they applied English law, including statute law, as it existed in 1726. But this principle was subject to two important exceptions. English law was only applicable subject to the Regulations which the local authorities were empowered to make in certain subjects[6]; and it was only applicable to the extent that it was possible in the particular conditions of India.[7] Lastly and above all, the jurisdiction of the English courts originally availed only in disputes involving an Englishman or for those who formally admitted it. In 1781 when the jurisdiction of the courts was broadened to include all disputes, it was provided that for matters involving Muslims or Hindus the court would adjudicate according to Muslim or Hindu law. The law based on English law, which was applied in the Presidencies, was nonetheless at the origin of what later became Anglo-Indian law.

472. Lex loci in the mofussil: first period

In the rest of India the sitation was different.[8] The courts in the *mofussil* were not royal courts; they were established by the East India Company which from 1765 had the right, in virtue of its privilege (*diwani* grant), to collect taxes in exchange for an annual payment of a prefixed sum to the Mogul emperor. With this right went that of administering justice in private matters. This situation continued until 1858 when the government of India was placed under the direct authority of the Crown.

In the *mofussil* there was no reason for English law to be applicable, and it would, in addition, have given rise to difficulties. A distinction therefore, dating from the plan[9] of Governor-General Warren Hastings (1732–1818) in 1772, was made. With respect to inheritance, marriage, caste and religious usages or institutions,

---

[6] These "Regulations" did not spell out rights within the private law but only provided how such rights would be sanctioned. Macaulay: *Speech in the House of Commons* (1853) as reported by Rankin (Sir G. C.), *Background to Indian law* (1946), p. 136.

[7] Thus the English statutes respecting Sunday observances were rejected, as well as the criminal sanctions in case of suicide, the rule prohibiting foreigners from owning land and many other technical rules. Setalvad (M. C.) in his *The Common Law in India* (1960), p. 53 speaks in this respect of a "selective" application of English law.

[8] There is no need for the purposes of this work to distinguish between these provinces directly administered by the English ("British India") and the Indian States—these latter, before Independence, covered one-third of India and included a quarter of the population.

[9] His Regulation for the Administration of Civil Justice.

the rules of Hindu or Muslim law were, according to the case, to be applied. In other matters decisions would be rendered according to general principles of "justice, equity and good conscience." This formula was employed in a Regulation of 1781 creating two superior courts, one for private law matters (*Sadar Diwani Adalat*), the other for criminal matters (*Sadar Nizamat Adalat*) for the provinces of Bengal, Bihar and Orissa. It was used again in the Indian High Courts Act of 1861 which reorganised the administration of justice throughout India.[10] As a result the situation in the *mofussil* was as follows: on the one hand, Muslim and Hindu law, applicable only in certain subject matters, did not have the same breadth of application as in the Presidency Towns; apart from them, the applicable law was not (as in the Presidency Towns) English law: the courts had to find the applicable rule of law by seeking the solution most in agreement with general principles of justice, equity and good conscience.

How did the judges interpret this formula? As an author has explained,[11] the point of it was not to provide a cover for the importation of English law but rather to exclude the application of the Common law. In a first phase much was left to the individual appreciation and wisdom of those who were called upon to decide disputes. No "reception" of English law under the cover of the expression employed in the law took place at this time, at least in any general sense.[12] Justice at this period was administered by civil administrators (Revenue Officers) who had no legal training or knowledge of English law; they often adjudictated in one of the Indian languages. English law was hardly appropriate of course to populations in which the English were in a very small minority. It seems therefore that a variety of customary or religious rules, which appeared to these officers to be most suitable in virtue of religious and other factors, was principally applied, and that these were drawn from Hindu or Muslim law, local customs or were

---

[10] The distinction made between the royal courts and the company courts then disappeared, but the phraseology of the old regulations was reproduced in the new law, 1861, 24 & 25 Vict. c. 104.

[11] Derrett (J. D. M.), "Justice, Equity and Good Conscience" in Anderson (J. N. D.) ed; *Changing Law in Developing Countries* (1963), pp. 114–153.

[12] Regulation 7 of 1852, for Bengal, specified that the formula "justice, equity and good conscience" was not to be interpreted so as to justify the application of English law or some other foreign legal system. The judges in each case were called upon to decide whether the rule they intended to apply was suitable to the requirements of justice such as it was to be understood in the Indian milieu.

simply dictated by the individual judge's notion of equity and good sense. As one writer has pointed out, the sitation in India was characterised by a remarkable dearth of indigenous legal principles.[13]

473. Second period: codification

The Charter Act of 1833[14] marks the opening of the second period. Codification, which had triumphed in France and had gained supporters even in England, was thought to be particularly serviceable for India. It would give certainty to Indian law and achieve its unification, and this would be in the interest of justice as well as a contribution to national development. Moreover it was also seen as the means for allowing the reception of a systematic, simplified and modernised English law adapted to Indian conditions.

In 1833 a *Law Member*—in effect a minister of justice—was added to the three member council assisting the governor-general of India in his task of governemnt.[15] The first person named to this post, the future Lord Macaulay (1800–1859), was, like many of his contemporaries, a fervent admirer of Bentham and codification. And codification was, moreover, formally anticipated in section 53 of the Charter Act. Under his direction the first Law Commission worked from 1833 to 1840 at which time it submitted its famous report known as the *Lex Loci Report*. The Commission planned to draw up three codes: one for a systematic exposition of Muslim law, a second for Hindu law and a third to contain the territorial law (*lex loci*) applicable in all cases when either Muslim or Hindu law was not. It was hoped this third code would end the legal diversity then existing in the different parts of India, and especially that between rules and principles observed in the Presidency Towns and the *mofussil*. As its basis, the Commission proposed that this code employ English law but with some restrictions and exceptions. A general clause would safeguard the established local customs and immemorial usages.

The suggestions of the first Commission, and in particular the

---

[13] Gledhill (A.), *The Republic of India* (*The British Commonwealth series*: *The Development of its Laws and Constitutions*) (2nd ed., 1964), Vol. 6, p. 211.

[14] 3 & 4 Wm. 4, c. 35.

[15] And today in India, unlike England, there is a minister of justice (Minister of Law).

draft penal code prepared, were not acted upon immediately. Even the recommendation as to the principle of codification met with resistance from Common law lawyers and the plans for Hindu and Muslim law codes also gave rise to serious objections. A second Commission, created in 1853, abandoned these two projected codes in favour of concentrating its efforts on the establishment of a *lex loci*.[16] Nevertheless it was only with the shock of the Indian Mutiny of 1857, and the constitutional reforms which followed, that real progress was made.[17]

From 1859 to 1882, an intensive legislative movement produced a vast body of Indian law and, with the co-operation of two new Commissions, it replaced the authority of English law in the Presidencies and the system obtaining in the *mofussil*. The movement then slackened although it did not stop altogether.

Indian law is thus principally made up of these various codes and important statutes. It is curious to note that the appellation *code* was only given to those Indian statutes which, by their content, corresponded to one of the Napoleonic codes. There is thus an Indian Code of Civil Procedure (1859, now replaced by a Code of 1908), a Criminal Code (1860) and a Code of Criminal Procedure (1861). The other important statutes which did in fact codify the Common law of India are not however so entitled (thus, the Limitation Act 1859; the Succession Act 1865 now replaced by a statute of 1925; Contract Act 1872[18]; Evidence Act 1872; Specific Relief Act 1872; Negotiable Instruments Act 1881; Transfer of Property Act 1882 amended in 1929; Trusts Act 1882, and so on). Just as in France or England, the general law on civil liability or torts has never been codified; a draft prepared by Sir Frederick Pollock (1845–1937) on the subject was not acted upon.

474. Reception of English law

A true reception of English law was brought about by means of these various laws drawn up by English jurists who often in fact

---

[16] In 1882, the Commission observed, and quite rightly, that the code envisaged for Muslim law could not, because of the nature of this law, succeed. It maintained that the legislature should not compromise its authority in the country by undertaking such a plan.

[17] However well before this date it had been considered necessary to reform completely the criminal law which was barbarous and left far too much to the individual discretion of the judges; the Cornwallis Code of 1793 and the Elphinstone Code of 1827 had already accomplished a good deal.

[18] The Indian Contract Act of 1872 has 269 articles of which the first 66 make up a "general part" on the law of contract.

worked only in London.[19] And this reception was subsequently confirmed when the special status of the East India Company ended in 1858 with the abolition of the nominal Mogul sovereignty and when, following a re-organisation of the courts in 1861, justice was more regularly administered throughout the whole of India by judges trained in the Common law.[20] The latter, very naturally, completed the work of reception begun by the legislature, and they considered, contrary to the historical truth, that by "principles of justice, equity and good conscience" one was to understand the rules of English law. By 1887 this evolution was complete for at this time the Judicial Committee of the Privy Council, the final court since 1833 for the administration of Indian law, felt itself able to say that "equity and good conscience" could generally be interpreted to mean the rules of English law if applicable to Indian society and circumstances.[21]

475. Originality of Indian law

Indian codes and statutes are founded on English legal concepts, but they are far from being merely a consolidation of English law. Codification was used as an instument of legal reform, not merely to achieve a systematic rearrangement of earlier rules. Thus, for example, the authors of the Criminal Code declared that they were influenced by the French *Code pénal*[22] and by the Criminal Code of Louisiana—and this is an admission that would never have been made in England. Nor were the codifiers of Indian law inhibited from introducing reforms judged suitable to English law itself: in the law of contract, for example, new rules have been provided touching the concept of consideration, contracts concluded by minors, contracts under seal, impossibility of performance and contractual liability. Now too there is different understanding of the cocept of public policy. For these reasons Indian codification

---

[19] In particular the second Commission sat in London from 1853 to 1855.

[20] The High Courts Act of 1861 abolished the *Sadar Adalats* as well as the Supreme Courts of the presidencies either by replacing them with High Courts or by attributing analogous functions to "judicial commissioners" until such courts could be set up.

[21] *Waghela* v. *Sheikh Masludin* (1887) L.R. 14 Ind. App. 89 at p. 96. Prior to 1870 the Judicial Committee expressed itself much less clearly, *cf.* Rankin (Sir G. C.), *Background to Indian Law* (1846), p. 39; Gledhill (A.), "The Influence of Common Law and Equity on Hindu Law since 1800" (1955) Int. & Comp. L.Q. 576–603.

[22] Anantanarayanan (M.) and Balasubrahmanyam (V.), "Criminal Law in India," *Revista del Instituto de derecho comparado*, Nos. 8–9 (1957), pp. 149–155. In fact a Scottish influence, rather than any other, is most noticeable.

appeared at the time as an improvement over English law, and was used as a model by a number of other countries (especially in eastern Africa[23] and the Sudan) wishing to codify their laws while still remaining within the Common law tradition.

The special circumstances prevailing in India were very naturally taken into account in the codification. This observation is borne out, for example, in respect of which crimes were retained in the criminal code and the elimination of the jury system in civil matters[24]; again, in the law of contract, in the rules relating to coercion or duress, the rendering of assistance to litigants (maintenance), the sharing of the proceeds of litigation (champerty) and agreements in restraint of trade; and in the law of inheritance, the abolition of the distinction between real and personal property and that of the principle of the return of gifts; there has also been a simplification in the rules dealing with the English forms of wills.

476. Membership in the common law family

Despite these reforms and the reliance on the technique of enacted law and codification, the law of India was, before Independence in 1947, very much part of the Common law family.

This was so, above all, because of its vocabulary and legal concepts. The rules of Indian law could not be any but those of English law. They have been shaped by the context of, and make use of the concepts derived from, the Common law system. Many traditional Indian law concepts, on the other hand, have been eliminated.[25]

Indian law is attached to the Common law tradition, in the second place, because of its techniques and its concept of the legal rule. Codification may very well have been the method used, but Indian codes are nonetheless Common law codes and they are used by Indian jurists in the same way that legislative materials are used in Common law countries.

---

[23] *East African Law Today*, conference report of the British Institute of International and Comparative Law, No. 8 of the *Commonwealth Law* series (1966).

[24] Even in criminal matters the jury is only imposed by the Criminal Code in the Presidency Towns. Each province is free to admit this institution or not, as judged best. In fact practice has varied enormously on this point. The law commission of 1955 recommended the abolition of the jury on the ground that it was an English practice that had never developed or taken root in India.

[25] *Cf.* those singled out by Mr. Justice Field in 1883 as mentioned by Sir G. C. Rankin, in his work *Background to Indian Law* (1946), p. 139, who concludes that there was nothing either "Indian" or oriental about the Indian codes.

The rule of precedent has not only been admitted, it has been made official in a way never envisaged in England. Different series of judicial reports have been published privately; the publication of the official series, begun in 1861, has always been considered a task falling properly to government because it was responsible for making known all law, whether legislative or judicial in origin.

The concepts and legal techniques of any law are the factors determinining its classification in one family or another. Indian law, shaped by English lawyers and judges, is necessarily a part of the Common law family. The example of the Indian Criminal Code is quite characteristic on this point. Macaulay, who fathered it, thought that English criminal law of his own period barbaric and backward, and his intention was to create a criminal code independent of any existing criminal legal system. The Law Commission in its report introducing the new code rejected the whole of the Muslim, Hindu and English laws on the subject. Even some of the terminology of English law was replaced. Nevertheless, when the code was finally completed in 1860, it appeared to be a Common law code because, while it had indeed rejected all the outmoded rules of English law, it was still rooted in the concepts and attitudes of English lawyers. For these reasons it could have been considered a model code for use in England itself. As the Indian Attorney-General M.C. Setalvad, has pointed out, Macaulay and his colleagues attempted to free themselves of established legal systems and endeavoured, in particular, not to follow English law in order that they might arrive at a solution truly adapted to the needs of India; they nevertheless—unconsciously but inevitably—followed the line of principles in which they had been educated and to which they were accustomed.[26]

India is attached to the Common law tradition not only by its concepts and techniques but also because of its concept of the judicial function and the importance which it attaches to the administration of justice, matters of procedure and the idea of the supremacy or rule of law. Indians rely upon good procedures, and these are based on English practice, in order to arrive at what is a substantively just solution. The psychological attitude of Indian lawyers and judges is the same as the English, and the judicial

---

[26] Setalvad (M. C.), *The Common Law in India* (1960), pp. 127–128; Rankin (Sir G. C.), *Background to Indian Law* (1946), p. 208.

function is clothed with the same prestige.[27] An eminence similar to that of the English is attached to judicial power in India and, in the same way, it implies that there is no distinction drawn between public law and private law. The courts must, according to this reasoning, exercise a general control over the whole range of legal disputes and without distinguishing whether the author of some misconduct or he who violates some legal provision, is a private citizen or an official of the government.

477. Differences compared to English law

The above conclusions must not, however, be pushed too far. There are, from a number of different points of view, factors which have always significantly distinguished the two laws.[28] For example, the English distinction between Common law and Equity does not exist in India and the reason is easy to understand. India has never had special courts for the application of Equity rules: both Common law and Equity have always been administered by the same courts. Thus India from the very beginning reached the same conclusion to which the English courts, ever since the reforms of the Judicature Acts of 1873–75, have irreversibly been led—that Common law and Equity constitute a single system. According to the expression of one author, Equity has found its place in India within rather than in opposition to the Common law.[29] This fusion has in fact led to a quite different understanding of the trust in India. On this point Indian law does not draw the English distinction between legal *rights* and equitable *interests*; for the Indian lawyer, if the "ownership" belongs to the trustee, the beneficiary of the trust is nonetheless vested with a true right.[30]

In the law of real property English legal vocabulary has been retained. However it is used in the regulation of a land tenure sys-

---

[27] This is true even though Indian judges have traditionally been recruited in two ways, either proceeding from the Bar (as in England) or being raised to the bench from the ranks of the civil service.

[28] English authors and the Privy Council itself have, on a number of occasions, warned the Indian courts about their tendency to follow too slavishly English precedents that are inappropriate to India. *Cf.* Setalvad (M. C.), *The Common Law in India* (1960), pp. 69, 86.

[29] Setalvad (M. C.), *op. cit.*, p. 57: "In India equity worked through and not in opposition to the common law."

[30] Thus instead of an *equitable estate* there is a *statutory right to enforce the trust*—that is, a right in virtue of which the trustee can be required to execute the trust. The Indian law of trusts does not regulate the relations within the group holding joint family property; and this exclusion is specified expressly by the statute.

tem so different from that in England that one may well ask whether this identity in terminology is really anything more than façade. The Indian concepts expressed by means of English terms very often seem quite different.

The Specific Relief Act of 1877 offers another example of Indian law's originality. This statute groups a number of rules of different origin and therefore seems to the English to be altogether heteroclite in character: it brings together Equitable rules of relief such as specific performance of contractual or other obligations, those relating to the rectification or cancellation of written instruments, rules dealing with the restitution of property of which a possessor is unjustly deprived or which has been illegally received, and even special remedies such as *mandamus*.

Indian private international law is also inspired by English law, but the attention of Indian lawyers and judges is particularly centred around conflicts between laws of "personal status," problems which do not have either the same characteristics or even the same importance for English jurists.[31]

478. Independence: confirmation of previous law

The independence of India, acquired in 1947, did not undermine the ideas established during the period of British rule, nor did it endanger the legislation already enacted. The Constitution of 1950 formally provides for the maintenance of the former law (s.372). India continues to be a member of the Commonwealth and remains a Common law country. Its connection with English law is, however severed in a number of respects. Quite apart from the subjects falling within the law of personal status in which respect membership in one community or another is the decisive consideration, Indian law exhibits an unquestionable originality within the Common law family comparable to that of American law when contrasted to English law.

479. Constitutional law

The originality of Indian law is particularly striking in its constitutional law.[32] The Indian Constitution, promulgated in 1950, has

---

[31] Rama Rao (T. S.), "Influence of English Law on Indian Private International Law" *Revista del Instituto de derecho comparado*, Nos. 8–9 (1957), pp. 128–148.
[32] Doré (F.), *La Republique indienne* (1970).

395 sections, divided into two parts, and eight schedules. The very existence of this document, and the union of states it has created,[33] immediately distinguish India from England where there is no written constitution and no federal state structure. The differences although somewhat less marked when contrasted to the United States which, of course, has both, are nonetheless real.

India and the United States are not easily comparable otherwise. Consider the language factor: a basic unity exists in the United States because of the common use of English, whereas in India there are 15 officially recognised languages which belong to four basic language groups.[34] The Constitutional provision that Hindi will be the official language of the Union is far from being realised in this sub-continent which resembles, in this regard, Europe much more than the United States.[35] But apart from this, the relationship of the states and federal power in the two countries is also different, particularly in respect of the form and manner of sharing legislative authority. There is no provision in the Indian Constitution similar to that of the American whereunder state jurisdiction is the principle and federal jurisdiction the exception. The Constitution enumerates those subjects falling within Union jurisdiction (97 sections), those within that of the state (66 sections) and others, finally, in which jurisdiction is shared (44 sections) because in their regard unification appears to be desirable although not absolutely necessary. The drafting of a uniform Civil Code for the whole country figures in this last category.

Very extensive powers are attributed to the federal authorities, in a way without parallel in the United States, to intervene in the affairs of a state when circumstances require the maintenance of peace and order. These provisions are invoked when a state becomes ungovernable, or in order to suspend fundamental rights

[33] The division of India into states, established by the 1950 Constitution, has been changed a number of times. It is now divided into 22 states and a number of territories. Prior to 1947, and apart from British India, there were 549 princely states, varying enormously in geographic size and population.

[34] According to linguists, there are 179 languages and 544 dialects spoken in India, all of which can be grouped within four large families.

[35] The Constitution of 1950 provided that Hindi would replace English as the official language in 1965, but this provision was changed in 1963 and again in 1968. It has, moreover, always stated that English will remain the official language in legal matters (legislation and in proceedings before the courts) until a date to be fixed by the central Parliament. A commission is at work modernising the Hindi language in order to adapt it to the expression of Common law concepts.

of citizens when public order or the security of the country is threatened.[36]

Having been subject to foreign ruling powers for centuries, Indians today are deeply united by, and are justly proud of, the independence they gained through the non-violent means required by their religious beliefs. Their Constitution of 1950 is not, however, of the same type as the American Constitution; the relative ease with which it can be amended by the dominant political party (40 times in 25 years) suggests an instability not known in the United States.

The judicial review of the constitutionality of legislation by the Supreme Court means, therefore, in these circumstances, something other than it does in the United States. One cannot speak of a "government by judges" in India because decisions of the Court which are contrary to the desires of the central government, or those of certain states, are easily negated through a constitutional amendment. This happened, for example, when the Patna High Court and the Supreme Court declared unconstitutional (as radical violations of property rights) a number of agricultural reforms legislated in the states of Bihar and West Bengal.[37] The fourth amendment to the Constitution, voted in 1955, overturned these decisions in order to enable the states and the Union to implement their "socialist" agrarian policies (and, for greater certainty, the same amendment expressly ratified 64 statutes already enacted in the subject matter).

Deeply tolerant, but confronting crushing poverty, India hesitates between liberal and socialist policies, and is attempting to reconcile these two philosophies. Their problems are thus very different from those in a country of such wealth and abundance as the United States, and the Indian Constitution itself sets off these differences. It has, for example, tempered the principle of "equal protection" under the law by recognising that certain castes, tribes or economically weak social groups should possess a special status, and some 40 per cent. of the population enters into one or another

---

[36] Pasbecq (C.), "L'état d'urgence en République indienne" *Rev. int. dr. comparé* (1977), p. 301.

[37] *State of West Bengal* v. *Bela Banerjee* [1954] S.C.R. 558. *Kameshwar Sing* v. *State Bihar* (1951) 30 Pat. 454. The Lands Reform Act, promulgated in 1950 in Bihar, provided that the compensation payable to the dispossessed proprietor would vary according to his own personal wealth. In various states since that time radical reform measures have limited private ownership of arable land to approximately five to eight hectars.

of such categories.[38] The Constitution moreover specifies that
"due process of law" only means observation of laws properly
enacted but does not authorise judges to pronounce upon their
wisdom or morality.

480. Judicial organisation and rule of precedent

The organisation established for the administration of justice
and the functioning of the rule of precedent are two other aspects
in which Indian law differs from English law.

India, given its size and population, is unable to have a centralised administration of justice such as that in England. And yet the
system it does have is also very different from that found in the
United States. With the exception of a federal Supreme Court sitting in New Delhi (composed of a chief justice and thirteen judges,
appointed after consultation by the President of the Republic),
there are only state or territorial courts.[39]

The main task of the Supreme Court[40] is to ensure respect for
the Constitution, when the constitutionality of legislation of the
states or the central government is in question. It also hears cases
in which it is alleged that there has been contravention of a "fundamental right" guaranteed by the Constitution. As part of its
general civil jurisdiction, the Court may hear appeals from any
decision of a High Court when the amount involved exceeds
20,000 rupees and it can hear appeals, upon special leave, from
any decisions of any court in India, except those of military tribunals.

The Court is empowered to establish its own rules of practice
and procedure for cases before it, which must, however, be
approved by the President of the Republic. The Constitution provides that at least five judges shall sit in cases falling within the first
two categories listed above. The same number must also sit in matters upon which the President has requested, as authorised by the
Constitution, an advisory opinion.

The Indian Supreme Court, like the American, can effect

---

[38] Doré (F.), *op. cit.*, pp. 78 *et seq.*

[39] *Cf.* Doré, *op. cit.*, pp. 397 *et seq.* as to the organisation of judicial administration in the
states. Apart from the lower courts there are District Courts for civil matters, Sessions Courts
for criminal matters and, above them, High Courts. The territorial jurisdiction of these High
Courts exceptionally includes several states or territories.

[40] Appeals to the Judicial Committee of the Privy Council in London were abolished in 1947.

changes in its own established case law. But the ease with which Parliament can amend the Constitution has made such reversals rather rare. One famous case should, however, be mentioned as illustrative of this power. The Court, reversing its own earlier position, decided in a much debated case of 1967 that only a future constituant assembly, and not Parliament, could impinge upon fundamental rights guaranteed by the Constitution.[41]

According to the Constitution (section 141), courts other than the Supreme Court must observe the decisions of the latter. As for the decisions rendered by such other courts themselves, the point is debated in India, just as it is in the United States, whether or not, in order to simplify the administration of justice and promote uniformity among the state laws, it is desirable either to abandon altogether, or at least to relax, the rule of precedent such as it had operated under British rule. A Commission established in 1955 considered, however, that practice in this regard is so linked to the psychology of lawyers and judges that it was impossible to open the matter up again even though it appeared desirable.[42] The important role devolving to legislation and the progress of the idea of codification may nonetheless bring about in India, as in other countries, changes on this point.

---

[41] *I. C. Golak Nath* v. *State of Punjab* [1967] S. C. R. 1643.
[42] *Report of the Law Commission of India*, pp. 628–629, cited by Setalvad (M. C.), *The Common Law in India* (1960), p. 50.

TITLE III

LAWS OF THE FAR EAST

481. General remarks

The laws of the Far East, whether their history or present day character is considered, offer considerable variety. But over and above all such variations, it is nonetheless possible, at least from a western point of view, to detect a number of characteristics common to all countries of the Far East. Unlike western peoples, those of the East do not see law as a vehicle for assuring peace and social order. Law does, of course, exist but it plays only a minor role; its function is subsidiary. Law itself is only applied, and the courts only hear cases, when other available means for resolving conflicts and re-establishing social peace have failed. Both the definitive solution and the resort to force which the law implies are frowned upon. The maintenance of social order rests primarily upon persuasion, on mediation, the constant appeal to self-criticism as well as upon an attitude of conciliation and moderation.

While this overall perspective is common to the different countries of the Far East, it does not obliterate the very great differences between them. The social pressures exerted upon individuals is in each of them now directed towards the creation of very different conceptions of society. Geography and history had already profoundly differentiated China, Japan, Mongolia, Korea and the Indochinese states long before the western intrusions of the nineteenth and twentieth centuries forced them to question their traditional structures. In appearances at least these intrusions brought about a complete change in society. Most far eastern countries adopted codes[1] and it appeared that they thereby rejected their traditions in favour of Romano-Germanic law as the

---

[1] Malaya and Burma were, however, subject to British rule and the customary laws of these countries, already influenced by Muslim and Hindu law, were greatly changed, in many respects, by the institutions and ideas taken from the Common law.

basis for social relations. At later moments in time, some of these countries, moreover, have indicated a desire to transform society through Communism.

The effect of these changes has been considerable. But those accomplished, as well as those now underway, are far from having wiped out all traces of special traditions. The western structures and institutions in many instances are no more than a façade, behind which social relations continue to be ruled in large part by the traditional models. And apart from that, it is very clear that mental attitudes anchored in traditional ways of thinking must be taken into account by present day ruling authorities. Thus China, for example, has embarked upon a very different route than that of the Soviet Union, in the construction of Communism.

In the last two chapters of this title, an examination will be made of the law of two of the principal countries of the Far East, China and Japan, the first representing a society which has embraced the Communist ideal and the second a society that has opted for the principles of a free democracy.

CHAPTER I

CHINESE LAW

482. Cosmic order and harmony

The traditional Chinese concept of the social order, which had developed until the nineteenth century apart from any foreign influence, is completely different from that of the West. The fundamental idea (distinct from any religious dogma) is that there is a cosmic order of things involving a reciprocal interaction between heaven, earth and men.[1] Heaven and earth observe invariable rules in their movement, but men are masters of their own acts; and according to the way in which men behave, there will be order or disorder in the world.

The harmony upon which world balance and man's happiness depend has two aspects. It is first of all a harmony between men and nature. Human behaviour must be co-ordinated with the order of nature. To avoid epidemics, poor crops, floods, earthquakes and other natural disasters, one must take into account the cycle of the seasons, the position of the stars and other events of nature when proceedings to various acts of public and private life. Persons in authority must set the example of lives conforming to the order of nature; that indeed is their essential role. Virtue and morality are thus more important in administrators than any technical expertise.

The second harmonious relationship that must exist is that between men. The ideas of conciliation and consensus must be primary in social relations. All condemnations, sanctions, majority decisions must be avoided. Contestations and disputes must be *dissolved* rather than *resolved* or decided; the solution proposed must

---

[1] Gernet (J.), *Le Monde chinois* (1972). But the same idea emerges in the conceptions of proof in medieval Europe: Coing (H.), *Die historischen Grandlegen der europeischen Rechtseinheit, J. B. der Max-Planck Gesellschaft zur Forderung der Wissenschaften.* (1973), pp. 24–36.

be freely accepted by each because he considers it to be just; no one, therefore, should come away with the feeling that he has lost face. Education and persuasion, not authority or force, must prevail.

483. Minor role of law

This way of thinking leads the Chinese to view unfavourably our western idea of law, with all of its abstraction and strictness.[2] Man must not assert his rights since his duty is to co-operate in the work of reconciliation and, if need be, renounce his position in the interest of all. Jurists are not trusted; they are likely, in referring to abstract rules, to create obstacles on the path to seeking solutions through compromise; whether they wish it or not, they thus encourage blameworthy behaviour that is contrary to society's interests. Any solution must, above all, and apart from legal considerations, be in agreement with equity and feelings of human sentiment. Damages awarded, for example, must be such that they do not reduce the author of some wrong, or his family, to a state of misery.[3]

Legislation, therefore, is not the normal instrument for resolving disputes among men. It may occasionally have a useful role to play, in so far as it suggests models of conduct or holds out threats to those who pursue anti-social conduct, but there is no question that anyone should observe the letter of the law and much discretion must be used in the handling and application of laws. The ideal is that laws never be applied and that the courts never render decisions.

In the traditional Chinese concept law is not excluded but it plays only a minor role. Law, we are told, is good for barbarians[4]: for those who have no concern for morality or society, for incorrig-

---

[2] Even the word "law" (*droit*), as R. Dekkers observes, evokes a certain rigidity; justice, in its symbolic representation, is blindfolded and does not see the parties.

[3] Tsien (T.-H.), "La responsabilité civile délictuelle en Chine populaire" Rev. int. dr. comparé 1967, pp. 875–882. Tsao (W.-Y.), "Equity in Chinese Customary Law" *in Essays in Jurisprudence in Honour of Roscoe Pound* (1962), pp. 24–43, at p. 32: "It is a time-honored tradition of the Chinese to settle disputes by resorting first to *Ch'ing*, human sentiment, then to *Lii*, reason, and lastly to *Fa*, law."

[4] According to legend, law (*fa*) was invented by a barbarous tribe (the *Miao*) in the time of the prophet Shun (23rd century B.C.) and God later exterminated them: *cf.* Bodde (O.) and Morris (C.), *Law in Imperial China* (1967).

ible criminals, other peoples or foreigners who do not share the values of Chinese civilisation. The Chinese, on the other hand, normally live outside or apart from the law. They don't seek out whatever rules the law contains or claim their day in court, but settle their disputes and regulate their dealings with others according to their own idea of what is proper, without assertion of their rights and with conciliation and harmony as goals in mind. The reestablishment of harmony is made easier because of the fact that the education of all concerned naturally prompts them to seek the reasons for conflicts in their own deficiencies, carelessness or blunders rather than to attribute them to the bad faith or fault of an adversary. Typical of this point is the attitude of the civil servant who, observing difficulties in his department, would confess to the emperor or even commit suicide and thus stimulate citizens into asking themselves whether they weren't those really responsible.[5] In such an atmosphere, where each is ready to recognise his faults, it is easy to lead people into making concessions and to accept the intervention of a mediator. This acceptance may, however, be more forced than voluntary, given the fear of public opinion.

This aversion for law was traditionally enhanced by a range of factors, among which figures prominently the poor organisation—perhaps intentional but, in any event, blithely accepted by the ruling powers—of judicial administration.[6] The official called upon to judge a dispute was removed from the litigants: not legally trained, recruited as a matter of principle from another province, he was not familiar with either the dialect or the custom of the region in which he acts. The clerks with which the pleader has to deal were corrupt and purposely prolonged the litigation from which they drew fees; the litigant was subjected to countless humiliations and

---

[5] T'ung-tsu-Ch'u, *Law and Society in Traditional China* (1961), pp. 226 *et. seq.* Vu Van Mau, "Influence du bouddhisme sur le droit" Rev. asienne de droit comparé, 1964, pp. 3–26.

[6] The great 7th century Emperor K'ang Hsi is reported to have openly said, as cited by S. Van de Sprenkel, *Legal Institutions in Manchu China* (1962), p. 77: "Law suits would tend to increase to a frightful amount, if people were not afraid of the tribunals, and if they felt confident of always finding in them ready and perfect justice. As man is apt to delude himself concerning his own interests, contests would then be interminable, and the half of the Empire would not suffice to settle the lawsuits of the other half. I desire, therefore, that those who have recourse to the tribunals should be treated without any pity, and in such a manner that they shall be disgusted with law, and tremble to appear before a magistrate."

the outcome of the trial was, in all events, very doubtful. According to popular maxims, "of ten reasons for which a magistrate may decide a case, nine are unknown to the public" and "a case won is money lost." Everything discouraged the Chinese from using the courts and encouraged the use of extrajudicial techniques for the settling of disputes.[7]

484. Confucianism: primacy of rites

The form of social order which for centuries represented the ideal in China was that proposed by Confucianism. According to the teachings of Confucius (551–479 B.C.), the fundamental social unit is the family, organised in a hierarchy under the almost absolute authority of its head. Public bodies and the state itself were patterned along the same model and refrained from interfering in the many aspects of social life reserved to the family. In communities and collectivities of various kinds, the individual's duty was to live according to the rite or "style of life" which fell to each according to his status. The observance of these rites, as laid down by custom, was, in China, the principle that took the place of law.

In such an essentially static concept of society, the ideas of filial piety, of submission to one's superiors and the prohibition of any type of excess or revolt were fundamental principles. The exercise of authority was, however, not arbitrary; it too was carried out in respect for rites and tempered by a morality which required that explanations precede any command, that arbitration precede judgment and that warning precede punishment.[8]

China existed for many centuries according to these precepts and without any form of organised legal profession. Justice was rendered by administrators acceding to their functions without any study of law who relied upon the advice of scribes belonging to an hereditary caste. Those who were trained in the law were only consulted clandestinely. No legal doctrine ever developed and no doctrinal writer established a name for himself in the long history of China.

---

[7] Cohen (J. A.), "Chinese Mediation on the Eve of Modernisation" 54 Cal. L. Rev. 1201–1226 (1966).
[8] Tsien (T. H.), *loc. cit.* p. 432.

485. The legalists

While the validity of these principles was contested, the movement was highly exceptional. In the third century B.C., during a turbulent period of Chinese history, the school of legalists, basing itself on the idea of man's natural tendency towards bad behaviour, repudiated traditional theory and emphasised the need to obey prescriptions of law (government by law) rather than relying on the virtues of rulers (government by men). The legalists' theories, as expounded in the works of Han-Fei-tzû (*d*. 233 B.C.) stated the need for permanent laws which would be known by servants of the state and to which individuals would, without exception, be subject. On the whole, these theories express a concept of legislation (*loi*) and law (*droit*) very close to the western idea. J. Escarra[9] observed that the theories of Han-Fei-tzû seem to express ideas so common with us that they appear to be somewhat "naive." These theories have remained however completely foreign to the Chinese mentality in general. They were too radical a departure from accepted thinking, and the legalists had only a passing success. They did not gain any general acceptance in China for the notion of permanent rules and the concept of sovereign law.

Re-established as a favoured philosophy during the Han dynasty (206 B.C.), Confucianism has ever since dominated Chinese thought. The Mongols, it is true, to show their scorn for it in the thirteenth century, ranked the Confucian scholars in the tenth and lowest social caste along with beggars and prostitutes, but this official attitude had no lasting effect. Confucian thought has prevailed right up to the twentieth century and law has never appeared important to the Chinese who have followed other paths in their search for justice. Legislation was never anything but complementary in their social order, based as it was upon the notion of a social *statut*.[10] To study what in the West would be called Chinese private law, one must thus look to Chinese custom.[11] The Chinese codes, which appeared in the Han dynasty, contain only administrative or criminal matters, and private law only figures in

---

[9] Escarra (J.), *Le droit chinois* (1936), p. 55.

[10] T'ung-tsu Ch'u, *Law and Society in Traditional China* (1961) states that law exists in order to maintain each person's status within the family rather than to determine what is right and what is wrong.

[11] McAleavy (H.), "Chinese Law" in Derrett (J. D. M.) ed., *An Introduction to Legal Systems* (1968), p. 115.

so far as customary rules may carry criminal sanctions.[12] A person wishing to obtain state intervention in a matter of "private law" thus had to accuse the other party of a crime. But public opinion might well condemn even this behaviour and the complainant himself risked punishment in the event that he failed to establish the accusation.

486. Codification

The ideal of a society without law appeared to be put into question following the Revolution of 1911. The desire to be freed of western domination led the Chinese to adopt a series of codes manifestly based on western models: a Civil Code in 1929–1931 (encompassing private and commercial law), a Code of Civil Procedure in 1932 and a Land Code in 1930.[13] In appearances, therefore, Chinese law has been Europeanised and can be ranked within the family of laws deriving from the Romanist tradition. In China, as in Europe, there is no lack of persons interested in the theoretical study of law.

487. Persistence of traditional ideas

Behind this façade, however, traditional concepts have persisted and, several exceptions apart, have continued to dominate the realities of Chinese life. The work of a few men wishing to westernise their country could not possibly have resulted in the sudden transformation of Chinese mentality or accustom the people and jurists of China, in only a few years, to the Romanist concept of law which itself had developed only after a thousand years in the hands of the Christian jurists of the West. The Chinese codes and

---

[12] The early codes have been lost. The oldest in existence, that of the T'ang dynasty, dates from the 7th century A.D. The later codes adopt its plan according to which there are two parts: criminal law (*lü*) and administrative measures (*ling*). The code in force at the fall of the Empire, the *Ta'Ching lü-li* code, was first published in 1646. The first part contained 457 basic rules (*lü*), complemented or amended by about 1800 other rules (*li*). The whole was grouped under six titles according to whichever one of the six imperial administrative offices they were relevant. Complete editions of the Code contain glosses, a commentary and examples serving as illustrations of the text. *Cf.* McAleavy, *op. cit.* pp. 119–122. An abbreviated version was published in French by G. Boulais, *Manuel du Code chinois* (1924); and P. L. F. Philastre, *Le code annamite* (2nd ed., 1909).

[13] These codes are still in force in Formosa. As to Hong Kong, annexed by the English in 1843, where they were never in force, *cf.* McAleavy (H.), "Chinese Law in Hong Kong: The Choice of Sources" in Anderson (J. N. D.) ed., *Changing Law in Developing Countries* (1963), pp. 258–269.

laws were traditionally only applied to the extent that they corresponded to the popular ideas of equity and propriety. When they
conflicted with tradition they were in fact ignored. In the early
period, no resort was had to the courts, either because one was
unaware of one's rights or because there was a wish to avoid the
disapproval of society. Social relationships continued to be governed in this way, as they were in the past. If, in exceptional cases,
one did go before the courts, the Chinese judges still decided
according to the standards set by Confucius rather than by an
application of the rules of written law. They would for example
refuse to evict a poor tenant who had committed no fault if the
landlord were well-off and not in need of the premises; they
granted delays to borrowers in embarrassed circumstances if their
creditors were rich. And, as feared, the enactment of new codes
resulted in an increased number of trials and this, to the Chinese,
was a sign of decadence. Even the most advanced thinkers considered a return to the principles of Confucius to be desirable.[14]

488. Communist China

China became a people's republic on October 1, 1949, as a result
of the Communist Party victory under Mao-Tse-Tung
(1893–1976). Like the U.S.S.R., it has from that date adhered to
Marxist-Leninist teaching.

The U.S.S.R. and European people's republics have willingly
resigned themselves, in a transitional phase, to accept the principle
of social legality. For centuries, in these countries, law has had a
primary role; there is, then, no great embarrassment in relying
upon the technique of law as the most effective means for building
and organising a new egalitarian and classless society. In China, on
the contrary, the principle of law is detracted; it represents for the
Chinese nothing more than a brief period of their history, an episode of the western imperialism of which they are now free.[15]
China is also more ready than the U.S.S.R. to ephasise moral
development and civic education among its citizens even though
the link formerly established between social harmony and the
natural order is no longer recognised.

---

[14] Chu Chong, *On the Reconstruction of the Chinese System of Law* (1947).
[15] Shao-Chuan Leng, *Justice in Communist China* (1957).

489. First years: the Soviet model

The "common programme" of 1949 abolished in one stroke all existing laws, decrees and courts (s.17). It was thus urgent to rebuild the framework of society with all speed.

In the first years following the arrival of the communists in power, it appeared that, as in the Soviet Union, the primacy of law and legislation would be (reluctantly) accepted because in them, it was thought, lay the quickest and most effective means for totally transforming society and preparing for the advent of communism. A series of fundamental laws was adopted from 1949 onwards, in line with the Soviet model for this social reorganisation. A people's Supreme Court was created to direct the work of all the new courts and a Prokuratura was also established, which seemed to proclaim the triumph of the principle of legality. Major legislation was enacted in 1950 (on marriage, land reform, unions) and in 1951 (provisional organisation of the judicial system, repression of counter-revolutionaries). A codification commission was created within the central government and began the work of drafting codes in 1950.

In the absence of a suffecent legally experienced personnel,[16] the operation of these new institutions encountered very great difficulty. The police and public security forces often assumed tasks properly belonging to the courts; special courts functioned in the place of ordinarily competent people's courts which were sometimes controlled by the soviets. The Prokuratura, in the absence of legislation, was barely able to organise itself and hardly knew what to do. The principle of legality was thus established only with difficulty and, in 1952–1953, attacks were launched against it and the separation of law and politics, the principles of the independence of the judiciary and equality before the law, against the formalism and non-retroactivity of legislation, and against such concepts as *nulla poena sine lege* and the limitation of actions.

The Soviet model nevertheless appears to have been followed in the end and the principle of socialist legality to have become established. The 1954 Constitution based on the Soviet Constitution of

---

[16] A major purge was carried out during 1952–53 in the judiciary; about 80 per cent. of the judges who had served under the previous regime (6,000 out of 28,000) were eliminated and 6,500 new judges were named from among the "activists."

1936, shows this to have been the case.[17] Many institutions became more stable. The courts and the Prokuratura were reorganised in September 1954: more than 2700 people's courts were set up by 1957 and 94,000 "correspondants" were assisting the prosecutors by September 1956. Reactions set in to previous excesses: a regulation of December 1954 provided guarantees against arbitrary arrest and detention.

490. Marxism-Maoism

The Chinese revolution took a new turn in 1957, when the first difficulties with the U.S.S.R. were encountered before the final rupture in 1960. China at this time resolutely decided to pursue a path towards communism different from that of the U.S.S.R.[18]

While Chinese criticism was directed against those in the Soviet Union who succeeded to the place of Stalin, it was really the entire political line observed since 1917 that was rejected in China. The collectivisation of the means of production in the U.S.S.R., a basic step required by Marxist teaching, was also accomplished in China, but it was not sufficient in itself nor even, perhaps, essential. Marx and Lenin had seen this clearly and both had said that the working class should not limit itself merely to taking power; it should also destroy the means of production which is directly linked to the domination by the middle class and in which the worker is no more than an isolated but living accessory exploited for the creation of wealth. In their concern for increasing production, Soviet leaders had neglected the basic reforms required in the management of the means of production and thus perpetuated the essence of the ideology of capitalist productivity. China meant to depart from this model (nothing other than a state capitalism, in reality) and had no intention of substituting a struggle for the immediate satisfaction of material needs as proposed by the Soviet revisionists to the struggle for the total emancipation of the working class and the liberation of humanity as required by Marxism.

In China, priority was to be given to social transformation rather than economic growth; a new relationship between men was to be

---

[17] The Constitution contains a developed Declaration of Rights. Section 78 guarantees the independence of the judiciary.
[18] Kazol (K. S.): *La deuxième Révolution Chinoise* (1973); Macciocchi (M. A.): *De la Chine* (1971).

established in order to end any possibility or trace of exploitation. Development of one sector (heavy industry) was not to be emphasised, as in the Soviet Union, to the detriment of the peasants who, as the mass of the population, were to be made to realise that, henceforth, things have changed and that they were no longer exploited. No *élite* made up of intellectuals (those in the liberal professions, engineers or civil servants) was to be allowed to raise itself above the workers. Not only will the latter participate in the management of enterprises but the managers and directors will themselves work in the production ateliers in order that the distinction between intellectual and manual workers will disappear. In the abiding preoccupation to establish equality, the method of payment by the article or through the attribution of work-points, as practised in the Soviet Union, will be abandoned: in the place of this economic criterion based on productivity, a subjective political measure will be substituted which takes into consideration the devotion of each worker in the job of accomplishing a common task. The remuneration of each will be established by the collectivity after each worker has stated how much he himself, after examining his conscience, thinks he should receive.[19] It may happen that productivity will suffer because of these innovations and that the raising of the Chinese standard of living will be delayed, but this is far from certain and it will not, in any event, be too expensive a price to pay if it does usher in an atmosphere of fraternity.

On yet another matter the Chinese intend to strike out on a different path than that of the Soviets. The principle of "democratic centralism" admitted in the U.S.S.R., and the authoritarian methods and repressive police measures practised there, are regarded as inappropriate in China, a state where the proletariat has assumed power. Emphasis is to be put on persuasion much more than upon force which, in China, has always been frowned upon. It is admitted that there are right, centre and left wings to the Communist Party and these contradictions are seen as normal and even as necessary features of any living organisation. It is also admitted further that there is always some risk that the party will atrophy, that its leaders will become isolated from the masses and then prepare a restoration of capitalism to their own profit. Thus tolerance is advocated, and an adversary is not treated as beyond

---

[19] This system has only been instituted in a limited number of sectors.

redemption. But the masses are invited to be vigilant in respect of the party leaders at all levels including the Central Committee, and they are expected to participate actively in the definition of future policies. Mao himself invited the Central Committee to practise self-criticism by placing at the entrance to his conference room a sign which said "Fire on Headquarters!" (*ta-tsu-bao*); and he invited the people to advance criticisms and stimulate discussion in every organisation with the slogan "May a hundred flowers bloom and a hundred schools debate!" At the end of the workers' "cultural revolution" of 1966–1969, when the party was shaken by new popular movements from the roots, the tenth Congress of the Chinese Communist Party promised (August 1973) to promote, in the future, upheavals of a similar sort to those which had just occurred. The new statutes of the Party said as much in their first chapter.

491. Rejection of legality

While an effort was thus being made to build a truly new society (and not simply a new economy), a return to tradition was also taken up in China by reversing the roles recognised respectively to education and to law.

The principle of legality, which had never gained any intellectual hold, nor become established in practice, was repudiated. Efforts to bring about codification were abandoned; party directives henceforth took the place of strict laws. The courts were restricted in their activities and made subordinate to the soviets of different levels: law, as well as economics, were thus subordinated to political considerations. In all these developments there was a return to the ancient traditions of China. Social peace was to be sought through education; the consensus of all was to be obtained in order to establish the new order. "Patriotic agreements" were concluded in which citizens promised to obey the law and observe social discipline. Conciliation regained its place of honour, and law was given only a minor role. Mao so declared in a speech of February 27, 1957 in which he said that law was not suitable for everyone. Two ways were seen to be open for the resolution of the contradictions of which society is the victim. One was the appeal to the use of law and its sanctions, and this was seen as amounting to dictatorship. It was formerly thought suitable for barbarians; now it would be applied to counter-revolutionaries when all hope for their reform was abandoned. But law was not, on the other hand, suitable to resolve merely internal, rather than antagonistic, social contradictions. The masses do not have to suffer the dictatorship which they themselves exercise. If a citizen commits some wrong-doing, there is no need to treat him as a criminal, cite him before a court for judgment and punishment. Such degradation and shame must be spared the citizen; he probably did not fully realise what he was doing. It is more appropriate to undertake his education and apply persuasion rather than subject him to the indignity represented by a civil or criminal condemnation.

492. New tendencies

The settlement of disputes, the dissipation of litigation and repentance for wrongs committed remain, therefore, today as in the past, of the highest importance. It is in this formal or technical sense only, however, that we can speak of a "return to tradition" in China because in other respects there are fundamental differences between the China of yesterday and today.[20]

The first essential difference is that the idea of a cosmic order, inherent in nature, encompassing natural phenomena as well as man's behaviour, has disappeared. It is no longer believed that droughts, floods or plagues of grasshoppers are linked to human conduct or that the cycle of the seasons is the model upon which to base the maintenance of world social order. Today the Chinese look rather to the doctrinal teachings of Marxism as interpreted in the thought of Chairman Mao. The wish to create a new, dynamic social order has replaced the static view of former times.

A second difference is linked to the transformation just mentioned, the replacement of the former methods of mediation by new processes. One formerly appealed to the family, the clan, neighbours or local notables to resolve disputes. Such groups have today been abandoned. Mediation, and the incitement thereto, are naturally the business of those who are politically involved because it is political doctrine, and not the order of nature, that serves as model. More than 200,000 quasi-official "people's mediation committees" have been set up and settle millions of disputes.

---

[20] Lubman (St.), "Mao and Mediation: Politics and Dispute Resolution in Communist China" 55 Cal. L. Rev. (1967) p. 1284 at p. 1349.

In addition to these committees a large number of potential trials are eliminated through the intervention of mediators of many kinds (unions, social organisations, street committees, party cells, activists, police, etc.).[21] The role of these facilities for mediation may well explain the absence in China of a system of public arbitration analogous to that found in the U.S.S.R.

There is a third and final difference. Formerly, it was thought that a compromise was the best way to resolve any dispute and each party was therefore encouraged to sacrifice something of his own claim or rights, in order that harmony be re-established. This view of things, without doubt, continues to animate dispute settlement in many instances. But another consideration has also taken on very great importance. Today, it is admitted that assuring the success of some policy may well be more important than the amicable resolution of a dispute and so a less important place is given to mediation and settlement. In many cases, the conflict will be resolved by scolding the parties, enjoining them to abandon their feudal ways of thinking and appealing to their consciences in order that they subordinate their own conduct to the needs of production. But general and abstract rules are not invoked as they would be in the West. Any problem can be resolved through the application of the teachings of Mao, the correct interpretation of the Marxist-Leninist doctrine.

In both traditional and modern communist China, therefore, many matters which in the West would find their way into a court of law are resolved outside the law. With very great patience, every attempt is made to lead citizens into recognising their own faults and correcting their own behaviour whether in matters civil or criminal. The person who has erred is not brought before a judge; those with whom he is in contact discuss the matter with him, indicate their disapproval and put him on the right path.

Trials, as such, are therefore rather rare, except where enemies of the people, incorrigibles and other outcasts are concerned. Legal sanctions are not applied to those who, despite their possible errors, are nonetheless good citizens. Law is only the ultimate remedy for cases where other means for dispute settlement have, exceptionally, failed. The business of the courts, it is reported, is largely (about 50 per cent.) concerned with disputes arising in con-

---

[21] Cohen (J. A.), *loc. cit.* p. 1202.

nection with the 1950 law on marriage. It is, apparently, difficult for the various mediation bodies to bring about the social transformation expected in this legislation in respect of so intimate a part of the life of all citizens.

493. Legislation, judicial decisions, doctrine

Little legislation was enacted in China after 1949 and up to the death of Mao in 1976. The reason does not lie, as one might think, in the revolutionary climate of the country and the resulting impossibility of formulating rules that would soon not be overtaken by events. It is rather because the Chinese have a traditional antipathy towards the clear cut forms of legislative statement. There is, then, for the same reason, only a small body of judicial decisions; very few decisions of the Supreme Court have been reported; the concept of binding judicial precedents is quite unknown. Nor has there been any real volume of doctrinal writing. A study entitled *Fundamental Problems of Private Law of the People's Republic of China*, prepared before the break with the U.S.S.R. and published in 1958, remains the sole work of its kind; the two legal periodicals which particularly dealt with law, *Legal Science* and *Research in Politics and Law* have both ceased publication, the first in 1959 and the second in September 1966.

494. Developments after Mao

After the death of Chairman Mao in 1976 a further change occurred. In the aftermath of the arrest of the "gang of four," legality and juridicism became matters of importance and, with the enactment of the 1978 Constitution, legislation began to appear once more. Since 1979 laws have been adopted on the following topics: elections, organisation of the courts, joint ventures, Chinese and foreign capital investment, marriage (in order to relax the institution of late marriages instituted in 1950 as a means for solving the demographic problem), local government, the environment; a criminal code (192 sections) and a code of criminal procedure (164 sections). Much other legislation is forthcoming. This new legislation is often based on western models.

What are the reasons for this change? The present Chinese leaders, humiliated during the cultural revolution, felt the need to pacify the people and think that the existence of legislation could help curtail injustices. In showing themselves to be more legalistic, they thereby indicated that they were opposed to the policies of their predecessors and also gave some reassurance to foreign interests invited to invest in the country. By adopting a criminal code, it was also intended to fight a growing criminality among the people by means of a body of dissuasive rules.

But the application of a range of enacted laws will really only be carried through when the number of courts, judges and lawyers is considerably increased and legal education therefore expanded,[22] and, above all, when the ways of thinking, traditionally hostile to the rigidity of law, have themselves evolved. It seems, however, most unlikely for some time yet to come that the principle of legality and the idea of law will have the same roles to play in this great country that they now have in the West.

495. Chinese concept of international law

Mediation, encouraged in respect of internal relations, is seen as no less desirable in the sphere of international legal matters.[23]

In 1954, China established a Foreign Trade Arbitration Commission, as part of the Chinese Council for Expansion of Foreign Trade.[24] The provisional procedures prepared for this body in 1956 are largely based upon those of the corresponding Soviet institution. In practice, however, the situation is different from that in either the U.S.S.R. or the European people's republics. Chinese tradition has been perpetuated in the field of international trade relations as well: mediation is preferred to the failure which the application of law represents. According to a German study of 1960, of the 61 cases heard by the Arbitration Commission at Peking, not one ended in an arbitral award; a settlement was reached in all instances.[25] It is true, of course, in this area, that the drafting of the contracts themselves, and the uncertainty surrounding the

---

[22] *Cf.* Macdonald (R.), "Legal Education in China" (1980) 6 Dal. L.J. 313; Bing Ho, "Chinese Legal Education" (1984) 8 Dal. L.J. 32.

[23] On the Chinese concept of public international law, *cf.* Hungdah Chiu, "Communist China's Attitude Toward International Law" 60 Am. J. Int. Law 245 (1966).

[24] Crespi-Reghizzi (G.), "Legal Aspects of Trade with China: The Italian Experience" 9 Harvard Int. L. J. 85 (1968).

[25] *Ibid.* p. 124. In most of the cases the Chinese appeared as vendors. When they are buyers, an arbitration agreement frequently stipulates arbitration in some other country, and in such cases it is not established that the arbitration procedures result in an equal number of settlements. *Adde* Pettit (C.), "Dispute Resolution in the People's Republic of China" (1984) 39 Arbitration Law J. 3.

applicable law, often blur the distinction, at best difficult to establish, between arbitration and mediation. There is nonetheless a difference between them which is of capital importance to the Chinese: the dispute is ended by an agreement of the parties rather than an arbitral award rendered upon the authority of an arbitrator.

CHAPTER II

JAPANESE LAW[1]

496. Historical factors

Until 1853, Japan had no contact with the West. Its traditional ways of thought, very far removed from those of western civilisation, were influenced however at different periods of its history by those of China with which it did have relations. And yet Japanese civilisation has remained distinct from the Chinese, partly because of the particular character of the Japanese themselves and partly because of the isolation in which the country was maintained by its rulers for the 250 years preceding its "opening-up" in 1853.

The first landmarks in Japanese law appear in the Taika era which began in the year A.D. 646. Under Chinese influence, a form of state and moralistic planning was introduced by means, in particular, of a system of periodic distribution of the state rice plantations in proportion to the numbers to be fed and a strict division of society into "ranks." Each class was required to perform some specific task for the state, and legal compilations based on Chinese models known as *ritsu-ryō* spelled out the duties of each.[2] They contain principally a series of prohibitions (*ritsu*) and rules of administration (*ryō*). These collections were commented upon in schools of law and administration for the enlightenment of the people. They contain no suggestion of the idea of *rights* but there is some notion of law in so far as they constitute a recording in writing of the duties of each person.

The land sharing system found in the *ritsu-ryō* of the seventh century, also based on Chinese ideas, functioned poorly in Japan.

---

[1] Noda (Y.), *Introduction au droit japonais* (1966) translated by A. H. Angelo as *Introduction to Japanese Law* (1976). *Cf.* also the interesting work published under the direction of A. Von Mehren: *Law in Japan. The Legal Order in a Changing Society* (1963) in which the changes brought about in Japanese law through American influence since 1945 are examined.
[2] *Taihō Ryō* (701), *Yōrō Ryō* (718).

In the ninth and tenth centuries a seigneurial system developed to the detriment of the system of sharing of public land previously practised. The Japanese seigneurial unit (*shō*) appears to have been an inviolable domain enjoying certain fiscal privileges; the master of the *shō* changed his right to receive the products of the land, which he enjoyed as an hereditary public official, into a right of full ownership of extensive tracts of land; within the *shō* he had the powers of a sovereign.[3]

Weaknesses in criminal justice, resulting insecurities and a series of civil wars led to the superimposition of a new feudal system at the end of the twelfth century. The emperor was deprived of any real power and his decline carried with it that of the courtier class (*kuge*) as well. Because of his sacred rights the emperor remained an important and revered figure but he no longer held any real power. He was above—but also quite outside—the military caste, unknown in China,[4] which henceforth governed. The military caste (*buke, bushi, samurai*) lived according to its own personal, customary law (*buke-hō*). The ruling "code of chivalry"[5] was founded on the idea of the duty of absolute faithfulness on the part of the vassal towards his overlord. There is once again no concept whatsoever of legal rights or duties. The vassal had no guarantee against the arbitrary action of the overlord; there was never any system of judgment by one's peers in Japan. Even the very idea that the vassal might have rights exercisable against his suzerain would have been shocking; their relationship was very much like that of father and son. There was, then, no concept of contract between them: "feelings such as affection, fidelity, abnegation, devotion to one person, the spirit of sacrifice to an idea, these lose their force as soon as they are placed within rigid limits, no matter how reasonable."[6]

---

[3] Joüon des Longrais (F.), *L'Est et l'Ouest. Institutions du Japon et de l'Occident comparées (Six études de sociologie juridique), 1958.*

[4] The egalitarian philosophy of ancient Chinese society was unknown in Japan. The Chinese system of examinations for entry into the civil service, for example, never penetrated Japan.

[5] The *Goseibai shikimoku*, the custom of the *buke* dating from 1232, has been published in French by Appert (G.), "Un code de la féodalité japonaise au XIIIe siècle" 24 Nouv. Rev. Hist. de droit (1900), pp. 338–365.

[6] Joüon des Longrais (F.), *op. cit.* pp. 144 *et seq. Cf.* as well the interesting comparison drawn between France and England, and the evolution of European feudalism upon the revival of Roman law.

497. Decadence of the Ritsu-Ryō

For several centuries the warrior class ethic of the *buke* existed alongside the more detailed regulation of the *ritsu-ryō*; the latter continued to apply to those who did not belong to the warrior class. During the period of the Ashizaka Shoguns (1333–1573), following the Kamakura era (1185–1333), a period of anarchy and civil war ended with the triumph of the so-called "unitary" feudalism. The superiority of the warrior over the peasant was established; the local representatives of the military class (*jitō*) whose duty it was to ensure public order and collect taxes, secured for themselves the revenues of the *shō* which, until that time, they had shared. Japan, now divided between several powerful local and independent lords (*daymyō*) to whom the *jitō* were infeudated, was plagued by a series of private wars. The rules of the *ritsu-ryō* fell into a desuetude; only the ancient personal law of the *buke* remained in force and they soon replaced the territorial customs.

Until that time there were different social classes in Japan each ruled by its own particular *statut*. This inegalitarian structure was replaced in the fourteenth century by a strictly conceived hierarchy which in its own way excluded any idea of rights of an inferior as against his superior. Since there was no concept of contract or reciprocal legal obligations between the members of the warrior class, there were none, *a fortiori*, between the lords and those who tilled the land.[7]

This hierarchical structure, in which any notion of rights was absent, was further re-enforced during the era of Tokugawa Shoguns (1603–1868) when the policy of isolation was inaugurated. As a reaction against European influences,[8] Confucianism was made the official religion. A policy of close supervision and a system of denunciation began in 1597 with the organisation throughout the country of groups of persons, five in number called *goningumi*, charged with reporting all crimes, maintaining public order, informing the police of the movements of others or the presence of foreigners. The group, treated as an entity for fiscal and criminal purposes, had to agree before any form of judicial procedure could be instituted by one of its members. It intervened in the family

---

[7] Joüon des Longrais (F.), *op. cit.* p. 256.

[8] The Portuguese had penetrated Japan by 1542 and the resulting predication of Christianity endangered the Japanese social order.

affairs of each member by supplying either counsellors or witnesses, and it controlled the cultivation of land. This institution so deeply marked the Japanese mentality during the Tokugawa period that its traces are present even today.

This established order was considered at the time to be a natural and immutable social organisation. It was based on a strict separation of social classes (warriors, peasants, merchants) and their arrangement into a hierarchy. The whole way of life of a Japanese was determined on the basis of the class to which he belonged; the type of house inhabited, the type and colour of cloth worn and type of food consumed were all predetermined. The Shōgun of Ido, who was possessed of real power, did not consider that acting as a judge formed a normal part of his functions, and only in exceptional cases would he intervene in such capacity. His jurisdiction only developed in the eighteenth century; according to a decision of 1767, it covered 53 types of cases classified into two categories: major disputes and money disputes. But the policy of the central administration was always directed to maintaining rather than usurping the jurisdiction of the local courts. Justice continued, however, to be administered by the shōgun rather against his will and private persons were never recognised as having the right to institute an action. Judicial functions were never distinguished from other public duties. And in Japan, there were no law schools, no professional magistrates, judicial administration or legal professionals.

498. Absence of the idea of law. The giri

Whatever at this period might be considered law, or merely written rules, amounts really to no more than instructions given by superiors to inferiors. The inferior had only to obey; the mass of people, systematically kept in ignorance, was not protected in any way against any form of arbitrary action. There was no question of rights in the relations of persons from an inferior class with those of a superior class. And the idea of law, altogether absent with respect to persons belonging to different classes, was no more evident in relations between those of the same class. Just as in China, there was a sentiment amounting to abhorrence at the finality of solutions and the absence of shades of meaning which the very idea of law implies. A whole series of rules, in nature much closer to rules of propriety than morality, was developed in order to specify the conduct to be observed on all occasions when one individual came into contact with others. These rules of behaviour, analogous to the Chinese rites, were known as *giri*. There was thus the *giri* of father and son, the *giri* of husband and wife, that between uncle and nephew, or brothers among themselves and, outside the family, that of landowner and farmer, lender and borrower, merchant and customer, employer and employee, more senior employee to more junior employee, and so on. As F. Joüon des Longrais has written, "The Asia of Confucius preferred the ideal of a filial relationship based on attentive protection and respectful subordination to that of equality."[9]

The *giri* therefore replaced law and, according to some Japanese, even morality. It was spontaneously observed not so much because it corresponded to a series of moral values or strict duties but rather because social reprobation attached to its non-observance. It would be a source of shame, a loss of face, for a Japanese not to respect one of the *giri* in which he was involved. A code of honour, wholly customary, thus determined all forms of behaviour. Until recent times, the system of the *giri* made any intervention of law in the western sense useless and even offensive.

499. Meiji Era: westernisation of Japanese law

Such was the picture of Japanese society at the beginning of the Meiji era in 1868. All these ancient structures then seemed to disappear as a result of a complete re-shaping of Japanese society. A democratic state of the western type replaced the former feudal state; and an extraordinary development has placed Japan at the forefront of the world's trading nations. And now there is modern legislation linking Japanese law to the laws of the West, in particular the Romanist laws of the European continent. The legal works written in Japan confirm the impression that the legal system, legal thought and indeed the whole of society have been thoroughly westernised. The studies devoted to the philosophy of law written by Japanese expound western jurisprudential theories without making any mention of traditional and specifically Japanese ideas. A complete break between the ancient and the modern Japanese laws apparently exists. It is extremely rare for any reference ever

---

[9] *Op. cit.* p. 256.

to be made to the former law which has, moreover, never yet been completely described in a single work. Modern Japanese law is wholly attached to western law; Harada, a Japanese Romanist, has been able to establish that without exception *all* the articles of the Japanese Civil Code are derived from some western or Roman law.

This process of westernisation was decided upon as the country's course of action at the beginning of the Meiji era and in order to terminate the unequal commercial treaties imposed in 1858 by a number of western powers (United States, United Kingdom, Russia, France and Holland) which Japan considered a national humiliation. It was easier to achieve a rapid modernisation by adopting a series of codes than to turn to the Common law. As early as 1869 the translation of French codes was undertaken and the work completed within five years despite all the difficulties involved, in particular the absence of qualified Japanese jurists. New words had to be found to express such elementary notions as "right" (*droit subjectif*) rendered as *kenri*, or "legal duty" (*obligation juridique*) rendered as *gimu*, which until that time were foreign to Japanese thought. With the help of a number of jurists, the Frenchman G. Boissonade[10] and a number of others, German and even English,[11] a series of codes was prepared by 1872.

A Penal Code and a Code of Criminal Procedure, both based on the French models, were enacted in 1882. In 1890 a law on judicial organisation and another on civil procedure based on German law were enacted. The adoption of the Civil Code proved more difficult. The original draft prepared by Boissonade, altered with respect to the law of persons and successions, was adopted in 1891 but not put into force because of opposition from different quarters. A new draft code was prepared. Although in theory merely an adaptation of the first, it was really quite different because of the considerable influence of the new German code on its authors. The Japanese code was finally adopted and put into force in 1898 (July 16).[12] Eclectic in content, in so far as it took into account a number of different European codes, it was in the

[10] Noda (Y.), "Gustave Boissonade, comparatiste ignoré" in *Problèmes contemporains de droit comparé*, t. II (1962), pp. 235–256.

[11] Although he was not called upon to participate in the work, the American jurist John H. Wigmore spent some years in Japan at this time. His passages on Japanese law in his *Panorama of the World's Legal Systems* (1928) are still valuable.

[12] An annotated English translation was published by de Becker (J. E.) in 4 vols. in 1909.

end nonetheless drawn up essentially along German lines. It was completed by a commercial code with the same characteristics in the following year.

This series of codes was paralleled in the public law area by a complete reform of the nation's public institutions. The freedom of agriculture was established in 1871, that for the sale of land in 1872. A constitution was enacted in 1889. The administrative structure was modernised by means of a new division of the country into departments (*kin*) and by a series of laws on such departments (1890) and on municipal structures (1888).

The law of Japan based on these various texts underwent very considerable change after 1945. There was no question at that time of returning to rules more in harmony with the genius of Japanese civilisation. The reforms introduced in a spirit of democratisation were American rather than Japanese in inspiration. A new constitution (1946), reforms in administrative organisation, the status of public officials, administrative jurisdictions and procedure resulted. There was also a radical re-organisation of the court structure and police, and some changes to the then existing codes were also made.

500. Westernisation of Japan

Since 1945, therefore, an Anglo-American influence has been at work on, and is sometimes in competition with, the Romanist influence. But the question is still very much open whether, behind this façade of westernisation, Japan really has undergone any kind of fundamental transformation and whether it has accepted the idea of justice and law such as understood in the West.

This question can be asked as readily in the field of private as in public law. In both cases the law is wholly state-made, copied from the West, and really only governs a very small part of Japan's social life. Western law does, after all, suppose a middle class, capitalist society made up of free individuals who establish their various relations on the basis of this liberty. Such a state of things is very far removed from the realities of Japan. It is true that Japanese *mores* are evolving, and they are approaching more and more, especially in urban society and among members of the younger generation, those presupposed by their law. But from all points of view Japanese society is still far from being a western society. The former habits and ways of thinking are still very much alive among the majority of Japanese, even those living in cities, the working classes and in commercial dealings. A state capitalism, or one developed by a small number of important businessmen, has grown up beside a very little changed peasant class closely linked to the industrial working class. A socially critical spirit has been slow to develop; the Confucian idea of an ordered hierarchy based on natural scheme of things is still very much alive. Individualism has never had very strong roots in Japan. Thus the social structures and the free atmosphere pre-supposed by western laws are present only to a very slight degree in Japan. Western laws were made for a rationalist milieu and their abstract conceptual structures are the product of a Cartesian outlook. In Japan the application of modern law runs counter to Japanese mystical sentimentalism, the outcome more of a poetic than a logical spirit, which has rendered the Japanese historically indifferent to the ideals of individual freedom and human dignity entertained in the West.

501. Public law

In the area of public law, the legally perfected democratic institutions are distorted in actual operation because of the fact that the Japanese do not really like becoming involved in public affairs. They prefer to leave the business of government to a small and powerful minority. Even today the Japanese people still do not realise that they are the masters of their own destiny. A specialist in the history of political ideas, Professor Oka, has not hesitated to speak of the "apparent constitutionalism" characterising the Japanese political order. Arbitrary action by the police excites few objections; the public authorities consider it their duty to arrange things in such a way that the police do not lose face and this means that a guilty person must be found—by any means possible whenever a crime has been committed. The judges are summary in the reasons provided in their judgments because they consider it unnecessary to justify their decisions. The judicial review of the constitutionality of legislation is exercised with extreme prudence, even reticence, by the Supreme Court.[13]

---

[13] Tanaka (K.), "Democracy and Judicial Administration in Japan," 2 *Journal of the International Commission of Jurists*, 7–19 (1959–1960).

502. Private law

Practice is just as far removed from theory in the field of private law. The Japanese still consider law as the means by which the state can forcibly impose the more or less arbitrary will of its political leaders; law as an idea is still associated with punishments and prison; in the popular conception good people stay out of the reach of the law because law is a hateful thing. To be brought before a court, even in a civil or private matter, is a source of shame; and this fear of shame—the loss of face—rather than any morality is the determining motive in Japanese conduct.

The concept of law has thus not penetrated the daily life of Japan. Even the logical character of law, and the necessary abstraction which its rules must have, are ideas foreign to this country which, until very recently, was unaware of the work of Aristotle. Still essential for the Japanese are the rules of behaviour (*giri-ninjō*) for each type of personal relation established by tradition and founded, at least in appearance, on the feelings of affection (*ninjō*) uniting those in such relationships. A person who does not observe these rules is seeking his own interest rather than obeying the nobler part of his nature; he brings scorn upon himself and his family. Apart from the contacts arising between large but depersonalised business and industrial concerns, one does not attempt to have one's rights enforced in a court of law even though this is permitted by the various codes. The creditor will thus request his debtor to be gracious enough to perform voluntarily the obligation he was kind enough to undertake in order to spare him any embarrassment; the victim of some accident, resigned to his misfortune, will spontaneously renounce pressing rights and will accept with grateful acknowledgment the nominal indemnity, as well as the apologies, of its author. To behave otherwise would imply that there was a guilty person—that is to say, a dishonest man. To have recourse to the law in order to enforce a legally legitimate claim is hardly distinguishable in Japan from extortion. The whole concept of *rights* depersonalises human relations; it places all men on an equal footing without regard to the hierarchy which, in Confucian teaching, the basis of Japanese tradition, exists in nature. It is, in a word, simply distasteful to the feelings of the Japanese, and they, as a people, allow themselves to be guided more by their feelings than by reason. The courts in Japan are far from being inactive, but the most important part of their activity, at least among private persons, consists of conciliation rather than adjudication.

503. Importance of conciliation

Several types of conciliation are envisaged by law.[14] The first, known as *jidan* is, traditionally, a pre-trial procedure. The Japanese still consider that going to court is blameworthy behaviour and, before doing so, will employ every effort to settle amicably any dispute that arises by appealing to mediators of various kinds. This form of reconciliation is, necessarily, not susceptible of statistical measurement[15] but it would appear in this connection that the police play a very important role—the Tokyo municipal police in 1958 had 21,590 *civil* cases and in 59 per cent. of them, it was able to obtain an amicable settlement between the parties.

In most cases the dispute ends there. But in the absence of a settlement the parties can, these days, go to court; and even there the possibility of reconciliation is not exhausted. According to the Code of Civil Procedure (art. 136), the judge must, throughout the proceedings, endeavour to bring the parties to a settlement. The ideal conclusion to the litigation is not a judgment with which both parties can agree, but rather a discontinuance of their suit which will result in a compromise or settlement between them. For the judge, therefore, in such a context, there are numerous occasions when he can assume the role of a mediator.[16]

Of course, the very fact of judicial intervention is, in itself, the sign of social disturbance and in Japan every effort is made to avoid it. Alongside the procedure just described (*wakai*), another is also available to the parties, known as *chotei*.[17] Instead of seeking judgment based in law, the parties may request the court to appoint a panel of conciliators which is charged with proposing an equitable settlement. This panel is normally composed of two conciliators and a judge, although the latter will refrain from taking an

---

[14] Henderson (D. F.): *Conciliation and Japanese Law: Tokugawa and Modern* (1964).

[15] It may be noted, however, that in 1955 more than 90 per cent. of recorded divorces (68,514 of 75,267) were passed on the parties' agreement.

[16] Discontinuances of suits rose to 40 per cent. in 1959. Even the Supreme Court attempts, sometimes with success, to promote the discontinuance of suits at its level.

[17] *Chotei* was established gradually between 1920 and 1930 in legislation on relations between land-owners and tenant farmers, and then for commercial matters, money debts, etc. At the present time it is regulated by legislation of 1951 on reconciliation in civil matters.

active part in the procedure because appearances must not suggest that the dispute has been resolved through the intervention of judicial authority. Disputing parties, with an eye to their reputations, often prefer to seize the courts through this *chotei* procedure rather than seek a settlement from the start. In respect of some types of disputes (family or labour matters) the law itself obliges the parties to resort to it.

Supposing further that the conciliation panel had proposed a solution, but that one or both parties refuse to accept it and, after several months devoted to the procedure, it must be said to have failed. It was then open to either party to go before the court within a two week delay and Japanese law then used to give the court an option: it could decide the case in strict law or homologate the compromise settlement proposed *ex aequo et bono* by the conciliators.

The question arose whether these provisions were constitutional in Japanese law. The Supreme Court delayed rendering its decision for some considerable time. It decided in 1960 that the Constitution was violated by this procedure. A majority of nine judges against six held the procedure to be contrary to section 32 (which guarantees free access to the courts) and section 82 (which establishes that judicial proceedings must be public) of the Constitution. The *chotei* procedure is, therefore, now only possible if the solution to which it gives rise is voluntarily accepted by the parties.

There has been, moreover, since 1958, something of a decline in the use of the *chotei* procedure. Statistics show that the courts are requested to decide in law more frequently than previously was the case. But the Japanese are far from having rejected their traditions: statistics also suggest that they are not litigiously minded. Lawyers remain few in number (in 1964 there were 7,136) and in the lower courts most litigation takes place without any lawyer present; the possibility that the judge will lead the parties to a settlement or decide, more or less openly, in equity, is increased correspondingly.

The anti-legalist attitude of the Japanese discourages resort to arbitration (*chusai*) in the proper sense of the term. It appears improper to them to anticipate that a contract will give rise to a dispute and, if it were to happen, that it could not be resolved by an agreement prompted by the parties' common goodwill. Arbitration agreements, while often found in contracts involving external trade, are, in respect of domestic business contracts, replaced by a clause stating that the parties will seeek a solution through reconciliation.

504. Social realities and law. Future of Japanese law

The Japanese are ready to accept all modern ideas proposed to them. They are very little concerned about the foreign origin of such ideas or with the contradictions sometimes existing between them. There is, of course, no essential contradiction in building a legal system on the western model while persevering in a way of life which ignores the rules of such system. Law is never—in any country—the only source of rules governing human affairs, and most people agree that this is, indeed, a good thing. Law does no more than propose a means of solving disputes for those cases in which it is impossible to come to some kind of friendly settlement or agreement. How then, one may ask, are matters settled in fact when there is such an amicable arrangement? Is it brought about by agreement on the model offered by the law or in some other way? It is well known that sociologists have no easy answers to these questions. The difference in the case of Japan and the West is that in the latter we endeavour to have the law reproduce the series of solutions which best corresponds to our sense of justice and our own social manners. The law artificially imported into Japan, on the other hand, is clearly not suited to, or even in harmony with, present Japanese social norms.

Unlike the situation in the socialist countries, Japanese leaders have never had any intention of transforming the way of life of the people through the enactment of codes. On the contrary, the desire to develop the country in economic matters, which led to the adoption of western legal forms, co-existed with a wish to conserve these traditional ways. No contradiction between the two ideas was seen to exist and the task of the future was accordingly thought to be to bring about their reconciliation. Until 1945 the Japanese continued to live, as they had in the past, quite unaware of the new law.

The events of 1945 were a shock for the Japanese; the precise consequences of this terrible moment in their history are still somewhat difficult to assess. Modern techniques are transforming all aspects of the relations and dealings between East and West.

The idea of equality of all men, which in the West finds its greatest support in the equality of all men before God, has been adopted on the secular level by individualist doctrines; and socialist theory, on this point at least, has followed suit. At the present time however Japan, among all the industrialised nations, is isolated by its attachment to a concept of a social hierarchy which, in the minds of its people, is imposed by the natural order. Industrialisation and urban development have put these structures into question; the defeat of 1945 and the foreign military occupation of Japan, which was without precedent, have created serious doubts about its continuing value. The older generation complains that Japanese youth no longer observes the *giri*. The progress of democratic ideas and the intensification of contacts with other parts of the world may result, however, in the end, in a gestation of the idea that law is a necessity—and that the rule of law is a necessary condition for the inauguration of the reign of justice. But even this can be no more than an hypothesis.

TITLE IV

LAWS OF AFRICA AND MALAGASY

505. Outline

The laws of Africa and Madagascar or, as it is now, the Mala-gasy Republic, deserve the special notice of contemporary jurists. The colonial period is over and Africans and Malagasies are now directing their own destinies. It is appropriate therefore to exam-ine first of all the state of the applicable law as it was both before and at the time of independence and then to enquire into the post-independence tendencies and present orientation of the law as now directed by the leaders of these new nations.

CHAPTER I

CUSTOMARY BASIS OF THE LAW

506. Importance and variety of customs

The parts of Africa south of the Sahara—"black" Africa, Ethiopia, Somaliland, the Sudan and Madagascar—were ruled for centuries by their own ancestral customary laws. Observance of custom was generally spontaneous since it was thought that one was obliged to live as one's ancestors had; the fear of supernatural powers and of group opinion were most often sufficient to assure a respect for the traditional ways of life. The fairly complex social system was able to provide for the resolution of disputes or to establish rules of conduct when new circumstances created fresh problems for the community in question.

There were of course many ancestral customs in this vast African territory.[1] Contacts between different groups were minimal and each community, largely self-sufficient, had its own customs and social habits. The differences between customs in the same region, or as between related ethnic groups, were largely secondary or even negligible in importance, but outside such general groupings these customs were sometimes very distinctive. In Africa there are tribes with monarchical or democratic social structures, and there are others so primitive that it is difficult even to discover any elements of social organization at all. The family is sometimes patrilineal, sometimes matrilineal, but even within these two general types there may be many variant structures. The land system varies from region to region as well. For these reasons it is difficult, if indeed not altogether arbitrary, to speak in general terms of an African and Malagasy customary law.

---

[1] In the former French Equatorial Africa and Belgian Congo there were about 1500 ethnic groups; in the Sudan alone there are 579; 200 in British East Africa; and 19 in Madagascar. In Senegal, 68 customs have been officially recognised by a decree of February 28, 1961, 20 of which are qualifed as Islamic and seven as Christian.

Does this mean, then, that there is no *legal* unity among these various communities, that there is no "African" law properly speaking? Opinions have in fact differed on this question. While acknowledging the great diversity of customs in a continent divided into so many communities, there is, however, now general agreement that certain characteristics common to all African laws do set them off from the laws of Europe. An English author, summarising the commonly received opinion, has put it this way: "[African law] is not . . . a single system, even one with variant schools, but rather a family of systems which share no traceable common parent. . . . But, more fundamentally, African laws reveal sufficient similarity in procedure, principles, institutions, and techniques for a common account to be given of them."[2]

507. African concept of the social order

In the African mind, ancestral custom is linked to a mythical order of the universe. To obey custom is to pay respect to one's ancestors whose remains are fused with the soil and whose spirits watch over the living.[3] Violations of custom will release unknown but certainly unfavourable consequences in a world where forces natural and supernatural, man's behaviour and the movements of nature, are all linked.[4]

African custom is thus based upon notions entirely different from those which have dictated modern western thinking. The African conception of the world is essentially static; it rejects the idea of progress and, therefore, frowns upon any act (such as the sale of land) or institution (such as prescription or usucapion) which has the effect of changing a previously established situation. The principal concern is for those social groupings (tribes, castes, villages, blood lines) which endure throughout time, rather than, as in the West, those which are more transient (individuals,

---

[2] Allott (A. N.), "African Law" in Derrett (J. D. M.) ed., *An Introduction to Legal Systems* (1968), p. 131.

[3] Verdier (R.), "Chef de terre et terre de lignage" in *Etudes de droit africain et de droit malgache* (J. Poirier, ed.) (1965), pp. 333–359.

[4] Deschamps (H.), "Les fondements du droit quotidien malgache," *ibid.* pp. 19–25. The etymology of the Malagasy word *fomba*—ancestral custom— is the protective cover or lid of the world order. Any violation of *fomba* is a sin (*fady*) and a danger for the universe, and, in particular, for the person who broke the custom and for his group.

couples, households).[5] Land belongs to one's ancestors and to future generations as much if not more than to those living. Marriage is an alliance between two families rather than a union of two people. The individual is not ignored, and his personality is recognized, but the group is the visible basic unit.[6]

Such a view of the world leaves little place for the notion of private rights deriving from the notion of individual personality. Much greater emphasis is placed upon the *obligations* of each person according to his social condition; and obligations properly juridical in character are not clearly distinguished from those which may be classed as simply moral. While this distinction can be drawn in respect of African customs themselves by European jurists,[7] it is, for the Africans, one difficult to understand in a country where there are no jurists and no legal scholarship. In the same way, the distinctions between public and private law, civil and criminal law, law and equity are, *a fortiori,* unknown; the law of property, contract and tort, linked to the notion of status, derive from, or form part of, the law of persons.[8] In the face of this apparently considerable disparity of ideas, European authors have asked themselves whether it is artificial to attempt to seek out our western idea of law and whether the customary laws of Africa and Malagasy ought not, more properly, to form the subject of anthropological rather than legal research.[9]

508. Procedures

Consider what happens when someone is accused of having violated custom or when there is some kind of dispute. Custom may well contain relevant rules but often these do no more than establish the basis of discussion from which an appropriate mechanism will emerge for its resolution. Justice will not always consist of what we know as the application of substantive rules; its role is to

---

[5] Alliot (M.), "Les Résistances traditionnelles au droit moderne dans les Etats d'Afrique francophone et à Madagascar" in *Etudes de droit africain et de droit malgache* (J. Poirier, ed.) (1965), pp. 235–256.

[6] Allot (A. N.), "African Law" in Derrett (J. D. M.) ed., *An Introduction to Legal Systems* (1968), p. 147.

[7] Gluckman (M.), *Politics, Law and Ritual in Tribal Society* (1965), p. 197.

[8] Gluckman (M.), *The Ideas in Barotse Jurisprudence* (1965), pp. 94, 170. Maine in his *Ancient Law* (1861) had already observed as much.

[9] Gluckman (M.), *Politics, Law and Ritual in Tribal Society* (1965), pp. xxii, 112; Allott (A. N.), *New Essays in African Law* (1970), p. 148.

bring about an amicable settlement between the parties rather than to see to the enforcement of their "rights."[10] The end in view is not to attribute to each his due. "Justice," in the African context, consists, above all, in assuring whatever is necessary for the cohesion of the group and restoring peace and understanding among its members.

Law and justice in the context of the small, pre-colonial societies of Africa and Malagasy were inevitably different from what they were in the vast communities of the European states. Native justice was an institution for peace rather than a means for the strict enforcement of law; its purpose was to reconcile the parties and to restore harmonious relations within the community. Searching for an agreement was all the more necessary in view of the lack of procedures for the enforcement of judgments which, in any event, because they are based only on some principle of authority, might well be of no effect whatsoever. Moreover, it is not rare, we are told, for the successful party, acting in that generous spirit characteristic of African society, to forego the enforcement of his judgment.[11]

509. Ascertainment of customs

It is very difficult for an outside observer to gain any thorough knowledge of these customs, and considerable linguistic difficulties are encountered when efforts are made to describe them. To apply the methods and to attempt to establish the categories of western laws is to distort totally the concepts of African custom.[12] This is particularly so in family relations. The African family is a group distinct from the western family unit; the range of relationships is conceived quite diffently; the African marriage settlement bears no resemblance to that of Muslim law and even less to the dowry (*dos*) of Roman law; the devolution of inheritances obeys

---

[10] Allott (A. N.), *Essays in African Law* (1960), p. 73; Gluckman (M.), *The Ideas in Barotse Jurisprudence* (1965), pp. 10, 22. The latter underscores the total absence of formalism in African procedure: there have never been procedural rules limiting either the jurisdiction or the powers of those bodies charged with the administration of justice; the ruling principle is *ubi ius ibi remedium* (*ibid.* p. 1).

[11] Van Velsen (J.), "Procedural Informality, Reconciliation and False Comparisons" in Gluckman (M.), *Ideas and Procedures in African Customary Law* (1969), pp. 137–152.

[12] Gluckman (M.), "Legal Aspects of Development in Africa" in Tunc (A.) ed., *Les Aspects juridiques du développement économique* (1966), p. 59, at p. 61.

rules we sometimes find hard to understand; the idea that an individual may own land runs counter to deeply engrained African notions.[13] Further problems are encountered respecting the extent to which the description of the custom provided by a member of the group in question really corresponds to actual practice or, even more so, to its application by the courts. The native interlocutor may distort it in order not to appear to contradict the investigator or, again, in his desire to show that his tribe is civilised.

No indigenous writings exist to simplify an investigation of these customs or any analysis of their major principles. In Africa a purely oral customary tradition has been preserved. Malagasy codes and legislation[14] do not constitute a true exception; they do no more than supply a number of special provisions or introduce a kind of administrative regulation. The social order was, in general, and in its detail, ruled apart from them, by the *fomba* or custom, comparable to Chinese ritual practices or the *giri* of Japanese law.

Numerous collections of customs (about 150 altogether) were compiled in colonial times through the efforts of the French African colonial administrators, but only about one-half of them was ever published and they are of very uneven quality.[15] In English Africa, on the other hand, there was very little interest in local custom[16]; only recently have the studies of ethnologists and jurists opened up the field, revealing their great diversity and enabling us to understand their structure and spirit.

510. Christian and Islamic influences

Even in the pre-colonial period there were non-African influences at work in Africa and Malagasy and among these the Christian and the Islamic were of most significance.

The conversion of Africa to Christianity took place in two

---

[13] *Cf.* on these matters Keba M'Baye, "Droit et développement en Afrique francophone de l'Ouest" in Tunc (A.) ed., *op. cit.* pp. 121–165.

[14] Thebault (E. P.), *Les lois et coutumes malgaches* (1960), contains the Malagasy text and the French translation of the code of 305 articles, published in 1881. The earlier codes were shorter: that of 1828 contains only 48 articles.

[15] On the history of the redaction of French West African customs, *cf.* the introduction by B. Maupoil to *Coutumiers juridiques de l'A.O.F.* (1939, 3 vols.). *Adde* Poirier (J.), "L'avenir du droit coutumier négro-africian" in *L'avenir du droit coutumier en Afrique* (Symposium-Colloque, Amsterdam, 1955), pp. 155–169.

[16] Cotran (E.), "The Place and Future of Customary Law in East Africa" in *East African Law Today* (1966), pp. 72–92.

stages. Ethiopia was Christianised at the start of the fourth century but elsewhere the conversion came about principally during the nineteenth century, at the time of the establishment of European settlements. It is now estimated that about 30 per cent. of Africans south of the Sahara are Christian. Islamicisation was more progressive. From the eleventh century, the countries of western Africa were partly converted, and in the fourteenth and fifteenth centuries Islam had conquered Somaliland and reached the shore of the Indian Ocean. About 35 per cent. of the inhabitants of black Africa (and about 45 per cent. in western Africa) are now Muslim.[17] While neither of these groups was totally successful in its efforts of conversion, both have gradually had a considerable influence on most of the peoples of both Africa and Madagascar. The question of most interest is the extent to which they exerted an influence on the customs. Whether Christian or Islamic, the extent of this influence varied considerably. Some customs were still observed despite the fact that they may have been contrary to either of the newly adopted faiths—man is a sinner and African societies, like many others, are not yet the city of God.[18]

Quite apart from the particular points on which the customs underwent transformation, both Christianity and Islam exerted a considerable influence in a general way as well. While still observed, much of the custom did lose its formerly necessary or supernatural quality in the eyes of the people. No longer seen as having been imposed by the natural world order, it became the symbol of an imperfect society. Because there was insufficient virtue to bring about complete reform, life continued to be regulated very much as it was in the past. But it was realised that God's Law—*the Law*—was not being followed. As a matter of fact therefore the customs did retain their sociological importance, but their authority ended the moment it was realised that there was another social and moral order both different and superior. In a sense the situation was roughly analogous to that in Europe at the time of the revival of the studies of Roman law; there too local and

---

[17] Monteil (V.), *L'Islam noir* (2nd ed., 1971). Anderson (J. N. D.), *Islamic Law in Africa* (2nd ed., 1970).
[18] Froelich (J. O.), "Droit musulman et droit coutumier" in Poirier (J.) ed., *Etudes de droit africain et de droit malgache* (1965), pp. 301–389. Anderson (J. N. D.), "Islamic Law in Africa: Problems of Today and Tomorrow" in Anderson (J. N. D.) ed., *Changing Law in Developing Countries* (1963), pp. 164–183.

regional customs remained a force, but true law was thought to lie in another body of rules. The idea of law has grown in Africa just as it did in Europe. Christianity and Islam deprived custom of its magical and supernatural basis, and thus began the process of its decay.

511. The example of Ethiopia

In the above respects, Ethiopia may serve as a typical example. This country even though dominated by a variety of Christian peoples—Amharas, Tigreans, and converted Gallas—has until now lived in observance of a wholly customary and extremely frag-mented[19] law. Custom had no religious or sacred character; for the Christian Ethiopians law was contained in a nomocanon, drafted in Egypt in the thirteenth century and translated from the Arab into the *ge'ez* language in the sixteenth century, known as the *Fetha Nagast* or "The Law of Kings."[20] Through the initiative of the Emperor Haile Selassie I (1892–1975) important reforms were undertaken. The new codes established completely new law in a number of areas or thoroughly reformed the customs in others. No voice was raised in protest at this. If there is still some attachment to the Ethiopian customs it is a matter of sentiment or self-interest. But custom, often criticised even by the religious sectors of Ethiopian society, has no sacred character in the eyes of the population.[21]

[19] *Cf.* the works of Conti-Rossini (C.), *Trattato di diritto consuetudinario dell'Eritrea* (1916) and Ostini (F.), *Trattato di diritto consuetudinario dell'Eritrea* (1956).

[20] It has been translated into English by A. P. Tzadua and edited by P. L. Strauss (1968) and published in *ge'ez* and in Italian by Guidi (I.), *Il Fetha Negast o Legislazione dei Rè Codice ecclesiastico e civile di Abissinia tradotto e annotato* (1899). Sand (P. H.), "Roman Law in Ethiopia." *Problèmes de droit contemporain. Mélanges L. Baudouin*, ed. A. Popovici, (1974), p. 511.

[21] David (R.), "A Civil Code for Ethiopia" 37 Tulane L.R. (1963), p. 187; *adde* "Un Code civil pour les Etats africains" in *Recueil Penant*, 1962, pp. 352–364 (also published in *Annales africaines*, 1962, pp. 160–170). As to Ethiopian criminal law, Lowenstein (S.), *Materials on Comparative Criminal Law as based upon the Penal Codes of Ethiopia and Switzerland* (1965). Beckstrom (J. M.), "Transplantation of Legal Systems: An Early Report on the Reception of Western Laws in Ethiopia" 21 Am. J. Comp. L., 557–583 (1973).

CHAPTER II

COLONIAL PERIOD

512. Colonial attitude

All Africa came under European rule in the nineteenth century.[1] What was the position of the colonial powers with respect to law?

The attitudes of the English and the various Latin colonial powers were different as a matter of principle. The French, Spanish and Portuguese followed a policy of "assimilation" based on the double postulate that all men were of equal worth and that the European civilisation was superior to the African. This policy continued until the end of the colonial period.[2] The 1946 French Constitution declared that the native populations would retain their *statut personnel* but only "so long as they do not renounce thereto." The French tendency is clearly shown by this exemption. The situation would seem to have been more or less the same in the Belgian Congo, except that in that case the respect for native custom was textually declared as early as the foundation of the independent Congo state in 1885 and later by the colonial Charter of October 18, 1908. In the Belgian Congo, as in the French possessions, assimilation was considered the normal result of the civilising policy, upon the mother countries taking the administration of the country directly into hand. The English on the other hand adopted a policy of "indirect rule" and, generally speaking, did not make so much of an effort to install their own ideas in the territories they established; in principle, they allowed the native populations to continue self-rule, according to their customs, but under British control.

---

[1] The Republic of Liberia was set up in 1847, peopled by Negroes repatriated from the United States from 1821. The special case of Ethiopia is excepted.
[2] Many of the French African leaders were députés to the French parliament (*Assemblée nationale*) and have acted as cabinet ministers in France.

The differences separating these two policies are quite clear in the public law area. The system whereby the colony was submitted to the direct control of the mother country was adopted by Latin countries whereas the English more willingly developed administrative structures along the lines of a simple protectorate. With respect to the type of local governing organ, each very naturally transposed to the colonial arena the centralist or decentralist concepts applied in their respective home countries.

Behind these different administrative systems, however, very similar work was in fact carried out.[3] The results prove the truth of this statement: the states that emerged from the former British Empire now consider themselves to be Common law countries, and those issuing from the French Empire or Belgian Congo, as well as Rwanda and Burundi and the former Spanish and Portuguese possessions, now belong to the Romanist legal system.

A two-fold development explains this result and what, in fact, has happened to African and Malagasy customs in the process. There was first of all a reception of a modern legal system needed to regulate the many questions arising because of the transition to a new civilisation and for which native customs were unable to provide any practically useful solutions. Secondly, a transformation of customary law took place in those areas where it already constituted a complete system of rules and concepts, either because the colonial power in question may not have considered it sufficiently civilised or because the law itself may have been forced to adapt to the changes taking place in other fields. Both the modern law and the traditional law will now be considered.

Section I—Modern Law

513. Need for new law

Custom was originally sufficient for the regulation of all aspects of social life in Africa and Malagasy. It settled all social, political and economic problems as well as family matters, commodity exchange and criminal law and procedure. The concept of society, as understood by the tribe or the village, was reflected in the tra-

---

[3] Gonidec (P. F.), *Les droits africains* (2nd ed., 1976).

ditional law on a wide variety of subjects. It was clearly not suited, however, to bring about, with all the speed that was desirable, an adaptation to the entirely new social order in the process of formation in the nineteenth and twentieth centuries.

Enactment of new law was necessary in a number of fields, especially in modern commercial law where there was no indigenous basis at all. Customary law anticipated only a limited number of contracts, those known to rural life. The whole of the law of business and commercial associations, bills of exchange, maritime law, and even the whole of contract law itself, had to be imported from the West. According to traditional notions, work was not so much a means of earning a living as it was a way of life established in communion with natural forces and involving the observance of ritual practices—the idea of a contract in which one undertook to work for a stranger for a wage was unthinkable.[4] A new labour law had therefore to be established, once there was a salaried labour force.

Custom had, on the other hand, developed as the means for regulating the relations of members of the same community leading the traditional native life. For Europeans, however, who lived very differently, it was again necessary to accept a western type of law. And to settle relations between natives and Europeans, or as between natives belonging to different groups or those who had left their own communities, a *ius gentium* had to be created.

The application of this law newly imported from the West could not be entrusted to the court system or the procedures already established by custom. In all the countries of Africa and Malagasy, courts of the European type, therefore, distinct from the native tribunals, were set up to deal with these cases—where custom could not apply, where disputes involving non-African or Africans with modern status occurred, and where new questions arose as the result of the many new matters for which the customs provided no rules.

514. Limitation of the scope of application of custom

The evolution however did not stop there. Trade with other African nations and national development, necessary to raise the

---

[4] Gonidec (P. F.), *op. cit.*; *adde* Keba M'Baye, "Droit et développement en Afrique francophone de l'Ouest" in Tunc (A.), ed., *Les aspects juridiques du développement économique* (1966), p. 131.

standard of living, made a modern administration imperative. Throughout the whole continent, therefore, administrative systems, marking a break with customary institutions, were set up. The local districts were either re-organised (and placed under control) or even suppressed. New local assemblies were constituted. Financial institutions, police, health and educational services and public works were all newly created since the traditional structures provided no foundation for them.

In criminal law the colonial powers attempted from the very beginning to stamp out a number of cruel practices and to end abuses of various kinds. Their active intervention in this area gradually increased. The French *Code pénal* came into force in 1946 in the whole of French Africa and Malagasy saving certain exceptions which took into account a number of local factors; the French law courts thus acquired exclusive jurisdiction in criminal matters. In British West Africa criminal codes and codes of criminal procedures based on English law were introduced, except in Sierra Leone where the original non-statutory criminal law was adopted.

This new body of law has had the effect of limiting the possible domain of customary law in French Africa and Malagasy to the rights and duties of private law, and in areas such as family relations and land tenure systems—the matters belonging to the area of pure *droit civil*. A similar development occurred in other colonies; in the Belgian Congo and in the English possessions, on the other hand, customary law seems to have retained more importance in criminal law matters.

Even where it has been retained custom may still possibly be replaced by some law of European inspiration. The natives in the French, Belgian and Portuguese possessions, were given the choice of submitting themselves to European status.[5] Moreover through registration they might, in French Africa, place their lands under regimes entirely different from those of the custom. The same held true of the British colonies. They could not, by way of a general option, place themselves wholly under "modern law" but this choice was open in respect of a limited number of acts or a par-

---

[5] The legislation of the Belgian Congo drew a distinction between civil status (*statut civil*) obtained through registration and an intermediate status (*statut civique*) given to those holding a *carte du mérite civique*.

ticular status. They could, for example, enter into a contract or marry "in the European style" with all the consequences attached thereto.

515. Modern African law and the families of western law

The law applicable in colonial Africa, modelled on western systems, very obviously reflected the legal ideas of the colonising nation in question. But a number of further specific points must be made in this connection. The application of French law throughout French Africa and Malagasy was neither complete nor automatic. The metropolitan country's codes and legislation only applied to the extent specified by decree and these or other similar regulatory measures might also bring into force particular rules in certain specified portions of the territory from time to time. The same system was used in the Spanish and Portuguese possessions as well as the Belgian Congo in each of which, however, a distinct *Code civil* was in force.

In territories under British control, British subjects and those to whom British protection was extended—as distinct from the native population—were subject to the regime established by way of order in council and local legislative measures. In West Africa, Northern Rhodesia (Zambia), Nyasaland (Malawi) and British Somaliland, English law (that is to say, the Common law, Equitable doctrines and statutes of general application[6]) was in force as it stood at a specified date—1874 for the Gold Coast (Ghana); 1880 for Sierra Leone; 1888 for Gambia; 1900 for Somaliland; 1902 for Nyasaland (Malawi); 1911 for Northern Rhodesia (Zambia). In East Africa reference was made to the law of British India as it stood in 1897 for Kenya, in 1902 for Uganda and in 1920 for Tanganyika, English law, as such, applying only subsidiarily. To the south of the Zambesi, the law applicable in principle was Roman-Dutch law and the statutes of general application as they stood on a specified date in each colony, Cape of Good Hope in Southern Rhodesia, Botswana (formerly Bechuanaland), Lesotho

---

[6] The difficulties to which this expression gave rise are discussed by Allott (A. N.), *New Essays in African Law* (1970), pp. 28–69. Among them were such questions as whether reference was made to English Common law only or some more general notion; whether the date of reference was to only statutes of general application or to the Common law as well; which statutes were indeed of "general application," etc. Another vexed question was the authority to be attributed to cases decided after the date fixed for the reception in any given country; *cf.* Allott (A. N.), *ibid.* pp. 87–92.

(formerly Basutoland),[7] the Transvaal in Swaziland (Ngwana). In Liberia, the Common law and practices of English and American courts, as expounded in Blackstone, Kent and other works of authority, were declared applicable.

The reception of European law, in the above scheme of things, was not, therefore, either final or total. Local legislative authority could in principle modify the received law.[8] Moreover, the courts were empowered to exclude any rule the application of which was inappropriate in local conditions. Through the effects of this two-fold development—legislative and judicial—African law may now, therefore, be distinguished, and sometimes strikingly so, from that which at the given dates was made applicable. New laws have thus issued forth from what now can be considered as no more than a common source.[9]

Section II—Traditional Law

516. Evolution of customary law

The colonial powers were not content with drawing up new law for matters for which custom made no provision or where it provided no adequate basis for the increasingly urgent need for new kinds of regulation. As indicated above they also removed its application from a number of areas where existing rules were unsatisfactory to European governments. In French Africa, for example, measures were introduced to free individuals from various forms of servitude or to improve the status of women, although these reforms have often remained a dead letter.[10] In British Africa, the courts were empowered to exclude custom when its application appeared contrary to justice, equity or good conscience, but little use was made of this power.[11]

[7] Poulter (S.), "The Common Law in Lesotho" (1969), 13 J. African Law 127–144.

[8] In 1930, a new penal code in East Africa replaced the Indian penal code; the English Law of Property Act was adopted in Tanganyika in 1902, etc.

[9] Allott (A. N.), *New Essays in African Law* (1970), pp. 68–69. Roberts-Wray (K.), *The Adaptation of Imported Law in Africa*, 4 J. of African Law 66–78.

[10] The Mandel decree (June 15, 1939) and the Jacquinot decree (September 14, 1951), for example, sought to introduce a number of principles found in the western law of marriage: Keba M'Baye "Droit et développement en Afrique francophone de l'Ouest" in *Les aspects juridiques du développement économique* Tunc (A.), ed., (1966), p. 128.

[11] Allott (A. N.), *New Essays in African Law* (1970), p. 158. The reserve was dropped in Ghana and Tanzania after independence.

There remains to be examined what fate befell customary law in respect of those subject matters where it was admitted that it was in force and should remain so. Customary law is certainly not incapable of evolution. Even before the colonial period it underwent some change when new political groupings came into existence (in Buganda, Basutoland or in the case of the Zulus, for example) and, even more so, under the influence of Christianity and Islam (family structure moved from the matriarchal to the patriarchal, for example, in some countries). With the new ideas and structures introduced by the colonial powers, this evolution was to be hastened forward. The introduction of a monetary economy, urbanisation, the creation of a labour market, the spread of education, the growth of democratic ideas and individualism, an increased ease in communications and greater contacts with Europeans—all these factors brought about a "hot-house" atmosphere which prompted many Africans to question the basis of their traditional law. Most Africans may well have continued to live as did their ancestors, but a growing number put into question their customary practices and institutions.

If there had been any real desire to preserve the traditional system, it was not sufficient merely to proclaim the principle that native custom was to be respected. Such an affirmation was altogether meaningless so long as no steps were taken to enable it to survive. Positive measures such as the clarification, reform and systematising of the customs would have ensured its place next to European law. Little effort was made, however, along such lines. The colonial powers did declare, as a matter of principle, their intention to respect customary law, but the actual measures implemented with a view to guaranteeing its application resulted in its complete deformation.

517. Role of native courts

The real state of things is especially clear if consideration is given to the case of French Africa and Malagasy. There the composition of the courts entrusted with the application of customary law has been fundamentally changed—those traditionally vested with authority were replaced by civil servants assisted by mere assessors of native custom.

It might well have been expected, on the other hand, that customary law would have evolved more naturally in English Africa since there the policy of "indirect rule" left the administration of justice in the hands of the traditional authorities acting under English supervision. But the difference was not so great as it might seem because the British administration often supported chiefs who had lost their recognised place or relied upon native institutions that were discredited.

All of that is not, however, the essence of the matter. In Both French and British Africa, the important point is that customary law, and its application, became distorted because of the view which held that it could be treated as though it were a western law. In the desire to rid African society of arbitrary action and establish a new security in legal relations, the very role and working conditions of the native courts were altered. By attempting to make them the guarantors of the rights of individuals, the courts lost their traditional function which was to compose conflicts and bring about reconciliations. They thus became mere statutory creations having little or no connection with traditional legal custom.[12]

518. Role of modern law courts

Modern law courts in Africa, staffed by jurists trained in the European tradition, have naturally tended to reinforce the tendency to see "legal rules" of the European type in customary law and thus they too distort its true nature. In those exceptional instances where they have been called upon to apply custom or to supervise its application, they have not approached the task in the spirit dictated by custom in respect of which, in any event, such intervention is, in principle, wholly inappropriate.

The modern courts in English Africa, in particular, have been disoriented by custom. When custom was stated and applied by native courts, the modern courts saw the existence and content thereof as a matter of simple fact and, by an "inverted rule of precedent,"[13] admitted that the native courts' findings were conclusive. When they themselves were called upon to apply native custom, they attempted to apply English rules of evidence in

---

[12] Allott (A. N.), "La place des coutumes juridiques africaines dans les systèmes juridiques africaines modernes" in Poirier (J.), ed., *Etudes de droit africain et malgache* (1965), pp. 257–266.
[13] The expression is Professor Allott's, *New Essays in African Law* (1970).

respect of the proof of foreign law or that of local or commercial custom. No such way of thinking was really suitable to reveal the true nature of custom and its application was, as a consequence, perverted. And the application of the rule of precedent, in those instances where the custom was notorious in law, was especially unsatisfactory in the African milieu where the need that custom should evolve is much more pressing than that there be some foreseeability in judicial decisions or security of jural relations.[14] The ways of thinking about the sources of law in one country are not always suitable to another.

519. Conclusions

Apart from having discarded the traditional ways in which disputes were solved, the greatest change in customary law in the colonial period was brought about by the overall influence of the new view of the social order—a rigid and formalistic one, incomprehensible to the African.[15]

The results are today severely criticised. By wishing to install prematurely the rule of law, such as it is understood in the West, we have upset the old order in societies which were not ready to receive modern western legal ideas. African civilisation was founded on certain values: a sense of community, respect for the aged, the absence of class antagonisms; it has been too readily accepted that these values could be destroyed without assuring that new ones will take their place. Unconsciously, perhaps, we have thus contributed to the breaking-up of the ties of family and clan, and we have been incapable of replacing them with a sense of solidarity binding African society as a whole.

---

[14] Allott (A. N.), *New Essays in African Law* (1970), pp. 151, 253.
[15] Cotran (E.), "The Place and Future of Customary Law in East Africa" in *East African Law Today* (1966), p. 77.

CHAPTER III

THE INDEPENDENT NATIONS

520. Confirmation of existing law

On the whole the African and Malagasy peoples have considered the evolution which has taken place in their countries since the beginning of the colonial period to be inevitable. No reactionary movement has set in since these countries gained their independence—indeed, the leaders of the new nations have shown their intention to carry the evolution through to completion.

The law of western inspiration established by the colonial powers has been confirmed in all the new states; as yet no voice has been raised in favour of its abrogation, even in those states which have declared themselves to be socialist. No important legislation has been repealed with a view to returning to the past. Various steps taken in different parts of the continent clearly indicate the intention to retain, and to perfect, the "modern law" put into place during colonial times.

Independence, however, has brought new men to power and has led to seeing many problems in a new light. The leaders of newly independent African states, much more so than their European predecessors, have been concerned about transforming their countries and affirming the values offered by their several different traditions. A significant reform movement has begun in respect of both public and private law.

With respect to public law, the pluralist democratic model provided by western European constitutions has shown itself to be ill-suited to African society. It has been abandoned in favour of presidential systems, often no more than a one-party dictatorship excluding citizens from any exercise of power. This situation is seen as provisional, and it is hoped that it will permit a modernisation of economic and social structures and attitudes necessary for a democratic regime to function.[1]

In private law contradiction is also noticeable. On the one hand custom is to be rehabilitated and attachment to customary principles to be affirmed because of a new emphasis on its moral value. On the other hand, however, there has been some movement toward repudiating many rules and structures that were seen as compromising national development. A way to reinforce an often precarious national unity, it has been thought, is to provide the country with a national law. Law in these circumstances has become an instrument for radical social change and it has correspondingly moved away from traditional custom.

521. Recovery of traditional values

Independence ushered in a new attitude towards traditional law. The leaders of the new African states were raised in milieux where custom was observed; because of this background they intend to affirm and maintain certain of its moral values which they hold in high esteem. They profess the belief that when purged of certain abusive elements custom may be able to form the basis of African private law. All the traditional social values are not to be rejected. The poet-president of Senegal, L. S. Senghor, exalts "negritude." The sense of social solidarity which custom establishes among the members of the clan is, in particular, a positive element to be preserved. Africa and Malagasy[2] do not intend to fall under the spell of excessive individualism which today is condemned even in the West. The idea of "African socialism" now enjoys a place of honour.[3]

De-colonisation was frequently accompanied by declarations

---

[1] Lavroff (D. G.), *Les systèmes constitutionnels en Afrique noire. Les Etats francophones* (1976). Tchirkin (V.) and Youdin (Y.), *L'Etat à orientation socialiste: instrument de transformation révolutionnaire* (1974).

[2] *Cf.* the *Recueil des lois civiles* (t. I: Dispositions génefrales. Droit de la famille), published in 1964 by the Ministère de la Justice de la République malgache, including the extremely interesting report by A. Ramangasoavina (pp. 7–76).

[3] On African socialism and the influence of Marxism in Africa, *cf.* Hazard (J. N.), "Marxian Socialism in Africa" (1969) 2 *Comparative Politics* 1–15 and "Marxist Models for West African Law" in *Ius privatum gentium. Festschrift für Max Rheinstein* (1969), Vol. 1, pp. 285–297. *Adde* by the same author "La familia de sistemas juridicos de inspiración marxista en Africa" in *Libro-homenaje a la memoria de R. Goldschmidt* (1967), pp. 131–146. Institut Gosudarstva i prava Akademii nauk S.S.S.R.; *Pravo v nezavysimyh stranah Afriki: Stanovlenie i razvitie* (1969).

that justice should be rendered according to customary law. If the new leaders are to be believed, their intention is to rehabilitate the traditional legal system. On this point there has been a reaction to the condescending and sometimes disdainful attitude which, it is thought, was prevalent in the colonial era.

Some very worthwhile efforts have been undertaken in order to bring about a better knowledge of customary law. In Malagasy, as early as 1957, a resolution of the representative assembly ordered that a collection and codification of customs be made. Similar work has been undertaken in Senegal. In Tanganyika, comparable efforts have been under way since 1961; the district councils have reduced many official customs into the Swahili language with a view to achieving some unification of customs.[4] In Nigeria, the regional assemblies have been encouraged to take the initiative in drafting authoritative compilations. An ambitious plan for a systematic exposition of African customary law (*Restatement of African Law Project*) has been undertaken by the School of Oriental and African Studies of the University of London with the support of the Nuffield Foundation and the co-operation of interested states. A number of volumes have now been published—on the laws of marriage and inheritance in Keyna (1968–1969), on the laws of marriage, property, inheritance, contract and tort in Malawi (1970–1971) and on family law in Botswana (1972).[5]

522. Policy of African leaders

The various measures just referred to have not, however, succeeded in preserving African law.[6]

The leaders of the new states, drawn from the evolved segments of African society which have modelled themselves on western patterns, have certainly exalted negritude and affirmed their africanism in their public speeches. Their several nations have struck

---

[4] Marriage law was completely reformed in Tanzania by the Law of Marriage Act 1971.

[5] The laws of 17 ethnological groups, representing 90 per cent. of the population of Kenya, have been studied by the English expert, E. Cotran; those of nine in Botswana by S. Roberts. The work of J. O. Ibik in respect of Malawi also considers a variety of such groups, except that for the law of civil liability only the Tumbaka group has been studied.

[6] Keba M'Baye, "Droit et développement en Afrique francophone de l'Ouest" in Tunc (A.), ed., *Les aspects juridiques du développement économique* (1966), p. 121, at p. 146. The author analyses the factors which have prompted a re-thinking of the earlier and overly theoretical position and have led to a renewal of customary law in a number of areas. *Adde* Kuper (H. and L.) eds., *African Law: Adaptation and Development* (1965).

out on different paths, some following the model of the free economies and others that of a collectivised economy. But in whatever way they have set about modernising their countries in order to develop them into nations, all of them have, however, in the end, acted in a manner detrimental to the survival of custom.[7]

No doubt, in the long term, it would have been difficult to maintain a modern public law founded on one set of principles and a private customary law founded on different principles. National unity will not easily be achieved when the cohesion of the tribe remains too strong; economic development requires that the individual be freed from too great a dependence upon his family or his ethnic group. African leaders therefore had to make a choice. Custom is the law of a group, the dimensions of which cannot be arbitrarily changed; by attempting to unify the law at the national level, custom was inevitably altered. Customary law is based on the ideas of harmony and reconciliation; the attempt to introduce the rule of law, seen as the guarantor of individual rights through legislation and judicial decisions, and the view that the latter contained rules to be followed strictly rather than a point of departure for the amicable settlement of disputes, has led to the repudiation of the very essence of custom.

It has counted for little in the end that statute law or decided cases have on occasion taken up and adopted any particular rule of customary law. If there had been a real desire to respect and perpetuate African legal tradition, it would have been necessary to do more than that—to restore the supple methods by which it was applied and developed. In other words, a pluralist concept of society would have had to be admitted: the groups that had developed a custom should have been entrusted with its continued administration, because without this there can be no real customary law. Once, however, the state assumes the place of the original group in the function of articulating and applying custom, its destruction is certain.

The policy, suggested above, was not that followed in the new

---

[7] Tunc (A.), ed., *op. cit.* The articles there published by K. M.'Baye, B. O. Nwabueze and the introductory study by A. Tunc are especially to be noted. While one can agree with M. Gluckman and A. A. Schiller in deploring the loss of the customs and in noting the many inconveniences created by the defective adaptation of modern law to the African context, would it be preferable, and possible, in order to avoid them, to maintain in Africa what one author has called an "anthropoligcal zoo"?

states, and there were good enough reasons to explain this course of action. Thus, while the new law may well have been based in some measure upon custom, this new state law is not customary law, even though it has been thought desirable to retain the term in official terminology.[8]

523. Reforms of judicial administration

In the colonial period, there were, generally speaking, two types of courts: those applying customary law exclusively and those applying only the modern law. This duality was questioned once the African countries gained their independence. It was thought somewhat shocking to have two kinds of justice in the same state, one of which (rightly or wrongly) was considered inferior to the other. In various countries, therefore, an important reform of judicial administration was carried through, and the result was the integration of the native courts into a unitary system of judicial administration. The distinction between modern and customary law courts does remain in place however in many English-speaking and French-speaking countries.[9]

These steps will in all likelihood have extremely important consequences with repect to customary law. That such will be the case has been observed many times before: the concepts of lawyers and of custom are very different. When applied directly by legally trained judges, and therefore with a rigidity contrary to its nature, custom will inevitably become distorted and bring about the decline of traditional law.

In the English-speaking African countries, until independence, custom was ascertained and applied by native courts and was considered to be no more than a fact when invoked before the super-

[8] Allott (A. N.), *New Essays in African Law* (1970), p. 145. The author underscores the difficulty of assuring that a fully equal treatment is given to customary and modern law on the one hand and, on the other, to the preservation of the traditional character of customary law (p. 278). Customary law may well be "law" (p. 148) but it is, essentially, a law that escapes jurists and one which is poorly adapted to the English rule of precedent (*cf.* the author's *Law and Language*, 1965).

[9] It remains in Liberia and Togo. Muslim law, in some states, is also applied by courts that are not yet integrated into the ordinary judicial system. *Cf.* Allott (A. N.), *Judicial and Legal Systems in Africa* (2nd ed., 1970). Lampue (P.), "La justice civile dans les Etats d'Afrique francophone et à Madagascar" Rev. jur. et pol. Ind. et Coop. (1966), pp. 155–184 and, by the same author, "La justice administrative dans les Etats d'Afrique francophone" Rev. Jur. et pol. Ind. et Coop. (1965), pp. 3–31. "Actes du Congrès de l'I.D.E.F. au Canada" Rev. jur. et pol. Ind. et Coop. (1969), p. 451.

ior courts. Today, in some countries at least, it has been declared to be a matter of law. It may seem that "custom," now that it is "law," has been, as it were, promoted. In practice, this means that custom will henceforth be applied and, in this application, amended by judges who, in all probability, will soon be aided by jurists trained in the Common law tradition and for whom custom is an unknown subject.[10]

The increasingly extensive publication of restatements and judicial decisions is carried forward with the professed object of saving customary law; it may well, however, contribute to its further decline. The truth is that while custom has become law it has lost its soul. There must be no illusions on this point: the custom which is now fully law has very little in common with traditional custom. De-colonisation has not contributed to the rehabilitation of custom, it has sounded its death knell.

524. Custom and modern society

While modern African legal systems do incorporate some elements of traditional customary law, they inevitably tend to reject what was of the real essence of custom. Christianity and Islam had already undermined customary legal thinking by substituting the idea of divine law to that of a cosmic balance which would be disturbed by the breaking of traditional interdicts. With the introduction of modern rationalist thought, which dissociates law from ancient beliefs and myths, the very basis of customary law thus gave way.

Customary law was a law of closed societies, turned in upon themselves. Modern law, on the contrary, is necessarily a *ius gentium* made for a society in which the numerous communities of other times have been fused. It cannot be the law of any single one of such former groups.[11] The leaders of many African countries wish to make a national law out of customary law and thus rein-

---

[10] Richardson (D. S.), "Whither Lay Justice in Africa?" in Gluckman (M.), ed., *Ideas and Procedures in African Customary Law* (1969), pp. 123–136.

[11] *Cf.* The statement of the Minister of Justice of the Ivory Coast, as cited by the first president of the Supreme Court of Senegal: whatever choice may be made, and whatever the subject matter, four fifths of the population will know nothing of the law applied to them, which will be as foreign as, say, French or Italian law. Why, then, be deprived of the benefits of a modern legislation, when there is this added advantage that no tribe or clan will be able to assert that its law predominates? (A. Tunc, ed., *Les aspects juridiques du développement économique* (1966), p. 146).

force, in the legal sphere, a national unity which, in the case of many of them, is still far from established.

Customary law was suitable to static peasant societies. The leaders of the present states wish to bring about reform in the very structure of society, to bridge the cultural gap which now separates the inhabitants of the cities from those of the country on the one hand and, on the other, the intellectuals and other evolved sectors of society from the mass of people. They mean further to stimulate new sectors of the economy and to promote land reform. The new law cannot therefore be based on custom because its aim is precisely, to change, on many fronts, the traditional ways of the population. The purpose of the law, says the Malagasy minister of justice, is to bring about those changes in tradition that will promote social and economic emancipation; it will therefore be in conflict with custom.[12] Very much as in the socialist states, the new law will thus be an expression of the will of the nations' leaders who intend to revolutionise society.

525. Codification of African law

A considerable reform of existing legislation has been accomplished in the former British, French and Belgian possessions, and in Ethiopia. Since their independence, more than 100 codes have been promulgated in the French-language states.[13] In Ethiopia, five codes were promulgated between 1957 and 1965, the contents of which correspond to the Napoleonic codes.[14] Major legislation has also been enacted in the English-speaking African countries, particularly Ghana, Nigeria and in East Africa.

The reform movement was directed first of all to the modern law. New codes were drafted in criminal law; the judicial organisation was reformed; in Senegal and Madagascar, in Ghana and Uganda, the law of obligations and contracts was re-formulated. The movement has also been carried forward in areas which intimately affect the personal status of Africans; important changes in

---

[12] Ramangasoavina (A.), "Les impératifs de la justice dans les pays en voie de développement" in (1965) Ann. Univ. Madagascar (Droit), Vol. 2, p. 18.

[13] Alliot (M.), "Problèmes de l'unification des droits africains" (1967) J. of African Law 86–98.

[14] Penal Code, 1957; Civil Code and Commercial Code, 1960; Code of Criminal Procedure, 1961; Code of Civil Procedure, 1965. Singer (N. J.), "Modernisation of Law in Ethiopia," 11 Harv. Int. J. 73 (1970).

the landed property systems of Senegal, Ghana and Kenya have also been introduced. In a number of francophone countries, and also in Tanganyika, there has been little hesitation in introducing reform, sometimes revolutionary in nature, in family law.[15]

Two questions arise in respect of this new legislation. The first is to ascertain to what extent it is, in fact, observed; the second is to decide whether or not Africa has followed too closely the models offered by western law.

526. Continuance of traditional ways of life

There must be no misconceptions. Much of the new legislation especially that which purports to reform the whole fabric of the family structure, affects the general population very little and has not yet changed the traditional African way of life. Behind the facade which this legislation really is, the peasants, in particular, continue to live the life of their ancestors, wholly unaware of the law of the cities and the new institutions set up.[16] According to well informed observers, 80 or 90 per cent. of the population still lives by the old ways quite oblivious to the whole movement towards modernisation. Ancient custom is in fact still followed and the state courts are by-passed in favour of arbitration or, even more frequently, conciliations according to traditional pro-cedures.[17]

But this does not mean that the new legislation is of no use. Although in advance of public opinion and the social manners it aspires to reform, the new legislation can have an important part to play in education and in the work of persuasion similar to that of the *ius commune* taught in European universities in the middle ages. The new laws provide the picture of the society which it is

---

[15] Keba M'Baye, ed., *Le droit de la famille en Afrique et à Madagascar* (1968). Blanc-Jouvan (X.), "La codification du droit du marriage dans les pays d'Afrique noire franchophone" *Ius privatum gentium, Festschrift für Max Rheinstein* (1969), Vol. II, p. 909. Verdier (R.), "Evolution et réformes foncières de l'Afrique noire francophone" 15 Journal de droit africain (1971), p. 85.

[16] This statement is, however, true only in a general way—it may be that custom itself in some areas has been completely reformed, *cf.* Roberts (S. A.), "The Settlement of Family Disputes in the Kgatha Customary Courts. Some New Approaches" (1971) J. of African Law 60.

[17] Poirier (J.), "L'analyse des espèces juridiques et l'étude des droits coutumiers africains" in Gluckman (M.), ed., *Idées et procédures dans les systèmes légaux africains* (1969), p. 97. Ollennu (N. A.), "The Structure of African Judicial Authority and Problems of Evidence and Proof in Traditional Courts" *ibid*. p. 110. "Evidence and Proof in Traditional Courts" *ibid*. p. 110. Krzeczunowicz (G.), "The Present Role of Equity in Ethiopian Civil Law" (1969) 13 J. of African Law 145.

hoped will come about. It cannot be expected that they will apply in their entirety and immediately, as would occur in the West. And so, in order to avoid any possibility of compromising its authority, the new legislation should be carefully framed and be implemented with some considerable prudence, leaving the judges charged with its application a large degree of latitude. The new legislation should be seen sometimes as a model intended to guide citizens' conduct rather than as a commandment to be strictly obeyed.

527. Primacy of the idea of development

One may well ask, moreover, whether in legal matters there has been too close an observance of the model provided by European countries. Some observers maintain that the whole of the law in Africa and Malagasy must be completely re-thought in order to put it fully in the service of the work of development and that all other considerations must be treated as secondary when compared with this principal objective.[18]

There is certainly no question in Africa of sacificing moral values or the dignity of man but, in under-developed countries, it is, on the other hand, legitimate, at least to a greater extent than one in the West is prepared to admit, to subordinate the individual to the community—this, moreover, was the spirit of the traditional customs.

Upon this basis there will probably develop in Africa a differently structured relationship between public law and private law when contrasted to what they are in Europe. Progressive initiatives are to be more expected on the part of the state than on that of individuals too poor or too ignorant to rise above their traditional habits and prejudices. The national rights of man must be guaranteed but they may nevertheless be more severely limited than they are in the West; the almost sacred character of the right of ownership must not be an obstacle to agrarian reforms required for an ordered development of the country; the fiscal legislation

---

[18] Granger (R.), "Problèmes d'application du droit moderne dans les pays en voie de développement" Ann. Univ. Madagascar, Vol. 2 (1965), p. 113. Gendarme (R.), "Problèmes juridiques et développement économique" in Tunc (A.), *Les aspects juridiques du développement économique* (1966), p. 25. Petit-Pont (M.), *Structures traditionelles et développement* (1968). Allott (A. N.), "Legal Development and Economic Growth in Africa" in Anderson (J. N. D.), ed., *Changing Law in Developing Countries* (1963), p. 194.

promoting agriculture must take into account the fact that the peasants are very often in debt and must contain measures which, for example, prevent loans from being used to reimburse abusive creditors or for unproductive expenses such as marriage and funeral ceremonies.

528. Problems in the application of law

In the developing countries, the circumstances, so unlike those in the West, in which the law is to receive application must be considered.[19] It will certainly be useful to extend legal education, publish legislative texts, judicial decisions and legal writings, and to make the documentation in legislative and administrative matters generally more available. Much work of this kind is accomplished by the various African institutes and the associations of African jurists. Taking advantage of the structures available through the one-party system, they are able to promote the new legislation as news through radio, the press and the organisation of conferences. Such work will not however produce the same results in Africa as it does in Europe. In the absence of professional organisations and legal practitioners in sufficiently large numbers, the law runs the very serious risk of becoming a dead letter or used only to the profit of the more evolved elements of society whose already privileged position will thereby be reinforced and not, as desired, reduced. Even in the industrialised nations it has been realised, only recently, that the economically weak classes of society are often unable to ascertain what their rights are and how to enforce them.[20] In the last few years, there has been a complete rethinking of the legal aid or legal assistance structures in many western countries. The same problem but in a more aggravated state exists in Africa. It would be worthwhile, therefore, that the needs of this continent be examined in the light of the experience gained in this respect in England, France and the United States, as well as in the socialist countries where this problem is said to have been beaten. It might also be useful to examine the laws drawn up by less highly developed countries. Apart from the socialist countries, the

---

[19] Boni (A.), "La mise en pratique des lois dans les nations en voie de développement" *Recueil Penant* (1963), p. 449. Gonidec (P. F.), "Problèmes d'application de la législation en Afrique" *Bull. Inst. int. d'administration publique* (1967), No. 2, p. 7.
[20] Cappelletti (M.), *Giustizia e società* (1972).

example of Mexico might be considered: the Federal Civil Code of 1928, as well as a number of civil codes of the Mexican States, dispense Mexican judges from applying the rule *ignorantia iuris haud excusat* (ignorance of the law is never an excuse) if, in the social circumstances of the parties, the application of the rule would amount to an injustice.[21]

529. Danger of European legislation and treaties

Too often, and in too many areas, the countries of Africa have adopted laws inappropriate to their own needs and conditions because they have simply copied those made for the circumstances of European countries. The colonial administrators themselves can be blamed for having adopted such an overly simple method. But the dangers inherent in this practice have increased rather than diminished since de-colonisation. Africa and Malagasy are too poor, and have far too few jurists, to be able to study effectively for themselves which law would be best in their own context. Even more than before independence they may adopt, without the necessary discernment, inappropriate models.

The same holds true with respect to international treaties and conventions. It is certainly desirable that there be African and Malagasy participation in international affairs, but it must also be realised that their interests are not represented—or at least are only very poorly represented—during the preparation of international agreements. The presence of their delegations at conferences where conventions are signed is really no more than a purely formal guarantee that their interests are protected.

530. Need for co-ordinated efforts

The true interests of the African countries can, in fact, be determined, and it is also possible that a country obtain good laws by making use of experts who are sufficiently conscientious to take into account its particular needs and who will have the good sense not to suggest laws which, in their own countries, would fulfil merely their own theoretical ambitions. It is very much to be regretted, however, that these efforts are carried on without any

---

[21] Aguilar Gutiérrez (A.) and Dérbez Muro (J.), *Panorama de la legislación civil de México* (1960), pp. 7, 15.

co-ordination. Too often several jurists in various countries are called upon to carry out work which might have been more profitably accomplished by one alone for the benefit of several countries. The fragmentation of Africa into something more than 40 distinct states is very regretable at a moment in time when reasonable chances of development are open only to rather larger collectivities.[22] This balkanisation of Africa is all the more unfortunate in that it very often amounts to no more than a prolongation of the arbitrarily established territorial divisions set up by the colonial powers; it may well prove disastrous if the result is a corresponding fragmentation of private law which, in the colonial period, was avoided to a large extent. At this moment in our history when European states are attempting to re-kindle the idea of a *ius commune,* the African states must not, through an ignorance of history, slip into a state of juridical provincialism contrary to both their own interests and the idea of law itself.

The danger has been realised by some of them. In industrial and intellectual property, in maritime law, some collaboration has begun between francophone states; private concerns have also promoted reports of judicial decisions common to several of the English-speaking states. These efforts remain, however, insufficient. It is to be hoped that the Organisation for African Unity, or the smaller organisations in Africa already in existence, or the International Commercial Law Commission of the United Nations or other similar groups, will take suitable steps to avoid a senseless fragmentation of African law.

The gaining of independence in Africa has engendered a great deal of enthusiasm. The essential tasks however are still to be accomplished—in all spheres and at all levels the new independent states require much development. In certain respects this development has been facilitated by de-colonisation, but this phase in itself will by no means assure it and, in certain respects, may even render it more awkward. And in terms of law alone, independence exposes the new states to a narrow nationalism which must be rejected. The legal development of Africa and Malagasy, so necessary to their progress, will be considerably facilitated if these

---

[22] Guernier (M.), *La dernière chance du tiers-monde* (1968), Alliot (M.), "Problèmes de l'unification des droits africains" (1967) J. of African Law 86. M'Baye (K.), "L'unification du droit en Afrique" Rev. sénégalaise de droit (1971), p. 65. David (R.), "Un code civil pour les Etats africains" *Recueil Penant* (1962), p. 352 and also *Ann. africaines* (1962), p. 160.

countries remain true to what is at once the better tradition of both Romanist and Common law countries—in otheir words, if they "de-nationalise" their laws and seek in common the fulfilment of their own civilisations through the constant quest for the realisation of justice.

APPENDIX I

BIBLIOGRAPHICAL INFORMATION

This bibliography does not include what may be called the "working tools" used in different countries to determine the actual legal rules applicable to a particular legal problem, nor the many various individual studies in comparative law published throughout the world. Its coverage is limited to the general scope of the present work and, therefore, its principal if not only purpose is to draw attention to those books and publications particularly useful to those undertaking an introductory study of an individual system of law or the use of the comparative method. Moreover, it is limited to English, French, German, Spanish and Italian publications.

Consultation of the works themselves listed in Section I, Bibliographical Tools, will to a great extent remedy the insufficiencies just mentioned.

SECTION I—BIBLIOGRAPHICAL TOOLS

The *Register of Legal Documentation in the World/Catalogue des sources de documentation juridique dans le monde* (2nd ed., 1957) published by UNESCO lists bibliographies, collections of laws and judicial reports, legal journals and the principal centres of legal documentation for each country.

Association of American Law Schools: *Law Books Recommended for Libraries.* Those numbers to be especially consulted are Nos. 2 (Comparative Law) and 45 (Foreign Law) by C. SZLADITS (1962), as well as No. 39 (African Law, by A.A. SCHILLER), No. 40 (Chinese Law, by S. SORICH), No. 41 (Islamic Law, by C. SZLADITS), No. 42 (Latin American Law, by H.L. CLAGETT) and No. 44 (Russian Law, by H.J. BERMAN).

MALCLÈS (L.N.), *Les sources du travail bibliographique* (2nd

577

ed., 1969) is a fundamental work indicating essential bibliographical sources in all subjects.

SZLADITS (Ch.), *Bibliography on Foreign and Comparative Law* (Books and Articles in English), 4 vols. (1955, 1962, 1968, 1975). This work indicates all the books and article published since 1790 in the English language on the subject of comparative law and laws other than the Common law. It is continued by annual supplements published under the auspices of the Parker School of Foreign and Comparative Law, Columbia University in the City of New York.

Introduction bibliographique à l'histoire du droit et à l'ethnologie juridique, under the direction of GILISSEN (J.), 8 vols. promised: (A) *Antiquité;* (B) *Europe médiévale et moderne (Partie généralé);* (C) *Europe occidentale (médiévale et moderne);* (D) *Europe centrale (médiévale et moderne);* (D.–l) *Europe orientale (médiévale et moderne);* (E) *Asie;* (E–1) *Afrique;* (F) *Amerique et Océanie.* Altogether, 118 parts are promised, extending to some 8,000 pages. By October 1, 1977 75 parts had appeared.

Index to Legal Periodicals and *Index to Foreign Legal Periodicals.* These two important publications indicate the *articles* published in the world's principal legal reviews: in the English language in the first mentioned and in languages other than English in the second. The publication of the *Index to Legal Periodicals* began in 1907, and that of the *Index to Foreign Legal Periodicals* in 1960. Cumulative volumes, appearing every two years and every five years, facilitate considerably the research on any particular question.

SECTION II—COMPARATIVE LAW REVIEWS

Any review may, on occasion, publish articles involving one or more foreign laws. Reviews mentioned here, however, are those which specialise in questions relating to foreign laws and the comparison of laws. The reviews dealing with only one particular family of law are indicated in the section devoted to such family.

(a) In English

International and Comparative Law Quarterly, 1952 (quarterly).

A continuation of the Journal of Comparative Legislation, 1896–1951.
American Journal of Comparative Law, 1952 (quarterly).
Inter-American Law Review. Revista jurídica interamericana, 1959 (semi-annual) published by the Tulane Institute of Comparative Law.
Korean Journal of Comparative Law 1973 (annual).
[*Comparative Juridical Review* (Clark Gables, Florida), 1964.]
Annual Survey of Commonwealth Law, 1970.
Review of Socialist Law, 1975 (quarterly).

(b) In French

Revue internationale de droit comparé, 1949 (quarterly). A continuation of the *Bulletin de la Société de législation comparée* (1869–1948).

The Société de législation comparée also embarked upon the publication of a new collection, called *Journées juridiques,* devoted to the work of the meetings of jurists which it organises periodically. Irregular since 1961.

Annuaire de législation française et étrangère, 1952 (annual). This is a continuation of the *Annuaire de législation étrangère* of 1872–1951. This *Annuaire* contains a series of articles showing the legislative changes brought about in the preceding year in a large number of countries and some comparative law studies.

Revue de droit international et de droit comparé, 1908 (quarterly). This review absorbed the *Revue trimestrielle de l'Institut-belge de droit comparé* which, under various titles, was published from 1908 to 1914 and from 1922 to 1939.

Revue hellénique de droit international, 1948 (quarterly) (Athens).

Annales de l'Institut de droit comparé d'Istanbul, 1950 (annual). The *Annales* publish articles in French, English and German.

Revue de la Commission internationale des juristes, 1957 (semi-annual). The International Commission of Jurists defends the principles of the free domocracies. The review mainly publishes articles relating to issues of judicial organisation and civil rights.

Revue de droit contemporain, 1954 (semi-annual, French version) published by the Association internationale des jurists démocrates, of Communist tendency.

(c) In German

Rabels Zeitschrift für ausländisches und internationales Privatrecht, 1927 (quarterly).

Brunz's Zeitschrift für ausländisches öffentliches Recht und Völkerrecht, 1927 (quarterly).

Zeitschrift für vergleichende Rechswissenschaft, 1878 specialising in primitive and oriental laws.

Zeitschrift für Rechtsvergleichung, 1960 (quarterly), published by the Institute of Comparative Law of the University of Vienna and by the Österreichische Gesellschaft für Rechtsvergleichung.

(d) In Spanish

Boletín mexicano de derecho comparado, 1968, a continuation of the *Boletín del Instituto de derecho comparado* (Mexico), 1948–1967 (quarterly).

Revista del Instituto de derecho comparado (Barcelona), 1953 (quarterly).

Inter-American Law Review. Revista jurídica interamericana, 1959 (Tulane University, New Orleans).

(e) In Italian

Annuario di diritto comparato e di studi legislativi, 1927 (annual).

SECTION III—GENERAL INTRODUCTORY WORKS ON COMPARATIVE LAW AND FOREIGN LAWS

(a) In English

GUTTERIDGE (H.C.), *Comparative Law* (2nd ed., 1949). This work examines the general problems of comparative law, compares the methods of English and French jurists and, in its last three chapters, studies the problems of the unification of law.

WIGMORE (J.H.), *A Panorama of the World's Legal Systems,* 3 vols. (1928); Library Edition, 1 vol. (1936). This work is perhaps too large in scope, but its value is that it was one of the first to popularise comparative law by showing the different kinds of legal thinking and the world's different legal systems.

D<small>ERRETT</small> (J.D.M.) ed., *An Introduction to Legal Systems* (1968). Seven articles written by eminent scholars on Roman law, Jewish law, Islamic law, Hindu law, Chinese law, African law and English law.

E<small>OSCI</small> (G.), *Comparative Civil (Private) Law* 1979.

I<small>NDIAN</small> L<small>AW</small> I<small>NSTITUTE</small>, *An Introduction to the Study of Comparative Law* (1971). The third portion of this work (pp. 57–149) has studies on the laws of Sri Lanka (Ceylon), China, Indonesia, Afghanistan, Malaya, Japan.

K<small>AGAN</small> (K.K.), *Three Great Systems of Jurisprudence* (1955). Roman law, Common law, Jewish law.

L<small>IEBESNY</small> (H.J.), *Materials on Comparative Law* (1976).

W<small>ATSON</small> (A.), *Legal Transplants* (1974).

S<small>CHLESINGER</small> (R.), *Cases and Materials on Comparative Law* (4th ed., 1980).

—— (ed.), Formation of Contracts. A Study of the Common Core of Legal Systems (1968).

Z<small>WEIGERT</small> (K.) & K<small>ÖTZ</small> (H.), *An Introduction to Comparative Law* I: The Framework. II: The Institutions of Private Law (1977). Translation from the German.

E<small>HRMANN</small> (H.W.). *Comparative Legal Cultures* (1976).

M<small>ERRYMAN</small> (J.H.) & C<small>LARK</small> (D.S.), *Comparative Law: Western European and Latin American Legal Systems. Cases & Materials* (1978).

The British Commonwealth. The Development of its Laws and Constitutions (directed by G.W. K<small>EETON</small>) is designed to provide an introduction to the laws of the different Commonwealth countries; up to the present time, volumes respecting the following countries have appeared:

Australia	G. W. P<small>ATON</small> (1952)
Ceylon	S<small>IR</small> I<small>VOR</small> J<small>ENNINGS</small> & H. W. T<small>AMBIAH</small> (1952)
India	A. G<small>LEDHILL</small> (2nd ed., 1964)
New Zealand	J. L. R<small>OBSON</small> (2nd ed., 1967)
United Kingdom	G. W. K<small>EETON</small> & D. L<small>LOYD</small> (1955)
Pakistan	A. G<small>LEDHILL</small> (2nd ed., 1967)
Union of South Africa	H. R. H<small>AHLO</small> & E. K<small>HAN</small> (1960); supplement (1962)

Malaya, Singapore, Borneo	L. A. Sheridan (1961)
Ghana & Sierra Leone	T. O. Elias (1962)
Scotland	T. B. Smith (2nd ed., 1962)
Republic of India	A. Gledhill (2nd ed., 1964)
Tanganyika	J. S. R. Cole & W. N. Denison (1964)
Uganda	J. S. Read & H. F. Morris (1966)
Nigeria	T. O. Elias (1967)

Ansay (T.) & Wallace (D.), *Introduction to Turkish Law* (1966).

(b) In French

David (R.) & (Jauffret-Spinosi (C.), *Les grands systèmes de droit contemporairis* (8th ed., 1982). The French language version of the present work.

David (R.), *Traité élémentaire de droit civil comparé. Introduction à l'étude des droits étrangers et à la méthode comparative* (1950). It is still interesting to read the first part of this work dealing with the general problems of comparative law.

Gutteridge (H.C.), *Le droit comparé* (1953). Translation of the 2nd edition (1949) of the English work, *Comparative Law*.

Arminjon (P.), Nolde (B.) & Wolff (M.), *Droit comparé*, 3 vols. (1950–52). This work differs from the preceding items in that it describes the basis of the law, and particularly the private law of a number of laws of different legal families. It is largely out of date now.

Livre du Centenaire de la Société de Législation comparée: Vol. I: *Un siécle de droit comparé en France* (1869–1969). *Les apports du droit comparé au droit positif français* (1969). Vol. II: *Evolution internationale et problèmes actuels du droit comparé* (1971).

Ancel (M.), *Utilité et méthodes du droit comparé* (1971).

Constantinesco (L.J.), *Traité de droit comparé.* Vol. I—*Introduction au droit comparé* (1972). Vol. II—*La méthode comparative* (1974).

Rodiére (R.), *Introduction au droit comparé* (1979).

Les systémes de droit contemporains. This collection, published by the Institut de droit comparé, Université de Paris, is a series of works intended to provide jurists of French formation with studies of various foreign laws. The following volumes have been published:

I   David (R). Gutteridge (H.C.) & Wortley (B.A.),

Introduction à l'étude du droit privé de l'Angleterre (1948).

II MILLIOT (L.), *Introduction à l'étude du droit musulman* (1953).

III ZAJTAY (I.), *Introduction à l'étude du droit hongrois. La formation historique du droit civil* (1953).

IV & V TUNC (A. & S.), *Le système constitutionnel des Etats-Unis d'Amérique.* Vol. I: *Histoire constitutionnelle:* Vol. II: *Le système constitutionnel actuel* (1954–1955).

VI TUNC (A. & S.), *Le droit des Etats-Unis d'Amérique. Sources et techniques* (1955).

VII & VIII DAVID (R.) & HAZARD (J.N.), *Le droit soviétique* Vol. I: *Les données foundamentales du droit soviétique;* Vol. II: *Le droit et l'évolution de la société dans l'U.R.S.S.* (1954).

IX LAPENNA (I.), *Conceptions soviétiques de droit international public* (1954).

X LEMASURIER (R.), *Le droit de l'île de Jersey* (1956).

XI & XII DAVID (R.) & COLLABORATORS, *Le droit français.* Vol. I: *Les données foundamentales du droit fr40çais;* Vol. II: *Principes et tendances du droit français* (1960).

XIII JAMBU-MERLIN (R.), *Le droit privé en Tunisie* (1960).

XIV STOYANOVITCH (K.), *Le régime socialiste yougoslave* (1961).

XV & XVI CATALA (P.), GERVAIS (A.) & Collaborators, *Le droit libanais* (1964).

XVII BAUDOUIN (L.), *Les aspects généraux du droit public dans la province de Québec* (1965).

XVIII GOUR (C.G.), *Institutions constitutionnelles politiques du Cambodge* (1965).

XIX NODA (Y.), *Introduction au droit japonais* (1966).

XX LINGAT (R.), *Les sources du droit dans le système traditionel de l'Inde* (1967).

XXI BAUDOUIN (L.), *Les aspects généraux de droit privé dans la province de Québec* (1967).

XXII TSIEN (TCHE-HAO), *Le droit constitutionnel et les institutions politiques de la République populaire de Chine* (1970).

XXIII   David (H.), *Introduction à l'etude du droit écossais* (2nd ed., 1972).

XXIV   Fromont (M.) & Rieg (A.), *La Republique fédérale allemande* t.I. (1977), t.2 (1982).

The collection *Comment ils sont gouvernés,* directed by Burdeau (G.) explains the principles of government in a number of countries. It features the following volumes at the present time:

I   Tunc (A.), *Etats-Unis d'Amerique* (3rd ed., 1973).

II   Chambre (H.), *Union soviétique* (2nd ed., 1966).

III   Gignoux (C.J.), *Suisse* (1960).

IV   Mast (A.), *Benelux* (1960).

V   Maranini (G.), *Italie* (1961).

VI   Debbasch (C.), *Tunisie* (1962).

VII   Buchmann (J.), *Afrique noire indépendente* (1962).

VIII   Rozmaryn (St.), *Pologne* (1963).

IX   Robert (J.), *La monarchie marocaine* (1963).

X   Tixier (G.), *Ghana* (1965).

XI   Knapp (K.) & Mlynar (Z.), *La Tchécoslovaquie* (1965).

XII   Fusilier (R.), *Les pays nordiques* (1965).

XIII   Lavroff (D.G.), *La republique du Sénégal* (1965).

XIV   Cadoux (C.), *L'Afrique du Sud* (1966).

XV   Djordjevic (J.), *La Yougoslavie* (1967).

XVI   Langrod (G.) & Clifford Vaughan (M.), *Irlande* (1968).

XVII   Wyrwa (T.), *Le Mexique* (1969).

XVIII   Waeles (R.), *Israël* (1969).

XIX   Dore (F.), *La République indienne* (1970).

XX   Robert (J.), *Le Japon* (1970).

XXI   Esen (B.N.), *La Turquie* (1970).

XXII   Pajot (L.), *Le Portugal* (1971).

XXIII   Wyrwa (T.), *Les républiques andines* (Bolivia, Chili, Columbia, Equador, Peru, Venezuela) (1972).

XXIV   Spassov (B.), *La Bulgarie* (1973).

XXV   Charvin (R.), *La République démocrate allemande* (1973).

XXVI   Krieger (A.), *Le Pakistan* (1974).

XXVII   Prouzet (M.), *Le Cameroun* (1974).

XXVIII Tsien Tche-Hao, *La Chine* (1977).

(c) In German

ZWEIGERT (K.) & KÖTZ (H.), *Einführung in die Rechtsvergleichung auf dem Gebiete des Privatrechts:* Bd. I: *Grundlagen* (1971), Bd. II: *Intitutionen* (1969).

RHEINSTEIN (M.), *Einfürung in die Rechtsvergleichung* (1974). A collection of his articles with an excellent bibliography.

CONSTANTINESCO (L.J.), *Rechsvergleichung:* Bd. I: *Einführung in die Rechsvergleichung* (1971).

DAVID-GRASMANN, *Einführung in die grossern Rechtssysteme der Gegenwart* (1966). This is a translation and adaption for a German public of the present work.

SCHNITZER (A.), *Vergleichende Rechtslehre,* 2 vols. (2nd ed., 1961). The most interesting feature of this work is the third part in which the present differences between the concepts and solutions of different laws are reviewed.

Die Zivilgesetze der Gegenwart, a collection published in Germany, before 1939, but still useful. It features volumes relating to the laws of France, England, Brazil, U.S.S.R. and Nordic countries (Sweden, Finland).

The collection *wie man in . . . Recht spricht,* published in Switzerland (Geist und Gesetz der Völker und Länder) contains the following volumes:

JUSTICE MCLEARY, *England* (1945).

FRITZSCHE (H.), *Schweiz* (1948).

EKELÖF (P.O.) *Schweden* (1949).

ESEN (B.N.), *Türkei* (1950).

A new collection, *Einführungen in das fremdländische Recht* has been initiated by the *Wissenschaftliche Buchgesellschaft,* Darmstadt. Works on the laws of the following countries have been published or announced:

Bulgaria	GEILKE (G.) & CHRIST (J.), 1975.
Poland	GEILKE (G.), 1971.
U.S.S.R.	GEILKE (G.), 1966.
U.S.A.	HAY (P.), 1976.
England	HEINRICH (D.), 1971.
Italy	LUTHER (G.), 1968.
France	SONNENBERGER (H. G.), 1972.
Fed. German Republic	BAUR (F.), 1974.

Rechtsvergleichung	EBERT (K. H.), 1978.
Einführung in die	
Grundlagen	DILGER (K.).
Nordic Countries	KORKISCH (F.).
Austria	KREJCI (H.).
Yugoslavia	LIPOWSCHEK (A.).
Japan	ROHL (W.).
Netherlands	SCHMINCK (A.).
Switzerland	SCHNYDER (B.).

(d) In Spanish

SOLÁ CAÑIZARES (F. DE), *Iniciación al derecho comparado* (1954).

MARTINEZ PAZ (E.), *Introducción al estudio del derecho comparado* (1934). This work, originally published in the Argentine Republic, was re-edited in 1960 by the Institute of Comparative Law of Mexico.

The work by GUTTERIDGE (H.C.), mentioned above, has been translated into Spanish: *El derecho comparado* (1954). There is also a translation of DAVID (R.), *Tratado de derecho civil comparado* (1953). Also translated into Spanish is the work mentioned below by SARFATTI (M.), *Introducción al estudio del derecho comparado* (1936).

The original French edition of the present work has also appeared in Spanish: *Los grandes sistemas de derecho del mundo contemporaneo* (1968).

(e) In Italian

ASCARELLI (T.), *Studi di diritto comparato* (1952).

SARFATTI (M.), *Introduzione allo studio del diritto comparato* (1933).

DAVID (R.), *I grandi sistemi giuridici contemporanei* (1967) Translation of the original French edition of the present work.

ROTONDI (M.), *Scritti giuridici:* Vol. II: *Studi di diritto comparato e teoria generale* (1973).

ANCEL (M.), *Utilità e metodi del diritto comparato. Elementi d'introduzione generale allo studio comparato dei diritti* (1974).

(f) In several languages

ROTONDI (M.), ed., *Inchieste di dirrito comparato* t. 2: *Buts et méthodes du droit comparé* (1973). The work contains 42 articles written in English, French, German, Spanish and Italian.

ZWEIGERT (K.) & PUTTFARKEN (H.J.) (eds.), *Rechtsvergeleichung* (1978). The work has 22 articles in English, French and German.

SECTION IV—ENCYCLOPEDIAS OF COMPARATIVE LAW; MISCELLANIES

(A) Encyclopedias

International Encyclopedia of Comparative Law, published under the auspices of the International Association of Legal Science, in 17 volumes, under the direction of ZWEIGERT (K.):

I	KNAPP (V.), *National Reports.*
II	DAVID (R.), *The Legal Systems of the World: Their Comparison and Unification.*
III	LIPSTEIN (K.), *Private International Law.*
IV	GLENDOW (M.A.), *Persons and Family.*
V	NEUMAYER (K.), *Successions.*
VI	YIANNOPOULOS (A.N.), *Property and Trusts.*
VII	VON MEHREN (A.T.), *Contracts in General.*
VIII	ZWEIGERT (K.), *Specific Contracts.*
IX	ZIEGEL (J.), *Commercial Transactions and Institutions.*
X	VON CAEMMERER (E.), *Restitution, Unjust Enrichment & negotiorum gestio.* ·
XI	TUNC (A), *Torts.*
XII	RODIERE (R.), *Law of Transport.*
XIII	CONRAD (A.) *Business and Private Organisations.*
XIV	ULMER (U.), *Copyright and Industrial Property.*
XV	HEPPLE (B.A.), *Labour Law.*
XVI	CAPPELLETTI (M.), *Civil Procedure.*
XVII	BLAGOJEVIĆ (B.T.), *State and Economy.*

Publication of the separate parts began in 1971.

SCHLEGELBERGER, *Rechsvergleichendes Handwörterbuch,* 7 vols. (1929–1939). The work contains 262 articles arranged alphabetically, but was to have had 300, it is complete to the word *Vermächtnis*. It deals with only private law (civil and commercial law) and is, to a large extent, now out of date.

Mention should be made of the French language *Jurisclasseur notarial, Droit comparé*—concerning matters of foreign law of interest to the notarial profession. It contains a number of sections in which many foreign laws are described.

In English, an equivalent but more complete work is MARTIN-DALE-HUBBLE, *Law Dictionary,* published in the United States, in annual editions, since 1931. The parts of this encyclopaedia of interest to comparatists are volumes III and IV: *Law Digests*.

Encyclopaedia Universalis. This work, published between 1968 and 1974, contains a large number of articles on subjects of private and public law. The part devoted to *droit privé* (private law) was under the direction of TUNC (A.), that related to *droit public* (public law) under the direction of BURDEAU (G.).

(B) Miscellanies

Introduction à l'étude de droit comparé. A collection of studies in honour of Edouard Lambert, 3 vols. (1938).

Mélanges offerts à Jacques Maury, 2 vols. (1960). The last article of Volume I and the whole of Volume II contain articles on comparative law.

LAWSON F.H.), *Selected Essays 2 vols. 1977.*

RHEINSTEIN (M.), *Einführung in die Rechtsvergleichung* (1974). A collection of the author's articles, with an excellent bibliography.

KAHN-FREUND (O.), *Selected Writings* (1978).

Multitudo legum Ius unum. Mélanges en l'honneur de W. Wengler (1973).

Problèmes contemporains de droit comparé, 2 vols. (1962). A collection of articles published by the Institut japonais de droit comparé, Université Chuo.

Festschrift für Ernst Rabel, 2 vols. (1954). Volume I contains articles on private international law and comparative law written in English, French and German.

XXth Century Comparative and Conflicts Law. Legal Essays in honour of Hessel E. Yntema (1961).

Essays in Jurisprudence in honour of Roscoe Pound (1962).

Von deutschen zum europäischen Recht. Festschrift für HANS DÖLLE, 2 vols. (1963). Articles in German, French and English.
Studi in memoria di TULLIO ASCARELLI, 3 vols. (1968).
Ius privatum gentium. Festschrift für MAX RHEINSTEIN, 2 vols. (1969).
Mélanges de droit comparé en l'honneur du doyen ÅKE MALM-STRÖM, Acta Inst. Upsaliensis Jurisprudentiae Comparativae XIV (1972).
Acta Academiae universalis jurisprudentiae comparativae. Mémoires de l'Académie internationale de droit comparé, 2 vols. (1928, 1934–1935).
Congreso internacional de juristas (Lima, December 8–10, 1951). Reports presented at a conference held to mark the Fourth Centenary of the Universidad major de San Marcos (1953).
Rapports généraux au Ve Congrès international de droit comparé (International Congress of Comparative Law) (Bruxelles, August 4–9, 1958), published under the direction of J. LIMPENS, 2 vols. (1960).
Rapports généraux au VIe Congrès international de droit comparé (International Congress of Comparative Law) (Hamburg, July 30–August 4, 1962), published under the direction of J. LIMPENS by the Centre interuniversitaire de droit comparé (1964).
Rapports généraux du VIIe Congrés international de droit comparé (Uppsala, August 6–13, 1966). Acta Inst. Upsaliensis Jurisprudentiae Comparativae, IX (1968).
Rapports généraux au IXe Congrés international de droit comparé (Teheran, September 27–October 4, 1974) published by the Institut de droit comparé de Téhéran (1977).
Rapports généraux au Xe Congrés international de droit comparé (Budapest, August 22–29, 1978) published in Budapest, 1981.

SECTION V—ROMANO-GERMANIC FAMILY[1]

(A) Reviews and Periodicals

Travaux de l'Association Henri Capitant pour la culture juridique française, 1946 (annual). The Association organises conferences of jurists from different countries whose laws are related to French

---

[1] See also Sections I to IV of this Appendix.

law. Each year it publishes a volume of *Travaux* containing the reports and discussions on the particular matters studied.

Annales de la Faculté de droit de Toulouse, 1953 (annual). In addition to other articles this publication includes the reports delivered during the "Journées de droit franco-espagnoles," organised annually by French and Spanish law faculties.

(B) Formation and History of Romanist Laws

MERRYMAN (J.M.), *The Civil Law Tradition. An Introduction to the Legal System of Western Europe and Latin America* (1969).

VILLEY (M.), *Leçons d'histoire de la philosophie du droit* (2nd eds., 1962), pp. 1–106.

—— *Cours d'histoire de la philosophie du droit* (1961–62 and following years).

SCHULZ (F.), *Principles of Roman Law* (1936). This work is less a description of Roman law rules than an explanation of certain special features of that law perpetuated in persent day Romanist laws. The same book appeared earlier in German: *Prinzipien des römischen Rechts* (1934), but the more recent English edition is preferable.

BUCKLAND (W.) & MCNAIR (A.D.), *Roman Law and Common Law* (2nd ed. by F.H. LAWSON (1953)).

A General Survey of Events, Sources, Persons and Movements in Continental Legal History, by different authors (*Continental Legal History Series,* Vol. 1, 1912, re-issued 1968). An excellent work containing studies of the principal laws of the European continent in their historical perspective.

KOSCHAKER (P.), *Europa und das römische Recht* (3rd ed., 1958). This excellent work has been summarised in English by J.K. WYLIE, "Roman law as an Element in European Culture," in *South African Law Journal,* Vol. 65, pp. 4–13, 201–212, 349–361 (1948).

WIEACKER (F.), *Privatrechtsgeschichte der Neuzeit* (2nd ed., 1963).

NICHOLAS (B.), *An Introduction to Roman Law* (1962).

JOLOWICZ (H.F.), ed., NICHOLAS (B.), *Historical Introduction to the Study of Roman Law* (3rd ed., 1972).

VINOGRADOFF (P.), *Roman Law in Medieval Europe* (3rd ed., de Zuleuta, 1961).

L'Europa e il diritto romano. Studi in memoria di P. Koschaker, 2 vols. (1954). These two volumes contain articles written in German, English, French and Italian.

COING (H.), *Handbuch der Quellen und Literatur der neuren europäischen Privatrechsgeschichte,* 3 vols. (1973–1977).

(C) Laws of Continental Europe (except the Nordic Group)

Bibliographies compiled under the sponsorship of the Association internationale des sciences juridiques (31, rue Saint-Guillaume, Paris VII):

Germany—(Gesellschaft für Rechsvergleichung, 1964 and supplements).

France—(R. David, 1964).

Luxembourg—(Comité national luxembourgeois de l'A.I.S.J., 1967).

SZLADITS (C), *Guide to Foreign Legal Materials: France Germany, Switzerland* (1959). An excellent guide of the sources and bibliography of French and Swiss law.

GRISOLI (A.), *Guide to Foreign Legal Materials: Italy* (1965).

GRAULICH (P.), GLASTRA VAN LORN (J.), VAN HOLK (L.E.), *Guide to Foreign Legal Materials: Belgium, Luxembourg, The Netherlands* (1968).

VAN DIEVOET (E.), *Le droit civil en Belgique et en Hollande de 1800 à 1948. Les Sources du droit* (1948).

AMOS (SIR MAURICE) & WALTON (F.P.), *French Civil Law,* 3rd ed. by H.F. LAWSON, A.E. ANTON, & L. NEVILLE BROWN (1967). An excellent description in English of French civil law.

NEVILLE-BROWN (L.) & GARNER (J.F.), *French Administrative Law* (2nd ed., 1973).

DAVID (R.), *English and French Law* (1980).

LAWSON (F.H.), *A Common Lawyer looks at the Civil Law* (1953).

MEHREN (A. VON) & GORDLEY (J.R.), *The Civil Law System: An Introduction to the Comparative Study of Law* (2nd ed., 1977).

SCHWARTZ (B.), *The Code Napoleon and the Common Law World* (1956).

ZEPOS (P.J.), *Greek Law* (1949).

CAPPELLETTI (M.), MERRYMAN (J.H.) & PERILLO (J.M.), *Introduction to the Italian Legal System* (1967).

DE VRIES (H.P.) & SCHNEIDER (G.A.), *Civil Law and the Anglo-American Lawyer. A case-illustrated Introduction to Civil Law Institutions and Methods* (1976).

WATSON (A.), *The Making of the Civil Law* (1981).

NICHOLAS (B.), *French Law of Contract* (1982).

CALHOUN (G.M.) & DELAMERE (C.), *A Working Bibliography of Greek Law* (1968).

KOKKINI-IATRIDOU (D.), *Introduction au droit hellenique* (1968).

RYAN (K.W.), *An introduction to the Civil Law* (1962).

DAVID (R.) & KINDRED (M.), *French Law. Its structure, Sources and Methodology.* (1972).

KAHN-FREUND (O.), LEVY (C.), RUDDEN (B.), *A Source Book on French Law* (1973).

COHN (E.J), *Manual of German Law,* 2 vols. (2nd ed., 1968, 1971).

FRAGA IRIBARNE (M.), *General Introduction to Spanish Law* (1967).

ANSAY (T.) & WALLACE (D.), *Introduction to Turkish Law* (2nd ed., 1978).

CONSTANTINESCO (L.) & HÜBNER (U.), *Einführung in das französische Recht* (1974).

SONNENBERGER (H.L.), *Einführung in das französische Recht* (1972).

HUBRECHT (G.), *Grundzüge des französischen Rechts* (1973).

FERID (M.), *Das französische Zivilrecht,* 2 vols. (1971).

(D) Laws of the Nordic Countries

Bibliography compiled under the sponsorship of the Association internationale des sciences juridiques:

Pays Nordiques (Denmark, Norway, Sweden, Finland, Iceland) by IUUL (S.), MALMSTRÖM (A.), SONDERGAARD (J.), HAUKAAS (K.), SNAEVARR (A.), JOKELA (H.) (1961).

EEK (H.), Evolution et structure des droits scandinaves, *Revue hellénique de droit international* (1961), p. 33.

Danish and Norwegian Law. A General Survey (1963).

ORFIELD (L.B.), *The Growth of Scandinavian Law* (1953).

Einführung in das schwedische Rechtsleben (1950).

Scandinavian Studies in Law. Yearbook 1957—Published under the auspices of the Faculty of Law of the University of Stockholm.

Periodically there is a list of articles published in English, French and German on the laws of Sweden, Denmark and Norway.

FRYKHOLM (L.), *Swedish Publications in English, French and German*, 1935–1960 (1961), also in the above series, merits special mention.

DANISH COMMITTEE OF COMPARATIVE LAW, *Danish and Norwegian Law. A General Survey* (1963).

Union of Finnish Lawyers (VOTILA (J.) ed.), *The Finnish Legal System* (1966).

(E) Laws of Latin America

KARST (K.L.) & ROSENN (K.J.), *Law and Development in Latin America. A Case-Book* (1975).

LAMBERT (J.), *Amérique latine. Structures sociales et institutions politiques* (2nd ed., 1968).

EDER (P.J.), Law in Latin America, in *Law: A Century of Progress*, 1835–1935, Vol. I, pp. 39–82 (1937).

—— *A Comparative Survey of Anglo-American and Latin-American Law* (1950).

—— *Principios caracteristicos del "common law" y del derecho latinamericano* (Con concordancias entre los códigos argentinos y la legislación del Estado de Nueva York) (1960).

DE VRIES (H.P.), *The Law of the Americas* (1965).

CLAGETT (H.), *Administration of Justice in Latin America* (1952).

DUMON (F.), *Le Brésil: Institutions politiques et judiciares* (1964)

VANCE (J.T.), *The Background of Hispanic-American Law: Legal Sources and Juridical Literature of Spain* (1943).

VILLALON-GALDAMES (A.), *Bibliografia juridica de America Latina (1819–1965)*. Vol. I: *Introduction, Argentina, Bolivia* (1969). The Editiorial jurdica de Chile, which publishes this work, promises 5 volumes and quinquennial supplements.

ELOLA (J.) ed., *Bibliografia sumaria de derecho mexicano*, by M. de la Villa & J.L. Zambrano (1957).

Universidad de Brasilia, *Noticia do direito brasileiro* (1970). Annual.

The Library of Congress, Washington D.C., has published a series entitled *Guide to the Law and Literature of* . . . , containing explanatory bibliographies of Latin-American countries. The

Legal Division of the Organisation of American States has published pamphlets on the business law of each Latin-American country, entitled *A Statement of the Laws of . . . in Matters Affecting Business.*

(F) Canon Law

ANDRIEU-GUITRANCOURT (P.), *Introduction à l'étude du droit en génénal et du droit canonique contemporain en particulier* (1963).

(G) "Mixed" Laws

WALKER (D.M.), *The Scottish Legal System* (3rd ed., 1969).
—— *Principles of Scottish Private Law* (3rd ed., 1982).
DAINOW (J.), ed., *The Role of Judicial Decisions and Doctrine in Civil Law and in Mixed Jurisdictions* (1974).
HAHLO (H.R.) & KAHN (E.), *The South African Legal System and its Background* (1968).
SMITH (T.B.), *British Justice. The Scottish Contribution.* The Hamlyn Lectures, series 13 (1961).
BAUDOUIN (L.), *Le droit civil de la province de Québec, modéle vivant de droit comparé* (1953).
CLARENCE SMITH (J.A.) & KERBY (J.): *Le droit puvé au Canada. Etudes comparatives. I. Introduction général Private Law in Canada. A Comparative Study. I. General Introduction* (1975).
LASKIN ((B.), *The British Tradition in Canadian Law* (1969).
McWHINNEY (E.) ed., *Canadian Jurisprudence. The Civil Law and the Common Law in Canada* (1958).
Livre du Centenaire du Code civil (Québec). T. I: *Le droit dans la vie familiale* (1969). T. II: *Le droit dans la vie économique et sociale* (1970).
BADIOU (E.), *Le droit romano-hollandais. Son évolution, ses caractéres généraux, son avenir* (1951).
LEE (R.W.), *Introduction to the Roman-Dutch Law* (5th ed., 1961).
Annual Survey of South Africa Law (1947).
Bibliography compiled under the sponsorship of the Association internationale des sciences juridiques (International Association of Legal Science). *Canada* (R. Boult, 1966).
Etudes de droit français et mauricien (1969).

GAMBOA (M.J.), *An Introduction to Phillipine Law* (6th ed., 1955).

NADAJARA (T.), *The Legal System of Ceylon in its Historical setting* (1972).

CHLOROS (A.), *Codification in a mixed Jurisdiction.* The Civil & Commercial Law of Seychelles (1977).

SECTION VI—FAMILY OF SOCIALIST LAWS[2]

(A) Bibliographies

Bibliographies compiled under the auspices of the International Association of Legal Science/Association internationale des sciences juridiques:

Hungary 1945–1965 (L. Nagy, 1966).
Poland 1944–1956 (W. Czachórski, 1958).
Rumania 1944–1973 (T. Ionasco, D. Rusu, 1969–1974).
Czechoslovakia 1945–1958 (V. Knapp, 1958)
U.S.S.R. (U.S.S.R Academy of Sciences, Institute of State Law, 1960).
Yugoslavia 1945–1967 (B.T. Blagojević, 2nd ed., 1968).

The Library of Congress, Washington, D.C. published a series of annotated bibliographies entitled *Legal Sources and Bibliography of . . .* for the following countries:

Bulgaria (I. Sipkow, 1956).
Hungary (K.A. Bedo, G. Torzsay-Biber, 1956)
Baltic States (Estonia, Lithuania, Latvia) (J. Klesment, D. Krivickas, V. Riismandel, A. Rusis, 1963)
Poland (P. Siekanowicz, 1964)
Rumania (V. Stoicoiu, 1964)
Czechoslovakia (A. Bohmer, J. Jira, S. Kocvara, J. Nosek, 1959)
Yugoslvaia (F. Gjupanovich, A. Adamovitch, V. Gsovski, 1964).

BUTLER (W.E.) ed., *Writings on Soviet Law and Soviet International Law. A Bibliography of Books and Articles published since 1917 in Languages other than the East European* (1966).

---

[2] See also Sections I to IV of this Appendix.

Association of American Law Schools, *Law Books Recommended for Libraries*. No. 44: "Russian Law," H.J. Berman.
Bibliographie juridique de la République démocratique allemande, 2 vols. 1974–1975.

(B) Reviews and Periodicals

Soviet Studies, 1949 (quarterly).
Slavic Review. American Quarterly for Soviet and East European Studies, 1942. Previously called *The Slavonic Yearbook* (Vol. 1), then *The Slavonic and East European Review* (Vols. II and III) and, from 1945 to 1960, *The American Slavic and East European Review* (Vols. IV to XX).
There are two reviews published by the Soviet cultural services:
Soviet Statutes and Decisions (1965).
Soviet Law and Government (1963). Translations of articles published in Soviet reviews.
Law in Eastern Europe, 1958 (irregular). A publication of the University of Leyden (the Netherlands) containing articles, in either English or French, on the laws of the European socialist countries (20 vols. published by 1976).
Review of Socialist Law ed., Feldbrugge (The Netherlands) 1974 (quarterly).
Ost-Europa Recht, 1955 (semi-annual).
Jahrbuch für Ostrecht, (1960 (semi-annual).
Berichte des Ost-Europa Instituts an der Freien Universität Berlin, Reihe Wirtschaft und Recht (79 pamphlets published from 1952 to 1967).
Studien des Instituts für Ostrecht (Munich) (18 volumes to 1967).
Recht in Ost und West (1957—published by the Freie Universität of Berlin (West Germany).
Annuaire de l'U.R.S.S. et des pays socialistes européens (law, sociology, culture, economy). Published by the Université des sciences juridiques, politiques et sociales de Strasbourg, Centre de recherches sur l'U.R.S.S. et les pays de l'Est.
Revue de l'Est. Economie et technique de plannification. Droit et sciences sociales, 1970 (quarterly).
Bulletin de droit tchécoslovaque, 1925 (quarterly).
Droit yougoslave, 1975 (three issues p.a.).
Revue de droit hongrois, 1958 (three issues p.a.).

Droit polonais contemporain, 1963.

Revue roumaine des sciences sociales. Série de Sciences juridiques, 1964.

Droit bulgare (Doctrine, Jurisprudence, Legislation) No. 2–3 (1971).

Revue de droit et de législation de la République démocratique allemande, 1965 (twice yearly).

Acta juridica Academiae Scientiarum hungaricae and *Acta Universitatis Szegediensis* (Acta juridica et politica) and the *Annales Universitatis Scientiarum Budapestinensis* occasionally contain articles in French.

The Polish review *Państwo i Prawo* contains summaries in French of the main articles, and issues a monthly pamphlet of them. The other principal reviews published in the people's democracies often also contain summaries in English and in French.

(C) General Works

(a) In English

Fundamentals of Marxism-Leninism (1961). The authorised manual explaining the Marxist-Leninist doctrine by a group of Soviet professors and published by the Foreign Languages Publishing House, Moscow. This is the basic work to be read by all those interested in Soviet matters.

HAZARD (J.N.) & SHAPIRO (I), *The Soviet Legal System. Post-Stalin Documentation and Historical Commentary* (1962). The twenty chapters of this work contain an excellent summary description of the evolution of Soviet law. The historical part of each chapter is followed by documents, extracts of laws, judicial decisions and Soviet legal works or reviews which illustrate the application of Soviet law. Recommended "Selected Readings," at the end of its three parts, are listed.

A revised edition was published by HAZARD (J.N.), SHAPIRO (I.) & MAGGS (P.B.) and a 3rd edition in 1977: HAZARD (J.N.), MAGGS (P.B.) & BUTLER (W.E.): *The Soviet Legal System. Fundamental Principles and Historical Commentary.* The illustrative documents vary from one edition to another. The 3rd edition is also complemented by BUTLER (W.E.), *The Soviet Legal System. Selected Contemporary Legislation and Documents* (1978).

HAZARD (J.N.), *Communists and Their Law. A Search for the Common Core of the Legal Systems of the Marxian Socialist States* (1969).

—— *The Soviet System of Government* (5th ed., 1980).

—— *Settling Disputes in Soviet Society, The Formative Years of Legal Institutions* (1960).

HAZARD (J.N.) & BABB (H.W.), *Soviet Legal Philosophy* (1951). A translation of a work by Pachoukanis and Soviet articles, with an introduction by J.N. HAZARD.

NOVE (A.) *Soviet Economy. An Introduction* (3rd ed., 1968).

ZILE (Z.L.), *Ideas and Forces in Soviet Legal History* (1970).

CONQUEST (R.) ed., *Justice and the Legal System in the U.S.S.R.* (1968).

JOHNSON (E.L.), *An Introduction to the Soviet Legal System* (1969).

KUCHEROV (S.), *The Organs of Soviet Administration of Justice: Their History and Operation* (1971).

FELDBRUGGE (F.J.M.), *Encyclopedia of Soviet Law* 2 vols. (1974).

Contemporary Soviet Law. Essays in honour of John N. Hazard, ed. by D.B. Barry, W.E. Butler, G. Ginsburgs (1974).

BERMAN (H.), *Justice in the U.S.S.R. An Interpretation of Soviet Law.* Revised ed. (1963).

GRZYBOWSKI (K.), *Soviet Legal Institutions: Doctrines and Social Functions* (1962).

IOFFE (O.S.) & MAGGS (P.B.), *Soviet Law in Theory and Practice* (1983).

BUTLER (W.E.), *Soviet Law* (1983).

—— ed., *Anglo-Polish Legal Essays* (1982).

NAGY (L.) ed., *Register of Legal Documentation of Socialist States.* 3 vols.

(b) In French

Les principes du marxisme-léninisme (2nd ed., 1964). The French version of the work mentioned above.

CHAMBRE (H.), *L'évolution du marxisme soviétique. Théorie économique et droit* (1974).

LESAGE (M.), *Les institutions soviétiques* (1975).

—— *Le droit Soviétique* (1975).

DEKKERS (R.), *Introduction au droit de l'Union soviétique et des Républiques populaires* (2nd ed., 1971).

BLAGOJEVIČ (B.T.), CZACHORSKI (W.), IONASCO (T.), KNAPP (V.), KROUTOGOLOV (M.A.), SZABO (I), TOUMANOV (V.A.), *Introduction aux droits socialistes* (1971).

ROZMARYN (St.) ed., *Introduction à l'étude du droit polonais* (1967).

SZABO (I.) ed., *Introduction au droit hongrois* (1975).

CHARVIN (R.), *Les Etats socialistes européens* (1975).

STOYANOVITCH (K.), *La pensée marxiste et le droit* (1974).

(c) In Spanish

DAVID (R.) & HAZARD (J.N.), *El derecho soviético*, 2 vols. (1964).

IOFFE (R.O.), *El derecho civil sovietico* (1960). A translation of those parts dealing with the civil law of a work published by the University of Leningrad on the fortieth anniversary of the 1917 Revolution.

(d) In German

PFAFF (D.), *Die Entwicklung der sowjetischen Rechtslehre* (1968).

MEDER (W.), *Das Sowjetrecht. Grundzüge der Entwicklung 1917–1970* (1971).

GEILKE (G.), *Einführung in das Sowjetrecht* (1966).

—— *Einführung in das Recht der polnischen Volksrepublik* (1971).

MAMPEL (S.), *Das Recht in Mitteldeutschland* (1966).

ARLT (R.) & STILLER (G.), *Die Entwicklung der sozialistischen Rechtsordnung in der D.D.R.* (1973).

PETEV (V.), *Sozialistisches Zivilrecht* (1975).

REICH (N.) & REICHEL (H.C.), *Einführung in das sozialistische Recht* (1975).

BRUNNER (G.), *Einführung in das Recht der D.D.R.* (1975).

(b) In Italian

NAPOLI TANO (T.), *Istituzioni di diritto sovietico. I presupposti e gli ordinamenti* (1975).

Section VII—Common Law Family[3]

(a) In English

1. With respect to England, apart from those works included in the bibliography of English law provided above, the following works deserve special mention:

KIRALFY (A.K.R.), *The English Legal System* (7th ed., 1984).

SMITH (P.F.) & BAILEY (S.H.), *The Modern English Legal System* (1984).

CHLOROS (A.G.) ed., *A Bibliographical Guide to the Law of the United Kingdom, the Channel Islands and the Isle of Man* (2nd ed., 1973).

DAVID (R.), *English Law and French Law* (1980).

Dictionary of English Law, under the direction of LORD JOWITT, 2 vols. (1959).

JACKSON (R.M.), *The Machinery of Justice in England* (6th ed, 1972).

2. For the United States of America, apart from the general works and reviews mentioned above, the following should be noted:

ANDREWS (J.L.), CHARPENTIER (A.A.), MARKE (J.J.) & STERN (N.B.) eds., *The Law in the U.S.A.—A Bibliographical Guide* (1966).

HAY (P.), *An Introduction to U.S. Law* (1976).

FARNSWORTH (E.A.), *An Introduction to the Legal System of the United States* (2nd ed., 1975).

SIGLER (S.A.), *An Introduction to the Legal System* (1968).

Annual Survey of American Law, 1942. This annual publication of New York University describes the main developments of the current year in the different branches of American law.

Law: A Century of Progress, 1835–1935, 3 vols. (1937). A collection of articles describing the evolution and tendencies of different branches of American law.

(b) In German

PARKER (R.), *Das Privatrecht der Vereinigten Staaten von Amerika* (1960).

---

[3] See also Sections I to IV of this Appendix.

—— *Das öffentliche Recht der V.S.A.* (1963).

SCHLESINGER (R.), *Die Rolle der Supreme Court in Privat und Prozessrecht der Vereinigten Staaten* (1965).

LOWENSTEIN (K.), *Verfassungsrecht und Verfassungspraxis der Vereinigten Staaten* (1959).

FULDA (C.), *Einführung in das Recht der V.S.A.* (1966).

HENRICH (D.), *Einführung in das englische Privatrecht* (1971).

BLUMENWITZ (D.), *Einführung in das anglo-amerikanische Recht* (1971).

RIEGERT (R.A.), *Das amerikanische Administrative Law* (1967).

(c) In Spanish

TUNC (A. & S.), *El derecho de los Estados Unidos. Instituciones judiciales, fuentes y tecnicas* (1957). A translation of the third volume and a chapter of the first volume of the work by the same authors, in the French language collection "Les systèmes de droit contemporains."

CHOMMIE, *El derecho de los Estados Unidos*, 3 vols. (1963).

(d) In French

COING (M.), *Bibliographie des études publiées sur le droit des Etats-Unis en des langues autres que l'anglais* (1967).

DAVID (R.), *Le Droit anglais* (4th ed. 1981).

TUNC (A. & S.), *Le droit des Etats-Unis* (3rd ed., 1974).

STONE (F.F.), *Institutions foundamentales du droit des Etats-Unis* (1965).

LEVY-ULLMANN (H.), *Le système juridique de l'Angleterre* t. I: *Le système traditionel* (1928).

ANCEL (M.) & RADZINOWICZ (L.), *Introduction au droit criminel de l'Angleterre* (1959).

MATHIOT (A.), *Le Régime politique britannique* (1955). (Cahiers de la Fondation nationale des sciences politiques, no. 68).

PACTET (P.), *Les institutions politiques de la Grande-Bretagne* (1960).

SCHWARTZ (B.), *Le droit aux États-Unis* (1979) *Le droit administratif américain. Notions générales* (1952).

CRABB (J.H.), *Le système juridique anglo-américain* (1972).

(e) In Italian

SERENI (A.P.); *Studi di diritto comparato. I. Il diritto degli Stati Uniti* (1958).

ILIFFE (J.A.), *Lineamenti di diritto inglese* (1966).

SECTION VIII—OTHER CONCEPTIONS OF LAW AND THE SOCIAL ORDER[4]

(A) In General

ANDERSON (J.N.D.) ed., *Changing Law in Developing Countries* (1963).

—— *Family Law in Asia and Africa* (1967).

BUXBAUM (D.C.) ed., *Traditional and Modern Legal Institutions in Asia and Africa* (1967).

DIAMOND (A.S.), *Primitive Law, Past and Present* (1971).

(B) Islamic Law and Muslim Countries

Index Islamicus, 1906–1955 (1958). A bibliography of articles dealing with Islam published in languages other than Arabic; under the direction of J. D. PEARSON with the collaboration of J.F. ASTON; pages 101–141 deal with Islamic law. In the supplement, for 1956–1960, published in 1962, Nos. 876–1294 concern Islamic law.

Encyclopédie de l'Islam, 4 vols. (1913). A second edition by B. LEWIS, CH. PELLAT & J. SCHACHT, 3 vols. published 1954, 1965, 1971. A fourth volume, in the course of publication ceased publication with issue no. 74.

BOUSQUET (G.H.), *Le droit musulman* (1963).

—— *Précis de droit musulman principalement malékite et algérien,* 3rd ed. (1950)

—— *Du droit musulman et de son application effective dans le monde* (1949).

CHARLES (R.), *Droit musulman* (1956).

LINANT DE BELLEFONDS (Y.), *Traité de droit musulman comparé,* 2 vols. (1965).

---

[4] See also Sections I to IV of this Appendix.

TYAN (E.), *Institutions du droit public musulman,* 2 vols. published: I. *Le Califat;* II. *Sultanat et califat* (1954–1956).

―― *Historie de l'organisation judiciaire en pays d'Islam,* 2 vols. 2nd ed. (1961).

COULSON (N.J.), *History of Islamic Law* (1964).

SCHACHT (J.), *An Introduction to Islamic Law* (1964). The work has an excellent bibliography on Islamic law.

ANDERSON (J.N.D.), *Islamic Law in the Modern World* (1959).

―― *Islamic Law in Africa* (2nd ed., 1970).

SANTILLANA (D.), *Instituzioni di diritto musulmano malichita, con riguardo arche al sistema sciafiita,* 2 vols. (1938).

KHADDURI (M.) & LIEBENSY (H.J.), *Origin and Development of Islamic Law* (1955), Vol. I of the series *Law in the Middle East.*

CHEHATA (CH.), *Droit musulman. Applications au Proche-Orient* (1970).

―― *Etudes de droit musulman* (1970).

ASSOCIATION OF AMERICAN LAW SCHOOLS: *Law Books recommended for Libraries.* No. 41. *Islamic Law,* by C. Szladits.

Studia Islamica, under the direction of R. Brunschwig & J. Schacht.

LOPEZ ORTIZ (J.), *Derecho musulmán* (1932).

FYZEE (A.A.A.), *Outlines of Mohammadan Law,* (4th ed., 1975).

(C) Jewish Law and the Law of Israel

LIVNEH (E.), *Israel. Legal Bibliography in European Languages* (1973). Annual supplements.

COHEN (B.), *Law and Tradition in Judaism* (1959).

―― *Jewish Law and Roman Law. A Comparative Study* 2 vols. (1966).

ELMAN (P.), *An Introduction to Jewish Law* (1958).

TEDESCHI (G.), *Studies in Israel Law* (1960).

International Lawyers' Convention in Israel, 1958 (1959). Collection of articles on Jewish law and the law of Israel.

Biennial Survey of Israel Law, 1958–59 and following years. Published by the Institute for Legislative Research and Comparative Law of Hebrew University of Jerusalem Faculty of Law.

BAKER (H.E.), *The Legal System of Israel* (1961)

—— *Connaissance du droit israélien* Revue d'études juridiques (1976).

(D) The Law of India

ALEXANDROWICZ (C.), *Bibliography of Indian Law* (2nd ed., 1974).

LINGAT (R.)., *The Classical Law of India.* Translated with additions by J.D.M. Derrett (1973).

DERRETT (J.D.M.), *Introduction to Modern Hindu Law* (1963).

—— *Religion, Law and the State in India* (1968).

—— *A Critique of Modern Hindu Law* (1970).

SETALVAD (M.C.), *The Common law in India* (1960).

—— *The Role of English Law in India* (1966).

MARSH (N.S.) ed., *Some Aspects of Indian Law Today* (1964).

JAIN (M.P.), *Outlines of Indian Legal History* (2nd ed., 1966).

(E) Laws of the Far East

Association of American Law Schools: *Law Books Recommended for Libraries,* No. 40, *Chinese Law,* S. SORICH.

RABINOWITZ (R.N.), "Materials on Japanese Law in Western Languages" 4 Am. J. Comp. L. pp. 97–104 (1955).

Chinese Law and Government (1968).

Studies in Chinese Law, Harvard Law School.

Law in Japan (1966) annual.

LI (V.), "The Role of Law in Communist China" *The China Quarterly,* No. 44, pp. 66–111 (1970).

Revue bibliographique de sinologie, 1955. Published by the Ecole pratique des Hautes Etudes, 6e section (Sorbonne).

ESCARRA (J.), *Le Droit chinois* (1936).

MEHREN (A. VON), *Law in Japan. The Legal Order in a Changing Society* (1963).

JOÜON DES LONGRAIS (F.), *L'Est et l'Ouest. Institutions du Japon et de l'Occident européen. Six études de sociologie juridique* (1958).

BODDE (D.), *Chinese Law: A selected Bibliography* (1961).

T'UNG-TSU CH'U, Law and Society in Traditional China (1961).

BODDE (D.) & MORRIS (C.), *Law in Imperial China* (1967).

BUTLER (W.E.) ed. *The Legal System of the Chinese Soviet Republic 1931–1934* (1983).

SHAO-CHUAN LENG, *Justice in Communist China* (1968).

HENDERSON (D.F.), *Conciliation and Japanese Law: Tokugawa and Modern*, 2 vols. (1964).

HAHM (P.C.), *The Korean Political Tradition and Law* (1967).

FU-SHUN LIN, *Chinese Law Past and Present. A Bibliography of Enactments and Commentaries in English* (1966).

COHEN (J.A.), *The Criminal Process in the People's Republic of China 1949–1963. An Introduction* (1968).

BLAUSTERN (A.P.) ed., *Fundamental Legal Documents of Communist China* (1962).

COLEMAN (R.) & HALEY (J.), *An Index to Japanese Law. A Bibliography of Western Langauge Materials 1867–1973.* (An annual special issue of "Law in Japan," 1975).

TSIEN (T.), *Les institutions chinoises et la Constitution de 1978* (1979).

La République populaire de Chine: cadres institutionnels et realisations. Vol. 1: *L'historire et le droit* by ENGELBORGHS-BERTELS (M.) & DEKKERS (R.), (1963); vol. II; *La planification et la croissance économique,* by GINSBURGH (V.) (1963).

CHEN (P.M.), *Law and Justice. Legal System in Communist China 2400 B.C.—A.D. 1964* (1974).

LENG (S.C.), *Justice in Communist China. A Survey of the Judicial System of the Chinese People's Republic* (1968).

NODA (Y.), *Introduction to Japanese Law* (1976).

WANG (D), *Les sources du droit japonais* (1978).

—— *Les sources du droit de la République populaire de Chine* (1982).

BARTHOLOMEW (G.), *Sources and Literature of Singapore Law,* [1975] Malaya L.R. 314–345.

KAISHER BAHADAN (K.C.), *Judicial Customs of Nepal* (2nd ed., 1971).

NADARAJA (T.), *The Legal System of Ceylon in its Historical Setting* (1972).

TAMBIAH (H.W.), *Principles of Ceylon Law* (1972).

MÜNZEL (F.), *Das Recht der Volkrespublik China* (1982).

HEUSER (R.), *Zur Einführung: Recht und Rechtstheorie in der Volkrespublik China* (1973).

TOMSON-JYUN-HSYONG SU, *Regierung und Verwaltung der Volkrespublik China* (1972).

KITAGAWA (Z.), *Die Rezeption des Europäischen Zivilrechts und seine Fortbildung in Japan* (1970).

Vu Van Mau, "Introduccion al derecho vietnamita" Rev. del Instituto de derecho comparado (Barcelona) (1964), pp. 38–71.

(F) Laws of Africa and Malagasy (Madagascar)

Association of American Law Schools, *Law Books Recommended for Libraries*, No. 39, *African Law*, A.A. Schiller.

Vanderlinden (J.), Bibliographie de droit africain 1947–1966 (1972).

(a) Reviews and Periodicals

The rapid evolution of these laws makes it particularly necessary to consult the following specialised reviews:

Annual Survey of African Law (1967). (French-speaking African countries are not generally reported on in this publication.)

Journal of African Law, 1956 (quarterly).

Journal of African Administration, 1949 (quarterly).

Revue juridique et politique Indépendance et coopération, 1947 (quarterly). This review was formerly called *Revue juridique et politique de l'Union française*, and then *Revue juridique et politique d'Outre-mer*.

Recueil Penant, Revue de droit des pays d'Afrique, 1891 (quarterly). First brought out as *Tribune des colonies*, then as *Recueil général de jurisprudence, de doctrine et de législation d'Outre-mer*.

Annales africaines, 1954 (annual). Published by the University of Dakar.

Annales malgaches, 1963. Published by the Université de Madagascar. Faculté de droit et des sciences économiques.

Revue juridique de Madagascar, 1951 (quarterly).

Revue judiciaire congolaise, 1962 (quarterly). Published by Lovanium University, Kinshasa (formerly Léopoldville).

(b) In English

The Legal Systems of Africa Series (Virginia Legal Studies):

I Redden (K.R.), *The Legal System of Ethiopia* (1968).

II Salacuse (J.W.), *An Introduction to Law in French-Speaking Africa*. Vol. I: *Africa South of the Sahara* (1969) Vol. II: *Africa North of the Sahara* (1975).

III Crabb (J.H.), *The Legal System of Congo-Kinshasa* (1970).

IV Palmer (V.V.) & Poulter (S.M.), *Lesotho* (1972).

Other volumes are promised (Somalia, Sudan, Ghana, Congo, Nigeria, Zambia, Malawi).

Law in Africa Series: 35 works published from 1962 to 1975 on different aspects of African law or the law of a number of African states (Sweet & Maxwell, London).

RUBIN (N.) & COTRAN (E.) eds., *Readings in African Law:* I. The Customary Judicial Process. Crimes and Civil Wrongs. The Law of Contract. Land Law. II. The Law of Persons. The Law of Marriage and Family. The Law of Succession and Inheritance.

African Systems of Thought. Preface by M. Fortes & G. Dieterlen (1965).

African Agrarian Systems. Studies presented and discussed at the second international African seminar. Lovanium University Léopoldville. Edited with an introduction by D. Biebuick (1963). Articles by 20 different authors.

FORTES (M.) & EVANS-PRITCHARD (E.E.) eds., *African Political Systems* (1940).

MILNER (A.) ed., *African Penal Systems* (1969).

ALLOTT (A.N.), *Essays In African Law* (1960).

—— *New Essays In African Law* (1970).

—— ed., *Judicial and Legal Systems in Africa* (2nd ed., 1970).

PHILLIPS (A.) & MORRIS (H.F.), *Marriage Laws in Africa* (1971).

KUPER (M. & L.), *African Law: Adaptation and Development* (1965).

BAADE (H.W.) & EVERETT (R.O.) eds., *African Law* (1963).

RADCLIFFE-BROWN (A.R.) & FORDE (D.), *African Systems of Kinship and Marriage* (2nd ed., 1962).

HUTCHISON (T.W.) ed., *Africa and Law. Developing Legal Systems in African Commonwealth Nations* (1968).

EKOW DANIELS (W.C.), *The Common Law in West Africa* (1964).

CONTINI (P.), *The Somali Republic. An Experiment in Legal Integration* (1970).

GLUCKMAN (M.). *The Ideas in Barotse Jurisprudence* (1972).

HAJI N.A. NOOR (M), *The Legal System of the Somali Democratic Republic* (1972).

HARVEY (W.B.), *Law and Social Change in Ghana* (1966).

MUSTAFA (Z.), *The Common Law in the Sudan. An Account the Justice, Equity and Good Conscience Provision* (1971).

UNIVERSITY OF IFE, *Integration of Customary and Modern Legal Systems in Africa* (1972).

(c) In French

Association Internationale des sciences juridiques: *Le droit de la terre en Afrique* (South of the Sahara) (1971).

Systèmes politiques africains (1964), French language version of the work above by FORTES (M.) & EVANS-PRITCHARD (E.E.).

Systèmes familiaux et matrimoniaux en Afrique (1953), French language version of the work above by RADCLIFFE-BROWN (A.R.) & FORDE (D.).

ELIAS (T.O.), *La nature du droit coutumier africain* (1961).

GONIDEC (P.F.), *Les droits africans, Evolution et sources* (2nd ed., 1976).

—— *L'Etat africain* (Evolution. Federalisme. Centralisation et décentralisation. Panafricanisme) (1970).

—— *Les systèmes politiques africains* (1971).

Les aspects juridiques du développement économique/Legal aspects of economic development under the direction of TUNC (A.) (1966).

GASSE (V.), *Les régimes fonciers africains et malgache. Evolution depuis l'indépendance* (1971).

GLUCKMAN (M.) ed., *Idées et procédures dans les systèmes legaux africains/Ideas and Procedures in African Customary Law* (1971).

M'BAYE (K.) ed., *Le droit de la famille en Afrique noir et à Madagascar* (1968).

Etudes de droit african et malgache under the direction of POIRIER (J.) (1965).

MASSERON (J.P.), *Le pouvoir et la justice en Afrique noire francophone et à Madagascar* (1966).

Université Libre de Bruxelles, Institut de sociologie, GILISSEN (J.) ed., *L'organisation judiciaire en Afrique noire* (1969).

RUBBENS (A.), *Le droit judiciare congolais* (1970).

VANDERLINDEN (J.), *Introduction au droit de l'Ethiopie Moderne* (1971).

LAVROFF (D.G.), *Les systèmes constitutionnels en Afrique noire. Les Etats francophones* (1976).

(d) In Italian

SACCO (R.) *Introduzione al diritto privato somalo* (1973).

SECTION IX—UNIFICATION AND HARMONISATION OF LAW
International Encyclopaedia of Comparative Law, Vol. II,
Chap. V: *International Unification of Private Law*, DAVID (R.)
(1971)

The International Institute for the Unification of Private Law
(Institut international de Rome pour l'unification du droit privé)
(UNIDROIT) (Villa Aldobrandini, 28 via Panisperna, Rome) in
its annual volume *Unification of Law/L'Unification de droit*, publishes a very complete bibliography of all works published in different countries relating to problems of the unification of law.

Le Service des publications des Communautés européennes, in
Luxembourg, has edited a work entitled *Publications juridiques
concernant l'intégration européenne* (1962), which is kept up to
date by supplements.

GRAVESON (R.H.) *Selected Essays.* II: *On Jurisprudence and the
Unification of Law* (1971).

APPENDIX II

USEFUL INFORMATION AND REFERENCES

Section I—Centres of Comparative Law

A list of centres of comparative law has been published by the *Revista del Instituto de derecho comparado*, Barcelona, Nos. 6–7 (1956), pp. 165–488—*Catálogo de centros de derecho comparado en el mundo*.

The information given in this publication is kept up to date by different comparative law reviews—in particular by the usual section devoted to news and events ("Actualités et Informations") in the *Revue internationale de droit comparé*.

Bulletin d'information des organismes français et associés de droit comparé, 1957 (annual), completed by information sheets published at irregular intervals by the Centre français de droit comparé (28 rue Saint-Guillaume, Paris VII), in manifold form, No. 26 (1980–81).

The Institut de la communauté européenne pour les études universitaires (244, rue de la Loi, Bruxelles) has also published a list of *Etudes universitaires sur l'intégration européenne* (No. 6, 1970). This brochure lists the centres interested in European unity and the studies undertaken and published under its aegis.

UNESCO, *Guide des centres nationaux d'information bibliographique* (3rd ed., 1970).

Section II—Comparative Law Studies

The *Faculté internationale pour l'enseignement du drio t comparé, Université de Strasbourg*, organises two sessions every year designed to introduce students to the study of comparative law. These sessions, each lasting for five weeks, take place in March-

April and August-September of each year; the spring session is always held in Strasbourg, whereas the summer session is generally held in some other French or foreign university centre. The teaching programme of the *Faculté internationale* is divided into three cycles; the first is given in French, German and English. Professors and students at the *Faculté* come from many different countries; formal lectures are complemented by seminars and practical assignments. Information may be obtained from: Secrétariat de la Faculté, Esplanade 67000 Strasbourg, France.

A programme similar in nature is offered by the *Faculté internationale de droit comparé de Luxembourg* but the courses are not so varied and take place only in Luxembourg: Secretariat, 13 rue Rost, Luxembourg.

Introductory courses in *Italian law* of one month (August-September) are given each year, in the French language, at the *Università degli studi d'Urbino.*

An introduction to English law, German law and the law of the European Economic Community is organised under the auspices of the *British Institute of International and Comparative Law* and the *German Academic Exchange Service* in London in the month of July: German Academic Exchange Service, 11–15 Arlington Street, London S.W.1.

Summer courses providing an introduction to English Common law are given every year in July-August at the City of London Polytechnic, Summer School, 84 Moorgate, London E.C.2, M6 SQ and every second year (even years) at Cambridge University: Board of Extramural Studies, Stuart House, Cambridge.

Summer courses providing an introduction to the law of the United States are given every year at the Salzburg Seminar of American Studies, Schloss Leopoldskrone, Salzburg, Austria, and by agreement between the Dutch Universities of Leyden and Amsterdam and Columbia University: *Summer Program in American Law*: Juridisch Studiecentrum II, Hugo de Grootstraat, 27, Leyden.

Other universities organise special study sessions to provide an introduction to their national laws. A year's programme in American law is offered at New York University, Washington Square, New York, N.Y. John Hopkins University offers a programme in international relations in Bologna, Italy.

Further information may be obtained from the *Bulletin d'infor-*

mation des organismes français et associés de droit comparé mentioned above and the bi-monthly bulletin *Nouvelles universitaires européennes* (2, rue Mérimée, Paris, XVI) for studies in European law organised by such centres as the Institut universitaire européen de Florence, the Collège d'Europe in Bruges, Belgium, the Institut européen de Turin, the Centre d'études européenes de Nancy, the Institut für europäisches Recht in Sazzbruck, and others.

Scholarships

Under the title *Study Abroad/Etudes à l'étranger*, the United Nations Educational, Scientific and Cultural Organisation (U.N.E.S.C.O., place de Fontenoy, Paris VIIe, France), publishes a brochure indicating scholarships available to students wishing to pursue their studies in a foreign country. Vol. XIX: 1972–1973 and 1973–1974 (1969). This publication is complemented by *Echanges universitaires* (2nd ed., 1967).

Section III—Comparative Law Libraries

Large foreign law collections are contained in the principal university or law faculty libraries in most English-speaking countries. In the United States both the Law Library of Congress and Harvard University have collections estimated at over 400,000 volumes; the Universities of Michigan, Columbia and Yale, in the United States, as well as the Los Angeles County Library, California, U.S.A., have large collections. In the United Kingdom, the Institute of Advanced Legal Studies in London has an especially fine collection of foreign materials. This Institute publishes *A Catalogue of Foreign Legal Periodicals held in United Kingdom Libraries* and a *List of Current Legal Research Topics*.

In France the principal libraries containing such materials are located in Paris: Faculté de droit et des sciences économiques; the Centre français de droit comparé (28 rue Saint-Guillaume, Paris VIIe), the Société de législation comparée, 31 rue Saint-Guillaume, Paris VIIe. The *Bulletin d'information des organismes français et associés de droit comparé*, mentioned above, contains information concerning the materials received by the principal

French faculties of law. See also Olivier (M.), *Répertoire des bibliothèques et organismes de documentation* (1971). Supplement 1973.

INDEX

[References are to paragraph number]

[References are to paragraph number]

[References are to paragraph number]

[References are to paragraph number]

[References are to paragraph number]

[References are to paragraph number]

[References are to paragraph number]